7th Edition

EFFECTIVE PUBLIC RELATIONS

Scott M. Cutlip

Dean Emeritus, Henry W. Grady School of Journalism
  and Mass Communications
The University of Georgia

Allen H. Center

Distinguished Resident Lecturer
San Diego State University
Vice President of Public Relations (retired),
  Motorola, Inc.

Glen M. Broom, Ph.D.

Professor, School of Communication
San Diego State University

Prentice

ISBN 0-13-245523-4

To   Erna Cutlip
      Nancy Center, and
      Betty Broom

© 1994, 1985, 1982, 1978, 1971, 1964, 1958, 1952
Prentice-Hall, Inc.
A Paramount Communications Company
Englewood Cliffs, NJ 07632

Printed in the United States of America

10 9 8 7 6 5 4 3 2 1

ISBN 0-13-245523-4

Prentice-Hall International (UK) Limited, *London*
Prentice-Hall of Australia Pty. Limited, *Sydney*
Prentice-Hall Canada Inc., *Toronto*
Prentice-Hall Hispanoamericana, S.A., *Mexico*
Prentice-Hall of India Private Limited, *New Delhi*
Prentice-Hall of Japan. Inc., *Tokyo*
Simon & Schuster Asia Pte. Ltd., *Singapore*
Editora Prentice-Hall do Brasil, Ltda., *Rio de Janeiro*
Prentice-Hall, *Englewood Cliffs, New Jersey*

Brief Contents

PART I: **CONCEPTS, PRACTITIONERS, CONTEXTS AND ORIGINS**

Chapter 1   Introduction to Contemporary Public Relations 1
Chapter 2   Practitioners of Public Relations 26
Chapter 3   Organizational Settings 56
Chapter 4   Historical Origins 89

PART II: **FOUNDATIONS**

Chapter 5   Ethics and Professionalism 129
Chapter 6   Legal Considerations 164
Chapter 7   Theoretical Underpinnings 198
Chapter 8   Communication and Public Opinion 227
Chapter 9   Media and Media Relations 259

PART III: **THE MANAGEMENT PROCESS**

Chapter 10   Step One: Defining Public Relations Problems 316
Chapter 11   Step Two: Planning and Programming 345
Chapter 12   Step Three: Taking Action and Communicating 379
Chapter 13   Step Four: Evaluating the Program 406

PART IV: **THE PRACTICE**

Chapter 14   Business and Industry 436
Chapter 15   Government and Politics 462
Chapter 16   Nonprofit Organizations, Health Care, and Education 494
Chapter 17   Trade Associations, Professional Societies, and Labor Unions 527

Contents

Preface   xiii

PART I   CONCEPTS, PRACTITIONERS, CONTEXT, AND ORIGINS

Chapter 1   Introduction to Contemporary Public Relations   1

Evolution of the Concept   2
Defining the Concept in Practice   3
Confusion with Marketing   6
Parts of the Function   8
  Publicity   8,   Advertising   10,   Press Agentry   11,
  Public Affairs   14,   Issues Management   16,   Lobbying   17,
  Investor Relations   19,   Development   20
Toward Recognition and Maturity   21
Additional Readings   24
Notes   25

Chapter 2   Practitioners of Public Relations   26

Number and Distribution   26
Where They Work   27
Education and Preparation   29
The New Majority: Women   30
Salaries   31
Work Assignments 33
Roles   42
  Communication Technician   42,   Expert Prescriber   42,
  Communications Facilitator   43,   Problem-Solving Facilitator   43
What Roles Research Tells Us   44
  Technicians versus Managers   44,   Environmental Influences   45,
  Scanning and Evaluation   46
The Glass Ceiling Effect   46
Minorities   47
Professionalism   48
Requirements for Success   50
Additional Readings   53
Notes   53

Chapter 3   Organizational Settings   56

Origins within Organizations   57
Public Relations Starts with Top Management   59
Staff Role   60
Decision-Making Role   62
The Internal Department   64,
  *The Department's Advantages   64,   The Department's
  Disadvantages   65,   Titles and Reporting Relationships   66*
Working with Other Departments   68
  *Marketing   70,   Legal Counsel   71,   Human Resources or
  Personnel   72,   Organizational Development   73*
The Outside Counseling Firm   74
  *Public Relations Firms   74,   Advertising Agency Ownership   75,
  Specialization   76,   Reasons for Retaining Outside Counsel   78,
  The Client-Firm Relationship   79,   The Counselor's Advantages   82,
  The Counselor's Handicaps   83,   Counseling Firm Costs   84*
Integrating the Function   86
Additional Readings   87
Notes   88

Chapter 4   Historical Origins of Public Relations   89

Ancient Genesis   89
Born in Adversity and Change   90
American Beginnings   91
The Middle Years   94
  *Press Agentry   94,   Political Campaigning   96,
  Business Practices   96,   Other Activities   98*
Evolution to Maturity   99
Seedbed Era: 1900–1917   100
  *Early Firms   101,   Early Pioneers   103,   Others of
  Influence   105,   Growth in Other Areas   107*
World War I Period: 1917–1919   109
Booming Twenties Era: 1919–1929   111
Roosevelt Era and World War II: 1930–1945   116
Postwar Boom: 1945–1965   120
Global Information Age: 1965–Present   122
Additional Readings   123
Notes   124

PART II   FOUNDATIONS

Chapter 5   Ethics and Professionalism   129

Ethical Foundations   129
  Professional Ethics   130,   The Imperative of Trust   130,
  Professional Privilege   131,   Social Responsibility   132,
  Positives   133,   Negatives   133
Other Professional Foundations   135
Professional Education   136
  Degree Programs   l36,   Continuing Education   138
Research and the Body of Knowledge   138
  Body of Knowledge Project   l39,   Support for Research   139,
  The Literature   140
Licensing and Accreditation   142
  Legal Considerations   143,   Accreditation   144
Professional Organizations   145
  Public Relations Society of America (PRSA)   145,   International
  Association of Business Communicators (IABC)   147,   Canadian
  Public Relations Society (CPRS)   147,   Institute of Public Relations
  (United Kingdom) (IPR)   147,   Public Relations Consultants
  Associated (United Kingdom) (PRCA)   148,   International Public
  Relations Association (IPRA)   148,   Specialized, Regional, and
  Local Associations   148,   Student Organizations   150
Codes of Ethics   151
Toward New Horizons   157
Additional Readings   160
Notes   161

Chapter 6   Legal Considerations   164

Public Relations and the First Amendment   165
  Commercial Speech   167,   Corporate Political Expression   168,
  Elections   169,   Referenda and Political Issues   170
Lobbying: The Right to Petition   172
  Lobbying   172,   Grass-roots Lobbying   173,   Foreign Agents   174
Communication between Labor and Management   175
  Representation Elections   175,   Collective Bargaining   l75
Financial Public Relations   176
  Disclosure   177,   Securities Trading   178,   Fraud   180
Access to the Media   182
  Print Media   182,   Broadcast Media   183
Access to Government Information and Meetings   185
Libel and Privacy   187
  Libel and Slander   187,   Privacy   188
Copyright and Trademarks   190
  Copyright   190,   Trademarks   192
Additional Readings   193
Notes   194

Chapter 7   Theoretical Underpinnings: Adjustment and Adaptation   198

The Ecological Approach   199
Some Basic Trends and Changes   200
  *Protecting the Environment   200,   Health Care Reform   201,
  AIDS   202,   Globalization of Business and Economies   202,   Global
  Communication in the Information Age   203,   Realignment of the
  Family   204,   Civil Rights and the Empowerment of Individuals   204*
Tracking the Trends   206
A Systems Perspective   206
  *Environmental Change Pressures   208,   Subsystems and
  Suprasystems   209,   Organizations as Systems   211*
Open and Closed Systems   212
Cybernetics in Open Systems   214
An Open Systems Model of Public Relations   219
Additional Readings   224
Notes   225

Chapter 8   Theoretical Underpinnings: Communication and Public Opinion   227

The Battle for Attention   228
Dissemination versus Communication   228
Elements of the Ccxrmunication Model   230
  *The Sender   230,   The Message   231,   The Medium or Channel   233,
  The Receivers   235,   Context of the Relationship   236,
  The Social Environment   237*
Effects of the Process   238
  *Creating Perceptions of the World Around Us   238,
  Setting the Agenda   239,   Diffusing Information and
  Innovations   240,   Defining Social Support   241*
Publics and Their Opinions   242
  Definition of Public Opinion   243,   The Publics   245
Individual Orientations and Coorientation   247
  *Orientation   247,   Coorientation   249,   Coorientational
  Consensus   250,   Coorientational Relationships   252*
Additional Readings   254
Notes   254

Chapter 9   Media and Media Relations   259

Media for Internal Publics   260
Printed Words   263
    *Organizational Publications   263,   Letters   267,   Inserts and
    Enclosures   268,   Reprinted Speeches, Position Papers, and
    "Backgrounders"   268,   Bulletin Boards   269*
Spoken Words   270
    *The Grapevine   270,   Meetings   271,   Speeches and Speakers'
    Bureaus   272*
Images and Words   273
    *Teleconferencing   273,   Closed Circuit Television (CCTV)   275,
    Videotape, Film, and Slide Presentations   276,   Displays and
    Exhibits   277*
Media for External Publics   279
    *Newspapers   280,   Wire Services and News Syndicates   285,
    Magazines   288,   Radio   290,   Television   293
    Cable Television   298*
Working with the Media   299
    *The Person in the Middle   300,   Guidelines for Good Media
    Relations   304,   Guidelines for Working with the Press   309*
Additional Readings   311
Notes   312

PART III   MANAGEMENT PROCESS
Chapter 10   Step One: Defining Public Relations Problems   316

Management Process   316
Role of Research in Strategic Planning   319
Research Attitude   320
Listening as Systematic Research   320
Defining Public Relations Problems   321
    Problem Statement   322,   Situation Analysis   323
Research Process   328
Informal or "Exploratory" Methods   329
    *Personal Contacts   329,   Key Informants   330,   Focus Groups and
    Community Forums   330,   Advisory Committees and Boards   332,
    Ombudsman   333,   Call-In Telephone Lines   334,
    Mail Analysis   335,   Field Reports   336*
Formal Methods   336
    *Secondary Analysis and On-Line Databases   338,
    Content Analysis   339,   Surveys   340*
Additional Readings   342
Notes   343

Chapter 11   Step Two: Planning and Programming   345

Strategic Thinking   345
  Public Relations as Part of Strategic Thinking   346,
  Management Expectations   347
Strategic Management   349
  Mission Statements   350,   Management by Objectives   352,
  Strategy and Tactics   353,   Reasons for Planning   354
Writing the Program   355
  The Program Plan   356,   The Role of Working Theory   358,
  Defining Target Publics   360,   Writing Program Objectives   362
Planning for Program Implementation   365
  Writing Planning Scenarios   365,   Anticipating Disasters and
  Crises   366,   Establishing an Information Center   370,
  Budgeting   371,   Pretesting Program Elements   374,
  Selling the Plan   375
Additional Readings   376
Notes   377

Chapter 12   Step Three: Taking Action and Communicating   379

Action and Communication   379
The Action Component of Strategy   380
  Acting Responsively and Responsibly   380,
  Coordinating Action and Communication   381,
  Action as an Open Systems Response   383
The Communication Component of Strategy   386
  Framing the Message   386,   Semantics   390,   Symbols   392
  Barriers and Stereotypes   394,   Putting It All Together in a
  Campaign   396,   Disseminating the Message   397,
  Reconsidering the Process   400
Implementing the Strategy   402
Additional Readings   403
Notes   404

Chapter 13   Step Four: Evaluating the Program   406

The Push for Measurable Results   407
Evaluation Research Process   410
Levels of Program Evaluation   413
  Preparation Criteria and Methods   415,   Implementation Criteria
  and Methods   420,   Impact Criteria and Methods   426
Interpreting and Using Results of Evaluation   431
Additional Readings   433
Notes   434

PART IV   THE PRACTICE

Chapter 14   Business and Industry   436

Public Relations in the Competitive Setting   436
Titles in Corporate Settings   437
Corporate Social Responsibility   438
   Prelude to the Present: The Uneasy 1960s and 1970s   439,
   A New Era of Corporate Social Responsibility: The 1980s   441,
   Public Relations Challenges in the 1990s   443
Corporate Philanthropy   446
Corporate Financial Relations   450
Consumer Affairs and the "Marketing Mix"   455
The Quest for Quality   456
Corporate Practice as the Model   457
Additional Readings   458
Notes   459

Chapter 15   Government and Politics   462

The Role of Public Relations in Government   462
Maintaining an Informed Citizenry   466
   United States Information Agency (USIA)   466,
   Citizen Participation   469
Barriers to Effective Government Public Relations   472
   Public Apathy   472,   Legislative Hostility to the Function   475
Government-Media Relations   478
   Media Access to Government   478,   Government Dependence on
   Media   480,   Media Reporting on Government   483
Military Public Relations   483
Government as Business   488
Public Relations in Politics   489
Additional Readings   491
Notes   491

Chapter 16   Nonprofit Organizations, Health Care, and Education   494

The Role of Public Relations in Nonprofit Organizations   497
*Voluntarism and Philanthropy   498,   Changing Climate   499,
Changing Function   500*
Health Care   501
*Health Care in Crisis   501,   Public Relations as Marketing   504,
Role of the News Media   506*
Social Welfare   507
Education   511
*Accountability   512,   Public Relations in Public Schools   512,
Higher Education   516,   The College President's Public
Relations Role   521*
Churches and Other Nonprofit Organizations   522
Additional Readings   524
Notes   525

Chapter 17   Trade Associations, Professional Societies, and Labor Unions   527

Types of Associations   527
Associations and Societies   528
*The Problem of Serving Many Masters   530,   An Era of Change and
Gain   531,   The Growing Importance of Public Relations   532,
The Nature of Programming   535*
Labor Unions   539
*The Role of Public Relations   540,   The Problem of Strikes   541
The Challenge for Labor   544*
Additional Readings   544
Notes   545

Index   547

Preface

Forty-two years is a long time for a book to dominate a field, but *Effective Public Relations (EPR)* has done just that. For six editions, *EPR* defined the practice of public relations, schooled generations of practitioners, and provided a ready reference for those in the calling. It occupies a position few books in any field enjoy: Many view it as "the bible" of public relations. As a result, **Scott Cutlip** and **Allen Center** have defined and shaped the study and practice of public relations since 1952. Not many people in any field have had more impact in their respective fields than have my coauthors. The same can be said of the book commonly referred to as "Cutlip and Center." I can say these things because they aren't writing this preface to the seventh edition.

Fast forward to the present: **Cutlip** and **Center** are still dominant figures in contemporary public relations, but the role and function of *EPR* have changed. *EPR* can no longer be the encyclopedia of public relations, in part, because of its contributions over the previous four decades. The body of knowledge has outgrown the bounds of a single book. *EPR* cannot cover all you need to know about public relations. No single book can do that. All the same, *EPR* remains the basic reference for the field, it continues as the most frequently used textbook, it is the book used by those preparing for accreditation exams, and it is the book most frequently cited in public relations literature.

So what does *EPR* do in its seventh edition? First of all it introduces you to the principles and practice of public relations, from defining the concepts and function to reporting its application in specific settings. Second, it provides you with a foundation of theory and process, recognizing that other books and other courses now cover in depth such topics as writing and techniques, research and evaluation, and management issues and case studies. *EPR* introduces and explores all of these areas, but can no longer be the only reference book in your professional library.

This edition is divided into four parts: Part I describes the field, basic concepts, the practitioners, their work settings, and the origins of what they do. Part II introduces the principles and theory that underpin and guide the practice. Part III applies theory to practice by outlining what is known as the four-step public relations process. Part IV gives context to the practice by illustrating what public relations does and how it functions in business, government, associations, and nonprofit organizations.

You also need to know what *EPR* does not do. First, it does not reconstruct history. The history chapter continues to be the definitive exposition on the origins of public relations. With each edition, more is added to the body of historical knowledge, as scholars explore and explain more about the origins of the practice. However, contemporary values and terminology have not been "retrofitted" to the people and events of the past just to be "politically correct." Rather, *EPR* attempts to be an objective and bias-free introductory textbook that is global in perspective.

Second, *EPR* does not trivialize public relations by presenting oversimplified "what-would-you-do-if" case studies. A few paragraphs, or even a few pages, cannot provide enough detail and background information for readers to be able to devise recommended solutions to complex problems. Rather, *EPR* provides the foundation upon which subsequent courses and books can build for developing strategy and tactics to solve problems. In short, although there are many sections that deal with applications in practice, this is not a "how to" manual for public relations. Be wary of those books that claim to show how to succeed in public relations without first providing a foundation derived from the body of knowledge.

And finally, this is not a new book. The seventh edition represents a major revision, to be sure, but not a major change in concept or direction. In many ways, it is consistent with the early editions, widely recognized as having helped define the field both as an academic field of study and as a professional practice. "Ecology" is expanded to a systems theory perspective. The concept of a management function is extended to increase the odds that public relations will be at the table when decisions are being made. Tasks performed by practitioners are categorized as organizational roles. Listening and feedback are developed as research and evaluation to meet contemporary demands for evidence and accountability. Of course, there are many new ideas, sources, and examples in the seventh edition, but the course was set in 1952 with the first edition of "Cutlip and Center."

Along the way, many contributed to both setting direction and to making midcourse corrections. This seventh edition is no exception, because many influenced both the substance and style of what you are about to read. Colleagues in academe provided valuable reactions and useful suggestions on drafts of chapters. Only they will recognize how their feedback changed and improved the book. I hope that Prentice Hall rewarded them amply for their counsel. I can demonstrate my gratitude by listing them here and hoping that if you know one or more of these professors you will thank them for their contributions: **Ronald B. Anderson**, University of Texas at Austin; **Marilyn Kern Fox-Worth**, Texas A&M University; **Carroll J. Glynn**, Cornell University; **Larissa A. Grunig**, University of Maryland; **Stanley Harrison**, University of Miami; **Michael D. Slater**, Colorado State University; **Eliza-**

beth Tidwell, Ferris State University; **JoAnn Myer Valenti**, Brigham Young University; **Gary L. Werner**, University of South Florida; and **Frank W. Wylie**, California State University-Long Beach (retired). **Kent R. Middleton**, University of Georgia, helped with the previous edition of the law chapter, but much of his work is reflected in the seventh edition of the same chapter. San Diego State University colleagues **David M. Dozier** and **Martha M. Lauzen** will recognize their contributions throughout the book.

Former and current students form a pipeline of new information and examples. I cannot list all who contributed, in part because the passage of time dims my recollection of who gave me what. Those I most associate with this edition include: **Vicki Hoffman Beck**, UCLA Medical Center, Los Angeles; **Donna Chandler**, Tracy-Locke/Pharr Public Relations, Dallas; **Marilyn Kendall**, formerly with Cable and Wireless, London; **JoNell Meittinen**, Stanford University (graduate student); **Vicci Rodgers**, The Rodgers Group, Chicago; **MaryLee Sacks**, Hill and Knowlton, London; **Dawn Soper**, Operation Lifesaver, Inc., Washington, D.C.; and **Bill Trumpfheller**, Nuffer, Smith, Tucker, Inc., San Diego. Among the students in classes while I revised, several stepped forward with ideas and suggestions that made their way into the seventh edition. At the risk of offending many not named, I want to thank **Ellen Jackson** and her husband **John** who took it as a challenge to find the perfect photograph of a cuttlefish to illustrate the analogy used in Chapter 7; and **Donald E. Roberts, Jr.,** a voracious reader who provided critical reviews and frequent "have-you-seen-this?" introductions to sources that helped broaden the perspective of the seventh edition.

As is the case with former students, I cannot list all the practitioners who contributed to this edition, sometimes indirectly but no less importantly. I want to acknowledge several who responded to my requests for help: **Tom Biederbeck**, Caterpillar Inc.; **Bob Delaney**, SIRIS Consulting Ltd.; **Lori A. Folts**, E. I. Du Pont De Nemours and Company; **Christine Foschetti**, Holt & Ross, Inc.; **Tom Gable**, The Gable Agency, Inc.; **Lorri Lee**, American Society of Association Executives; **Richard K. Long**, Weyerhaeuser Company; **James E. Lukaszewski**, The Lukaszewski Group; Rear Admiral **Kendall Pease**, U.S. Navy; **David B. Saddler**, American Chamber of Commerce Executives; **Steven V. Seekins**, American Medical Association; **Charles Sengstock, Jr.**, Motorola Inc.; **Alvie L. Smith**, General Motors (retired); **Kerry Tucker**, Nuffer, Smith, Tucker, Inc.; and **John C. West**, Phillips Petroleum Company.

Four collaborators made extraordinary contributions to the seventh edition: **William C. Adams**, Associate Professor, Florida International University, helped with the chapter on business and industry (Chapter 14); **Mark S. Cox**, Director of Public Relations, City of Chesapeake, Virginia, helped update the chapter on government and politics (Chapter 15); and **Kenneth G. Trester**, Director of Planning and Marketing, University of Michigan Medical Center, and **Catherine J. Smillie,** Director of Sales and Marketing, MCARE, Ann Arbor, helped revise the chapter on nonprofit organizations, health care, and education (Chapter 16). The seventh edition presents an up-to-date portrait of the challenges practitioners face in each of these settings because of these contributors.

Editors and coauthors deserve special acknowledgment in this preface. They make things possible and they make things difficult. In the final analysis, however, the seventh edition got done and is a better book because of their prodding and contributions. Prentice Hall senior editor **Sandra M. Steiner** provided able assistance and firm direction as the one in charge of getting the seventh edition produced. Production editor **Karen S. Fortgang** of bookworks was the one who skillfully supervised turning the manuscript into a book. Copy editor **Kathleen Lafferty** caught most of the typos, mistakes, and careless wording, thereby making the seventh edition more readable than was my original manuscript. In spite of their seemingly unrelenting push to meet deadlines, their not-so-veiled threats about the consequences of my tardiness, and their marks all over my finished manuscript, I am indebted to them and appreciate their valuable assistance in producing the seventh edition. Their influence and skills are reflected from cover to cover.

So also are the contributions of my coauthors, **Cutlip** and **Center.** They have been patient, yet anxious; supportive, yet frustrated by how long it was taking me to revise; and demanding, yet committed to doing it right, not just fast. At stake was their four-decade investment in making *EPR* the field's leading text and reference. I hope that they now share my satisfaction with the seventh edition. For my part, I am forever in their debt for giving me the opportunity and the challenge of revising "Cutlip and Center." I could not be prouder of my associations with them and with this book.

And finally, I must address the charge that I have not been carrying my full share of household chores and responsibilities. In my defense, a major revision of a text like this requires dedication and singleness of purpose. (As I wrote those words, I can almost hear the hoots and howls of laughter from coauthors, editors, and coworkers.) My accuser, however, has signed a contract to do a similar revision of a major text in her nursing specialty, so our roles are about to reverse. She can look forward to staring into her monitor for endless hours, dealing with pushy editors, soothing anxious coauthors, and burning the midnight oil to meet deadlines. I, on the other hand, look forward to grocery shopping and sorting the laundry. (Now that you remind me, it has been a long time since I did either of those joyous chores.) For that time and support, I thank **Betty,** my wife, and wish her the same joy and satisfaction as I now feel with the completion of *EPR*7.

Glen M. Broom
San Diego State University

CHAPTER

1

Introduction to Contemporary Public Relations

Public relations is the management function that establishes and maintains mutually beneficial relationships between an organization and the publics on whom its success or failure depends.

To satisfy human needs and wants, individuals and social groupings establish and maintain relationships with others. These relationships require varying degrees of interaction and interdependence and, therefore, different levels of social, political, and economic exchanges. Even though this has always been the case, modern society consists of increasingly interdependent, complex, and often conflict-laden relationships.

Human relations and *interpersonal relations* describe the study and management of relations among *individuals*. Likewise, *international relations* deals with relationships among *nations*. *Public relations* applies when the level of concern is an *organization*'s relationships with others.

People use the term *public relations* to refer to many things, however, paying little attention to concise definitions. Our purpose in this chapter is to clarify the definition by establishing the meaning of the concept and distinguishing it from other organizational functions and activities. We begin by reviewing how the concept has changed over the years.

EVOLUTION OF THE CONCEPT

Differing concepts of public relations reflect the evolution of this maturing function in organizations and society. They also indicate the struggle of an emerging profession seeking its unique identity. Highlights of the evolution illustrate how the concept took on its current meaning. (See Chapter 4 for a more detailed analysis.)

In the early 1900s powerful business interests employed public relations to defend their special interests against muckraking journalism and government regulation. There were many positive uses of public relations during this period, but the emphasis was on "telling-our-story" counterattacks designed to influence public opinion and to prevent changes in public policy toward more regulation of business.

The concept as one-way persuasive communication dominated as the United States entered World War I and created the Committee on Public Information. Headed by George Creel, the committee's goal was to unite public opinion behind the war effort through a nation-wide propaganda campaign. During those early years, public relations took the form of publicity designed to influence others.

Many still define the concept as merely persuasive publicity. For example, a recent dictionary defined public relations as "*inducing* the public to have understanding for and goodwill" (emphasis added). This concept also reflects the title of an influential book written by Edward L. Bernays, *The Engineering of Consent* (1955). Bernays's title stuck. As a result, even today many practitioners find themselves dealing with managers and clients holding exclusively this concept of public relations: persuading others.

During the several decades following World War II, the concept evolved to include notions of two-way communication: reciprocity and relationships. Definitions include such words as *reciprocal*, *mutual*, and *between*, indicating change to an interactive view of the function. This concept appears in *Webster's Third New International Dictionary*: "The art or science of developing reciprocal understanding and goodwill." The British Institute of Public Relations defines the function as an effort to establish and maintain "mutual understanding between an organization and its publics."

Previous editions of this text reflect the interactive concept: "the planned effort to influence opinion through good character and responsible performance, based on mutually satisfactory two-way communications." Another recent text emphasizes communication in yet another version of this interactive concept: "the management of communication between an organization and its publics."[1]

In the late 1930s, however, Harwood L. Childs introduced an even more advanced concept, which only recently reemerged as part of contemporary thought. Going against the conventional wisdom,

Childs concluded that the essence of public relations "is not the presentation of a point of view, not the art of tempering mental attitudes, nor the development of cordial and profitable relations." Instead, he said the basic function "is to reconcile or adjust in the public interest those aspects of our personal and corporate behavior which have a social significance."[2] In short, Childs said that public relations helps organizations *adjust* to their environments.

The organizational adjustment concept suggests a management-level, policy-influencing role. This concept of the function also calls for *corrective action* in addition to the communication. Reflecting Childs's notions, the International Public Relations Association definition (adopted in 1978) includes "counseling organization leaders" and implementing "planned programs of action."

In summary, the one-way concept of public relations leads to propaganda or persuasive communication, the two-way concept emphasizes communication exchange and mutual understanding, and the organizational adjustment concept puts the function in the role of counseling management on corrective actions. In practice, contemporary public relations reflects a mix of all three concepts.

DEFINING THE CONCEPT IN PRACTICE

Another way to understand the concept is to analyze the specific tasks and responsibilities included under the title. By describing what public relations includes and what it does in practice, we develop operational definitions of the function.

One of the most persistent efforts to define public relations has been that by *Public Relations News*, one of several commercial newsletters serving the field:

Public relations is the management function which evaluates public attitudes, identifies the policies and procedures of an individual or an organization with the public interest, and plans and executes a program of action to earn public understanding and acceptance.

Notice that this definition focuses on *activities*. Hundreds have written definitions attempting to capture the essence of public relations by listing the major activities that make up the practice. Longtime public relations scholar and professional leader, the late Dr. Rex F. Harlow, collected definitions written since the early 1900s, identified the major elements in each, and classified the central ideas. From his analysis of 472 definitions, he produced a definition that includes both conceptual and operational aspects:

> Public Relations is the distinctive management function which
> helps establish and maintain mutual lines of communication,
> understanding, acceptance and cooperation between an organiza-
> tion and its publics; involves the management of problems or
> issues; helps management to keep informed on and responsive to
> public opinion; defines and emphasizes the responsibility of
> management to serve the public interest; helps management
> keep abreast of and effectively utilize change, serving as an early
> warning system to help anticipate trends; and uses research and
> sound and ethical communication as its principal tools.[3]

In November 1982, the Public Relations Society of America formally adopted an even longer "Official Statement on Public Relations." The
statement represents the work of a blue-ribbon panel of leaders who
attempted to provide society members a definition of the field. In addition to the conceptual definition stressing public relations' contributions
to society, the definition describes a collection of activities, results, and
knowledge requirements. (See Exhibit 1–1.)

EXHIBIT 1-1

Public Relations Society of America's "Official Statement on Public Relations"

(Formally adopted by PRSA Assembly, November 6, 1982)

Public relations helps our complex, pluralistic society to reach decisions and function more effectively by contributing to mutual
understanding among groups and institutions. It serves to bring
private and public policies into harmony.

Public relations serves a wide variety of institutions in society
such as businesses, trade unions, government agencies, voluntary
associations, foundations, hospitals, schools, colleges, and religious
institutions. To achieve their goals, these institutions must develop
effective relationships with many different audiences or publics
such as employees, members, customers, local communities, shareholders, and other institutions, and with society at large.

The management of institutions need to understand the attitudes and values of their publics in order to achieve institutional
goals. The goals themselves are shaped by the external environment. The public relations practitioner acts as a counselor to management and as a mediator, helping to translate private aims into
reasonable, publicly acceptable policy and action.

As a management function, public relations encompasses the
following:

▶ Anticipating, analyzing, and interpreting public opinion, attitudes, and issues that might impact, for good or ill, the operations and plans of the organization.

▶ Counseling management at all levels in the organization with regard to policy decisions, courses of action, and communication, taking into account their public ramifications and the organization's social or citizenship responsibilities.

▶ Researching, conducting, and evaluating, on a continuing basis, programs of action and communication to achieve the informed public understanding necessary to the success of an organization's aims. These may include marketing, financial, fund raising, employee, community or government relations, and other programs.

▶ Planning and implementing the organization's efforts to influence or change public policy.

▶ Setting objectives, planning, budgeting, recruiting and training staff, developing facilities—in short, *managing* the resources needed to perform all of the above.

▶ Examples of the knowledge that may be required in the professional practice of public relations include communication arts, psychology, social psychology, sociology, political science, economics, and the principles of management and ethics. Technical knowledge and skills are required for opinion research, public-issues analysis, media relations, direct mail, institutional advertising, publications, film/video productions, special events, speeches, and presentations.

In helping to define and implement policy, the public relations practitioner uses a variety of professional communication skills and plays an integrative role both within the organization and between the organization and the external environment.

Similar notions in many definitions suggest that public relations:

1. Conducts a planned and sustained program as part of management
2. Deals with the relationships between an organization and its publics
3. Monitors awareness, opinions, attitudes, and behavior inside and outside the organization
4. Analyzes the impact of policies, procedures, and actions on publics
5. Adjusts those policies, procedures, and actions found to be in conflict with the public interest and organizational survival
6. Counsels management on the establishment of new policies, procedures, and actions that are mutually beneficial to the organization and its publics
7. Establishes and maintains two-way communication between the organization and its publics
8. Produces specific changes in awareness, opinions, attitudes, and behaviors inside and outside the organization
9. Results in new and/or maintained relationships between an organization and its publics

The evolution of the concept and the numerous descriptions of the practice lead us to the following conceptual definition:

> Public relations is the management function that establishes and maintains mutually beneficial relationships between an organization and the publics on whom its success or failure depends.

This conceptual definition unifies the broad range of activities and goals identified with the practice. It also identifies building and maintaining the mutually beneficial relationships essential to modern society as the moral and ethical basis of the profession. At the same time, it suggests criteria for determining what is and what is *not* part of the function.

CONFUSION WITH MARKETING

Marketing is the *management function* most often confused with public relations. Advertised openings for "public relations representatives" turn out to be positions as door-to-door sales representatives or telephone solicitors. In many small organizations, you might see the same person doing both functions. After observing this situation, some have concluded that there is no difference between the two.

Probably the greatest confusion occurs in nonprofit organizations and government when "nonprofit marketing" and "social marketing" refer to building and maintaining relationships with members, donors, and other constituents. In one such case, a practitioner in a major hospital found a new "Marketing Communication Department" sign on her door. Much to her surprise, management had changed the title of the "Public Relations Department" without telling her!

Those in the practice add to the confusion. Many public relations practitioners' business cards identify them as doing "marketing communications" or "marketing support programs." Some public relations firms have "marketing communications" or "marketing public relations" in their titles and on their letterheads. The principal of one such firm wrote a book describing "public relations that supports the marketing of goods and services," calling the practice "marketing public relations."[4] Many of those hired into public relations find themselves doing marketing work simply because both they and their managers confuse the two functions. Others do marketing support publicity because that is what their firm or agency gets paid to do.

Given the widespread confusion, it is understandable when people assume that public relations work entails promotion and sales of goods and services. After considering the public relations–marketing distinction, a principal in a public relations firm observed that if sales is not the mission of public relations, then "75 percent of public relations people are really in marketing."

If not always differentiated in practice, the two functions can be distinguished conceptually and their relationship clarified. First, *human needs and wants* are fundamental to the concept of marketing. What people require or desire gets translated into *demand*. Second, marketers offer *products and services* to satisfy the demand. Consumers select the products and services that provide the most *utility, value, and satisfaction*. Third, the marketer delivers the product or service to the consumer in *exchange* for something of value. This *transaction* distinguishes the marketing function: two parties trading values.[5] This is expressed in a form similar to the conceptual definition of public relations:

> Marketing is the management function that identifies human needs and wants, offers products and services to satisfy those demands, and causes transactions that deliver products and services in exchange for something of value to the provider.

In practice, marketing consists of a coordinated program of research, product design, packaging, pricing, promotion, and distribution. The goal is "to attract and satisfy customers (or clients) on a long-term basis in order to achieve an organization's economic objectives. Its fundamental responsibility is to build and maintain a market for an organization's products or services."[6]

Product publicity is part of marketing promotion. Because many think that publicity is synonymous with public relations, product publicity contributes to the confusion between marketing and public relations. Public relations specialists help in the marketing effort by writing product publicity stories and by arranging media coverage of new products. They are called on because of their expertise in writing and placing "news" stories and in dealing with the news media, but their efforts are part of the marketing strategy to cause the transaction between the organization and customers.

Some organizations treat exchange relationships with customers as only one of many organizational relationships. On their organization charts, marketing is part of the larger public relations function. Other organizations view marketing as the basic function, paying attention only to those noncustomer relationships seen as important to the marketing effort. Public relations is subordinate to marketing in these organizations. A few put "customer relations" under public relations, making it responsible for nonmarketing concerns of customers such as complaints, instructions for product use, safety information, and repair service. In many organizations, however, marketing and public relations are separate management functions with different but complementary goals.

These two major management functions deal with an organization's many publics, yet their roles often result from historical precedence and reflect little understanding of their differences. A major difference is that marketing is typically a *line management function* engaged in turning organization inputs into outputs of value to others.

Public relations operates as a *staff management function* providing counsel and other services to support line functions. As a result of the line-staff relationship, public relations practitioners often provide publicity and media support for marketing efforts. In too many organizations, however, neither senior line management nor public relations and marketing practitioners clearly distinguish between the two concepts or understand the relationship between the two organizational functions.

In summary, marketing focuses on exchange relationships with customers that lead to quid pro quo transactions, meeting customer demands and achieving organizational economic objectives. Public relations covers a broad range of relationships and goals with many publics: employees, investors, neighbors, special-interest groups, governments, and many more. Effective public relations contributes to the marketing effort by maintaining a hospitable social and political environment. Likewise, successful marketing and satisfied customers make good relations with others easier to build and maintain.

To achieve organizational goals, every organization must attend to its public relations and marketing functions. Each contributes by building and maintaining the different relationships essential for organization survival and growth.

PARTS OF THE FUNCTION

People also confuse public relations with its activities and parts. For example, many think that "publicity" is all that constitutes public relations. Publicity is often the most visible part, but seldom the only program strategy. Similarly, in Washington, D.C., and state capitals, often the most noticeable public relations activity is "lobbying." Lobbying typically represents only part of a larger public relations effort, however, with the lobbyists themselves reporting to the organization's top public relations executive.

Our conceptual definition helps show how each of the following activities relate to the contemporary meaning of public relations.

Publicity

Much information in the media originates outside the media, often from public relations sources. These sources have little or no control over if, when, and how it will be reported, however, because they do not pay for the placement. Media decision makers use the information because they think that it has news value and will be of interest to their audiences. They may change the original information or how it is presented, usually without identifying the source. In the eyes of readers, listeners, or viewers, each medium carrying the information is the source.

Publicity is information from an outside source that is used by the media because the information has news value. It is an *uncontrolled* method of placing messages in the media because the source does not pay the media for placement.

Examples of publicity include a story in the financial section about increased earnings for a major corporation, a columnist's item on the progress of a charity fund-raising campaign, a feature story in the health section announcing the latest scientific findings from a cancer research center, an entertainment calendar listing of the local appearance of your favorite music group, and television news coverage of the new civic center dedication ceremony. These stories no doubt were originated by the corporation's public relations department, charitable organization's director of donor relations and development, university medical center news bureau, music group's publicist, and the mayor's director of media relations (sometimes called "press secretary").

Publicity Materials

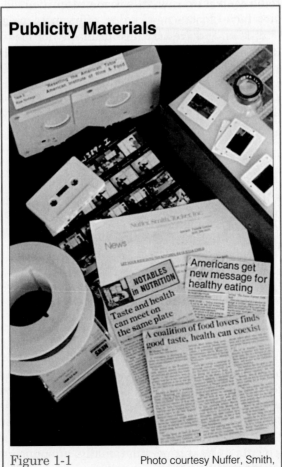

Figure 1-1   Photo courtesy Nuffer, Smith, Tucker, Inc., San Diego.

Print media probably received a press release, feature story with photographs, or press kit including detailed background information. Broadcast media may have received a broadcast-style news script, recorded interview, video new release (VNR), or press kit including material suitable for broadcast (see Figure 1–1). To get publicity, the source must know what types of information will attract media attention, identify a newsworthy lead, and write and package the information in a form acceptable to each medium. It helps to have a reputation among journalists as a trustworthy news source.

Another publicity method uses newsworthy events to attract media coverage. Groundbreaking ceremonies, ribbon cuttings, anniversary open houses, reunions, dedications, telethons, marathons, ceremonial appointments, honorary degrees, contract and legislation signings, organized protests, press conferences, and other special events are designed primarily as "news." By staging and managing such events, sources attempt to gain some control over what is reported in the media. Successful publicity events have obvious news value, offer photo, video, or sound recording opportunities, and are arranged primarily for media coverage.

Understandably, some confuse publicity with the broader concept of public relations. Public relations evolved from publicity. Much of contemporary practice is directed to generating publicity. In fact, some organizations use publicity releases and special events as the major strategies for achieving public relations objectives. There is more to the public relations function than publicity, however.

Advertising

Whereas the source typically cannot control publicity, advertising sponsors can control content, placement, and timing by paying for the media time and space. Like publicity, advertising is mediated, nonpersonal communication. We define it as follows:

> Advertising is information placed in the media by an identified sponsor that pays for the time or space. It is a *controlled* method of placing messages in the media.

Many associate advertising with selling goods and services as part of the marketing function, but it is not limited to that purpose. Other parts of the organization use this controlled means of placing messages in the mass media for nonmarketing purposes. For example, personnel departments place advertisements in newspaper classified and Sunday business sections to announce job openings. And legal departments place advertisements in newspapers of record to conform with public notification requirements. Eastman Kodak Company lawyers placed advertisements in newspapers nationally, announcing settlement of the "Kodak Instant Camera" class action lawsuit. The advertisements described settlement terms and provided a return form to be completed by those who purchased instant cameras from Kodak.

Public relations uses advertising to reach audiences other than the customers targeted by marketing. Investor relations places advertisements to assure stockholders and financial analysts that the corporation has thwarted a hostile takeover attempt. Community relations places an advertisement announcing its gift to the local symphony, yet not a single member of the intended audience buys the wing assemblies and air frames the company manufactures. The public relations committee of a local charity buys a full-page advertisement to thank contributors to the new homeless center fund drive.

Mobil Oil has used "advertorials" (see Figure 1–2) for more than 20 years for public relations purposes.[7] The *Minnesota Law Review* described such corporate advertising as "a hybrid creature designed to use the means of paid advertising to accomplish the goals of PR." Toshiba Corporation placed advertisements in major newspapers across the nation expressing "Its Deepest Regrets to the America People" and admitting that one of its divisions had violated trade agreements. San Diego Gas and Electric (SDG&E) ran advertisements explaining why its board of directors unanimously voted to merge with Tucson Electric Power Company (TEP) and unanimously rejected SCEcorp's (Southern California Edison) unsolicited takeover. When the TEP merger fell through, SDG&E's advertisements explained why being acquired by SCEcorp was suddenly a good thing for employees and the community, as well as customers.

Organizations use advertising when they are not satisfied with what is being said in the editorial sections of media, when they feel that their publics do not understand issues or are apathetic, or when they are trying to add their voices to a cause. In the final analysis, however, organizations turn to advertising when they want control over message content, placement, and timing.

So, organizations use publicity and advertising for both marketing and public relations purposes. In the case of publicity, the source does not pay for media time or space because media gatekeepers think that the information has relevance and news value. However, the information source does not control what is said, how it is said, or when it is said. If the source has the budget to purchase media time and space, advertising gives control over communications placements. In summary, publicity and advertising are different methods for placing *both* marketing and public relations messages in the mass media.

Other activities and specialties that cause confusion include *press agentry, public affairs, issues management, lobbying, investor relations,* and *development.*

Press Agentry

In the first chapter of *Walking the Tightrope*, Hollywood publicist Henry Rogers captures the essence of press agentry: "When I first

Public Relations Advertisement

A voice for the multinationals

It's become popular in recent years to bang on bigness as though it were inherently "bad." And, if you happen to be a company that's big and a multinational to boot, the problem is compounded.

But, in the words of the old Gershwin tune, "It ain't necessarily so."

To prove it, we would like to explode a few myths about big American companies with foreign interests:

For example, they're making gizmos and gadgets overseas more than ever before. And that obviously means they're hiring more people "there" and fewer people here. Right?

Wrong.

And to add insult to injury, they probably sell all those foreign-made things back to us in the U.S.A. Right?

Wrong.

And that must be why we've got this enormous trade deficit.

Wrong, wrong, WRONG.

Let's look at some of the facts:

● America's multinational corporations are the biggest contributors to the plus-side of the U.S. economy, according to soon-to-be-released findings of the Emergency Committee for American Trade.

● From 1989 to 1991, exports accounted for approximately 90 percent of U.S. real economic growth, and American multinationals generated about two-thirds of those exports.

● As America continues to struggle with a deep trade deficit, America's multinationals have a hefty and growing trade surplus. In 1990, the surplus in their overall balance of payments—a combination of repatriated income and the value of exports less imports—reached $130 billion.

● American companies that invest overseas the most also export the most. It stands to reason: Most of their foreign operations rely on American components, services and technology. Where investment leads, trade will follow.

● Over 90 percent of sales by American-owned manufacturers in foreign countries, excluding Canada, goes to markets outside the U.S. And those foreign operations are largely financed by their own earnings, not by windfalls from their U.S. parents.

● In fact, a great deal of what is not reinvested by those foreign affiliates finds its way back to this country. Some $48 billion in net income was repatriated to the U.S. in 1992, thus providing additional investment funds and creating jobs here at home.

What does all this mean for American jobs? Many American multinationals may have had to lay off workers because of declining revenues, or lagging productivity. But not because they're moving jobs overseas.

On the contrary, American multinationals and their growing trade surpluses create American jobs. Every billion dollars in manufactured exports creates more than 14,000 manufacturing jobs in the U.S. In 1990, they accounted for 2.4 million jobs. And that was just in manufacturing. Manufactured exports also stimulate job creation in trade, service, transportation and other sectors. In 1990, that meant five million American workers owed their jobs to manufactured exports by American multinationals.

Globalization is the ticket to the future, particularly as overseas markets continue to grow at higher rates than our own. That's why our country must vigorously support an open system of global trade and investment. The positive contribution of U.S. foreign investment to our economy is in jeopardy. Many well-intended policymakers want to put foreign investment on a tighter leash. They think that's the way to keep dollars and jobs in America. But that's wrong. Not just in theory, but in fact.

Mobil®

Figure 1–2   Courtesy Mobil Corporation

started, I was in the publicity business. I was a press agent. Very simply, my job was to get the client's name in the paper."[8] He candidly reports how in 1939 he lied to the West Coast editor of *Look* magazine about Rita Hayworth's extensive wardrobe, resulting in a cover and ten pages of photographs of the then-relatively unknown actress. Following this attention in a major national magazine, she became the talk of Hollywood, and Columbia Pictures extended her contract. To the extent that the mass media confer status on those covered, one might conclude that early stardom for Rita Hayworth was unfortunately at least partly the result of her press agent's lie about the extent of her wardrobe.

> Press agentry is creating newsworthy stories and events to attract media attention and to gain public notice.

Press agentry plays a major role in record companies, circuses, tourist attractions, motion picture studios, television, concert promotions, and the business enterprises headed by "media personalities." Considerable press agentry goes into political campaigns and national political party conventions to build name recognition and attract large audiences. Successful press agents gave us the legends of Davy Crockett and Hulk Hogan; promoted the Indianapolis 500 Memorial Day auto race into a national event; made Miami Beach and Puerto Vallarta internationally known resorts; turned Florida's Disney World into a vacation destination even before opening day; made *Batman Returns*, *Unforgiven*, and Disney's *Aladdin* must-see movies before the editing was completed; and opened our hearts to killer whales ("Shamu") and an invader from outer space ("E.T.").

Press agents work more to attract public notice than to build public understanding. Publicity is the major strategy of press agents. They base their approach on the "agenda-setting theory," which says that the amount of mass media coverage subsequently determines the relative importance of topics and people on the public agenda. In the candid words of a veteran press agent, "We stoop to anything, but our stuff gets printed." And it can pay off. A musical group's earning power may be as much a tribute to the skill of its press agent to build the right contacts through publicity as to its musical abilities. A career-launching appearance on a network talk show may result more from the work of a press agent than from the talent of the guest. Likewise, the new "in place" club or restaurant may be more the product of a press agent's publicity than of the ambiance, food, and entertainment of the place itself.

There are full-time press agents, and most public relations practitioners engage in a little press agentry at some time or another to achieve public awareness objectives through publicity. There is more to public relations than press agentry, however. Confusion results when press agents use the term *public relations* to describe what they do or to give themselves and their agencies more prestigious—if less accurate—titles.

Public Affairs

Some corporations, the armed services, and many governmental agencies use the "public affairs" title for the public relations function. In the armed services and governmental agencies, the public affairs title is part of the name game caused by the 1913 Gillett Amendment to an appropriation bill in the House of Representatives. The amendment stipulates that federal agencies cannot spend for publicity unless specifically authorized by Congress. This legislative hostility was reaffirmed in Public Law 92-351, Section 608(a), enacted July 13, 1972. This law expressly prohibits government spending on "publicity or propaganda purposes designed to support or defeat legislation pending before the Congress."

Neither the 1913 amendment nor the 1972 law refer to "public relations." Nevertheless, many federal, state, and local governmental officials apparently confuse publicity with the larger concept of public relations. As a result, agencies typically use other terms to describe the function of building and maintaining relationships with their constituents. It is nothing more than a name game, however, as thousands of government public relations specialists work under titles such as "public affairs," "public information," "communications," "constituent relations," and "legislative liaison."

In many corporate public relations departments, the public affairs section attends to public policy and "corporate citizenship": political education for employees, civic volunteer service by employees and managers, and active participation in community development. Corporate public affairs specialists serve as liaisons with governmental units; implement community improvement programs; encourage political activism, campaign contributions, and voting; and volunteer their services in charitable and community development organizations (see Figure 1–3). Many public relations counseling firms use the public affairs label to identify their lobbying and governmental relations departments.

Motivation for the growing interest in public affairs is recognition of the power of grassroots movements and increasingly independent local politicians. Another reason for the renaissance of public affairs in the 1990s is that many corporate managers are more sensitive to public opinion and public policy related to the environment and social equity, in part because they were in school during the activist-dominated 1960s and 1970s.[9]

Confusion between public affairs and public relations exists because some organizations use the terms interchangeably to represent the larger public relations concept. In these organizations, management views public affairs as a more acceptable title for the public relations function. In other organizations, public affairs represents a specialized part of public relations. Even in these organizations, however, only 43 percent use public affairs as the title for this specialized department, with others using the titles corporate affairs and external affairs.[10]

Our definition establishes public affairs as a part of the public relations function:

Public affairs is the specialized part of public relations that builds and maintains mutually beneficial governmental and local community relations.

Public Affairs Job Description

Public Affairs Managers

Times Mirror Cable Television, one of the largest multi-cable systems in the nation, has maintained its commitment to bring quality entertainment and services to the marketplace. This continued demand for excellence coupled with new growth has created 3 additional openings for Public Affairs Managers.

The successful candidates will work with field management to develop and implement broad-based public affairs programs at subsidiary cable TV systems nationwide. Other responsibilities will include insuring franchise compliance, producing press releases and other media, developing and implementing strategies to resolve regulatory problems, and conducting a community relations program. In addition, to be effective in this position, it is crucial that applicants are willing to work in a staff support role.

For this position, we are seeking public policy-oriented individuals with a BA degree and a minimum of 5 years direct hands-on experience in at least 2 of the following: government relations, public relations, community affairs or the cable industry. Grad work and/or a law degree would be a definite plus. Other requirements include: strong oral and written communications skills as well as knowledge of local government and/or public sector regulatory functions.

We are a subsidiary of The Times Mirror Company and offer an attractive compensation and benefits package including free dental insurance and a company paid pension plan. If you are a talented, assertive and skilled professional, we encourage you to explore our career opportunities. For immediate consideration, please send your resume and salary requirements to the **Human Resources Department, Times Mirror Cable Television, P.O. Box 19398, Irvine, CA 92713. (No phone calls please.)**

TIMES MIRROR
CABLE TELEVISION

We are an equal opportunity employer and encourage women and minorities to apply.

Figure 1–3   Courtesy Times Mirror Cable Television

Issues Management

By the mid-1970s, corporations had engaged public relations specialists to identify emerging public policy issues and to develop corporate responses. The process became known as "issues management." Rather than waiting until issues reach the legislative or regulatory stages of the public policy formation process, this process emphasizes an active role in formulating public policies. Two elements capture the essence of the concept of issues management: (1) early identification of issues with potential impact on the organization and (2) a strategic response designed to mitigate or capitalize on their consequences.[11]

> Issues management is the proactive process of anticipating, identifying, evaluating, and responding to public policy issues that affect organizations and their publics.

Because issues management operates in areas of public policy, it is part of public affairs, which in turn is part of the larger public relations function. As originally introduced by public relations consultant W. Howard Chase, issues management includes identifying issues, analyzing issues, setting priorities, selecting program strategies, implementing programs of action and communication, and evaluating effectiveness. He says the process "aligns corporate principles, policies and practices to the realities of a politicized economy."[12]

Even though issues management has been held out as a new approach that gives practitioners new status, many practitioners do not see it as different from what they already do. Others express concern that the term suggests something most unlikely—that an organization can "manage" a major public issue—and unacceptable because it sets up visions of manipulation. One definition in the literature suggests such powers, saying that issues management

> seeks to identify potential or emerging issues (legislative, regulatory, political, or social) that may impact the organization, and then mobilizes and coordinates organizational resources to strategically influence the development of those issues. The ultimate goal of issues management should be to shape public policy to the benefit of the organization.[13]

Many major corporations, however, have created issues management units, or "task forces," either by establishing specialized sections or by renaming existing sections of the public relations department. They concern themselves with how to respond to public concerns about biotechnology (genetic engineering), damage to the ozone layer (greenhouse effect), offshore oil drilling, toxic waste disposal, health care costs, maternity and paternity leaves, day care, an aging population, and corporate support for education. They build coalitions with other interested parties, accelerate issues of opportunity, eliminate or redirect potential threats, and make internal adjustments to manage change. As Manville Corporation Vice President of Corporate Relations Donald Ferguson puts it, "Dealing with this year's issue is good public relations. The future is issues management."

Conceptually, if not always administratively, issues management is part of the public relations function. When viewed merely as persuasive communication to influence public policy, however, it becomes part of *tactical decision making*, not part of an organization's *strategic planning*. When concerned with adjusting the organization and building relationships with stakeholders to achieve mutual goals, it makes public relations part of management.[14]

Lobbying

An even more specialized part of public affairs, lobbying, attempts to influence legislative and regulatory decisions in government. Even though the U.S. Constitution protects the right to petition the government, some view lobbying as an attempt to manipulate government for selfish ends. Movies and television shows depicting smoke-filled rooms and payoffs by lobbyists working for powerful corporate and special interests perpetuate the cynical view of lobbying. News stories sometimes report unmarked envelopes stuffed with cash, lavish parties, and weekend outings designed to corrupt the democratic process or competitive forces in free enterprise.

Federal and state laws open most lobbying to public scrutiny by requiring those whose principal activity is petitioning the government to register and to report income sources and expenses. Registration laws and their enforcement vary a great deal from state to state. In spite of occasional abuse and public rebuke, lobbying remains a legal and accepted way for citizen groups, associations, labor unions, corporations, and other public and special-interest groups to influence government decision making.

> Lobbying is the specialized part of public relations that builds and maintains relations with government primarily for the purpose of influencing legislation and regulation.

You see the term used primarily in Washington, D.C., and state capitals. Similar efforts at county and municipal levels often are part of and undifferentiated from public affairs, community relations, or other public relations efforts.

Lobbyists at all levels of government must understand legislative process, know how government functions, and be acquainted with individual lawmakers and officials. Because such topics are not part of many public relations practitioners' educational preparation or work experience, lobbying often gets delegated to well-connected lawyers and professional lobbyists (typically ex-legislators and political insiders).

The number of lobbyists has increased dramatically in recent years. For example, between 1975 and 1990, the number of lobbyists registered with the U.S. Senate increased from about 3000 to more than

33,000. About three of every four companies with sales of $100 million or more have staffs engaged in lobbying. One publication lists more than 14,000 people and firms who represent 12,500 domestic and foreign businesses, trade associations, unions, and other advocacy groups.[15]

Because lobbying deals with relations with government, it is conceptually part of the public relations function of an organization. In practice, lobbying must be closely coordinated with other public relations efforts directed to nongovernmental publics. Sophisticated communication attempts to mobilize like-minded constituents so that their voices are heard by lawmakers and officials in government. Computerized mailing lists, software for individualizing letters, and fast high-quality printers make possible direct mail programs that can produce a flood of mail, phone calls, and personal visits from constituents. Lobbying becomes "grassroots lobbying," getting the folks back home to take up the cause.

EXHIBIT 1-2

Lobbyists

"I personally believe lobbyists have a very useful role. If you want to find out the real information, if you want a breadth of opinion, call the lobbyists who are for it and the lobbyists against it. You'll get an education in a hurry. They'll give you all the best arguments on both sides. I think the system works."

Senator James A. McClure, Republican of Idaho, quoted by Bernard Asbell in *The Senate Nobody Knows* (Baltimore: The Johns Hopkins University Press, 1978), p. 198.

In its primary roles as credible advocate and reliable source of information, lobbying takes the form of information designed to persuade (see Exhibit 1–2). Lobbyists succeed or fail in part based on their traditional public relations skills: their abilities to construct and present convincing communications to both government officials and to grassroots constituents. In addition to those abilities, a sophisticated knowledge of government, legislative process, public policy, and public opinion processes is needed. As one Washington, D.C., public relations specialist said, "Yesteryear's lobbyist—with a large bankroll and a promise of frolicsome times for appreciative legislators—wouldn't recognize today's professional."[16]

Lobbying is an outgrowth of our democratic system functioning in a pluralistic society, keeping government open to those affected by proposed legislation and government regulation. However, the money and power of special interests sometimes pose a serious threat to the integrity of the governmental process and to the larger public good. Laws cannot stop everyone who is determined to abuse or corrupt the right that all citizens have to participate in government.

Investor Relations

Also referred to as financial relations, investor relations is another specialized part of the larger public relations function in many publicly held corporations. "IR" specialists work to enhance the value of a company's stock and to reduce the cost of capital by increasing shareholder confidence and making the stock attractive to individual investors, financial analysts, and institutional investors.

Investor relations is the specialized part of corporate public relations that builds and maintains mutually beneficial relationships with shareholders and others in the financial community.

The investor relations practitioner keeps shareholders informed and loyal to the company so as to maintain a fair valuation on the company's securities. Here is an example of how it might work to benefit both the company and investors:

A new biotechnology company has 10 million shares outstanding and each share sells for $20. The company has a market value of $200 million. Let's assume that the stock becomes more attractive to institutional investors, financial analysts, and individual investors as they learn more about the company, its management, and plans. If the price moves to $25 a share, the market value of the company is $250 million! Now assume that the company needs $10 million to support expansion or research on promising new products. At $25 a share, it needs to issue only 400,000 new shares, versus 500,000 shares at $20, to raise the $10 million to finance the expansion or research. Not only are investors' holdings worth more, but it takes fewer shares to raise additional capital.

On the other hand, imagine what happens to the value of investments and the cost of new capital after a corporation loses shareholder confidence, fails to respond to analysts' concerns about the latest quarterly earnings report, or receives negative coverage in the financial press. The potential impact on the market value and cost of new capital for large corporations amounts to millions, even billions, of dollars.[17]

Investor relations specialists must know corporate finance, accounting, Wall Street, international equities trading (the Tokyo Stock Exchange is the world's largest), international business trends, the Securities Exchange Commission and stock exchange financial reporting requirements, business journalism, and much more. And in our global economy, it helps to know several languages, to be widely traveled, and to have studied the rapidly changing international political scene. Because of such expertise, investor relations specialists are highly paid.

Development

If investor relations is critical for financing publicly held corporations, then fund-raising and membership drives are equally vital to health, educational, political, special-interest, art, theater, and other private nonprofit organizations. The term frequently used to identify this aspect of public relations is "development." Many hospitals, museums, zoos, symphony orchestras, and universities have a "director of development." Groups that rely more on memberships for their revenues—professional societies, unions, trade associations, and citizen action groups—might have a "director of member services and development."

> Development is the specialized part of public relations in private nonprofit organizations that builds and maintains relationships with donors and members for the purposes of securing financial and volunteer support.

Development specialists work for public broadcasting stations, disease prevention and research foundations, community arts groups, youth clubs, and religious organizations. Because these groups depend on donations, membership fees, or a combination of the two, they rely heavily on annual campaigns and special events to call attention to their needs and to solicit public support and contributions.

An annual telethon, 10-K run, open house, homecoming, or celebrity auction, however, represents only a small portion of a year-long program designed to establish and maintain relationships with volunteers, alumni, members, donors, and prospects. Fund-raising activities and membership services make up part of an overall program to build and maintain relationships with various publics. This makes development a significant part of the larger management function—public relations—in nonprofit organizations.

The terms discussed in the preceding sections all deal with an organization's relationships with specific groups or publics. They are all parts of the broader function known as public relations. Some organizations split the function based on *internal* and *external* publics. *Internal relations* staff deals with publics concerned about or involved in the internal workings of the organization, such as employees, families of employees, and volunteers. Relations with publics outside the organization—neighbors, consumers, environmentalists, investors, and so forth—are the responsibility of *external relations*.

Title confusion is further complicated when the total function is given one of many other labels such as *corporate relations, university relations, hospital relations, public information*, or *corporate communications*. By whatever name, the basic concept and function of public relations are similar from one organization to the next—large or small, local or global—as all effective organizations identify, establish, and maintain relationships important to survival and growth. In practice, however, too often employers and clients narrowly or wrongly define public relations by the various tasks they assign to it. In one organization, public relations takes the form of candid, open communication with many publics. In another, it attempts to maintain a silent, low profile. In one organization the purpose can be to provoke controversy and to maintain an adversarial relationship that motivates and activates members. In yet another, the intent may be to reconcile or compromise with an important public, as between management and a labor union.

Likewise, practitioners define public relations every day by the limits of what they are qualified to do and by what they call "public relations." For example, many think of public relations as product publicity, because that is what they are paid to do under the rubric of public relations. Others see it as "getting ink" or exposure in the mass media, because that is their experience with former journalists now claiming to be public relations practitioners.

Concerned citizens see frequent references to "PR," "public relations," and "flacks" in press coverage of oil spills, industrial toxic waste leaks, legislative or regulatory inactivity, city hall corruption, and so forth. Media coverage seldom associates public relations with positive stories of organizations and their accomplishments.

In short, *most people know public relations by what they see organizations and practitioners do, or are reported to have done, in the name of public relations*. Few study the concept itself or the roles public relations plays in organizations and society. The challenge to practitioners is to perform public relations consistent with the contemporary definition of this vital organizational and social function.

TOWARD RECOGNITION AND MATURITY

Some scholars credit public relations for the heightened attention to public accountability and social responsibility among government administrators and business executives. Other scholars point to the function's role in making organizations responsive to public interests and its contribution to the public information system so essential to democratic society.

Public relations deserves credit for establishing and sustaining the connection between public support and top management's heightened attention to social responsibilities and to leadership in personal standards of behavior. As one business leader long ago said, "We know perfectly well that business does not function by divine right, but, like any other part of society, exists with the sanction of the community as a whole. . . . Today's public opinion, though it may appear as light as air, may become tomorrow's legislation for better or worse."[18]

Public relations also helps organizations anticipate and respond to public perceptions and opinions, new values and lifestyles, power shifts among the electorate and within legislative bodies, and other changes in the environment. This contributes to making the democratic process—as well as the social, economic, and political systems—more effective in meeting social needs. Without the public relations function, organizations tend to become insensitive to changes occurring around them and become dysfunctional as they get further and further out of step with their environments.

Another social utility of public relations is making information available. Practitioners increase public knowledge and understanding by promoting expression and competition in the marketplace of ideas regarding, for example, the causes of ozone depletion, the impact of international trade barriers, or the need for blood donations and disaster relief. They serve the public interest by providing a voice in the public forum for every point of view, including the views of those, such as the homeless, that would not otherwise be heard because of limited media attention.

The practice serves society by mediating conflict and by building relationships essential to the dynamic consensus needed to maintain social order. Its social function—its mission—is served when it replaces ignorance, coercion, and intransigence with knowledge, compromise, and adjustment. In other words:

> Public relations facilitates adjustment and maintenance in the social systems that provide us with our physical and social needs.

In the final analysis, an organization's relationships are the responsibility of top management. Henry DeVries, vice president of public relations at Independent Order of Foresters mutual insurance company, rephrased our definition in more down-to-earth words: "Public relations is the boss's job to build and keep strong bonds with key groups that the organization needs to grow and thrive." Once this type of thinking is embraced at the top, it spreads and becomes part of an organization's culture.

Those professionally engaged in helping organizations establish and maintain mutually beneficial relationships perform an essential management function that has impact on the larger society. The social responsibility of organizations motivates top managers' increasing interest in the function and a general growing recognition of the essential nature of public relations in maintaining social order. *Inherent in the function is a moral thrust toward harmonious adjustment among interdependent elements of society.*

Even though the policies and activities of employers, clients, and practitioners often define the day-to-day practice, the evolution of the concept and the professional calling reflects changing needs of the larger society. In its advanced form, the function responds to long-term social needs, not to immediate special interests while ignoring negative side effects or consequences for society. As practitioners accept this social responsibility and act accordingly, others will understand and value public relations' contributions to organizations and society.

EXHIBIT 1-3

The Role of Public Relations in Johnson & Johnson's Tylenol Crisis

Courtesy Lawrence G. Foster and reprinted with permission from *Public Relations Journal.*

The public relations decisions related to the Tylenol crisis and the product's strong comeback came in two phases.

Phase one was the crisis phase, which began . . . with the grim news of the cyanide poisonings. Since the extent of the contamination was not immediately known, there was grave concern for the safety of the estimated 100 million Americans who were using Tylenol. The first critical public relations decisions, taken immediately and with total support from company management, was to cooperate fully with the news media. The press was key to warning the public of the danger.

Later it was realized that no meeting had been called to make that critical decision. The poisonings called for immediate action to protect the consumer, and there wasn't the slightest hesitation about being completely open with the news media. For the same reasons the decision was made to recall two batches of the product, and later withdraw it nationally. During the crisis phase of the Tylenol tragedy, virtually every public relations decision was based on sound, socially responsible business principles, which is when public relations is most effective.

Almost immediately, planning began for phase two, the comeback, and this involved a more detailed and extensive public relations effort that closely followed important marketing decisions and reached out to many audiences. The comeback began officially with a 30-city video press conference via satellite, an innovative approach suggested by Burson-Marsteller, a public relations agency responsible for Tylenol product publicity.

The video conference and all other key decisions were discussed and debated by a seven-member strategy committee formed by Chairman and CEO James E. Burke to deal with the Tylenol crisis. The committee included a public relations executive and met twice daily for six weeks. The decisions it made dealt with every aspect of the problem—from packaging to advertising to appearances on network television. Many required follow-up by the public relations staff at corporate and McNeil Consumer Products Company—the subsidiary that manufacturers Tylenol.

The Tylenol tragedy proved once again that public relations is a business of basics, and that the best public relations decisions are closely linked to sound business practices and a responsible corporate philosophy.

Lawrence G. Foster
Corporate Vice President-Public Relations (retired)
Johnson & Johnson

ADDITIONAL READING

Brody, E. W. "The Domain of Public Relations." *Public Relations Review* 18, no. 4 (Winter 1992): 349–64. Advances impact-oriented concept of public relations over traditional message-delivery model.

Center, Allen H., and Patrick Jackson. *Public Relations Practices: Managerial Case Studies and Problems*, 4th ed. Englewood Cliffs, N.J.: Prentice-Hall, Inc., 1990. Collection of classic case studies illustrating problems and opportunities in managing public relations.

Coates, Joseph F., Vary T. Coates, Jennifer Jarratt, and Lisa Heinz. *Issues Management: How You Can Plan, Organize and Manage for the Future*. Mt. Airy, Md.: Lomond Publications, Inc., 1986. Quick read on concepts, processes, techniques, and methods of issues management as "futures research."

Cutlip, Scott M. *Fund Raising in the United States*. New Brunswick, N.J.: Transaction Publishers, 1990. Reprinting of definitive study of fund raising and its role in American philanthropy. New preface and introduction add current perspective.

Grunig, James E., ed. *Excellence in Public Relations and Communication Management*. Hillsdale, N.J.: Lawrence Erlbaum Associates, Publishers, 1992. Summary of public relations theory and research literature as part of International Association of Business Communicators (IABC) Research Foundation project.

Grunig, James E.., and Larissa A. Grunig. "Conceptual Differences in Public Relations and Marketing: The Case of Health-Care Organizations." *Public Relations Review* 17, no. 3 (Fall 1991): 257–78.

Grunig, James E. and Todd Hunt. *Managing Public Relations*, 2d ed. New York: Holt, Rinehart and Winston, forthcoming.

Hiebert, Ray Eldon, ed. *Precision Public Relations*. New York: Longman, Inc., 1988. Collection of articles describing theory and practice.

Newsom, Doug, Alan Scott, and Judy VanSlyke Turk. *This Is PR: The Realities of Public Relations*, 5th ed. Belmont, Calif.: Wadsworth Publishing Co., 1993. One of several useful introductions to the field.

Seitel, Fraser P. *The Practice of Public Relations*, 5th ed. New York: Macmillan Publishing Company, 1992. Another introductory text written by a former public relations executive at Chase Manhattan Bank.

Sharpe, Melvin L., and Sam Black, eds. "Special Issue: International Public Relations" *Public Relations Review* 18, no. 2 (Summer 1992). Eleven articles on the impact of global change on public relations practice.

Toth, Elizabeth L., and Robert L. Heath, eds. *Rhetorical and Critical Approaches to Public Relations*. Hillsdale, N.J.: Lawrence Erlbaum Associates, Publishers, 1992. Discussion of public relations as rhetorical dialogue and of critical theorists' methods for assessing public relations.

White, Jon. *How to Understand and Manage Public Relations*. London: Business Books Limited, 1991. A British scholar's jargon-free guide for managers.

Wilcox, Dennis L., Phillip H. Ault, and Warren K. Agee. *Public Relations Strategies and Tactics*, 3d ed. New York: Harper and Row, 1992. Yet another introductory text.

Witenberg, Ernest, and Elisabeth Witenberg. *How to Win in Washington: Very Practical Advice about Lobbying, the Grassroots, and the Media*. Cambridge, Mass.: Basil Blackwell Inc., 1989. Washington consultants discuss role of lobbying and grassroots constituencies in issues management.

NOTES

[1]James E. Grunig and Todd Hunt, *Managing Public Relations* (New York: Holt, Rinehart and Winston, 1984), 6.

[2]Harwood L. Childs, *An Introduction to Public Opinion* (New York: John Wiley and Sons, Inc., 1940), 3 and 13.

[3]Rex F. Harlow, "Building a Public Relations Definition," *Public Relations Review* 2, no. 4 (Winter 1976): 36.

[4]Thomas L. Harris, *The Marketer's Guide to Public Relations* (New York: John Wiley and Sons, Inc., 1991). Examples on the first page of the first chapter illustrate the use of publicity and other sales promotion activities in marketing. It is not a book about public relations. Rather it describes how public relations practitioners apply their understanding and skills in the marketing function.

[5]Philip Kotler, *Marketing Management*, 6th ed. (Englewood Cliffs, N.J.: Prentice-Hall, Inc., 1988), 3–9.

[6]Glen M. Broom and Kerry Tucker, "An Essential Double Helix," *Public Relations Journal* 45, no. 11 (November 1989): 39. See also Glen M. Broom, Martha M. Lauzen, and Kerry Tucker, "Public Relations and Marketing: Dividing the Conceptual Domain and Operational Turf," *Public Relations Review* 17, no. 3 (Fall 1991): 219–25.

[7]Gerri L. Smith and Robert L. Heath, "Moral Appeals in Mobil Oil's Op-Ed Campaign," *Public Relations Review* 16, no. 4 (Winter 1990): 48–54.

[8] Henry C. Rogers, *Walking the Tightrope: The Private Confessions of a Public Relations Man* (New York: William Morrow and Company, Inc., 1980), 14.

[9]Lloyd B. Dennis, "Public Affairs: Deja Vu All Over Again," *Public Relations Journal* 46, no. 4 (April 1990): 14–17.

[10]*The State of Corporate Public Affairs* (Washington, D.C.: Foundation for Public Affairs, 1992). Report of national survey of 163 senior public affairs executives.

[11]A useful survey of major corporations' definitions of issues management appears in Brad Hainsworth and Max Meng, "How Corporations Define Issues Management," *Public Relations Review* 14, no. 4 (Winter 1988): 18–30.

[12]W. Howard Chase, "Public Issue Management: The New Science," *Public Relations Journal* 33, no. 10 (October 1977): 25–26.

[13]Brad Hainsworth and Max Meng, "How Corporations Define Issue Management," *Public Relations Review* 14, no. 4 (Winter 1988): 28–29.

[14]For the theoretical basis of issues management, see Robert L. Heath, "Corporate Issues Management: Theoretical Underpinnings and Research Foundation," *Public Relations Research Annual* 2 (1990): 29–65.

[15]*Washington Representatives*, 15th ed. (Washington, D.C.: Columbia Books, 1991).

[16]From an article by Peter Hannaford, "Lobbyists Go Legit," in *PR Week* 34 (October 24–30, 1988): 8. (*PR Week* is no longer published in the United States.)

[17]For detailed analysis of investor relations program impact on stock prices, see Kenneth A. Saban, "Demasking Wall Street's Influence on Stock Prices," *Public Relations Review* 13, no. 3 (Fall 1987): 3–11.

[18]Quote from former General Electric Company President Ralph J. Cordiner, as reported in Scott M. Cutlip and Allen H. Center, *Effective Public Relations*, 2d ed. (Englewood Cliffs, N.J.: Prentice-Hall, Inc., 1958), 6.

Practitioners of Public Relations

The way to gain a good reputation is to endeavor to be what you desire to appear.

SOCRATES

This chapter discusses the number of public relations practitioners, who they are, what they do, the roles they play, and their professional aspirations. Compared with accounting, law, medicine, nursing, and other more established professions, the relatively young practice of *public relations is an emerging profession.* Unlike the more established professions, public relations does not yet require a prescribed educational preparation, government-sanctioned qualifying exams, and peer review to assure competent and ethical practice. Nor do its practitioners operate in clearly defined roles recognized widely as essential for the common good. And because there are no complete official lists, estimates of who and how many practice public relations are based on membership data from the major professional societies and statistics from the U.S. Department of Labor.

NUMBER AND DISTRIBUTION

The number of practitioners continues to increase as organizational, social, economic, and political forces change the role and stature of the function worldwide. For example, the 1991 edition of *Reed's Worldwide Directory of Public Relations Organizations* reports that approximately 150,000 *members* belong to 215 public relations associations, societies, clubs, and other groups worldwide.

Different organizational titles and job descriptions, however, make accurate counts impractical even within the United States. As pointed out in Chapter 1, what one organization calls "marketing communication" may actually describe a public relations position. What another organization calls a "public relations representative" would be more accurately titled "sales" or "customer service representative." Little agreement on the underlying concept and inconsistent use of titles complicate attempts to determine the size and scope of the field.

The U.S. Department of Labor reports public relations employment statistics in its monthly *Employment and Earnings* under the occupational headings "Managers: marketing, advertising and public relations" and "Public relations specialists." These categories do not include all who work in the field, however. For example, artists, graphic designers, photographers, lobbyists, and researchers working in public relations departments and firms may be counted in other work categories. As a result, the department's figures probably include half or less of those working in public relations. Public relations managers are combined with other managers, so separate counts are not available. Even though the data are incomplete, Table 2–1 clearly illustrates the rapid growth of public relations.

TABLE 2–1

PUBLIC RELATIONS EMPLOYMENT TREND	
Year	Number of "Public Relations Specialists"[a]
1950	19,000
1960	31,000
1970	76,000
1980	126,000
1990	162,000
2000 projected[b]	197,000

[a]U.S. Department of Labor Category and statistics from *Employment and Earnings* reports.
[b]Projected total computed using linear regression model.

WHERE THEY WORK

Employment opportunities for public relations specialists exist in almost every community but are concentrated in major population centers. For example, the greatest numbers of PRSA members are in California, New York, Texas, Ohio, Michigan, Pennsylvania, and Illinois. New York has the largest Public Relations Society of America (PRSA) chapter with almost 800 members. Washington, D.C., is second with almost 550. The Chicago and Atlanta chapters each have more than 500 members.

About half (52 percent) work in business and commercial corporations: financial, consumer goods, utilities, manufacturing, and industrial; 20 percent in public relations firms, advertising agencies, and individual consultancies; 10 percent in associations, foundations, and educational institutions; 8 percent in health care: hospitals, medical agencies, and other health services; 5 percent in government: federal, state, and local; and 5 percent in charitable, religious, and other not-for-profit organizations (see Table 2–2).[1]

TABLE 2–2	TYPES OF PUBLIC RELATIONS EMPLOYERS	

Organizations	Estimated Percent of Practitioners[a]
Corporations: manufacturing, industrial, consumer goods, financial, insurance media, and entertainment	52
Public relations firms, advertising agencies, and individual practitioners	20
Associations, foundations, and educational institutions	10
Health care: hospitals, clinics, home health care agencies, and mental health facilities	8
Government: local, state, and federal	5
Charitable, religious, and social welfare organizations	5

[a]Composite profile from surveys of professionals by PRSA, IABC, and newsletters serving the field.

The single largest employer for public relations is the federal government. According to the U.S. Office of Personnel Management, almost 3300 "public affairs" specialists work under various titles. The total jumps to almost 22,000 in the "information and arts" category, however, when the count includes photographers, writers and editors (not including technical writers and editors), visual information specialists, and others working in public communication for the government.[2] Presumably, this figure includes the 8566 persons working for the U.S. Information Agency: 4215 in the United States and 4351 abroad.[3] However, because the function is often camouflaged to hide it from Congress and the press, no reliable figures on the number of public relations specialists in government are available.

The growing number of public relations firms range in size from an independent counselor (who may use "and Associates") to the large national and international firms with staffs of hundreds. For example, Burson-Marsteller, although third in net fees worldwide, has more than 2500 employees. The two largest public relations firms—Shandwick and Hill and Knowlton, Inc.—each employ about 2000. Shandwick employs more than 500 in its London headquarters office alone. Hill and Knowlton and Burson-Marsteller, with offices worldwide, both have headquarters in New York. Burson-Marsteller has almost 500 employees in New York, 150 in Washington, D.C., and 120 in Chicago. Hill and Knowlton employs more than 400 in New York, 280 in Washington, D.C., and 110 in Chicago. Fleishman-Hillard, an international firm based in St. Louis, employs 225 in its headquarters office. The largest firm in Los Angeles—Rogers and Cowan of Shandwick—employs almost 100.[4]

Several major corporations have 100 or more public relations specialists in headquarters and branch offices. "Downsizing" in the late 1980s and early 1990s greatly reduced the number of large staffs and shifted work to rapidly growing external firms. Practitioners work in global corporate headquarters, in headquarters of operating subsidiaries, and in branch offices around the globe. Survey results indicate, however, that more than half of all practitioners work in firms or departments with fewer than five public relations professionals.

EDUCATION AND PREPARATION

Ninety-five percent of practitioners are college graduates, including almost 25 percent with some postgraduate studies, almost 25 percent with master's degrees, and 2 percent with doctoral degrees. PRSA and International Association of Business Communicators (IABC) membership surveys show that practitioners entered the field from many academic majors and work experiences. Approximately 40 percent of both groups of practitioners majored in journalism, with news-editorial graduates outnumbering public relations graduates two to one. English, speech, communications, and business (in that order) follow journalism as college majors of those entering public relations.

Increasingly, employers look for specialized public relations degrees and advanced degrees emphasizing research and social science. Professional development programs stress updating skills and career planning. In addition to the more than 300 colleges and universities offering public relations undergraduate and graduate programs, PRSA, IABC, and other professional groups sponsor continuing education courses, institutes, seminars, and conferences.

Newspaper journalism experience is no longer required preparation for public relations employment. Some journalistic media experience, however, gives practitioners an understanding of media gatekeepers' values and ways of working. It also has a negative impact when the experience leads to a "journalist-in-residence" approach, making news dissemination the working definition of public relations practice. Twenty-eight percent of IABC members worked for newspapers, magazines, radio stations, or television stations before being hired in public relations. An equal number entered the profession immediately after graduating from college. Almost two thirds of PRSA members, who tend to be older and more experienced practitioners, worked in the media prior to their current career in public relations. As more and more employers and public relations managers change their "journalist-in-residence" definition of the practitioner's role, public relations students will find it easier to move directly into the field after graduation. Given the choice, however, most employers still value media experience even if it is only with the school newspaper.

Many employers also look for someone with education or experience in a specialized field in addition to public relations. About half of all practitioners worked in some "noncommunication" business before entering public relations. The most difficult positions to fill are those requiring specialized preparation and backgrounds such as health care, computer technology, corporate finance, and agriculture. For example, students who combine public relations education with a minor in health care or hospital administration have a clear advantage when applying for hospital public relations openings. Likewise, graduates who minored in computer science while completing their public relations education have a competitive advantage in the world of high-tech public relations.

THE NEW MAJORITY: WOMEN

According to U.S. Department of Labor statistics, in 1968 only 25 percent of those in the public relations occupational category were women. By the end of 1983, women held more than 50 percent of public relations jobs. In 1992, almost three of every five practitioners were women. The U.S. Department of Labor reported in January 1993 that 58.4 percent of "public relations specialists" were women.[5]

When the late Rea Smith wrote "Women in Public Relations: What They Have Achieved" in 1968, only one in ten members of PRSA was female.[6] The ratio was one in seven in 1975 when Sondra Gorney concluded that "the walls of the traditional 'man's world' have not tumbled yet."[7] Apparently, the walls had tumbled by 1990 when PRSA membership was 54 percent female and IABC membership 60 percent female.[8]

The trend toward an even greater proportion of women is reflected in statistics from public relations education. Surveys of colleges and universities indicate that there are two female students for every male student planning to enter the profession. In the late 1980s, 68 percent of students in public relations were women and 62 percent of those getting degrees from journalism and mass communication programs were female.[9]

SALARIES

Table 2–3 illustrates the range of practitioners' salaries. PRSA reports the highest salaries for industrial and manufacturing companies. *pr reporter* newsletter shows practitioners in the financial services sector as the highest paid, attributing the $75,000 median salary to "in-trouble industry" competition for top public relations counsel. Industrial companies, consulting firms (other than public relations), public relations firms, and utilities make up the other top-paying fields. IABC reports salaries by major product or service, showing that the highest paid practitioners worked in petroleum, automotive, metals and mining, communications utility, and aerospace companies.

Many experienced practitioners earn $100,000, $200,000, or more. They typically work for multibillion-dollar corporations where top public relations executives often are corporate officers, either elected or appointed. These officers typically receive stock options, bonus or profit-sharing checks, and lucrative retirement programs in addition to six-figure salaries. Fringe benefits and perquisites add considerable value to their positions. Employers do not frivolously dispense high salaries or extra benefits, however. Just as in other fields, employers must compete for top public relations professionals and managers. For example, when Time Warner, New York, hired a new senior vice president to head the public relations function, one newsletter reported a "compensation package in the hundreds of thousands." The competition for management-level talent is so intense that specialized search firms (sometimes called "head-hunters") are retained to identify, screen, and recruit finalists for top public relations positions.

Salaries tend to be highest in the Northeast and Middle Atlantic, led by New York and Washington, D.C. The West also pays relatively high salaries, with northern California's Silicon Valley leading that part of the country. Salaries in the Midwest and South are below the national median.

Salary survey results show a pay difference in public relations that deserves special attention: In 1989, IABC found a $12,000 gap between men and women's salaries in the United States. *pr reporter* newsletter survey results show an even greater pay disparity, $14,000. PRSA's 1993 salary survey put the gap at $18,935, with the difference tied to age and years of experience. For example, PRSA found that men younger than 35 are more likely to earn more than $45,000 than are women who are younger than 35 (28% versus 6%).

TABLE 2–3

SALARIES			
Type of Organization	PRSA Survey[a]	IABC Profile[b]	pr reporter Newsletter[c]
ALL RESPONDENTS	**$46,204** (Median)	**$40,300** (Median)	**$45,500** (Median)
Industrials/manufacturing	62,303		
Automotive		54,500	
Consumer Products			48,750
Industrials			57,900
Metals/Mining		51,800	
Manufacturing		40,100	
Petroleum		58,900	
Public relations firms	53,728	39,600	55,000
Utilities	52,672		53,000
Communications utility		49,500	
Financial/insurance	49,602		
Banks			42,000
Insurance		36,500	
Media/communications	49,473		
Telecommunications			42,850
Scientific/technical	44,351		
Computer technology		42,300	
Government	44,019	35,500	
Federal			45,000
State			43,650
Local			42,000
Associations/foundations	43,388		45,000
Transportation/hotel/ resorts/entertainment	41,843		
Travel/tourism			36,000
Health care	41,550		
Medical/hospital		34,500	
Health care hospital			41,000
Health care—other			46,250
Advertising agency	41,066		42,000
Education	41,008	34,000	42,600
Religious/charitable	35,545		
Non-profit		33,800	
Social/non-profit			32,000

[a]"Salary Survey," *Public Relations Journal*, Vol. 49, No. 7 (July 1993), p. 13.
[b]*Profile '89* (San Francisco: International Association of Business Communicators and IABC Research Foundation, 1989)
[c]*pr reporter*, Vol 33, No. 39 (October 1, 1990)

Although 55 percent of all women in public relations older than 35 make more than $45,000, the comparable figure for men older than 35 is 82 percent.[10]

In a study that surveyed the same practitioners in 1979 and again in 1985, the salary gap worsened between surveys. The results show that women earn less than men even when they have equal education, professional experience, and tenure in their jobs. Over the 6-year period, men's annual raises averaged more than 9 percent, while women averaged less than 6 percent annually.[11] That disparity appears to have lessened in the 1990s, however, as both PRSA and IABC membership salary surveys show that more women than men receive raises and that women receive larger percentage raises than do men. Furthermore, a comparison of men's and women's salaries in 1979 with 1991 salaries shows the gap all but closed after removing the differences accounted for by years of experience and participation in management decision making in the manager role.[12]

WORK ASSIGNMENTS

One way to describe public relations work is to list the specialized parts of the function: media relations, investor relations, community relations, employee relations, government relations, and so forth. These labels do not describe the day-to-day work, however. Ten categories summarize the many and diverse work assignments in public relations:

1. **Writing and Editing:**   Composing print and broadcast news releases, feature stories, employee and external newsletters, correspondence, shareholder and annual reports, speeches, brochures, film and slide-show scripts, trade publication articles, institutional advertisements, and product and technical collateral materials.

2. **Media Relations and Placement:**   Contacting news media, magazines, Sunday supplements, freelance writers, and trade publications with the intent of getting them to publish or broadcast news and features about or originated by the organization. Responding to media requests for information, verification of stories, and access to authoritative sources.

3. **Research:**   Gathering information about public opinion, trends, emerging issues, political climate, media coverage, concerns of consumer and environmental special-interest groups, and so forth, to plan programs responsive to its publics and problem situations. Monitoring program implementation and assessing program impact to evaluate program effectiveness.

4. **Management and Administration:** Programming and planning in collaboration with other managers; determining needs, establishing priorities, defining publics, setting goals and objectives, and developing strategies. Administering personnel, budget, and program schedules.

5. **Counseling:** Advising top management on the social, political, and regulatory environments; consulting with the management team on how to respond to crises; and working with key decision makers to devise strategies for managing organizational responses to critical and sensitive issues.

6. **Special Events:** Arranging and managing news conferences, 10-K runs, conventions, open houses, ribbon cuttings and grand openings, anniversary celebrations, fund-raising events, visiting dignitaries, contests, award programs, and other special observances.

7. **Speaking:** Appearing before groups, coaching others for speaking assignments, and managing a speakers' bureau to provide platforms for the organization before important audiences.

8. **Production:** Creating communications using multimedia knowledge and skills, including art, typography, photography, layout, and computer desktop publishing; audio and video recording and editing; and preparing audiovisual presentations.

9. **Training:** Preparing executives and other designated spokespersons to deal with media and other public appearances. Helping introduce changes in organizational culture, policies, structure, and procedures.

10. **Contact:** Meeting, greeting, and hosting people important to the organization. Serving as the liaison with media, community, and stakeholder groups, both internal and external.

Although last on this list, being "good with people" is often the first thing many associate with public relations. This is true enough, as public relations people often find themselves dealing with sensitive people problems and relationships, but do not be misled by this commonly held stereotype of public relations work.

The mix of assignments and responsibilities varies greatly from organization to organization, but one task dominates as the common denominator: *writing.* (Study the job descriptions in Exhibit 2–1.) An ability to write remains a requirement throughout one's career. The typical workday logs of a corporate public affairs specialist, an assistant account executive, a public relations officer of a city, and a public affairs manager in federal government in Exhibits 2–2, 2–3, 2–4, and 2–5 illustrate the need for good writing skills.

Assignments vary across positions, departments, and organizations. Over time, however, individual practitioners develop strategies and approaches for doing their jobs. In other words, they assume *roles.*

EXHIBIT 2-1

Descriptions of Public Relations Jobs

- Managing the organization, development and coordination of print media relations policies/programs.
- Creating, developing and implementing management's opportunities to interface with print media.
- Advocating the corporation's viewpoints and emphasizing positive aspects of its positions.
- Preparing appropriate corporate responses to the media as required.
- Providing assistance in formulating, writing and/or editing articles for the general news media and/or trade press.

PUBLIC RELATIONS SPECIALISTS

Position open

Communication assistant to help with all facets of employee communication, pr, including 8-page tabloid. Should have layout, writing, design experience. Nationally known, North Carolina-based textile company, plants in four southern states. Excellent salary, benefits. Send resume, work

Director Of University Relations

The director oversees all activities of the department in areas of internal and external communications, campus events and community and media relations. The director also works closely with the university's central administration, making recommendations on university communications efforts and on the university's response to situations affecting public opinion and support.

Public Relations Specialist

Experience in public relations activities (arranging promotional tours and book promotions; assisting in placement of radio and television programs; arranging press conferences; writing press releases, familiarity with public interest environ

You will act as a Public Relations Generalist, writing for special projects, banking trade publications, financial journals, news magazines, radio and TV media. You will also perform a wide variety of typical PR duties as well as planning and arranging special events and programs.

You will need a BA degree with 7-10 years' PR experience. This should encompass a strong communications background. Journalistic experience and demonstrated creative ability. Because the emphasis of this position is on leadership, you should have 5-7 years' public relations management experience with excellent communications and people skills. Candidate will bring to this highly-visible position the ability to implement PR programs from concept through all aspects of implementation...on time and within the

Hospital Public Relations

Positions Available

Position requires a strong public affairs orientation, a working knowledge of PAC administration, overall familiarity with current issues & solid research, oral & written communication skills. Diplomacy & the ability to handle high pressure situations is a must.

TOP-QUALITY WRITER

Large Southeastern corporation needs versatile, energetic, articulate writer, preferably with some speech-writing experience. Must have proven ability to explain complex subjects through easy-to-read, easy-to-cat tive with cap Ma req

Defense/Aerospace Public Relations Specialist

We need a public relations professional with at least 3-5 years of direct experience handling publicity and related PR activities in defense, aerospace or high technology industries. Must be able to write feature articles for technical (trade) journals as well as news releases. Should have media contacts within the technical markets mentioned above. U.S. Citizenship and degree in journalism or English required.

This perso public rela including p

Director of Public Relations

Established organization has need for director who is a competent writer, a photographer, and experienced in public service, foundation or corporate public relations. Unique, challenging opportunity in an interesting dynamic position. Please send resume and history in strict confidence to:

PUBLIC RELATIONS FIELD REPRESENTATIVE

The desired candidate will have strong writing skills with a degree in Journalism or Public Relations, and a minimum of five years experience. Special events experience, beverage industry experience, and knowledge of local media are also desired.

MANAGER, CORPORATE COMMUNICATIONS

media company based has a unique opportunity. Business communications experience in writing, publications production. In corporate communications, including production of annual reports and news releases daily.

OR WRITER

Position requires 3-5 years experience in corporate or agency PR and/or high technology publishing. In addition, you must possess established business and technological press and media contacts, plus strong written and presentation skills.

If you're the accomplished, talented individual we seek, please forward your resume and salary history to:

Director of Employee Communications

You'll be responsible for all oral and written programs to ensure their effectiveness; keep management abreast of employee concerns, and employees informed of Company matters; assist top management with special communications projects as they arise; plus produce the Company's in-house publication.

Specific experience with in-house publications and in public speaking is important to this key position; previous Human Resources exposure would be an asset. BA or equivalent desired; MBA preferred.

EXHIBIT 2–2

Day in the Life of a Corporate Public Relations Officer

8:30   Review overnight faxes that arrived from Hong Kong and Tokyo offices. One from the Hong Kong corporate affairs officer requests more details on the freelance photographer we sent to Southeast Asia to get photos for a number of articles we're commissioning for the corporate external magazine.

9:10   Write note to all executive directors regarding events and entertainment in conjunction with International Telecommunications Union in Geneva. (Our office is organizing the construction and management of a two-tiered stand at this exhibition of worldwide telecommunications held every 4 years.)

10:00   Attend weekly managers meeting of corporate affairs department. Discuss events of the coming week and staff's current projects.

11:15   Marketing executive from our Europe region drops by to tell me about meeting she attended last week in Germany. She relayed to me some questions our German office had about the new customer magazine. Called the public relations executive there to discuss these issues and set up a meeting when he next visits headquarters.

12:30   Lunch in company cafeteria with corporate affairs colleagues, discussing implications of management structure changes we learned about in this morning's meeting. Press release will be issued tomorrow because the changes could affect international mobile telephony and the company's strategy for handling this growing part of our business.

2:00   Received call from our Washington office saying that they will fax me the final changes on the article for our external magazine we have been jointly writing for the last 5 weeks.

2:30   Attend meeting with our employee magazine editor and independent research company representative to discuss possible readership survey. Discuss numbers for the pilot survey and methods of interviewing readers in the Caribbean and Hong Kong areas.

4:20   Receive call from marketing executive in Dublin office. He needs advice on corporate identity design for their new company vehicles. Agreed to have artwork prepared by our corporate identity design team.

5:15   Write and send fax to Hong Kong corporate affairs officer giving details of our photographer's objectives. Thank him for giving photographer guided tour of our new transponder facility and ask him for local hotel recommendations for photographer.

5:30   Tuck weekly PR and advertising trade magazine in briefcase to read on train ride home.

Marilyn Kendall, Corporate Affairs Officer
Corporate Affairs Department
Cable and Wireless
London, England

EXHIBIT 2–3

Day in the Life of an Assistant Account Executive

8:00   Check mail and phone messages. Return calls and start time sheet to record billable hours of day's activities.

8:10   Call print and broadcast media to announce news conference with Governor Ann Richards and client. (Client is sponsoring new literacy program.)

9:30   Take call from client requesting proposal for promotional publicity. Meet with account supervisor to discuss objectives, strategies, and media hook.

10:30	Receive news release writing assignment from account supervisor. Determine audience and objectives, then write draft of release, including quotes from client. Get account supervisor's approval and fax release to client for review, changes, and approval.
12:15	Go to lunch and brainstorming session with account team to exchange ideas for planned client product promotion.
1:15	Read two newspapers from client's community to identify possible tie-ins for new projects. Call staff writer to get more information about item in "Health Watch" column related to client's product.
2:30	Log morning activities on time sheet.
2:45	Call public relations director at recycling company (client's partner) to confirm approved use of artwork in client's direct mail piece. Receive approval and fill out work order for creative section.
3:15	Write news media advisory announcing client's sponsorship of Boys Choir of Harlem. Prepare media list for account supervisor's approval.
4:15	Meet with potential printing vendor. Get assignment to introduce vendor's ideas and strategies to client in a letter. Write first draft of letter for account supervisor's review.
5:05	Try again to reach print media and broadcast media contacts about the literacy program news conference with Governor Richards.
5:15	Log afternoon activities on time sheet and write "to do" list for next day.

Donna Chandler, Assistant Account Executive
Tracy-Locke / Pharr Public Relations
Dallas, Texas

EXHIBIT 2–4

Day in the Life of a City Public Relations Director

8:15	Scan morning newspapers for items related to city, including local, state, and real-estate sections; op-ed page; and letters to the editor.
8:45	Check electronic mail and in-box for messages. Sign purchase requisitions for office supplies. Route items of interest to other staff.

9:00   Attend city manager's staff meeting. Point out potential public relations implications of issues on agenda for next city council meeting. Review possible topics for next monthly lunch meeting with city hall reporters.

9:45   Meeting (impromptu) with assistant planning director who is about to be interviewed by TV reporter about new billboard ordinance. Outline basic advice for how to handle interview.

10:00   Called department staff together to begin planning next month's "Chesapeake Magazine" television program. List potential segments: Seat Belt Awareness Month, city's curbside recycling program, award-winning high-school cheerleaders, and lifelong resident who restores antique player pianos.

10:45   Review two news release drafts written by staff. One announces new assistant economic development director and the other warns that next week's planned road repairs will slow traffic on a major thoroughfare. Suggest minor revisions and ask that road repair costs be included.

11:00   Return phone calls: (1) citizen complaining that funds for city newsletter would be better spent hiring more school-teachers, (2) recreation department requesting help with brochure, (3) salesperson offering coffee mugs imprinted with city logo, and (4) city manager asking me to represent him at a Thursday night reception welcoming new commander of the Navy's Atlantic fleet (need to present gift and make brief comments on behalf of the city).

11:30   Drive to city's cable television studio to anchor weekly "Newsbreak" program. Record program for cablecast prior to tonight's televised city council meeting.

12:15   Meet over lunch with local newspaper advertising representative. She wants help contacting city departments about placing ads in city anniversary tabloid insert.

1:15   Meet with staff to review bids for graphic design for public utilities department brochure featuring new water treatment and storage system. Decide to schedule interviews with two bidders with lowest prices.

1:45   Write memo for city manager's signature to update city council on status of customer service program.

2:15   Write summary of findings from recently completed survey of city residents. Will use report as the basis for updating city council on the public relations program during the upcoming budget process.

3:00   Make presentation to Chamber of Commerce board of directors on the survey of city residents. Use graphs generated on the computer desktop publishing system to relate findings to the business community.

4:30   Check in-box for afternoon mail and return phone calls: (1) police chief requesting publicity for junior high school antidrug forum, (2) public relations practitioner new to the area seeking leads on possible employment (suggested he attend next meeting of PRSA chapter), and (3) radio reporter wanting to know if anything "newsworthy" is likely to happen at tonight's city council meeting. She says she does not want to invest time attending "unless there is something controversial to cover."

4:50   Check with staff in television production control room next to city council chambers as they prepare for live telecast of meeting.

5:00   Attend city council meeting. Stay ready to answer questions about public relations aspect of every item on the agenda, but no questions arise this evening.

8:10   Arrive home too late for dinner but in time to tuck the kids in bed and read them two chapters of *The Merry Adventures of Robin Hood*.

Mark S. Cox, APR
Director of Public Relations
City of Chesapeake, Virginia

EXHIBIT 2-5

Day in the Life of a Federal Government Public Affairs Officer

7:30   Review daily reports of accidents and incidents while one of the staff prepares a message for the codaphones. (The press call these to get updated information.)

7:45   Check computer bulletin board for clippings, calendar, and other messages.

8:00   Return to revising the public affairs plan for a facility consolidation—a controversial issue. "Graffiti wall" next to desk contains every comment received about the proposal. Use these comments as a basis for developing message strategy.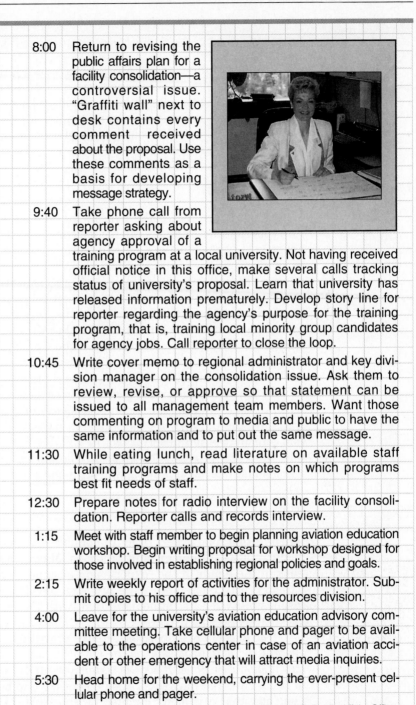

9:40   Take phone call from reporter asking about agency approval of a training program at a local university. Not having received official notice in this office, make several calls tracking status of university's proposal. Learn that university has released information prematurely. Develop story line for reporter regarding the agency's purpose for the training program, that is, training local minority group candidates for agency jobs. Call reporter to close the loop.

10:45   Write cover memo to regional administrator and key division manager on the consolidation issue. Ask them to review, revise, or approve so that statement can be issued to all management team members. Want those commenting on program to media and public to have the same information and to put out the same message.

11:30   While eating lunch, read literature on available staff training programs and make notes on which programs best fit needs of staff.

12:30   Prepare notes for radio interview on the facility consolidation. Reporter calls and records interview.

1:15   Meet with staff member to begin planning aviation education workshop. Begin writing proposal for workshop designed for those involved in establishing regional policies and goals.

2:15   Write weekly report of activities for the administrator. Submit copies to his office and to the resources division.

4:00   Leave for the university's aviation education advisory committee meeting. Take cellular phone and pager to be available to the operations center in case of an aviation accident or other emergency that will attract media inquiries.

5:30   Head home for the weekend, carrying the ever-present cellular phone and pager.

Joette Storm, APR, Public Affairs Officer
Federal Aviation Administration, U.S. Department of Transportation
Anchorage, Alaska

ROLES

Practitioners adopt roles in organizations by taking on patterns of behaviors to deal with recurring types of situations and to accommodate others' expectations. Four public relations roles describe the practice. At one time or another, practitioners play all these roles to varying degrees, but a dominant role emerges for each as he or she goes about day-to-day work and dealings with others.

Communication Technician

Most practitioners enter the field in the communication technician role. Entry-level job descriptions call for someone with communication and journalistic skills, such as writing and editing employee newsletters, writing news releases and feature stories, and dealing with the media. When operating in this role, practitioners are not present when management defines problems and select solutions. Rather than being part of the management team, they produce the communications and implement the program, sometimes without full knowledge of either the original motivation or the intended results. The effectiveness of the communications and program depends on the adequacy of others' problem definitions, strategic decisions, and ability to communicate these to those charged with implementation.

Practitioners not only begin their careers in this role, but spend much of their time in the technical aspects of communication, as illustrated by the list of work assignments presented in the preceding section and by the job descriptions in Exhibit 2–1. When limited to this role, however, practitioners typically do not contribute significantly to management decision making and strategic planning.

Expert Prescriber

When in this role, expert practitioners are seen as the authority on both public relations problems and solutions. Management leaves public relations in the hands of the "expert" and assumes a relatively passive role. Expert practitioners define the problem, develop the program, and take responsibility for its implementation, with management content to get back to business as usual.

The expert prescriber role seduces practitioners because it is personally gratifying to be viewed as the authority on what needs to be done and how it should be done. It seduces employers and clients because they want to feel secure and may think they do not have to bother with public relations now that it is being handled by an expert. Limited participation by key top managers, however, means that their relevant knowledge does not get factored into the problem-solving process. Public relations becomes compartmentalized, apart from the mainstream of the enterprise.

By not participating themselves, managers remain dependent on the practitioner. Commitment to the program and responsibility for its success or failure also are left with the practitioner. Whereas the expert prescriber role is called for in crisis situations and periodically throughout any program, in the long run it hinders the diffusion of public relations thinking throughout the organization. It also often leads to dissatisfaction with practitioners, as they are held solely accountable for program results even though they had little or no control over critical parts of the situation.

Communication Facilitator

The role of communication facilitator casts practitioners as sensitive listeners and information brokers. Communication facilitators serve as liaisons, interpreters, and mediators between the organization and its publics. They maintain two-way communication and facilitate exchange by removing barriers in the relationship and keeping channels of communication open. The goal is to provide both organizational management and publics the information they need for making decisions of mutual interest.

Practitioners in the communication facilitator role find themselves acting as information sources and official channels between organizations and their publics. They referee interactions, establish discussion agendas, summarize and restate views, call for reactions, and help participants diagnose and correct conditions interfering with communication relationships. Communication facilitators occupy boundary-spanning roles and serve as links between organizations and publics. They facilitate communication so to improve the quality of decisions related to the policies, procedures and actions of both publics and organizations.

Problem-Solving Facilitator

When practitioners assume the role of problem-solving facilitator, they *collaborate* with other managers to define and solve problems. They become part of the strategic planning team. Collaboration and consultation begin with the first question and continue until the final joint evaluation of program success or failure. Problem-solving practitioners help other managers and the organization apply to public relations the same management step-by-step *process* used for solving other organizational problems.

Line managers provide much of the *content*, as they are the ones most knowledgeable of and most intimately involved with the organization's policies, procedures, and actions. They are also the ones with the *power* to make needed changes. As a result, they must share in the evolutionary thinking behind public relations decisions. If other managers do not participate, they remain unaware of program motivations and objectives, they do not understand the thinking behind strategic decisions, and they do not make the commitments necessary for achieving program goals. They see public relations as a sometimes necessary staff function that handles pesky problems not directly related to the organization's main mission. On the other hand, practitioners operating in the problem-solving facilitator role get invited to join the management team when decisions are being made.

WHAT ROLES RESEARCH TELLS US

Beginning in the late 1970s, researchers began studying the factors that lead practitioners to play different roles. Research also centered on how different roles affect professional advancement and participation in management.[13]

Technicians versus Managers

Research findings show that practitioners play several roles, but that one emerges as dominant for most. For example, in a study of PRSA members in the United States, 48 percent rated themselves dominant in the expert prescriber role and 27 percent scored communication technician as their dominant role. Another 14 percent scored the problem-solving facilitator role as dominant, 7 percent scored two or three roles equally as dominant, and only 4 percent put themselves in the dominant role of communication facilitator.[14]

In a similar study of Canadian Public Relations Society and Canadian IABC members, 42 percent rated themselves in the dominant role of communication technicians, 16 percent as expert prescribers, 15 percent as problem-solving facilitators, and 12 percent as communication facilitators. Fifteen percent weighted two or three roles equally.[15] The differences observed in the U.S. and Canadian surveys probably reflect PRSA's older, more experienced membership. In cross-sectional surveys, a practitioner's dominant role appears associated with sex, age, and years of experience (see Table 2–4).

Role differences help explain the disparity in men and women's salaries. Fifty-one percent of the women in the PRSA sample scored communication technician as their dominant role, compared with only 21 percent of their male counterparts. Fifty-eight percent of the men operate in the expert prescriber dominant role, whereas only 34 percent of the women see this as their primary role. Even after accounting for differences in age and years of professional experience, there remain significant differences in the roles played by men and women. As salaries are clearly associated with dominant roles, the differences in roles played help explain the salary gap (see Table 2–4). Questions remain, however, about why differences in roles and salaries exist.[16]

TABLE 2–4

	ROLE DIFFERENCES				
Dominant Role	**Percentage of Mean Salary[a]**	**Years of Full-time Experience**	**Years in Current Job**	**Percent in each Dominant Role[b]** Men	Women
Expert prescriber	116	16	6.6	58	34
Problem-solving facilitator	104	15	6.5	16	11
Communication facilitator	97	13	6.6	5	4
Communication technician	69	10	4.6	21	51

[a]Index base of 100 equal to average salary for entire sample, *n* = 458.
[b]Subsample (417) does not include 33 with tied scores and 8 who did not identify sex.

High scores on the communication technician role tend to stand alone. For the other three roles, however, high scores on one tend to go with high scores on the other two. In other words, practitioners whose dominant roles are expert prescriber, communication facilitator, or problem-solving process facilitator also tend to score relatively high on the other two roles. The high correlations among the three roles suggest that they go together to form a single, complex role. If so, the simplest way to describe the dominant roles in practice is as either *technicians* or *managers*.

Environmental Influences

As Tables 2–4 and 2–5 illustrate, however, important distinctions are lost when three of the conceptual roles are combined. For example, roles are related to organizational environments. Communication technicians tend to work in organizations with relatively stable, low-threat environments. Communication facilitators predominate in organizations with relatively turbulent settings that pose little threat. Problem-solving process facilitators and expert prescribers work in organizations with threatening environments. In relatively stable settings, the problem-solving process facilitator role dominates. Expert prescribers dominate in rapidly changing environments.[17]

TABLE 2–5

	ORGANIZATIONAL ENVIRONMENTS AND ROLES	
	Low Threat	**High Threat**
Little change	Communication technician	Problem-solving facilitator
Much change	Communication facilitator	Expert prescriber

In short, the expert prescriber role appears when immediate action is imperative, whereas the problem-solving process facilitator role is preferred when there is time to go through the process of collaboration and joint problem solving. High-paid problem-solving process facilitators and expert prescribers work for organizations most subject to competition, government regulation, labor conflicts, and public scrutiny. As Table 2–3 indicates, these practitioners work for automotive, consumer products, petroleum, and other industrial and manufacturing companies. They also work for the public relations firms retained to counsel such companies. By contrast, the lower-paid communication technicians and communication facilitators work for charitable and nonprofit organizations, government, education, and the hospitality industry.

Scanning and Evaluation

The impact of practitioner use of research consistently appears in studies of roles. In a 6-year panel study, practitioners who used all types of research and information gathering were the ones most likely to have moved into management roles. Practitioners in the technician role after 6 years were also the ones least likely to use research in their work.[18] The relationship between using research and role also appears in the findings of an international sample of IABC members. Operating in the manager role correlates with the use of scientific, informal, and mixed approaches to research, whereas operating in the technician role does not.[19]

The research shows that all types of information gathering helps practitioners move into management roles. The obvious conclusion is that practitioners must be actively gathering information to be used in decision making before they are invited to the management table. Furthermore, becoming part of the management team does not happen simply because of years on the job. Rather, moving into a management role happens more as a result of how much research practitioners do.[20]

Many factors influence the roles practitioners play, including education, professional experience, personality, supervision, and organizational culture. Practitioners who understand the causes and consequences of the various roles can develop strategies for dealing with different situations and with others' views of practitioner roles. This understanding may be particularly important for women, as research shows that role differences are associated with both salaries and access to the organizational decision-making process.

THE GLASS CEILING EFFECT

Studies of women in public relations suggest both a salary gap and a "glass ceiling" on promotions to management positions. As one researcher put it, there is a "million-dollar penalty for being a woman," noting the effect of male-female salary differences over the course of a career.[21]

Roles research shows that annual income and participation in management decision making increase when practitioners change from the technician role to one of the managerial roles. The other finding is that these role changes occur for men more readily than for women. For example, the percentage of practitioners in the technician role decreased significantly and the percentage in the management role increased significantly over the 6-year period. Detailed analyses revealed, however, that women tended to remain in the communication technician role whereas men moved out of that dominant role to one of the management roles. Whereas in the first survey 38 percent of the communication technicians (dominant role) were women, 6 years later 52 percent of the technicians were women. Not only did the role differences mean that the salary gap widened, but also that during the 6 years between surveys more men gained access to and participation in management than did women.[22]

Those who study the glass ceiling problem suggest the following strategies:

1. Women aiming for top management must develop career plans and select employers with care, not plan on "being in the right place at the right time." "Women have to get into the game and be as aggressive and determined as any male counterpart."

2. Women must develop management skills: goal setting, analysis, planning, research, program execution, measurement, and evaluation. They must also know how to communicate with managers. As one female manager put it, "I think as time goes on, and this is especially critical for women, communicators are going to have to think like managers, talk like managers, and communicate with other managers."

3. Women must aim higher. One study found that when women are asked to estimate what salary they will be making in 10 years, they project only 60 percent of what men project. Rather than undervalue themselves, they should research salaries in the area and in comparable organizations before accepting an offer. Researchers also found that women may forget to negotiate "perks": professional dues, conference expenses, and other benefits in addition to salary.[23]

The research evidence suggests, however, that for women trying to break through the glass ceiling in public relations, conducting research—environmental scanning and program evaluation—promotes movement into management decision making.[24]

MINORITIES

Surveys of the field show that minorities represent a little more than 7 percent of all practitioners. U.S. Department of Labor statistics show a marked increase of minorities in the "public relations specialists" category, from slightly more than 3 percent in 1979 to more than 11 percent in 1991.[25] Demographic trends and the increasing marketplace power of minorities call for an even greater presence in the years to come, however. Recognition of the importance of building and maintaining relationships with all racial and ethnic segments of the community has prompted increased opportunities for individual practitioners as well as for an increasing number of minority-owned firms.[26]

Experts point to the growing need for both internal and external public relations directed to minority audiences. As one public relations executive put it, "Agencies and corporate public relations staffs that don't have these capabilities will find themselves at a competitive disadvantage."

In the meantime, surveys continue to show that minorities are underrepresented in corporate departments, firms, and other major organizations' public relations staffs. Educational opportunities are opening to minority students, scholarships and internship programs encourage participation, and employment opportunities reward those who take advantage of them. Within the next few years, however, minority practitioners with public relations training and skills will be in high demand because all organizations will need to communicate with the many publics in an increasingly pluralistic society.[27]

PROFESSIONALISM

When practitioners get together at professional meetings, discussions typically turn to the extent to which public relations qualifies as a profession and its practitioners as professionals. The topic of professionalism dominates many conferences. The many publications and newsletters serving the field all address concerns about professionalism and the professionalization of public relations. Most recently, concerns about professional status motivated PRSA to require continuing education for its accredited members.

Notions of what constitutes a profession date back to preindustrial England. Sons of wealthy landowners went to either Cambridge or Oxford to receive liberal arts education before taking exams to enter the practices of law and medicine. Wealth was a prerequisite because professional practice provided little, if any, remuneration.

By the late 1800s the "status professionalism" of England began to give way to "occupational professionalism." Specialized skills and knowledge became the basis for entry, opening the way for the growing middle class. Although under attack in some fields, many of the values associated with the professions of the earlier time persist today: "personal service, a dislike of competition, advertising and profit, a belief in the principle of payment in order to work rather than working for pay and the superiority of the motive of service."[28] Many have attempted to define contemporary professions, but no definition satisfies all fields. The characteristics used in some appear to argue the cases for particular occupational groups while excluding others. There is general consensus, however, that the following criteria are basic to all professions:

1. **Requires specialized education to acquire a body of knowledge and skills based on theory developed through research.** The practice is based more on unique knowledge than on performance skills.
2. **Provides a unique and essential service recognized as such by the community.** Practitioners are identified with their profession: "She's a lawyer" or "He's the accountant."
3. **Emphasizes public service and social responsibility over private interests.** Private economic gain and special interests are subordinate to the public good. There is "nobility of purpose."
4. **Gives autonomy to and places responsibility on practitioners.** Freedom to decide and act carries with it individual accountability.
5. **Enforces codes of ethics and standards of performance through self-governing associations of colleagues.** Values are interpreted and enforced by disciplining those who deviate from accepted norms and prescribed behaviors. Professional societies provide standards for preparation, admission, and status.

The discussion of practitioners' educational backgrounds makes it clear that entry into public relations does not require specialized educational preparation. Only a minority of practitioners belong to the major "professional" associations. An even smaller number are "accredited" by their associations, meaning that they have passed a battery of tests and been judged competent by a panel of their professional peers. No state requires those entering the practice to be licensed. There even is disagreement *within* the field as to what constitutes public relations, notwithstanding the varied and often bizarre notions held by others.

Frequent examples of self-serving behavior and advocacy on behalf of special interests bring into question the extent to which public service and social responsibility guide the practice. Only a small percentage of practitioners work as truly independent counselors. In fact, most function in staff positions accountable to line management, so autonomy and personal responsibility are not commonly associated with their roles. And because only a small portion of practitioners belong to strong professional associations, the vast majority are not subject to enforced codes of conduct.

These issues are discussed more in Chapter 5, but clearly a strict interpretation of the criteria would preclude calling public relations a "profession." In fact, if required to completely adhere to the standards in the previous list, few fields would pass the test. Many in public relations, on the other hand, qualify as "professionals" on many or most criteria and strive to meet professional standards. Concerted efforts in education and associations advance the calling and professionalize the field. *Professionalism is an important concern and goal for those entering the emerging profession of public relations.*

EXHIBIT 2–6

Requirements for Success

Skills

▶ Effective writing
▶ Persuasive speaking

Knowledge

▶ In-depth knowledge of various media
▶ Understanding of management process
▶ Business, financial acumen

Abilities

▶ Problem solver
▶ Decision maker
▶ Deft in handling people, generates confidence
▶ Assumes responsibility

Qualities

▶ Stability and common sense
▶ Drive and enthusiasm
▶ Wide-ranging interests and intellectual curiosity
▶ Good listener
▶ Tolerance for frustration
▶ Style

Courtesy Jo Proctor and reprinted with permission from *Public Relations Journal.*

REQUIREMENTS FOR SUCCESS

A survey of top public relations executives shows that they think communication skills, knowledge of media and management, problem-solving abilities, motivation, and intellectual curiosity are needed for success (see Exhibit 2–6). Exhibit 2–7 presents Bill Cantor's list of personality traits required for success in public relations. Weyerhaeuser public relations executive Richard Long lists five qualities of those on the career fast track:

1. **Results:**   The single most important key to success is a reputation for getting results. Employers and clients pay for *results*, not *hard work* and *effort*.

2. **Conceptualizing:**   Those on the fast track have an ability to focus on the employer's or client's needs. The strong conceptualizer is a "quick study" who is a good listener and thorough note taker.

3. **Human Relations:**   The person on the fast track is a team player who balances personal goals with those of the organization. This person also knows how to deal with management, including times when not agreeing with the boss.

4. **Style:**   The most important style-related trait is a "can-do" attitude. Another is constructive competitiveness. Those on the fast track translate confidence into persuasive advocacy and substantive public relations contributions.

5. **Intangibles:**   This quality almost defies description, but charisma, presence, and moxie affect the way other managers evaluate people in public relations. Go to school on the boss. The bottom line with bosses, however, is to find ways to make their jobs easier. Know what your boss expects of you.[29]

Among other traits sought by employers are understanding how the business works (whatever a particular organization's business is), being goal oriented, having a broad education, being well read, keeping up with current events, and having a an ability to deal with frustration and to improvise. One trait tops every list, however. *An ability to write is number one by a wide margin.* As one executive put it, "Too often, clear writing is not stressed sufficiently and the public relations professional goes through his or her career with one hand tied behind. Learn how to write before you start to climb the public relations ladder."[30]

In short, *writing grammatically correct, forceful, easy-to-read, informative, and persuasive copy for publication and speech is a requirement for both entry-level employment and long-term career success.*

EXHIBIT 2–7

Cantor's Traits for Success

1. **Response to tension.**   Most successful public relations executives are intense people, although it may not always be evident even to themselves. Often they are at their best under fire, and rather than solving problems by abstract analysis, will reach practical solutions by direct action.

2. **Individual initiative.**   The successful public relations executive will usually take immediate action before a situation becomes blown out of proportion. He or she usually will not wait for instructions, but takes the initiative to solve the problem; seeks to anticipate and adjust to change; leads the public relations effort.

3. **Curiosity and learning.** The public relations professional should have an inquiring mind, should want to learn everything possible about the product, service, client or organization, and the competition. Since public relations is not an exact science, frequently the public relations executive must try a number of approaches in order to solve a problem, some of which might not work. If and when they don't work, the professional does not regard them as personal blunders, but as learning opportunities. Problems are solved by persistence and intelligence. He or she never stops learning.

4. **Energy, drive and ambition.** The successful public relations person has energy, drive and ambition. He or she works rapidly and is not afraid to take a calculated risk, This is a very important element in the personality of public relations executives. Most of the top practitioners are stimulated by the problems to be solved, and are willing to work the hours it takes to reach their goals.

5. **Objective thinking.** Public relations executives must be as objective and factual as possible and above all, have excellent judgment. They must know what to do and say, and when. They must have a sense of timing. They must have a capacity for intense concentration and attention to intricate detail, and keen powers of observation. This is especially critical in counseling.

6. **Flexible attitude.** It is crucial that public relations executives have the ability to see things from someone else's viewpoint, *e.g.*, executive management's, a publication editor's or a hostile audience's.

7. **Service to others.** Most successful public relations executives have a natural desire to help people. Pleasure in the success of others is a major motivation for the service behavior.

8. **Friendliness.** Public relations people generally are perceived as likable, friendly and genuinely interested in others, rarely as resentful, bitter, or hostile. They develop and maintain a wide range of personal contacts.

9. **Versatility.** The successful public relations executive is often able to perform well in a variety of areas because he or she has a venturesome spirit and a lively interest in the world at large. The best practitioners are generalists with a specialty. The desire to learn and the ability to focus on varied subjects helps them adjust rapidly to new tasks and multiple client problems and needs.

10. Lack of self-consciousness. Successful public relations executives are much less self-conscious than other executives, perhaps because they often function as catalysts. Although some practitioners have large egos, they often are self-effacing, functioning in the background while projecting others into the limelight. This trait is indigenous to the public relations professional.

Courtesy Bill Cantor and reprinted with permission from *Public Relations Journal*.

ADDITIONAL READINGS

Cantor, Bill and Chester Burger, eds. *Experts in Action: Inside Public Relations*, 2d ed. New York: Longman, Inc., 1989. Thirty-eight authors discuss what successful public relations practitioners do in a variety of organizations.

Hon, Linda Childers, Larissa A. Grunig, and David M. Dozier. "Women in Public Relations: Problems and Opportunities." In *Excellence in Public Relations and Communication Management*, edited by James E. Grunig, 419–38. Hillsdale, N.J.: Lawrence Erlbaum Associates, Publishers, 1992.

Creedon, Pamela J., ed. *Women in Mass Communication: Challenging Gender Values*. Newbury Park, Calif.: Sage Publications, 1989. Collection of writings explores feminist theory and the women's movement in mass communication.

Dilenschneider, Robert L. *Power and Influence: Mastering the Art of Persuasion*. New York: Prentice Hall Press, 1990. Insider's view of the workings of public relations written by the former president and chief executive officer of Hill and Knowlton.

Grunig, Larissa A., ed. "Special Issue on Women in Public Relations." *Public Relations Review* 14, no. 3 (Fall 1988). Overview and seven articles describe status of and prognosis for women in field.

Lauzen, Martha M. "Public Relations Roles, Intraorganizational Power, and Encroachment." *Journal of Public Relations Research* 4, no. 2 (1992): 61–80.

Lauzen, Martha M., and David M. Dozier. "The Missing Link: The Public Relations Manager Role as Mediator of Organizational Environments and Power Consequences for the Function." *Journal of Public Relations Research* 4, no. 4 (1992): 205–20.

Serini, Shirley A. "Influences on the Power of Public Relations Professionals in Organizations: A Case Study." *Journal of Public Relations Research* 5, no. 1 (1993): 1–25.

Toth, Elizabeth L. and Carolyn G. Cline. "Public Relations Practitioner Attitudes Toward Gender Issues: A Benchmark Study." *Public Relations Review* 17, no. 2 (Summer 1991): 161–74.

NOTES

[1] Estimates based on PRSA and IABC membership data and descriptive statistics from other surveys of practitioners.

[2] Office of Workforce Information, U.S. Office of Personnel Management, *Federal Civilian Workforce Statistics: Occupations of Federal White-Collar and Blue-Collar Workers* (Washington, D.C.: Government Printing Office, October 31, 1985), 7, 18, and 68.

[3] Statistical Analysis and Services Division, U.S. Office of Personnel Management, *Federal Civilian Workforce Statistics: Employment and Trends* (Washington, D.C.: Government Printing Office, July 1990), 37.

[4] For data on employee numbers, see current editions of *O'Dwyer's Director of Public Relations Firms* and *O'Dwyer's Directory of Corporate Communicators.*

[5] *Employment and Earnings* (Washington, D.C.: U.S. Department of Labor, Bureau of Statistics, January 1993).

[6] Rea W. Smith, "Women in Public Relations," *Public Relations Journal* 24 (October 1968): 26, 27, and 29.

[7] Sondra K. Gorney, "Status of Women in Public Relations," *Public Relations Journal* 31 (May 1975): 10–13.

[8] PRSA and IABC statistics in this chapter are taken from 1990 PRSA membership profile; David Y. Jacobson and Nicholas J. Tortorello, "Salary Survey," *Public Relations Journal* 46, no. 6 (June 1990): 18–25; and *Profile '89* (San Francisco: International Association of Business Communicators and IABC Research Foundation, 1989).

[9] Paul V. Peterson, "Journalism and Mass Communication Enrollment Leveled Off in 1987," *Journalism Educator* 43, no. 1 (Spring 1988): 4–10; and Gerald M. Kosicki and Lee B. Becker, "Annual Census and Analysis of Enrollment and Graduation Enrollment," *Journalism Educator* 47, no. 3 (Autumn 1992): 68.

[10] Nicholas J. Tortorello and Elizabeth Wilhelm, "Eighth Annual Salary Survey," *Public Relations Journal* 49, no. 7 (July 1993): 10–19.

[11] Glen M. Broom and David M. Dozier, "Advancement for Public Relations Role Models," *Public Relations Review* 12, no. 1 (Spring 1986): 37–56. Much of the roles research reported here was supported by grants from the Institute (formerly Foundation) for Public Relations Research and Education.

[12] David M. Dozier and Glen M. Broom, "Evolution of the Managerial Role in Public Relations Practice." (Paper presented to the Public Relations Division, Association for Education in Journalism and Mass Communication Annual Convention, Kansas City, August 1993.)

[13] For the original conceptual definitions of the roles, see Glen M. Broom and George D. Smith, "Testing the Practitioner's Impact on Clients," *Public Relations Review* 5, no. 3 (Fall 1979): 47–59.

[14] Glen M. Broom, "A Comparison of Sex Roles in Public Relations," *Public Relations Review* 8, no. 3 (Fall 1982): 17–22.

[15] Jennie M. Piekos and Edna F. Einsiedel, "Roles and Program Evaluation Techniques Among Canadian Public Relations Practitioners," *Public Relations Research Annual* 2 (1990): 95–113.

[16] Broom, "Roles in Public Relations," 21.

[17] Lalit Acharya, "Public Relations Environments," *Journalism Quarterly* 62, no. 3 (Autumn 1985): 577–84.

[18] Broom and Dozier, "Public Relations Role Models," 51–52.

[19] David M. Dozier, "The Innovation of Research in Public Relations: Review of a Program of Research," *Public Relations Research Annual* 1 (1990): 16–21.

[20] Broom and Dozier, "Public Relations Role Models," 54.

[21] Carolyn Garret Cline, "Public Relations: The $1 Million Penalty for Being a Woman," in *Women in Mass Communication: Challenging Gender Values*, edited by Pamela J. Creedon (Newbury Park, Calif.: Sage Publications, 1989), 263–75.

[22] Broom and Dozier, "Public Relations Role Models," 45–49.

[23]Adapted and quoted from Cline,   "The $1 Million Penalty for Being a Woman,"
272–74.

[24]Dozier,   "The Innovation of Research in Public Relations," 22.

[25]*Employment and Earnings* (Washington, D.C.: U.S. Department of Labor,
Bureau of Statistics, January 1980 and January 1991).

[26]Marilyn Kern-Foxworth,   "Status and Roles of Minority PR Practitioners,"
Public Relations Review 15, no. 3 (Fall 1989): 39–47.

[27]Marilyn Kern-Foxworth,   "Minorities 2000: The Shape of Things to Come,"
Public Relations Journal 45, no. 8 (August 1989): 14–18, and 21–22.

[28]Philip Elliott,   *The Sociology of Professions* (London: Macmillan and Co.,
1972), 52–53. Useful reference on the origins and evolution of professions.

[29]Adapted from a speech to East-Central District Conference, Public Relations
Student Society of America, Louisville, Kentucky, April 5, 1986, by Richard K.
Long. At that time, Long was director of corporate communication at Dow
Chemical Company, Midland, Michigan. He is now vice president–corporate
communications with Weyerhaeuser, Tacoma, Washington. Used with
permission of the author.

[30]From speech to Black Public Relations Society of Greater New York by
Kenneth R. Lightcap, managing director, Manning Selvage and Lee, New
York, April 17, 1991.

CHAPTER 3

Organizational Settings

The nature of an executive decision itself shapes the uses and quality of intelligence because it affects the number, kinds, and organization of experts called to serve.

HAROLD L. WILENSKY

Organizational settings of public relations underwent great changes in the late 1980s and early 1990s. Corporate restructuring, "downsizing," mergers, and acquisitions; budget deficits in government; and funding problems in many not-for-profit organizations all reshaped the function *within* organizations. All types of organizations reorganized the public relations function, reduced department staff size, or tried to do more with the same people.

Many organizations shifted part of or all the workload to *outside* counseling firms and agencies, producing dramatic increases in business and profitability. Public relations firms merged, bought out others, or were acquired by bigger firms. Large, cash-rich advertising agencies purchased public relations firms, promising clients "one-stop-shopping" at "communication supermarkets." Large public relations firms became even larger by opening national or international branches, or through acquisitions and mergers.

Practitioners work within these turbulent organizational settings, whether in internal departments or external firms. Many work at the highest levels of management, reporting directly to chief executive officers. This chapter discusses the origins and place of the function in organizations, its responsibilities, and its working relationships with other departments.

ORIGINS WITHIN ORGANIZATIONS

To understand why public relations practitioners occupy certain positions and roles, you need to know some of the ways in which the function comes into being. For example, top managers in a growing corporation discover that they have lost touch with employees, and face-to-face communication with all employees is no longer possible or fast enough. The human resources department gets approval to hire an editor to produce a new employee newsletter.

The publication successfully keeps everyone abreast of what is happening in the corporation and of business plans. Then the energetic and ambitious editor gets the additional task of writing occasional news releases about employee achievements and corporate successes. Soon the editor takes on duties as speech writer for the chief executive officer and as the corporation's media contact. The editor hires an assistant to handle the growing number of internal and external publications.

Because the function has expanded beyond its employee publication origins, it is moved out of the personnel department and given the title Public Relations Department. The new department's manager reports directly to the chief executive officer to improve communication and to build better relationships with all the corporation's key publics.

As the corporation grows, the public relations function takes on responsibilities for maintaining relationships with investors and financial analysts, government agencies at all levels, community groups, environmental and other special-interest groups, plus an increasingly diverse work force. The manager gets promoted to vice president and appoints managers for each of the specialized areas. The new vice president is elected to the executive committee and participates in corporate decision making at the highest level.

From its origin as a low-level communication support function in the personnel department, the function developed to become an integral part of the management team. As with others on the team, to stay there it must contribute to achieving organizational goals and demonstrate accountability through measurable results.

Other common starting points include doing product and service publicity, news support for national advertising campaigns, fundraising, and membership drives. In other organizations, public relations' humble beginning can be traced back to someone answering letters from customers or members; to someone writing copy for direct mail, institutional advertising, or the annual report; to someone handling visitors, conducting tours, or arranging the annual meeting; or to someone serving as an organization's ombudsman for employees or neighbors.

Creation does not always spring from a welcome opportunity, however. In many cases, emergencies or crises attract considerable public and media attention. If there is no one on the staff qualified to deal with the media and to handle public information, the function begins under the pressure of crisis conditions. Those brought in, either as staff members or outside counsel, subsequently may be hired or retained on a continuing basis. Long after the emergency or crisis subsides, public relations is defined and redefined to fit changing missions, needs, problems, opportunities, values, and a succession of chief executive officers' views of the function.

As a result, some large organizations have only small public relations departments, whereas some relatively small enterprises employ many practitioners, even supplementing their work with outside counsel. While most departments stand alone and report directly to the chief executive officer (CEO), some report to human resources or marketing officers. Some organizations retain outside counselors when internal staff seems the more appropriate choice. In others, the internal staff gets assignments for which outside counsel would be the better choice. Large public relations departments in some organizations have generous budgets, even though the original motivations for the function have long been forgotten. Departments in other organizations strain to marshal public support, to neutralize well-organized public opposition, or to build new relationships across international borders even though there is neither staff nor funds to meet the need or to achieve program goals.

Such mismatches often represent nothing more than delays in adapting to change. But practitioners also disagree about what is the best or right structure and place for the function in various types of organizations. As a result, each internal public relations department is tailor-made to suit a particular organization and its unique circumstances.

Likewise, client relationships with outside counseling firms begin in quite simple and unexpected ways. For example, an outside firm (sometimes called an "agency") is retained to undertake a special project, such as conducting a survey of community opinions. The survey results lead to proposals to take advantage of an opportunity or to solve a public opinion problem discovered by the survey. Success in the follow-up project leads to a continuing and expanding relationship as the client draws on the full range of the firm's capabilities.

The client pays the firm a monthly retainer fee, ensuring access to outside counsel when needed and covering a set number of hours of service each month. Above and beyond regular counsel and services, the firm takes on special projects such as the annual report, the grand opening and dedication of the new headquarters building, and the new corporate video. The client pays for these projects on an hourly fee basis or through a single fixed fee covering all costs associated with the project.

The firm's account executive and the internal department's management work as a team to plan and carry out the public relations function. The account executive meets periodically with the CEO and public relations management to discuss plans and to assess progress. The client-firm relationship becomes so close that there is potential for taking each other for granted.

Occasional friction develops, however, when the account executive is not available because of work demands from other accounts or, more commonly, when the firm's monthly charges are for more hours than the public relations vice president anticipates. A hastily called meeting to discuss the invoice reminds both the account executive and internal public relations management that outside counsel is a variable cost and that the two have different economic incentives. The relationship continues, but with frequent reminders that clients and outside counselors work from different perspectives. But of course, one of the reasons the client organization retained the counseling firm in the first place was to provide an outsider's view of the situation.

PUBLIC RELATIONS STARTS WITH TOP MANAGEMENT

One of the few safe generalizations in public relations is that *an organization's public reputation derives in substantial part from the behavior of its senior officials.* As those in top management act and speak, so go the interpretations and echoes created by the public relations function. Thus, public relations is inescapably tied, by nature and by necessity, to the management function.

For example, recall how Source Perrier responded when traces of benzene were found in its bottled water. Perrier's top management first suggested that it resulted from a single, isolated cleaning accident and that contaminated bottles were limited to only the few being recalled in North America. The next installment of top management's story came when scientists found benzene-tainted products in Europe. This time management attributed the benzene to a simple problem with the filter system. Finally, red-faced Perrier management announced a worldwide recall. Tests showed that consumers around the world had been drinking contaminated products for months. Media blasted Perrier, questioning management's integrity and raising concern for public safety.

Johnson & Johnson's handling of the Tylenol$_{TM}$ tampering crisis stands in stark contrast. Top management put customer safety first, immediately pulling the product off retail shelves and recalling capsules in the United States and abroad, even though the tampering cases appeared only in the Chicago area. Media coverage praised the company's socially responsible actions, reported the company's cooperation with federal agencies, and gave full coverage to announcements of new tamper-resistant packaging. Unlike Perrier, Johnson & Johnson's crisis became a classic case study in how to handle such crises.

Both cases potentially involved and affected many stakeholder groups: customers who consume products, employees, wholesalers and retailers, consumer action groups, government agencies, stockholders and investment analysts, media worldwide, and concerned citizens around the world. The Perrier case probably contributed to the subsequent series of investigations and media disclosures about the quality and purity of all bottled waters, so even competing brands were affected. The Johnson & Johnson response positioned it as a leader in safe packaging, forcing competing brands to follow suit.

These two cases illustrate the generalization that public relations credibility starts with management integrity and socially responsible action. In addition, long-term success in public relations calls for the following from top management:

1. Commitment to and participation in public relations
2. Retention of competent public relations counsel
3. Incorporation of public relations perspectives in policy making
4. Two-way communication with both internal and external publics
5. Coordination of what is done with what is said
6. Clearly defined goals and objectives

The first task, and a continuing one, is to earn and hold broad support for the public relations function within the organization. Unless support is earned, there will be conflict, not coordination and cooperation. Conflict soon begets friction and frustration. Support and understanding develop with time and on the basis of a track record of achievements that contribute to organizational success.

Executives in top management determine long-term goals, set policies, and approve procedures to guide the entire organization. In the process they decide, at least tentatively, on the scope and the place of all office and field management functions. Intentionally or not, they determine the role of each and the relationship each has with the others.

STAFF ROLE

Public relations is a *staff* function, one of several that advise and support the *line* managers who have responsibility and authority to run the organization. Thus, practitioners need to understand the staff role.

The line-staff management model originated in the military but now is used in most large organizations. Line functions in industry include the product- and profit-producing functions: engineering, production, and marketing. Staff functions include those that advise and assist line executives: finance, legal, human resources (formerly personnel), and public relations. These functions become increasingly necessary as organizations increase in size and complexity. Line executives have the authority and responsibility to set policy and to see that the work gets done, but they need assistance in the form of plans, advice, support services, and suggestions from staff executives. *The job of staff officers is to advise top officials and to support and assist line officers.*[1] In other words, staff officers contribute to the main line of business rather than complete self-contained tasks or produce the organization's end products. As one executive put it:

> In public relations—and I now know that I share this frustration with other staff officers—you're always spending somebody else's money. You're always doing something for them; you're bailing them out, or you're writing a piece for them, or putting out a publication that deals with *their* subject, not yours. The result is a built-in requirement for an extensive approval process.[2]

Line management and public relations staff have a right to expect certain things from each other. Management can reasonably expect the following from the public relations staff:

1. Loyalty
2. Help with the public relations aspects of decisions
3. Skill in articulating principles and in enhancing public understanding of the organization
4. Inspiration to help all members do their best
5. Influence in restraining other members from saying or doing anything detrimental to the organization's welfare

Staff should expect the following from management:

1. Positive public relations leadership
2. Support of approved communications policy
3. Strategic plans embracing all policies and programs
4. Adequate budget to do the job, including funds for adequate public opinion research, analysis, and program evaluation
5. Reasonable availability for consultation and for public appearances

Each also has the right to expect of the other character and performance that will stand public scrutiny and fulfill the organization's social responsibility.

Differences between line and staff management, however, call for different roles in the relationship. *Line management determines the ground rules and sets the course. Once all points of view have been aired and debated, the resulting decisions may result from a consensus or from choices made by line management. Both line and staff managers must participat but final decisions are the province of senior line management. Public relations works within those rules and with others on matters having an impact on the organization's relationships with others, inside and outside.*

Because managing organizational relationships is an increasingly important and central function, an increasing number of public relations practitioners are advancing from staff positions to line management. A few have become chief executive officers. As the Perrier and Johnson and Johnson examples make clear, public opinion and public response to an organization's actions may have as much influence on the bottom line as the performance of engineering, research, marketing, manufacturing, and other executives. As a result, public relations executives increasingly participate in making important strategic decisions. Some eventually find themselves chairing these decision-making meetings.

The move from public relations staff into line management is typically applauded in public relations circles, whereas the reverse is viewed with alarm. In a bit of semantic tyranny, the Task Force on the Stature and Role of Public Relations labeled movement into public relations management from outside as "encroachment," identifying it as a threat to the profession.[3] Concern centers on who will make public relations program decisions and recommendations and who will be left with the tasks of implementing programs.[4] But not all agree that there is an encroachment problem.

Line managers often move through a variety of assignments before reaching the top. Seldom, however, do they acquire public relations experience during their regular rotation of assignments. One view is that such moves add to public relations' credibility as a management function, demystify the function for other managers, and expand career opportunities for those now viewed as communication technicians who have no role in management.[5] In the meantime, demarcations between line and staff management guide decision making in most organizations.

DECISION-MAKING ROLE

Traditional and somewhat rigid distinctions between line and staff managers—giving orders versus giving advice—do not always represent their respective *roles in decision making*. For example, practitioners operating in the expert prescriber role often have power to choose among public relations program alternatives, with line management later endorsing the selections or exercising veto power. When in the problem-solving process facilitator role, practitioners collaborate with line managers to make decisions. The bottom line, however, is that relatively few practitioners hold policy decision-making positions in the "dominant coalition," a term used to describe those who hold power in organizations.[6]

In addition, *characteristics of the practitioners* themselves contribute to their exclusion from the dominant coalition. Researchers have identified practitioners' lack of broad business experience, passivity, naiveté about organization politics, technical educations, gender, and tenure in their organizations as factors contributing to public relations' relatively limited power in organizations.[7]

Public relations participation in organizational decision making also depends on the *extent to which the function is involved in various kinds of research*. Researchers have called such research "organizational intelligence-gathering," "environmental scanning," "scanning for planning," and "formal versus informal research." Regardless of labels, survey results consistently show that when the function engages in various types of research, there is a greater likelihood that it will be involved in decision making and other management planning activities.[8]

The major determinant of public relations' role in organizational decision making, however, is the *degree to which line managers and practitioners themselves view the function as part of the management team*. When top management views the function as marginal and outside the main line of business, it remains outside the dominant decision-making coalition.

In organizations in which public relations is seen as communication output only, the function becomes routine and highly structured. Practitioners work primarily as communication technicians in these settings, dealing with "programmed decisions," such as issuing weekly news packets and publishing the monthly employee newsletter. Programmed decisions dominate in most organizations so as to free valuable management time and money for "nonprogrammed decisions" that deal with the "novel, unstructured, and consequential."[9]

When public relations operates in the realm of programmed decisions, it is seen as part of organizational routine and overhead. On the other hand, when it participates in nonprogrammed decision making, it is seen as an important player in achieving organizational goals and contributing to the bottom line. Management by objectives (MBO), management by objectives and results (MOR), and management by key results guide public relations program planning and management as the function becomes increasingly concerned with impact and accountability.

Public relations must become part of an organization's structure and process for adapting to changes. It must take on responsibilities in helping organizations identify, assess, and adjust to its turbulent economic, political, social, and technological environments. In the words of one corporate chief executive officer:

> The public relations professional who can help a company or client meet the new challenges that will result from these radical changes, and facilitate communications among diverse peoples will have a solid place in 21st century management.[10]

THE INTERNAL DEPARTMENT

The internal department is the most common structure for serving the public relations needs of organizations. The unit of specialists within the organization may consist of only one person, as in a small hospital, or a staff of 500, such as at IBM. Probably even more work in public relations in the Department of Defense, but the actual number there remains elusive. A public relations department may be concentrated in the organization's headquarters or scattered among many locations. Size, role, and place in the organization chart vary from one organization to the next.

The Department's Advantages

The internal department has at least four factors working in its favor:

1. Team membership
2. Knowledge of the organization
3. Economy to the organization for many ongoing programs
4. Availability to associates

Team membership is the department's greatest advantage over outside counsel. In some organizations the top public relations executive's office is next door to the chief executive's office. As an example of the close working relationship, the top public relations executive at Eastman Kodak begins most workdays in a meeting with the CEO and board chairman.[11]

Frequent contact between the public relations department and top line management is the rule rather than the exception. *pr reporter* newsletter's annual survey of practitioners shows that 60 percent discuss public relations issues with their CEOs at least once each week. Confidence, trust, and support of management can result from this frequent contact. The close relationship between the department and chief executive's office in most organizations leads to first-team membership for the function. The price of admission is loyalty.

Knowledge of the organization means an intimate, current knowledge that comes from being insiders and participants. Staff members know the relationships among individuals and departments. They know the undercurrents of influence and politics, can call on key people to make decisions, can avoid those who put personal ambition and expedience above organizational and public interests, and are aware of who can serve as able and articulate spokespersons versus tongue-tied, media-shy persons who do not perform well on camera.

Some trusted outside counselors are able to acquire such knowledge, but insiders are in the best position to do so and to do most about it most *continuously*. Department staff can advise when and where needed, conciliate, and provide a full range of services while taking into account the organizational history and culture of which they are a part.

Economy results from lower overhead costs and efficient integration in an organization. When the need for public relations is continuous—and in most organizations it is—then a full-time, permanent staff is typically more cost-effective than outside counsel and services. For example, the marginal costs of the department's rent, heat, and light are typically a small portion of overhead costs in a large organization. The outside firm's overhead can be higher than that for an internal department simply because outside firms are typically smaller than the client organizations they serve.

Start-up costs for projects often are less because internal staff members already have the necessary background, access, and understanding. Routine aspects of the work, such as weekly news releases, monthly publications, quarterly reports, and so forth, are efficiently handled by those closest to the sources and other departments in the organization. Efficiency contributes to cost effectiveness.

Availability of staff practitioners has many facets. When things go wrong, practitioners are only a minute away from a face-to-face meeting with the organization's officials. And as deputies, they can be entrusted with delicate matters. For example, if a senior executive defects in a huff, the CEO wants a public relations specialist on the spot who knows the background, understands the dangers of mishandling the news, and has credibility with the news media and other key players.

Availability means being on call for all departments, divisions, or even decentralized units. Staff members can be called into meetings on short notice. In some organizations, public relations is also decentralized, with specialists assigned to each operating unit. In others, a centralized function operates from headquarters much in the fashion of an outside firm, treating operating units and other departments as "clients." The difference, of course, is that the on-site internal staff members are relatively handy for consultation.

The Department's Disadvantages

Team membership can get in the way on occasion. Loyalty can lead to being exploited. Availability can cast the function as a catch-all without clearly defined roles and missions.

A *loss of objectivity* happens ever so slowly and unwittingly as practitioners become part of the team and are subject to day-to-day forces in the work place. In supporting and being supported, they tend to be absorbed and compromised by group views. Their ability to see other points of view

gives way to the subjectivity that afflicts those they were hired to counsel. They lose their ability to do the boundary spanning needed to avoid or solve problems in the organization's relationships with others. In effect, practitioners run the risk of becoming part of the problem.

Domination and subservience result when the function is co-opted—becomes a group of "yes" men and women—in its staff support role. Being team players and helping others is one thing; being diverted from goals, planning, and strategy to run errands for others is another. Practitioners walk a narrow line between rendering professional services that are valuable, helpful, and appreciated and rendering low-level support that is easily replaced. Successfully making this distinction in practice tends to sort out potential staff executives from those who cannot or will not attain executive status. Detractors like to describe this in oversimplified terms such as "organizational politics" or "playing the political game." There is much more to it. The key is team play, but with retention of one's individuality and professionalism. It is not easy.

Confused roles and mission can result from being readily available. Practitioners often find themselves serving as stand-ins for top executives who make commitments but do not or cannot follow through themselves. For example, the CEO accepts an invitation to serve on a community organization board or committee but finds it difficult to attend the meetings. The practitioner often gets a call to attend in the CEO's place. Such groups are seldom pleased to have the public relations practitioner instead of the CEO but usually accept the switch as a price for the organization's support and for permission to use the CEO's name on the letterhead and in other public communications.

Another example of confused roles and mission is the case of the director of public relations of a state bar association who was given responsibilities for supervising the housekeeping staff and for handling the homeless and others who entered the main reception area wanting to use restroom facilities. How did the practitioner get such duties? Being the only nonlawyer at the director level did not help. Having a open-ended job description also made the function vulnerable. He also was the most available, as other directors were often out of the office conducting programs and services for the membership. It became a vicious cycle: The more miscellaneous assignments he got, the less time he had for the association's public relations effort. Soon, the executive director was questioning his effectiveness.

Titles and Reporting Relationships

Titles and positions of departments in organizations vary greatly. *O'Dwyer's Directory of Corporate Communications* lists titles for 5500 departments in companies, associations, and governmental units. Recent editions of this annual directory show that about 30 percent use

"public relations," making it the most commonly used title. Another 20 percent use "corporate communications" or "communications." Slightly less than 10 percent use "public affairs," and about the same number combine functions in the title, "advertising/public relations." Other commonly used titles include "corporate relations" and "public information."

There is no compelling reason to conclude that some other title will replace "public relations." To the contrary, "public relations" has survived almost a century in spite of the many attempts by practitioners themselves to find an alternative, in spite of the occasional taint of malpractice by individual practitioners, and in spite of public relations bashing by the media. Meantime, both news media and publics worldwide have come to understand the term and to use it to describe this function in organizations. Switching labels does not change 100 years of history.

More significant than the department's title, however, is where the top public relations executive fits in the chain of command in policy decisions. Too often, one former corporate public relations executive argues, public relations is not included in the corporate decision circle. That group typically brings together the CEO, president (if not the same person serving as CEO), and the heads of manufacturing, finance, marketing, engineering/research and development, and legal. Public relations joins administration and personnel/human resources functions as outsiders to the decision-making executive group. As a result, external implications of decisions and communication needs do not reach the table as decisions are made.[12]

Even if not included in the decision circle meetings, the top public relations executive typically reports directly to the CEO. For example, when Jeanne Golly was named vice president of corporate communications at Kmart Corporation, she reported directly to the Kmart chairman and CEO, Joseph Antonini. In municipal government, the organizational chart typically shows the top public relations specialist reporting directly to the city's CEO, either the mayor or city manager. For example, in Chesapeake, Virginia, Mark Cox (see Exhibit 2–4) reports to the city manager, who in turn reports to the city council, much as a corporate president and CEO reports to the board of directors. *O'Dwyer's Directory of Corporate Communications* reports that about half of the corporate departments report to the CEO, typically the chairman or president.

Reporting relationships and job functions are included in organization charts and job descriptions. These lay the groundwork for division and specialization of work, communication up and down the chain of command, and acceptance of various functions throughout the organization. Some practitioners, however, become preoccupied with trying to change the charts and edit their job descriptions, as though these, with no other changes, will elevate the public relations function or somehow change how it is performed. As one long-standing opponent of organization charts—the late Clarence Randall, innovator in management approaches when he was head of Inland Steel—pointed out:

Line and Staff Organization Chart

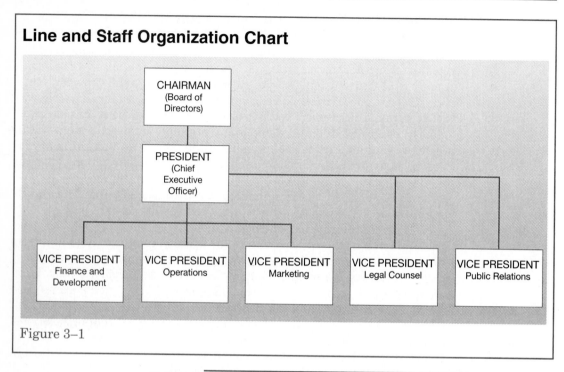

Figure 3–1

> To know who is to do what and to establish authority and responsibility within an institution are the basic first principles of a good administration, but this is a far cry from handing down immutable tablets of stone from the mountaintop. . . . It is not the preparation of the organization chart that I condemn, but its abuse: this blowing up its significance to a point where guidance ceases and inhibition sets in.[13]

Organization charts are, at best, approximations, but they do help clarify the role and relationships of various functions. Figure 3–1, for example, shows an organization chart in which public relations and legal counsel are staff functions reporting to the CEO, but separate from the line managers. Figures 3–2 and 3–3 detail the public relations departments at a university and a corporation, illustrating typical reporting relationships within the function.

WORKING WITH OTHER DEPARTMENTS

Public relations staffers work most closely with the line functions of marketing and finance. They also work in collaboration with the staff functions of human resources (or personnel), industrial or employee relations, and legal. All functions intertwine and overlap in varying degrees, and sometimes the department finds itself in unavoidable confusion over

University Public Relations Department

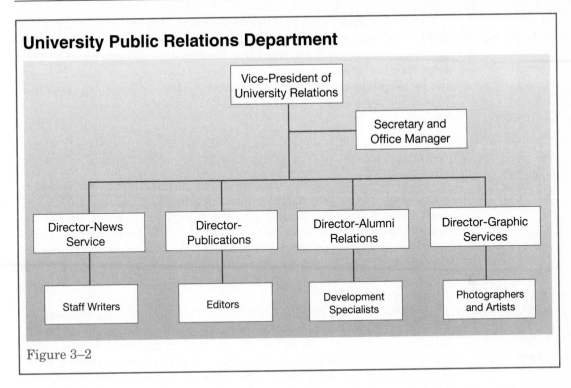

Figure 3–2

Corporate Public Relations Department

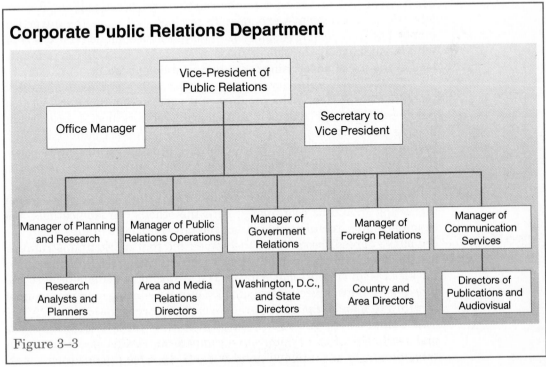

Figure 3–3

roles and in conflict with another department. Disruptive and costly friction occurs particularly in relations with marketing, legal counsel, human resources, and development. To discharge obligations effectively, each function needs the support and cooperation of the others. But with the potential for conflict, practitioners should be aware, alert, and ready to redefine the mission of public relations and to mend fences.

Marketing

As Chapter 1 points out, public relations is most often confused with marketing. These two major communication and outreach functions must work in harmony in dealing with an organization's many publics. Conflict usually arises in corporations over which should be responsible for institutional advertising and product publicity. In nonprofit organizations, the bone of contention is allocation of resources—budget and people—for fund-raising, membership drives, or public education and persuasion campaigns.

Confusion also results from mistaken notions that advertising is the sole province of marketing and that public relations *is* publicity. Advertising designed to establish, change, or maintain relationships with key publics (usually by influencing public opinion) should, by its objectives and strategic nature, be supervised by the public relations department. Advertising for public relations purposes will require the advertising department's expertise to produce and place the advertisements, but the outcome sought has more to do with public relations than with consummating the sale of goods or services. Mobil Oil for years has lead in the use of advertising for public relations purposes.

Conversely, publicity about products and services designed to increase sales is clearly the province of the marketing function. Because public relations staff members are typically more skilled at writing and placing publicity, they often are enlisted to help with publicizing new products, product changes, price changes, product recalls, and special promotional activities in the marketing effort. Such publicity is part of marketing, however.

Advertising and publicity produced by either public relations or marketing should be coordinated with the other's communications. For example, public relations should not tell environmental groups about the company's "green" products at the same time that marketing is running a nationwide sale to clear out the last of the "nongreen" product lines. Backlash is an ever-present danger. The growth of articulate protest and consumer groups, investigative and consumer reporting, and government scrutiny all mandate public relations–marketing cooperation.

Competition, and even conflict, between these two functions is understandable. Practitioners often compete on parallel career tracks for recognition, job advancement, and budgets. In some organizations, marketing and public relations report to the same executive in an attempt to coordinate efforts. Usually, however, they are separate departments, with public relations in a staff relationship to the chief executive officer and marketing as part of the line management chain of command.

Legal Counsel

The conflict between public relations and legal staffs is an old one. In the days of the muckrakers, corporate executives turned first to their lawyers to fix things. Some still do. Ivy Lee felt strongly about this:

> I have seen more situations which the public ought to understand, and which the public would sympathize with, spoiled by the intervention of the lawyer than in any other way. Whenever a lawyer starts to talk to the public, he shuts out the light.[14]

Traditionally, legal and public relations counselors approach situations from different perspectives. Lawyers tend to favor "no comment," pointing out that what you say may come back to haunt you and that you are not obliged to say anything. Public relations practitioners, on the other hand, espouse the virtues of openness, of sharing information as soon as possible, of cooperating with media, and of responding to people's claims to their right to know. Lawyers are accustomed to getting extensions, protracting the process in private, and delaying responses as long as possible. Public relations specialists routinely meet deadlines, recognize media time constraints as real, and respond immediately to media requests.

Public relations practitioners work to build and maintain mutuality and harmony in relationships. If public relations succeeds, then top management assumes that things are going smoothly and that there is no need for counsel. Lawyers, on the other hand, are called on when conflict and discord dominate an organization's relationships. Under conditions of threatened or actual legal action, top management turns to legal counsel for advice and protection. Hence lawyers gain power when organizations face conflict and discord with publics that turn to the courts for redress.

Practitioners with good writing skills can help make legal documents more understandable. In doing so, they could save organizations the costs of being misunderstood because of obscure or needlessly harsh language in touchy situations. Cooperation between these two functions can protect the organization legally while at the same time serving the public interest, as when Sentry Insurance led the way in the insurance industry by rewriting policies and literature in plain English. The new policy descriptions meet the test of legal counsel and greatly increase information value to policyholders and prospective customers.

Coordination of legal and public relations counsel can benefit organizations in many areas. For instance, close cooperation between the two is critical during labor contract negotiations, product recalls, layoffs or other sensitive personnel matters, consumer protests or boycotts, and other legally based or explosive situations. Additionally, legal and public relations counsel must be coordinated on such matters as booklets explaining benefits to employees, legality of advertising or publicity claims, plant security, and disclosure of financial information.[15]

Once a concern primarily in business and industry, now close cooperation between legal and public relations counselors is necessary in most organizations. A few examples make the point. Universities defend themselves both in the courts of justice and public opinion when campus date rapes become national news. The presidents of Stanford, MIT, and other major universities call in both lawyers and public relations specialists when excessive overhead charges on federally funded research projects make headline news. Executives at Red Cross and other blood banks nationwide consult both legal and public relations staff when news of contaminated blood in Oregon activates lawsuits and erodes public confidence in the nation's blood supply. Too late, but mayors and city managers call in both lawyers and public relations staff when the evening news leads with out-of-court settlements involving large sums of tax dollars and secrecy agreements about discrimination, sexual harassment, police brutality, or other misconduct on the part of public officials. Even church leaders consult lawyers and public relations practitioners after news reports of a priest admitting to molesting children in a church school program.

Increasingly, legal and public relations specialists collaborate when counseling CEOs and coordinate their responses in courts of law and in courts of public opinion. As one lawyer advised fellow legal counselors, however, "Make sure you are the lawyer and that public relations is handled by a public relations professional."

Human Resources or Personnel

In 1989, the American Society of Personnel Administrators changed its 40-year-old name to the Society for Human Resources Management. Some predict that the emerging conflict between public relations and human resources will become a "turf war" similar to the one public relations and marketing experienced in the 1980s and early 1990s. Lines are blurred and opportunity for friction is high.

Fundamental problems concern (1) whether human resources' role in strategic planning in personnel matters during downsizing, mergers, and acquisitions extends to areas outside employee relations; (2) the extent to which communication efforts within the community constitute an extension of the organization-employee relationship; and (3) whether programs directed to the employee public draw more on public relations concepts than on those developed from the traditions of personnel and extended to the new function of human resources. Control of employee communications (not the whole of employee relations) is the most frequent source of conflict between these two functions. Compromise comes when practitioners and human resource specialists realize that internal relationships inevitably reverberate externally.

Surveys of the field indicate the nature of overlapping assignments. Seventy percent of *pr reporter* newsletter's readers report that employee communication is handled by the public relations department, while only 22 percent indicate employee communication falls under the human resources function. Of course, the newsletter's readers are primarily public relations practitioners.

In contrast, the results of a survey of 2000 companies by the Wyatt Company, which deals primarily with human resources and personnel departments, indicated a quite different picture. More than half—53 percent—of the responding companies place employee communication under human resources, whereas only 30 percent put it under public relations.

Strategic management of employee relations, however, requires close cooperation and collaboration between public relations and human resources. At Alcoa, for example, successful management of employee communication results from the two departments working in partnership. In some other organizations, however, the conflict intensifies as employee communications and various public relations roles such as community relations, media relations, and other strategic communication functions are assigned to human resources. In some cases, top public relations executives have resigned when reorganizations put their departments under human resources.

Organizational Development

Beginning in the late 1960s, organizations increased efforts to develop their major resource, people. Organizational development (OD) departments accepted assignments such as helping introduce organizational changes, management team building, leadership development, and management consulting on strategic planning. In many organizations, OD specialists took over traditional training departments and annexed other functions. For example, among the primarily training-oriented tasks listed in one article appears "maintaining organization relationships."[16] The potential for confusion and conflict with the public relations function is apparent.

To increase their own effectiveness, some employee communication specialists are studying OD concepts and techniques. As the number of OD departments increases, however, public relations practitioners will have to coordinate their programs with overall organization change efforts and other OD programs designed for employees, managers, and key outside groups. Otherwise, organizations run the risk of splitting such programs into too many parts over several departments. Learning the language and techniques of OD and group facilitation helps practitioners demystify the process and collaborate with OD specialists to achieve common goals.[17]

THE OUTSIDE COUNSELING FIRM

Beginning in the 1980s, many public relations agencies switched their titles to "public relations firms." The change in titles reflects the increased emphasis on counseling and strategic planning services, viewed as more professional than those of press agents and publicity agencies. Another reason for the switch is to position the firm as something different from advertising agencies and other vendors of services working on commissions. Although many still use "agency," most in the field prefer the association with law firms, management consulting firms, certified public accounting firms, architectural firms, and consulting engineering firms.

Public Relations Firms

The more than 2000 public relations counseling firms and agencies in the United States range widely in size and scope of service.[18] New York leads all cities in the number of firms, with Chicago a distant second. The three largest firms each employ more than 2000 people worldwide, but there are uncounted thousands working as individual counselors. Many work as "So-And-So and Associates," often meaning, "If I can't handle the project alone, I know other practitioners I can bring in on the project."

O'Dwyer's Directory of Public Relations Firms provides the most complete listing of U.S. firms by location and specialty, plus almost 500 in 55 other countries. According to the leading professional publication in London, *PR Week*, Shandwick has about 850 employees in its European offices and Burson-Marsteller about 750. These numbers could increase dramatically as the European Community's economy improves and nationalistic barriers subside.

Phone directories in every major city list firms under "Public Relations" and "Publicity." For example, the London yellow pages directory contains more than 500 listings under "Public Relations Consultancies." Another 70 listings appear under "Publicity Consultants."

Many of the London firms are branches or affiliates of large international firms. For example, the world's largest firm (more than 100 offices worldwide), Shandwick, has its headquarters office in London, which is also the city's largest firm. London's second largest firm is a branch of New York–based Burson-Marsteller. Chicago-based Edelman Public Relations Worldwide and St. Louis–based Fleishman-Hillard both have large London branches. The world's largest public relations conglomerate—WPP Group PLC—is also based in London. WPP owns both Hill and Knowlton and Ogilvy Public Relations Group, both based in New York. Hill and Knowlton's London office usually ranks among the top five or six firms in London, based on annual billings and number of employees.

Large public relations firms are opening branches, acquiring smaller firms, and affiliating with firms in major cities around the globe. As client organizations deal in the global community, so must their public relations firms. Firms use different approaches to "globalization," however. For example, each of Shandwick's 100 offices has its own name and approach to serving its clients. Each is staffed by nationals who know the media and cultures in the area served. Following a similar approach, the loosely affiliated international network of 60 firms known as The Worldcom Group, Inc., says it provides "global access, local focus."

Both Burson-Marsteller and Hill and Knowlton, on the other hand, have strong corporate cultures and procedures that guide, even control, operations in offices worldwide. James H. Dowling, New York–based Burson-Marsteller president and CEO, describes his firm's common vision, values, and approach internationally as "seamless." Similarly, Hill and Knowlton uses its name worldwide, moves executives among offices, and directs international operations from its New York headquarters.

Whatever the approach, going global was the major development of the late 1980s and early 1990s. As markets and economies became global, as global alliances formed, as global media delivered messages around the world within seconds, public relations and every other aspect of corporate business became global enterprises. Public relations firms now serve clients with new approaches to communication and sophisticated counsel in a global village.

Advertising Agency Ownership

Of the 20 largest firms, ten are subsidiaries of large advertising agencies; most were acquired as advertising agencies bought out founders and principals of closely held public relations firms. The trend began in 1978 when Foote, Cone and Belding purchased Carl Byoir and Associates. The largest U.S.-based firms are now owned by advertising agencies: Hill and Knowlton, Inc., by J. Walter Thompson Co. (which in turn is owned by London-based WPP Group PLC); Burson-Marsteller by

Young & Rubicam, Inc.; Ogilvy Public Relations Group by WPP Group; and Omnicom PR Network by Omnicom Group.

Those who work in firms owned by large advertising agencies point to greater cooperation between the marketing and public relations functions being served by the "full-service" team, better research provided by the more experienced and sophisticated research departments of advertising agencies, greater communication production resources and capabilities, and better management.

Critics of advertising agency ownership believe that public relations firms lose their independence and clients lose the benefit of the counselor's alternative view in communication planning. They also point to diminished budgets and power for public relations as it inevitably becomes subservient to marketing-driven budgets and goals of the advertising team. Problems also arise when two strong institutions with different histories and cultures try to perform as a team, especially when historically they were competitors. Even though under the umbrella of common ownership, they remain competitors for the client's budget. Because each unit of a large conglomerate is rewarded based on how much business it generates, in effect advertising and public relations units compete for the client's business. Also, critics question the value of the offer of one-stop shopping. Few clients use them as communication supermarkets. Rather, most large clients prefer to spread their business over several agencies and firms, expanding the range of perspectives and client experiences.

History suggests that forces work against the advertising agency–public relations subsidiary arrangement. Advertising agencies have found it difficult to determine what public relations services to offer, how to organize the function effectively, and how to sustain it apart from the advertising side of the shop, from which it derives the vast majority of dollar billings. The N. W. Ayer advertising agency pioneered in 1920, and the Albert Frank-Guenther Law agency took the next step when it began offering full-fledged public relations and publicity services. In the 1930s, J. Walter Thompson, Young & Rubicam, and Benton & Bowles soon followed. By the mid-1940s, 75 agencies provided publicity service for clients, according to an *Advertising Age* survey.

Specialization

The full-service firm still dominates, but there is a trend toward firms carving out their own specialized client-service market niches. One such specialty is demonstrated by the dramatic growth of Washington, D.C., firms that specialize in lobbying, public affairs, legislative affairs, and other government relations. The client lists at many such firms include foreign governments and foreign corporations who follow developments in the U.S. capital and who want their points of view considered. An example is "Citizens for Free Kuwait" retaining Hill and Knowlton while the United States contemplated going to war with Iraq to end its occupation of Kuwait. The tab was almost $6 million.

At the other extreme, the service can be nothing more than putting out news releases about a visiting dignitary or providing updates on legislation of interest to a foreign client. Regardless of the assignment, individuals who represent foreign interests must register with the U.S. Department of Justice. The Foreign Agents Registration Act of 1938 requires registration by any "public relations counsel, publicity agent, information-service employee, or political consultant that acts within the U.S. in the interest of a foreign principal." Globalization and increased international commerce of all kinds suggest that this will continue as a growth area for public relations firms specializing in government relations.

Unfortunately, the "Beltway" (Washington, D.C.) set also includes influence-peddling operations that rise and fall with administrations and as the public-service–private-power revolving door produces more Michael Deavers and Lyn Nofzigers. Commenting on the antics of these and others from the Reagan administration who turned government service into profitable public relations and lobbying practices, one editorial writer asked, "Has the murky 'profession' of public relations turned to sleaze?" In fact, for some it meant prison time and hefty fines for illegal lobbying. That approach aside, there remains a large and growing need for legitimate public relations counsel on legislative affairs and lobbying in the nation's capital, as well as in every state capital and major city.

Other specialties include agriculture, financial public relations and investor relations, health care, high-tech, sports, and travel and tourism, to name only a few. In agriculture, for example, the John Volk Company (Chicago) serves clients such as Ralston Purina, National Livestock and Meat Board, and Caterpillar. The world's largest financial public relations firm, the Financial Relations Board (Chicago, New York, San Francisco, Dallas, and Sherman Oaks, California), provides financial, investment, and other business communication services to a long list of clients. The client list at Wang Associates Health Communications (New York) includes pharmaceutical, biotechnology, and health care organizations such as Abbott Laboratories, Barnes Hospital, and Warner-Lambert. In the high-tech setting of Santa Clara, California, the client list at Cunningham Communication, Inc., includes C-Cube Microsystems, Hewlett-Packard, and Metaphor Computer Systems. Alan Taylor Communications, Inc. (New York) specializes in sports publicity, special events, and media tours for clients such as General Mills (Wheaties$_{TM}$), U.S. Golf Tour, and Women's Tennis Association. And as a final example of specialization, M. Silver Associates, Inc. (New York) serves travel clients American Express, Cunard Hotels and Resorts, and Stouffer Presidente Hotels (Mexico).

Other consulting firms such as Daniel H. Baer, Inc. (Sherman Oaks, California) and James E. Arnold Consultants (New York) specialize in helping clients select public relations firms and evaluate their performance. For example, IBM retained the Arnold firm during the process of evaluating proposals from firms being considered for additional work for the giant computer manufacturer. (See Exhibit 3–1.)

EXHIBIT 3-1

Check List for Selecting a Firm

Competence and reputation

- Years in business
- Size – people and billings
- Full service – specialties
- Reach – local, regional, national, international
- Growth pattern/financial stability
- Types of accounts
- Experience with accounts similar to yours – any conflicts
- Samples of work
- Sample list of suppliers used

Staff

- List and qualifications of staff – full time, project clients, free lance/consultants
- Names of several former employees
- Staff to be assigned to your account – qualifications and longevity with firm
- Percent of their time to be devoted to your account – other accounts they will handle
- Staff or personnel backup available
- Staff turnover in the past two years

Clients

- Existing client list
- Past clients
- Average number of clients during past three years – retainer clients, project clients
- Oldest clients and length of service
- Average length of client/firm relationships
- Clients lost in last year

Results and measurement

- Does firm understand your objectives/needs?
- How will progress be reported?
- How will results be measured?
- What will it cost – billing process, hourly rate, expenses billed, approval process?

Courtesy Harland W. Warner, Manning, Selvage & Lee, and reprinted with permission of *Public Relations Journal.*

Reasons for Retaining Outside Counsel

Chester Burger, long-time consultant to the public relations industry, lists six reasons why organizations retain firms, even though some have internal departments:

1. Management has not previously conducted a formal public relations program and lacks experience in organizing one.
2. Headquarters may be located far from communications and financial centers.
3. The firm has a wide range of up-to-date contacts.
4. An outside firm can provide services of experienced executives and creative specialists who would be unwilling to move to other cities or whose salaries could not be afforded by a single organization.
5. An organization with its own public relations department may need highly specialized services that it cannot afford or does not need on a full-time, continuous basis.
6. Crucial policy matters require the independent judgment of an outsider.

As an example, GTE Diversified Products retained Hill and Knowlton to help plan and conduct the global public relations program for its joint venture with Siemens A.G. of then–West Germany. The vice president of public affairs charged with coordinating internal and external communication throughout operations in the United States and 22 other countries enlisted experienced outside help:

> By retaining their (Hill and Knowlton) services, we benefited from an existing network of media contacts, saving us some of the trouble of tracking down outlets we needed to contact with news of the joint venture. We also used their capabilities in resolving problems in translating, designing, and delivering documents in a manner appropriate to each of our markets.
>
> . . . If you don't have a structure in place, you should consider hiring the services of an outside firm that can provide you with the necessary expertise. . . . In a global setting, doing all this requires more effort, more forethought, and more skills than ever. There are simply more variables to contend with. And this puts ever greater demands on public affairs staff.[19]

The Client-Firm Relationship

Sometimes counseling firms seek clients they can help. In other circumstances, clients seek help from counseling firms. For instance, an oil company may have a persistent problem with government regulation of offshore drilling, a long-planned enterprise in which millions of dollars have been invested. However, plans are held up because of opposition to exploration by environmental groups, investor concern that stock value will drop because of unfavorable reports in the business press, and public skepticism that the oil company will protect fragile ocean ecosystems. Added to that are memories of Exxon's public relations mishandling of the *Exxon Valdez* oil spill off Prince William Sound in Alaska. The internal department convinces the chairman and CEO that it is time to seek the best outside help available to help manage a complete overhaul of the public relations program. In some cases, it takes a *Valdez* oil spill or stock sell-off to get top management's attention.

It is not uncommon for the client-firm relationship to begin with an emergency, as was the case when Arizona Economic Council officials called on Hill and Knowlton. After Arizona voters defeated a ballot initiative establishing a state holiday honoring Martin Luther King, Jr., the National Football League announced that it would move the 1993 Super Bowl game from Tempe. In such emergencies, counsel provides advice and helps the client manage the crisis. Depending on the outcome, the firm may be retained on a long-term basis to prevent such crises in the future. In the Arizona situation, however, the Super Bowl game was moved to the Rose Bowl in Pasadena and Hill and Knowlton lost the Arizona Economic Council as a client.

Under more typical circumstances a counseling firm begins its service after being invited to present a proposal. It begins by researching the client's problem situation and relationships with publics affected by or involved in the situation. Called a public relations audit, this initial exploration can take several days or even months. When it is completed, the counselor may report that there is no real problem or threat that requires outside assistance or that the problems disclosed by the research are outside the counselor's area of expertise. More likely, however, the counsel arranges to make a presentation outlining the following:

1. Research findings and situation analysis of the problem or opportunity
2. Potential harm or gain to the organization
3. Projected difficulties and opportunities, given various courses of action or nonaction
4. Overall program goals, as well as objectives for various publics
5. Immediate action and communication responses, if needed to meet a crisis
6. Long-range plan for achieving the goals and objectives
7. Evaluation plans
8. Staffing plans and budget

Usually, competing firms make presentations, with one selected on the basis of demonstrated capabilities and the presentation proposal. Once retained, the counselor usually functions in one of three ways:

1. Provides advice, leaving execution to the client's internal staff
2. Provides advice and works with the client's staff to execute the program
3. Provides advice and undertakes full execution of program

Counselor Presentation

Figure 3–4

Courtesy Kerry Tucker, President, Nuffer, Smith, Tucker, Inc., San Diego.

Occasionally, client-firm relationships take a turn the client does not anticipate. To get the business (win the account), usually an "A-Team" of experienced professionals makes the presentation (new business pitch). The client is duly impressed by the talent and depth of experience they assume will be applied to their problems. That may be the last time they see of many of these people, however. Instead, the account gets assigned to lower-level junior staff members who do not have the range of experiences represented by the new business development team. Critics justifiably refer to this practice as a bait-and-switch tactic. The firm's senior executives show up just often enough to assure the client that the business is not being neglected.

Occasionally, clients call for a review of the firm's work or even reopen the selection process by requesting proposals from competing firms. Such a review may simply be a cover story for a decision to change firms that has already been made. To soften the blow, the incumbent firm is given the "courtesy" of making the "short list" of finalists, but another firm gets the account. Or, clients sometimes call for reviews and entertain proposals from competing firms to remind the incumbent firm that the client's business should not be taken for granted or given anything less than prime attention. Newsletters serving the field and some counselors suggest yet another reason why some clients call for proposals: to get new ideas, free. The suspicion is that there is no real intention to retain a firm or to replace an incumbent. These published request for proposals (RFPs) or the invitations to selected firms represent an unethical search for new ideas without intending to pay for the counsel. For that reason, some firms will not do speculative pitches unless the client pays a fee that covers the cost of preparing the presentation.

The Counselor's Advantages

A Public Relations Society of America Counselors Academy survey of corporate members found that almost three out of four use outside counsel even though they have their own internal departments. In its 1991 survey of the profession, *pr reporter* newsletter reported that 31 percent of the responding organizations increased their use of outside counsel while 14 percent reduced their use of firms. Clearly, external counsel provides valuable services not readily available internally.

Counselors rank *variety of talents and skills* as their greatest advantage over internal staffing. *Objectivity*, relatively untrammeled by the politics within an organization, ranks second. *Range of prior experience* is third; *geographical scope of their operations*, fourth; and the *ability to reinforce and upgrade a client's internal staff*, fifth.

A number of counselors emphasize the *flexibility* of their staff and operations as a prime advantage. In their offices, or no farther away than the telephone, are skilled researchers, artists, models, copy editors, magazine feature writers, media coaches and placement specialists, talk show experts, photographers, and legislative experts. A client can request a highly technical and specialized service and an account executive can attend to the need immediately.

Flexibility is also tied to scope of operations and to range of experience. A firm based in New York, Washington, or Chicago can serve clients in Colorado, West Virginia, and California. One of the global firms' real assets is their network of branch offices or affiliated firms in London, Tokyo, and Melbourne, just as in Denver, Dallas, and Seattle. For example, Omnicom PR Network has more than 50 offices in 15 countries; Rowland Worldwide has 34 offices; Edelman Public Relations Worldwide has 22 offices; Ogilvy Public Relations Group has more than 50 offices throughout the United States, Europe, Asia, the Pacific, and Latin America; and Manning Selvage and Lee has more than a dozen offices plus a worldwide network of affiliated firms.

In the course of any year a counselor will work on many different problems. Typically the repertoire of experiences includes employee strikes; protests by activist groups; special events such as grand openings, annual meetings, anniversaries, award ceremonies, and dedications; quarterly and annual reports; and research on proposed legislation. In addition, a great deal of time is devoted to supporting marketing efforts: introducing new products and services, publicizing their uses, and promoting other aspects of the marketing effort. In practice, marketing support pays the bills for many public relations firms. As one firm principal put it, "Take away our work in marketing and you take away more than half our business."

In effect, a public relations firm is a repository of living case histories. Each project adds to its fund of knowledge. Experience and versatility of staff make this synergy possible. The counselor approaches each situation bolstered by experience with similar situations and knowledge of the success or failure that attended previous encounters.

The counselor's *reputation* can be a major advantage. Outside experts often can introduce ideas that internal staffers have struggled unsuccessfully to place on the agenda. Paying a hefty fee apparently increases top management's attention to public relations counsel. Knowing that the counselor's reputation and subsequent referrals are on the line also helps ensure performance.

The Counselor's Handicaps

With rare exceptions, intervention by outside counsel—and this applies to almost all consultants—meets with *internal opposition* ranging from nonacceptance to outright rejection. This is, at least in theory, the counselor's most serious handicap. Antagonism toward and resistance to outsiders are natural human traits. The old guard resists change—the new idea, the new approach, the new look—and sees it as a threat to security and established ways of doing business.

The counselor, more often than not, makes suggestions in the form of recommendations. Those originally responsible can take offense and be alienated by these suggestions. Their realm is being invaded; their judgment is being criticized. The offended ask, "What does this outsider know about our organization, our way of doing things?"

Counselors, however, do not rank this problem at the top. They overwhelmingly cite *questions of cost* as the most frequent problem with clients. They list *threat to old guard and set ways* as the second most persistent handicap. *Resistance to outside advice* comes in third, and fourth is *unforeseen conflicts of personality or conviction*.

Other problems expressed frequently by counselors include a stubborn *lack of understanding of public relations by clients* and *unavailability of clients*—presumably the decision makers—at times when counselors want decisions. This suggests a problem of priorities on the part of clients.

Threatened insiders can create problems not related to the actual quality of service. Under the guise of scrutiny and concern, they raise questions about cost, return on investment, or qualifications. They point to the counselor's *superficial grasp of the organization's unique problems*: the local and historical angles on problems, the sacred cows, the things we never talk about. When those in the client organization raise such questions, it is an uphill battle for external counselors. Dealing with the internal staff and others in the client organization calls for special consulting skills.

Counseling Firm Costs

Clients retain the services of a counseling firm for specific projects or for an indefinite period of continuing service, reviewable and renewable at intervals. Fees for specific projects are paid on an hourly fee basis or as a negotiated fixed fee covering the entire project. Fees for continuing services, on the other hand, are established in one of three ways:

1. A monthly retainer covering a fixed number of hours and services
2. A minimum retainer plus monthly billing for actual staff time at hourly rates or on a per diem basis
3. Straight hourly charges, usually on a scale representing the range of experience and expertise

Out-of-pocket expenses are generally billed at cost and are exclusive of the retainer fee. In some cases, the client deposits an advance with the firm to cover such expenses. Some firms, however, mark up actual costs of certain expenses by 15–20 percent to cover overhead costs. Ruder Finn (New York), for example, marks up advertising placements, photography, and printing by 20 percent, but bills actual cost for entertainment, clipping services, and postage.

Fees vary widely. Large counseling firms have minimum retainer fees, usually in the range of $1000 to $10,000, but up to $50,000 per month for major accounts. Hill and Knowlton's minimum retainer is $7500 per month. At the other end of the scale, small counseling firms may provide a minimal service, such as writing an occasional news release, for as little as $100. Hourly fees range from a low of $25 an hour for assistant account executives or other junior support staff, to several hundred dollars for every hour worked by senior counselors and firm principals. Ruder Finn, which does not charge fixed monthly retainer fees, reportedly charges an average of $250 per hour for senior counselors and in the $80–$150 hourly range for other project staff. These rates typically reflect salary markups in the range of 2.5 to 3.5 the actual hourly staff costs. Figures differ from city to city, but four elements are reflected in counseling fees and charges:

1. Actual cost of staff time devoted to the project
2. Executive time and supervision
3. Overhead costs
4. Reasonable profit for doing the work

EXHIBIT 3-2

Time Sheet

Reprinted with permission from *The PR Client Service Manual: Managing for Results and Profit*, San Diego, Calif.: The Gable Group, 1992.

TIMESHEET

Name: _____   Employee #: _____   Date: _____

⏱	JOB# PFC	JOB	OPER. CODE	TOTAL HOURS	COMMENTS	✓	JOB# PFC	JOB	OPER. CODE	TOTAL HOURS	COMMENTS
7:00						11:00					
7:06						11:06					
7:12						11:12					
7:18						11:18					
7:24						11:24					
7:30	684	342	100		Plan product	11:30					
7:36					launch event	11:36					
7:42						11:42					
7:48						11:48					
7:54						11:54				2.0	
8:00						12:00					
8:06						12:06					
8:12						12:12					
8:18						12:18					
8:24						12:24					
8:30						12:30	142	010	130		Follow-up on
8:36				.2		12:36					grand opening
8:42	684	342	110		meet w/client	12:42					pitch letter
8:48					re special	12:48					
8:54					event	12:54					
9:00						1:00					
9:06						1:06					
9:12						1:12					
9:18						1:18					
9:24						1:24					
9:30						1:30					
9:36						1:36					
9:42						1:42					
9:48						1:48				1.4	
9:54				1.3		1:54	201	010	110		Call re next
10:00	920	920			New business	2:00					year's program
10:06					hotel proposal	2:06				.3	
10:12						2:12	444	222	125		Brainstorm
10:18						2:18					special event
10:24						2:24					
10:30						2:30					
10:36						2:36				.5	
10:42						2:42	925	925			
10:48						2:48					
10:54						2:54					

The most common threat to client-firm relationships is conflict over the costs and hours billed. As a result, most firms use sophisticated accounting methods to record and track staff hours and project expenses. Within firms, "billable hours" often become a criterion for assessing employee productiveness. Some firms, formally or informally, expect each practitioner to bill a minimum number of hours each month, just as in most accounting and law firms. For example, it would not be unusual for an employee to "bill out" an average of more than 30 hours each week. In other words, the employee's time sheet—recorded in tenth- or quarter-hour units—documents 30 or more hours of work charged to specific client projects. (Exhibit 3–2 shows a typical form for recording hours.) Each client's monthly bill, then, reflects the total hours recorded on all staff time sheets designated to that account or project. Account executives monitor these time sheets and detailed expense records to keep costs in line with the client-firm agreement.

INTEGRATING THE FUNCTION

Increasingly, organizations are using a combination of internal departments and outside counsel to fulfill the public relations management function. Also, increasingly, top management recognizes the essential nature of public relations to organizational success. Top practitioners are increasingly joining the executive decision-making group, or at least are consulted on major decisions. Practitioners in firms are increasingly serving as counselors and strategic planners, rather than as press agents and communication technicians. Public relations has become an integral part of organization management.

According to Robert Dilenschneider, former president and chief executive officer of Hill and Knowlton, progress in integrating the function is threatened by the "seven deadly sins in this business." *First is overpromising*, making commitments for things they know they cannot deliver. *Second is overmarketing*, or overselling the client on the capabilities or expertise of public relations. *Third is underservicing*, referred to earlier as the bait and switch, listing senior people as part of the account team but using junior staff to do the work. *Fourth is putting the firm's financial results ahead of performance and results for the client. Fifth is the quick fix*, when public relations takes the form of a short-sighted response to a complex problem that requires a long-lasting solution. It is too easy to fall into the trap of client or management expectations that public relations has the power to fix problems without having to make important changes in the organization. *Sixth is treating public relations as simply a support function* charged with implementing strategies formulated by lawyers, financial officers, and top line managers. *Seventh is violating ethical standards*, as nothing has greater value than the function's reputation for ethical conduct and concern for social responsibility.[20]

Public relations has impact in an organization when people begin to tell each other that candor in communication is the best policy and that socially responsible actions are in the best interest of the organization. This means that public relations consciousness is gaining ground and there is growing confidence in the staff and outside counselors.

Exposing a clean organization to public gaze, operating in the mutual interests of itself and its publics, does not mean that everything about the organization should be made public knowledge. In business there are competitors to consider. In the military there are security considerations. In health institutions there are ethical limitations on disclosure of patient information. In government agencies there are political and regulatory factors. Everywhere there are legal pros and cons. Common sense helps, but organizations must have specialized staff or counsel to perform the public relations function in an ethical and professional manner. This is the lesson from public relations' history, the topic of the next chapter.

ADDITIONAL READINGS

Cantor, Bill, and Chester Burger, eds.   *Experts in Action: Inside Public Relations*, 2d ed. New York: Longman, Inc., 1989. See Bill Cantor, "Chapter 26: Finding and Keeping the Right People" and "Chapter 27: Public Relations/Public Affairs Job Guidelines" (pp. 283–326); James E. Arnold, "Chapter 28: A CEO's Expectations of Public Relations" (pp. 331–48); and Robert L. Ferrante, "Chapter 31: Using a Public Relations Firm" (pp. 392–405).

Dozier, David M., and Larissa A. Grunig.   "The Organization of the Public Relations Function." In *Excellence in Public Relations and Communication Management*, edited by James E. Grunig, 395–417. Hillsdale, N.J.: Lawrence Erlbaum Associates, Publishers, 1992.

Grunig, Larissa A.   "How Public Relations/Communication Departments Should Adapt to the Structure and Environment of an Organization . . . And What They Actually Do" and "Power in the Public Relations Department." In *Excellence in Public Relations and Communication Management*, edited by James E. Grunig, 467–501. Hillsdale, N.J.: Lawrence Erlbaum Associates, Publishers, 1992.

Nager, Norman R., and Richard H. Truitt.   *Strategic Public Relations Counseling*. New York: Longman, Inc., 1987. (now published by University Press of America, Lanham, Md.) Authoritative discussion of public relations counseling concepts, ethics, and practices. Includes numerous interviews.

Wilensky, Harold L.   *Organizational Intelligence*. New York: Basic Books, Inc., Publishers, 1967. Still-relevant exploration of factors affecting amount of attention and resources devoted to information gathering in organizations.

Wilson, James Q.   *Bureaucracy*. New York: Basic Books, Inc., Publishers, 1989. Scholarly discussion of the rules, regulations, and workings of bureaucracies in government, corporations, and other institutions.

NOTES

[1] R. Wayne Pace, *Organizational Communication: Foundations for Human Resource Development* (Englewood Cliffs, N.J.: Prentice-Hall, Inc., 1983), 16–17.

[2] Bruce R. Barstow, "An Insider's Outside View of Public Relations," in *Precision Public Relations*, edited by Ray Eldon Hiebert (New York: Longman, Inc., 1988), 58–59. (First published in *Public Relations Review* 10, no. 1: 10–17.)

[3] Philip Lesly, "The Stature and Role of Public Relations," *Public Relations Journal* 37, no. 1 (January 1981): 15.

[4] Martha M. Lauzen, "Public Relations Roles, Intraorganizational Power, and Encroachment," *Journal of Public Relations Research* 4, no. 2 (1992): 61–80.

[5] Barstow, "An Insider's Outside View of Public Relations," 65.

[6] James E. Grunig, ed., *Excellence in Public Relations and Communication Management*. Hillsdale, N.J.: Lawrence Erlbaum Associates, Publishers, 1992. The term *dominant coalition* is first introduced on p. 24 and then used throughout the book.

[7] Larissa A. Grunig, "Power in the Public Relations Department," *Public Relations Research Annual* 2 (1990): 115–55.

[8] For a detailed analysis, see David M. Dozier, "The Innovation of Research in Public Relations Practice: Review of a Program of Studies," *Public Relations Research Annual* 2 (1990): 3–28.

[9] Herbert A. Simon, *The New Science of Management Decision* (New York: Harper and Row, 1960): 5–6.

[10] William O. Bourke, "Reassessing the Public Relations Role," *Public Relations Journal* 46, no. 1 (January 1990): 40. Bourke is chairman and CEO of Reynolds Metals Company.

[11] Norman R. Nager and Richard H. Truitt, *Strategic Public Relations Counseling* (New York: Longman, Inc., 1987), 194.

[12] Roy T. Cottier, "Communication: A Management Strategy, Not a Professional Technique," *Vital Speeches* 53, no. 18 (July 1, 1987): 556–59. Speech to International Association of Business Communicators, Toronto. Cottier is former senior vice president of corporate relations at Northern Telecom Limited.

[13] Clarence Randall, *The Folklore of Management* (Boston: Little, Brown, 1959), 24.

[14] Ivy Lee, *Publicity: Some of the Things It Is and Is Not* (New York: Industries Publishing Co., 1925): 58–59.

[15] See Chapter 6 for more detailed discussion of legal considerations.

[16] Tod White, "Increasing Your Effectiveness as a Training and Development Professional," *Training and Development Journal* 33 (May 1979): 3–12.

[17] Warner Burke, *Organization Development: A Normative View* (Reading, Mass.: Addison-Wesley Publishing Company, 1987) provides overview of OD. A special issue of *Management Communication Quarterly* 3, issue 1 (August 1989), provides a similar introduction to group facilitation.

[18] See current edition of *O'Dwyer's Director of Public Relations Firms* published by J. R. O'Dwyer Co., Inc., New York, for listings, addresses, executive names, number of employees, billings, and specialties. The 1993 edition lists more than 2200 firms and departments of advertising agencies cross-listed with their 15,000-plus clients.

[19] Geoffrey L. Pickard, "Bridging the Gap in Joint Venture Communications: Global Public Affairs," *Vital Speeches* 53, no. 5 (December 15, 1986): 145–48.

[20] Robert L. Dilenschneider, "The Seven Deadly Sins," *PR Week* (November 14–20, 1988): 11. *PR Week* is no longer published in the United States. For similar perspective with extensive case examples, see Dilenschneider's book, *Power and Influence: Mastering the Art of Persuasion* (New York: Prentice Hall Press, 1990).

Historical Origins of Public Relations

> Those who cannot remember the past are doomed to repeat it.
>
> **GEORGE SANTAYANA**

Studying how public relations evolved provides helpful insights into its functions, its strengths, and its weaknesses. Many practitioners do not have a sense of their calling's history and thus do not fully understand its place and purpose in society. This lessens their professionalism. Published histories typically oversimplify what is a complex and dramatic story by emphasizing novelty and a few colorful personalities. But understanding public relations' historical context is a vital part of today's practice.

The history of public relations cannot be told by simply saying that it grew out of press agentry. Nor can it be fully told in terms of people such as Ivy Lee or Arthur Page. Efforts to communicate with others and to deal with the force of public opinion go back to antiquity; only the tools, degree of specialization, breadth of knowledge, and intensity of effort are relatively new.

ANCIENT GENESIS

Communicating to influence viewpoints or actions can be traced from the earliest civilizations. Archaeologists found a farm bulletin in Iraq that told farmers of 1800 B.C. how to sow their crops, how to irrigate, how to deal with field mice, and how to harvest their crops, an effort not unlike today's distribution of farm bulletins by the U.S. Department of Agriculture. Rudimentary elements of public relations also appear in descriptions of the king's spies in ancient India. Besides espionage, the spies' duties included keeping the king in touch with public opinion, championing the king in public, and spreading rumors favorable to the government.[1]

Greek theorists wrote about the importance of the public will, even though they did not specifically use the term *public opinion.* Certain phrases and ideas in the political vocabulary of the Romans and in the writing of the medieval period relate to modern concepts of public opinion. The Romans coined the expression *vox populi, vox Dei,* "the voice of the people is the voice of God." Machiavelli wrote, in his *Discoursi,* "Not without reason is the voice of the people compared to the voice of God," and he held that the people must be either "caressed or annihilated."

Public relations was used many centuries ago in England, where the kings maintained Lords Chancellor as "Keepers of the King's Conscience." There was an acknowledged need for a third party to facilitate communication and adjustment between the government and the people. So it was with the church, traders, and artisans. The word *propaganda* was born in the seventeenth century, when the Catholic Church set up its *Congregatio de Propaganda Fide,* "Congregation for Propagating the Faith."

BORN IN ADVERSITY AND CHANGE

The American beginnings of public relations appear in the American Revolution struggle for power between the patrician-led patriots and the commercial, propertied Tories. Later efforts to gain public support include the conflict between the trade and property interests led by Hamilton and the planter-and-farmer bloc led by Jefferson, the struggle between Jackson's agrarian pioneers and the financial forces of Nicholas Biddle, and the bloody Civil War.

Twentieth-century developments in this field are directly tied to the power struggles evoked by political reform movements. These movements, reflecting strong tides of protest against entrenched power groups, have been the catalytic agents for much of the growth of the public relations practice, since the jockeying of political and economic groups for dominance created the need to muster public support.

Public relations also grew in response to the need to gain public acceptance and utilization of swiftly advancing technology. For example, when the Bell Telephone System switched to all-number telephone dialing, it ran into a storm of public opposition on the West Coast from the Anti-Digit Dialing League, organized by Carl May against what he called the "cult of technology."[2] The U.S. Postal Service encountered similar resistance when it introduced zip codes.

The history of public relations is meaningful only when it is related to these power conflicts and recurring crises of change. It is not mere coincidence that, in the past, business interests took public relations most seriously when their positions of power were challenged or threatened by the forces of labor, the farmer, the shopkeeper, government regulators, or a maturing generation. Nor is it a coincidence that labor's programs intensified when an adverse public reaction to labor was crystallizing in regulatory legislation or waning public support. Similarly, the most intense developments in public relations within government came in periods of crisis: World War I, the Great Depression and New Deal, World War II, the Korean War, Vietnam, the uneasy Cold War years with the Soviet Union, the invasion of Panama, and the Persian Gulf War in Iraq and Kuwait.

So public relations practices must be examined in their historical context.

AMERICAN BEGINNINGS

Using publicity to raise funds, promote causes, boost commercial ventures, sell land, and build box-office personalities in the United States is older than the nation is. The American talent for promotion can be traced back to the first settlements on the East Coast in the seventeenth century. Probably the first systematic effort on this continent to raise funds was that sponsored by Harvard College in 1641, when that infant institution sent a trio of preachers to England on a "begging mission." Once in England, they notified Harvard that they needed a fund-raising brochure, now a standard item in a fund drive. In response to this request came *New England's First Fruits*, largely written in Massachusetts but printed in London in 1643, the first of countless public relations pamphlets and brochures.[3]

The tools and techniques of public relations have long been an important part of political weaponry. Sustained campaigns to move and manipulate public opinion go back to the Revolutionary War and the work of Samuel Adams and his cohorts. These revolutionaries understood the importance of public support and knew intuitively how to arouse and channel it. They used pen, platform, pulpit, staged events, symbols, news tips, and political organization in an imaginative, unrelenting way. Adams worked tirelessly to arouse and then organize public opinion, proceeding always on the assumption that "the bulk of mankind are more led by their senses than by their reason." Early on, he discerned that *public opinion results from the march of events and the way these events are seen by those active in public affairs.* Adams would create events to meet a need if none were at hand to serve his purpose.[4]

Far more than most realize, today's patterns of public relations practice were shaped by innovations in mobilizing public opinion developed by Adams and his fellow revolutionaries. In fomenting revolt against England, these propagandists, operating largely from the shadows, developed and demonstrated the power of these techniques:

1. The necessity of an organization to implement actions made possible by a public relations campaign: the Sons of Liberty, organized in Boston in January 1766, and the Committees of Correspondence, also born in Boston in 1775.[5]
2. The use of symbols that are easily identifiable and emotion arousing: the Liberty Tree.
3. The use of slogans that compress complex issues into easy-to-quote, easy-to-remember stereotypes: "Taxation without representation is tyranny."
4. Staged events that catch public attention, provoke discussion, and thus crystallize unstructured public opinion: the Boston Tea Party.[6]
5. The importance of getting your side of a story to the public first, so that your interpretation of events becomes the accepted one: the Boston Massacre.[7]
6. The necessity for a sustained saturation campaign using these techniques through all available channels of communication to penetrate the public mind with a new idea or a new conviction.

The enormous difficulty of mobilizing public opinion to fight a revolution and to form a government is little appreciated today.

> They knew that there was a wide gap between their public professions and American reality. They knew that there was bitter opposition to Independence and that the mass of the people were [sic] mostly indifferent. They knew, too, that there were deep rivalries and serious differences among the colonies.[8]

In weak contrast to the revolutionists' effective communication, the Tories, supporters of King George and the British Empire, relied not so much on propaganda as on legal and military pressures, to no avail. It is little wonder that an exuberant Sam Adams would exult when he heard the firing at Lexington, "Oh, what a glorious morning is this!" He and his fellow propagandists had done their work well.[9] The emotion-laden revolutionary campaign set patterns for the nation's political battles that were to follow.[10]

The next landmark in public relations in the new nation came with publication of 85 *Federalist* letters written to newspapers in 1787–1788 by Alexander Hamilton, James Madison, and John Jay. The letters urged ratification of the Constitution. David Truman says, "The entire effort of which *The Federalist* was a part was one of the most skillful and important examples of pressure group activity in American history." Morrison and Commager hold that "unless the Federalists had been shrewd in manipulation as they were sound in theory, their arguments could not have prevailed."

Historian Allan Nevins described these propaganda efforts as "history's finest public relations job." He wrote:

> Obtaining national acceptance of the Constitution was essentially a public relations exercise, and Hamilton, with his keen instinct for public relations, took thought not only to the product but to the ready acquiescence of thoughtful people; and he imparted his views to others. . . . Once the Constitution came before the country, the rapidity with which Hamilton moved was a striking exemplification of good public relations. He knew that if a vacuum develops in popular opinion, ignorant and foolish views will fill it. No time must be lost in providing accurate facts and sound ideas.[11]

The first clear beginnings of the public presidential campaign and of the presidential press secretary's function came in the era of Andrew Jackson. In the late 1820s and early 1830s, the common man won the ballot and the free public school was started. Literacy increased greatly and political interest was stimulated by a burgeoning, strident party press. As the people gained political power, it became necessary to campaign for their support. No longer was government the exclusive concern of the patrician few. "The new Democracy was heavily weighted with what gentlemen were pleased to call the rabble." With the rise of democracy in America came increasing rights for, and power of, *the individual*.[12] The ensuing power struggle produced an unsung pioneer in public relations, Amos Kendall.

As a key member of President Jackson's "Kitchen Cabinet," Kendall served Jackson as a pollster, counselor, ghost writer, and publicist. The "Kitchen Cabinet" was unexcelled at creating events to mold opinion. On all vital issues that arose, Jackson consulted these key advisers, most of whom, like Kendall, were former newspapermen.

Jackson, unlettered in political or social philosophy, had difficulty getting his ideas across. Like many of today's executives, he needed a specialist to convey his ideas to Congress and the country. Jackson's political campaigns and his government policies clearly reveal the influence of Kendall's strategy, sense of public opinion, and skill as a communicator.[13]

Likewise, Bank of the United States President Nicholas Biddle and his associates were fully alert to the methods of influencing public opinion in their political battles with Jackson and Kendall. In fact, banks were the first businesses to use the press for this purpose; by loans to editors and placement of advertisements, they influenced many newspapers and silenced others. John C. Calhoun asserted as early as 1816 that the banks had "in great measure, control over the press." Biddle's publicist, Mathew St. Clair Clarke, saturated the nation's press with press releases, reports, and pamphlets pushing the bank's case. In March 1831, the bank's board authorized Biddle "to cause to be prepared and circulated such documents and papers as may communicate to the people information in regard to the nature and operations of the bank." But the pamphlets, the many articles planted in the press, and the lobbying efforts by Biddle and his associates did not prevail over the forces of Jackson and Kendall.[14]

THE MIDDLE YEARS

Many of the generating forces had their origins in the nineteenth century, although the modern concept of public relations was little known in young America. There were few inducements for its full-scale development and no means of mass communication on a national basis. Group relationships were relatively simple; people were relatively self-sufficient and independent, the majority then living on farms.

The roots of modern public relations can be traced to these times, however. As Alan Raucher writes:

> Three major antecedents of twentieth-century publicity can be distinguished from their sometimes shady past. One of these was press agentry. Another was advertising. A third antecedent for publicity, rather unexpectedly, came from business critics and reformers. By the first decade of the century, those three elements, largely unnoticed by contemporaries, fused into a new compound.[15]

Press Agentry

To state that public relations has evolved from press agentry, although a gross oversimplification, contains a kernel of truth. Systematic efforts to attract or divert public attention are as old as efforts to persuade and propagandize. Much of what we define as public relations was labeled press agentry when it was being used to promote land settlement in our unsettled West or to build up political heroes.

Elements of press agentry are found in many public relations programs today, but not as strongly as critics assert. Press agentry, beginning with Phineas T. Barnum and the theatrical press agents who followed, developed as an adjunct to show business. Box-office enterprises are still the prime employers of press agents. Press agentry has reached its zenith in today's professional sports world, as illustrated with the promotions for the Super Bowl, championship boxing matches, and "Final Four."

Amos Kendall's time brought an effective demonstration of the "buildup" when Jackson's opponents created the myth of Davy Crockett in an effort to woo the frontier vote away from Old Hickory. Crockett's press agent was Mathew St. Clair Clarke. (The Davy Crockett legend was given an intensive if short-lived revival in the 1950s, when Walt Disney featured that "yaller flower of the forest" in movies, television programs, books, and records. Disney did not create the Crockett legend; he embellished it.)[16]

But the master of them all was Phineas Taylor Barnum, and he knew it. Barnum lived from 1810 until 1891, a period of great importance in the evolution of public relations, and his influence still lives today.

Barnum's showmanship was evident not only in a canny instinct that enabled him to give the masses what they wanted, but also in his ability to dictate to them a desire for what he thought they should want. . . . Every man has his star. Barnum's star was an exclamation mark.[17]

Promoter Barnum even employed his own press agent, Richard F. "Tody" Hamilton.[18]

Railroad publicists played an important role in settling our nation and in creating the romantic aura that still surrounds the West. Beginning in the 1850s, railroads and land developers used publicity and advertising to lure people westward. Charles Russell Lowell, who directed the Burlington Railroad's publicity campaign launched in 1858, wrote: "We are beginning to find that he who buildeth a railroad west must also find a population and build up business." He had good advice for today's practitioner: "We must blow as loud a trumpet as the merits of our position warrants."[19] From then until the American frontier closed near the end of the century, press agents' publicity was a major force moving people to new lands and new lives.

Other promoters were quick to recognize the power of publicity and advertising. When the promoters of the World's Columbian Exposition in Chicago of 1893 found their grandiose plans ridiculed and misrepresented in the American and European press, they quickly set up a Department of Publicity and Promotion and hired a newspaperman, Moses P. Handy, "to utilize the printing press in every possible way."[20] Success crowned Handy's efforts.

Success begot imitators. Barnum led the way, and others followed in an ever-increasing number. During the two decades before 1900, press agentry spread from show business to closely related enterprises. But as press agents grew in number and their exploits became more outrageous—although successful, more often than not—it was natural that they would arouse the hostility and suspicion of editors and inevitable that the practice and its practitioners would become tainted. This stigma remains as part of public relations' heritage.

Political Campaigning

Public relations strategists have played dominant roles in politics and political parties. Virginian John Beckley ranks among the first of a long line of political propagandists and organizers who have made the party system work. He was a devoted aide of Thomas Jefferson in building what was then known as the Republican party but today is the Democratic party. He was Jefferson's eyes and ears, his propagandist, "one of the leading party organizers of the 1790s."[21]

However, the development of modern political campaign methods and techniques, except insofar as these have been modified by television, satellite transmissions, and jet travel, is largely rooted in the last decades of the nineteenth century. Increasingly, "the activities of the public relations man [sic] have become a significant influence in processes crucial to democratic government."[22] In the 1880s and 1890s, techniques used by the political party managers followed from improved printing technology, abundant supply of cheap paper, and increasing literacy, factors that were also increasing the number of newspapers.

The need seen by both parties to "educate" new immigrants spurred the evolution of the "literary bureaus" into press bureaus, now a standard fixture of political campaigns.[23] The hard-hitting Bryan-McKinley campaign of 1896 marked the first use of political campaigning methods. Both parties set up campaign headquarters in Chicago, from whence flowed a heavy stream of pamphlets, posters, press releases, and other campaign propaganda, not unlike contemporary American political campaigns. William Jennings Bryan, a Democrat with little money, used the campaign train, an innovation that lasted until the jet age and that is revived occasionally in an attempt to demonstrate a candidate's commitment to take the campaign to the people.

By 1900, political press bureau managers, both national and state, had assumed most of the functions that characterize the roles of political practitioners. Mass communication inevitably assumed its central role in American politics with the introduction of radio in the mid-1920s and air travel in the 1930s.[24]

Business Practices

The last two decades of the nineteenth century brought other discernible beginnings of today's practice. Frenzied and bold development of industry, railroads, and utilities in America's post–Civil War era set the stage for public relations in the twentieth century.

In the 25 breathtaking years from 1875 to 1900, America doubled its population and jammed its people into cities, went into mass production and enthroned the machine, spanned the nation with rail and wire communications, developed the mass media of press and magazines, and replaced the plantation owner with the head of industry and the versatile pioneer with the specialized factory hand. All this laid the foundation for a mighty industrial machine.

The rise of powerful monopolies, the concentration of wealth and power, and the roughshod tactics of the robber barons brought a wave of protest and reform in the early 1900s. Contemporary public relations emerged out of the melee of the opposing forces in this period of the nation's rapid growth. Goldman observes, "Shouldering aside agriculture, large-scale commerce and industry became dominant over the life of the nation. Big business was committed to the doctrine that the less the public knew of its operations, the more efficient and profitable—even the more socially useful—the operations would be."[25] In this era of "the public be damned," exploitation of people and of natural resources was bound to bring, ultimately, protest and reform once people became aroused.

The prevailing hard-bitten attitude of business people toward the public—be they employees, customers, or voters—was epitomized in the brutal methods used by Henry Clay Frick to crush a labor union in the Carnegie-Frick Steel Company's Homestead, Pennsylvania, plant in 1892. The employees' strike was ultimately broken and the union destroyed by the use of the Pennsylvania state militia. Cold-blooded might won this battle, but the employees eventually won the war. Much of public relations history is woven into the unending struggle between employer and employee.[26]

The Carnegie-Frick Steel strike marked the transition from craft control to managerial control. Historian Merle Curti observed, "Corporations gradually began to realize the importance of combating hostility and courting public favor. The expert in public relations was an inevitable phenomenon in view of the need for the services he could provide."[27] Theodore N. Vail, who laid the public acceptance and public policy foundations of the nation's telephone system, recognized this as early as 1883 even though his buccaneering bosses did not. On December 20, 1883, Vail asked W. A. Leary of the Iowa Union Telephone and Telegraph Company these questions:

What has been the tendency of the relationship between the public and the local Co's. for the past year, i.e., are the relations between the public and the Co's. improving?

Where there has been any conflict between the local Exchange and the public, what has been the cause of the difficulties, and what has been the result?

A full and detailed reply to me would be of great service.[28]

In about 1888, the Mutual Life Insurance Company employed Charles J. Smith to manage a "species of literary bureau."[29] Although advertising and public relations are distinct in today's business enterprise, they developed along parallel lines, with overlapping functions, blurred distinctions, and confusion in the public mind. Advertising evolved to meet the marketing needs of business; public relations—or more accurately, publicity—evolved partly as a marketing support function, but mainly for other purposes.[30]

The *first corporate public relations department,* in the contemporary meaning of this term, was established in 1889 by George Westinghouse for his new electric corporation. Westinghouse had organized his company in 1886 to promote his revolutionary alternating-current system of electricity. Thomas A. Edison had earlier established Edison General Electric Company, which used direct current. The now-famous "battle of the currents" ensued.

Edison, aided by the astute Samuel Insull, launched a scare campaign against the Westinghouse alternating-current system. As McDonald records:

> Edison General Electric attempted to prevent the development of alternating current by unscrupulous political action and by even less savory promotional tactics. . . . The promotional activity was a series of spectacular stunts aimed at dramatizing the deadliness of high voltage alternating current, the most sensational being the development and promotion of the electric chair as a means of executing criminals.[31]

When the state of New York adopted electrocution in 1888, Westinghouse realized that he had to get his story to the public. He hired a Pittsburgh journalist, E. H. Heinrichs, who served as his personal press representative until Westinghouse died in March 1914. Heinrichs later said that he was hired not because of the "battle of the currents," but because Westinghouse, like today's executive, did not have time to deal with the press. Heinrichs was the company's main channel through which news about the company passed to the press.[32] Then, as now, it took specialized skill to gain a hearing in the public forum and to deal with media demands.

Other Activities

The fund-raising drive was born in the Civil War. Jay Cooke conceived and directed the first American fund-raising drive. Cooke sold war bonds for the Union by first selling patriotism and building a militant public opinion. Many of his techniques reappeared in the bond drives of World Wars I and II.

Also by the time of the Civil War, the U.S. Marine Corps was using advertising on a regular basis to attract recruits. And in the Spanish-American War of 1898, the work of Cuban propagandists did much to arouse American sympathies for Cuba and to discredit Spain. The Cuban junta used press releases and mass meetings to raise funds and promote support for the Cuban cause from 1895 on. Today, representation of foreign government interests in the United States, particularly in Washington, D.C., is an increasingly important, sometimes controversial, part of public relations.

Professional groups were paying attention to public opinion by the mid-1800s. In 1855, the American Medical Association (AMA) passed a resolution "urging the secretary of the Association to offer every facility possible to the reports of the public press to enable them to furnish full and accurate reports of the transactions." And in 1884, the AMA launched the first of its many programs to counter antivivisectionists' attacks, a problem that persists to this day as animal rights groups protest use of animals in research.

EVOLUTION TO MATURITY

Although the roots of today's practice lie far in the past, its definite beginnings date from the early 1900s, when the world entered the century that spanned from the horse and buggy to the space shuttle. The dividing lines blur a bit, but the growth can be traced through six main periods of development:

1. *Seedbed Era*   (1900–1917) of muckraking journalism countered by defensive publicity, and of far-reaching political reforms promoted by Theodore Roosevelt and Woodrow Wilson through the use of public relations skills.

2. *World War I Period* (1917–1919) of dramatic demonstrations of the power of organized promotion to kindle a fervent patriotism: to sell war bonds, enlist soldiers, and raise millions of dollars for welfare.

3. *Booming Twenties Era*   (1919–1929), when the principles and practices of publicity learned in the war were put to use promoting products, earning acceptance for changes wrought by the war-accelerated technology, winning political battles, and raising millions of dollars for charitable causes.

4. *Roosevelt Era and World War II*   (1930–1945) the Great Depression and World War II, with events profound and far-reaching in their impact, which advanced the practice of public relations. This period was dominated by Franklin D. Roosevelt and his counselor, Louis McHenry Howe.

5. *Postwar Era*   (1945–1965) of adjustment as the nation moved from a war-oriented economy to a post-industrial, service-oriented economy and shouldered leadership of the free world. This era brought widespread acceptance of public relations as the number of practitioners passed the 100,000 mark. It also brought strong professional associations, the beginnings of public relations education, and the emergence of television as a powerful communications medium.

6. *Global Information Society* (1965–present) with its accelerating high technology, multiplying channels of communication, and the transition from a national economy to a world economy that features global interdependence and global competition. Stresses from these profound changes place ever heavier burdens on the function and its role in mediating conflicting interests to bring about mutual adjustment and accommodation.

These periods of development followed what Edward Bernays calls the "public-be-damned" period of American enterprise, after the Civil War and lasting until about 1900. During public relations' seedbed era, Bernays suggests that the country had entered the "public-be-informed" period. He labels the period following World War I as the time of "mutual understanding." Recent history documents antiwar protests, the consumer movement, environmental activism, civil rights, and other demonstrations of the increasing power of individuals and special interests. Mutual understanding has no doubt given way to the period of "mutual adjustment," representing a dramatic change from the public relations early in the twentieth century.

SEEDBED ERA: 1900–1917

Muckraking journalists—David Graham Phillips, Lincoln Steffens, Upton Sinclair, Ida Tarbell, and others—effectively exploited the newly developed national forums made possible by popular magazines, national wire services, and feature syndicates. Regier says, "Muckraking . . . was the inevitable result of decades of indifference to the illegalities and immoralities attendant upon the industrial development of America."[33] The reform and protest period extended roughly from 1900 to 1912. The muckrakers took their case to the people and got action. The agitation before 1900 had been primarily among farmers and laborers; now the urban middle classes took up the cry against government corruption and the abuses of big business.

The muckrakers thundered out their denunciations in boldface in the popular magazines and metropolitan newspapers, which now had huge circulations. By 1900, there were at least 50 well-known national magazines, several with circulations of 100,000 or more. The *Ladies Home Journal*, founded only 17 years before, was approaching a circulation of one million. The impact of the mass media was growing.[34] "It was muckraking that brought the diffuse malaise of the public into focus."[35]

The work was dramatically begun by Thomas W. Lawson's *Frenzied Finance*, appearing as a series in *McClure's* magazine in 1903. Ida Tarbell's *History of the Standard Oil Company*, described at the time as "a fearless unmasking of moral criminality masquerading under the robes of respectability and Christianity," and Upton Sinclair's novel *The Jungle*, exposing the foul conditions in the meat-packing industry, both produced violent public reaction. Public protest and reform brought regulatory legislation and a wave of "trust-busting." Businesses were forced to take the defensive.

Long accustomed to a veil of secrecy, business leaders felt the urge to speak out in self-defense but did not know how. Their first instinct was to turn to their advertising planners and lawyers. In the first stages of the muckraking era, many great corporations sought to silence the attacks from the press by the judicious and calculated placement and withdrawal of advertising. U.S. Senator John F. Dryden, president of Prudential Insurance Company, by using the pressure of Prudential's advertising department, was able to squelch a critical article about himself and get published instead a highly complimentary one in *Cosmopolitan* magazine.[36]

In the wake of New York State's Armstrong Committee's exposure of wrongdoing in the insurance industry, the New York Mutual Life Insurance Company commissioned N. W. Ayer to carry out an advertising campaign to restore public confidence in the insurance business.[37]

Early Firms

The Publicity Bureau, the nation's first publicity firm and forerunner of today's public relations firm, was founded in Boston in mid-1900 by George V. S. Michaelis, Herbert Small, and Thomas O. Marvin "to do a general press agent business for as many clients as possible for as good pay as the traffic would bear." Michaelis, a Boston journalist once described by an associate as "a young man of many expedients," took the lead in organizing this new enterprise and was with it until 1909. One of the first people hired was James Drummond Ellsworth, who would later work with Theodore N. Vail in building the public relations program of American Telephone and Telegraph Company.[38]

The Publicity Bureau came into national prominence in 1906, when it was employed by the nation's railroads to head off adverse regulatory legislation then being pushed in Congress by President Roosevelt. Ray Stannard Baker reported:

> The fountainhead of public information is the newspaper. The first concern, then, of the railroad organization was to reach the newspaper. For this purpose a firm of publicity agents, with headquarters in Boston, was chosen. . . . Immediately the firm expanded. It increased its Boston staff; it opened offices in New York, Chicago, Washington, St. Louis, Topeka, Kansas . . . and it employed agents in South Dakota, California, and elsewhere.[39]

According to Baker, the Publicity Bureau operated secretly, "careful not to advertise the fact that they are in any way connected with the railroads." *This firm effectively used the tools of fact finding, publicity, and personal contact to saturate the nation's press, particularly weeklies, with the railroads' propaganda.* The campaign was to little avail, however, because the Hepburn Act, a moderately tough regulatory measure, was passed in 1906 after President Roosevelt used the nation's press and the platform to publicize a more persuasive case. Failure of their nationwide publicity effort caused railroad executives to reassess their public relations methods and, within a few years, to set up their own public relations departments. The Publicity Bureau faded into oblivion in 1911.

Other industries turned to the specialist who could tell business's story in the public forum: the news reporter. *Thus began the large-scale recruitment of journalists to serve as interpreters for corporations and other public institutions.* Some reporters took the Publicity Bureau's lead and organized similar firms. With waves of the popular revolt beating against Capitol Hill, the opportunity for such a firm in Washington became apparent. William Wolf Smith quit his job as correspondent for the *New York Sun* and the *Cincinnati Enquirer* to open a "publicity business" in the capital in 1902. A *New York Times* reporter later recalled that the Smith firm solicited "press-agent employment from anybody who had business before Congress."[40] Smith's agency also lasted little more than a decade.

During the seedbed era, former Buffalo reporter and veteran political publicist George F. Parker and Ivy Lee established a third New York firm in 1904, Parker & Lee. They formed their partnership after handling publicity for Judge Alton Parker's unsuccessful race against Theodore Roosevelt. The firm lasted less than 4 years, but Lee, the junior partner, left a lasting mark on the emerging craft of public relations.

The Hamilton Wright Organization, Inc., was founded in 1908 when Hamilton Mercer Wright, a freelance journalist and publicist, opened an office in San Francisco. He moved to New York City in 1917. Wright's first publicity work was for the California Promotion Committee. His agency's first account was the promotion of the Philippine Islands on behalf of U.S. business interests. His son and grandson, both carrying the same name, followed in the founder's footsteps by specializing in promotion of foreign countries in the United States, before ceasing operation in the late 1960s.

The fifth agency started during the first decade of this century lasted until 1988. Pendleton Dudley, who was to become an influential figure in public relations for half a century, took his friend Ivy Lee's advice and, in 1909, opened a publicity office in New York's Wall Street district. For 57 years, until he died at the age of 90, Dudley remained the active head of his firm, Dudley-Anderson-Yutzy Public Relations. In 1970, sisters Barbara Hunter and Jean Schoonover acquired the firm and changed the name to D-A-Y. The firm became a subsidiary of Ogilvy and Mather in 1983, and the separate identity and operation of D-A-Y was dropped in 1988.

Thomas R. Shipp organized the second firm in Washington, D.C. Shipp, like William Wolff Smith, was a native of Indiana and a former reporter. He set out on his own after spending 6 years learning publicity and politics under two experts, Theodore Roosevelt and Gifford Pinchot. Shipp opened his "publicity company" in 1914, as Smith was closing his to return to law school.

Early Pioneers

Rex Harlow

The need for publicity services became apparent in other parts of the country. *Rex F. Harlow* began a lifetime career in 1912 in Oklahoma City when he was hired by an older brother to promote *Harlow's Weekly*. Harlow's career spanned the evolution of this young, uncertain calling to its maturity in the 1980s and helped shape today's practice. While teaching at Stanford University in 1939, he began teaching public relations courses and founded the American Council on Public Relations (ACPR). In 1944 he started the monthly, *Public Relations Journal*, published today by the Public Relations Society of America, an organization was formed in 1948 when Harlow's ACPR merged with the National Association of Public Relations Council.[41] (Harlow died April 16, 1993, at 100 years of age.)

That same year that Harlow began his career—1912—Atlanta got its first publicity agency when Fred Lewis and William Seabrook, both reporters, formed the Lewis-Seabrook Company to do "advertising and publicity." This agency lasted a little more than 3 years.

For the most part, these ex-reporters in the employ of business countered the muckrakers with whitewash press agentry, demonstrating little grasp of the fundamental problems in the conflict. But there were exceptions. One was *Ivy Ledbetter Lee*, a native of Georgia. Lee, a Princeton graduate, was a reporter covering the business world who saw the possibility of earning more money in the service of private organizations who were seeking a voice. After 5 years as a reporter, Lee quit his low-paying job on the *World* in 1903 to work in Seth Low's campaign for mayor of New York. This led to a job in the press bureau of the Democratic National Committee during the 1904 presidential campaign.

Ivy Lee

Parker had directed the publicity for Grover Cleveland's three campaigns for the presidency, but Cleveland was not wise enough to use him as a press secretary during his two terms as president.[42] In 1904, Parker was recalled to political battle to direct publicity for the Democratic National Committee in the futile campaign to unseat President Theodore Roosevelt. Lee was hired to assist him. Out of their campaign association came the decision to form the Parker and Lee partnership, which dissolved in 1908, when Ivy Lee became the Pennsylvania Railroad's first publicity agent. That year, Parker set up another partnership with C. A. Bridge, then city editor of the *New York Herald*. The

Parker-Bridge partnership folded in 1913, presumably because that year Parker was appointed to handle publicity for the Protestant Episcopal Church, a position he held until 1919. In 1920, Parker returned to politics when General Leonard Wood hired him to provide counsel for his campaign for the Republican party's presidential nomination.[43]

Lee, when appointed to represent crusty George F. Baer and his associates in the anthracite coal strike, issued a "Declaration of Principles," which was to have a profound influence on the evolution of press agentry into publicity and of publicity into public relations. Eric Goldman observed that this declaration "marks the emergence of a second stage of public relations. The public was no longer to be ignored, in the traditional manner of business, nor fooled, in the continuing manner of the press agent."[44] It was to be informed. Lee's declaration, mailed to all city editors, reads:

> This is not a secret press bureau. All our work is done in the open. We aim to supply news. This is not an advertising agency; if you think any of our matter ought properly to go to your business office, do not use it. Our matter is accurate. Further details on any subject treated will be supplied promptly, and any editor will be assisted most cheerfully in verifying directly any statement of fact. . . . In brief, our plan is, frankly and openly, on behalf of business concerns and public institutions, to supply to the press and public of the United States prompt and accurate information concerning subjects which it is of value and interest to the public to know about.[45]

Lee put this new approach to work in the anthracite coal strike. The work of reporters assigned to cover the strike was enormously simplified because all channels of communication were open. Although reporters were not permitted at the strike conference, Lee did provide reports after each meeting. *Lee was among the first to use the "handout" system on a large scale.* His success in generating favorable press coverage for the coal operators led to the retention of Parker and Lee by the Pennsylvania Railroad in the summer of 1906. Lee handled this account.[46]

During this period Lee used the term *publicity* to describe what is now called public relations; the concept and Lee's success grew steadily. In December 1914, at the suggestion of Arthur Brisbane, Lee was appointed as a personal adviser to John D. Rockefeller, Jr. The Rockefellers were being savagely attacked for the strike-breaking activities of their Colorado Fuel and Iron Company. Lee served the Rockefellers until his death in 1934.

Ivy Lee did much to lay the groundwork for contemporary practice. Even though he did not use the term *public relations* until at least 1919, Lee contributed many of the techniques and principles that practitioners follow today. He was among the first to realize the fallacy of publicity unsupported by good works and to reason that performance determines the publicity a client gets. Lee propelled the growth of publicity departments and trained publicity advisers in many institutions. In his 31 years in public relations, Lee changed the scope of what he did from "pure agency" to serving as "a brain trust for the businesses we work with." One of the craft's most forceful representatives, he made public relations an occupation by his practice and preachments. However, Raucher warns, "Ivy Lee's reputation before World War I as the outstanding publicity specialist may easily obscure the general forces which created the new occupation. Lee built his career by exploiting problems of giant corporations in the early twentieth century."[47]

Lee's record, although substantial, is not free from criticism. When he died, he was under fire for his representation of the German Dye Trust, controlled by I. G. Farben. Lee advised the cartel after Adolf Hitler came to power in Germany and the Nazis had taken control. Although he never received pay directly from the Nazi government, Lee was paid an annual fee of $25,000 and expenses by the Farben firm from the time he was retained in 1933 until his firm resigned the account shortly after his death in 1934.[48]

Others of Influence

The part played by *Theodore Roosevelt* in spurring the evolution has been little noted. The colorful president was a master in the art and power of publicity, and he used his knowledge and skill to gain his political ends. Observers claimed that Roosevelt ruled the country from the newspapers' front pages. One of his first acts upon assuming the presidency was to seek an understanding with the press. Veteran reporter David S. Barry later observed that Roosevelt "knew the value and potent influence of a news paragraph written as he wanted it written and disseminated through the proper influential channels." Roosevelt's successful and well-publicized antitrust suit against the Northern Securities Company turned the tide against the concentration of economic power. His conservation policies, effectively promoted by Gifford Pinchot in the government's first large-scale publicity program, saved much of America's resources from gross exploitation.

As one historian observed, "Roosevelt's colorful, outgoing personality and shrewd sense of publicity had his name constantly in the papers, and in ways to make him a national hero."[49] He saw the White House as a "bully pulpit."

With the growth of mass-circulation newspapers, Roosevelt's ability to dominate the front pages demonstrated a newly found power for those with causes to promote. He had a keen sense of news and knew how to stage a story so that it would get maximum attention. His skill forced those he fought to develop similar means. He fully *exploited the news media as a new and powerful tool of presidential leadership,* and he remade the laws and the presidency in the process.

Business leader *John D. Rockefeller* never appeared to mind criticism, but philanthropist Rockefeller was cut to his Baptist quick by the accusation that his philanthropies were a means of buying public favor. When the "tainted money" issue flared yet again in 1905, he was hurt and angered. This led to his employment of Joseph Ignatius Constantine Clarke, colorful Irish reporter, at a then high salary of $5000 a year. Clarke, attached to the legal department and given a staff of one stenographer, one office helper, and a person to paste clippings, worked hard to lift the veil of secrecy from Standard Oil and its founder, and with some success. Rockefeller became more open and courteous with reporters, and, starting in October 1908, he published a series of autobiographical articles in *World's Work*. But as the legal and public attacks mounted, the company's executives quit giving Clarke information, and he resigned in frustration in 1913, the first in a long list of practitioners who have quit because of lack of administrative support.[50]

The period of 1900–1917 saw an intensive development of public relations skills by the railroads and the public utilities. These businesses, particularly the local transit companies, were the first to feel the heat of public anger and to be brought under public regulation. The Interstate Commerce Act set the pattern. In a 5-year period, 1908–1913, more than 2000 laws affecting railroads were enacted by state legislatures and by Congress.

From 1897 on, the term *public relations* appeared with increasing frequency in railroad literature and in speeches of railroad tycoons. In 1909, the *Railway Age Gazette* pleaded for "better public relations" in an editorial entitled "Wanted: A Diplomatic Corps." *J. Hampton Baumgartner*, another pioneer, was hired in 1910 to do publicity and public relations for the Baltimore & Ohio Railroad. In 1913, he told the Virginia Press Association that the railroads had tried to build closer relations with the public by working through the press.

Henry Ford pioneered in the positive use of public relations in the automobile industry. David Lewis, who has chronicled Ford's public relations story, says, "The industrialist is revealed . . . as perhaps the most astute self-advertiser in the whole history of a land that has produced its full share of promoters and showmen." From 1908 on, Ford and his associates sought publicity, in sharp contrast to their publicity-shy business contemporaries of that era, which may explain why Ford prospered as many competitors fell by the wayside.[51]

Another businessman, *Samuel Insull*, was equally innovative in the expanding utility field. In the late 1890s, his Chicago Edison Company relied on sales techniques, free wiring, and rate cuts to increase the use of electricity. In 1901, Insull created an advertising department to ensure specialized treatment of his many messages to the public; in 1902, he built a demonstration "Electric Cottage"; in 1903, he started *The Electric City*, an external community publication, "to gain understanding and good will" in Chicago. Insull began using films in 1909, perhaps making him the first to use movies for public relations purposes. He initiated "bill stuffers" in 1912, and in later years used these for political messages. Most utilities do this today. He and his associates made countless public speeches, many of which were reprinted for wider distribution. Insull knew well that those identified with an institution are the prime determinants of its public reputation.[52]

The former American Telephone and Telegraph Company pioneered in public relations as well as in communications. Although public relations got short shrift after *Theodore N. Vail* was forced out in 1887 until he was returned to power in 1902, the Bell company did organize a "literary bureau" in Boston around 1890 and was one of the first clients of the Publicity Bureau. After Vail returned as a director, the policies that became identified with AT&T began to take shape, and they were brought to the fore when Vail became president in 1907. Vail hired James *Drummond Ellsworth* and began a publicity and advertising program.

Efforts were undertaken to eliminate public criticism through efficient operation and consideration for the needs of subscribers. A systematic method of answering complaints was put into effect. Unlike other utilities, Bell did not fight public regulation, but accepted it as a price for monopoly. Vail and Ellsworth, in collaboration with the N. W. Ayer advertising agency, began an institutional advertising campaign that continues to this day. AT&T showed the way in public relations advertising and public relations.[53] (See Exhibit 4–1.)

Instructed by these examples, other business executives began to see the need for publicity assistance. In 1907, Jones and Laughlin Steel Company hired *W. T. Mossman* as public relations director because, F. F. Jones, Jr., son of the firm's founder, "had become uneasy over TR's (Theodore Roosevelt) attacks on business." Reflecting the confusion of concepts in this era, Mossman referred to himself as a "press agent," one "who got the facts for the newspapers." As the seedbed era ended in 1916, the duPont Powder Company hired Charles K. Weston, city editor of the *Philadelphia Ledger*, to become its publicity director, which *Editor and Publisher* reported deadpan "is something very different from a press agent."

Growth in Other Areas

Equally important public relations developments were taking place outside the business community. For instance, the seedbed years brought innovative publicity programs to colleges and universities. At Yale in 1899, Anson Phelps Stokes converted the office of secretary into an effective alumni and public relations office. At Harvard in 1900, Charles W. Eliot, who in his inaugural address of 1869 had voiced the necessity of influencing "opinion toward advancement of learning," retained the Publicity Bureau. The University of Pennsylvania's public relations program dates from 1904, when it set up the University Bureau of Publicity. That same year, Willard G. Bleyer, pioneer journalism educator,

EXHIBIT 4-1

Proposal for a Public Relations Bureau in AT&T in 1912, by Walter S. Allen

The establishment of a Public Relations Bureau in the American Telephone and Telegraph Company in which all information concerning the relations of the telephone companies to the public should be concentrated and made available for use, would serve to coordinate much of the work now done independently by various departments of that company and the operating companies.

This bureau could bring together a large sum of material at present scattered and a proper arrangement and collation of this would make it readily available and eliminate a considerable amount of duplication.

It would also be able to give its attention to the trend of public opinion and the drift of legislation and by a study of these, bring to the attention of executive officers in a condensed form the broader lines of public sentiment in time to enable the telephone company to meet new phases of legislation and in many cases to forestall legislation by remedying conditions which have been the cause of trouble.

By employing a central organization to collect, analyze and distribute material relating to these questions there will be a distinct saving in time of those actually engaged in work in the field and a broader and more efficient treatment of the problems.

All the available material can be brought together and everyone dealing with these questions be kept in touch with the trend of public opinion and action throughout the country. . . .

organized a press bureau at the University of Wisconsin at the direction of public relations-minded President Charles R. Van Hise. But it was William Rainey Harper, dynamic builder of the University of Chicago, who did more than any other educator to harness the power of publicity to the cause of higher education. His methods and his resulting success were observed and copied by many others.[54]

Churches, too, began to perceive the need for a public voice. One cleric wrote, "We will find that if we believe in the fruits of publicity we must believe also in the potential power of human nature to achieve goodness." Nonetheless, as in the case of business, it was the sharp attacks of critics that brought about the first programs. The Seventh Day Adventist Church, responding to public attacks on its opposition to Sunday laws, in 1912 established a publicity bureau with a former newspaper reporter in charge.[55] The Trinity Episcopal Church of New York City, under biting public attack since 1894 for its exploitation of renters in its church-owned tenements, in 1909 became one of the first clients of Pendleton Dudley.

The whirlwind high-pressure campaign to raise money for charitable causes was first fabricated in 1905 in Washington, D.C., by YMCA fund-raisers Charles Sumner Ward and Lyman L. Pierce. In their $350,000 drive for a new YMCA building, *they were the first to use full-time publicists in a fund drive*. The Y's successful techniques were soon used in the annual appeals of churches, colleges, civic centers, and health and welfare agencies.[56] The Ward-Pierce campaign format has endured the test of time and can be easily recognized in today's annual United Way drives.

Today's large-scale fund drives for health causes employ thousands of persons. The first health group to use publicity to raise funds was the National Tuberculosis Association, founded in 1908, forerunner of the National Lung Association. That same year the American Red Cross hired its first publicity agent. The U.S. Marine Corps established a publicity bureau in Chicago in 1907 under Captain William C. Harllee, thus showing the way for present-day public relations programs in the nation's military.

Publicity's considerable dimensions in these early years of the new century was reflected in growing concern of journalists about the "perils of publicity." Don C. Seitz, business manager of the *New York World*, reported to the 1909 convention of the American Newspaper Publishers Association that the number of press agents was growing and that some were making $6000 to $12,000 a year, very high pay in those years.

Everybody was employing them; even the New York Orphan Asylum was paying a publicity man $75 a month. The advertising agencies— Albert Frank and Company, Lord & Thomas, N. W. Ayer & Son, J. Walter Thompson—had set up publicity departments which took fees for their services, fees diverted from the advertiser's newspaper advertising budget. Automobile manufacturers were sending a page of material each day to the *World*, and the cement, food, insurance, utilities, and other businesses were equally busy.[57]

WORLD WAR I PERIOD: 1917–1919

The contemporary practice of public relations first emerged as a defensive measure, but World War I gave it great offensive impetus. *George Creel and his Committee on Public Information demonstrated, as never before, the power of publicity to mobilize opinion.* The Committee on Public Information (CPI)—often referred to as the Creel Committee—was set up by President Woodrow Wilson, who was keenly aware of the importance of public opinion. George Creel was made chairman. It was his task to mobilize public opinion in support of the war effort and Wilson's peace aims in a country in which opinion was quite divided when war was declared.

Creel had no campaign manual to guide him. He improvised as he went along. For example, he had no national radio or television to reach the nation quickly, so he created the "Four Minutemen," a network of volunteers covering the nation's some 3000 counties. These volunteers, alerted by telegrams from Washington, would fan out to speak to schools, churches, service clubs, and other gatherings. By the war's end nearly 800,000 of these 4-minute messages had been delivered to some 400,000 persons. The CPI effort headed by Creel and Carl Byoir is chronicled in Creel's *How We Advertised America* and by Mock and Larson in *Words That Won the War*.

Creel assembled as brilliant and talented a group of journalists, scholars, press agents, editors, artists, and other manipulators of the symbols of public opinion as America had ever seen united for a single purpose. The breathtaking scope of the huge agency and its activities was not to be equaled until the rise of the totalitarian dictatorships after the war. Creel, Byoir, and their associates were literally public relations counselors to the U.S. government, carrying first to the citizens of the country and then to those in distant lands, the idea that gave motive power to the stupendous undertaking of 1917–1918.[58]

The Liberty Loan drives were promoted by a separate campaign directed by Guy Emerson, later to pioneer in bank public relations, and John Price Jones, who later led the way in organized fund-raising. Their campaigns, based heavily on advertising techniques, taught many business people the values of public relations.

These successful demonstrations were to have a profound impact in the years ahead. Analyzing the influence of the Creel Committee, the *New York Times* commented in 1920:

> Essentially the species, if not a war product, is one which the war has mightily increased. Liberty Loans had to be advertised throughout the country. Publicity did that. Five times, at short intervals, the newspapers of the nation stepped into line and "put across" to the man at the breakfast table, and in his office, in the factory, in the mine—into every phase of commerce and industry, in fact, the need of digging down deep into his pocket and "coming across." It worked. Beautifully and efficiently. Not only did he have a staff of press agents working immediately under him in a central office, but Creel decentralized the system so that every type of industry in the country had its special group of publicity workers. In this manner, more than in any other, were the heads and directors of movements of every type introduced to and made cognizant of the value of concentrating on publicity in so-called "drives."[59]

To illustrate the *Times's* point, when America entered the war, the Red Cross had a membership of 486,194 in 372 chapters scattered across the nation and $200,000 in working funds. In September 1918, as the war neared its end, the Red Cross had 20 million members in 3864 chapters and had raised more than $400 million in gifts and membership dues. Another example: On May 1, 1917, there were only some 350,000 holders of U.S. bonds; 6 months later, after two organized publicity and sales drives for Liberty Bonds, there were 10 million bond holders.

Equally impressive was Herbert Hoover's reliance on public relations to encourage food conservation by the nation's households, hotels, restaurants, and food dealers. The Food Administration, under the public relations direction of Ben Allen, former Associated Press correspondent, transmitted appeals about saving food to the public by every available means of communication. The nation's media donated nearly $20 million in advertising space, and an estimated 20 million people pledged their support by returning coupons inserted in publications or distributed at countless local meetings.

After the war there emerged an overly optimistic belief in the power of mass communication. A noted political scientist, Harold D. Lasswell, observed, "When all allowances have been made, and all extravagant estimates pared to the bone, the fact remains that propaganda is one of the most powerful instrumentalities in the modern world."[60] Unfortunately, many organizations still invest large sums in the outmoded hypodermic model of mass communication that emerged from the World War I experience.

Carl Byoir

The Creel Committee trained a host of practitioners, who took their wartime experiences and fashioned a profitable calling. Among these were *Carl Byoir* and Edward L. Bernays. Byoir, who at age 28 had been associate chairman of the CPI, after a decade's tour into other endeavors founded in 1930 what would become one of the country's largest public relations firms. Bernays, who had a minor role in the CPI, beginning in the 1920s became one of the field's definers and tireless advocates.

BOOMING TWENTIES ERA: 1919–1929

Vigorously nourished by wartime developments, the public relations specialty quickly spread. It showed up in government, business, the churches, social work—now burgeoning in the war's aftermath—the labor movement, and social movements. The victory of the Anti-Saloon League in achieving national prohibition and the triumph of the women's suffrage movement, both in 1920, provided fresh evidence of the newly found power. And because the process of industrialization and urbanization had been pushed ahead several notches during the war, the growth and development of the practice, like much else in society, was accelerating.

Among those vying with Ivy Lee for prominence and for business in the 1920s was *Edward L. Bernays.* Prior to World Way I, Bernays had worked as a press agent. While he worked for the Creel Committee during the war, his busy mind envisioned the possibility of making a life's work of what he called "engineering public consent."[61] Bernays coined the term *public relations counsel* in *Crystallizing Public Opinion*, the first book on public relations, in 1923. He broke more new ground the same year when he taught the first public relations course at New York University. Bernays continued in his roles as author, lecturer, advocate, and critic into the 1990s. *Life* Magazine's 1990 special issue titled "The 100 Most Important Americans of the 20th Century" included Bernays. He celebrated his 102nd birthday November 22, 1993.

Edward Bernays

Bernays married *Doris E. Fleischman* in 1922. Together they ran their firm, Edward L. Bernays, Counsel on Public Relations, until formally retiring from active practice in 1962. She died in 1980. They counseled major corporations, government agencies, and U.S. presidents from Calvin Coolidge through Dwight Eisenhower, with Bernays taking the spotlight for most assignments. Although credited with being an equal partner with Bernays in the firm, with creating the first public relations newsletter, and with collaborating with Bernays to develop the term *public relations counsel,* Fleischman struggled for professional equality because of her sex.[62] For example, in one of her two books she wrote:

> Many men resented having women tell them what to do in their business. They resented having men tell them, too, but advice from a woman was somewhat demeaning. I learned to withdraw from situations where the gender of public relations counsel was a factor or where suggestions had to be disassociated from gender. If ideas were considered first in terms of my sex, they might never get around to being judged on their own merits.[63]

Bernays's book followed Walter Lippmann's 1922 *Public Opinion,* a book that reflected the growing interest in power and nature of public opinion. In all the years prior to 1917, only 18 books on public opinion and publicity were printed. At least 28 titles appeared between 1917 and 1925.

Scholarly interest also dates from this period. Social scientists began to explore the nature of public opinion and the role of mass communication in its formation. Although sophisticated opinion-measurement methods did not appear until the 1930s, the postwar work of social scientists contributed much to the development of market research, public opinion polls, and communication science.

Many other rapid-fire developments occurred during this postwar period. Several new counseling firms were established. In 1919, John Price Jones established his firm, Organization and Publicity Counsel, to direct fund-raising campaigns and to provide publicity service to corporations. Over the years, until he retired in 1956, Jones made more money and gained more fame raising funds than as a public relations counselor.

Harry A. Bruno was an aviation enthusiast and wartime flier. After the airline he was working for went broke in 1923, he set up a firm in partnership with Richard Blythe. Most of Bruno's early clients were makers of airplane motors and instruments, seeking to promote aviation. He gained national prominence when he and Blythe handled the press relations for Charles A. Lindbergh's historic flight across the Atlantic in May 1927. Bruno's publicity and public relations projects did much to speed America's acceptance of the air age.

There were only six public relations firms listed in the Manhattan telephone directory in 1926. In that year, William Baldwin, after serving an apprenticeship in a shipbuilding firm and as a fund-raiser, opened an agency that was to serve corporate and civic clients—many of the latter, gratis—over the next 35 years. In 1927, John W. Hill, a Cleveland journalists, started a firm in that city. In 1933, he formed a partnership with Don Knowlton, and shortly thereafter moved to New York to found Hill and Knowlton, Inc. Knowlton remained to run the Cleveland office. The two firms, connected only by overlapping ownership, operated independently until 1964, when Knowlton retired and the Cleveland office was sold to a successor firm. Hill died in 1977. In 1980, JWT Group, the holding company that owned J. Walter Thompson Company advertising agency, acquired Hill and Knowlton for $28 million dollars. The JWT Group of companies was acquired by the British conglomerate WPP Group PLC in 1989.

John W. Hill

Two years before Hill set up shop in Cleveland, Edward D. Howard II organized a public relations agency there that celebrated its 65th anniversary in 1990. Edward Howard and Co. is not only Ohio's oldest public relations firm, but is also the nation's longest surviving independently owned firm. It is now an affiliate of Hill and Knowlton.

Another little-known pioneer was Glenn G. Hayes of Chicago, who established Hayes, Loeb and Company in 1921, an agency specializing in farm public relations. His partner, Sidney C. Loeb, landed Sears, Roebuck and Co. as the first big account when Sears needed a program to counteract a movement by thousands of local merchants to fight mail-order competition.

This period also saw increased use of public relations advertising as a tool. Illinois Central Railroad started a campaign in 1920 that sought "promotion of a better understanding and closer relationship with the patrons of our lines." In 1922, Metropolitan Life Insurance Company started a good-health campaign. In 1923, General Motors

(GM) began to use advertising to sell itself as an institution. GM did not set up its own department until 1931, when it brought in *Paul Garrett*, another influential pioneer. At GM Garrett built an innovative corporate program, which was widely copied by other corporations.

Paul Garrett

In 1921, the American Association of Engineers held its *first national conference on public information.* Later it published the proceedings in a book entitled, *Publicity Methods for Engineers.*

Another development of the early 1920s was the wholesale adoption of the Creel Committee techniques. Beginning in 1919, for example, Samuel Insull and his cohorts in the utilities industry sparked a movement to persuade the American people of the blessings of privately owned utilities.[64] Despite the cloud that later crossed this program, it embodied some forward-looking concepts.

Quick-buck promoters also grasped the lessons taught by the success of wartime promotional campaigns. The disreputable Ku Klux Klan, born during Reconstruction, had been revived in Atlanta in 1915 as a "bottle club." By 1919, the club was floundering. Its promoter, William Joseph Simons, hired two publicists, Edward Y. Clarke and Bessie Tyler, who had formed the Southern Publicity Association as a firm to promote wartime fund drives. In just 3 years, the Clarke-Tyler campaign multiplied the Klan's membership from a few thousand members in 1920 to about three million, earning great sums for themselves at the expense of a bitter legacy to the nation.[65]

Arthur W. Page

Among the pioneers shaping today's practice, *Arthur W. Page* stands at the summit. Page built three successful business careers, yet found time to contribute his talent to many public service endeavors. He was a writer and editor of *World's Work Magazine* and other periodicals of Doubleday, Page and Company from 1905 until 1927. Then he accepted Walter Gifford's offer to become vice president of American Telephone and Telegraph Co. to succeed James D. Ellsworth. At the outset Page made it clear that he would accept only on the conditions that he was not to serve as a publicity man, that he would have a voice in policy, and that the company's performance would be the determinant of its public reputation. Page's philosophy is summed up in this statement:

> All business in a democratic country begins with public permission and exists by public approval. If that be true, it follows that business should be cheerfully willing to tell the public what its policies are, what it is doing, and what it hopes to do. This seems practically a duty.[66]

Page retired from AT&T in 1947, after integrating public relations concepts and practices into the Bell System. From then until his death in 1960, he served as a consultant to many large corporations and gave much of his time to the service of government, higher education, and other causes; but it was Page's work for AT&T that left his lasting imprint on public relations. His precepts and principles not only endure in the companies that used to be part of AT&T (broken up in 1984), but are being renewed and promoted by the Arthur W. Page Society. Founded in 1983, this society's membership includes senior corporate public relations executives and others who have demonstrated outstanding achievements in public relations.

After World War I, and in part as a response to the dislocations caused by war, interest in and use of publicity techniques spilled over into the Community Chest movement and the new field of social work. As more and more money had to be raised to meet more and more needs of an urban society, recognition of the importance of publicity and the need for trained publicists grew.

Advancement of social work publicity was spearheaded by Evart G. Routzahn and Mary Swain Routzahn of the Russell Sage Foundation. In the early 1920s, the Routzahns played key roles in the birth of the National Publicity Council for welfare agencies and of a Health Education Section in the American Public Health Association. What was first a committee on publicity methods in social work became, in 1922, the National Publicity Council for Welfare Services. From its inception until 1940, the council was used by the Routzahns to transport new ideas, new techniques, and missionary zeal to novices in health and welfare publicity work. This body, which attained 1200 members, went through several reorganizations and name changes. In 1975, it became the National Communications Council for Human Services and, in 1977, it was merged into the Public Relations Society of America.

Religious leaders also sensed the changing times. In 1918, the National Lutheran Council launched a strong national church publicity program. Later that same year, a Catholic organization, the Knights of Columbus, organized a publicity bureau with John B. Kennedy as its director. The *New York Times* noted at the time, "They are quite frank in admitting that the 'biggest and most practical human lesson learned from the war is that nothing requiring organized effort can succeed without publicity and plenty of it.'" The quote was attributed to Kennedy. The YMCA and YWCA had long had publicity staffs, and they formed something of a nucleus for the spread of organized church publicity. Astute leaders everywhere were observing this "most practical human lesson from the war."

It was also during this period that a sense of identification and professionalism began to emerge in this new craft. The first national public relations organization was established in Chicago on June 15, 1915, as a part of the Associated Advertising Clubs of the World. Seven bankers founded the new organization and called it the Financial Advertising Association, reflecting that banking public relations in the era of World War I was seen as advertising, and stiff, high-collar advertising at that. In its early years, the association was mainly an "idea exchange" for its members, but it changed its name in 1947 to the Financial Public Relations Association, in 1966 to the Bank Public Relations and Marketing Association, and again in 1970 to the Bank Marketing Association, to express its purpose more accurately.

The next group to organize better exemplified the evolution of public relations. A handful of major universities and colleges had set up press bureaus prior to the war. More did so in the early 1920s, generally as an adjunct to a capital fundraising drive. Owing mainly to the determined efforts of T. T. Frankenberg, then publicity director for the Western College of Women in Oxford, Ohio, the Association of American College News Bureaus had been organized in April 1917. It lapsed into inactivity during the war, but came alive again in the 1920s.

At the 1925 convention, the organization took on new strength, reflecting the growth of the practice in higher education. Symbolic of its growth in ensuing years, the organization's name was changed in 1930 to the American College Publicity Association, in 1964 to the American College Public Relations Association, and in 1974—after a merger with the American Alumni Council—to the Council for the Advancement and Support of Education (CASE). This merger reflected a shift in emphasis in college public relations from publicity to development and fund-raising. CASE was launched under the leadership of its first president, *Alice L. Beeman*. She had previously been general director of the American Association of University Women, based in Washington, D.C., and the AAUW Educational Foundation. In her new position as president of CASE, *Beeman was the first woman to head a national public relations association*.

Alice Beeman

ROOSEVELT ERA AND WORLD WAR II: 1930–1945

Propelled by wartime lessons and a changing America, the practice of public relations moved full speed ahead until the stock market crash in 1929. The ensuing Great Depression marks another milestone. That persistent economic catastrophe and Franklin D. Roosevelt's New Deal prompted development of the practice in many fields.

FDR combined strong leadership with consummate skill to harness the forces of protest into an effective political coalition. He won his battles on front pages and over the radio, a new medium he used with matchless skill. Roosevelt's adroit moves in the public arena can be credited in large part to his public relations mentor, Louis McHenry Howe. The astute, tough-minded Howe served FDR faithfully and effectively from 1912 until Howe's death in 1936. He gave his life to being Roosevelt's right-hand man and did much to advance him to the White House.[67] FDR's success in winning public support spurred the efforts of the conservative forces, particularly the business community, to counter his appeals. But such a cataclysmic event as the Depression was bound to produce a sharp readjustment of values, and a new trend set in, marked by wider acknowledgment of an institution's or industry's social responsibility. *It was increasingly realized that mutually beneficial public relationships could be built only by coupling responsible performance with persuasive publicity.*

Events flowing from the Depression and the New Deal brought home to every group the need to build informed public support. New Dealers soon found that this was essential to pave the way for their radical reforms, and government public relations had its greatest expansion under Franklin Roosevelt. School administrators were made to realize the dangers of an uninformed public as hard-pressed taxpayers chopped off "the frills" in education. The Depression brought a tremendous expansion in social welfare needs and agencies, whose administrators also came to realize the need for better public understanding. Military leaders, looking apprehensively at the buildup of the Nazi and Fascist war machines, began to promote support for more adequate armed forces. Colleges and universities, caught in the web of financial woes, turned more and more to public relations to raise funds.

Business leaders turned increasingly to public relations specialists for help in fighting against Roosevelt's biting criticisms and his legislative reforms. There was a marked trend away from occasional and defensive efforts and toward more positive and continuous programs, administered by newly established departments. A growing labor movement, too, found that it had problems and needed guidance. Growth was stimulated all along the line by the social and economic upheavals of the Depression.

This period also brought the tool that promised more precise, more scientific measurement and assessment of public opinion. The Roper and Gallup polls, begun in the mid-1930s, won wide respect in the presidential election of 1936. Perceptive practitioners began using this new tool to advise managements and to formulate programs. The public opinion poll, with the application of new sampling methods, has steadily improved in reliability and in utility. George Gallup, who did much to make polling a key tool of public relations, politics, marketing, and scholarship, died in 1984.

In 1934, the first minority-owned firm opened in Philadelphia. Joseph Varney Baker left his position as city editor of the *Philadelphia Tribune* to provide counsel to the Pennsylvania Railroad Company. Baker was the first black to serve as president of a PRSA chapter and the first to be accredited by PRSA. His firm's list of clients included Chrysler, Gillette, Procter & Gamble, NBC, RCA, and Scott Paper Company. One authority on minorities in public relations concluded that during the 40 years that Baker's firm existed, it "was hired to communicate only with the black consumer market, and the practice has continued to this day."[68]

This era also produced the forerunner of a major segment of today's practice: the political-campaign specialist. In 1933, husband and wife

Clem Whitaker and Leone Baxter formed the first agency specializing in political campaigns, headquartered in San Francisco. California, with its heavy reliance on the initiative and referendum and its weak political party organizations, provided fertile ground for the growth of political firms. From 1935 through 1958, the firm managed 80 major campaigns and won all but six. This agency brought a new approach to politics, including the media blitz in the final days of the campaign. Today it has countless imitators.

Leone Baxter

World War II produced more violent changes in the environment, accelerating the development of public relations. Once more the government led the way, with a breathtaking demonstration of the power of an organized informational campaign. This time the instrument was the Office of War Information.

When war broke out after the Japanese bombing of Pearl Harbor on December 7, 1941, the government's information machine, which had been built largely in the New Deal years, was in some disarray. Three major information agencies overlapped and jousted for dominance: the Office of Facts and Figures, headed by Archibald MacLeish, the poet; the Office of Government Reports, headed by Lowell Mellett, former Washington correspondent; and the Division of Information in the Office of Emergency Management, headed by Robert Horton. President Roosevelt was reluctant to create a central information agency, even with the chaos, fearing Congress and the press would interpret it as a "propaganda instrument to propel America into war." FDR knew well how the Creel Committee had become a whipping boy when its slogans of World War I turned to bitter irony in the 1920s. It was in that period that "propaganda" had become a sullied, useless word.

After Pearl Harbor, however, the urgency of the situation prompted Roosevelt to issue Executive Order 9182, in June 1942, creating the Office of War Information (OWI) and appointing Elmer Davis as its director.[69] George Creel, who had brilliantly directed the CPI in World War I, was never consulted by FDR. Davis, veteran news reporter and radio commentator, never effectively brought the warring forces in the OWI under control, nor did he play the role Creel did in counseling the president, but he and the OWI set the pace for extensive expansion of the practice in the armed forces, in industry, and in allied fields. OWI developed more techniques and trained many more practitioners than did the Creel Committee.

In the opinion of two public relations scholars, the OWI's greatest contributions derived from its work as the predecessor of the United States Information Agency. OWI was the agency that pointed out the danger in not countering distorted ideas of the United States throughout the world.[70] Other institutions learned this lesson during these tumultuous years.

Public relations in the armed forces today constitutes a major segment of the practice. Prior to the outbreak of World War II, however, it had been given scant support by authoritarian military leaders. In 1935, General Douglas MacArthur, then chief of staff, appointed a young major, Alexander Surles, to head up a public relations branch with the "dual job of getting before the public the War Department's anxiety over things to come in Europe and to help newsmen pry stories out of the War Department."[71] In January 1941, Surles was asked to draft a plan for "a man-sized bureau of public relations."

With the advent of war, this staff quickly grew from three to 3000 officers and civilians. Concurrently, the Navy Department moved to expand and strengthen its public relations. The Army Air Corps, under the imaginative leadership of General H. H. "Hap" Arnold, a former information officer, quickly recruited a host of skilled public relations and advertising specialists. Their task was to sell air power in an age of trench-minded generals. Even though the armed forces went into the war ill-equipped for public relations, they acquitted themselves well. The work was largely a matter of publicity, censorship, and assistance to war correspondents. In the process they trained countless numbers of practitioners for this work after the war and built a solid foundation for practice in the postwar boom.

The war years brought paid advertising to the fore as a major tool of public relations, now in its many forms: public relations advertising, public service advertising, issue or advocacy advertising, and institutional advertising. Two forces spurred this development. In World War I many makers of goods quit advertising because the products for the civilian market were in short supply and thus needed no advertising. When many of these manufacturers returned to the civilian market after the war, they found that many had forgotten brand names. Advertising executives pounded this lesson home in the 1920s. The second force at work was the advertising industry's concern with its tarnished reputation. In the wake of the 1929 market crash and the ensuing Depression, advertising was singled out as one of the villains. New Dealers sought legislation to eliminate fraud in advertising and to require government grade labeling. At the same time, several antiadvertising books became best sellers.

These forces gave birth to the War Advertising Council in 1942, which worked with industry and with the government to make advertising a major tool in getting citizens to produce for the war, to ration scarce resources, to buy war bonds, and to serve in the armed forces. In advocating the council, James Webb Young called for advertising's power to be used in open propaganda in international relations, to create understanding and reduce friction. Likewise, he advocated its application to the arts, music, and literature, and promoted it as a servant of "all the forces of righteousness."[72] Young reflected what Bernays called "a movement toward public responsibility in private business," a movement required if business were to work its way back to credibility. As a result of this wartime development, advertising is used widely as a major public relations tool.

POSTWAR BOOM: 1945–1965

World War II brought new opportunities; new demonstrations of public relations utility in motivating war production, military morale, and civilian support; and new techniques and channels of communication. The war also schooled about 75,000 persons in the practice. The tensions and problems of the uneasy years of conversion from a wartime to a peacetime economy and the transition from an industrial to a postindustrial, service-oriented society accentuated and extended these developments. For example, in the late 1940s, industry was wracked by a series of bitter, prolonged strikes as organized labor fought to redress grievances built up in the no-strike war period and to keep wartime gains in pay. These struggles and increased public criticism of big business placed heavy demands on the function in business and industry.[73]

Similarly, the postwar baby boom and the GI-fed enrollment bulge brought new and heavy demands on the nation's schools and colleges, forcing administrators to accept the need for public relations counsel. School districts had to promote one bond issue after another to build additional schools, and the nation's institutions of higher education had to scramble for funds for more teachers and buildings to meet the exploding demand for higher education and research.

Expanding world trade and political conflict extended the practice around the world, with American practitioners leading the way. Advances in telecommunication and transportation brought the peoples of the world into the closest contact in the history of civilization. The same ecological factors that compelled the development of public relations in the United States were now operating on a global scale, only faster. For example, the Cold War between the world's superpowers, the United States and the Soviet Union, necessitated conversion of the OWI to what today is the U.S. Information Agency (USIA) and the maintenance of large public relations staffs in the armed forces.

Today's USIA grew from several information and cultural exchange bodies born in World War II and the early postwar years. The Office of International Information and Educational Exchanges was created by the Fulbright Act in 1946. Heightening cold war tensions prompted passage of the U.S. Information and Educational Exchange Act of 1948, known as the Smith-Mundt Act. Dissatisfaction with the resulting split authority resulted in creation of the U.S. Information Agency on August 1, 1953, under President Eisenhower's Reorganization Plan No. 8. This made USIA independent of the State Department, which retained, until the Carter administration, authority over cultural and educational exchanges.

The advent of television as a powerful national forum and its consequent widespread impact on a more-educated society likewise brought new public relations opportunities and problems to institutions and their executives. Television's role in politics, for example, spawned the political campaign specialist, now a major role in the nation's political system. Eventually, television prompted many leaders in business, government, military, and so forth to undergo "media training" to become adept at talking in "sound bites," controlling the agenda in interviews, and fielding questions with answers based on a message strategy.

These and kindred developments during the postwar decades of rapid expansion brought increased stability and maturity to the field. This era saw the number of practitioners pass the 100,000 mark. This era also saw the foundations for a profession being put in place by strong professional associations and the beginning of public relations education in the nation's colleges. Both these developments were fed by rapid growth in books and journals, which were published to build a common body of knowledge for the field. The 1945–1965 boom period was highlighted by these developments:

1. Steady growth in the number of programs in industries, institutions, social agencies, government bureaus, and trade associations. Already-established programs tended to mature and to move beyond publicity.

2. Stabilization in the number of independent counseling firms, especially in the communication hubs of New York, Washington, Chicago, and Los Angeles.

3. A tremendous spurt in the number of books, articles, and journals devoted to the practice and its philosophy, problems, and techniques. The literature is voluminous, although somewhat repetitive.

4. Organization of new associations for practitioners and redirection or consolidation of those already established. Many of these are now mature.

5. Growth in the number of college courses and students and in the breadth and depth of the courses. Increased support for collegiate preparation from practitioners and great acceptance of young graduates in the job market.

6. Internationalization of the practice and its standards, reflected in the formation of the International Public Relations Association in 1955.

Another force pushing the practice toward professionalism came from campuses. In this period, public relations education, which had its origins in publicity courses in the 1920s, developed slowly because the function was suspect in the minds of many academicians. A 1946 survey identified 30 major institutions offering public relations courses.[74] Ten years later a Public Relations Society of America survey found 92 were offering courses designed to prepare students for this work, with 14 schools offering a major.[75] By 1964, as this era ended, 14 institutions offered a bachelor's degree in public relations, 29 had undergraduate sequences, and all told, 280 were offering instruction in various courses.[76]

Public relations education gained some cohesion with the formation of the Council on Public Relations Education at the 1956 convention of the Association for Education in Journalism meeting at Northwestern University. Approval came only after a spirited floor fight in which many traditional journalism teachers opposed the move. The council's purpose was "to promote fuller exchange of information and ideas among teachers" and to enlist the support of practitioners. That educators' group is now a large and recognized division in the expanded Association for Education in Journalism and Mass Communication. Later that same year the PRSA created the Foundation for Public Relations Research and Education. This foundation—no longer affiliated with PRSA and now known as the Institute for Public Relations Research and Education—has supported scholarly research, undergraduate and graduate student scholarships, preparation of the most comprehensive bibliography in the field of mass communication, and summer fellowships for educators and has in other ways advanced the field toward professionalism. A year later, in 1957, PRSA established an educational Advisory Council that served as a further bridge between the professional and academic communities.

Additional impetus for the growth of professionalism came with establishment of one strong general organization and emergence of a number serving specialized fields of practice. The Public Relations Society of America was born August 4, 1947, when representatives of the West Coast American Council on Public Relations and the East Coast National Association of Public Relations Counsel met in Chicago. The Washington-based American Public Relations Association voted not to come in at that time, but ultimately capitulated in 1961. Dr. Rex F. Harlow, who had organized the council, was the moving force in bringing this merger about. In 1945, while president of the council, Harlow had started the *Public Relations Journal*, which became the monthly magazine of PRSA after the merger.[77] In this and other ways, Rex Harlow played a major role in the professionalization of public relations.

GLOBAL INFORMATION AGE: 1965–PRESENT

From the mid-1960s, the function of public relations has increased in importance and complexity. Far-reaching trends running through our nation and world have made government affairs a main public relations task and brought "issues management" and management by objectives to the function's lexicon. Since the late 1960s, says Robert B. Reich, America's slowly unraveling economy has led to growing unemployment, mounting business failures, and falling productivity. He attributes the decline in America's political system to the decline of broad-based political parties, one-term presidents, and tax revolts.[78] In 1950, only 17 percent of our people worked in information jobs; by the early 1980s, more than 60 percent were similarly employed. In 1960, the United States had about 25 percent of the world market share in manufacturing; but by the 1980s, this had slipped to less than 17 percent. These trends presaged the end of the industrial era in the United States.

But the driving force in contemporary practice has been the onrush of the global information age. Although this new age had its roots in the 1950s, it really took off in the mid-1960s. Naisbitt sets the beginnings of "the information society" in 1956 and 1957. In 1956, for the first time in American history, white-collar workers outnumbered workers in industrial production. A year later, 1957, brought the Soviet satellite, *Sputnik*, and with it the era of global satellite communications. By the 1980s, the output of information was accelerating by some 40 percent annually. That means, says Naisbitt, "data will double every twenty months. The on-line information selection business is now a multi-billion-dollar enterprise." Computer technology is to the information age what the mechanized assembly line was to the industrial age.[79]

As then-president and chief executive officer of Dow Chemical Company, Frank Popoff, told the 1989 graduating class at Alma College (Michigan):

Twenty years ago people talked in terms of air travel shrinking space and time, making it possible to move among nations and continents in hours instead of days. Today, with the advent of telecommunications, business people in Japan, Europe and Midland, Michigan, can meet simultaneously without leaving their offices.

. . . Once people talked about industrialization, about nations developing the machinery and the skills to manufacture and distribute products on a large scale at affordable cost. Now we talk about globalization, about the world as a global community where nations and people can share one economy, one environment, one technology and, at least in commerce, one language.[80]

ADDITIONAL READINGS

Berens, Robert J. *The Image of Mercy.* New York: Vantage Press, 1967. History of public relations for the American Red Cross.

Creedon, Pamela J., ed. *Women in Mass Communication: Challenging Gender Values.* Newbury Park, Calif.: Sage Publications, Inc., 1989.

Cutlip, Scott M. "History of Public Relations Education in the United States." *Journalism Quarterly* 38, no. 2 (Summer 1961): 363–70.

Endres, Fred F. "Public Relations in the Jackson White House." *Public Relations Review* 2, no. 3 (Fall 1976): 5–12.

Foxworth, Marilyn Fern. "African-American Achievements in Public Relations." *Public Relations Journal* 47, no. 2 (February 1991): 18–19.

Golden, L. L. L. *Only by Public Consent: American Corporations' Search for Favorable Opinion.* New York: Hawthorn Books, 1968. Brief history of public relations programs at AT&T, General Motors, DuPont, and Standard Oil of New Jersey.

Hartung, Barbara W. "America's Era of Many Opinions." *Public Relations Review* 6, no. 2 (Summer 1980): 3–10. Years 1790–1830.

Gunther, John. *Taken at the Flood—The Story of Albert D. Lasker.* New York: Harper and Row, 1960. Biography of America's advertising pioneer responsible for many public relations innovations.

Hill, John W. *The Making of a Public Relations Man.* New York: David McKay and Co., 1963. Part autobiography, part philosophy by public relations pioneer.

Lyon, Peter. *Success Story: The Life and Times of S. S. McClure.* New York: Charles Scribner's Sons, 1963. Biography of architect of muckraking movement.

Maier, Pauline. *Political Lives in the Age of Samuel Adams.* New York: Alfred A. Knopf, Inc., 1980.

Olasky, Marvin N. *Corporate Public Relations: A New Historical Perspective.* Hillsdale, N.J.: Lawrence Erlbaum Associates, Publishers, 1987; or "The Development of Corporate Public Relations, 1850–1930." *Journalism Monograph* 102 (April 1987), by the same author. Critic's recasting of the historical role of public relations as an attempt by corporations to limit competition.

Paisley, William J. "Public Communication Campaigns: The American Experience." In *Public Communication Campaigns*, 2d ed., edited by Ronald E. Rice and Charles K. Atkin, 15–38. Newbury Park, Calif.: Sage Publications, Inc., 1989.

Pearson, Ron "Perspectives on Public Relations History." *Public Relations Review* 16, no. 3 (Fall 1990): 27–38.

"Public Relations in American History" (special issue). *Public Relations Review* 4 (Fall 1978). Lectures by historians Allan Nevins, Ray Allen Billington, Frank E. Vandiver, George F. G. Stanley, Eric F. Goldman, and Joe B. Frantz.

Raucher, Alan R. "Public Relations in Business: A Business of Public Relations." *Public Relations Review* 16, no.3 (Fall 1990): 19–26.

Schoch, Kathleen S. "Professional Unity in Public Relations Organizations." *Public Relations Review* 9 (Winter 1983): 3–13. Traces rise of professional organizations in public relations.

NOTES

[1] A. L. Basham, *The Wonder That Was India* (London: Sidgwick and Jackson, 1954), 122.

[2] John Brooks, *Telephone: The First Hundred Years* (New York: Harper and Row, 1976), 270–71.

[3] Samuel Eliot Morison, *The Founding of Harvard College* (Cambridge, Mass.: Harvard University Press, 1935), 303. Also see Hugh T. Lefler, "Promotional Literature of the Southern Colonies," *Journal of Southern History* 33 (1967): 3–25.

[4] Philip Davidson, *Propaganda and the American Revolution, 1763–1783* (Chapel Hill: University of North Carolina Press, 1941), 3.

[5] Cass Canfield, *Sam Adams' Revolution (1765–1776)* (New York: Harper and Row, 1976).

[6] Benjamin Woods Labaree, *The Boston Tea Party* (New York: Oxford University Press, 1966).

[7] For the account that imprinted the patriots' version on history, see James Bowdoin, Dr. Joseph Warren, and Samuel Pemberton, "Short Narrative of the Horrid Massacre in Boston," in *Tracts of the American Revolution, 1763–1776*, edited by Merrill Jensen (New York: Bobbs Merrill, 1967).

[8] Merrill Jensen, "The Sovereign States," in *Sovereign States in an Age of Uncertainty*, edited by Ronald Hoffman and Peter J. Albert (Charlottesville: University of Virginia Press, 1981).

[9] For the Tory side of the propaganda battle, see Carol Berkin, *Jonathan Sewall, Odyssey of an American Loyalist* (New York: Columbia University Press, 1974).

[10]William Baldwin, Jr., "Bicentenary of a Classic Campaign," *Public Relations Quarterly* 10 (Spring 1965).

[11]Allan Nevins, *The Constitution Makers and the Public, 1785–1790* (New York: Foundation for Public Relations Research and Education, 1962), 10. Also in *Public Relations Review* 4 (Fall 1978).

[12]T. Swann Harding, "Genesis of One 'Government Propaganda Mill,'" *Public Opinion Quarterly* 11 (Summer 1947): 227–35. (A history of public relations in the U.S. Department of Agriculture.)

[13]For one example of Kendall's work, see Lynn Marshall, "The Authorship of Jackson's Bank Veto Message," *Mississippi Valley Historical Review*, vol. L (December 1963). For an additional view of Kendall, see *Autobiography of Amos Kendall* (Micro-Offset Books, 1949, reprinted). For an estimate of Kendall's influence, see Arthur M. Schlesinger, Jr., *The Age of Jackson* (Boston: Little, Brown, 1945).

[14]For accounts of this epic public relations battle, see James L. Crouthamel, "Did the Second Bank of the United States Bribe the Press?" *Journalism Quarterly* 36 (Winter 1959); and Bray Hammond, *Banks and Politics in America* (Princeton, N.J.: Princeton University Press, 1957).

[15]Alan Raucher, *Public Relations and Business, 1900–1929* (Baltimore: Johns Hopkins University Press, 1968).

[16]For accounts of Davy Crockett's buildup, see James A. Shackford, *David Crockett, the Man and Legend* (Chapel Hill: University of North Carolina Press, 1956); Marshall Fishwick, *American Heroes: Myths and Realities* (Washington, D.C., 1954), 70–71; and Vernon Parrington, *Main Currents in American Thought* (New York: Harcourt Brace Jovanovich, 1930), vol. II, 173–78.

[17]Irving Wallace, *The Fabulous Showman: Life and Times of P. T. Barnum* (New York: Alfred A. Knopf, Inc., 1959).

[18]Dexter W. Fellows and Andrew A. Freeman, *This Way to the Big Show* (New York: Viking, 1936; Halcyon House, 1938), 193; and Phineas Taylor Barnum, *The Life of P. T. Barnum Written by Himself* (New York: Redfield, 1855), 154–74.

[19]Richard C. Overton, *Burlington West* (Cambridge, Mass.: Harvard University Press, 1941), 158–159.

[20]Rossiter Johnson, ed., *A History of the World's Columbian Exposition*, vol. II (New York: D. Appleton, 1897), 1–31.

[21]Noble E. Cunningham, Jr., "John Beckley: An Early American Party Manager," *William and Mary Quarterly* 13 (January 1956): 40–52.

[22]Stanley Kelley, Jr., *Professional Public Relations and Political Power* (Baltimore: Johns Hopkins University Press, 1956). (One of the first books to point out the growing role of public relations in politics gives examples from the late 1940s, and early 1950s.)

[23]Luther B. Little, "The Printing Press in Politics," *Munsey's Magazine*, 23 (September 1900): 740–44.

[24]For a full account, see Stanley L. Jones, *The Presidential Election of 1896* (Madison: University of Wisconsin Press, 1964).

[25]Eric F. Goldman, *Two-Way Street* (Boston: Bellman Publishing Co., 1948). (A sketchy potboiler.)

[26]For a concise account, see Leon Wolff, *Lockout* (New York: Harper and Row, 1965).

[27]Merle Curti, *The Growth of American Thought*, 3rd ed. (New York: Harper and Row, 1964), 634.

[28]Copied from original in AT&T Archives.

[29]"Manufacturing Public Opinion," *McClure's Magazine* 26 (February 1906): 450–52.

[30]Ray Ginger, *The Age of Excess* (New York: Macmillan, 1965), 25.

[31]Forrest McDonald, *Insull* (Chicago: University of Chicago Press, 1962), 44–45. (Biography of the utility magnate who blazed many public relations trails before he crashed in ruin.)

[32]"America's First Press Agent a Well-Known Pittsburgher," clipping in Westinghouse Company files, circa 1906.

[33]C. C. Regier, *The Era of the Muckrakers* (Chapel Hill: University of North Carolina Press, 1932). (Regier neglects the role of metropolitan newspapers in this muckraking.) For a generous sampling of newspaper articles, see Arthur Weinberg and Lila Weinberg, eds., *The Muckrakers* (New York: Simon and Schuster, 1961).

[34]Parrington, *Main Currents in American Thought,* vol. III, pp. 404–5. For details on the rise of the mass media, see Edwin Emery, *The Press and America* (Englewood Cliffs, N.J: Prentice-Hall, Inc., 1972); Theodore Peterson, *Magazines in the Twentieth Century* (Urbana: University of Illinois Press, 1964); and Stephen Fox, *The Mirror Makers* (New York: Morrow, 1984).

[35]Richard Hofstadter, *The Age of Reform* (New York: Alfred A. Knopf, Inc., 1955), 185.

[36]Robert D. Reynolds, Jr., "The 1906 Campaign to Sway Muckraking Periodicals," *Journalism Quarterly* 56. (Autumn 1979): 513.

[37]Ralph H. Hower, *The History of an Advertising Agency: N. W. Ayer & Son at Work, 1896-1939* (Cambridge, Mass.: Harvard University Press, 1939), 117. See also p. 95 of the 1949 revised edition.

[38]For details, see Scott M. Cutlip, "The Nation's First Public Relations Firm," *Journalism Quarterly* 43 (Summer 1966). (It was in fact a publicity agency, not a public relations firm.)

[39]Ray Stannard Baker, "Railroads on Trial," *McClure's Magazine* 26 (March 1906): 535–44. The story is also told in the Weinbergs' *The Muckrakers.*

[40]"Department Press Agents," Hearing Before Committee on Rules, House of Representatives, May 21, 1912, 62d Congress, 2d session (Washington, D.C.: Government Printing Office, 1912), 16. Also see William Kittle, "The Making of Public Opinion," *Arena* 41 (1909): 443–44.

[41]Rex F. Harlow, "Years of Challenge," an unpublished autobiography, 1982. Harlow's writings are cited elsewhere in this chapter and in Chapter 1. His American Council on Public Relations is discussed in Chapter 5.

[42]Gordon A. Moon II, "George F. Parker: A 'Near Miss' as First White House Press Chief," *Journalism Quarterly* 41 (Spring 1964): 183–90.

[43]Correspondence in Box 141, *General Leonard Wood Papers*, Library of Congress, suggests that the Parker and Bridge firm continued into the 1920s with Parker and Roy Mason as partners.

[44]Goldman, *Two-Way Street.*

[45]Quoted in Sherman Morse, "An Awakening on Wall Street," *American Magazine* 62 (September, 1906): 460.

[46]*Ivy L. Lee Papers*, Princeton University Library. Lee's correspondence of 1907 includes a letter from the president of Pennsylvania Railroad to a colleague in Southern Pacific, saying that he had concluded that the time had come to take measures to "place our case before the public."

[47]Raucher, *Public Relations and Business,* For the definitive biography see Ray Eldon Hiebert, *Courtier to the Crowd: The Story of Ivy L. Lee and the Development of Public Relations* (Ames: Iowa State University Press, 1966).

[48]For testimony on this case, see *Investigation of Nazi and Other Propaganda: Public Hearings before a Subcommittee of the Committee on Un-American Activities, Hearing Number 73-NY-7* (Washington, D.C.: Government Printing Office, 1934); and *Trials of War Criminals before the Nurenberg Military Tribunal, volumes VII and VIII, Case Six, U.S. v. Krauch,* "The I. G. Farben Case" (Washington, D.C.: Government Printing Office, 1963). See also *Activities of Nondiplomatic Representatives of Foreign Principals in the United States,* Hearings before Committee on Foreign Relations, U.S. Senate, parts 1–13 (Washington, D.C.: Government Printing Office, 1963).

[49]George Juergens, *News From the White House: The Presidential-Press Relationship in the Progressive Era* (Chicago: University of Chicago Press, 1981), 70.

[50]See full story in Joseph I. C. Clarke, *My Life and Memories* (New York: Dodd, Mead, 1955); and "A New Press Agent," *Editor and Publisher* 4 (May 12, 1906).

[51]For story of Ford's public relations, see David L. Lewis, *The Public Image of Henry Ford: An American Hero and His Company* (Detroit: Wayne State University Press, 1976).

[52]Samuel Insull, *Central Station Electric Service* (Chicago: privately printed, 1915), 356.

[53]See Noel L. Griese. "James D. Ellsworth, 1863–1940," *Public Relations Review* IV (Summer 1978): 22–31.

[54]For more on the development of public relations in higher education, see Scott M. Cutlip, "Advertising' Higher Education: The Early Years of College Public Relations," *College and University Journal* 9 (November 1970), part I, and vol. 10 (January 1971), part II.

[55]Howard Weeks, "The Development of Public Relations as an Organized Activity in a Protestant Denomination" (Master's thesis, American University, 1963).

[56]For a full account of public relations' role in fund-raising, see Scott M. Cutlip, *Fund Raising in the United States: Its Role in America's Philanthropy* (New Brunswick, N.J.: Rutgers University Press, 1965).

[57]Edwin Emery, *History of American Newspaper Publishers Association* (Minneapolis: University of Minnesota Press, 1950), 125–30.

[58]James O. Mock and Cedric Larson, *Words That Won the War* (Princeton, N.J: Princeton University Press, 1939), 4.

[59]*New York Times,* February 1, 1920, p. 9, col. 1.

[60]Harold D. Lasswell, *Propaganda Techniques in the World War* (New York: Alfred A. Knopf, Inc., 1927), 220.

[61]For a detailed chronicle of his own career, see Edward L. Bernays, *Biography of an Idea: Memoirs of Public Relations Counsel Edward L. Bernays* (New York: Simon and Schuster, 1965).

[62]Pamel J. Creedon, "Public Relations History Misses 'Her Story,'" *Journalism Educator* 44, no. 3 (Autumn 1989): 26–30.

[63]Bernays, Doris Fleischman, *A Wife Is Many Women* (New York: Crown, 1955), 171. As quoted by Creedon in "Public Relations History," p. 28.

[64]For this unsavory page in history, see *Utility Corporations: Efforts by Associations and Agencies of Electric and Gas Utilities to Influence Public Opinion,* Summary Report Prepared by Federal Trade Commission, 70th Congress 1st session, Senate Document 92, Part 71-A (Washington, D.C.: Government Printing Office, 1934). A popular summary is Ernest Gruening's *The Public Pays* (New York: Vanguard, 1931). For a kinder view, see McDonald, *Insull.*

[65]John M. Shotwell, "Crystallizing Public Hatred: The Ku Klux Klan in the Early 1920s" (Master's thesis, University of Wisconsin-Madison, 1974).

[66]George Griswold, Jr., "How AT&T Public Relations Policies Developed," *Public Relations Quarterly* 12, (Fall 1967): 13. (A special issue devoted to AT&T's public relations.) Also see Noel L. Griese, "He Walked in the Shadows: Public Relations Counsel Arthur W. Page," *Public Relations Quarterly* 21 (Fall 1976).

[67]For a balanced view of Howe's contributions to FDR's career and his public relations ideas, see Alfred B. Rollins, Jr., *Roosevelt and Howe* (New York: Alfred A. Knopf, Inc., 1962).

[68]Marilyn Kern-Foxworth, "Minority Entrepreneurs Challenge the Barriers," *Public Relations Journal* 45, no. 8 (August 1989): 19.

[69]Allan M. Winkler, *The Politics of Propaganda: The Office of War Information 1942–45* (New Haven, Conn.: Yale University Press, 1978), 4.

[70]For a quick study of the OWI, see Robert L. Bishop and LaMar S. Mackay, "Mysterious Silence, Lyrical Scream: Government Information in World War II," *Journalism Monographs* 19 (May 1971), based on their Ph.D. dissertations written at the University of Wisconsin.

[71]Information based on Colonel Sidney A. Knutson's thesis, "History of Public Relations Program of U.S. Army" (University of Wisconsin, 1953). Also see Gordon W. Keiser, *The U.S. Marine Corps and Defense Unifications 1944–47* (Washington: National Defense University Press, 1982).

[72]Thomas S. Repplier, "Advertising and 'The Forces of Righteousness,'" in *The Promise of Advertising*, edited by Charles H. Sandage (Homewood, Ill: Richard D. Irwin, Inc., 1961), 59.

[73]"Business Is Still in Trouble," *Fortune* 39 (May 1949) reflects business' postwar public relations problems. For a biting critique of some business efforts to deal with critics, see William H. Whyte, *Is Anybody Listening?* (New York: Simon and Schuster, 1952).

[74]Alfred McClung Lee, "Trends in Public Relations Training," *Public Opinion Quarterly* 11 (Spring 1947): 83–91.

[75]Public Relations Society of America, "Public Relations Education in American Colleges and Universities," August 1956. (Study was directed by Hale Nelson, chairman of PRSA Education Committee.)

[76]Ray E. Hiebert, "Public Relations Education in American Colleges and Universities 1964," report prepared for the Public Relations Society of America, 1964.

[77]Rex Harlow, "A Timeline of Public Relations," *Public Relations Review* 6 (Fall 1980): 5.

[78]For implications of transition from a post-industrial to an information society, see Robert B. Reich, *The Next American Frontier* (New York: Times Books, 1983); and Rosabeth Moss Kanter, *The Change Masters* (New York: Simon and Schuster, 1983).

[79]John Naisbitt, *Megatrends: Ten New Directions Transforming Our Lives* (New York: Warner Books, 1982); and John Naisbitt and Patricia Aburdene, *Megatrends 2000: Ten New Directions for the 1990s* (New York: William Morrow and Co., 1990) are useful in understanding implications of accelerating change.

[80]Frank Popoff, "The Incredible Shrinking World," in *The Point Is . . .*, no. 127 (May 18, 1989): Dow Chemical Company, Midland, Michigan.

CHAPTER 5

Ethics and Professionalism

If I have done my job well for the right purpose, my life has substance and meaning. If I have done my job poorly or for the wrong purpose, I have squandered my life, however much I have prospered.[1]

JOHN KULTGEN

We cannot discuss the professional status of public relations without first talking about ethics. In fact, adherence to a code of "professional ethics" separates professions from other skilled occupations. Ethical issues take on added importance because professionals with special expertise have unprecedented power in decisions that affect every aspect of society. In the global village, where information and influence reach most parts of the world with amazing speed and ease, their power does not stop at national or cultural boundaries. Ethics and professionalism are global concerns; social responsibility is no longer just a local matter.

This chapter explores the ethical and professional foundations of public relations practice. It also chronicles aspects of an occupation taking on the philosophy and trappings of a calling and an *emerging profession*.

ETHICAL FOUNDATIONS

You do not have to be a card-carrying cynic to question the ethical foundations of some established professions. Evening news reports tell of physicians prescribing unnecessary tests and medications sold by laboratories

129

and pharmacies that they themselves own, committing Medicare or insurance fraud, and performing costly (and sometimes risky) but unnecessary surgery. Critics point to some lawyers making top dollar as "hired guns" for special interests by filing lawsuits to harass and intimidate, to frustrate judicial process, or to obscure facts in "legalese." Others have been convicted for absconding with clients' estates. Investigative journalists and prosecutors expose television ministers living in luxury and lust while preying on those most susceptible to fund-raising appeals and least able to support bogus, but high-sounding, missionaries.

Absence of rigorous policing of such pretenders and charlatans erodes public confidence. Ideally, professional societies or associations engage in self-policing to deter malfeasance, to enforce the collective morality, and to ensure that professionals will engage in what one writer calls "right conduct."[2] Spike Lee said the same thing in his movie title *Do the Right Thing*. Surely, the primary goal is to protect the client of professional services. At the same time, however, self-policing in the professions protects the professional franchise and maintains public trust and support for professional privilege.

Professional Ethics

Right conduct suggests that actions are consistent with moral values generally accepted as norms in a society or culture. In professions, the application of moral values in practice is referred to as "applied ethics."[3] Established professions translate widely shared ideas of right conduct into formal codes of ethics and professional conduct. These statements of applied ethics guide professional practice and provide the basis for enforcement and sanctions.

Thus, professional conduct is based on what are generally considered virtuous motives, monitored and assessed against established codes of conduct, and enforced through concrete interpretation for those who deviate from accepted standards of performance. *The principle behind professional ethics is that one's actions are designed to create the greatest good for both the client and community as a whole, rather than to enhance the position and power of the practitioner.*

Why this concern for ethics and enforcement of codes of conduct? The answers are at the same time both simple and complex. The simple answer is to protect those who entrust their well-being to the professional. The more complex answer also includes concerns about protecting the profession itself: professional privilege, status, and collegiality.

The Imperative of Trust

Clients' relationships with professionals differ from their relationships with other providers of skills and services. For example, if you go to a hospital emergency room, it is unlikely that you will know the doctors and nurses who take care of you. Yet you will most likely have some degree of confidence that they are qualified and capable and, furthermore, that they will perform with your best interests in mind. Even if you are alert and able, it is unlikely that you will delay their performance while you check their transcripts to make sure they took the appropriate courses and passed all their exams, or ask them to justify their fee schedule or itemize anticipated costs. Contrast your relationship with these doctors and nurses with the one you establish with the mechanic or repair shop when your car needs major or emergency service.

The difference centers on the nature of "fiduciary relationships." When you seek the services of a professional, you put yourself—not just your things—at risk. Your well-being is subject to the judgment and actions of the professional. Except in extreme circumstances, you maintain ultimate control, but you typically must reveal aspects of your person and behavior that normally remain private. In other words, you *trust* the professional with information and access that often are withheld from even your closest friends and family. Often, you actually *entrust* yourself and your possessions to the professional. That is, you enter a *fiduciary relationship*, meaning the professional holds you, and possibly your possessions, in trust and is *obliged* to act in your best interest. This obligation differentiates the professional from other knowledgeable and skilled artisans.[4]

Professional Privilege

Because of the value and trust inherent in fiduciary relationships, professionals traditionally hold privileged positions in society. Additionally, professionals do work that is seen as especially valuable, in part because of the preparation and practice to develop the required knowledge and skills. Because money alone does not justly reward such work, society extends privileges to its practitioners. So not only must professionals invest a great deal of time to acquire and maintain their own knowledge and skills, but they must also commit themselves to uphold the profession by honoring its obligations and values.

When professionals violate fiduciary relationships or otherwise exploit clients, or when they perform substandard practice, they threaten not only their client's welfare but that of their entire profession. Professional privilege rests on the foundation of public trust and confidence in both the professional's expertise and right conduct.

To protect both clients and their own privileged positions in society, professions establish codes of ethics and standards of practice. These codes often have the weight of law and the power of state sanctions. The argument for codes and rigorous enforcement rests on the belief that professional work involves special and valuable knowledge and skill essential to the public good, and so esoteric and complex that only those deemed qualified may engage in practice.[5]

Professional privilege rests, therefore, on the implicit agreement among the profession, the public, and the state. As one writer put it:

> Protect my members from the unfettered competition of a free market, and you can trust them to put your interest before their own. I will select them carefully and train and organize them to provide competent and ethical service.[6]

Simply put, professional privilege extends beyond an individual practitioner's relationship with client and colleagues; it also includes obligations derived from an implicit contract with the larger society.

Social Responsibility

Professions, then, also must fulfill expectations and moral obligations at the level of society. Commitment to serve society applies to both individual practitioners and the profession collectively. It means that right conduct takes into account the welfare of the larger society as the professional helps clients solve problems. It also means that associations of professionals exercise collective power as moral agents and watchdogs for the betterment of society. To fulfill their social responsibilities, professionals are expected to do more than provide knowledge and skilled services; they are "held responsible for improving the institutions administering those services."[7]

Because public relations has impact well beyond the boundaries of client organizations, individual practitioners must be concerned with both the intended and unintended consequences of the function. Collectively, through their professional associations, they must take responsibility for prescribing standards of competence, defining standards of conduct, establishing educational and accreditation requirements, encouraging research to expand the body of knowledge that guides the practice, and representing the profession in matters affecting the profession's charter and social mission.[8]

Ultimately, public relations is judged on its impact on society. Public relations' social utility is enhanced when (1) it promotes the free, ethical competition of ideas, individuals, and institutions in the marketplace of public opinion; (2) it reveals the sources and goals underlying attempts to influence; and (3) it enforces high standards of conduct. Social utility is diminished when (1) it suppresses or otherwise limits competition of ideas, (2) it hides or ascribes to others the true sources of public relations efforts, and (3) it leaves unchallenged incompetent or unethical practice.

Positives

The major positives of socially responsible public relations include:

1. Public relations improves professional practice by codifying and enforcing ethical conduct and standards of performance.
2. Public relations improves the conduct of organizations by stressing the need for public approval.
3. Public relations serves the public interest by making all points of view articulate in the public forum.
4. Public relations serves our segmented, scattered society by using communication and mediation to replace misinformation with information, discord with rapport.
5. Public relations fulfills its social responsibility to promote human welfare by helping social systems adapt to changing needs and environments.

Much good can be credited to ethical public relations practice, and opportunities for serving the public interest abound. Public relations' benefits are apparent in the billions of dollars raised to construct buildings, endow professorships, and provide scholarships in universities; in campaigns to eradicate disease and substance abuse, reduce poverty, improve nutrition, and house the homeless; in the lessening of ethnic, racial, and religious discrimination and conflict; in responsive economic enterprises providing profit for investors, jobs for employees, and goods and services for consumers; and in greater understanding of global problems and relations. The potential good inherent in ethical, effective public relations is limitless. So is the potential for social dysfunction.

Negatives

Three major negatives can be attributed to the practice:

1. Public relations gains advantages for and promotes special interests, sometimes at the cost of the public well-being.
2. Public relations clutters already-choked channels of communication with the debris of pseudoevents and phony phrases that confuse rather than clarify.
3. Public relations corrodes our channels of communication with cynicism and "credibility gaps."

Too often the thrust of public relations is to obfuscate and obscure rather than to clarify complex public issues. Robert Heilbroner recognizes public relations as a social force and charges it with a major part "in the general debasement of communications from which we suffer." He says:

> No one can quarrel with the essential function that public relations fills
> as a purveyor of genuine ideas and information. No one denies that
> many public relations men, working for corporations as well as for col-
> leges or causes, honestly communicate things which are worth commu-
> nication. Nor can anyone absolve public relations for loading the com-
> munications channels with noise. We read the news and suspect that
> behind it lies the "news release." We encounter the reputation and
> ascribe it to publicity. Worst of all, we no longer credit good behavior
> with good motives, but cheapen it to the level of "good public relations."[9]

Practitioners also stand accused, with some validity, of loading our communication channels with noise and clogging them with the clutter of manufactured stories. Expressing these concerns, historian Daniel Boorstin argues that "pseudoevents" blur, rather than clarify, public issues. In his book *The Image*, Boorstin writes:

> The disproportion between what an informed citizen needs to know
> and what he can know is even greater. The disproportion grows with
> the increase of the officials' power of concealment and contrivance.
> The news gatherers' need to select, invent, and plan correspondingly
> increases. Thus inevitably our whole system of public information
> produces always more "packaged" news, more pseudoevents.[10]

Although Boorstin primarily blames journalists for this, practition-ers produce the majority of pseudoevents covered by the media. However, events planned to promote a cause in the public interest do have a legitimate place in public relations. This no one will deny. It is the phony events to promote dubious causes that come under fire. Precious news space or time given to a celebrity's honorary degree, a ribbon-cutting ceremony, or an orchestrated photo opportunity preempts explaining the complexities of the plight of the homeless, the national debt, the breakup of the Soviet Union, or international trade relations. Ethical public relations contributes to clarification of public issues, not to their displacement, distortion, or obfuscation.

This social aspect of right conduct reminds us that both individual practitioners and the profession as a whole are entrusted with the welfare of larger society as a condition on how they serve clients. This aspect of ethics is referred to as the profession's "social responsibility." When choosing such work and life, one also takes on the social responsibility of the profession, as well as its knowledge, skills, trust, and privileges.

In summary, to qualify as a profession, practitioners—both individually and collectively—must operate as moral agents in society. This requirement is *the ethical basis for professional practice: placing public service and social responsibility over personal gains and private special interests.*

OTHER PROFESSIONAL FOUNDATIONS

Concern for the ethical behavior in public relations addresses the emerging profession's effort to qualify *morally*. Other moves toward professional status derive from the caliber of training required of aspiring professionals and the conduct of basic research to guide the practice. These represent efforts to qualify through *knowledge and expertise*. In addition, practitioners and their organizations increasingly take on the institutional, procedural, and membership rules of other professions, in short, to qualify *functionally*.

Keep in mind, however, that the concept of a profession is not the product of logic. Rather, as legal historian Willard J. Hurst pointed out in an early issue of *Public Relations Journal*, "practice and experience in making society function have led to the definition of some occupations as professional, and have from time to time determined which ways of earning a living should fit the professional category."[11] Many callings—nursing, financial planning, and real estate, to name but a few—are striving for professional status. Few have earned it. Much of the effort is self-serving; some of it is public-spirited.

Attempts to achieve professional status might be considered selfish by some, but the results of increased professionalism benefits society as a whole. Professionalization institutionalizes the best practices and establishes standards of quality that serve the public interest. Professionalization has, by and large, brought us better health care; safer highways and bridges; better houses; faster cars and airplanes; and higher standards in business, banking, and accounting. We would add to this list more competent public relations counsel.

To assess the progress of contemporary practice and the calling toward achieving the status of a profession, we need criteria. In addition to the ethical foundation and moral imperative outlined in the previous section, other indicators of professional status include:

1. Specialized educational preparation to acquire unique knowledge and skills, based on a body of theory developed through research
2. Recognition by the community of a unique and essential service
3. Autonomy in practice and acceptance of personal responsibility by practitioners
4. Codes of ethics and standards of performance enforced by a self-governing association of colleagues

In summary, for public relations to achieve professional status, there must be specialized educational programs, a body of knowledge, community recognition, individual accountability, and commitment to abide by established codes that protect the public interest and spell out social responsibility.

PROFESSIONAL EDUCATION

As a leading public relations practitioner told students at Ball State University: "Public relations will never reach the status of a profession as long as people can get into the field and prosper without having completed a fairly rigorous course of study in the field."[12] True enough, established professions require extended periods of training to learn the knowledge and skills needed to practice; generally the more rigorous the training and esoteric the knowledge, the higher the professional status.

Because preparation is standardized and demanding, those entering professions go through similar initiations to the values and expectations of practice. Their common socialization experience not only standardizes the practice, but also encourages commitment to life-long careers and strong bonds with colleagues. Because of the commitment, time, and effort invested in acquiring the knowledge and skill base, professionals value achievement in the intellectual aspects of their fields.[13]

Degree Programs

University-level instruction in public relations dates from 1920. Concurrent with the beginning of the publicity boom of that era, Joseph F. Wright introduced a publicity course at the University of Illinois, frankly admitting that the course was created to bring prestige to his new calling. Two years later, in 1922, Frank R. Elliott introduced a publicity course at Indiana University. Both Wright and Elliot organized the first institutional publicity programs for their universities. Teaching the publicity courses on a part-time basis gave these pioneers the faculty status they needed to earn support among colleagues who looked askance at "propagandists."[14]

Edward L. Bernays, who had just written *Crystallizing Public Opinion*, offered the first public relations course in 1923. Bernays taught the one-semester-credit course for 2 years in the journalism department of New York University's School of Commerce, Accounts, and Finance. By 1946, 30 colleges offered 47 courses.[15] In 1956 the Public Relations Society of America (PRSA) made the first comprehensive survey of public relations education and found that the number of colleges offering courses had tripled in a decade.[16] Another survey financed by PRSA in 1970 identified 303 institutions offering one or more courses and increasing scholarly research activity.[17] The 1981 Commission on Public Relations Education estimated that 10,000 students were taking public relations courses at some 300 institutions.[18] In 1987, a similar commission found more than 160 colleges and universities offering public relations sequences or degree programs associated with journalism schools and departments, but made no estimate of how many programs reside in communication and speech departments.[19] PRSA's 1991 guide,

"Where to Study Public Relations," lists 212 colleges and universities in the United States, Canada, Puerto Rico, and Australia.[20] In addition, there are respected programs in Austria, England, and Germany.

Wherever it is housed, public relations education has attracted the attention of practitioners, as well as large numbers of students. The most recent commission recommends that undergraduate public relations programs contain no more than 25 percent course work in the major, with the rest devoted to liberal arts, sciences, and other general education courses. The commission also recommends that only half the course work in the major be specifically identified as public relations content. Without identifying specific courses, the commission lists five core content areas of study:

> Principles, practices, and theory of public relations: Introduces theories, managerial tasks, and ethical responsibilities. This is a concepts and principles course, not a skills or production course.
>
> Public relations techniques: Writing, message dissemination, and media networks: Stresses writing, designing, editing, and distributing written materials used in public relations practice. Includes print, broadcast, and audiovisual media.
>
> Public relations research for planning and evaluation: Introduces the use of research to identify problems and publics, to determine action and communication strategies, and to assess program results. Includes both fact-finding and evaluative research methods used in public relations decision making.
>
> Public relations strategy and implementation: Employs case-method and campaign-planning approaches to give students experiences in program planning, managerial analysis, and program administration. Applies decision theory and management theories to public relations strategic planning.
>
> Supervised public relations experience. Provides hands-on experience in an internship, practicum, or cooperative education setting. Typically takes the form of a carefully structured, supervised professional assignment in a public relations department or firm.[21]

The commission also suggests specialized advanced study in a specialized area of public relations practice, such as publicity and media relations, community relations, financial and investor relations, employee relations, or international relations. Additional recommended course work includes communication theory and process; history and structure of mass communication; and communication production: writing and editing, graphics and typography, photography, electronic media, and public speaking.

The recommended graduate curriculum includes either a thesis research project or comprehensive examinations and the following core courses:

> Communication Theory: Examines principal theories, processes, and models, including concepts and systems.
>
> Communication Research: Includes data analysis and logic related to research design and procedures.

Research Design and Critical Analysis: Examines contemporary research methodology and original research designs emphasizing hypothesis testing.

Communication in Society: Explores role and impact of communication (particularly mass media). Considers historical, legal, and economic issues.

Advanced Public Relations Case Studies: Examines representative public relations organizations, their problems, and their procedures.

Public Relations Management: Analyzes public relations as a primary management responsibility, emphasizing resolution of conflicts between private and public sectors of society.[22]

Continuing Education

Professions require continuing education to keep practitioners current in theory and skills. PRSA and International Association of Business Communicators (IABC) now encourage members to earn continuing education units (CEUs) for participating in some professional development seminars and workshops. For example, IABC program literature explains:

> CEUs allow you to build a permanent record of achievement which may be used as evidence of increased performance capabilities and job advancement. The CEU officially is defined as 10 contact hours of participation in an organized continuing education experience under responsible sponsorship, capable direction and qualified instruction.

As of 1993, all accredited (APR) members of PRSA must earn points from continuing education, professional development, and public service to maintain their accredited status. The requirement to maintain current expertise and skills and to perform public service moves the field even closer to the more-established professions. Continuing education also demonstrates commitment to the lifetime of learning needed to provide clients current and competent service, part of any profession's implicit contract with society.

RESEARCH AND THE BODY OF KNOWLEDGE

Ideally, professional higher education introduces aspiring practitioners to the body of theory and skills upon which the profession is based. Continuing education then keeps practitioners up to date on research developments that expand the body of knowledge. Not everyone, however, accepts the concept of a body of knowledge and the value of basic research. Few practitioners subscribe to or read the field's research journals. Even some board members of foundations and institutes ostensibly established to encourage basic research talk about scholarly research with disdain and try to divert resources to producing "news you can use."

One sure sign of advancement toward professional status is the increasing demand for research and critical examination of the conventional wisdom guiding the practice. Public relations problems in business and industry, for example, are every bit as tough and complicated as the problems faced by engineering, finance, production, or distribution. Practitioners must approach them as methodically and as thoroughly prepared as engineers, economists, and other managers approach their own. Such a scientific approach requires understanding based on a body of knowledge developed through extensive research. Hence, the oft said, "Nothing is more practical than a good theory."

Body of Knowledge Project

In 1986, the PRSA research committee headed by then–US West Communications public relations executive George Fowler began what became known as the "PRSA Body of Knowledge Project." This group took on the tasks of identifying relevant theory and research publications, abstracting the books and articles included in the inventory, and publishing updated bibliographies and abstracts.[23]

The literature serving the field reflects the gap between the immediate information needs of practitioners and the theory-building research conducted by scholars. For example, the content of PRSA's *Public Relations Journal* and IABC's *Communication World* reflect practitioners' primary interest in day-to-day problems and techniques related to designing and implementing programs. On the other hand, the scholarly journals—*Public Relations Review* and *Journal of Public Relations Research*—report research on the social context of public relations, professionalism, and theory development related to the practice. The literature mirrors classic concerns of other emerging professions: preoccupation and introspection during the search for collective identity, justification, and recognition.[24]

Support for Research

Because professions draw upon a specialized body of knowledge developed through research, practitioners are obligated to support the advancement of professional knowledge. Much credit for the advance toward professionalism goes to the Foundation for Public Relations Research and Education, a nonprofit organization established by PRSA in 1956 to foster basic research and education. In 1959 the foundation initiated a fellowship program that enabled teachers to work in counseling firms or corporations. A decade later it set up a graduate scholarship award. In 1961 the foundation began sponsoring a series of annual lectures. Perhaps its most important contributions, however, were in subsidizing much-needed books, publishing *Public Relations Review* (the field's first scholarly journal), and funding a series of public relations bibliographies.

During the 1980s, however, the foundation drifted from its original mission and began to exert its independence from PRSA. Directors funded failed attempts to introduce public relations education in business schools and pushed to broaden the appeal of *Public Relations Review* beyond the scholarly research audience. In 1988, culminating the long-running debate over the role of the scholarly journal, the foundation cut off financial support and transferred ownership to the founding editor's company. In the foundation's announcement of ownership change, it promised a new publication providing "information and ideas based primarily on the day-to-day experience of experts." Completing the change and separation from PRSA in 1989, the foundation changed its name to the Institute for Public Relations Research and Education. It also broadened its mission to "improve the effectiveness of organizational management by advancing the knowledge and practice of public relations and public affairs."

The institute continues to fund public relations research projects, publish important books for the field, recognize outstanding scholarship, and award undergraduate and graduate scholarships. Its annual Pathfinder Award recognizes outstanding research contributions to the body of knowledge. The annual master's thesis award and graduate research grants encourage advanced public relations studies.

During the late 1980s and early 1990s, however, the IABC Research Foundation became the major funding agency for public relations research. Estimated to total more than $400,000, its "Excellence in Public Relations and Communication Management" project explored the function's contributions to the bottom line and identified factors contributing to organizational success. Professor James Grunig at the University of Maryland led a team of researchers from the United States and the United Kingdom that produced comprehensive reviews of theory and research, as well as collected data from more than 200 organizations in the United States, Canada, and United Kingdom.[25]

The Literature

The University of Wisconsin Press published the first comprehensive bibliography of public relations books and periodical literature in 1957. The second edition, published in 1965, carried nearly 6000 entries of books and articles relevant to the practice. The third edition in 1974 added 4000 titles to the growing body of literature. The fourth issue of *Public Relations Review* in 1975 began that journal's series of updated bibliographies.[26] The first bibliography produced as part of the PRSA Body of Knowledge Project appeared in the spring 1988 issue of *Public Relations Review*.[27] Since then, abstracts of the major works are available in binders or on computer disks from PRSA.

Increases in the number of scholarly books and journals devoted to the field indicate a growing knowledge base for study and practice. An important advance came with public relations' first scholarly journal, *Public Relations Review*, launched in 1975 under the auspices of the then–Foundation for Public Relations Research and Education. The same foundation funded the start up of a second scholarly journal in 1984, *Public Relations Research and Education*. Although only three semiannual issues were published, it provided the impetus for three subsequent volumes of *Public Relations Research Annual* (1989–1991). Reflecting the continuing growth of scholarly research, the annual became a quarterly, *Journal of Public Relations Research*, in 1992. *Public Relations Review* and *Journal of Public Relations Research* are the primary publications sharing scholarly research, theoretical discourse, and criticism of the field.

The oldest professional or trade publication in the field, started in 1944 by Rex F. Harlow, is PRSA's *Public Relations Journal*. It emphasizes professionalism, discusses techniques used in practice, presents case histories, and provides a forum for debate on practice and ethics. *Public Relations Quarterly*, started in 1954 as the publication of the then-named American Public Relations Association (APRA), is similar in purpose and content, although its articles are somewhat longer and less "how-to" oriented. Since 1961, when APRA merged with PRSA, *Public Relations Quarterly* has been privately published. The International Public Relations Association began its quarterly journal, *International Public Relations Review*, in 1977. Edited in the organization's Geneva office and printed in the United Kingdom, this journal includes thoughtful commentaries, status reports on public relations around the globe, and a truly international perspective on the practice.

Four national weekly newsletters—the major ones in a growing field—report current news, opinions, and how-to information: *Public Relations News*, started in 1944; *pr reporter*, started in 1958; *Jack O'Dwyer's Newsletter*, started in 1967; and *Communication Briefings*, started in 1981. In addition, magazines such as *O'Dwyer's PR Services Report* and *PR Week* (U.K.), as well as numerous regional and specialized newsletters, publish news, features and how-to articles of interest to practitioners. (See Exhibit 5–1.)

Of course, the volumes of analyses and research reports that *do not* get published and widely disseminated would dwarf the literature of the field. Most research conducted by public relations departments and firms is considered proprietary, therefore not shared beyond the sponsoring organization. Often such research addresses specific issues and publics at a particular time and does not draw on or contribute to the body of theory. If publications do result from such case studies and descriptive surveys, they tend to take the form of "how-public-relations-saved-the-day" reports. As a result, much of what passes as "research" in the literature consists of selectively published narratives that do not test or build theory, therefore adding little to the body of knowledge as represented by the literature of the field.

Publications

Scholarly Journals

Journal of Public Relations Research, Lawrence Erlbaum Associates,
    Publishers, 365 Broadway, Hillsdale, NJ 07642 (Editors: James E. Grunig
    and Larissa A. Grunig, College of Journalism, University of Maryland,
    College Park, MD 20742)
Public Relations Review, JAI Press Inc., 55 Old Post Road—No. 2, P.O. Box
    1678,Greenwich, CT 06836 (Editor: Ray E. Hiebert, College of Journalism,
    University of Maryland, College Park, MD 20742)

Professional Periodicals

Communications World, International Association of Business
    Communicators, One Hallidie Plaza, Suite 600, San Francisco, CA 94102
    (monthly)
International Public Relations Review, International Public Relations
    Association, Case Postale 126, CH-1211, Geneva, Switzerland (quarterly)
O'Dwyer's PR Services Report, J. R. O'Dwyer Company, Inc., 271 Madison
    Avenue, New York, NY 10016 (monthly)
Public Relations Journal, Public Relations Society of America, 33 Irving Place,
    New York, NY 10003 (monthly)
Public Relations Quarterly, P. O. Box 311, Rhinebeck, NY 12572
PR Week, Haymarket Marketing Publications, Ltd., 22 Lancaster Gate,
    London W2 3LP

Newsletters

Communication Briefings, 700 Black Horse Pike, Suite 110, Blackwood, NJ
    08012
Jack O'Dwyer's Newsletter, 271 Madison Ave., New York, NY 10016
PR News, Phillips Publishing, Inc., 7811 Montrose Road, Potomac, MD 20854
pr reporter, PR Publishing Company, Inc., P.O. Box 600, Exeter, NH 03833

LICENSING AND ACCREDITATION

Pioneer counselor Edward L. Bernays was among the first to advocate
licensure. In 1953 he argued, "In the entire history of professions, licensing standards and criteria and finally codes of ethics in public conduct

have been necessary . . . to exclude those who are not properly qualified."[28] The indefatigable Bernays was still thumping the same drum more than 50 years later: "We must get the two words, public relations, defined by law with licensing and registration of practitioners, as is the case with lawyers, medical doctors and other professionals. Today the term 'public relations' is in the public domain and anyone—many without training, education, or ethical behavior—is welcome to use it to describe what he or she professes to do."[29] Yet, practitioners in the United States remain divided on the desirability of licensing.

Legal Considerations

The issue of occupational licensure—the permission granted by the state to engage in a specific occupation—raises three basic constitutional issues: (1) the right of freedom of expression, (2) the right of the states to regulate occupations, and (3) the right of individuals to pursue occupations without unjustified state interference. Licensure must be justified on the grounds that it is crucial to the well-being and preservation of society.

Two serious constitutional issues are raised in the matter of licensing. One is the problem of *demonstrating a compelling state interest*; the other is safeguarding the practitioner's *freedom of expression*. The right of the states to regulate occupations is based on the Tenth Amendment, which reserves for states (or people) all powers not specifically delegated to federal government. Of course, the First Amendment protects freedom of speech.

In recent years, the courts have raised the lower limits of what is defined as "compelling state interest." The two broad reasons generally given for public relations licensure—protection of society and professionalization of practitioners—must be considered carefully in the light of "compelling state interest."

The first of these reasons, that public relations can harm society by "corrupting the public channels of communications," is the stronger of the two, yet it is weak in the eyes of the courts. Although public relations has the potential for abuse, its actions may be no more dangerous to society as a whole than would be those exercised directly by the organization for whom the practitioner might act. And although public relations may be controversial, the courts have argued in cases such as *Adams* v. *Tanner*, 244 U.S. 590 (1917), and *Baker* v. *Daly*, 15 F. Supp.2d 881, that controversy is not sufficient cause to regulate. The argument that licensing would protect society is directly refuted in law. The courts have consistently found that even abusive communication merits protection under the First Amendment.

The second of these reasons, that licensure would professionalize the practice, also gets short shrift in the law. It may be a powerful professional argument, but it has no legal basis. In no case have the courts suggested that because licensing would be beneficial, it would be justifiable. Licensing cannot be imposed simply for the benefit of those in an occupational group, either to raise standards or to fence out competition.

Nor can the question of infringement of freedom of expression be easily dismissed. If the state did license practitioners, the exact degree of infringement of the practitioner's right of expression would most likely be minimal. What is at issue here is the right to the title "certified public relations counselor." The Supreme Court stated in *Time* v. *Hill,* 385 U.S. 374, that constitutional guarantees of free speech and press are not so much for the benefit of those concerned "as for the benefit of the citizens generally." In developing a measure of fitness that involves the competence to communicate, the state would be recognizing different competencies in individuals. Yet the right to freedom of expression is accorded to all, as contrasted with the privilege of practicing medicine, which is not guaranteed in the Constitution.

Advocates counter that licensing would be voluntary, thereby avoiding conflicts with the constitutionally protected rights. Likewise, organizations cannot be forced to hire only licensed practitioners. Instead, state licensing would limit only the use of the title "licensed public relations practitioner" or a similar title using the "licensed" label, not the right of free expression. Advocates also point out that employers and clients would soon learn the value of hiring licensed professionals. They also argue that states could work out reciprocity agreements whereby licenses issued by one state would be honored by other states, assuming similar examinations and criteria are established.[30]

A bill "to provide for the issuance of licenses for public relations counselors" was introduced in the Massachusetts legislature in late 1991 to commemorate Edward Bernays's 100th birthday. If passed, the bill would have established a licensing board; spelled out "good character, education and examination" as requirements for licensure; prohibited those without licenses from using titles that include "public relations," "communication," or "corporate communication"; and authorized use of current accreditation exams for the purposes of licensing. The 1992 legislative hearings made it clear that the bill was more symbolic and honorific of Bernays than representative of a consensus in the public relations community. On the whole, it appears that licensure will not soon provide a means of elevating and standardizing the preparation, ethics, and competence of practitioners.

Accreditation

In the absence of state licensing, PRSA, IABC, and several state and specialized associations—such as the Wisconsin Society for Hospital Public Relations—have programs to certify practitioners. Such accreditation programs usually require a written examination and an oral defense before a panel of qualified peers. Beginning in 1991, PRSA began an accreditation maintenance program, requiring accredited members to remain active in continuing education and public service. To retain their "Accredited Public Relations" designation (or APR, printed after their names), accredited members must earn ten points every 3 years through education, professional development, and public service activities.

Of the approximately 8000 eligible PRSA members—those in practice 5 or more years—about half are accredited. An even smaller number of IABC members, less than 5 percent of the membership, have attempted and passed that organization's accreditation exam. One survey of practitioners revealed that only 12 percent think that accreditation is "very important."

Proposals to consolidate the many accreditation programs under a single certification program usually die because of lack of interest and territorial jealousies among the professional organizations. One suggestion was to form a "public relations council" as a single accrediting body and to bring the combined weight of the many associations and societies to bear on practitioners who violate codes of ethics and professional behavior. Such a council would set and maintain high professional and commercial standards and arbitrate complaints about the conduct of individual practitioners, departments, and firms.

In summary, a single, well-publicized, and strongly enforced accreditation program is needed to move public relations toward professional status. Current practice is guided by weak voluntary codes, splintered efforts by different associations and societies, and no state licensing. This situation is not lost on the major professional associations and societies.

PROFESSIONAL ORGANIZATIONS

The growth of professional associations reflects the serious efforts being made by many practitioners to surround the function with status and to advance its competence. One directory lists 215 such groups in 72 countries with combined membership of more than 150,000.[31] Although these associations include only a small portion of all those working in the public relations field, they exert considerable influence through their publications, conferences, seminars, awards programs, and advocacy for the practice.

Public Relations Society of America (PRSA)

The largest professional organization is the Public Relations Society of America, with 15,000 members in 101 chapters. Headquartered in New York City, PRSA traces its origins to three older associations established to bring together practitioners of this growing vocation.

PRSA was formed February 4, 1948, by the merger of the National Association of Public Relations Counsel (NAPRC) and the American Council on Public Relations (ACPR). The NAPRC was first organized in 1936 as the National Association of Accredited Publicity Directors. Composed largely of New York City practitioners without any official accreditation process, it used the words *national* and *accredited* in a very loose sense. It changed its name in 1944 to reflect the shift of emphasis to public relations. The ACPR was started in San Francisco in 1939 as an association for West Coast practitioners.

The goal of forward-looking practitioners and educators for a strong national association, serving all fields of practice, was finally realized July 1, 1961, when the American Public Relations Association (APRA) merged into PRSA. Headquartered in Washington, D.C., and dominated by trade-association practitioners, APRA had been organized in 1944 after a 7-year effort by Washington practitioners. At the time of the merger in 1961, PRSA had 3359 members and the APRA 826; 100 practitioners held membership in both organizations.

APRA made two contributions to the advancement of public relations: its Silver Anvil Awards to recognize successful programs and its *Quarterly Review of Public Relations*, later renamed in turn *PR Quarterly* and *Public Relations Quarterly*. PRSA continued the Silver Anvil Awards program, but dropped APRA's quarterly publication in favor of the monthly *Public Relations Journal*, which ACPR began in 1944.

PRSA fosters the exchange of ideas through its publications and meetings, promotes a sense of professionalism, provides opportunities for continuing education, and encourages ethical behavior and high standards of practice. Its strength and scope were greatly enhanced in 1977 when the National Communication Council for Human Services, the organization of practitioners serving the health and welfare fields, voted to consolidate its membership and services with those of PRSA.

The counselors in the PRSA organized a "counselors' section" in 1960 as a means of dealing more effectively with the problems of special concern to public relations firms. This section studied counseling fees, issued a booklet defining the role of the counselor, and in 1963 gained PRSA's approval of a voluntary plan of self-accreditation, based on character, experience, and examination. This section is now the Counselors Academy and requires PRSA accreditation (APR) for membership. PRSA members who were engaged in association work followed suit in 1963 when they won approval for a "business and professional association section," now known as the Association Section. A government section—now Public Affairs and Government Section—was formed in 1970, and other interest groups have since organized. There are now 14 sections: Corporate, Educational and Cultural Organizations, Educators, Financial Services, Health Academy, Investor Relations, Professional Services, Social Services, Technology, Travel and Tourism, and Utilities.

Following the split with the Foundation (now the Institute) for Public Relations Research and Education in 1989, PRSA established another foundation to support research, to fund scholarships, and to publish materials. Its major project has been establishing the Body of Knowledge Project and updating the reference listings and abstracts.

International Association of Business Communicators (IABC)

Progress toward increased professionalism and higher standards in public relations has been greatly advanced by the emergence of the IABC as a strong organization. Founded in 1970, IABC grew from 3500 members to more than 13,000 members in just two decades. The association has 125 chapters and affiliates in 14 countries, including Canada, United States, United Kingdom, Philippines, and—most recently—Southern Africa. Headquarters is in San Francisco, with a branch office in London.

To advance the competence and ethics of this field, IABC has created a professional development guide for practitioners to help them identify skills and knowledge areas they need to acquire to attain their career goals and an ethics review committee to enforce its code of ethics. Its Gold Quill and EXCEL awards programs set standards for and recognize excellence in communication program design and implementation. Its monthly magazine, *Communication World*, serves as a news source on emerging issues and a reference on communication trends, theory, and practice. IABC's belief that communication should be a management function is supported with a program to reach key educators. IABC, like PRSA, has formed a foundation to support education and research.

Canadian Public Relations Society (CPRS)

Founded in 1948, the same year as PRSA, CPRS has 1800 members in 14 chapters. One third of the members are accredited. CPRS publishes a quarterly newsletter, *Communique*, and holds an annual conference. Headquartered in Ottawa, Ontario, CPRS closely parallels PRSA in philosophy and programming.

Institute of Public Relations (United Kingdom) (IPR)

Also founded in 1948, IPR has 12 regional groups and a total of 3500 members. It has long been a leader in establishing and enforcing codes of professional and ethical conduct and in encouraging academic preparation and professional development within the profession. IPR publishes *Public Relations* eight times a year and sponsors the Communication Advertising and Marketing Education Foundation.

Public Relations Consultants Association (United Kingdom) (PRCA)

This association of "consultancies"—called "firms" in the United States—was formed in 1969 to promote professional standards in consultancy practice, to act as a clearinghouse for clients seeking counseling in public relations, and to represent members' interests. Only its 165 member consultancies, representing almost 4000 staff, may use the title "registered public relations consultants." In addition to publishing consultancy costs and other research, the association works closely with IPR in promoting the profession and in establishing standards of practice. The association's charter, definitions, guidelines, codes, and arbitration and disciplinary procedures formed the basis for those adopted by the European Community nations.

PRCA guidelines for member consultancies suggest that all staff members pledge compliance with the association's charter requirements. Furthermore, the guidelines call for a clause of charter compliance in all employment contracts. As long-time professional leader Tim Traverse-Healy in London, told the authors, the guidelines indicate the way "responsible practitioners here are beginning to think and act."

International Public Relations Association (IPRA)

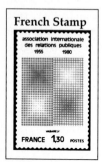

French Stamp

association internationale
des relations publiques
1955   1980

FRANCE 1,30 POSTES

When IPRA was formed in London in 1955, it had only 15 members in five countries. Membership now totals 1000 in 65 countries, with headquarters in Geneva, Switzerland. IPRA is formally recognized by the United Nations, and its members serve as consultants to the U.N. Economic and Social Council. In 1965 it adopted the Code of Athens, based on the U.N. Declaration of Human Rights. To commemorate IPRA's 25th anniversary in 1980, the French Post Office Authority issued the first and only stamp dedicated to public relations.

IPRA promotes professional recognition, high standards, and ethics among practitioners working in international aspects of public relations. In addition, it supports professional development and recognition in parts of the world where public relations is just developing and helps establish new national associations. IPRA meets twice each year, annually recognizes "outstanding contribution to better world understanding," publishes *International Public Relations Review* quarterly, and issues "Gold Papers" on major issues of interest to the global public relations community.

Specialized, Regional, and Local Associations

The growing memberships of several specialized national organizations attest to the field's growing sense of common interests, developing esprit de corps, and professionalism. For example, hospital practitioners formed a society affiliated with the American Hospital Association in 1964. Now almost 3000 members belong to the *American Society of Hospital Marketing and Public Relations* in a loosely structured network of 57 regional and local societies. It publishes a monthly newsletter, *Hospital Marketing and Public Relations*, and operates a job referral service for members.

Also typical of these specialized groups is the *National Association of Government Communicators* (NAGC). Organized in January 1976, it combined the memberships of the Government Information Organization and the Federal Editors Association. NAGC has 750 members, mostly in the Washington, D.C., area, but also in regional chapters in Frankfort, Kentucky; Minneapolis; Philadelphia; Denver, Susquehanna Valley, Pennsylvania; Austin, Texas; Hampton Roads, Virginia; and Chicago. Goals are to gain recognition for government communicators in the policy-making process and to advance professionalism among members through workshops, seminars, and annual meetings. It also works with the Civil Service Commission to update and write meaningful job standards. Another of NAGC's goals is to get Congress to repeal laws that restrict and hobble the public relations function in government.

Also growing is the network of *Black Public Relations Society* chapters in Atlanta, Chicago, Los Angeles, New York, Philadelphia, and Washington, D.C. The first chapters were formed in 1973, with the most recent formed in New York in 1991. Chapters provide mentoring and networking opportunities and encourage African-American students to enter public relations careers. Look for similar organizations for Hispanic practitioners, such as the *Hispanic Public Relations Association* founded in 1984 in Los Angeles.

Other specialized associations include:

Religious Public Relations Council	Founded 1929
National School Public Relations Association	1935
Agricultural Relations Council	1953
Baptist Public Relations Association	1954
National Society of Fund Raising Executives	1960
National Investor Relations Institute	1969
Council for Advancement and Support of Education (CASE)	1975
Issues Management Association	1982

Florida Public Relations Association, founded in 1938, is one of several state associations. Others include *Maine Public Relations Council*, *Public Relations Association of Mississippi*, and *Texas Public Relations Association*. Similar to the state groups, most major cities have public relations clubs, publicity clubs, and other associations not affiliated with PRSA, IABC, or other national and international organizations.

In addition, a number of "exclusive" groups have developed over the years, with varying degrees of impact in shaping the practice. These include the *Wise Men*, begun in 1938 by John W. Hill, Pendleton Dudley, and T. J. Ross; *Public Relations Seminar*, started in 1951 as an outgrowth of the National Conference of Business Public Relations Executives; and *Pride and Alarm*, founded in 1957 by New York–based practitioners who style themselves "junior Wise Men." Such groups function informally and hold their meetings in private. Exclusivity for the "in group" is their hallmark. The newest "by-invitation-only" group is the *Arthur W. Page Society*, formed in 1983 as the giant AT&T public relations unit anticipated being splintered among AT&T and seven newly formed regional telephone companies as a result of divestiture.

Outside the United States, there are more than 100 national and regional associations in some 70 countries, and the total is increasing as public relations gains recognition in the global community. Examples include *Public Relations Institute of Australia* (established in 1960; 2000 members), Brazil's *Federal Council of Public Relations Professionals* (1969; 8000 members), *French Public Relations Federation* (1971; membership composed of six separate associations of individuals and consultancies), *German Society of Public Relations* (1958; 1200 members), *Public Relations Society of India* (1958; 3000 members), and *Nigerian Institute of Public Relations* (1963; 3800 members).

Student Organizations

Development of the *Public Relations Student Society of America* (PRSSA) under the auspices of PRSA has strengthened education and recruitment into the field. PRSA's interest in organizing student chapters first surfaced in 1950, but it was not until April 1967 that now-retired Professor Walter Seifert of Ohio State University proposed such an organization to the PRSA assembly. The proposal won quick approval, and the first chapter was chartered in 1968. In 1992 there were PRSSA chapters on more than 150 campuses with almost 7000 members. PRSSA's purpose is "to cultivate a favorable and mutually advantageous relationship between students and professional public relations practitioners." To ease graduating PRSSA students' transition into the field, PRSA established a preassociate membership with reduced fees and special programs.

IABC also sponsors student chapters on 55 U.S. campuses and three in Canada. Student chapter membership totals more than 1500. IABC also invites students to join professional chapters. Territorial disputes between PRSA and IABC emerged when one university's student public relations club tried to affiliate with both PRSSA and IABC. PRSSA's rule forbidding dual affiliation illustrates the absence of common purpose and shared goals among the many professional associations and societies governing public relations.

CODES OF ETHICS

In addition to a self-governing organization, a basic requirement for professions is adherence to a set of professional norms, usually referred to as codes of ethics. As acceptance of professionalism and a sense of cohesiveness have developed, there has been increasing concern for standards of professional responsibility. Many practitioners are making an earnest effort to qualify morally. Others see codes of ethics as so much window dressing and high-sounding puffery.

Attempts to advance the ethics in this field are reflected in the number of codes of professional standards for public relations practice. In the United States, the principal code is that of the Public Relations Society of America. PRSA's first Code of Professional Standards was adopted in 1954 and revised in 1959, 1963, 1977, 1983, and 1988.

The 1963 revisions strengthened ethical guidelines for financial practice. Following several years of investigation, the Securities and Exchange Commission issued a biting indictment of the malpractices of a handful of practitioners. Revision of the code in 1977 responded to the threat of antitrust litigation against the PRSA by the Federal Trade Commission (FTC). The commission's Bureau of Competition had decided that code provisions barring contingency fees and banning one member from encroaching upon another member's clients were in violation of free competition. These provisions of the code were in contention:

> *A member shall not propose to a prospective client or employer that the amount of his fee or other compensation be contingent on or measured by the achievement of specified results; nor shall he enter into any fee agreement to the same effect.*

> *A member shall not encroach upon the professional employment of another member. Where there are two engagements, both must be assured that there is no conflict between them.*

The latter provision had long been a source of debate inside and outside PRSA because it did not apply to the many practitioners who did not belong to PRSA. Thus it appeared to protect only counselors who were PRSA members, making fair game of those who were not. In fact, the provision was never meaningfully enforced.

Although PRSA membership did not agree with the FTC's charges, the two provisions in question were deleted from the code April 29, 1977. Nevertheless, PRSA leaders made it clear that the society does not condone pirating accounts or contingency fees. The Federal Trade Commission, on October 27, 1977, accepted from PRSA an agreement containing a consent order that prohibits the society from "promulgating rules that affect fee arrangements or business solicitations." Thus the FTC approved the society's amended code.

Whereas the revised code also removed "sexist concepts and language," it retained another hotly debated provision:

> *A member shall adhere to truth and accuracy and to generally accepted standards of good taste.*

The phrase "generally accepted standards" remained a bone of contention among thoughtful practitioners. Its elasticity allowed more than one unethical practice to go unpunished until the 1988 revision of the code, after a case was brought before the grievance board.

The case involved a practitioner's disclosure of a potential client's plans to a competitor. Two articles were reworded to cover "potential" as well as past and present clients. The 1988 revision did not change the major provisions of the code. Rather, the Code of Professional Standards for the Practice of Public Relations was expanded to 17 articles and reworded to make them more understandable. In addition, revisions aligned PRSA's code with that proposed by the 13 member organizations of the North American Public Relations Council. (See Exhibit 5–2 for PRSA's Code of Professional Standards.)

EXHIBIT 5–2

Public Relations Society of America Code of Professional Standards for the Practice of Public Relations

(This code was adopted by the PRSA Assembly in 1988. It replaces a Code of Ethics in force since 1950 and revised in 1954, 1959, 1963, 1977, 1983, and 1988.)

DECLARATION OF PRINCIPLES

Members of the Public Relations Society of America base their professional principles on the fundamental value and dignity of the individual, holding that the free exercise of human rights, especially freedom of speech, freedom of assembly, and freedom of the press, is essential to the practice of public relations. In serving the interests of clients and employers, we dedicate ourselves to the goals of better communication, understanding, and cooperation among the diverse individuals, groups, and institutions of society, and of equal opportunity of employment in the public relations profession.

We pledge:

To conduct ourselves professionally, with truth, accuracy, fairness, and responsibility to the public;

To improve our individual competence and advance the knowledge and proficiency of the profession through continuing research and education;

And to adhere to the articles of the Code of Professional Standards for the Practice of Public Relations as adopted by the governing Assembly of the Society.

CODE OF PROFESSIONAL STANDARDS FOR THE PRACTICE OF PUBLIC RELATIONS

These articles have been adopted by the Public Relations Society of America to promote and maintain high standards of public service and ethical conduct among its members.

1. A member shall conduct his or her professional life in accord with the <u>public interest.</u>
2. A member shall exemplify high standards of <u>honesty and integrity</u> while carrying out dual obligations to a client or employer and to the democratic process.
3. A member shall <u>deal fairly</u> with the public, with past or present clients or employers, and with fellow practitioners, giving due respect to the ideal of free inquiry and to the opinions of others.
4. A member shall adhere to the highest standard of <u>accuracy and truth,</u> avoiding extravagant claims or unfair comparisons and giving credit for ideas and words borrowed from others.
5. A member shall not knowingly disseminate <u>false or misleading information</u> and shall act promptly to correct erroneous communications for which he or she is responsible.
6. A member shall not engage in any practice which has the purpose of <u>corrupting</u> the integrity of channels of communications or the processes of government.
7. A member shall be prepared to <u>identify publicly</u> the name of the client or employer on whose behalf any public communication is made.
8. A member shall not use any individual or organization professing to serve or represent an announced cause, or professing to be independent or unbiased, but actually serving another or <u>undisclosed interest.</u>
9. A member shall not guarantee the achievement of specified results beyond the member's direct control.
10. A member shall <u>not represent conflicting</u> or competing interests without the express consent of those concerned, given after a full disclosure of the facts.

11. A member shall not place himself or herself in a position where the member's personal interest is or may be in conflict with an obligation to an employer or client, or others, without full disclosure of such interests to all involved.

12. A member shall not accept fees, commissions, gifts or any other consideration from anyone except clients or employers for whom services are performed without their express consent, given after full disclosure of the facts.

13. A member shall scrupulously safeguard the confidences and privacy rights of present, former, and prospective clients or employers.

14. A member shall not intentionally damage the professional reputation or practice of another practitioner.

15. If a member has evidence that another member has been guilty of unethical, illegal, or unfair practices, including those in violation of this Code, the member is obligated to present the information promptly to the proper authorities of the Society for action in accordance with the procedure set forth in Article XII of the Bylaws.

16. A member called as a witness in a proceeding for enforcement of this Code is obligated to appear, unless excused for sufficient reason by the judicial panel.

17. A member shall as soon as possible sever relations with any organization or individual if such relationship requires conduct contrary to the article of this Code.

PRSA members agree to conduct their professional lives in accordance with the code. Compliance is enforced in confidential proceedings, following complaints of code violations by a PRSA member, by a nonmember, or through media exposure. A nine-member national Board of Ethics and Professional Standards acts somewhat as a grand jury, investigating complaints and deciding whether or not to file charges. Disciplinary cases are referred to either six-member judicial panels in each of PRSA's nine national districts or directly to PRSA's board of directors. Exhibit 5–3 outlines the rather cumbersome process.

In its first 35 years, the Board of Ethics and Professional Standards heard a total of 168 complaints, an average of almost five cases each year. Every article of the code was cited at least once, but the most frequent complaints (45 percent) involved charges of not dealing fairly with the public and clients. The other most frequent complaints charged members with intentionally communicating false or mislead-

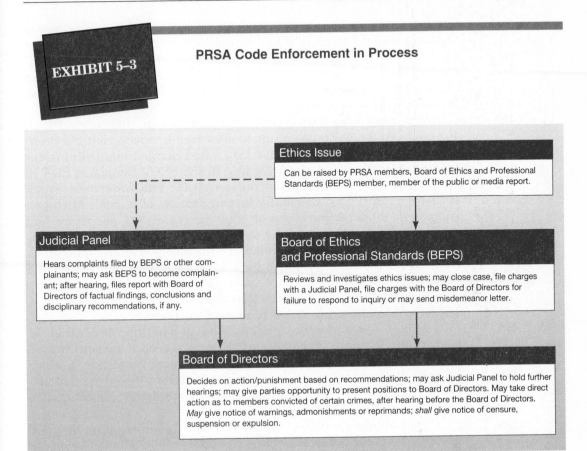

EXHIBIT 5–3

PRSA Code Enforcement in Process

Ethics Issue

Can be raised by PRSA members, Board of Ethics and Professional Standards (BEPS) member, member of the public or media report.

Judicial Panel

Hears complaints filed by BEPS or other complainants; may ask BEPS to become complainant; after hearing, files report with Board of Directors of factual findings, conclusions and disciplinary recommendations, if any.

Board of Ethics and Professional Standards (BEPS)

Reviews and investigates ethics issues; may close case, file charges with a Judicial Panel, file charges with the Board of Directors for failure to respond to inquiry or may send misdemeanor letter.

Board of Directors

Decides on action/punishment based on recommendations; may ask Judicial Panel to hold further hearings; may give parties opportunity to present positions to Board of Directors. May take direct action as to members convicted of certain crimes, after hearing before the Board of Directors. *May* give notice of warnings, admonishments or reprimands; *shall* give notice of censure, suspension or expulsion.

Courtesy Public Relations Society of America.

ing information, conduct not in the public interest, and failure to adhere to high standards of truth, accuracy, and good taste.

The ethics board is not without its critics. Reporting how one case was handled, *Jack O'Dwyer's Newsletter* (May 25, 1983) referred to the Board as "one of the more timid groups in the land." A later issue of the same newsletter (September 18, 1991) criticized PRSA's spending "$30,000 or so in legal bills each year so that a handful of members can rail at each other in private." According to the newsletter, "almost nothing emerges from the ethics board," pointing out that the board reviewed 12 cases in 1990 but sent none to a judicial panel.

Enforcement has been uneven over the years. The first penalty for violation was meted out in 1962, when a member was censured for attempting to take away the account of another member. Two members were censured in 1963 and another was suspended in 1964 in the wake of the Fulbright Committee's investigation of counselors representing foreign governments. Since those early cases, however, fewer than one out of five cases gets referred to judicial panels or the board of directors. Most cases are dismissed because of lack of evidence, settled to the satisfaction of all parties, or dropped because the charged member died or simply resigned. One of the quirks in the code is that it applies only to members.

The most notorious recent case occurred in 1986 when PRSA President Anthony Franco resigned after media reports that the Securities and Exchange Commission (SEC) had charged him with insider trading in a client's stock. According to the SEC's complaint filed in U.S. District Court in Washington, D.C., the American Stock Exchange noticed an unusually large purchase of a small Michigan company's stock. A purchase of 3000 shares at $41 per share had occurred the day before public announcement that a private investment group would buy the company for $50 per share. The stock exchange traced the purchase back to Franco, who had helped the company—his client—prepare an announcement of the impending sale. The SEC complaint alleges that Franco had denied the purchase, but later telephoned his broker to rescind the trade.[32]

Almost a year after the incident, without admitting or denying the allegations in the SEC complaint, Franco signed a consent decree accepting terms of a Final Judgment of Permanent Injunction in which he and his agents are "restrained and enjoined from, directly or indirectly" any practices designed to defraud, mislead or deceive, in connection with the purchase or sale of such security.[33]

Franco became PRSA president about 6 months after the SEC investigation and before the charges became public. Months before he told other PRSA officers about the SEC charges, however, Franco had signed a consent decree in which he neither admitted nor denied the charges. When Franco resigned his PRSA presidency, immediate past president David Ferguson, acting as interim president, stepped in to guide the judicial process outlined in the society's bylaws.

Before he dropped his PRSA membership, however, Franco requested an ethics board hearing. This action in effect silenced PRSA on the matter because its bylaws require that such hearings are closed and confidential. The *Wall Street Journal* headline read, "PR Society Receives Some Very Bad PR—From Its Ex-Chief."[34] The story went on to criticize PRSA for how it handled the case. President-elect John Felton, who began his presidency early as a result of the Franco resignation, defended the society's actions: "The need to protect the accused from harm requires confidentiality based on the basic American principle that we are innocent until we have had a chance to be heard by peers and proven guilty."[35] This principle was upheld in the early 1990s when the American Bar Association refused to bow to public pressure and rejected a proposal to make public its disciplinary records.

To remove the loophole that prevented prosecution after a member resigns, the bylaws were amended to allow continuing the investigation for up to 90 days after the resignation. Bylaw changes also allow the president or designated officer to notify the membership and make other public statements about such resignations and pending charges. This officer is also authorized to announce the results of the judicial proceedings, including "any disciplinary action which would have been taken had the member not resigned."

Most people recognize that the adoption of a code of ethics does not automatically bring morality to a calling. However, establishing a code reflects a sincere desire among a vast majority of leaders and members for raising standards of ethical practice and for providing yardsticks for guiding and judging individual behavior. A long-time leader and crusader for higher ethics in public relations, Frank Wylie, admonishes, "We shouldn't allow ourselves to accept the lowest common denominator of behavior—the negative and retrogressive 'it won't really hurt anyone' philosophy. We must aspire to a better level of ethics, and we must persevere to achieve that goal."[36]

As a distinguished Canadian counselor once pointed out, "Unfortunately, these codes have little real value unless they are accepted in turn by the employers of practitioners and applied to the conduct of the business itself."[37] Ethics scholar Donald Wright does not let individual practitioners off the hook, however: "Although there always will be some peer-imposed discipline based on codes of ethics, the bottom-line of ethical decision making in our field will continue to rest in the laps of individual practitioners."[38]

TOWARD NEW HORIZONS

Even after the considerable progress recorded since the mid-1900s, public relations still stands short of public acceptance as a true profession. The field lacks standardized educational requirements, mandatory certification or licensing, full-fledged devotion to serving the public interest, public acceptance of its social utility, and effective self-regulation. There is a growing consensus on a fairly standardized curriculum in the nation's schools and departments of journalism and communication, but still no educational requirements for entry to the practice. Although accreditation is encouraged by some professional associations and societies, proposals to certify or license practitioners are either rejected without serious consideration or posed as symbolic gestures. And whereas codes of ethics and standards of practice are held up as evidence of professional status, enforcement poses little threat or is easily subverted when the subject of enforcement simply drops his or her membership.

As a result, the field continues to be plagued with press agents parading as counselors and with those who are more interested in manipulating the opinions of others than in understanding them. There is still ample evidence that the function is not fully and widely understood, even among its practitioners. In sum, the field still takes in many who cannot qualify functionally, morally, or through knowledge and expertness. Fortunately, however, the ranks of those who can are growing at a faster rate.

The future looks promising, but there are still those who say that public relations is an art, not a profession. They apparently chose to ignore that the difference lies in the fiduciary relationship that is built into professional practice but not into art.[39] Likewise, they chose to ignore the growing body of knowledge and related specialized skills required to practice the mature concept of public relations. On the other hand, preoccupation with *professional status* may detract from the real value of *professionalism*: the ideal of providing competent and ethical service to those in need. One without the other falls short of the ideal: Ethics without competence is meaningless; competence without ethics is directionless. European scholar Hans-Martin Sass makes the point clearly:

> Ethics and expertise belong together; only together do they constitute true professionalism and provide a morally acceptable foundation for professional fiduciary services. The client . . . expects not general expertise . . . or general commitment to virtues or moral or religious principles from the expert; rather, he or she expects experienced expertise in making good technical and good moral judgments in concrete cases.[40]

Whether or not public relations qualifies as a profession is less important than the extent to which its practitioners do good and do no harm. If practitioners as a group are to measure up, they will have to practice positive public relations. They will have to stand for things. Professional status will not be achieved by singing hymns of faith and self-congratulations. In short, behavior speaks louder than words. As a respected practitioner, the late T. J. Ross, said many years ago in an interview with *Fortune* magazine, "Unless you are willing to resign an account or a job over a matter of principle, it is no use to call yourself a member of the world's newest profession . . . for you are already a member of the world's oldest."[41]

Not that long ago a handful of pioneers staked a claim on what we now know as public relations. Now is the time to strengthen educational programs, to build the body of knowledge, to toughen admission requirements, to raise the standards of ethics and acceptable behavior, and to accept the nobility of serving the public interest. Doing so will ensure public relations' position as an emerging profession and will provide opportunities to achieve professional status to those with the morality, knowledge, and skills. For in the final analysis, it is individuals committed to high standards of ethics and professionalism who will distinguish public relations from other occupations.

EXHIBIT 5-4

Public Relations Ethics in Practice

Situation 1: Your firm is one of several under consideration by a manufacturer planning to introduce a new service. The company anticipates severe opposition from certain groups and politicians. You are given confidential information as to the service and the company's plans so you can develop a proposal. The company awards the contract to a competing firm. Can you disclose the information to the manufacturer's opposition?

Answer: You are obligated by the PRSA code Article 13 to safeguard the confidences and privacy rights of present, former, and prospective clients or employers.

Situation 2: Your firm publishes a newsletter directed to brokerage houses. A corporate executive—one of your clients—asks you to help make the company better known among stock brokers. You publish a highly optimistic forecast of the company's business prospects, leaving out some information about problems. You also fail to indicate your firm's relationship with the company. Were you under any obligation to disclose this relationship? Should you print a correction that includes all the information you have about the company?

Answer: According to Article 5 of the code, you must immediately print a correction in your newsletter, giving all the facts and clarifying your relationship with the company. Not only is your incomplete and optimistic report in violation of federal security regulations, but you are also in violation of several articles of the code: Articles 1, 3, 4, 5, 7, and 8. Your publication clearly was not in the public interest, did not deal fairly with the public, and did not adhere to the highest standards of accuracy and truth. The code forbids disseminating false or misleading information and representing an undisclosed interest while professing to be independent or unbiased. The code also requires that you be prepared to identify clients or employers on whose behalf communication is made.

Situation 3: Your employer directs you to set up a supposedly independent citizens' organization to demonstrate support for a new real-estate development that requires planning commission approval. The new organization will be financed secretly by your company and a group of contractors who will participate in building the homes. Is there anything wrong with establishing this organization?

Answer: You may not set up an organization that purports to serve an independent cause but actually carries out a private or unannounced interest of a PRSA member, client, or employer (Article 8).

Situation 4: A pharmaceutical company arranges for your firm to arrange a press conference for an independent British scientist who has tested one of your client's new products and written a favorable research article. You are also to arrange speaking engagements for the visiting scientist. After your successful press

conference, which gained wide media coverage, you learn that the scientist is actually an employee of the pharmaceutical company's research subsidiary. What actions should you take?

Answer: You must sever relations with this client as soon as possible (Article 17) and cancel all speaking engagements you arranged for the scientist (Article 5). To continue the relationship and program would violate Articles 1, 2, 3, 4, 6, and 8: act in the public interest, exemplify high standards of honesty and integrity, deal fairly with the public, adhere to the highest standards of accuracy and truth, shall not corrupt the integrity of communication channels, and shall not use an individual purported to be independent to serve an undisclosed interest.

Situation 5: Your employer asks you to give a series of talks in communities served by your company. You are to discuss the new plant being built and its operations. You visit the plant before giving the speech prepared by your immediate supervisor. During the tour you learn that several claims in the speech are not true. Can you give the speech as originally written?

Answer: Knowingly presenting false or misleading information to the public is a clear violation of Articles 1, 2, and 5. If your employer insists that you give the speech as written, then your only choice is to resign (Article 17).

Situation 6: A client asks you to help arrange a public offering of stock. You decline because you have no experience in corporate finance or financial relations. Instead, you refer the client to your friend, a fellow PRSA member, who specializes in financial relations. The practitioner sends you a check for $500 in appreciation of the referral. Can you accept the money?

Answer: You may keep the payment from your appreciative friend only if your client knows about the payment and approves (Articles 11 and 12).

Adapted from article written by the late Donald B. McCammond, APR, while he served as chairman of PRSA's Board of Ethics and Professional Standards. "Ethics: The Right Choice," *Public Relations Journal* 43, no. 2 (February 1987): 8–10. Used with permission of *Public Relations Journal.*

ADDITIONAL READINGS

Baker, Lee. *The Credibility Factor: Putting Ethics to Work in Public Relations.* Homewood, Ill.: Business One Irwin, 1993.

Black, Jay, ed. *Journal of Mass Media Ethics* 4, no. 1 (1989). This issue is devoted to articles on ethics in public relations.

Cutlip, Scott M. "The Tobacco Wars: A Matter of Public Relations Ethics." *Journal of Corporate Public Relations* 3 (1992–1993): 26–31.

Donaldson, Thomas. *Ethics in the Global Market.* London: Oxford Press, 1989. Author outlines rights both multinational and domestic corporations are bound to respect as part of their moral mission.

VanLeuven, Jim, ed. "Special Issue: Education in Public Relations." *Public Relations Review* 15, no. 1 (Spring 1989).

Wakefield, Gay. "Caution: Public Relations Education Ahead." *Central States Speech Journal* 39, no. 2 (Summer 1988): 88–89. Argues that speech communication departments are the "natural home" of public relations education.

White, H. Allen, Carol E. Oukrop, and Richard Alan Nelson. "Literature of Public Relations: Curriculum for a Unique Career." *Journalism Educator* 46, no. 4 (Winter 1992): 38–43. Provides evidence that specialized public relations education has "a measurable effect" on future public relations practitioners, giving them unique skills and perspectives.

Wright, Donald K., ed. "Special Issue: Ethics in Public Relations." *Public Relations Review* 15, no. 2 (Summer 1989).

NOTES

1. John Kultgen, *Ethics and Professionalism* (Philadelphia: University of Pennsylvania Press, 1988), 371.
2. R. M. Veatch, "The Danger of Virtue," *Journal of Medicine and Philosophy* vol. 13 (1988): 445–46.
3. Baruch Brody, *Ethics and Its Applications* (New York: Harcourt Brace Jovanovich, 1983).
4. Robert Sokolowski, "The Fiduciary Relationship and the Nature of Professions," in *Ethics, Trust, and the Professions: Philosophical and Cultural Aspects*, edited by Edmund D. Pellegrino, Robert M. Veatch and John P. Langan (Washington, D.C.: Georgetown University Press, 1991), 23–43.
5. For more detailed discussion of the bases for professional privilege, see Eliot Freidson, "Nourishing Professionalism," in Pellegrino, Veatch and Langan, eds., *Ethics, Trust, and the Professions, 193–220.*
6. Ibid., 196.
7. Kultgen, *Ethics and Professionalism,* 248.
8. Ibid., 183–84.
9. Robert Heilbroner, "Public Relations: The Invisible Sell," in Reo M. Christenson and Robert O. McWilliams, *Voice of the People*, 2d ed. (New York: McGraw-Hill, 1967), 485.
10. Daniel Boorstin, *The Image* (New York: Atheneum, 1962), 17.
11. Willard J. Hurst, "The Professions of American Life," *Public Relations Journal* 13, no. 8 (August 1957).
12. David Ferguson, "A Practitioner Looks at Public Relations Education," 1987 Vern C. Schranz Distinguished Lecture in Public Relations (Ball State University, Muncie, Indiana).
13. Freidson, "Nourishing Professionalism," 195–97.
14. Scott M. Cutlip, "History of Public Relations Education in the United States," *Journalism Quarterly* 38 (Summer 1961).
15. Alfred McClung Lee, "Trends in Public Relations Training," *Public Opinion Quarterly* 11 (Spring 1947).
16. Hale Nelson, "Training for Public Relations," *Public Relations Journal* 12, no. 9 (September 1956).
17. Ray Eldon Hiebert, *Trends in Public Relations Education, 1964–1970* (New York: Foundation for Public Relations Research and Education, 1970). Also, see "PR in Classroom," *Public Relations Journal* 26 (September 1970).

[18]Kenneth O. Smith,   "Report of the 1981 Commission on Public Relations Education," *Public Relations Review* 8 (Summer, 1982): 66–68.

[19]William P. Ehling and Betsy Plank,   *Design for Undergraduate Public Relations Education* (Chicago: Commission on Undergraduate Public Relations Education, 1987).

[20]Public Relations Society of America,   *Where to Study Public Relations* (New York: Public Relations Society of America, 1991).

[21]Ibid., 23–27.

[22]Smith,   "Report of the 1981 Commission," 68.

[23]See James K. VanLeuven,   "Public Relations Body of Knowledge: A Task Force Report," *Public Relations Review* 13, no. 4 (Winter 1987): 11–18, for description of the project. See "Public Relations Body of Knowledge Task Force Report," *Public Relations Review* 14, no. 1 (Spring 1988): 3–40, for first listing of selected sources.

[24]Glen M. Broom, Mark S. Cox, Elizabeth A. Krueger, and Carol M. Liebler, "The Gap Between Professional and Research Agendas in Public Relations Journals," *Public Relations Research Annual* 1 (1989): 141–54.

[25]Other members of the team included Professor David M. Dozier, San Diego State University; Professor William P. Ehling, Syracuse University; Professor Larissa A. Grunig, University of Maryland; and public relations consultants Fred C. Repper, Ingram, Texas, and Jon White, Bedford, U.K. The project report is *Excellence in Public Relations and Communication Management: Contributions to Effective Organizations*, edited by James E. Grunig (Hillsdale, N.J.: Lawrence Erlbaum Associates, Publishers, 1992).

[26]Scott M. Cutlip,   *A Public Relations Bibliography* (Madison: University of Wisconsin Press, 1957 and 1965); Robert L. Bishop,   *Public Relations: A Comprehensive Bibliography* (Ann Arbor: University of Michigan Press, 1974); and Bishop's two updates published in *Public Relations Review* 1, no. 4 (Winter Supplement 1975–1976) and 3, no. 2 (Summer 1977). Albert Walker compiled the annual bibliographies for *Public Relations Review* from 1976 until 1986.

[27]PRSA Task Force,   "Public Relations Body of Knowledge," *Public Relations Review* 14, no. 1 (Spring 1988): 3–39.

[28]Edward L. Bernays,   "Should Public Relations Counsel Be Licensed?" *Printers Ink*, December 25, 1953.

[29]Edward L. Bernays,   "The Case for Licensing PR Practitioners," *Public Relations Quarterly* 28 (Spring 1983): 32.

[30]Raymond P. Ewing,   "Master Plan," *Public Relations Journal* 43, no. 7 (July 1987), review of Edward L. Bernays's book, *The Later Years: Public Relations Insights 1956–1986* (Rhinebeck, N.Y.: H and M Publishers, 1986). See Paul S. Forbes's letter to the editor response, "Pro test," in *Public Relations Journal* 43, no. 9 (September 1987): 6–7.

[31]John M. Reed, ed.,   *Reed's Worldwide Directory of Public Relations Organizations*, 2d ed. (Washington, D.C.: Pigafetta Press, 1991).

[32]*SEC* v. *Anthony M. Franco*, United State District Court, District of Columbia, Civil Action 86 Civ. 2382, Litigation Release No. 11206 (August 26, 1986).

[33]Final Judgment of Permanent Injunction as to Anthony M. Franco, *SEC* v. *Anthony M. Franco*, USDC, District of Columbia, Civil Action 86 Civ. 2382.

[34]Joanne Lipman,   "PR Society Receives Some Very Bad PR—From Its Ex-Chief," *Wall Street Journal*, September 26, 1986, pp. 1 and 16.

[35]From remarks by John W. Felton before PRSA Assembly, November 8, 1986, Washington, D.C. Copy mailed to all PRSA members December 11, 1986.

[36]Frank Wylie,   "Professional Ethics and Other Misconceptions." Address before the Publicity Club of Chicago, April 20, 1977.

[37]Leonard Knott,   *Plain Talk about Public Relations* (Toronto: McClelland and Stewart, 1961), 3. Written by one who pioneered and shaped the practice in Canada.

[38]Donald K. Wright,   "Ethics Research in Public Relations: An Overview," *Public Relations Review* 15, no. 2 (Summer 1989): 4.

[39]Sokolowski,   "The Fiduciary Relationship," 31.

[40]Hans-Martin Sass,   "Professional Organizations and Professional Ethics: A European View," *Ethics, Trust, and the Professions*, edited by Pellegrino, Veatch and Langan, 270–71.

[41]Quote from J. Handly Wright's 1979 Gold Anvil Award acceptance speech, Public Relations Society of America National Conference, 1979. Wright is retired vice president of the Association of American Railroads.

CHAPTER 6

Legal Considerations

It is the purpose of the First Amendment to preserve an uninhibited marketplace of ideas in which truth will ultimately prevail.

JUSTICE BYRON WHITE

To a great extent, the legal context defines, limits, and regulates modern public relations practice. An authority on public relations law says that "every area of public relations practice involves legal rights and restriction."[1] Yet, because the term *public relations* is not listed in commonly used legal dictionaries and encyclopedias, it has no "legal meaning," unlike "commercial speech," "advertising," and "advertisement."[2]

A communication law expert estimates that 35 percent of all statutes make reference to communication. Another media law textbook author pointed out that the U.S. Supreme Court handed down more than 20 media-related decisions in the 3 years leading up to the 1992 edition of his book.[3] As a result of the increasingly complex legal climate, most large communication businesses—public relations firms, advertising agencies, and news media—have specialized lawyers on staff or law firms on retainer.

Presidents Reagan, Bush, and Clinton ran for office on the promise of reducing government regulation, but the task was complicated by entrenched bureaucracies, special interests, and an entrenched and powerful legal establishment, as well as legitimate public calls for government protection. Despite political rhetoric to the contrary, many—if not most—regulatory agencies are necessary to protect the public.

This chapter outlines major areas of law relevant to public relations, but space does not permit exhaustive discussion of legal requirements imposed on practitioners. Practitioners should consult their attorneys or corporate counsel on specific questions about legal matters. This chapter will first outline the increasing impact of First Amendment decisions on public relations law and then discuss several areas of regulation.

PUBLIC RELATIONS AND THE FIRST AMENDMENT

Self-government is based on the philosophy of open, robust debate in a free marketplace of ideas. As Supreme Court Justice William O. Douglas wrote,

> When ideas compete in the market for acceptance, full and free discussion exposes the false and they gain few adherents. Full and free discussion keeps a society from becoming stagnant and unprepared for the stresses and strains that work to tear all civilization apart.[4]

Freedom of expression is protected from government control in the United States by the First Amendment to the Constitution. The First Amendment says that Congress shall make no law "abridging the freedom of speech, or of the press; or the right of the people peaceably to assemble, and to petition the Government for a redress of grievances."

Although adopted in 1791, the First Amendment was not interpreted by the Supreme Court until the twentieth century. In decisions since the early 1900s, the Supreme Court has ruled that the First Amendment restrictions on government interference with freedom of expression apply both to the federal government and to state governments.[5] The Court has also ruled that the First Amendment applies to most media, including newspapers, books, magazines, broadcasting, and film.[6] Thus publishers and broadcasters have a constitutionally protected right of expression just as individuals do. The Supreme Court has also ruled that charitable appeals for funds, on the street or door to door, are protected under the First Amendment because they involve the "communication of information, the dissemination and propagation of views and ideas, and the advocacy of causes."[7]

Not all content comes under First Amendment protection, however. "Fighting words" that provoke another to violence and certain symbolic actions that interfere with government, such as burning a draft card, have been ruled to be outside First Amendment protections.[8] Until recently, commercial advertising and most corporate expression was not protected by the First Amendment from government regulation or suppression. And no Supreme Court First Amendment decision ever specifically referred to "public relations."[9]

Expression that does come under the First Amendment is not protected absolutely. Persons or corporations whose expressions defame, invade the privacy, or disturb the peace of others may have to pay damages. Generally, a person will be held accountable for speech that damages another only after he or she expresses it, but in rare circumstances the government can block the dissemination of expression by issuing a prior restraint. However, prior restraints on expression are presumptively unconstitutional.[10]

The U.S. Supreme Court ruled in 1992 that so-called "hate speech" cannot be banned simply because of its content. In the case before the Court, the city of St. Paul, Minnesota, had prosecuted a youth under a law intended to punish those who burn crosses, display swastikas, or otherwise express racial or religious bigotry and hate. Justice Antonin Scalia wrote that governments may not punish those who "communicate messages of racial, gender or religious intolerance" simply because those targeted may be offended or emotionally distraught. The Court was unanimous in overturning the St. Paul "hate speech" law, thus broadening First Amendment protection and limiting use of the "fighting words doctrine" to suppress potentially offensive expressions of bigotry.[11]

Furthermore, governments cannot pass overly broad laws that infringe upon First Amendment rights by allowing law enforcement officers too much power to limit demonstrations or the circulation of fliers at reasonable hours and places.[12] The Court has ruled that it is a violation of the First Amendment for a city to prohibit charitable groups from soliciting contributions if more than 25 percent of the funds raised are used for administrative expenses and overhead.[13]

The Supreme Court has been most concerned about protecting political expression. For example, in *New York Times* v. *Sullivan* the Court said that the United States has

> a profound national commitment to the principle that debate on
> public issues should be uninhibited, robust, and wide-open, and that
> it may well include vehement, caustic, and sometimes unpleasantly
> sharp attacks on government and public officials.[14]

The Court's decisions foster a "marketplace of ideas" free of most government regulation. By contrast, the Constitution permits considerable regulation of the communication about commercial marketplace of goods and services. A conflict for communicators arises when businesses and organizations are not allowed to communicate public messages that would be protected by the First Amendment if originated by a newspaper or private individual. In recent years, however, the Court has extended limited First Amendment protections to commercial advertising and corporate speech.

Commercial Speech

In 1942 the Supreme Court summarily ruled that the First Amendment does not protect "purely commercial advertising."[15] The Court reconsidered its almost casual dismissal of commercial advertising in 1976. In *Virginia State Board of Pharmacy* v. *Virginia Citizens Consumer Council*, the Supreme Court ruled that the First Amendment bars a state from prohibiting pharmacists from advertising the prices of prescription drugs. In his opinion for the court, Justice Harry Blackmun came close to equating the traditionally protected marketplace of ideas with the more regulated commercial marketplace:

> Advertising, however tasteless and excessive it sometimes may seem, is nonetheless dissemination of information as to who is producing and selling what product, for what reason and at what price. So long as we preserve a predominantly free enterprise economy the allocation of our resources in large measure will be made through numerous private economic decisions. It is a matter of public interest that those decisions, in the aggregate, be intelligent and well informed. To this end the free flow of commercial information is indispensable.[16]

Since *Virginia Pharmacy*, the Court has struck down other statutes prohibiting commercial expression. Because of Supreme Court decisions, states may not bar attorneys from advertising the prices of "routine" legal services, home owners from advertising their houses by placing "for sale" signs in their yards, and drugstores from advertising contraceptives.[17]

When deciding commercial speech cases, the Court employs a four-part test. Initially the Court looks to see if the expression is protected by the First Amendment. To be protected, the expression must concern a lawful activity and not mislead. The Court also asks if the asserted governmental interest is substantial enough to justify regulation. If the expression is protected and the government interest is substantial, the Court then asks whether the regulation directly advances the governmental interest and whether the regulation is more extensive than necessary to serve that interest.[18]

The Court has not accorded the same degree of protection to commercial advertising that it insists upon for other protected content. Because of "common sense" differences between commercial speech and political expression, the Court says that advertising can be more heavily regulated by government and trade and professional associations. For example, in 1986 the Court ruled in *Posadas de Puerto Rico Associates* v. *Tourism Company of Puerto Rico* that it was constitutionally permissible for the government to forbid gambling casino advertising directed to local residents while promoting casino gambling directed to nonresidents. Although the 5–4 decision seemingly violates the four-part test from *Central Hudson*, the Court justified its position, saying, "In our view, the greater power to completely ban casino gambling necessarily includes the lesser power to ban advertising of casino gambling."[19]

The Court also abandons the presumption against the constitutionality of prior restraints when applying the First Amendment to commercial advertising. In addition, the tolerance normally shown for caustic, misleading, and even false charges in the political arena does not extend to commercial advertising. Regulatory bodies, the Court has said, are still free to require the inclusion of "additional information, warnings and disclaimers, as are necessary" to ensure that advertisements are not deceptive, such as in cigarette advertising.[20]

An advertising law scholar points out that deception in advertising is something of a paradox. On one hand, the law allows "puffery" because it does not work, meaning that reasonable people are not misled by such "legalized lying." On the other hand, why would advertisers use puffery if they truly think it does not work? However, concern about repressing advertising content that may be useful to some consumers and a cautious attitude about possible violation of First Amendment guarantees of free speech limit prosecution of what many might consider deceptive advertising.[21]

Thus, either by design or through neglect, a company's First Amendment protection for advertising its products and services, although extended, hardly represents a sturdy bulwark against government controls. Beginning in 1990, for example, the Federal Trade Commission (FTC) reversed its 1980s "hands-off" posture regarding questionable advertising practices. Under the direction of its new chairwoman, Janet Steiger, in 1992 the FTC was conducting as many as 20 investigations of environmental claims made by advertisers. In addition, other federal agencies with regulatory power over advertising include the Federal Communication Commission, Securities and Exchange Commission, U.S. Postal Service, and Bureau of Alcohol, Tobacco and Firearms. Although none of them has as much control over advertising as does the FTC, they generally monitor advertising content to protect the public against misleading, fraudulent, and even "obscene and indecent" ads.[22]

Corporate Political Expression

Corporate political expression is also more restricted than political expression by individuals and the media. Traditionally, newspapers and other news media have been the only corporations with the same "right" of free expression as an individual. Although all corporations enjoy the rights of due process like any private individual, courts and legislatures have prohibited unregulated corporate and union participation in the political arena. This is apparently out of fear that large organizations would use their immense resources to dominate what is supposed to be a free market of ideas. There has also been concern that stockholders, union members, and utility rate payers are unfairly coerced if their investments, dues, and utility bills are used to support political causes in which they may not believe. As a result of these concerns, the Labor Management Relations Act of 1947 (known as the Taft-Hartley Act and passed over President Harry S Truman's veto), prohibited corporations and unions from making either contributions to, or expenditures on behalf of, political candidates for federal office.[23]

Elections

The prohibition on corporate and union contributions and expenditures was incorporated into the Federal Election Campaign Act of 1971 and its amendments.[24] The Federal Election Campaign Act also placed limits on the amount that individuals could contribute to candidates and spend independently on behalf of a candidate. An *expenditure* is independent if it is not made in cooperation or consultation with the candidate. An expenditure made as part of and in coordination with a candidate's campaign is a *contribution*.

In 1976 the Supreme Court struck down the spending limits on individuals in *Buckley* v. *Valeo*. The Court ruled that individual expenditure limits violate the First Amendment because they put a substantial restraint "on the quantity and diversity of political speech."[25] But the Court did uphold the constitutionality of limits on contributions individuals could make to a candidate. Under the act, individuals cannot contribute more than $1000 to any one candidate and a total of $25,000 in any one year to all candidates.

Unlike limits on expenditures, the Court said, limits on contributions impose only a "marginal restriction upon the contributor's ability to engage in free communication."[26] Contributions are only a symbolic expression of support, the Court said, whereas expenditures by individuals are direct expression that cannot be limited without violation of the First Amendment. The Court also upheld the provisions of the Federal Election Campaign Act requiring political committees and candidates to report their contributions and expenditures to the Federal Election Commission, the regulatory body created by the act. These reports of who contributes, spends, and receives money are open to the public so that voters can learn which interests support which candidates.

The Supreme Court did not rule in *Buckley* on the constitutionality of prohibiting corporate contributions and expenditures in elections. It did note, however, that large contributions undermine "the integrity of our system of representative democracy" to the extent that they are given "to secure political *quid pro quo* from current and potential office holders."[27] The Court added that avoiding the "appearance of corruption" is of almost equal concern. Interpreting the statutory prohibitions on corporate contributions and expenditures, the Federal Election Commission has ruled that it is illegal for a corporation to grant a loan to a candidate without charging a normal rate of interest and requiring repayment at a normal due date. It is also illegal to allow the use of corporate facilities to produce election materials without reimbursement at usual commercial rates. Leave time used to aid a candidate, however, is not a contribution, even if paid, as long as the company granting leave does not direct an employee to aid a candidate.[28]

Whereas corporations and unions may not make contributions or expenditures in an election, they are permitted a narrow range of partisan and nonpartisan communications. Partisan messages by corporations can include extremely opinionated, even vitriolic, communication about candidates or elections. Delivery of such messages, however, must be restricted to a corporation's executive and administrative personnel, its shareholders, and their families. Unions may also distribute partisan communications to members and their families. Permitted, but closely regulated, nonpartisan activities include urging employees through posters and newsletters to register and vote, distributing registration materials, and buying newspaper ads urging citizens to vote.[29]

Corporations and unions can also help their employees and members make contributions and expenditures by setting up and administering separate segregated funds, or *political action committees*. A PAC, as these committees are called, can contribute up to $5000 to as many candidates as its members wish.

Political action committees play a powerful role in American elections, raising concern that their influence leads to "the best Congress money can buy." Whatever the danger or value of PACs, corporations and unions themselves are allowed very little communication in elections, but they are allowed more in referenda and other political issue campaigns where the chance of corruption is thought to be less.

Referenda and Political Issues

Massachusetts once had a statute prohibiting corporations from trying to influence a ballot question that did not relate directly to their businesses. In 1978 the Supreme Court struck down that law in *First National Bank of Boston* v. *Bellotti*. First National Bank and four other companies wanted to buy advertising to oppose a referendum on establishing a state personal income tax. Bellotti, the attorney general of Massachusetts, threatened action against the companies if they bought advertising opposing the proposal.

In striking down the statute, the Supreme Court appeared to establish a First Amendment right for corporations. Justice Lewis Powell, writing for the Court, said that the inherent worth of speech that informs the public "does not depend upon the identity of its source, whether corporation, association, union, or individual."[30] Justice Powell dismissed the argument that corporations are too powerful to be allowed participation in the marketplace of ideas. There is no evidence, he said, "that the relative voice of corporations has been overwhelming or even significant in influencing referenda in Massachusetts, or that there has been any threat to the confidence of the citizenry in government."[31] The Court also rejected the attorney general's argument that corporate advertising in a referendum amounted to a forced contribution by shareholders to support causes in which they did not necessarily believe.

But the Court stopped short of creating a First Amendment right of expression for corporations similar to that of individuals or media companies. As in the Court's earlier commercial advertising cases, Justice Powell placed the First Amendment protection on the content of the speech rather than on the speaker. Powell said that the proper question is not whether corporations have First Amendment rights, but whether the Massachusetts statute abridges free expression.[32] The Court struck down the statute because it prohibited political expression that "was at the heart of the First Amendment's protection." An advertisement expressing a view on a tax referendum "is the type of speech indispensable to decisionmaking in a democracy, and this is no less true because the speech comes from a corporation rather than an individual."[33]

The *Bellotti* decision opens the door for corporations to participate in government affairs. There are many referenda on taxes, rent control, beverage container deposits, and other issues on which corporations and public interest groups wish to state their views. But companies can also comment on political issues other than referenda. In 1980 the Supreme Court struck down a New York Public Service Commission ruling that barred utilities from including messages about public issues along with a customer's monthly bill. The Consolidated Edison Company had included a bill insert advocating the development of nuclear power. The Court said that the public service commission's prohibition "strikes at the heart of the freedom to speak."[34] In a companion case the Court held that an electric utility could not be barred from promoting the use of electricity.[35]

The Court has also ruled that contributions cannot be limited where they will be used to support ballot issues. In *Citizens Against Rent Control* v. *City of Berkeley*, the Court struck down an ordinance limiting to $250 contributions to an organization opposing a rent-control referendum proposal. In its decision the Court blurred the constitutional distinction between contributions and expenditures established in *Buckley* v. *Valeo*. In *Buckley*, the Court said that limits on contributions in an election are only a "marginal restriction" on expression because contributions are symbolic speech. But in *Citizens Against Rent Control*, the Court said limits on contributions in a referendum are "beyond question a very significant form of political expression."[36]

As a consequence, for example, large corporations such as the Walt Disney Company, Exxon Corporation, Mobil Oil Corporation, Philip Morris, ABC, CBS, and NBC were among the many large corporations contributing to a campaign to defeat California's Proposition 167 in 1992. The "tax the rich" measure would increase taxes on the wealthiest individuals and corporations while reducing sales taxes and giving renters tax credits. Less than 3 weeks before election day, Disney reportedly contributed $250,000 to the campaign to defeat 167, and Philip Morris gave $200,000. The courts have not explained why such contributions are protected expression in a referendum but not in an election.

If logic prevailed, the *Buckley* and *Bellotti* decisions would allow corporations to advertise their views in candidate elections. If independent election expenditures by individuals are pure speech, as the Court ruled in *Buckley*, so too, it could be argued, are independent expenditures by corporations. If the source of speech does not determine whether it is protected, as the Court ruled in *Bellotti*, then, arguably, corporate election advertisements could enjoy as much protection as corporate advertisements in referenda and political issues. At least one state court has been convinced by this logic.[37] Before other courts follow, however, they will have to be persuaded that the potential for corporate and union corruption of democratic processes is not greater in elections than in political issues where there are no candidates. In the meantime, companies may spend and contribute freely to advertise their positions on referenda and political issues, subject to media acceptance of their ads.

LOBBYING: THE RIGHT TO PETITION

Many practitioners represent clients or employers as lobbyists before federal and state legislatures. In fact, lobbying has been one of the fastest growing specialties in public relations practice. Lobbyists attempt to influence legislation and regulations, primarily by providing information. If they represent foreign governments or businesses, they may also be "foreign agents."

Lobbying

Lobbyists are required to disclose their activities under Title III, the Federal Regulation of Lobbying Act of 1946.[38] The law requires any person whose principal purpose is to influence legislation to register with Congress and file quarterly financial statements detailing lobbying expenses and sources of income. The Supreme Court narrowed the law, in decisions in 1953 and 1954, so that it applies only to people and organizations whose main purpose is to influence legislation through "direct communication with members of Congress on pending or proposed federal legislation."[39]

Lobbying is "representations made directly to Congress, its members, or its committees."[40] This includes direct pressure on members of Congress through an "artificially stimulated letter writing campaign."[41] But lobbying does not include general public relations campaigns that attempt to "saturate thinking of the community" about public issues.[42] Nor does it include testimony before a committee of Congress, or magazines and newspapers that, in the ordinary course of business, publish news items and editorials urging the passage or defeat of legislation.[43] Lobbying does not include contacts with a member of the executive branch who then contacts a member of Congress.

Registered lobbyists are supposed to report all contributions of $500 or more, along with the identity of the contributor; and all expenditures of $10 or more, the identity of the recipient, and the purpose of the expenditure. Lobbyists are also supposed to tell what legislation they have tried to influence and what articles they have caused to be published to further their goals.[44] The narrowing of the law by the Supreme Court, however, excludes many powerful lobbyists, such as unions, from the reporting requirements either because their "principal purpose" is not lobbying or because the lobbyists do not make "direct communications" with a member of Congress. Instead, they communicate with legislative staff members or officials in the executive branch.

Grass-Roots Lobbying

Successful lobbyists typically use "grass-roots lobbying" and other campaign techniques, such as issue or advocacy advertising, to mobilize public support outside the nation's capital and state capitals. The goals, of course, are to sway public opinion and activate constituents, and thereby increase pressure on legislators and government agencies. In effect, grass-roots lobbying combines the strengths of direct lobbying with the power of political movements.

For example, the American Nurses' Association, state nursing associations, and specialty nursing organizations mounted a successful campaign to lift some restrictions on direct reimbursement for nursing services. New federal rules in 1992 allow nurse practitioners and clinical nurse specialists to bill Medicare for some services directly, rather than having to bill through a physician. These advanced-practice nurses now can apply for Medicare provider identification numbers and bill for services they provide to patients in nursing facilities and to patients living in designated rural areas. Getting the change required coordinated lobbying and grass-roots lobbying to increase legislators' knowledge of what these specialized nurses do, to overcome bureaucratic inertia, and to counter other interest groups' reluctance to accept the new policy.

Grass-roots lobbying is part of an organization's First Amendment right to express itself on public issues. But if a powerful corporation uses a public relations campaign to do damage to another, it may run afoul of antitrust laws. In *Eastern Railroad Presidents Conference* v. *Noerr*, the U.S. Supreme Court ruled that antitrust laws, which prohibit anticompetitive restraints of trade, do not bar corporations from joining with public relations counsel in a "no-holds-barred" public relations campaign to affect legislation. In *Noerr*, the Court said that railroads could try through public opinion to kill legislation favored by truckers. However, the Court said there may be situations where a publicity campaign, "ostensibly directed toward influencing governmental action, is a mere sham to cover . . . an attempt to interfere directly with the business relationships of a competitor."[45] In such a case, the antitrust laws might apply.

Federal tax law treats lobbying as expression, not as a business expense. In other words, the U.S. Internal Revenue Service does not consider public lobbying a normal business expense for which a company can claim a tax deduction, as it can for product advertising. Even if the lobbying is for or against legislation that directly affects the advertiser's business, no deduction is allowed.

Foreign Agents

Counselors serving foreign governments must register under the Foreign Agents Registration Act of 1938, whether they are lobbyists or not.[46] Congress passed the Foreign Agents Registration Act to limit Nazi and Fascist propaganda in the United States and to identify foreign agents working here. In making the conference report to the House of Representatives, Congressman Emanuel Celler said, "We believe that the spotlight of pitiless publicity will serve as a deterrent to the spread of pernicious propaganda. We feel that our people are entitled to know the sources of any such efforts, and the person or persons or agencies carrying on such work in the United States."[47]

Under the amended Foreign Agents Registration Act, all persons who are working as agents of foreign governments, companies, or political parties must register within 10 days with the U.S. Attorney General. They also must report under oath every 6 months the names of the foreign interests for whom they work, the activities they carry out, and where they get and how they spend their money. The law defines "agent" as anyone in the United States who works as a public relations counsel, publicity agent, information-service employee, or political consultant for a foreign principal. However, diplomatic officers, officials of foreign governments, journalists for American publications, and those engaged in charitable or religious activities are exempted from registration.[48]

In addition, foreign agents must label lobbying materials and "political propaganda" as being distributed by a registered foreign agent. They also must provide copies to the attorney general. Political propaganda includes communication intended to influence public opinion about foreign policy; promote racial, religious, or social tensions; or advocate the forceful overthrow of other Western Hemisphere countries.[49]

COMMUNICATION BETWEEN LABOR AND MANAGEN

Public relations specialists in corporations and unions must be mind that the Taft-Hartley Act not only regulates communications during political elections, but also prohibits management from interfering with labor's right to organize and to bargain collectively once a union is established. The Taft-Hartley Act prohibits both unions and management from engaging in unfair labor practices.

Representation Elections

The National Labor Relations Act of 1935 required strict neutrality in communications to employees that involve organization of employees or collective bargaining. But in 1941 the Supreme Court ruled that an employer could not be barred "from expressing its view on labor policies." The employer, the Court said, is free "to take any side it may choose" on a controversial labor issue as long as the employer does not restrain or coerce the employees.[50] The Court views management's course of conduct, rather than any individual statement, as coercive.

The Supreme Court's holding was codified in the Taft-Hartley Act of 1947. Section 8(c) says that no management view, argument, or opinion will be an unfair labor practice as long as the expression contains "no threat of reprisal or force or promise of benefit."[51] The purpose of section 8(c), according to the legislative conference committee, was "to protect the right of free speech when what the employer says or writes is not of a threatening nature or does not promise a prohibited favorable discrimination."[52]

Management will not engage in an unfair labor practice if it communicates to employees through speeches, talks, and letters to tell workers about the strike history of the union, the likely dues and assessments, and the merits of working for a company without a union. But management cannot threaten to fire or punish employees because of union activities, make promises to influence votes, spy on union meetings, or call employees separately to discuss the union. Management also cannot urge employees individually to vote against the union.

Collective Bargaining

Section 8(d) of the Taft-Hartley Act requires companies and unions "to meet at reasonable times and confer in good faith with respect to wages, hours, and other terms and conditions of employment." This means that both parties are supposed to enter negotiations with open minds and with a willingness to reach an agreement. If management is unwilling to meet or is unreasonably firm in its offers, labor may file an unfair labor practice charge with the National Labor Relations Board (NLRB).

ie U.S. Court of Appeals for the Second Circuit upheld a NLRB
hat General Electric engaged in an unfair labor practice when it
d "take-it-or-leave-it' bargaining methods with a widely publi-
ince of unbending firmness" in its negotiations with the Interna-
nion of Electrical, Radio and Machine Workers Workers (IUE).[53]
ral years, General Electric had followed a firm policy vis-à-vis
is, backing up a hard-line policy with an intensive program of
employee communication. Union critics labeled the program as "Boul-
warism" because it was formulated largely by Lemuel R. Boulware.
Looking at the "totality of conduct," the NLRB hearing examiner said
General Electric flooded employees with:

> a constant stream of communications plugging the merits of its bar-
> gaining position. In some instances it advanced arguments not only
> more full but different from those presented to the union negotiators
> at the bargaining table, a circumstance found herein to constitute
> the clearest evidence of bargaining bad faith.[54]

Furthermore, the company stressed to employees the finality of the company's offer, the futility of further negotiations, the "selfish" and "irresponsible" motives of the union leadership, and the jeopardy of employees' jobs.[55]

Unfair labor practices by unions include mass picketing that physi-
cally prevents nonstriking employees from entering a plant, acts of violence on a picket line, threats to employees that they will lose their jobs
unless they support the union, and refusal to bargain in good faith.

FINANCIAL PUBLIC RELATIONS

Financial public relations, one of the highest-paid specialties in public
relations practice, requires both an understanding of corporate finance
and legal knowledge. Public Relations Society of America defines this
part of public relations as:

> The dissemination of information that affects the understanding of
> stockholders and investors generally concerning the financial position
> and prospects of a company, and includes among its objectives the
> improvement of relations between corporations and their stockholders.[56]

*Under the Securities and Exchange Commission's "integrated disclo-
sure system," corporations in which members of the public own shares
must continuously provide information about the health of the company.*
Investor relations specialists issue press releases, draft speeches, conduct
annual meetings, and write quarterly and annual reports to achieve the
"adequate and accurate information" required under federal law.

Investor relations practice is regulated by several statutes passed after the stock market crash of 1929. For example, the 1933 Securities Act restricts corporate communication before and during the period that new securities offerings are being registered with the Securities and Exchange Commission (SEC).[57] The Securities and Exchange Act of 1934, which regulates trading of securities after their initial distribution, requires periodic reporting about a company.[58] The Investment Company Act of 1940 and the Investment Advisers Act of 1940 regulate investment companies and advisers.[59] In addition, practitioners in financial public relations are subject to the disclosure rules of the stock exchange where their company is listed.

Disclosure

Disclosure takes two forms: that which is mandated by statute and that which is required to avoid fraud. The Securities Act of 1933 and the Securities and Exchange Act of 1934 mandate disclosure. The 1933 act requires filings with the Securities and Exchange Commission when securities are offered to the public.

The Securities Act of 1933 requires that companies provide "material information" about new security offerings so that investors can make purchasing decisions based on facts. Information is considered "material" if

1. The information is likely to have a significant effect on securities prices, or
2. The information (including relevant interpretation in some cases) is likely to be considered important by a reasonable investor in making investment decisions to buy, hold, or sell shares.[60]

The act requires a company to register its stock with the Securities and Exchange Commission and provide detailed information about its financial history and prospects.

Section 5 of the 1933 act prohibits a company from offering to sell or to buy a security before the security is registered with the SEC. During the prefiling period and 20-day waiting period after securities are filed, a company can distribute a "red-herring" prospectus that describes the stock but clearly indicates that it is not an offering for sale. Not until a securities offering is registered can brokers and dealers issue written offers to sell the stock. During the registration period, companies do continue the usual flow of advertising, informational press releases, quarterly and annual reports, and proxy statements. Two cases illustrate this disclosure requirement.

In a case held to violate section 5 of the 1933 act, two New York underwriters issued a press release before a registration statement was filed with the SEC. The press release touted more than 100,000 acres of prime Florida land "in the area of the Gold Coast" of Florida on which industrialist Arthur Vining Davis's Arvida Corporation would under-take a "comprehensive program of orderly . . . development." Within a short time the press release resulted in newspaper stories nationwide and stimulated investments totaling more than $500,000.

The SEC ruled that the references in the press release to the 100,000 acres on the Gold Coast illegally began the selling process before the securities were registered. Arvida's final prospectus, issued after registration, revealed that development might be more difficult than the press release had indicated. It turned out that much of the land was not conveniently located and that some of the money raised through the stock offering might have to be used to retire debt rather than to develop new properties.[61]

The SEC, in July 1984, published a report of an investigation of Howard Bronson and Co., a New York public relations firm, in which the agency and Thomas F. Pate, a vice president in the firm, were rebuked for dissemination of "false and misleading statements of mater-ial facts made in connection with the offer and sale of unregistered secu-rities of a foreign issuer whose common stock was traded over-the-counter." Pate, who supplied a report to some 50 broker-dealers recommending the stock of International Technologies Corporation, also failed to disclose that this was done for a "consideration of $3,000 per month," according to the SEC release dated July 12, 1984. This inves-tigative report was issued under provisions of section 21(a) of the 1934 Securities Exchange Act. The SEC release concluded:

Although the Commission does not consider public relations firms to be guarantors of the information they gather for distribution, such firms should not view themselves as mere publicists or communicators of information with no attendant responsibility whatsoever for the contents of such information. Indeed, these firms must be aware of their obligation not to disseminate information concerning their clients which they know or should have reason to know is materially false or misleading.[62]

Securities Trading

The Securities Exchange Act of 1934 mandates disclosure to ensure that investors have accurate information during the trading of securities. Section 13 of the act requires companies registered with the SEC to file quarterly, annual, and other reports with the SEC. Section 14 regulates the solicitation of proxies.

The annual report has long been regarded the most effective medi-um for disseminating corporate financial information to the investment community. There are two kinds of annual reports: the usually glossy publication sent to shareholders and the four-part report filed on Form 10-K with the SEC. For many years the content of these two reports was often quite different. The SEC demanded extensive disclosure of market information, financial data and 5-year summaries of sales and assets on Form 10-K, while the annual report to shareholders often contained much less. The 10-K was always available to the public, but investors seldom requested it. However, since 1982, annual reports to shareholders must contain most of the financial information and discussion required in Form 10-K.

Notable for the financial public relations practitioner is the required management discussion and analysis (MD&A) in which the SEC asks management to describe in detail company liquidity, capital resources, results of operations, and future prospects. Practitioners often write drafts of the MD&A after canvassing officers and directors for suggestions.

Besides writing annual reports, the public relations professional is likely to have an important role in issuing proxy materials and organizing the company's annual meetings. Proxies are the statements companies must provide under section 14 of the 1934 act to tell shareholders when and where the annual meeting will be held and what business will be conducted. Stockholders who cannot attend the meeting can vote their shares by proxy, giving specific direction in writing about how their votes are to be cast. The practitioner may have a hand in writing management policy proposals, publishing them in the proxy statements, and organizing and conducting the annual meeting at which proposals will be voted upon. In proxy fights, in which a group of shareholders tries to sway votes to oppose management, the public relations practitioner may help choose issues, plan appeals to stockholders, and buy editorial advertising to promote management's positions.

Practitioners also participate in the updating of information—"continuous disclosure"—required by the securities laws and the rules of the stock exchanges. Under section 12 of the 1934 act, companies must file quarterly reports on SEC Form 10-Q within 45 days of the end of the first three quarters and "current reports" on Form 8-K within 15 days of any material change in the company. Changes that must be reported on Form 8-K include shifts in the control of the company, acquisition or disposition of assets, bankruptcy or receivership, changes in the company's certifying accountants and financial statements, and resignations of directors.

In addition, the antifraud provisions of the securities laws—section 10(b) of the 1934 act and rule 10(b-5) in the Code of Federal Regulations—require corporate officers with access to nonpublic information ("insiders") to make "immediate disclosure" of material changes if the insiders plan to trade the company's stock. Furthermore, stock exchange rules also require immediate disclosure of material changes in a company.

Simply issuing a press release may not be sufficient to fulfill the disclosure requirements. The American Stock Exchange disclosure policies, for example, require a company, "at a minimum," to release announcements of material information simultaneously to the national business and financial news wire services, the national news wire services, the *New York Times*, *Wall Street Journal*, *Moody's Investors Service*, and Standard and Poor's Corporation. Appropriate disclosure procedure depends on the size of a company and the dispersion of its stockholders, but the basic principle remains the same: public statements must be truthful.

Fraud

Section 10(b) of the 1934 act and rule 10(b-5) prohibit fraud in securities trading. Rule 10(b-5) makes it unlawful, in connection with the purchase or sale of any security, (a) to employ any device, scheme, or artifice to defraud; (b) to make any untrue statement of a material fact or to omit to state a material fact; and (c) to engage in any act or practice that operates as a fraud or deceit.

For there to be fraud in the buying and selling of securities, it is usually necessary to show that insiders are using nonpublic information to help them trade securities profitably or that insiders are "tipping" friends and clients with information that gives them an unfair advantage over the average investor. "Insiders" barred from tipping or trading on information not available to the public include corporate executives, public relations personnel, and outside accountants, lawyers, public relations counsel, and other professionals with access to corporate plans.

The SEC charged a public relations firm with insider trading for the first time in early 1986. (Recall that the second case of Anthony Franco discussed in Chapter 5 occurred later in 1986.) In the first case, the SEC said that Ronald Hengen of R. F. Henegen Inc., a financial public relations firm, passed insider information about one of the firm's clients to a stockbroker. Based on the advance knowledge that Puritan Fashions Corporation (now part of C. K. Holdings, Inc.) would not achieve its sales and profit projections, the stockbroker advised another stockbroker and clients to sell Puritan stock amounting to some $2 million. The case illustrates that public relations practitioners "must not only know the law, they must take steps to ensure it will be followed."[63]

Because a public relations firm may be held liable, many insert clauses in client contracts to protect themselves should information provided by a client lead to charges of fraud. A typical clause reads as follows:

You agree to indemnify and hold harmless from and against any and all losses, claims, damages, expenses, or liabilities which [name of public relations firm] may incur based upon information, representations, reports, or data furnished by you to the extent such material is furnished or prepared by or approved by you for use by [name of public relations firm].

In the *Texas Gulf Sulphur* case, the Second Circuit Court of Appeals ruled that insiders and the company violated rule 10(b-5) by responding to rumors with a press release that misleadingly downplayed the importance of mineral samples taken at a Canadian mine. After the promising samples were found, but before the press release was issued, corporate insiders bought Texas Gulf Sulphur stock. At least one officer tipped outsiders, who also bought stock.[64]

In *Schlanger* v. *Four-Phase Systems, Inc.*, the courts held that the company had issued a misleading statement denying knowledge of any corporate development that would account for market activity in its stock. At that very time, however, the company was actively engaged in merger discussions.[65] In a similar case, the SEC decided that *Carnation Company* issued "materially misleading" statements when it said that there were no corporate developments that would account for unusual market activity in its stock. Carnation issued the statement while it was engaged in preliminary acquisition talks with Nestlé, S.A., which ultimately led to the Nestlé acquisition of Carnation.[66]

In its report of the Carnation Company ruling, the SEC encouraged public companies to respond promptly to market rumors concerning material corporate developments. Referring to the *Texas Gulf Sulphur* and *Four-Phase Systems* cases, the SEC concluded:

> Whenever an issuer makes a public statement or responds to an inquiry from a stock exchange official concerning rumors, unusual market activity, possible corporate developments or any other matter, the statement must be materially accurate and complete. If the issuer is aware of non-public information concerning acquisition discussions that are occurring at the time the statement is made, the issuer has an obligation to disclose sufficient information concerning the discussions to prevent the statements from being materially misleading.[67]

During the mid- to late 1980s national news headlines featured a litany of SEC prosecutions of securities fraud and insider-trading cases. In May 1986, SEC and federal prosecutors charged Dennis Levine of profiting $12.6 million through insider trading. In November 1986, Ivan F. Boesky agreed to pay a $100-million penalty to settle SEC charges of insider trading. In December 1987, Boesky was sentenced to 3 years in prison. In September 1988, the SEC charged Drexel Burnham Lambert and the now infamous Michael Milken of insider trading, stock manipulation, fraud, and other federal securities laws violations. In December the same year, the Drexel firm pleaded guilty to six felonies, settled the SEC charges, and paid a $600-million fine. The firm filed for bankruptcy-court protection in February 1990. In April that year, Milken pleaded guilty to six felonies and paid a $600 million fine. He began a 10-year prison sentence in November 1990. And these are just the major players in a series of scandals that reached from New York to Beverly Hills, contributing to the collapse of the junk-bond market and, some say, to the stock market crash of 1987.[68] It is little wonder that the SEC remains vigilant in the areas of financial public relations, stock manipulation, and insider trading.

ACCESS TO THE MEDIA

Public relations plays an important role in the marketplace of ideas. Its practitioners are responsible for making certain that the ideas, information, or causes of their employers or clients get a public hearing. The job requires access to the media, but the law allows media to refuse any story or advertisement they do not wish to run.

Print Media

Constitutional protection of freedom of the press has thus far blocked creation of a legal right of access to the print media for any particular cause, idea, or spokesperson. Some First Amendment scholars argue that the right of expression is rather thin if it can be exercised only by the managers of mass communication. It may have been appropriate, so the argument goes, in the eighteenth century to grant publishers absolute control of their publications under the First Amendment. At that time virtually anyone could start a newspaper. Contrast that situation with today, when most major cities are served by only one metropolitan newspaper. In a time of monopoly newspapers, protecting only the right to publish does not guarantee that the marketplace of ideas will be robust.[69]

So far, only one lowly court has recognized a right of access to the print media, and that was a long time ago, in 1919. In *Uhlman* v. *Sherman*, a lower court in Ohio held that public dependence on the community's only newspaper imposed an obligation on the publisher to open his advertising columns to the public on an equal basis.[70] However, courts since then have consistently held that a publisher can refuse any editorial or advertising copy, providing the publisher does not break a contract or violate the antitrust laws.[71] In the *Home Placement Service* v. *Providence Journal* decisions, the courts ruled that the newspapers involved violated antitrust laws by denying a would-be competitor the opportunity to buy advertising space.[72]

The U.S. Supreme Court has firmly refused to recognize a right of access to the print media. In 1974 the Court struck down a Florida statute requiring a newspaper to give a candidate for public office space to reply to criticism in the publication. Pat Tornillo, a teacher who had led a strike in Miami, brought suit against the *Miami Herald* when the paper refused to give him space to reply to an editorial calling him a "czar" and a lawbreaker while he campaigned for the state legislature.

The Supreme Court ruled the Florida access statute an unconstitutional abridgment of freedom of the press. In a unanimous opinion written by Chief Justice Warren Burger, the Court rejected the argument that the public needs a right of access to the print media. "A responsible press," the chief justice wrote, "is an undoubtedly desirable goal, but press responsibility is not mandated by the Constitution, and like many other virtues, cannot be legislated."[73]

Broadcast Media

Until the mid-1980s, there was stronger legal support for access to broadcast media than to print. Broadcasting has been subject to more government regulation since its inception than print has. The government has issued licenses for use of the limited broadcast band since the early 1900s. The Federal Communications Act of 1934, which established the current regulatory framework for broadcasting, requires that stations licensed by the government operate in the "public convenience, interest or necessity." Under this affirmative obligation, broadcast license holders have been required to provide public access to air time on radio and television stations. Broadcasters, unlike publishers, were obliged under the Fairness Doctrine and the Equal Time Rule to treat a wide variety of issues with balance.

Those obligations began to diminish during the "deregulation" era of the 1980s, however. First, the Supreme Court, in 1984, declared unconstitutional the federal law barring the public radio and television stations from broadcasting editorials (*F.C.C.* v. *League of Women Voters*, 468 U.S. 364). That case opened the door to a series of challenges and eventual changes in the FCC requirements.

The *Fairness Doctrine*, first enunciated by the Federal Communications Commission in 1949, was incorporated into section 315 of the Federal Communications Act 10 years later. Section 315 required broadcasters to afford reasonable opportunity for the discussion of conflicting views on issues of public importance. To fulfill their fairness obligations, broadcasters were required to seek out controversial issues and then treat all sides fairly.

In deciding in favor of the League of Women Voters, the Supreme Court overturned for the first time federal content restrictions on broadcasters' First Amendment rights. Although not a direct test of the Fairness Doctrine, Justice William J. Brennan's footnote to the majority ruling questioned the scarcity rationale that had so long justified restrictions on broadcast content:

> The prevailing rationale for broadcast regulation based on spectrum scarcity has come under increasing criticism in recent years. Critics, including the incumbent Chairman of the FCC, charge that the advent of cable and satellite television technology, communities now have access to such a wide variety of stations that the scarcity doctrine is obsolete. We are not prepared, however, to reconsider our long-standing approach without some signal from Congress or the FCC that technological developments have advanced so far that revision of the system of broadcast regulations may be required.[74]

When the FCC abolished the Fairness Doctrine in 1987, FCC Chairman Dennis Patrick concluded "that the Fairness Doctrine chills free speech" and that doing away with it will "extend to the electronic press the same First Amendment guarantees that the print media have enjoyed since our country's inception."[75] When some in Congress pushed to reinstate the Fairness Doctrine in 1989, President Bush announced that he would veto such legislation. When the Supreme Court declined to review a case in 1990, the Fairness Doctrine was put to rest, at least for the time being.

The case began before the FCC had abolished the Fairness Doctrine. The FCC had ruled that a Syracuse, New York, television station had violated the Fairness Doctrine when it refused to provide air time to a group opposed to the construction of a nuclear power plant. The station had carried commercials in favor of the plant. The station appealed the FCC's ruling. The federal court sent the case back to the FCC, ordering it to take into account the First Amendment. The FCC responded by abolishing the Fairness Doctrine. Backed by pro–Fairness Doctrine groups, the opposition group challenged the FCC's right to abolish the Fairness Doctrine. The Court of Appeals ruled that the FCC acted within the law. By simply refusing to review the case, rather than ruling it unconstitutional, however, the Supreme Court left open the possibility that Congress some day could restore the Fairness Doctrine.[76]

Although the controversial Fairness Doctrine is no longer in effect, section 315 of the Communications Act still requires broadcasters to provide equal access to the airways for political candidates during election campaigns. Under the Equal Time Rule, or "equal opportunity provision," if a broadcaster permits any public office candidate to appear on the station, *the broadcaster must give all other bona fide candidates for the same office in the same election equal opportunity to appear*. The requirement for nonfederal elections differs from the requirement for federal elections.

For example, a broadcast station may choose to sell advertising time only to major party candidates running for local office in the primary race, because minor party candidates are not running against the major party candidates. In the general election, however, all candidates for the same office must be given the opportunity to buy equal amounts of advertising time at the same rates. Section 312(a)(7) of the Communications Act requires stations to provide "reasonable access" to all candidates for federal office.[77]

After studying broadcasters' sales practices during election campaigns, the FCC determined that not all candidates were being offered the lowest rates. This practice was in violation of the lowest unit charge provision of section 315(b). The FCC rewrote the rules in 1991 to require all broadcasters to offer all candidates the lowest cost air time sold to any other advertiser in all the classes of available air time. News coverage of candidates and debates among major candidates—considered bona fide news—are exempt from the Equal Time Rule.[78]

The Equal Time Rule also requires broadcasters to carry advertisements from political candidates *without censorship*, even when some might consider the content offensive. In the 1992 campaign, for example, some "pro-life" candidates included pictures of dead fetuses in their campaign ads. Some candidates used "character assassination" tactics, but stations were required to run the ads. The Supreme Court has ruled, however, that since under section 15 they cannot censor or otherwise limit what politicians say in their ads, after carrying the advertisements broadcasters have immunity from libel and slander suits.[79]

The Equal Time Rule applies even when an on-air employee of a station runs for office. In other words, if an on-air reporter or disk jockey runs for public office, the station must give other candidates for the same office equal broadcast time at no charge. For example, when a Sacramento television reporter wanted to run for city council in his community, the station said he would have to take unpaid leave to avoid other candidates getting equal air time. When the reporter appealed, the FCC and courts sided with the station.[80] So even though legislators and broadcasters periodically call for its repeal, as was the case with the Fairness Doctrine, the Equal Time Rule remains in effect with no indication that it will be weakened any time soon.

ACCESS TO GOVERNMENT INFORMATION AND MEETINGS

To encourage open government and an informed electorate, the federal government and all 50 states have open records and meeting laws. The federal Freedom of Information Act, enacted in 1966 and strengthened in 1976 by the Government in the Sunshine Act, has significantly increased public access to government records and proceedings.[81]

The Freedom of Information Act was amended in 1974, requiring agencies to publish lists of records and fee schedules for making requested copies. In 1986 Congress reduced fees agencies were charging news organizations and educational institutions and raised fees charged to commercial businesses. Businesses requesting information now must not only pay the costs of copying documents, but also must cover the time spent searching for and reviewing documents. Instead of citizens and journalists being the major benefactors of the act, lawyers are the most frequent users. Historians and other academicians also are frequent users.[82]

The act gives "any person" access to all records of all federal agencies unless those records are exempt. Agencies do not have to release information that would jeopardize national security, reveal business trade secrets, invade an individual's privacy, or interfere with a law enforcement investigation. Nor are regulatory agencies required to release reports dealing with banking and other financial institutions or oil and gas exploration data and maps. Internal agency memoranda and information specified by federal statutes are also exempted from disclosure. Interpretation of these exemptions continues to be controversial and a way for agencies to withhold information.

The courts have etched away at the power granted to those outside government under the Freedom of Information Act. For example, in 1980 the Supreme Court ruled that reporters could not have former Secretary of State Henry Kissinger's diary of official telephone calls because he took the diary home with him. Unless the government compelled him to return it, the diary was beyond the reach granted under the act.[83] Many of the Central Intelligence Agency's records were excluded in a case decided by the Supreme Court in 1985.[84] In 1989 the Court restricted access to the Federal Bureau of Investigation's records, ruling out public access to criminal histories on the basis that such information "can reasonably be expected to invade that citizen's privacy."[85]

The Government in the Sunshine Act requires about 50 federal agencies' central policy-making and governing boards to announce and open meetings to the public. The limitations on this requirement, however, roughly parallel the exemptions allowed under the Freedom of Information Act. When an agency does hold a closed meeting, it must record the proceedings or document what happened in detailed minutes. After the meeting, the agency must report what happened and the results of any votes taken, including how each of those present voted. The act excludes most informal gatherings and unofficial meetings.[86] And none of the rights granted under the open meetings act applies to private businesses, except under the provisions of the Securities Exchange Act discussed in previous sections.

Even with the sometimes controversial exemptions and limitations, the Freedom of Information Act and Government in the Sunshine Act, and their counterparts at lower levels of government, have opened the files and meetings of government to public scrutiny. Public relations practitioners in government must make sure that officials are aware of their obligations under these two acts and must respond appropriately to press requests for access to information and meetings. In fact, public affairs officers in government work often confront the conflict between government agencies' desire to work in relative secrecy and journalists' demand for full disclosure. Claims of "national security" and "individual privacy" too often have been covers for concealing official abuses of position and other misconduct in government.

LIBEL AND PRIVACY

Practitioners responsible for writing news releases, speeches, corporate reports, newsletters, house organs, and other communications are constantly watchful for pictures and statements that might defame or invade privacy. Libel and privacy are two related areas of civil law that become increasingly important as aggressive lawyers pursue and generous juries encourage by voting large damage awards. Both practitioners and their employers can be held liable for tort violations.

Libel and Slander

Defamation occurs as *libel (published written defamation)* and *slander (distributing spoken defamation)*. It includes statements or communications that diminish the respect, goodwill, confidence, or esteem; or produce other adverse feelings about a person or institution. Related laws are designed to protect the reputations of persons and institutions. Four conditions—sometimes five—must be met before a statement is held legally libelous. The statement must:

1. Hurt someone's reputation; be *defamatory.*
2. *Identify* the victim by name or by some other way obvious to others.
3. Be *communicated*—published or broadcast—to an audience other than the victim.
4. Contain an element of *fault*, proof of a falsehood being disseminated with either malice or negligence.
5. Or, in the absence of the fourth condition, cause provable *damages or injury.*[87]

Newsletters covering public relations periodically report cases of practitioners suing in state courts under libel laws because of statements made after they were fired from public relations firms or other organizations. Similarly, practitioners responding to press inquiries about terminated executives must be aware of their own state's libel laws, as statements may be seen as damaging someone's reputation or future employment opportunities. Common law defenses, however, are well established as the following:

1. *Truth* is the oldest and strongest defense. The burden of proving falsity is on the one bringing suit. The plaintiff must not only prove that the statement is false, but also that it was done with malice or negligence.
2. *Privilege* protects otherwise libelous statements that are fair and accurate accounts of what occurs in government proceedings and documents.
3. *Fair comment* includes opinions about the performance of those in the public limelight: actors, politicians, sports stars, musicians, and other celebrities.[88]

Any individual has the right to sue for libel, as do corporations. In some states, nonprofit organizations and other small groups can sue for libel. Governments cannot sue for libel, but public officials may sue as individuals when they think their reputations have been subjected to defamatory statements that cause injury or actual damages. Suing may not be the wisest course, however.

Corporations and executives considering suits against critics who they feel have defamed them must consider the public relations ramifications of their suits in the court of public opinion, as well as their chances of winning in a court of law. Also, practitioners must remind thin-skinned executives about the constitutional protection for caustic and even false comments in the public arena. Educational institutions, manufacturers, art galleries, advertising agencies, public relations firms, and others who offer their work to the public are subject to "fair comment."

Privacy

Citizens express increasing concern about protecting their private lives as computers make it increasingly easy to identify specific individuals and associate them with records of past and current behavior. For example, if you donate to a favorite cause, your name and other vital information may be sold or traded to organizations pushing similar causes. Soon after your first check is cashed, similar organizations begin soliciting you for donations. Telephone calls during dinner hours and an avalanche of mail solicitations make it clear that the first organization shared information about you with others. Your response may be feeling that your right to privacy has been violated and you "just want to be let alone."

Such concern is reflected in statutes and court cases that place limits on what information can be collected about citizens, how errors can be corrected in their information, and who has access to the information. Several states have passed laws severely limiting the use of electronic surveillance devices, the results of medical and substance-abuse tests, and personal data. Public relations practitioners have increasing responsibilities to safeguard the privacy of employees.

Legal scholar William L. Prosser divided the law of privacy into four different torts, each of which is "an interference with the right of the plaintiff . . . 'to be let alone,'" The four categories include:

1. *Intrusion* upon the plaintiff's seclusion or solitude, or into his or her private affairs;
2. *Public disclosure* of embarrassing private facts about the plaintiff;
3. Publicity that places the plaintiff in a *false light* in the public eye; and
4. *Appropriation,* for the defendant's advantage, of the plaintiff's name or likeness.[89]

Each of the four categories affects public relations. For example, *intrusion* is the tort of invading a person's solitude or seclusion, usually through illegal entry, unlawful search, or electronic eavesdropping. Secretly taping conversations, whether in person or over the phone, may lead to privacy claims.[90]

Public disclosure of private facts is similar to libel in that it violates the personality and may cause mental anguish. But the private facts tort differs from defamation in that the communications in a disclosure case are true, but embarrassing, and reputation is not necessarily damaged. Courts have found the private facts tort when intimate medical information, sex-crime victim identity, or name of juvenile offender is revealed, as well as when photographs show someone in an embarrassing pose. Practitioners working at public institutions, particularly where medical information is stored, should be familiar with statutory limitations on the release of client or patient information. Most such organizations have written guidelines for releasing information. As a general rule, a public relations practitioner should get written permission before releasing personal information. Parents must give permission for the release of private information about minors.

A person is placed in a *false light* when he or she is made to appear other than he or she is. Like libel, this tort involves false statements or portrayals, but unlike libel, a person's reputation need not be harmed. False light results when personal humiliation and mental anguish are demonstrated. For example, the false light tort has been found when captions accompanying photographs mislead or misrepresent. The "general rule," according to one authority, is:

A photograph is reasonably safe if the caption is not misleading. . . .
However, if the caption creates a false impression about the people in the picture, or if it is used for commercial (i.e., non-editorial) purposes, the risk of a lawsuit for invasion of privacy is much greater.[91]

Appropriation occurs when someone uses the name or picture of another for advertising or trade purposes without consent. Appropriation occurs, for example, where an advertiser uses a celebrity's picture without permission. Practitioners should get a signed release from anyone whose name or picture is being used in commercial promotions or other publications. Employees may provide an implied consent when they willingly offer information and photos for in-house news publications. But employees have claimed appropriation where employers used employees' pictures in publications outside the corporate "family."

A legal spin-off of the appropriation tort is violation of a person's right of publicity. This is the right to exploit one's own talents. For example, in 1992 the Supreme Court refused to review a 1989 award of $400,000 to singer Bette Midler. Midler had sued Young and Rubicam for using a singer who intentionally sounded like Midler in advertisements produced for Ford's Mercury Sable.[92] Courts also have held that companies violate a person's right of publicity when they record an entertainer's entire act or sell memorabilia capitalizing on his or her personality without permission. Courts in some states have held that the right of publicity can be passed to one's heirs, making it a inheritable property right rather than a personal right. Such a case in California involved sales of souvenirs using the likeness of Bela Lugosi, star of the original *Dracula* film.[93] In Elvis Presley cases in Tennessee, however, a series of court decisions ended with the court concluding that Presley's right of publicity did not survive his death, and in fact passed to the public domain.[94] Of course, this decision is moot for those who claim to have seen Elvis shopping last week at their local Kmart or Kroger store.

In summary, organizations cannot use a living person's name or likeness for advertising or commercial purposes without consent, and in some states, the same applies to deceased celebrities' names and likenesses. Practitioners must get consent before using someone's name, voice, photograph, or other portrayal. It is an oversimplified statement, but people generally have a legal right to their privacy.

COPYRIGHT AND TRADEMARKS

Public relations communicators frequently use the words and pictures of others in brochures, news releases, pamphlets, reports, and speeches. Sometimes public relations officers use excerpts of others' work; sometimes they hire outside contractors to write copy or take pictures. Publishing and selling the creative work of others and protecting property rights in one's own work is the province of copyright and trademark law.

Copyright

The copyright statute was revised in 1976 to take into account developments in photocopiers, videotapes, motion pictures, broadcasting, cable television, and other technologies since the original act was adopted in 1909. It has been amended many times since. For example, in 1988 Congress enacted the National Film Preservations Act to regulate movie colorization and in 1990 passed the Visual Artists Rights Act to give sculptors, painters, and other visual artists control over whether or not their names can be used on works that have been altered with or without their permission.

Copyright law provides that the copyright owner "shall have exclusive right" to reproduce, distribute, and use original works of expression fixed in a tangible medium. You can copyright written, musical, dramatic, pictorial, graphic, and sculptural works. You cannot copyright ideas, methods of operation, concepts, or utilitarian objects such as lamps or typefaces. For example, you can copyright the photograph of a famous landmark building on your campus, but your copyright does not prevent others from photographing the same building. The copyright protects only your photographic image from being used without your consent.[95]

A public relations practitioner writing stories and taking pictures during the regular course of employment creates "works made for hire" that belong exclusively to the employer. However, contracts must be written to define an employer's rights in works created by employees during off-hours or by outside contractors and freelancers. A freelancer who sells a work without a contract usually gives up only rights to first publication.

Claiming formal copyright requires attaching a copyright notice to the work and registering with the Copyright Office of the Library of Congress in Washington, D.C. Within 3 months of publication, the owner must file a four-page form, include two copies of the material to be copyrighted, and pay a fee based on the number of pages in the document. Registration is not necessary for the copyright to be valid, but is necessary if a copyright owner is to bring suit for infringement.

The copyright notice on the work consists of the following: (1) the word "Copyright," the abbreviation "Copr.," or the copyright symbol ©; (2) the date of publication; and (3) the name of the copyright owner. For example: "Copyright 1994 by [your name here]." Copyright for an individual lasts for the life of the author plus 50 years. For a work made for hire, copyright lasts for 75 years from the date of publication or 100 years from the date of creation, whichever is shorter.

Limited or "fair use" of copyrighted works is not an infringement. Critics, scholars, news reporters, and public relations professionals can quote briefly from copyrighted works while evaluating or commenting upon them. But use of a substantial portion of another's work may be an infringement, particularly if that use lessens the potential market for the copyright owner. For example, copying and distributing chapters of this book violates the publisher's copyright protection of the material. Distributing photocopies of magazine articles to several corporate departments to save subscription costs also infringes upon a publisher's copyright.

Determining whether use of copyrighted material qualifies as fair use under the statute involves the following criteria:

1. The purpose and character of the use, including whether such use is of a commercial nature or is for nonprofit educational purposes.
2. The nature of the copyrighted work.
3. The amount and substantiality of the portion used in relation to the work as a whole.
4. The effect of the use upon the potential market for or value of the copyrighted work.[96]

For example, in 1991 a federal court ruled that the widespread practice of copying and selling packets of course readings does not qualify as fair use. As a result, Kinko's Graphics and other campus copying services must now get permission to copy and agree to pay royalties (if required) on previously published materials such as journal articles and book chapters.[97]

Practitioners and broadcast news monitoring service executives testified in 1992 before a Senate Judiciary Committee subcommittee in favor of a bill that would extend the fair use exception to the broadcast equivalent of print clipping services. Some broadcast monitoring services record news and public affairs programming about or of interest to their client organizations. Broadcasters have charged that these recordings constitute infringement of copyrighted material. Not surprisingly, public relations professionals and monitoring service executives argue that such use falls under the fair use exemption. So far, broadcast monitoring services do not have to pay royalties to broadcast stations.

Trademarks

The Lanham Trademark Act of 1946 and its amendments protect *trademarks*: words, names, and symbols used by companies to identify and distinguish their goods or services from those of another. A trademark can be a product brand name such as Kleenex. A *trade name*, on the other hand, identifies the commercial name of the producer. Kimberly Clark Corporation, a trade name, manufactures Kleenex tissues, a trademark.

Trademark rights are created through adoption and use of the mark on goods in trade. Trademark rights are protected under common law, but registration of a trademark with the U.S. Patent and Trademark Office creates presumptions of ownership that are important should infringement be claimed. Application for trademark registration can be filed before or after the mark is used in commerce, but usually after a commercial research firm has confirmed that no other party has registered the name, phrase, or logo intended as a trademark. Applications include (1) a written application form, (2) a drawing of the trademark, (3) the registration fee ($175), and (4) three examples of how the trademark is being used. The ® symbol or the phrase "Registered in U.S. Patent and Trademark Office" indicates a registered trademark. Often the "TM" subscript is used when the registration is pending. The first registration lasts for 5 years, with 10-year renewals for as long as the mark is used in commerce.

Owners of trademarks frequently run advertisements reminding journalists and public relations practitioners to use trademarks as adjectives, not as nouns or verbs, and to use capital letters when referring to their product. You may use a *Xerox* photocopier, or simply a photocopying machine; you do not "Xerox" a document.

Trademark infringement occurs when someone other than the owner uses the mark or a confusingly similar one on the same or closely related goods. Under the Trademark Law Revision Act of 1988, trademark owners may sue those who falsely malign their products or services in comparative brand advertising. It awards damages three times the actual damages. The revision also allows a company to register and protect a trademark for up to 3 years before they actually begin marketing a product carrying the trademark.[98]

Corporations with valuable trademarks have legal staffs to police their use. Infringement can lead to public relations problems; the Coca-Cola Company made network news when it brought suit against a popular pizza parlor in California for misrepresenting the soft drink. Corporations frequently use advertising in news media journals to remind journalists of the proper use of protected trademarks, reminding them to capitalize "Xerox" and to use trademarks as adjectives followed by the generic product category, such as "Dolby sound system" or "Kodak color film." These policing efforts are designed to avoid losing exclusive use of a trademark by allowing it to fall into common usage as a generic word itself.

Legal issues also guide the business practices of public relations professionals. Contract law in particular calls for frequent specialized legal counsel. For example, since an advertising agency successfully sued when more than half the employees left with most of the agency's business in 1954, employment contracts routinely contain "noncompete" clauses. The threat of malpractice suits has even spawned a modest interest in professional malpractice insurance policies. These examples suggest that to work in public relations, one must know enough about legal matters to be sensitive to potential problems and to recognize when to seek legal counsel.

A single chapter in this introductory book can only open a small array of issues that cut across many areas of practice. It is rare, however, that public relations problems are settled in a court of law. More likely they are resolved in the court of public opinion, the topic of our next chapter.

ADDITIONAL READINGS

Collins, Erik L., and Robert J. Cornet. "Public Relations and Libel Law." *Public Relations Review* 16, no. 4 (Winter 1990): 36–47. Examines how public relations activities have led courts to apply the "public figure" designation to executive seeking redress for defamatory statements.

Kupperman, Theodore R., ed. *Privacy and Publicity* (Westport, Conn. Meckler, 1990). Collection of readings from *Communications and the Law*.

McClure, James A. "Communicating During Union Negotiations." *Public Relations Journal* 47, no. 8 (August 1991): 24–25. Outlines how to coordinate public communication with labor relations and legal staffs during collective bargaining.

Lawrence, John Shelton and Bernard Timberg, eds.   *Fair Use and Free Inquiry: Copyright Law and the New Media*, 2d ed. Norwood, N.J.: Ablex Publishing Corporation, 1989. Nineteen contributing authors cover history and trends in copyright law as well as contemporary problems with "new media," such as off-air taping, and fair use of films, broadcasts, photos, and research.

Smith, Craig R.,   *All Speech Is Created Equal.* Long Beach, Calif.: The Freedom of Expression Foundation, 1990. A conservative perspective on extending First Amendment protection to commercial speech and on resisting attempts to resurrect the FCC's Fairness Doctrine. Author uses summaries of many of the cases cited in this chapter to argue his points.

Sneed Don K., Tim Wulfemeyer, and Harry W. Stonecipher.   "Public Relations News Releases and Libel: Extending First Amendment Protections." *Public Relations Review* 17, no. 2 (Summer 1991): 131–44.

Walton, Wesley S., and Charles P. Brissman.   *Corporate Communications Handbook: A Guide for Managing Unstructured Disclosure in Today's Corporate Environment.* New York: Clark Boardman Co., Ltd., 1989. The authors—both lawyers—present case studies, case law, and SEC guidelines to illustrate legally required disclosure.

NOTES

[1] Frank Walsh,   *Public Relations and the Law*, 2d ed. (Sarasota, Fla.: Institute for Public Relations Research and Education, Inc., 1991), 1.

[2] Catherine A. Pratt,   "First Amendment Protection for Public Relations Expression: The Applicability and Limitations of the Commercial and Corporate Speech Models," *Public Relations Research Annual* 2 (1990): 207.

[3] Wayne Overbeck,   *Major Principles of Media Law* (Fort Worth: Harcourt Brace Jovanovich College Publishers, 1992), preface.

[4] *Dennis* v. *United States*, 341 U.S. 494, 584 (1951).

[5] *Near* v. *Minnesota*, 283 U.S. 697 (1931). This famous case actually only *limited* the *kind* of government interference.

[6] For example, *Red Lion Broadcasting Co.* v. *Federal Communications Commission*, 395 U.S. 367 (1969) (broadcasting): *Burstyn* v. *Wilson*, 343 U.S. 495 (1952) (film).

[7] *Village of Schaumburg* v. *Citizens for a Better Environment*, 444 U.S. 620, 632 (1980). The Independent Sector played a major role in this case.

[8] For example, see *Chaplinsky* v. *New Hampshire*, 315 U.S. 568 (1942) (fighting words); and *Miller* v. *California*, 413 U.S. 15 (1973) (obscenity).

[9] Pratt, "First Amendment Protection for Public Relations Expression," 207.

[10] *New York Times* v. *United States*, 402 U.S. 713 (1971).

[11] *R.A.V.* v. *St. Paul*, 112 S.Ct. (1992). See Overbeck,   *Major Principles of Media Law*, 62–63.

[12] For example, *Skokie* v. *National Socialist Party of America*, 69 Ill.2d 605, 373 N.E.2d 21 (1978).

[13] *Village of Schaumburg* v. *Citizens for a Better Environment*, 444 U.S. 620 (1980). In 1984 the Court also ruled that state-imposed limits on the amount of money charities may spend on fund-raising violate the charities' constitutional right of free speech in *Maryland* v. *Munson*, 467 U.S 947 (1984). The vote was five to four.

[14] *New York Times* v. *Sullivan*, 376 U.S. 255, 270 (1964).

[15] *Valentine* v. *Chrestensen*, 316 U.S. 52, 54 (1942).

[16]*Virginia State Board of Pharmacy* v. *Virginia Citizens Consumer Council*, 425 U.S. 748, 765 (1976).

[17]*Bates* v. *State Bar of Arizona*, 433 U.S. 350 (1977) (legal advertising); *Linmark Associates, Inc.* v. *Township of Willingboro*, 431 U.S. 85 (1977) (signs); and *Carey* v. *Population Services International*, 431 U.S. 678 (1977) (ads for contraceptives).

[18]*Central Hudson Gas and Electric Corp.* v. *Public Service Commission of New York*, 447 U.S. 557, 563–64 (1980).

[19]*Posado de Puerto Rico Associates* v. *Tourism Company of Puerto Rico*, 478 U.S. 328 (1986).

[20]*Virginia State Board of Pharmacy* v. *Virginia Citizens Consumer Council*, 425 U.S. 748, 771–72, n. 24 (1976).

[21]Ivan L. Preston,   *The Great American Blow-Up: Puffery in Advertising and Selling* (Madison: University of Wisconsin Press, 1975).

[22]Overbeck, *Major Principles of Media Law*, 410–19.

[23]29 U.S.C. sec. 141 *et seg.* (1988).

[24]2 U.S.C. sec. 441(b) (1988).

[25]*Buckley* v. *Valeo*, 424 U.S. 1, 19 (1976).

[26]Id. at 20–21.

[27]Id. at 26.

[28]See 2 U.S.C. sec. 441(b) (1988). See also 11 C.F.R. secs. 100.7 and 114.9 (1992).

[29]2 U.S.C. sec. 441(b), 11 C.F.R. sec. 114, and Federal Election Commission Advisory Opinion 1980–20.

[30]*First National Bank of Boston* v. *Bellotti*, 435 U.S. 765, 777 (1978).

[31]Id. at 789–90.

[32]Id. at 776.

[33]Id. at 777.

[34]*Consolidated Edison Co. of New York, Inc.*, v. *Public Service Commission of New York*, 447 U.S. 530, 535 (1980).

[35]*Central Hudson Gas and Electric Corp.* v. *Public Service Commission of New York*, 447 U.S. 557 (1980). In December 1983, the California Public Utilities Commission ordered Pacific Gas and Electric to include a fund-raising appeal from a watchdog group, TURN, in its bills four times a year.

[36]*Citizens Against Rent Control* v. *City of Berkeley*, 102 S.Ct. 434, 438 (1981).

[37]*Kentucky Registry of Election Finance* v. *Louisville Bar Association*, 579 S.W.2d 622 (Ky.Ct.App. 1979).

[38]2 U.S.C. sec. 261 *et seq.* (1988).

[39]*United States* v. *Harris*, 347 U.S. 612, 620 (1954). See also *United States* v. *Rumely*, 345 U.S. 41 (1953).

[40]*Rumely*, 345 U.S. at 47.

[41]*Harris*, 345 U.S. at 620.

[42]*Rumely*, 345 U.S. at 47.

[43]2 U.S.C. sec. 267 (1988).

[44]2 U.S.C. sec. 262–67 (1988).

[45]*Eastern Railroad Presidents Conference* v. *Noerr*, 365 U.S. 127, 144 (1961).

[46]22 U.S.C. sec. 611 *et seq.* (1988).

[47]83 *Cong. Rec.*, 7, 8022 (1938).

[48]22 U.S.C. sec. 611(c)(1)(iii), (1988).

[49]*Id.*, secs. 611 and 614.

[50]*National Labor Relations Board* v. *Virginia Electric and Power Co.*, 314 U.S. 469, 477 (1941).

[51]29 U.S.C. sec. 158(c) (1988).

[52]National Labor Relations Board, 1, *Legislative History of the Labor Management Act*, 549 (1948).

[53]*National Labor Relations Board* v. *General Electric Co.*, 418 F.2d 736, 762 (2d Cir. 1969).

[54]National Labor Relations Board, "General Electric Company and International Union of Electrical, Radio and Machine Workers, AFL-CIO, Case No. 2-CA-7851," April 2, 1963.

[55]*Intermediate Report*, appended to *General Electric Co. and International Union of Electrical, Radio and Machine Workers*, AFL-CIO, 150 N.L.R.B. 192, 277 (1964).

[56]"Code of Professional Standards for the Practice of Public Relations: An Official Interpretation of the Code As It Applies to Financial Public Relations," *Public Relations Journal* (1992–93 Register Issue) 48, no. 6R (June 1992): xix.

[57]15 U.S.C. sec. 77(a) *et seq.* (1988).

[58]15 U.S.C. sec. 78(a) *et seq.* (1988).

[59]15 U.S.C. sec. 80(a-1) *et seq.* (1988) and 15 U.S.C. sec. 80(b-1) *et seq.* (1988).

[60]Walsh, *Public Relations and the Law*, 2d ed., 62–63.

[61]*Securities and Exchange Commission* v. *Arvida Corp.*, 169 F. Supp. 211, 213–14 (S.D.N.Y. 1958).

[62]Securities and Exchange Commission Release of July 12, 1984, "In the Matter of *Howard Bronson & Co. and Thomas F. Pate*," 10. See also Scott M. Cutlip, "Attendant Responsibility: Public Relations and the SEC," *Public Relations Journal* 41, no. 1 (January 1985): 26–31.

[63]Frank Walsh, "Public Relations Firm Charged with Insider Trading," *Public Relations Journal* 42, no. 5 (May 1986): 10.

[64]*Securities and Exchange Commission* v. *Texas Gulf Sulfur Co.*, 401 F.2d 833 860-2 (2d Cir. 1968) (*en banc*) *cert. denied*, 394 U.S. 976 (1969).

[65]*Schlanger* v. *Four-Phase Systems, Inc.*, 582 F. Supp. 128 (S.D.N.Y. 1984).

[66]Securities and Exchange Commission Release No. 22214 of July 8, 1985, "In the Matter of *Carnation Company.*"

[67]*Ibid.*, 7.

[68]James B. Stewart, "Scenes From a Scandal: The Secret World of Michael Milken and Ivan Boesky," *Wall Street Journal* (Marketplace Section), October 2, 1991, pp. B1 and B8. The article was adapted from James B. Stewart's book, *Den of Thieves* (New York: Simon & Schuster, 1991).

[69]Jerome Barron, *Freedom of the Press for Whom?* (Bloomington: Indiana University Press, 1973). See also Benno C. Schmidt, Jr., *Freedom of the Press vs. Public Access* (New York: Praeger, 1976).

[70]*Uhlman* v. *Sherman*, 22 Ohio N.P.N.S. 225, 31 Ohio Dec. 54 (1919).

[71]*Shuck* v. *Carroll Daily Herald*, 215 Iowa 1276, 247 N.W. (1933); *Chicago Joint Board, Amalgamated Clothing Workers of America* v. *Chicago Tribune Co.*, 435 F.2d 470 (7th Cir. 1970).

[72]*Home Placement Service* v. *Providence Journal Co.*, 682 F.2d 274 (1st Cir. 1982), *cert. denied*, 103 S.Ct. 1279 (1983).

[73]*Miami Herald Publishing Co.* v. *Tornillo*, 418 U.S. 241, 256 (1974).

[74]Overbeck, *Major Principles of Media Law*, 344.

[75]*Ibid.*, 341.

[76] *Syracuse Peace Council* v. *Federal Communications Commission*, 867 F.2d 654 (D.C. Cir. 1989).

[77] Section 312(a)(7) was upheld in *Columbia Broadcasting System, Inc.* v. *Federal Communications Commission*, 453 U.S. 367 (1981).

[78] Overbeck, *Major Principles of Media Law*, 335–38.

[79] *Farmers Educational and Cooperative Union of America* v. *WDAY, Inc.*, 360 U.S. 525 (1959).

[80] *Branch* v. *Federal Communications Commission*, 824 F.2d 37 (D.C. Cir. 1987). In 1988 the Supreme Court refused to review the decision of the U.S. Court of Appeals.

[81] Freedom of Information Act, 5 U.S.C.§ 552 (1966), and Government in Sunshine Act, 5 U.S.C.§ 552(b) (1976).

[82] Overbeck, *Major Principles of Media Law*, 260–71.

[83] *Kissinger* v. *Reporters Committee for Freedom of the Press*, 445 U.S. 136 (1980).

[84] *Central Intelligence Agency* v. *Sims*, 471 U.S. 159 (1985).

[85] *U.S. Department of Justice* v. *Reporters Committee for Freedom of the Press*, 489 U.S. 749 (1989). This decision was extended in *John Doe Agency* v. *John Doe Corp.* 493 U.S. 146 (1989) to include many other government documents obtained by the FBI during investigations.

[86] *Federal Communications Commission* v. *ITT World Communications*, 466 U.S. 463 (1984). For a summary of the Government in the Sunshine Act, see Overbeck, *Major Principles of Media Law*, 276–88.

[87] Overbeck, *Major Principles of Media Law*, 89–90.

[88] *Ibid.*, 90.

[89] William L. Prosser, 48 *Calif. L. Rev.* 383 (1960).

[90] Kent Middleton, "Journalism and Tape Recorders: Does Participant Monitoring Invade Privacy?" 2 *Communication/Entertainment L. J.* 287 (1980).

[91] Overbeck, *Major Principles of Media Law*, 159.

[92] *Midler* v. *Ford Motor Company* 849 F.2d 460 (9th Cir. 1988).

[93] *Lugosi* v. *Universal Pictures,* 25 Cal.3d 813, 603 P.2d 425, 160 Cal. Rptr. 323 (1979).

[94] *Memphis Development Foundation* v. *Factors*, 616 F.2d 956 (6th Cir. 1980), and *Factors* v. *Pro Arts, Inc.*, 652 F.2d 278 (2d Cir. 1981).

[95] Walsh, *Public Relations and The Law*, 27–28.

[96] *Ibid.*, 31.

[97] *Basic Books* v. *Kinko's Graphics Corp.*, 758 F. Supp. 1522 (S.D.N.Y. 1991).

[98] Overbeck, *Major Principles of Media Law*, 199–203. See also Walsh, *Public Relations and the Law*, 32–34 for an overview of trademark law.

CHAPTER 7

Theoretical Underpinnings: Adjustment and Adaptation

Organizations as systems strive toward an equilibrium with other systems, an equilibrium that constantly moves as the environment changes. Systems may attempt to establish equilibrium by controlling other systems; by adapting themselves to other systems; or by making mutual, cooperative adjustments.[1]

JAMES E. GRUNIG AND JON WHITE

Critics say that public relations cannot become a profession because it lacks an integrating conceptual model or theory. Without one, the field has no framework for understanding, organizing, and integrating the many activities and purposes of public relations. The professionalization of any field requires a body of knowledge grounded in theory.

This chapter presents such a theoretical model for public relations. As defined in Chapter 1, public relations deals with the relationships that organizations build and maintain with publics. These relationships occur in and are influenced by political, social, economic, and technological change pressures. Careful assessment of these ever-changing forces is essential if organizations are to steer a safe, steady course through the increasingly turbulent global environment. In fact, to paraphrase Darwin, it is not the powerful organizations that will survive in the new millennium, it is those able to adjust and adapt to a changing world.

Part of this scenario is free trade among nations. Linking the 12 European Community countries in 1992 was simply the most visible indicator of the move toward free trade worldwide. At the same time, economic alliances are breaking down regional trade barriers in North America, South America, Latin America, the South Pacific, Southeast Asia, the Persian Gulf, and West Africa. It is conceivable that talk of trade imbalances and trade deficits between countries soon will be no more meaningful than trade imbalances between New York and Chicago, Los Angeles and San Francisco, Kyoto and Tokyo, or Munich and Stuttgart. For example, in 1991 more than 1000 Japanese-owned factories in 49 U.S. states employed more than 350,000 people. Japanese automobile companies manufactured automobiles in Tennessee, Ohio, and Illinois. Sony manufactured television sets in southern California. At the same time, Coca-Cola and Pepsi bottled their "American soda pops" around the globe. In other words, even past barriers often were more political than real.

Speeding the demise of the last vestiges of protective barriers are millions of miles of fiber-optic cables linking computers, fax machines, telephones, and local communication networks worldwide. The global marketplace thrives on this rapidly developing global telecommunication system. Being "out of the loop" takes on new and real meaning when talking about world trade and the global economy. Few organizations can truly isolate themselves from these global economic forces. In fact, most will have to link their activities and products just to stay in business.

Global Communication in the Information Age

Some reports had both Saddam Hussein and George Bush tuned to Cable News Network monitoring developments in the Persian Gulf conflict, providing ample evidence of the revolution in information flow and access. Few could have imagined that Marshall McLuhan's notion of a "global village" would include the heads of two warring states simultaneously following live coverage of their high-tech war on Ted Turner's Atlanta-based international television network. Likewise, founders of the modern Olympics could not have imagined that the games would become the world's largest media event, transforming the global village into the largest audience in history.

An array of fixed-position satellites provides two-way communication anywhere in the world. Pocket-sized transmitter-receivers that were once science fiction within the reader's lifetime are now commonplace in international commerce, government, and even social exchange. Even though English is the language of international business, computers are extending the reach of the new information age by translating documents, transcribing voice communication, and empowering those formerly excluded from international discourse. And the messages, whatever their intended content, tell distant peoples about each other and events of common interest. Simply put, the window on the world is opening wider and wider to more and more people.

Communication satellites and fiber-optic networks deliver electronic mail, television and radio coverage, newspaper and magazine content, and "secure" commercial transactions and government communications. No doubt some of the information is about the latest developments in artificial intelligence, virtual reality, robotics, and other technology spawned by computers and the information age. What organization can operate without regard to these developments?

Realignment of the Family

No longer do most American families look like the families portrayed in old movies: Dad drives off to work in *the* family car; mom gets the kids (one girl and one boy) ready for school; the kids hold hands and walk a short distance to their neighborhood school; mom goes about her daily chores, paying particular attention to getting the "ring around the collar" out of dad's shirts; after school, the boy delivers newspapers while the girl helps mom prepare dinner; dad returns from work in time to loosen his tie and to rest with the evening paper before dinner; and finally, the family spends the evening together reading, playing board games, or doing school homework. It is safe to say that you probably do not know a family like this now.

Variations on family structure are too numerous to describe, but a few examples will help make the point: families headed by single parents, mixed families that include children from previous marriages and stepparents, extended families in which grandparents are parenting their grandchildren, and even "bicoastal" families in which one parent works "back East" and the other works "out West." Experts point out that almost one fourth of all children live with only one parent (usually the mother) and that one third of those families live in poverty. What organization can ignore the impact of family life on its most important public, its employees? What organization can ignore the impact of these same forces on customers, clients, neighbors, and others in the community?

Civil Rights and the Empowerment of Individuals

Amnesty International makes a point of keeping the spotlight on countries that violate individual rights and freedom. Global communication networks make the spotlight bright indeed. Under the glare of global attention, even South Africa's apartheid began to give way to a new public policy recognizing the rights of all citizens. And following the well-established pattern, increased literacy and education continue to spur greater individual rights and freedom worldwide.

In no small way, the demise of the Soviet-style socialism around the world will ultimately enhance individual opportunities to participate in the emerging global economy. Even with their obvious potential for abusing individuals, the new democratic economies will benefit more individuals than did centrally controlled production and distribution. Unlike economies run by governments, those driven by individual enterprise—entrepreneurship—and individual consumers will empower individuals. Even formerly die-hard socialists now call for "market-driven socialism" and "free-market socialism." Regardless of the new labels designed to gloss over fundamental change, however, capitalism is replacing socialism because of relentless pressure by individuals who want to participate in the global economy.

EXHIBIT 7–1

Tracking Trends and Issues

Picture yourself as the captain of the starship *Enterprise*.

You want to be sure that you have a radar system that can accurately anticipate fast-moving meteors and the location of nearby planets to avoid impending disasters.

While moving through space at warp speeds, you don't want to wait until these obstacles are in sight to adjust your course and keep the ship out of danger.

The same is true about an organization—your organization—facing a meteor shower of issues in today's rapidly changing environment.

As issues affecting your organization arise, it is best to have a radar system in place that will help management *anticipate* trends and issues likely to affect your organization and its publics, rather than waiting until it's too late to do anything except react defensively.

If you are in public relations, you must start being more systematic in the tracking and management of issues. If you don't, someone else in your organization will. It's a prerequisite for organizational survival in the 90s.

Even the starship *Enterprise* would find it difficult to navigate through the turbulent issues environment most organizations face today.

From speech by Kerry Tucker, President, Nuffer, Smith, Tucker, Inc., San Diego, California, to Public Relations Club of San Diego, April 14, 1992. Used with permission.

TRACKING THE TRENDS

This discussion of major trends and changes is far from complete, but should indicate some of the major forces that affect organizations. It simply is not possible to build one omnibus list that would cover all situations. Instead, the role of public relations is to track and analyze the specific trends and forces at play in particular situations.

For example, how will the growing animal rights movement affect an organization's ability to accomplish its mission? The *Los Angeles Times Magazine* reports that the-Maryland-based animal rights group, People for the Ethical Treatment of Animals (PETA), "has grown from humble origins to an 800-pound gorilla . . . the largest organization of its kind in the country, claiming more than 350,000 members."[10] Cosmetics manufacturers, medical research laboratories, meat packers, and even federal government agencies have had to factor the views of this new activist force into their decision making.

The animal rights movement forced Avon, Estée Lauder, Benetton, and Tonka Toy Company, among others, to stop testing products on rabbits, guinea pigs, and other animals. It forced the National Institutes of Health to close a research clinic that used animals in research and the Pentagon to halt wound tests on animals. A slaughterhouse in Texas was ordered shut after PETA pressure. PETA is also winning the battle for public opinion, as an overwhelming majority support animal rights and think it should be illegal to kill animals for fur or use animals in cosmetics research.

Consider the issue of education reform: As more and more Americans enter the job market without basic writing, math, and problem-solving skills, American industry slips further behind in the competitive global marketplace. At the same time, parents must cope with ever-increasing costs for post-secondary education. RJR Nabisco Corporation in 1992 began matching employees' annual contributions to an tax-deferred educational savings plan. RJR Nabisco contributes up to $4000 toward the costs of college, everything from a 2-year college to an Ivy League university. Many other companies have "adopted" schools to help promote improvement in the educational system. Others have started their own basic education programs in an attempt to equip employees with basic job skills. Few organizations escape problems brought on by the education crisis, or the changing family, or new technology such as Prodigy® and CompuServ®, or the changes in the balance of global competition.

A SYSTEMS PERSPECTIVE

This discussion of changes and their impact on organizations suggests a systems perspective for public relations. The systems perspective applies because mutually dependent relationships are established and maintained between organizations and their publics.

The concepts of adjustment and adaptation, as well as our definition of public relations, employ concepts and propositions from *systems theory*. For example, a university is part of a system composed of alumni, donors, neighbors, employers, high-school counselors and teachers, and other universities in the area, to name but a few of the many publics. Even the simplest definition of a system—a set of interdependent parts—illustrates this perspective. However, an elaborated definition better serves our analysis:

> A system is a set of interacting units that endures through time within an established boundary by responding and adjusting to change pressures from the environment to achieve and maintain goal states.

In the case of public relations, the set of interacting units includes the organization and the publics with which it has or will have relations; they are somehow mutually affected or involved. Unlike physical and biological systems, however, definitions of social systems are not especially dependent on the physical closeness of component parts. Rather, specification of organization-public interactions defines systems. In other words, an organization-publics system consists of an organization and the people involved with and affected by the organization. Whereas the organizational component in the system is relatively easy to define, publics are abstractions defined by the public relations manager applying the systems approach. In fact, different publics, and therefore a different system boundary, must be defined for each situation or problem.

This principle of systems theory can be illustrated by comparing a university's publics when the goal is recruiting students versus when the goal is raising money for a new business school computing center. The student recruitment campaign might include college-bound high-school students, their parents, high-school counselors, students currently enrolled at the university, and alumni. Because the university tends to attract students from a particular region or segments of the population, program planners would have to identify the geographic and sociographic "territory" to be covered in the recruitment effort. In effect, each of these decisions defines the components and boundary of the system for the student recruitment program.

The capital campaign for the new computing center at the same university, on the other hand, calls for a different definition of the organization-publics system. Program planners would determine what groups or entities are most interested in such a facility or most likely to benefit from its presence on campus. Surely the local business community would include potential donors. In cities far from the campus, corporate foundations that have historically funded innovative educational programs would be included as prospective contributors. More specifically, computer hardware and software companies that hire computer scientists would be identified as a third public for this campaign. Not all alumni are likely contributors, but those who have succeeded in professions calling for computing skills could be selected from the alumni list to make up a fourth public.

In both situations, definitions of the publics include those with whom the organization must establish and maintain enduring and mutually beneficial relationships. Most relationships, however, extend well beyond the period of such specific campaigns. Therefore, even though relationships must be defined specifically for each situation and program goal, they also must be viewed in the larger context of the university's overall public relations program.

Public relations efforts, then, are part of an organization's *purposive* and, therefore, *managed* behavior to achieve goals. For example, a fire that destroys a museum certainly has an impact on the museum's relationships with donors and others. Such an unplanned event, however, clearly is not part of the public relations program. On the other hand, the fund-raising campaign, ground-breaking ceremony, and grand opening gala are public relations responses to the situation created by the fire. These events are intended to establish or maintain relationships necessary for rebuilding the museum.

In some cases, goals can be achieved by simply maintaining existing relationships in the face of changing conditions. More likely, however, organizations must continually adjust their relationships with publics in response to an ever-changing social milieu. Because organization-publics systems exist in changing environments, they must be capable of adapting their goals and relationships to accommodate change pressures from their complex and dynamic settings. A classic case of adjustment and adaptation is the redirection of March of Dimes fund-raising and research to birth defects after polio vaccine eliminated the disease for which the organization-publics system was originally created.

Environmental Change Pressures

Systems theorists typically define the environment as anything that generates change pressures—information, energy, and matter inputs—on a system. Environmental inputs to organization-publics systems take many forms. For example, news reports about abuses by top executives at United Way—lavish lifestyles, high salaries, consulting fees paid to associates, limousine and luxury hotel expenses, and even Concorde flights to Europe—certainly affected the charity's relationships with donors and local United Way chapters. And the impact was not limited to United Way, as all charities braced for a donor backlash, greater public scrutiny, and even government investigations of high salaries and generous benefits packages of nonprofit organizations executives. For example, soon after the United Way case made headlines in the nation's news media, the biweekly *Chronicle of Philanthropy* reported that more than one fourth of the nation's largest 117 charities paid top executives $200,000 or more annually.

Changes in educational levels and values of those entering the local work force affect relationships between a local manufacturing company and labor unions, community groups, local government, and other employers in the area. Shifts in university students' majors—from history to business, for example—put stress on the rather rigidly structured faculty and resources at a university. Changes in the university in turn affect relationships with its various publics: prospective students, current students, faculty, alumni, trustees, donors, legislators, and prospective employers of graduating students. Relationships with other institutions of higher education will change as they compete for history majors and refer business students to each others' campuses.

Even "an insignificant leak" of radioactive water in a power utility's nuclear generating reactor puts stress on a utility's relationships with regulators, antinuclear citizen groups, and the financial community. Or, recall the media coverage of protest groups picketing tuna-canning companies because their fishing practices killed dolphin. Almost immediately sales slumped, government scrutiny increased, children and parents alike erroneously accused the companies of killing "Flipper" for profit, and protest stickers were attached to the product on grocery story shelves. "Socially conscious" investors sold "tuna stock" as prices plummeted.

These examples illustrate that change pressures on organization-publics systems come from many types of environmental sources. In turn, organization-publics relationships change in response to these environmental pressures. If they do not change, old relationships become dysfunctional because the organization acts and reacts in ways inappropriate to the new circumstances. If unmanaged and nonpurposive in their responses to environmental changes, systems tend to degenerate to maximum disorder, what systems theorists call "entropy." In social systems this means that coordinated behavior to attain mutually beneficial goals is no longer possible. In effect, systems break up. *Public relations management is charged with keeping organizational relationships in tune with the mutual interests and goals of organizations and their publics.*

Subsystems and Suprasystems

To this point we have defined the system as the organization and its publics. Similarly, the organization is itself composed of a set of interacting units. From this perspective, the organization also can be viewed as a system. Because organizations exist in dynamic social settings, they must modify internal processes and restructure themselves in response to changing environments. In the absence of such adjustment and adaptation, organization—just as any other social system—become out of step with the world around them. As counselors to line management, the public relations staff is charged with keeping the organization sensitive to environmental changes, anticipating as well as reacting to change pressures.

Likewise, the organization-publics system can be part of a larger set of interacting units, thus viewed as a component of a higher-order social system. For example, a local United Way–publics system is but one component of the community's charitable social service system. It is also only one subsystem in the national system of affiliates, which in turn is but one component of the nation's charitable social service system. Eventually, of course, one could project this series of ever-larger systems to the highest level on earth, the "world." Many public relations specialists work at the level of the private enterprise system, health care system, educational system, or international development system, to name but a few examples of regional, national, or international systems.

The systems perspective, then, suggests that *the level and definition of the system must be appropriate to the concern or the problem situation.* A component—a subsystem—in one system may be itself analyzed as a system in another context. Likewise, a system defined as such for one purpose may be but a component or subsystem in a higher-order suprasystem when the reason for the analysis changes.

For example, when reorganizing the local United Way's *internal* structure and programming, the organization is viewed as the system and the publics viewed as parts of the environment. When the United Way scandal made the headlines, however, for some purposes each of the 2100 local United Way organizations and their publics became local systems within an even larger environmental context. Likewise, the national United Way of America made up of national headquarters and all 2100 local units can be viewed as but one component in the national or international charity system. And the charities taken as a group are but one component in the larger set of tax-exempt, nonprofit organizations some have referred to as the "third sector" of the economy.

The United Way scandal illustrates the latter level of systems analysis, as news of national United Way President William Aramony's high salary and extravagant lifestyle produced change pressures on all tax-exempt charitable, religious, and educational groups and foundations. Individual donors called for more accountability and greater scrutiny of what charities do, as did the National Committee for Responsive Philanthropy. A congressional subcommittee called for more Internal Revenue Service staff members to monitor the more than one million tax-exempt organizations. (The one million total does not include almost 350,000 churches and other national groups such as 4-H, Boy Scouts, Girl Scouts, and Boys and Girls Clubs!) Television evangelists, national foundations, universities, and even local charities all felt the heat of media attention and increased public scrutiny.

Systems theorist James G. Miller uses the concept of higher-order systems to define a system's environment:

The immediate environment is the suprasystem minus the system itself. The entire environment includes this plus the suprasystem and systems at all higher levels which contain it. In order to survive, the system must interact with and adjust to its environment, the other parts of the suprasystem. These processes alter both the system and its environment. It is not surprising that characteristically living systems adapt to their environment and, in return, mold it. The result is that, after some period of interaction, each in some sense becomes a mirror of the other.[11]

Organizations as Systems

Miller says "living systems" engage in exchanges with their environments, producing changes in both the systems and their environments. Such imagery of exchange processes, structural change, and adaptation captures the essence of the public relations function in organizations. Specifically, public relations is part of what organization theorists call the *adaptive* subsystem, as distinct from the *production, supportive/disposal, maintenance,* and *managerial* subsystems.[12] In this context the managerial subsystem is defined as "direction, adjudication, and control" of the other subsystems.

Adaptive subsystems vary in sensitivity to their environments, just as do the public relations functions within organizations. Some organizations actively monitor their social environments and make adjustments based on what is learned. An example is a church that begins offering single-parent counseling and social events in response to the growing number of households headed by divorced and single parents. On the other hand, given public concerns about health care costs and excessive corporate profits, how sensitive was the pharmaceutical company that charged 100 times more for a drug used to treat human cancer than when the same drug was sold as an antiparasitic agent in farm animals?

The amount of resources, time, and effort an organization devotes to monitoring its environment is determined by:

1. The degree of conflict or competition with the external environment, typically related to the extent of involvement with and dependence on government.
2. The degree of dependence on internal support and unity.
3. The degree to which internal operations and external environment are believed to be rationalized, that is, characterized by predictable uniformities and therefore subject to planned influence; and affecting all of these.
4. The size and structure of the organization, its heterogeneity of membership and diversity of goals, its centralization of authority.[13]

Organizational adjustment and adaptation to new conditions depend in part on how open organizations are to their environments.

Differences in how sensitive organizations are to their environments provide a useful basis for further systems analysis of the public relations function.

OPEN AND CLOSED SYSTEMS

All systems—mechanical, organic, and social—can be classified in terms of the nature and amount of interchange with their environments. The continuum ranges from closed systems on one extreme to open systems on the other. *Closed systems* have impermeable boundaries so they cannot exchange matter, energy, or information with their environments. *Open systems*, on the other hand, exchange inputs and outputs through boundaries that are permeable. Of course, social systems cannot be completely closed or totally open, so they are either *relatively open* or *relatively closed*. The distinction is important.

The extent to which systems are closed is an indication of their insensitivity to their environments. Closed systems do not take in new matter, energy, or information. In short, closed systems do not adapt to external change and eventually disintegrate. On the other hand, open systems are responsive to environmental changes. Survival and growth of open systems depend on interchange with its environment. Noting this open system tendency in successful corporations, Peters and Waterman conclude that "innovative companies are especially adroit at continually responding to change of any sort in their environments."[14]

Open systems adjust and adapt to counteract or accommodate environmental variations. Inputs from the environment can be reactions to a system's own outputs or the result of changes independent of system outputs. In either case, inputs have an impact on system goal states, those conditions the system holds as "ideal" or "desired." Inputs can cause deviations from these system goal states. When that happens, feedback within a system causes adjustments in both system *structure* (what the system *is*) and *processes* (what the system *does*). The adjustments are intended to reduce, maintain, or increase the deviations. The output of adjustments can be directed internally or externally, or both. Internal outputs change or maintain goals states. External outputs change or maintain environmental conditions. Which type of output should public relations stress? That depends, for "there is no property of an organization that is good in any absolute sense; all are relative to some given environment, or to some given set of threats and disturbances, or to some given set of problems."[15] And does it mean that an open system will adjust effectively? Not necessarily, for "there is maladjustment as well as adjustment; the function concept only poses the question of adequacy but does not settle it beforehand."[16] (Figure 7–1 represents the cyclical nature of an open system's interchange with

Open Systems Model

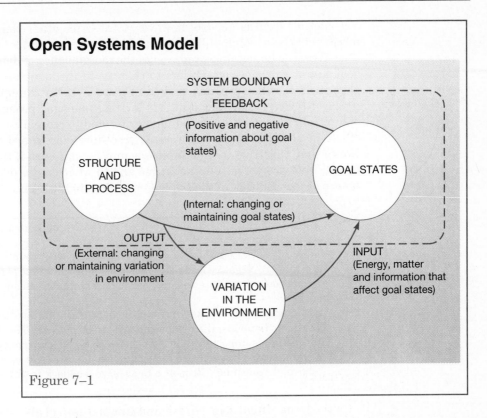

SYSTEM BOUNDARY

FEEDBACK

(Positive and negative information about goal states)

STRUCTURE AND PROCESS

GOAL STATES

(Internal: changing or maintaining goal states)

OUTPUT

(External: changing or maintaining variation in environment

VARIATION IN THE ENVIRONMENT

INPUT

(Energy, matter and information that affect goal states)

Figure 7–1

its environment, assessment and reassessment, and adjustment and adaptation essential to the system maintenance and change.)

The ultimate goal of systems, of course, is survival. But because they exist in changing environments, open systems must continually adjust to maintain states of equilibrium or balance. The conditions necessary for survival are represented as the "goal states" in the model. Paradoxically, open systems must continually change to remain the same, an enduring set of interacting units. To differentiate the *dynamic* states of relatively open systems from the *static* states of relatively closed systems, systems theorists refer to the changeable goal states as *homeostasis*. This term is used "to avoid the static connotations of equilibrium and to bring out the dynamic, processual, potential-maintaining properties of basically unstable . . . systems."[17] The person credited with coining the term *homeostasis* said it "does not imply something set and immobile, as stagnation," but rather "a condition which may vary."[18]

Homeostasis, then, refers to goal states that, while *relatively stable*, are subject to change as a result of system inputs. For example, your academic department attempts to maintain a certain student population, but that goal may change if the state reduces the university's budget. The student census goal could be increased if new resources are added, such as a newly endowed lectureship made possible by wealthy alumni.

Yet another term is needed, however, to describe other changes characteristic of open systems that adjust and adapt to environmental inputs.

Whereas homeostasis represents the maintenance of dynamic system goal states, *morphogenesis* refers to changes in the structure and process element in the open systems model in Figure 7–1. For example, press and public criticism of how the state fair is being managed prompts the board of directors to appoint a new administrator and to reorganize the business office. In addition, the board revises procedures for awarding contracts. Notice that the structure and processes may change even if the goal states do not, and vice versa. What changes and to what extent depends on the nature of the feedback in the system. According to Littlejohn:

> Feedback can be classified as positive or negative, depending on the way the system responds to it. *Negative feedback* is an error message indicating deviation; the system adjusts by reducing or counteracting the deviation. Negative feedback is the most important type of feedback in homeostasis because negative feedback maintains a steady state.
>
> A system can also respond by amplifying or maintaining deviation. When this happens, the feedback is said to be *positive*. This kind of interaction is important to morphogenesis, or system growth (e.g., learning). . . . The response to negative feedback is "cut back, slow down, discontinue." Response to positive feedback is "increase, maintain, keep going."[19]

Systems, then, can adjust and adapt their goals, structures, or processes, depending on the kind and amount of feedback. Open systems not only generate different types of feedback as a result of system inputs, but they exhibit more flexibility in adjusting to inputs. Choices among alternative adaptive strategies are made on the basis of which ones are most effective in helping the system maintain or achieve system goals in the context of environmental change pressures. As one systems theorist put it," All systems are adaptive, and the real question is what they are adaptive to and to what extent."[20]

CYBERNETICS IN OPEN SYSTEMS

Study of this input-output self-regulation process in systems is referred to as *cybernetics*. Buckley's general cybernetic model (Figure 7–2) portrays what tends to occur or would occur ("were it not for complicating factors") in goal-seeking systems. The model contains five elements: (1) goals established in a control center; (2) outputs related to the goals, which have impact on the state of the system and its environment; (3) feedback to the control center on the effects of the output; (4) a comparison of the new system state with the goal state; and (5) control center determination of the need for corrective output.[21]

General Cybernetic Model

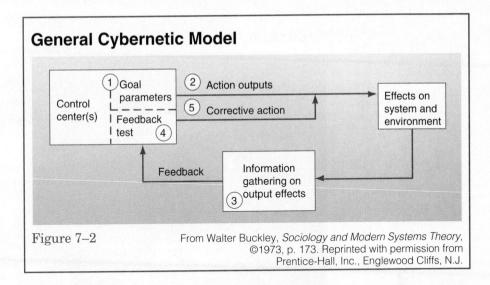

Figure 7–2

From Walter Buckley, *Sociology and Modern Systems Theory*, ©1973, p. 173. Reprinted with permission from Prentice-Hall, Inc., Englewood Cliffs, N.J.

Cybernetic control systems used for navigation on space shuttles, airplanes, and ships are good examples. Early in the twentieth century, sailors called the first such navigational system "iron mike." This relatively simple cybernetic system contained a course-setting device, a course indicator to signal discrepancies from the set course, and a mechanism for activating the rudder to make course corrections. Compare that with the sophisticated cybernetic control system on the most advanced and largest sailing ship, *Club Med 1*:

A hard gust of wind generates pressure on the sails. The extent of that increase in pressure is measured, and the computer instructs the sheets, which are attached to the clews of the sails, to slacken off— spilling the incremental wind and thereby easing the tension. Simultaneously, the computer instructs the windward seawater ballast to ingest more water, while the leeward ballast chamber rushes to empty its supply of water. It is most terribly important to do all of this before the ship lists over more than two degrees, that being, on *Club Med 1*, the limit of official toleration. If the ship were to heel more than two degrees, passengers might notice that they were under sail, and that isn't really the idea, on the world's largest sailboat. So that everything described above happens within approximately three seconds.[22]

Even a thermostat-furnace system can be described as a cybernetic system. Just as does *Club Med 1*, this system responds (corrective actions) to deviations from the goal state (the temperature set in the thermostat). Its responses, however, include either production or cessation of heat only: turning on or off the furnace. Similarly, relatively simple organisms have limited options for dealing with variations in their

Cuttlefish

Figure 7–3   Photograph courtesy Gerhard Saueracker, Morley, Western Australia

environments. For example, the cuttlefish (Figure 7–3)—a squidlike marine mollusk—indiscriminately squirts an inklike fluid when it encounters something in its surroundings.

Organizations, much like the *Club Med 1*, have so many sophisticated options available for dealing with environmental change that they make turning on the heat and squirting ink seem primitive. Or do they? Some public relations programs are routinized to the point that, regardless of the problem and without regard to environmental conditions, the response is to get out a press release "telling our story." In other words, the response is both predetermined and applied indiscriminately from situation to situation. Maybe the cuttlefish's strategy for squirting ink at problems is not unique to that species!

Simple mechanical cybernetic systems and living organisms typically do not change structurally except when pushed to the limit of system tolerance. For example, even though the cuttlefish makes cosmetic changes to blend in with its environment, structural change is not an option when confronting threats in its surroundings. Social systems and complex cybernetic systems such as those used in "smart buildings," on the other hand, have the capacity to use cybernetic self-regulation to make relatively major structural changes. Such changes occur to adapt to new environmental conditions or to modify outputs to change or neutralize the sources of change pressure. This interchange between systems and their environments is characteristic of open systems and makes morphogenesis—purposive changes in structure and process—possible. In short, open systems have the capacity to adjust and adapt to constantly changing environments.

Another quality of open systems becomes apparent when social systems are compared with mechanical systems and many living organisms. Simple, relatively closed systems *react* to outside events only if the input—change pressure—is sufficient to penetrate the system boundary. Complex, relatively open systems monitor—and in some cases, actively probe—their environments to detect and predict changing conditions. In other words, sophisticated open systems *anticipate* changes in their environments and initiate corrective actions designed to counteract or neutralize the changes before they become major problems.

Public relations exhibits a similar range of closed versus open approaches. When public relations practitioners get together, they often use "reactive" and "proactive" to describe programs. *Reactive programs employ relatively closed systems approaches to program planning and management.* Like the cuttlefish ink squirting, a reactive public relations program activates only when disturbed. For example, *Forbes* suggested that Weyerhaeuser's management philosophy "minimizes outside pressures for performance on management." The magazine went on to say, "The company is structured in ways that once made sense but no longer do." According to *Forbes*, the longtime chairman's (the founder's great-grandson) "reaction to criticism was to shrug it off," hiring from the outside "was nearly taboo," and "change moves at a glacial pace in this company." Completing the picture of a relatively closed systems approach, the magazine reported that company representatives "declined to talk with *Forbes* for this story, citing among other things a negative story that ran 13 years ago. Like an elephant, Weyerhaeuser never forgets. Like an elephant, it is also hard to turn around."[23]

Proactive programs, in contrast, use their early-warning "radar" to gather information, to make adjustments, and to generate internal and external output to prevent or avoid problems. Digital Research, Inc.'s announcement that it would no longer merely issue a steady stream of press releases is an example of an organization changing from a closed systems approach to public relations to a more open systems model. Instead of indiscriminately squirting ink like a cuttlefish, the computer software company adopted a proactive open systems approach. To that end Digital Research not only retained a public relations firm, but also added the firm's head to its board of directors. The first step in the new approach was a series of strategic planning sessions. Sounds rather proactive, right?

Similarly, even a power utility, long thought of as the corporate equivalent of an elephant, can behave as a proactive open system. For example, while other utilities were fighting acid rain regulations and legislation, Minneapolis-based Northern States Power Co. had already factored pollution control and reduction into operations. "Their policy is to exceed every environmental requirement that's placed on them," according to a Minnesota antipollution agency program chief. Northern States, for example, to comply with new emission regulations started buying low-sulfur Western coal years before it needed to. By doing so it locked in prices and transportation costs well beyond the year 2000. Meanwhile, other Midwest utilities continued to burn the cheaper, high-sulfur Midwestern and Eastern coals. As a result, these coal-burning utilities now pay premium prices for the cleaner-burning Western coal. Northern States also installed scrubbers to clean sulfur from smoke and gases emerging from its furnaces in the early 1970s and improved their efficiency since then. Utilities that waited until the 1980s and 1990s paid more than five times as much for scrubbers. The company's president and chief executive takes the long view, "You have to be environmentally responsible to have a hope for success or longevity." In the early 1990s, Northern States ranked among the nation's top 200 most profitable companies.[24]

EXHIBIT 7-2

Adjustment and Adaptation, "Ma Bell" Style

Maybe no organizational change received as much attention as did the court-ordered divestiture of the Bell System. January 1, 1984, the then 107-year-old American Telephone and Telegraph split into eight separate companies: AT&T and seven regional companies. The old AT&T had been the world's largest company, secure in its position as a virtual monopoly, and the employer of almost a million "telephone people." It began with the famous words of Alexander Graham Bell, "Mr. Watson, come here. I want to see you." Its transformation stands as an extreme example of system adjustment and adaptation to a changed environment.

Whereas changes in its legal environment made headlines during the nearly nine-year court battles leading to divestiture, change in the structure and business of the giant was inevitable. New telecommunication technologies opened the long-distance business to competitors such as MCI, GTE's Sprint, and ITT's Longer Distance. Short-distance communication changed also. City and county governments, corporations, and other high-volume users installed their own microwave systems, bypassing local telephone companies and monthly "phone bills."

AT&T's new Phone Center stores signaled a new age of competition among phone equipment suppliers. And even though AT&T had been building its own computers for years, it could not enter that market because of legal restraints. In short, the Bell System was vulnerable to competition and constrained by regulations and size. Change was the only alternative in an increasingly dynamic and competitive world.

During AT&T's long court fight against divestiture, it was planning for the inevitable order to change. When it happened, its advertisements announced, "We've been working to make the biggest change in our lives a small change in yours." In fact, some financial analysts said that AT&T gave in to the courts too easily. AT&T's chairman decided that the fight would have gone on for years with little hope of avoiding the breakup. Instead, he and AT&T devised a new structure to respond to the new legal, social, economic, and technological environments. The response should have been anticipated: Theodore N. Vail, twice chairman of AT&T—1878 to 1887 and 1907 to 1920—pioneered in making the corporation responsive to its social setting. He did not fight public regulation and hired James D. Ellsworth to begin a public relations program that responded to public interests. Ellsworth was succeeded by Arthur W. Page, whose philosophy of public relations and corporate social responsibility endures (see Chapter 4).

By the early 1990s, AT&T and the seven regional companies had broadened their missions and product lines well beyond what was once thought of a "the telephone company." They manufactured computers and other communication equipment, expanded their publishing businesses, diversified their communication services, and became leaders in the generation and transmission of information. Cable television companies, other manufacturers, publishers, and the other telephone companies faced not one, but eight competitors.

AT&T joined the newspaper industry and other information providers in 1992 to push for legislation limiting entry of the seven "Baby Bells" to long-distance, information, and security-alarm services. The seven regionals have opposed such legislation and joined with other companies in joint ventures to develop medical and educational information services, home-shopping services, video entertainment, and dial-up classified and yellow-pages advertising.

In short, a corporate dinosaur transformed itself into eight thriving, competing communication giants. The old AT&T adjusted and adapted rather than follow the other dinosaurs into extinction.

AN OPEN SYSTEMS MODEL OF PUBLIC RELATIONS

Output of a steady stream of press releases and other traditional reactive public relations responses is suggestive of closed systems thinking. This all-too-common approach to the function is apparently based on two assumptions: (1) that the purpose of public relations is limited to effecting changes in the environment, and more mistakenly, (2) that organizations have the power to change their environments, thereby eliminating the need to change themselves. Does this kind of thinking remind you of the cuttlefish and thermostat-furnace system? On the other hand, an open systems approach casts public relations in the role of bringing about changes both in environments and in organizations as a result of environmental inputs.

Bell and Bell refer to the first approach to public relations as *functionary* and the second as *functional*. In their view, the functionary role is similar to a closed systems approach:

> Public relations functionaries attempt to preserve and promote a favorable image of the organization in the community on the hypothesis that if the organization is "liked" the public will continue to absorb the organization's outputs. Such functionaries are only concerned with supplying information about the organization to the environment and not with supplying information to the organization about the environment. Because functionaries do not supply feedback information, they do not function in decision-making or even in advisory roles in relation to environmental concerns. Therefore, *they have little to say about "what" is said; they are mainly concerned with "how" things are said.*[25]

Reactive Public Relations

Figure 7–4   Courtesy Doug Marlette, *The Charlotte Observer.*

In this approach to public relations, the emphasis is on maintaining the status quo within the organization while effecting change in the organization's publics. The goal of building and maintaining relations between the organization and its publics is to bring the publics into line with the organization's plans.

In contrast, a functional view of public relations calls for an open systems approach, changing both the organization and the environment. Relations between the organization and its publics are maintained or changed on the basis of reciprocal output-feedback-adjustment. In the functional approach, public relations:

> has the potential to act in an advisory capacity and to have impact on decision-making. This potential in turn leads to some control over its own domain in times of crisis and, as a sensing device, public relations can be effective in preventing many potential crisis situations. Management properly remains the "large wheel" but the small wheel that is public relations may occasionally be capable of influencing the larger one. If observations of external and internal environments indicate that a policy or practice is detrimental to the best interests of the organization (and, increasingly, society) management can be encouraged to adjust.[26]

The functionary approach casts public relations practitioners in the technician role discussed in Chapter 2. In this limited role, they monitor the environment (if at all) to make communication output more effective, not to make changes within the organization. In organizations in which public relations operates in the functional mode, on the other hand, practitioners become part of top management, "the dominant coalition."

> Practitioners with the knowledge, training, and experience to practice a two-way model of public relations are more likely to be included in the organization's dominant coalition. They also are more likely to have power in that coalition rather than to serve it in an advisory role. When public relations managers have power in the dominant coalition, they can influence organizational ideology and the choice of publics in the environment for which strategic public relations programs are planned. At that point, public relations practitioners can fulfill a communication counseling and management role—and truly practice the profession defined for them in public relations textbooks but seldom fulfilled in the real world.[27]

In effect, public relations practiced in the closed systems (functionary) model attempts to maintain the status quo within organizations while directing change efforts at the environment. When public relations is part of organizations' strategic attempts to adjust and adapt to their dynamic environments, the practice reflects the open systems (functional) model.

The open systems approach radically changes the practice from how it is widely practiced. Whereas the more common functionary version attempts to exercise control over environmental forces, the open systems model suggests adjustment and adaptation as the more realistic and appropriate responses. Most definitions of organizational environment suggest that it includes factors outside organizational boundaries and often outside organizations' control. An organization's *specific environment* includes those "constituencies that can positively or negatively influence the organization's effectiveness. It is unique to each organization and it changes with conditions."[28]

The open systems model uses "two-way symmetric" approaches, meaning that communication is two-way and that information exchange causes changes on both sides of organization-public relationships. The one-way versus two-way distinction leads the Grunigs to propose yet another way to describe closed and open systems approaches to public relations: *craft public relations* versus *professional public relations*.

Practitioners of craft public relations seem to believe that their job consists solely of the application of communication techniques and as an end in itself. To them, the purpose of public relations simply is to get publicity or information into the media or other channels of communication. Practitioners of professional public relations, in contrast, rely on a body of knowledge as well as technique and see public relations as having a strategic purpose for an organization: to manage conflict and build relationships with strategic publics that limit the autonomy of the organization.[29]

Both approaches emphasize the primary role of communication in social systems. As Buckley put it, "the interrelations characterizing higher levels (of systems) come to depend more and more on the transmission of *information*—a principle fundamental to modern complex system analysis."[30]

Applying the open systems approach to public relations first and foremost calls for purposeful sensing of the environment to anticipate and detect changes that affect organizational relationships with publics. Following an open systems approach, public relations must be selectively sensitive to specifically defined publics that are mutually affected and, or, involved by organizational policies, procedures, and actions. *The open systems model of public relations calls for research skills to monitor publics and other environmental forces, as well as forces within organizations.*

Open systems public relations also has the capacity to initiate corrective actions within organizations and direct programs to affect knowledge, predispositions, and behaviors of both internal and external publics. The outcomes sought are maintenance or achievement of goals that reflect the mutual interests of organizations and their publics. Those found in conflict with mutual interests are changed or eliminated, *before* they become issues or problems. Proactive corrective action may be the major and most useful aspect of the open systems model of public relations. Steps taken in advance reduce both the amount of effort required and the trauma associated with crisis-oriented reactive public relations.

Thus organizations employing open systems public relations maintain their relationships by adjusting and adapting themselves and their publics to ever-changing social, political, and economic environments. (Figure 7–5 illustrates the open systems model applied to public relations.)

As early as 1923, in one of the earliest public relations books, *Crystallizing Public Opinion*, Edward L. Bernays wrote about the role of the "public relations counsel" in a democratic society. Expressing a model of public relations similar to our open systems approach, he said that the public relations counsel recognizes changes in the organization's social setting and advises clients or employers how the organization should change itself and respond so as to establish a "common meeting ground." Not many years later, Harwood Childs said that the function of public relations is to "reconcile or adjust in the public interest" those aspects of organizations that have social significance. This concept of public relations, based on the open systems theoretical model, serves as the basis for the many activities used under the banner of public relations and spells out its essential role in organizations and society.

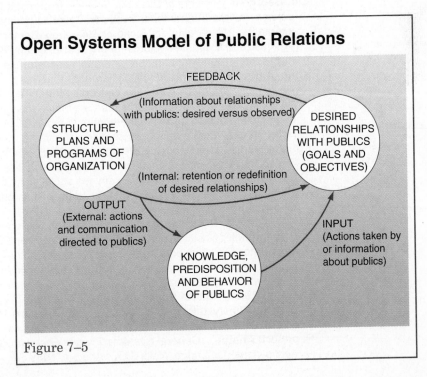

Open Systems Model of Public Relations

FEEDBACK
(Information about relationships with publics: desired versus observed)

STRUCTURE, PLANS AND PROGRAMS OF ORGANIZATION

DESIRED RELATIONSHIPS WITH PUBLICS (GOALS AND OBJECTIVES)

(Internal: retention or redefinition of desired relationships)

OUTPUT
(External: actions and communication directed to publics)

INPUT
(Actions taken by or information about publics)

KNOWLEDGE, PREDISPOSITION AND BEHAVIOR OF PUBLICS

Figure 7–5

In the final analysis, public relations practitioners are applied social and behavioral scientists. Working on behalf of their organizations and in the public interest, they are *managers of change*. They plan and facilitate organizational and social adjustment and adaptation, using primarily communication, the topic of the next chapter.

ADDITIONAL READINGS

Baker, Frank, ed. *Organizational Systems: General Systems Approaches to Complex Organizations.* Homewood, Ill.: Richard D. Irwin, Inc., 1973. Readings oriented to an open systems approach to organizational research and theory.

Cadwallader, Mervyn L. "The Cybernetic Analysis of Change in Complex Social Organizations." in *Communication and Culture: Readings In the Codes of Human Interaction,* edited by Alfred G. Smith. New York: Holt, Rinehart and Winston, 1966.

Churchman, C. West. *The Systems Approach.* New York: Dell Publishing Co., Inc., 1979. Applies systems approach to management and decision making.

Hage, Jerald. *Theories of Organizations: Form, Process, and Transformation.* New York: John Wiley and Sons, Inc. (Wiley-Interscience), 1980. Seminal work on organizations as adaptive systems.

Jelinek, Mariann, Joseph A. Litterer, and Raymond E. Miles. *Organizations by Design: Theory and Practice.* Plano, Tex.: Business Publications, Inc., 1981. Readings in organization design, "the basic alignment or fit of the organization with its environment."

Klir, George J. *Facets of Systems Science.* New York: Plenum Press, 1991. Volume 7 of the International Series on Systems Science and Engineering, International Federation for Systems Research. Contains 11 chapters that synthesize and update systems theory in science and 35 reprinted articles representing significant authors and publications of the field.

Kuhn, Alfred J. *Organizational Cybernetics and Business Policy: System Design for Performance Control.* University Park: Pennsylvania State University Press, 1986. Presents a seven-phase model for applying systems theory to the design and management of complex business organizations. Uses General Motors as a case study.

Kuhn, Alfred J., and Robert D. Beam. *The Logic of Organization: A System-Based Social Science Framework for Organization Theory.* San Francisco: Jossey-Bass Publishers, 1982. Examines social systems concepts—information, decisions, communication, transactions, and power—to develop theory of organization.

Laszlo, C. A., M. D. Levine, and J. H. Milsum. "A General Systems Framework for Social Systems." *Behavioral Science* 19 (March 1974): 79–92.

Monge, Peter R. "Systems Theory and Research in the Study of Organizational Communication: The Correspondence Problem." *Human Communication Research* 8 (Spring 1982): 245–61.

Pearson, Ron. "Ethical Values or Strategic Values? The Two Faces of Systems Theory in Public Relations." *Public Relations Research Annual* 2 (1990): 219–34.

Rapoport, Anatol. *General Systems Theory: Essential Concepts and Applications.* Tunbridge Wells, U.K.: Abacus, 1985.

NOTES

[1] James E. Grunig and Jon White, "The Effects of Worldviews on Public Relations Theory and Practice," in *Excellence in Public Relations and Communication Management*, edited by James E. Grunig (Hillsdale, N.J.: Lawrence Erlbaum Associates, Publishers, 1992), 43–44.

[2] Alvin Toffler, *The Third Wave* (New York: Bantam Books, 1980), paperback, 9. See also Toffler's *Future Shock*.

[3] Frederick Williams, *The New Communications*, 3d ed. (Belmont, Calif.: Wadsworth Publishing Company, 1992), 340.

[4] Some of this information adapted from Marvin Cetron and Owen Davies, *Crystal Globe: The Haves and Have-Nots of the New World Order* (New York: St. Martin's Press, 1991). See also Cetron and Davies, "Trends Shaping the World," *The Futurist* 25, no. 5 (September–October 1991): 11–21.

[5] Faith Popcorn, *The Popcorn Report* (New York: Doubleday Currency, 1991), 86. Written by the marketing forecaster who named and predicted the stay-at-home syndrome called "cocooning," this book outlines ten basic trends and shows how they will change consumer demand, lifestyles, and organizations.

[6] "Special Report: Whooooo cares?," *Weyerhaeuser Today* (Weyerhaeuser Company, August 1991): 1–4.

[7] Edith Weiner, "Business in the 21st Century," *The Futurist* 26, no. 2 (March–April 1992): 13–17. The concept of stewardship is credited to Aldo Leopold, who joined the U.S. Forest Service in the Southwest in 1909, moved to Wisconsin in 1933 to manage the Forest Products Laboratory, took on various conservation leadership posts in Wisconsin, and was a professor at the University of Wisconsin–Madison before his death in 1948.

[8] Data from Associated Press report, "New Study Predicts 25 Million Will Have AIDS by Year 2000," *San Diego Union-Tribune*, June 4, 1992. The full report, *AIDS in the World 1992*, was published by Harvard University in late 1992.

[9] John Naisbitt and Patricia Aburdene, *Megatrends 2000: Ten New Directions for the 1990's* (New York: William Morrow and Company, Inc., 1990), 22. A useful summary of the rather obvious developments that make up the evening television news and magazine cover stories.

[10] Howard Rosenberg, "Fighting Tooth & Claw: Ingrid Newkirk's Combative Style and Headline-Grabbing Stunts Have Shaken Up the Animal-Rights Movement," *Los Angeles Times Magazine*, March 22, 1992, p. 18.

[11] James G. Miller, *Living Systems* (New York: McGraw-Hill Book Company, 1978), 29–30.

[12] For complete explications of these subsystems see Chris Argyris, *Integrating the Individual and the Organization* (New York: John Wiley and Sons, Inc., 1964), and Daniel Katz and Robert L. Kahn, *The Social Psychology of Organizations* (New York: John Wiley and Sons, Inc., 1966), 39–47.

[13] Harold L. Wilensky, *Organizational Intelligence: Knowledge and Policy in Government and Industry* (New York: Basic Books, Inc., Publishers, 1967), 10.

[14] Thomas J. Peters and Robert H. Waterman, Jr., *In Search of Excellence* (New York: Harper and Row, 1982), 12.

[15] R. Ashby, "Principles of the Self-organizing System," in *Principles of Self-organization*, edited by H. Von Foerster and G. W. Zopf (New York: Pergamon Press, 1962), 266.

[16] Siegfried F. Nadel, *Foundations of Social Anthropology* (London: Cohen and West, 1951), 375.

[17]Walter Buckley, *Sociology and Modern Systems Theory* (Englewood Cliffs, N.J.: Prentice-Hall, Inc., 1967), 14.

[18]Walter B. Cannon, *The Wisdom of the Body* (New York: W. W Norton and Company, Inc., 1939), 24.

[19]Stephen W. Littlejohn, *Theories of Human Communication*, 4th ed. (Belmont, Calif.: Wadsworth Publishing Company, 1992), 47. Chapter 3 presents a good summary of systems concepts and their application to communication. The most complete reference on systems theory is Miller's 1100-page *Living Systems*, previously cited. More readable and probably most cited is Ludwig von Bertalanffy, *General Systems Theory: Foundations, Development, Applications*, rev. ed. (New York: George Braziller, Inc., 1968).

[20]Lotfi A. Zadeh, as quoted by George J. Klir, *Facets of Systems Science* (New York: Plenum Press, 1991), 143.

[21]Buckley, *Sociology and Modern Systems Theory*, 172–76. Cybernetic theory of self-regulating systems was first detailed in Norbert Wiener's *Cybernetics* (Cambridge, Mass.: MIT Press, 1948) and revised in a 1961 second edition (New York: John Wiley and Sons, Inc.).

[22]William F. Buckley, Jr., "Haut Boat," *Forbes FYI* (March 16, 1992), 88 and 90.

[23]John H. Taylor, "Rip Van Weyerhaeuser," *Forbes* 148, no. 10 (October 28, 1992): 38–40. The story goes on to report changes in top management, structure, and incentive programs to make the company more responsive and profitable.

[24]Steve Weiner, "Profit without Pollution," *Forbes* 139, no. 11 (May 18, 1987): 46.

[25]Sue H. Bell and Eugene C. Bell, "Public Relations: Functional or Functionary?" *Public Relations Review* 2, no. 2 (Summer 1976): 51–52.

[26]Ibid., 53.

[27]James E. Grunig and Larissa Schneider Grunig, "Toward a Theory of the Public Relations Behavior of Organizations: Review of a Program of Research," *Public Relations Research Annual* 1 (1989): 60.

[28]Stephen P. Robbins, *Organization Theory: Structure, Design, and Applications*, 3d ed. (Englewood Cliffs, N.J.: Prentice-Hall, Inc., 1990), 207.

[29]James E. Grunig and Larissa A. Grunig, "Chapter 11—Models of Public Relations and Communication," in *Excellence in Public Relations and Communication Management*, edited by James E. Grunig (Hillsdale, N.J.: Lawrence Erlbaum Associates, Publishers, 1992), 312.

[30]Buckley, *Sociology and Modern Systems Theory*, 47.

8

Theoretical Underpinnings: Communication and Public Opinion

No human capability has been more fundamental to the development of civilization than the ability to collect, share, and apply knowledge. Civilization has been possible only through the process of human communication.[1]

FREDERICK WILLIAMS

The force of public opinion has steadily gained strength around the world as mass communication has become a global phenomenon. Governments and institutions formerly somewhat isolated from the glare of media attention and public scrutiny now see their actions or nonactions reported via international news media. For example, international pressure was marshalled against Saddam Hussein because of media portrayals of his troops' invasion of and atrocities in Kuwait, never mind that some of the so-called atrocities turned out to be unsubstantiated fabrications!

Television pictures of oil-coated birds and sea otters on even the most remote beaches stir emotions and activate protests against those seen as responsible, whether it is Saddam Hussein's troops or Exxon's leaking oil tanker. Those same television satellite signals carry pictures of starving children in Mozambique, Malawi, Somalia, Zimbabwe, and Zambia, or war-torn Sarajevo, causing an outpouring of sympathy and aid from around the world. Few successfully hide from the peering eye of the world's media: not the despotic dictator, not the crooked savings and loan executive, not the U.S. Navy officer engaged in sexual harassment, not the government official living a life of luxury within a nation of starving children, not the university president using public funds to purchase and maintain a yacht, not the corporate executive drawing millions of dollars in salary and benefits while investors and employees witness the demise of their company.

Nor can the world's audiences ignore the constant stream of messages about the people, events, and places in the global village. Media have expanded the "world outside" and increased the number of "pictures in our heads," to borrow from Walter Lippmann in *Public Opinion*.[2] The media themselves have multiplied to the point that competition for audience attention is greater than ever.

THE BATTLE FOR ATTENTION

Each year U.S. book publishers issue more than 50,000 new titles. During the same period, a typical U.S. child sees 20,000 television commercials. There are some 12,000 magazines, approximately 10,000 radio stations, almost 2000 newspapers, more than 1200 television stations, and new media technologies too numerous to count in the United States. Each attempts to attract an audience. Estimating how many messages each of us is exposed to each day by all these media has become something of a guessing game. Suffice to say that each of us is exposed to or seeks out hundreds, even thousands, of messages each day.

You chose to read this section of *Effective Public Relations*, but more likely during the rest of the day you were exposed to or will be exposed to many more messages, many of which you did not or will not seek out. You will probably screen out many because you have little or no interest in the content. You will skip some because you do not have time to pay attention. You will miss others simply because you were preoccupied with something else and had "tuned out." In short, your attention is the object of fierce competition. The contenders are many. To defend against the onslaught of attention seekers, you may become choosy, even resistant. Few messages get through. Even fewer have an impact. No wonder one communication scholar refers to "the obstinate audience."[3]

Public relations communications compete in this crowded message environment. The first task is to get the *attention* of target publics. Second is to stimulate *interest* in message content. Third is to build a *desire* to act on the message. And fourth is to direct the *action* of those who behave consistent with the message. Unfortunately, the communication process is not as simple as many apparently believe.

DISSEMINATION VERSUS COMMUNICATION

The myth of communication suggests that sending a message is the same as communicating a message. In essence, *dissemination is confused with communication*. This confusion is apparent in public relations when practitioners offer media placements (clippings and broadcast logs) as evidence that communication has occurred. These practitioners probably subscribe to the communication model introduced by information scientists Shannon and Weaver, based on their work for Bell Telephone Laboratories in the late 1940s.[4]

Shannon and Weaver's model consists of an information source, message or signal, channel, and receiver or destination. Not surprisingly, because of their telephone perspective, the communication process produces relatively few and simple problems. *Technical* problems arise when the signal or channel limits or distorts the message being transmitted from the source to the sender. *Semantic* problems occur when the receiver's perception of the message and meaning are not the same as those intended by the sender. *Influence* problems indicate that the sender's message did not produce the desired result on the part of the receiver. As Weaver wrote,

> The questions to be studied in a communication system have to do with the amount of information, the capacity of the communication channel, the coding process that may be used to change a message into a signal and the effects of noise.[5]

But as public relations practitioners will tell you, communication with target publics is much more complicated than this set of questions suggests. As the late Wilbur Schramm pointed out, communication is complicated by people:

> Communication (*human* communication, at least) is *something people do*. It has no life of its own. There is no magic about it except what people in the communication relationship put into it. There is no meaning in a message except what the people put into it. When one studies communication, therefore, one studies people—relating to each other and to their groups, organizations, and societies, influencing each other, being influenced, informing and being informed, teaching and being taught, entertaining and being entertained—by means of certain signs which exist separately from either of them. To understand the human communication process one must understand how people relate to each other.[6]

This is no simple task. In fact, Schramm's concept of communication requires a two-way-process model in which sender and receiver operate within the contexts of their respective frames of reference, their relationship, and the social situation.

As Figure 8–1 illustrates, *communication is a reciprocal process of exchanging signals to inform, instruct, or persuade, based on shared meanings and conditioned by the communicators' relationship and the social context.*

Communication Process Model

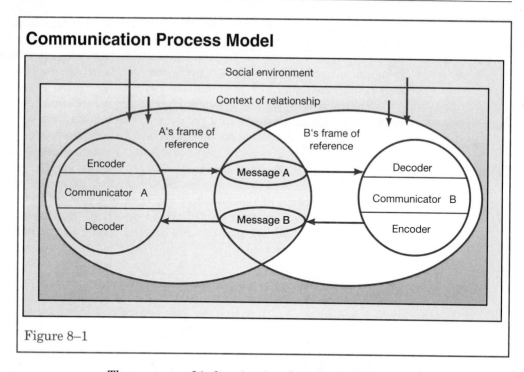

Figure 8–1

The process of *informing* involves four steps: (1) attracting attention to the communication, (2) achieving acceptance of the message, (3) having it interpreted as intended, and (4) getting the message stored for later use. The more demanding process of *instruction* adds a fifth step: stimulating active learning and practice. The process of *persuasion* goes beyond active learning to the sixth step of accepting change: yielding to the wishes or point of view of the sender. Clearly, barriers to achieving the outcomes of informing, instruction, and persuasion increase with the addition of the fifth and sixth steps in the processes.[7]

ELEMENTS OF THE COMMUNICATION MODEL

Early communication researchers studied the individual elements in the communication process model to determine the effect of each on the effectiveness of the process. Most studies dealt with persuasion as the desired outcome, but more recent studies have expanded the range of effects studied.

The Sender

Characteristics of message sources affect receivers' initial acceptance of the message, but have little effect on long-term message impact. Hovland and his colleagues called this long-term source impact the "sleeper effect."[8] For example, according to the theory of source credibility and attractiveness, safe-sex messages promoting prevention of HIV infection among college students are more readily accepted as believable when presented by highly credible sources, such as a recognized medical authority, than when presented by peers. In a few weeks, however, recipients of the message will retain about the same amount of information whether they got it from a credible source or from a fellow college student.

More recent research suggests both short-term and long-term source impact. Source credibility amplifies the value of information, according to one scholar. The theory suggests that the perceived status, reliability, and expertness of the source add "weight" to messages. Multiplying the three source characteristics by each other yields the "weight" factor of the source in the communication process.[9]

Researchers have concluded that although the source characteristics affect the communication process, their impact varies from situation to situation, topic to topic, and time to time. At a minimum, however, source characteristics affect receivers' initial receptivity to messages.

The Message

First of all, recognize that whereas message characteristics surely have an impact in the communication process, many communication scholars agree that "meaning is in people, not words." This observation leads naturally to the conclusion that different people receiving the same message may interpret it differently, attribute different meanings to it, and react to it in different ways. There is little doubt, however, that message characteristics have powerful effects, even if they do not conform to simple and direct cause-and-effect explanations. As suggested by the notion of the "obstinate audience," message effects are mediated by receivers, thereby frustrating the search for "rules" that apply in all communication situations.

Early persuasion research on message characteristics produced few such rules, but did provide guidance still used in public relations today. For instance, if you wish to persuade, should the message contain only on side of the issue, or should it address both sides of an argument? Research findings generally support the following recommendations:

1. If receivers oppose your position, present arguments on both sides of the issue.
2. If receivers already agree with your position, your message will have greater impact—probably reinforcement—if you present only arguments consistent with the receivers' views.
3. If receivers are well educated, include both sides of the argument.
4. If you use messages containing both sides of the argument, do not leave out relevant arguments on the opposing side, or receivers who notice the omission will grow suspicious of your presentation.[10]
5. If receivers are likely to be exposed later to persuasive messages countering your position, use two-sided messages to "inoculate" the audience to build resistance to the later messages.[11]

Recent message research suggests that gaining compliance is a complicated process, however. If the message source has little power or control to exercise over the receiver, then persuasion becomes the primary strategy. If, on the other hand, the sender has power or control, then instruction or direction becomes the relevant strategy. Researchers list four major approaches to gaining compliance through communication:

1. **Sanction strategies** use rewards and punishments controlled by the sender, controlled by the receiver, or the result of the situation.
2. **Altruism strategies** call upon the receiver to comply so as to help or come to the aid of the sender or some third party represented by the sender.
3. **Argument strategies** employ (a) *direct requests*, in which the sender does not give the receiver the rationale or motivation for the request; (b) *explanations*, in which the sender gives the receiver one or more reasons for complying; and (c) *hints*, in which the sender sets up the situation or suggests circumstances from which the receiver draws the desired conclusion and compliance.
4. **Circumvention strategies** misrepresent the situation, give false rationales, or promise rewards and punishments not within the sender's power to deliver.[12]

Research on the impact of message characteristics supports the general conclusion from the previous section: Message impact is mediated or conditioned by receivers. For example, the classic study of order of presentation—"primacy" versus "recency"—demonstrated that the first part of the message has the greatest effect on receivers with low initial interest. The last part of the message has the greatest effect on those with high initial interest.[13]

Another line of message research initiated by Hovland and his associates at Yale deals with the use of fear to achieve compliance. After conducting an experiment using messages about dental hygiene, Janis and Feshback concluded that low-fear messages produce more compliance than do high-fear messages. High-fear messages apparently produce defensive reactions in the receiver that led to distortion, denial, or rejection of the message.[14] Some recent research on fear appeals, however, suggests a much more complicated relationship in which several factors influence the relationship between fear messages and subsequent compliance.

For example, high-fear messages about the dangers of smoking and of venereal disease, when combined with believable recommendations, produce high scores on intended compliance. Three factors affect the impact of fear messages: (1) the seriousness or harmfulness of the subject, (2) the likelihood or probability of the feared event, and (3) the efficacy of the recommended course of action. Apparently, receivers evaluate fear-producing messages on these three characteristics before making a decision to adopt recommended courses of action. Researchers refer to this decision process as "protection motivation."[15]

In the final analysis, however, many characteristics of the source, receiver, and the communication situation mediate the impact of messages on receivers. One writer concluded:

> When main-effect findings demonstrated relationships between
> the selected variable and some measure of attitude/behavior
> change, additional variables such as source characteristics, power,
> and receiver variables were investigated.[16]

The Medium or Channel

New technologies for delivering messages challenge conventional wisdom. For example, widespread adoption of fax machines during the 1980s revolutionized business communication. The same can be said about all phone communication with the introduction of answering machines, cordless and cellular phones, and voice mail. Now, for the increasing number of people who work with computers, E-mail is changing communication within organizations and across other networks.

For example, at Unisys, almost six out of ten employees "access" the company's electronic newsletter at their own workstation terminals. Rather than having to wait for the next issue of a printed newsletter or until announcements get posted on bulletin boards, employees "sign on" to the company's mainframe computer to get news that can be updated at any time. Employees ranked the Unisys News Network as their preferred information source, ranking it over their bosses, over printed newsletters, and even over the ever-popular grapevine. Because of the success of the electronic newsletter, Unisys dropped its printed newsletter. No one complained.[17]

Surprisingly, Unisys employees selected the electronic newsletter over interpersonal communication with their bosses. Communication scholars and practitioners historically have considered face-to-face interpersonal communication the most direct, powerful, and preferred method for exchanging information. In contrast with mass communication, interpersonal communication involves as few as two communicators (typically in close proximity), uses many senses, and provides immediate feedback. This description of the interpersonal communication situation, however, does not take into account the possibility that mass media messages may be directed to only a few (or only one!) in the audience. Likewise, physical proximity can be less important than the nature of the relationship between communicators, what one scholar calls the "intimacy-transcends-distance phenomenon." What begins as impersonal communication when people initially exchange messages can become interpersonal communication as the communicators develop a relationship.[18]

Extending time and distance, however, often requires using message delivery systems other than in-person presentations. In much of contemporary society, face-to-face contacts give way to mediated transmissions. Spoken words give way to written communication. Individually addressed letters give way to printed messages. Printed publications give way to broadcast words and pictures. Broadcast messages give way to networks of computers carrying digital signals translated into all manner of information. Choosing the "right" *medium* (singular) or *media* (plural) requires an understanding of media and media effects.

Interest in media selection intensified after Marshall McLuhan's famous assertion that "the medium is the message."[19] Untangling media effects from those of other elements of the process, however, remains an unfinished task. Attempts to demonstrate "all-powerful" media effects— sometimes referred to as the "hypodermic model"—have largely failed to do so. For example, concern about powerful media effects on children usually motivates both criticism and research.[20] First the 1929–1932 Payne Fund studies of how movies influenced children led to production codes and reinforced the prevailing "legacy of fear." Next, publication of *Seduction of the Innocent* in 1954 led to the "great comic book scare." The book's author concluded that comic books lead children to delinquency, cruelty, violence, and undesirable sexual behavior, but not all children, however. And not all these conclusions were supported by the evidence, but that did not keep the author from concluding that comic books are "definitely and completely harmful."[21]

Soon after, comic books gave way to television as the object of concern and study. Between 1959 and 1960, Stanford University researchers studied almost 6000 students, almost 2000 parents, and hundreds of teachers and others in 11 communities, comparing television communities with those without television, urban communities with suburban communities, and industrial communities with agricultural communities. The researchers wanted to learn how television affects children. They learned, however, that most children are not sitting targets for television. Instead, it was children who used television for entertainment, for information, and for social purposes. Not surprisingly, the researchers found that many factors in the communication process and context mediate the effects of television on children.[22]

One media effects theory suggests that print and television have different effects because of characteristics of the media themselves. "High-involvement" print media tend to produce effects that follow a "see-learn-feel-do" sequence. Television, as a "low-involvement" medium, produces gradual shifts in perceptions, often through repetition. Latent effects on perceptions are later activated when the situation demands a decision or other response, such as when making a purchase. In other words, television effects on subsequent behavior may not appear for some time. Additionally, attitude changes may follow the behavior. The explanation is that the left hemisphere of the brain processes high-involvement print media messages, whereas low-involvement media messages are processed by the right hemisphere.[23]

Notice that explanations of low-involvement and high-involvement media effects rely on differences in receivers' brain activities. Research using recent advances in brain-wave measurement technology, however, do not support this explanation. Researchers tested the media involvement model, asking: "Do television viewing subjects show a larger amount of beta (conversely, a smaller amount of alpha) in the right brain hemisphere than in the left?" They found that neither hemisphere dominates during television viewing, concluding that television viewing produces brain-wave patterns much like other activities. In other words, according to the researchers, "television viewing appears to be nothing special."[24]

The Receivers

Communication models—and public relations programs—often position the audience as passive recipients at the end of a message transmission process. This tradition continues even though research evidence and constant references to "two-way" suggest a different model and role for the audience.

In early mass communication studies, however, "mass society" audiences were viewed as vulnerable to messages and media manipulated by those in control. As a consequence of industrialization, urbanization, and modernization, concerned critics saw people as alienated and isolated from the kind of strong social and psychological forces found in traditional societies. It was this notion of vulnerable audiences that motivated both early research on media effects and the growing concern of critics.[25]

The evidence gathered on audience effects, however, suggests a different type of receiver. Apparently children are not as uniformly vulnerable to film, comic books, and television as media critics feared. And the Yale persuasion experiments demonstrated that receivers are not uniformly influenced by messages designed to change attitudes. For example, receivers who value group membership are relatively unaffected by messages espousing positions counter those of the group. Those who are persistently aggressive toward others tend to be resistant to persuasive messages. On the other hand, receivers with low self-esteem and feelings of social inadequacy are influenced more by persuasive messages than are people with high self-esteem and feelings of indifference toward others.[26]

In short, the notion of a monolithic and passive mass audience does not describe reality. Rather, the more accurate description suggests selected active receivers processing messages designed for the few, not the masses:

Since audiences are known to be evasive at best and recalcitrant at worst, every effort is made to communicate artfully and well. While communication is conceptualized as a one-way flow, efforts are directed at targeting messages for different audience segments and promoting audience involvement wherever possible.[27]

Context of the Relationship

Communication occurs within the context of the communicators' relationship. The range of such relationships includes close and intimate relationships such as in friendships and marriage, as well as formal, competitive, and conflictual interpersonal relationships in a variety of settings. The point, of course, is that the relationship itself affects much about the communication process.

For example, one theory of friendships suggests that four dialectical factors influence the nature and amount of communication between friends. The first is *independence versus dependency*. Communication between friends occurs under contradictory pressures: to let each other make his or her own decisions while at the same time providing support and help. The second is *affection versus instrumentality*. Friends communicate within the context of giving affection as an end in itself, versus using the friendship to achieve some other end. The third dialectic is *judgment versus acceptance*. For example, friends are supposed to accept each other without conditions, but what kind of friend are you if you do not provide "constructive criticism" to help your friend? (Good luck on that one!) The fourth dialectic influencing communication between friends is *expressiveness versus protectiveness*. The conflict here is between spontaneity and honesty versus strategy and caution. Overriding all of these cross pressures is the notion that friendship is a private relationship played out within a set of public expectations. No wonder communication is a complicated process even between friends.[28]

Conflict provides a similarly complicated context for communication. Conflict occurs when two or more people have the power to inflict sanctions on each other while trying to achieve mutually exclusive objectives. The combatants may have different values and may define the conflict situation differently. Each has the means or resources to engage the other. Conflict ends when the combatants sense victory or defeat, or that the probable outcome does not justify the cost of continuing.[29]

All relational communication reflects four basic dimensions: (1) emotional arousal, composure, and formality; (2) intimacy and similarity; (3) immediacy or liking; and (4) dominance-submission.[30] For example, your supervisor announces changes in scheduled work hours for student assistants without consulting with the students (the first dimension) by posting the new schedule on the office bulletin board (the second dimension). The notice also expresses the supervisor's hope that the new schedule does not inconvenience any of the assistants (the third dimension), but that the supervisor has the power to establish work schedules (the fourth dimension).

Not surprisingly, nonverbal behaviors play important roles in relational communication. *Proximity* communicates intimacy, attraction, trust, caring, dominance, persuasiveness, and aggressiveness. *Smiling* communicates emotional arousal, composure, formality, intimacy, and liking. *Touching* suggests intimacy. *Eye contact* intensifies the other nonverbal behaviors.[31] Of course, these interpretations of nonverbal behaviors do not take into account cultural differences. For example, in some cultures, such as Arab and Latin American cultures, close proximity does not necessarily indicate dominance or aggressiveness. Likewise, in Navajo and some Asian cultures eye contact can be interpreted as a sign of disrespect or challenge. In some cultures, touching in public is practically forbidden.

Whether verbal or nonverbal, communication in relationships helps the parties make predictions about others in the relationship. Communication reduces uncertainty about the probable outcomes of future exchanges and provides a basis for the continuing relationship. Understanding the communication process, however, requires not only an understanding of the relationship between communicators, but also the larger social context within which communication occurs.

The Social Environment

Communication affects and is affected by the social setting. Thus communication occurs as a structured process within evolving systems of related components and activities. Social systems include families, groups, organizations, and all kinds of collectivities that are at the same time both producers and products of communication.

For example, when people think they can achieve something through joint action that cannot be accomplished individually, they form groups. Communication in groups depends on the nature of the group (primary versus secondary, formal versus informal, task-oriented versus experiential), characteristics of group members, group size, group structure, group cohesiveness, and group purpose.[32] Apart from understanding the determinants and consequences of group communication, researchers and practitioners alike are concerned with group effectiveness in making decisions.

Successful group decision making requires accomplishing four tasks: (1) developing an adequate and accurate assessment of the problem, (2) developing a shared and complete understanding of the goal and criteria for success, (3) agreeing on the positive outcomes of decisions, and (4) agreeing on the negative outcomes of decisions. Decision-making effectiveness, therefore, depends on the extent to which members' communication helps achieve these group functions.[33]

Organizations impose additional layers of complexity and constraints on communication. But nobody said this was going to be easy. Recall that the forces at play in the larger society (outlined in Chapter 7) affect how all communicators—individuals, groups, and organizations— approach their publics, shape the content of their messages, define communication goals, and condition audience responses. Recall also the central point of the last chapter: All elements of a system are interdependent and mutually influenced by forces in their environment. In short, communication—when it occurs—results from a complex reciprocal process in which communicators try to inform, instruct, or persuade within the contexts of their relationships and the larger social setting.

EFFECTS OF THE PROCESS

Communication effects have long been the object of concern and study. The range of effects run the gamut from early concerns about "all-powerful" media to "no effects." Hypothesized unlimited effects of movies on helpless children motivated the Payne Fund studies of the 1920s. Maybe critics simply feared too much. After ambitious public persuasion and political campaigns in the 1940s and 1950s produced disappointing results, many concluded that mass communication has almost no impact. Maybe the campaign planners simply asked too much of mass communication. More recent evidence supports theories in which mass communication effects occur under specified conditions. Apparently, the answer depends on what question you ask.

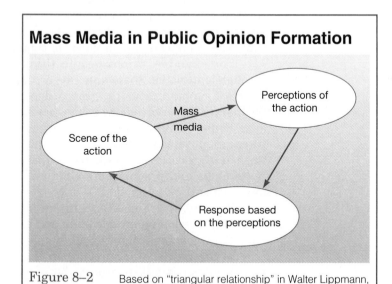

Mass Media in Public Opinion Formation

Figure 8–2   Based on "triangular relationship" in Walter Lippmann, *Public Opinion*, New York: Harcourt, Brace and Company, 1922, pp. 16–17.

Creating Perceptions of the World Around Us

Early theorists cast mass communication in the role of telling us about events, things, people, and places we could not experience directly ourselves. Walter Lippmann said it best when he wrote about "the world outside and the pictures in our heads." He described a "triangular relationship" between the scene of action (interpreted to include people, places, actions, and the entire range of possible phenomena), perceptions of that scene, and responses based on the perceptions. The last side of the triangle is complete when the responses have impact on the original scene of action. Mass media fit in the model between the scene of action and audience perceptions (see Figure 8–2).[34]

Lippmann pointed out that most of us cannot or do not have direct access to much of the world; it is "out of reach, out of sight, out of mind." The mass media help us create a "trustworthy picture" of the world that is beyond our reach and direct experience. His notions of media impact on public perceptions not only set the stage for studying mass communication effects, but arguably established the conceptual basis for much of what later became public relations.

Setting the Agenda

The "agenda-setting" theory of mass communication effects builds on Lippmann's notion of media impact by distinguishing between *what we think about* and *what we think*. The difference is that the former includes what we know about (cognition), whereas the latter refers to our opinions and feelings (predisposition). Agenda setting suggests that mass media can have substantial and important impact on the cognitive level without affecting predisposition.[35] But it should be clear that, even if media are limited to this one effect, setting the agenda is not a trivial consequence.

For example, early explorations of agenda setting by the press during presidential elections found that relative media emphasis on issues has a cumulative effect on the electorate. The same issues, with the same relative emphasis as that given by the media, make up the voters' agenda. In other words, the issues considered least-to-most important by voters reflect patterns of media coverage rather than a particular political agenda. Furthermore, the relative number of people concerned about issues parallels the relative media emphasis of those issues. Media and public agendas were most similar during the early stages of the campaign and for those issues least likely to be within peoples' direct experience.[36]

Imagine the potential consequences of media agenda setting. First of all, media coverage can elevate the public standing of issues, people, organizations, institutions, and so forth. Second, changes in the amount of media attention can lead to changes in public priorities. Third, the more concerned people are about something, the more they tend to learn about it, they stronger their opinions of it, and the more they tend to take action on it. (Notice, however, that the agenda-setting theory does not predict what information, which way their opinions will change, or what types of actions they will take.) Fourth, media coverage can affect the agenda priorities of some specific and important publics, such as legislators, regulators, and other policy makers.

In summary, mass communication can affect public opinion by raising the salience of issues and positions taken by people and groups in the news.[37] And, as does Lippmann's theory of media effects, the agenda-setting theory contributes to the conceptual foundation for public relations mass communication.

Diffusing Information and Innovations

Beyond setting the issue agenda, research in a variety of settings shows that mass communication facilitates social interaction and change. For example, some people use mass media to get information from sources unlike themselves. The sources may come from different social, economic, and educational backgrounds but are accessible through the media. The media, then, provide information from sources that would otherwise not be available through interpersonal networks in which "like talks to like." Once people get information from the media, however, they enter conversations armed with useful new information. What we learn from mass media often determines what we talk about with others, providing the common ground needed to begin conversation: "Did you see in this morning's paper that . . . ?" or "Wasn't Jay Leno funny last night when he said . . . ?" In effect, mass media provide information to those who seek it and supply information needed for subsequent interpersonal communication.[38]

Originally, communication scholars referred to the mass media-interpersonal sequence of communication as the "two-step flow" model. This model of communication effects suggests that ideas flow from the media to opinion leaders, who in turn inform others through interpersonal conversations. Most now agree, however, that communication is a "multistep flow" process in which media are more effective than interpersonal conversations in spreading information. Interpersonal communication is more effective than mass media, however, in forming or changing predisposition toward an issue of innovation. On a wide range of issues and innovations, people are more likely to turn to their interpersonal networks of "near-peers" for subjective evaluations than to mass media sources.[39] Of course, mass media can extend the reach of "peers," thus the care with which spokespersons are chosen.

Characteristics of the innovation or new idea, as well as characteristics of the adopters, influence the adoption process. Ideas or innovations are more readily adopted if they are (1) more advantageous than the current situation, (2) compatible with previous experience and other aspects of the situation, (3) simple, (4) easily tried, and (5) observable with readily apparent outcomes. "Innovators" are the first to adopt, followed by "early adopters," "early majority," "late majority," and "laggards." Characteristics of the individuals in each of the categories vary with the nature of change being adopted and the context.[40]

Diffusion and adoption processes illustrate the impact that mass communication has on interpersonal communication and networks. More importantly, they show how mass and interpersonal communication interact in social systems and in social change.

Defining Social Support

The *spiral of silence* theory suggests a phenomenon referred to as "the silent majority." Individuals who think their opinion conflicts with the opinions of most other people tend to remain silent on an issue. Carried to an extreme, even if a majority actually agree but do not individually recognize the social support, their silence and inactivity can lead to the erroneous conclusion that not many people support a particular view. On the other hand, individuals who think that many others share their view, or that the number of people who agree is growing rapidly, are more likely to express their views. Under these conditions, a vocal minority that sees itself on "the winning side" can appear to represent a widely shared perspective.[41] In either case, as Lippmann pointed out more than 50 years before the spiral of silence theory appeared, people "respond as powerfully to fictions as they do to realities, and that in many cases they help to create the very fictions to which they respond."[42]

In essence, *public opinion arises as individuals collectively discern about support for their views through personal interaction and by attending to the mass media*. Individuals observe and assess their social environments, assessing the distributions of opinions, estimating the strength and chances of success for each, and determining the social sanctions and costs associated with each. The spiral begins when individuals choose to remain silent or to express their views. It continues as others observe the presence or absence of support for their own views. It gains apparent legitimacy when increasing numbers of individuals translate their observations into public silence or expression. It is reinforced when media cover the views being displayed most forcefully and most frequently and do not make an effort to determine the actual distribution of views.

Media coverage can reflect, enforce, or challenge the spiral of silence effect on public opinion. But understanding the dynamics of individuals' collective observations of their social environments and public opinion translates rather directly into public relations practice. Examples include public information campaigns designed to break the spirals of silence associated with smoking, drinking and driving, substance abuse, domestic violence, sexual harassment, and safe sex, to list only a few. In each instance, and for many other public issues, mass communication played a key role in redefining socially accepted expression and behavior.

Sociocultural Model of Persuasion

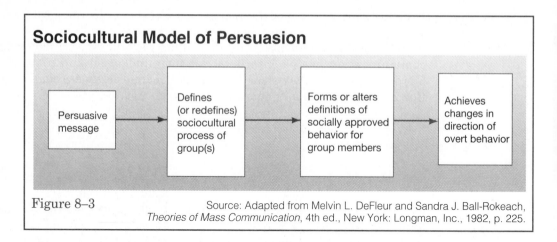

Figure 8–3   Source: Adapted from Melvin L. DeFleur and Sandra J. Ball-Rokeach,
Theories of Mass Communication, 4th ed., New York: Longman, Inc., 1982, p. 225.

As illustrated in Figure 8–3, mass media messages can provide individuals pictures of their social environment, whether there is social
approval or disapproval of their views or actions. This "sociocultural
model" of communication effects suggests that "messages presented via
the mass media may provide the appearance of consensus regarding orientation and action with respect to a given object or goal of persuasion."[43]

PUBLICS AND THEIR OPINIONS

Nineteenth-century writer and first editor of *Atlantic Monthly* James
Russell Lowell said, "The pressure of public opinion is like the atmosphere. You can't see it, but all the same it is sixteen pounds to the
square inch." Lowell's words have even more relevance now. Public opinion has never been more powerful, never been more fragmented, never
been more volatile, and never been more exploited and manipulated. For
example, public opinion of "family values" played a major role in the
1992 presidential campaign. Public opinion of health care costs prompted reform movements. Public opinion polls have long guided politics,
government programs, entertainment programming, and even corporate
decision making. In short, much as Lowell suggested, public opinion is
an always-present, dynamic force. It is part of public relations' mission
to help organizations recognize, understand, and deal with this powerful
influence in their environments.

It is not an easy task, however. As the former vice president of
AT&T says:

> Public opinion is not necessarily logical; it is amorphous, ambivalent,
> contradictory, volatile. Consequently, those of us who would hope to
> influence public opinion can only expect that our efforts, over time, may
> nudge the consensus toward some reasonable perception of the issues.[44]

His experience led him to conclude that publics have "an astounding ability to ignore very material facts when those facts don't interest them, and increasing the supply of information does not necessarily increase public knowledge."[45]

Nevertheless, public opinion is a powerful force in modern society. Organizations of all types must deal with *real* and *perceived* public opinion as they establish and maintain relationships with their many internal and external publics.

Definition of Public Opinion

The common notion of public opinion holds that it is simply the aggregation of individual views on some issue. This "individual agreement" approach to defining public opinion, however, misses the point that it is *public*. Individual cognition may or may not represent the *consensus*, or "thinking together," that more fully represents the kinds of opinions that form and are formed by public discussion among those sharing a "sense of commonness."

Thus public opinion represents more than the collected views held by a particular category of individuals at one point in time. Public opinion is not adequately defined as simply a *state* of individual cognition. Instead, it reflects a dynamic *process* in which ideas are "expressed, adjusted, and compromised en route to collective determination of a course of action."[46]

It occurs within groups of communicating people, who together determine what the issue is, why it is a cause for public concern, and what can be done about it. While the process unquestionably involves private cognition, individuals' thoughts about a social issue are largely dependent for both form and content on public discussion. This is why communication is so often metaphorically equated with externalized cognition: Communication requires "thinking together."[47]

In practice, however, both researchers and public relations practitioners take "snapshots" of public opinion, essentially freezing the process at one point in time so as to describe it at one time and compare it with other times. Their surveys too often measure only direction and intensity, leaving other important dimensions out of the picture.

The *direction* of opinion indicates the evaluative quality, telling us the "positive-negative-neutral," "for-against-undecided," or "pro-con-it-depends" quality of predisposition. In its simplest form, direction is a "yes-no" answer to a survey question. You frequently hear public opinion survey results reported as simply the percentages for or against some issue, proposition, or candidate. (Recall the many times you heard the percentages supporting Bush and Clinton during the 1992 presidential campaign.) Direction clearly represents the most basic and most frequently used measure of public opinion.

Intensity provides measures of how strongly people feel about their opinions, whatever the direction. For example, right up until the November 1992 election, pollsters asked registered voters to indicate "on a scale of 1 to 10" how strongly they supported either the Bush-Quayle or Clinton-Gore ticket. Likewise, surveys often ask respondents to mark "strongly agree, agree, neutral, disagree, or strongly disagree" to indicate both direction and intensity of feelings. Intensity measures provide an initial estimate of the relative strength of predisposition, even if often only indicating "loudness" on one side versus the other on issues such as abortion, prayer in schools, and clear-cutting forests.

Stability refers to how long respondents have held or will hold the same direction and intensity of feelings. Measures of stability require observations taken at two or more points in time. Think of this dimension as something like the charts that track stock prices or temperature patterns over time. Remember the "bump" in support for each of the 1992 presidential candidates after the two national conventions? Support for a Clinton presidency jumped rather dramatically following the Democratic convention, as did support for a second term for President Bush even before the Republican convention came to a close.

Informational support refers to how much knowledge people hold about the object of opinion. To carry through with the 1992 presidential election campaign examples, some partisan voters held strong opinions of their respective candidates, yet did not hold much information to back up their predisposition. In a study of a mayoral election, researchers found that those more informed about issues hold stronger opinions about the issues, but the direction of the opinions are not easily predicted. And those with more knowledge and strong opinions are more likely to vote and to contact local officials.[48]

Absence of such "mass" behind an opinion in less partisan situations can indicate that the direction and intensity are susceptible to change. For example, if Monsanto finds that public opinion against field testing of genetically engineered plants is not well informed, the company can mount a public information campaign designed to educate community members about the risks and benefits involved.

Measures of *social support* provide evidence of the extent to which people think their opinions are shared by others in their social milieu. The persuasion model in Figure 8–3 indicates the power of perceptions of social approval or disapproval. Pollsters probing this dimension of public opinion ask respondents to report their impressions of what significant others think about an issue, or to estimate the distribution of public opinion on the issue under study. In effect, measures of social support show how people define the nature of the consensus on issues.

Think of both informational and social support as giving predisposition "weight" or inertia. If, for example, people with a strong opinion on an issue hold a lot of information—pro and con—about that issue and see their particular position as being widely shared, then the direction and expression of the opinion are not likely to change. Much like the direction of a bowling ball is little affected by the air movement created by air conditioner and furnace fans, opinions with much informational and social support have great mass and are not susceptible to easy or quick change. On the other hand, even strongly held opinions can change if they are not backed by information and perceived social support. They can change direction as frequently and rapidly as a Ping-Pong™ ball in a wind storm!

In other words, describing and understanding public opinion requires greater measurement sensitivity and depth than the simple "yes-no" questions often used in telephone polling. Public opinion reflects a dynamic process of interpersonal and media communication on issues among groups and collectivities of people who have the capacity to act in similar ways. "Thinking together" often leads to "acting together," the real reason for understanding public opinion.

The Publics

First of all, discard notions about "the general public." The mosaic of the many different ethnic, racial, religious, geographic, political, occupational, social, and special-interest groupings that would be included make the general public concept of little, if any, value in public relations. Rather, effective programs that communicate and build relationships call for specifically defined "target publics." Without such specific definitions and detailed information about intended audiences of messages, how do program planners measure public opinion, establish program objectives, develop meaningful message and action strategies, select media to deliver messages selectively and effectively, and determine if the program worked?

Specific contemporary approaches to defining publics are discussed in Chapter 11, Planning and Programming, but the basic concept traces back to the early 1900s. Philosopher and educator John Dewey defined a public as an active social unit consisting of all those affected who recognize a common problem for which they can seek common solutions. He wrote that publics are formed by "recognition of evil consequence brought about a common interest." Without communication, however, it "will remain shadowy and formless, seeking spasmodically for itself, but seizing and holding its shadow rather than its substance."[49]

Grunig expands on Dewey's concept by outlining three factors that move *latent* publics to become communicating *active* publics:

1. **Problem recognition**   represents the extent to which people are aware that something is missing or amiss in a situation, thereby knowing that they need information.

2. **Constraint recognition**   represents the extent to which people see themselves limited by external factors, versus seeing that they can do something about the situation. If people think they can make a difference or have an effect on the problem situation, they will seek information to make plans for action.

3. **Level of involvement**   represents the extent to which people see themselves being involved and affected by a situation. In other words, the more they see themselves connected to a situation, the more likely they will communicate about it.[50]

After testing his "situational theory" of publics on a variety of environmental issues, Grunig concludes that environmental publics defined according to their communication behavioral similarities are not the same as those identified by demographic attributes or attitudes.[51] He consistently finds four types of publics:

1. **All-issue publics**   are active on all issues.
2. **Apathetic publics**   are inattentive and inactive on all issues.
3. **Single-issue publics**   are active on one or a limited number of related issues. (Such publics include the pro-life and animal rights groups.)
4. **Hot-issue publics**   are active after media expose almost everyone and the issue becomes the topic of widespread social conversation. ("Family values" during the 1992 presidential campaign and "global warming" created publics after attracting extensive media attention.)[52]

As suggested by Grunig's situational theory of publics, cross-situational definitions do not apply readily in specific situations. For example, useful definitions of publics go beyond demographics or "psychographics" to include relevant indicators of common recognition of mutual interests and situational variables that tie certain individuals, but not others, to specific situations or issues. In other words, publics result from specific issues or situations, not shared cross-situational traits. Dewey said that when

a church, a trade union, a business corporation, or an educational institution conducts itself so as to affect large numbers outside of itself, those who are affected form a public which endeavors to act through suitable structures, and thus to organize itself for oversight and regulation.[53]

Dewey's concept of a public logically extends to include structures, rules, sanctions, and punishments imposed by those affected when "it is deemed necessary to have those consequences systematically cared for."[54]

Specific issues and situations determine each public's composition, size, and range of responses. For example, an organization's philanthropic donation to support construction of a controversial abstract sculpture in a park can activate many individuals to respond in a variety of ways. Some, if not most, of those who see themselves "affected" by the organization's charity probably have no direct contact with the organization making the donation and do not live near the park. On the other hand, if the same organization proposes a complex restructuring of management and of its long-term debt, then only a few top executives who fear being laid off as a result of "right sizing," financial analysts, and institutional investors may respond to the proposed changes. From the perspective of the publics that come into existence in the two situations, a wider range of and more individuals are moved to react in a variety of ways by the charitable contribution than by the restructuring proposals. It is conceivable, however, that the "evil consequences" of restructuring will be much greater in the community than the existence of an avant-garde piece of public art.

INDIVIDUAL ORIENTATIONS AND COORIENTATION

The different publics and reactions stimulated by the two situations in the previous scenarios suggest both individual and shared orientations. Individual orientations, however, do not become "public opinion" until they are shared—or perceived to be shared—by others. The realization, rightly or wrongly, that an individual's views of a situation are similar to those held by others evokes a sense of identification among individuals and the perception of a common interest. In other words, individual orientations include perceptions of issues or objects in one's environment, as well as perceptions of significant others' views of those same issues or objects. When two or more individuals' orientations include the same issues or objects and each other, they are in a state of "coorientation."

Orientation

Individuals hold opinions of varying degrees of relevance and intensity. Individuals assign value to objects in their environment on the basis of both their previous history with the objects and their assessment of the objects in the current context. (See Figure 8–4.) The former value is *salience*, or the feelings about an object derived from an individual's experiences and reinforcements from previous situations. Salience refers to what the individual brings to a situation as a result of history. The second source of value is *pertinence*, which refers to the relative value of an object on the basis of object-by-object comparisons on the basis of some attribute or attributes. Pertinence value can vary depending on which attribute is used to make the comparison or what other objects are used in the comparison.[55] In other words, salience indicates how individuals feel about an object, independent of the situation, whereas pertinence depends on how the individual defines the situation. To describe and understand an individual's opinion about some object, then, you have to measure both salience and pertinence. The distinction helps clarify the relationship between attitudes and opinions.

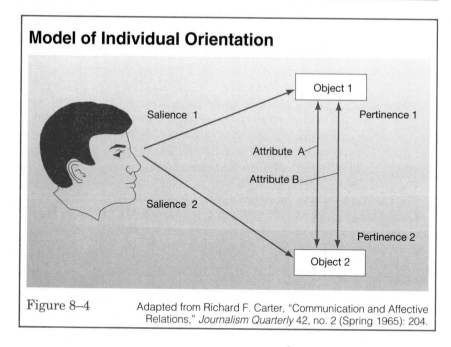

Model of Individual Orientation

Figure 8–4   Adapted from Richard F. Carter, "Communication and Affective
Relations," *Journalism Quarterly* 42, no. 2 (Spring 1965): 204.

An attitude is the cross-situational predisposition or preference with respect to an object. Attitudes predispose individuals to respond in certain ways toward objects from one situation to another, based on a lifetime of accumulating and evaluating information and experiences. *An opinion, on the other hand, is the judgment expressed about an object in a particular situation or given a specific set of circumstances.* Opinions tend to reflect an individual's related attitudes, but also take into account aspects of the current situation.

Scholars have generally distinguished between attitudes and opinions in two ways:

> First, opinions are generally considered to be verbal, or otherwise overt responses to a specific stimulus (an issue), while attitudes are more basic global tendencies to respond favorably or unfavorably to a general class of stimuli. While opinions are largely situational, attitudes are more enduring with a person across situations. Second, opinions are considered to be more cognitive and somewhat less affective in their makeup. . . . An attitude is an immediate, intuitive orientation while an opinion is a thought-out, reasoned choice between alternatives for action in a social matrix.[56]

The notion that opinions are expressed makes them important to the formation and study of public opinion. On the other hand, intrapersonal predisposition does not affect public opinion formation. Not until attitudes get expressed through opinions in discussion or other public com-

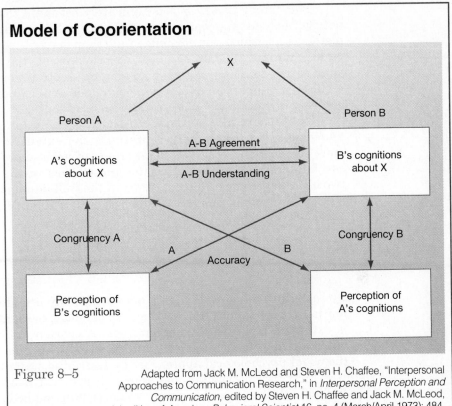

Model of Coorientation

Figure 8–5   Adapted from Jack M. McLeod and Steven H. Chaffee, "Interpersonal Approaches to Communication Research," in *Interpersonal Perception and Communication*, edited by Steven H. Chaffee and Jack M. McLeod, special edition of *American Behavioral Scientist* 16, no. 4 (March/April 1973): 484.

munication do they have an impact on the processes of forming and changing public opinion. That opinions are public expressions establishes public opinion as a social phenomenon.

Coorientation

The social or interpersonal concept of public opinion requires two or more individuals oriented to and communicating about an object of mutual interest. In other words, they are "cooriented" to something in common and to each other.

The coorientational model in Figure 8–5 illustrates the intrapersonal and interpersonal elements of communication relationships.[57] First, the *intrapersonal* construct of *congruency* describes the extent to which your own views match your estimate of another's views on the same issue. Some refer to this variable as "perceived agreement." On the basis of this estimate, you formulate strategies for dealing with the other person or for spontaneously responding in interactions.

The extent to which you accurately estimate the other's views determines the appropriateness of your actions. You surely recall instances in which you misjudged another person's position on some issue of mutual interest. *Accuracy*, then, represents the extent to which your estimate matches the other person's actual views. Because it requires a comparison of observations taken from two different people, accuracy represents an *interpersonal* construct.

The other interpersonal constructs include *agreement* and *understanding*. Agreement represents the extent to which two or more persons share similar *evaluations* of an issue of mutual interest. Understanding measures the similarities in the definitions of two or more persons. In terms used in the individual orientation paradigm, agreement compares saliences, whereas understanding compares pertinences.

Coorientational Consensus

By including many individuals simultaneously oriented to issues of mutual concern and interest, the interpersonal coorientational model is extended to large social groupings. A coorientational concept of public opinion in communities and society provides an alternative to the usual psychological approaches to describing states of consensus.

First, the coorientational approach does not use the traditional "individual agreement" approach to describing public opinion, that is, an aggregation of individual orientations to some issue or topic. Instead, the coorientational approach casts public opinion as the product of both individual perceptions on an issue and their perceptions of what significant others think about the same issue.

Social scientists long ago recognized the need to take into account *perceptions of agreement* in addition to *actual agreement*. Scheff, for one, argued that perceptions of agreement can be independent of actual agreement and that perceptions of agreement more likely affect public behavior than does actual agreement. In fact, it is often the case that those involved in issues of public debate do not know the state of actual agreement, operating instead on their perceptions of agreement.[58]

Conceiving public opinion—or consensus—in this way makes it a complex social phenomenon that can be described using coorientational concepts. For example, the state of *monolithic consensus* represents high levels of actual agreement accurately recognized as such by those involved. *Dissensus* exists when high levels of actual disagreement are accurately perceived as such. (See Table 8–1.)

Public opinion based on inaccurate perceptions of agreement are more troublesome in relationships. Unlike actual agreement or disagreement, however, inaccurate perceptions are at least subject to change as a result of effective communication. For example, after extended interac-

TABLE 8-1	TYPES OF COORIENTATIONAL CONSENSUS	
	Perceive that majority also agrees on issue	Perceive that majority does not agree on issue
Majority actually agree on issue	Monolithic Consensus	Pluralistic Ignorance
Majority does not agree on issue	False Consensus	Dissensus

Source: Adapted from Thomas J. Scheff, "Toward a Sociological Model of Consensus," *American Sociological Review* 32, no.1 (February 1967): 39.

tion, two or more persons may simply agree to disagree. At least they know where each other stands on the issue. The same cannot be said about situations based on inaccurate perceptions of each others' views.

False consensus exists when there is actual disagreement but the majority of those involved think they agree. *Pluralistic ignorance* represents the state of public opinion in which a majority perceive little agreement, but in fact there is widespread agreement. When those involved do not accurately recognize the state of actual agreement, they act on the basis of their inaccurate perceptions. In the cases of false consensus and pluralistic ignorance, their responses and public expressions (that is, public opinion) are not consistent with the actual distribution of individual orientations on issues of common interest. Accurate perceptions of others' views, however, are surely the most likely outcome of public communication and the greatest motivation for maintaining communication in society and in relationships.

What may appear as logical in the context of this discussion, however, apparently is not widely recognized by those who commission or practice public relations. Instead of trying to increase the accuracy of cross perceptions in social relationships, most communication efforts attempt to influence levels of agreement, or to "engineer consent." But actual agreement can exist independent of perceptions of agreement, leading to Scheff's more useful definition of coorientational public opinion:

> Complete consensus on an issue exists in a group [read "public"] when there is an infinite series of reciprocating understandings between the members of the group [read "public"] concerning the issue. I know that you know that I know, and so on.[59] (Words in brackets added.)

In the context of public relations, the coorientational approach to consensus and relationships also is useful for describing the nature of organization-public relationships.

Coorientational Relationships

The coorientational approach helps identify three public relations problems that call for rather straightforward communication strategies:

1. An organization and a public hold different definitions of an issue. They simply are not talking about the same thing when they engage in communication about "the issue." They are talking about different issues.

2. The organization's perceptions of a public's views of an issue (evaluations and/or definitions) do not match the public's actual views. Organizational management makes decisions about a public based on inaccurate estimates of the public's views. Not surprisingly, the relationship suffers when members of that public are subjected to the organization's actions and communications.

3. Members of a public hold inaccurate perceptions of an organization's positions on an issue of mutual concern. Public responses to the organization's management, its products, its actions and procedures, and so forth are based on inaccurate estimates of management policy and values.

Note that in all cases, the nature of the organization-public relationship is threatened by differing definitions and inaccurate perceptions, not disagreement over the issue itself. None of the situations calls for communication designed to change the level of agreement-disagreement on the issue. Communication that helps create shared definitions and increase accuracy improves the relationship and makes each side's dealings with the other more appropriate. (See Figure 8–6.)

For example, even though the Army Corps of Engineers communicated the advantages of a proposed flood-control project to the various publics who would be affected, they apparently did not do the same for the project's disadvantages. Convinced that the various publics supported the project, the Corps scheduled what was to be the final public hearing for project approval. Project planners were surprised by the suspicions, concerns, objections, and uncertainties expressed at the hearing. The project was delayed for the additional meetings and negotiations needed to improve accuracy in both the Corps's and publics' perceptions, of the project and each other's views.[60] Had the Corps initially used the coorientational approach to assess public opinion of the project, they might have identified their relationship problems and taken steps to avoid the costly delays.

As this example illustrates, the coorientational approach serves three major purposes in public relations planning. First, coorientational measures provide the information needed to identify and describe problems in organization-public relationships. Rather than defining problems in ways that limit strategies to those designed to increase agreement by changing public perceptions, this approach calls for an assessment of all parties' views to understand relationships.

Coorientational Model of Organization-Public Relationships

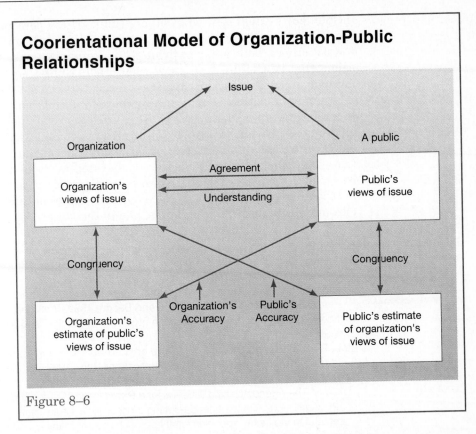

Figure 8–6

Second, coorientational measures provide useful guidance for planning appropriate messages and responses to correct organization-public relationship problems. Coorientational assessments of relationships can lead to atypical, yet efficient, solutions. For example, imagine that the analysis shows that management has an inaccurate perception of a public's views on an issue and, as a result, is proposing what will be an inappropriate action or response. Simply reporting the public's actual views on the issue to management may be the only corrective action needed.

Third, repeated use of coorientational measures indicates how the relationship changes as a result of the communication and other corrective actions. In other words, agreement, understanding, congruency, and accuracy serve as outcome criteria for assessing the impact of public relations efforts on organization-public relationships.[61]

In conclusion, public relations establishes and maintains relationships between organizations and their publics by—but not limited to—facilitating two-way communication. The communication, however, may have less impact on the extent to which parties agree or disagree than on the accuracy of their cross perceptions of each other's views. In the final analysis, Lippmann's "pictures in our heads" of the "world outside" include our estimates of what others think. These perceptions of social reality lead to the formation of active publics and condition actions toward others, both other individuals and organizations. As Lippmann said, "That is why until we know what others think they know, we cannot truly understand their acts."[62]

Communication, then, not only moves information from one party in a relationship to another, but also defines the relationships and social environment within which we all function: as citizens, employees, managers, and policy makers. Not surprisingly, the media of communication—the topic of the next chapter—play essential roles in shaping both issues and their social contexts. Mass media make possible the "thinking together" that shapes and represents the states of consensus in complex organizations, in communities, and in the larger global society.

ADDITIONAL READINGS

Hennessy, Bernard. *Public Opinion*, 5th ed. Monterey, Calif.: Brooks/Cole Publishing Company, 1985.

Knapp, Mark L., and Anita L. Vangelisti. *Interpersonal Communication and Human Relationships*. Boston: Allyn and Bacon, 1992. Summary of literature and theory related to dialogue, interaction rituals, relationships, and other aspects of relational communication.

Rice, Ronald E., and Charles K. Atkin, eds. *Public Communication Campaigns*, 2d ed. Newbury Park, Calif.: Sage Publications, Inc., 1989.

Rogers, Everett M., James W. Dearing, and Soonbum Chang. "AIDS in the 1980s: The Agenda-Setting Process for a Public Issue," *Journalism Monographs* 126 (April 1991). Traces agenda-setting process for a single issue over time, in contrast to the usual cross-sectional approach used in many agenda-setting studies.

Salmon, Charles T., ed. *Information Campaigns: Balancing Social Values and Social Change*, Sage Annual Reviews of Communication Research, vol. 18. Newbury Park, Calif.: Sage Publications, Inc., 1989.

Van Leuven, James K., and Michael D. Slater. "How Publics, Public Relations, and the Media Shape the Public Opinion Process." *Public Relations Research Annual* 3 (1991): 165–78.

NOTES

[1]Frederick Williams, *The New Communications*, 3d ed. (Belmont, Calif.: Wadsworth Publishing Company, 1992), 9.

[2]Walter Lippmann, *Public Opinion* (New York: Harcourt, Brace and Company), 1922, 3 and 4.

[3]Paul F. Lazarsfeld, Bernard Berelson, and Hazel Gaudet, *The People's Choice: How the Voter Makes Up His Mind in a Presidential Campaign*, 3d ed. (New York: Columbia University Press, 1968), 151.

[4]Warren Weaver, "The Mathematics of Communication," in *Communication and Culture: Reading in the Codes of Human Interaction*, edited by Alfred G. Smith (New York: Holt, Rinehart and Winston, 1966), 17. Reprinted from *Scientific American*, 181 (1949): 11–15. Original theory published in Claude E. Shannon and Warren Weaver, *The Mathematical Theory of Communication* (Urbana: University of Illinois Press, 1949).

[5]Ibid., 17.

[6]Wilbur Schramm,   "The Nature of Communication Between Humans," in *The Process and Effects of Mass Communication*, rev. ed., edited by Wilbur Schramm and Donald F. Roberts (Urbana: University of Illinois Press, 1971), 17.

[7]Ibid., 38–47.

[8]Carl I. Hovland, Irving L. Janis, and Harold H. Kelley,   *Communication and Persuasion* (New Haven, Conn.: Yale University Press, 1953). The World War II "Yale studies" provided the foundation for persuasion theory still used for designing both persuasion effects research and public communication campaigns.

[9]Norman H. Anderson,   "Integration Theory and Attitude Change," *Psychological Review* 78, no. 3 (May 1971): 171–206.

[10]Adapted from Carl I. Hovland, Arthur A. Lumsdaine, and Fred D. Sheffield,   "The Effect of Presenting 'One Side' versus 'Both Sides' in Changing Opinions on a Controversial Subject," in *Experiments on Mass Communication* (Princeton: N.J.: Princeton University Press, 1949), 201–27. Also in Schramm and Roberts,   *The Process and Effects of Mass Communication*, 467–84.

[11]Arthur A. Lumsdaine and Irving L. Janis,   "Resistance to 'Counterpropaganda' Produced by One-Sided and Two-Sided 'Propaganda' Presentations," *Public Opinion Quarterly* 17, no. 3 (1953): 311–18. See also William J. McGuire, "Persuasion, Resistance, and Attitude Change," in *Handbook of Communication*, edited by Ithiel de Sola Pool and others (Skokie, Ill.: Rand McNally, 1973), 216–52.

[12]Adapted from Richard L. Wiseman and William Schenck-Hamlin,   "A Multidimensional Scaling Validation of an Inductively-Derived Set of Compliance-Gaining Strategies," *Communication Monographs* 48, no. 4 (December 1981): 257–58.

[13]Carl I. Hovland, ed.,   *The Order of Presentation in Persuasion* (New Haven, Conn.: Yale University Press, 1957). Reports series of experiments from the Yale studies of message effects in persuasion. The order of presentation, however, turned out to be a relatively minor factor in the communication process, inspiring little research over the years.

[14]Reported in Hovland, Janis, and Kelley,   *Communication and Persuasion.*

[15]Ronald W. Rogers,   "A Protection Motivation Theory of Fear Appeals and Attitude Change," *Journal of Psychology* 91 (September 1975): 93–114. See also Rogers and C. R. Mewborn,   "Fear Appeals and Attitude Change: Effects of a Threat's Noxiousness, Probability of Occurrence, and the Efficacy of Coping Responses," *Journal of Personality and Social Psychology* 34, no. 1 (July 1976): 54–61.

[16]Michael Burgoon,   "Messages and Persuasive Effects," in *Message Effects in Communication Science*, Sage Annual Reviews of Communication Research vol. 17, edited by James J. Bradac (Newbury Park, Calif.: Sage Publications, Inc., 1989), 157.

[17]From letter to the editor, "Success Story for On-Line News," by Katharine Marshall, director, Internal Communications, Unisys, Blue Bell, Penn., in *IABC Communication World* 9, no. 6 (May–June 1992): 5.

[18]See Gerald R. Miller,   "Interpersonal Communication," chapter 5 in *Human Communication: Theory and Research*, edited by Gordon L. Dahnke and Glen W. Clatterbuck (Belmont, Calif.: Wadsworth Publishing Company, 1990), 91–122, for a review of interpersonal communication.

[19]Marshall McLuhan,   *Understanding Media: The Extensions of Man* (New York: McGraw-Hill, 1965), 7.

[20]Shearon A. Lowery and Melvin L. DeFleur, *Milestones in Mass Communication Research: Media Effects*, 2d ed. (New York: Longman, Inc., 1988). Summarizes 13 major studies that attempted to document media effects.

[21]Frederic Wertham, *Seduction of the Innocent* (New York: Rinehart, 1954). See Lowery and DeFleur, *Milestones in Mass Communication Research*, 213–43, for a summary of Wertham's all-out condemnation of comic books.

[22]Wilbur Schramm, Jack Lyle, and Edwin B. Parker, *Television in the Lives of Our Children* (Stanford, Calif.: Stanford University Press, 1961). See Lowery and DeFleur, *Milestones in Mass Communication Research*, 245–70, for a summary.

[23]Herbert E. Krugman, "The Impact of Television Advertising: Learning without Involvement," in *The Process and Effects of Mass Communication*, edited by Schramm and Roberts, 485–94. (First published in *Public Opinion Quarterly* 24: 349–56.) See also Krugman, "Memory without Recall, Exposure without Perception," *Journal of Advertising Research* 17, no. 4: 7–12.

[24]William Miller, "A View from the Inside: Brainwaves and Television Viewing," *Journalism Quarterly* 62, no. 3 (Autumn 1985): 508–14.

[25]Summary of "Developing Frameworks for Studying Mass Communication," chapter 1 in Lowery and DeFleur, *Milestones in Mass Communication Research*, 1–29.

[26]Lowery and DeFleur, *Milestones in Mass Communication Research*, 151–61.

[27]Brenda Dervin, "Audience as Listener and Learner, Teacher and Confidante: The Sense-Making Approach," in *Public Communication Campaigns*, 2d ed., edited by Ronald E. Rice and Charles K. Atkin (Newbury Park, Calif.: Sage Publications, Inc., 1989), 69.

[28]William K. Rawlins, "A Dialectical Analysis of the Tensions, Functions and Strategic Challenges of Communication in Young Adult Friendships," in *Communication Yearbook 12*, edited by James A. Anderson (Newbury Park, Calif.: Sage Publications, Inc., 1989), 157–89.

[29]Michael E. Roloff, "Communication and Conflict," in *Handbook of Communication Science*, edited by Charles R. Berger and Steven H. Chaffee (Newbury Park, Calif.: Sage Publications, Inc., 1987), 484–536. See also Charles Watkins, "An Analytical Model of Conflict," *Speech Monographs* 41, no. 1 (1974): 1–5.

[30]Stephen W. Littlejohn, *Theories of Human Communication*, 4th ed. (Belmont, Calif.: Wadsworth Publishing Company, 1992), 265–66. Good survey of communication theory. See also Judee K. Burgoon and Jerold L. Hale, "The Fundamental Topoi of Relational Communication," *Communication Monographs* 51 (1984): 193–214.

[31]Littlejohn, *Theories of Human Communication*, 265–66.

[32]Marvin E. Shaw and Dennis S. Gouran, "Group Dynamics and Communication," in *Human Communication: Theory and Research*, edited by Gordon L. Dahnke and Glen W. Clatterbuck (Belmont, Calif.: Wadsworth Publishing Company, 1990), 123–55.

[33]Randy Y. Hirokawa, "Group Communication and Decision Making Performance: A Continued Test of the Functional Perspective," *Human Communication Research* 14, no. 4 (Summer 1988): 487–515.

[34]Walter Lippmann, "The World Outside and the Pictures in Our Heads," chapter 1, *Public Opinion* (New York: Harcourt, Brace and Company, 1922).

Reprinted in *The Process and Effects of Mass Communication*, rev. ed., edited by Schramm and Roberts, 265–86.

[35]Maxwell E. McCombs and Donald L. Shaw,   "The Agenda-Setting Function of Mass Media," *Public Opinion Quarterly* 36, no. 2 (Summer 1972): 176–87. First of many reports of media agenda-setting effects on a variety of issues in a variety of settings.

[36]Maxwell McCombs, Edna Einsiedel, and David Weaver,   *Contemporary Public Opinion: Issues and the News* (Hillsdale, N.J.: Lawrence Earlbaum Associates, Publishers, 1991), 12–17.

[37]Ibid., 17–21.

[38]Steven H. Chaffee,   "The Interpersonal Context of Mass Communication," in *Current Perspectives in Mass Communication Research*, vol. 1, edited by F. Gerald Kline and Phillip J. Tichenor (Beverly Hills, Calif.: Sage Publications, Inc., 1972), 95–120.

[39]Everett M. Rogers,   "Communication and Social Change," in *Human Communication*, edited by Dahnke and Clatterbuck, 259–71.

[40]Ibid.

[41]Elisabeth Noelle-Neumann,   "The Theory of Public Opinion: The Concept of Spiral of Silence," in *Communication Yearbook 14*, edited by James A. Anderson (Newbury Park, Calif.: Sage Publications, Inc., 1991), 256–87. Noelle-Neumann first published her theory in "The Spiral of Silence: A Theory of Public Opinion," *Journal of Communication* 24, no. 2 (Spring 1974): 43–51, and later in book form, *The Spiral of Silence: Public Opinion—Our Social Skin* (Chicago: University of Chicago Press, 1984).

[42]Lippmann,   *Public Opinion*, 14.

[43]Melvin L. DeFleur and Sandra J. Ball-Rokeach,   *Theories of Mass Communication,* 4th ed. (New York: Longman, Inc., 1982), 226.

[44]Edward M. Block,   "How Public Opinion Is Formed," *Public Relations Review* 3, no. 3 (Fall 1977): 15.

[45]Ibid., 10.

[46]Vincent Price and Donald F. Roberts,   "Public Opinion Processes," in *Handbook of Communication Science*, edited by Berger and Chaffee, 784.

[47]Ibid., 782–83.

[48]Dan Drew and David Weaver,   "Media Attention, Media Exposure, and Media Effects," *Journalism Quarterly* 67, no. 4 (Winter 1990): 740–48.

[49]John Dewey,   *The Public and Its Problems* (New York: Henry Holt and Company, 1927), 15–17.

[50]James E. Grunig and Fred C. Repper,   "Strategic Management, Publics, and Issues," in *Excellence in Public Relations and Communication Management*, edited by James E. Grunig (Hillsdale, N.J.: Lawrence Erlbaum Associates, Publishers, 1992), 135–37.

[51]See also James E. Grunig,   "Communication Behaviors and Attitudes of Environmental Publics: Two Studies," *Journalism Monographs* 81 (March 1983): 40–41.

[52]Grunig and Repper,   "Strategic Management, Publics, and Issues," 139.

[53]Dewey,   *The Public and Its Problems*, 28–29.

[54]Ibid., 16.

[55]Concepts and paradigm of individual orientation adapted from Richard F. Carter,   "Communication and Affective Relations," *Journalism Quarterly* 42, no. 2 (Spring 1965): 203–12.

[56]Price and Roberts, "Public Opinion Processes," 787.

[57]Model and coorientational concepts from Jack M. McLeod and Steven H. Chaffee, "Interpersonal Approaches to Communication Research," in *Interpersonal Perception and Communication*, edited by Steven H. Chaffee and Jack M. McLeod, special edition of *American Behavioral Scientist* 16, no. 4 (March/April 1973): 483–88.

[58]Thomas J. Scheff, "Toward a Sociological Model of Consensus," *American Sociological Review* 32, no. 1 (February 1967): 32–46.

[59]Ibid., 37.

[60]Keith R. Stamm and John E. Bowes, "Communicating During an Environmental Decision," *Journal of Environmental Education* 3, no. 3 (Spring 1972): 49–56.

[61]Glen M. Broom, "Coorientational Measurement of Public Issues," *Public Relations Review* 3, no. 4 (Winter 1977): 110–19. See also Glen M. Broom and David M. Dozier, *Using Research in Public Relations* (Englewood Cliffs, N.J.: Prentice-Hall, Inc., 1990): 36–39.

[62]Lippmann, *Public Opinion*, 13.

CHAPTER 9

Media and Media Relations

Every newspaper when it reaches the reader is the result of a whole series of selections as to what items shall be printed, in what position they shall be printed, how much space each shall occupy, what emphasis each shall have. There are no objective standards here. There are conventions.[1]

WALTER LIPPMAN

Practitioners of public relations use printed words, spoken words, images, and combinations of all these communication forms. They use both *controlled media* and *uncontrolled media* to communicate with their organizations' many publics. Controlled media include those in which practitioners have the say over what is said, how it is said, when it is said, and—to some extent—to whom it is said. Uncontrolled media are those over which practitioners have no direct role in decision making about media content. Instead, media gatekeepers decide what is reported, how it is reported, when it is reported, and to whom it is reported.

Technology is changing our notions about media, especially the concept of "mass media." As one scholar concluded, "The net effect of all these technologies will be to make channels, and the kinds of content they carry, differentially available to the public."[2] Notions about mass, undifferentiated passive audiences are also being outdated as interactive media replace conventional one-way channels. Technology that was originally developed to increase output has often resulted in more individualized communications.

For example, computerized word processing and high-speed printers began by generating large numbers of letters with the *appearance* of being addressed to individuals. Now, more sophisticated software programs linked to databases produce letters that address individuals by name and with respect to specific information needs. Individually targeted direct mail has changed the media mix in many advertising budgets and is increasingly being used to reach individuals with important public relations messages. Some meeting and convention planners are incorporating interactive audience response systems such as IRIS to get immediate feedback on topics being discussed. Movie producers are experimenting with audience participation in determining story lines and outcomes with interactive systems to replace passive movie viewing. Faxes and call-in polls have made even magazines and television two-way media. Fiber-optic systems hold promise for creating veritable information freeways that can change communication, commerce, and social relationships at all levels. In short, media are undergoing rapid change and "demassification."

What follows is a snapshot of the major media as they are now used and some of the developments that hold promise for the future. The first part of this chapter examines the media used primarily for—but not limited to—communicating with internal publics. The second section reviews media used for reaching large and dispersed, primarily external, publics. The chapter concludes with a discussion of media relations, one of public relations' primary assignments.

MEDIA FOR INTERNAL PUBLICS

An organization's most important relationships are those with employees at all levels. The terms *internal publics* and *employee publics* refer to both the supervisors as well as those being supervised. These publics represent an organization's greatest resource, its people. According to Alvie Smith, former director of corporate communications at General Motors, two factors are changing employee communication and enhancing management's respect for this part of the public relations task:

1. The value of understanding, teamwork, and commitment by employees in achieving bottom-line results. These positive aspects of worker behavior are strongly influenced by effective, way-of-life interactive communications throughout the organization.

2. The need to build a strong manager-communication network, one that makes every supervisor at every level accountable for communicating effectively with his or her employees. This needs to be more than just job-related information and should included key business and public issues affecting the total organization.[3]

In Smith's view, organizations miss out on a sizable share of their human resource potential because they do not put a high priority on effective, two-way communication as the foundation for management-employee relations and overall job performance. He calls the consequence of result "slothing on the job":

The ugly truth is that employee disloyalty and lack of commitment to organizational goals may be costing American businesses more than $50 billion a year. This is probably a conservative figure when you include the cost of absenteeism, labor grievances, production interruptions, poor quality, repair and warranty expenses for fixing poor quality and—highly important—owner disloyalty, loss of repeat customer sales and credibility. Perhaps most costly of all is inaction by employees who withhold their best efforts and ideas; who cruise along with just passable performance.[4]

The coordination and mediation necessary for dealing with employees today puts the public relations staff, with its communication savvy and skills, square in the middle of managing internal relationships. Apple Computer, for example, sees employee communication "as a key factor in maintaining a wide-open progressive work environment as well as the most important channel in keeping a far-flung, empowered and decentralized organization aligned and coordinated."[5] Delta Air Lines chairman and CEO, Ronald W. Allen, who rose through the ranks by running departments such as personnel and training, sees his primary job as cultivating a motivated and loyal work force.[6]

Day-to-day working relationships involve a great deal of contact, but effective employee communication develops in a climate of trust. Ideally, working relationships are characterized by at least seven conditions:

1. Confidence and trust between employer and employees
2. Candid information flowing freely up, down, and sideways
3. Satisfying status and participation for each person
4. Continuity of work without strife
5. Healthful surrounding
6. Success for the enterprise
7. Optimism about the future

The chief executive must establish that climate and underwrite it as formal policy. Even with such support from the top, however, many barriers stand in the way of free-flowing, two-way communication in organizations.

Opinion Research Corporation has tracked employee opinions of organizational internal communication since 1950. Large majorities consistently give their organizations favorable scores on *credibility*, but less than half say their organizations do a good job of letting them know

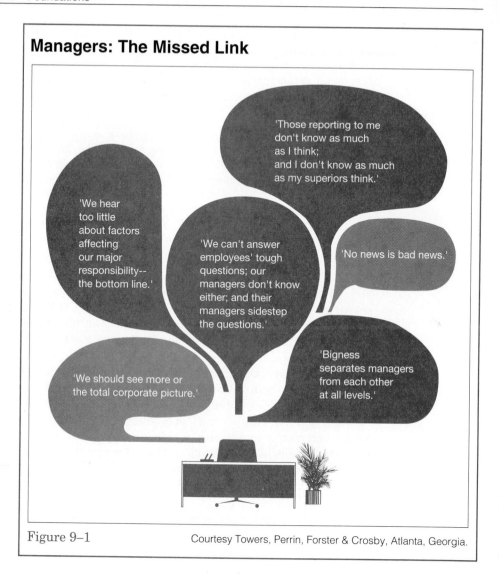

Managers: The Missed Link

'Those reporting to me
don't know as much
as I think;
and I don't know as much
as my superiors think.'

'We hear
too little
about factors
affecting
our major
responsibility--
the bottom line.'

'We can't answer
employees' tough
questions; our
managers don't know
either; and their
managers sidestep
the questions.'

'No news is bad news.'

'Bigness
separates managers
from each other
at all levels.'

'We should see more or
the total corporate picture.'

Figure 9–1   Courtesy Towers, Perrin, Forster & Crosby, Atlanta, Georgia.

what is going on, or *downward communication*. Similarly, less than half give high marks to their organizations' willingness to listen to their views, or *upward communication*. A similar survey conducted by the consulting firm Towers, Perrin, Forster and Crosby found the grapevine second only to immediate supervisors as employees' major source of organizational information. Nine out of ten surveyed ranked their immediate supervisor as the "preferred source" and ranked the grapevine as the least preferred source. (See Figure 9–1.)

The Wyatt Company survey of corporate readers of its employee communication newsletter identified "help employees understand business direction/mission" as the number one objective of employee communication programs. Employee publications, bulletin boards, group meetings, personnel handbooks, and memos are the most frequently used media for management communication directed to employees. Face-to-face communication with an "open-door policy" is the primary medium for encouraging upward communication and building good working relationships with employees.

Balancing the needs for employee satisfaction with the success of the enterprise is but one aspect of the continuous adjustment and reconciliation in the employer-employee relationship. As a part of the larger public relations function, however, *the goals of employee communication are to establish and maintain mutually beneficial relationships between an organization and the employees on whom its success or failure depends.*

PRINTED WORDS

Even with the advance of computers and other communication technology, printed publications remain the primary media for internal communication in most organizations. For example, telecommunication giant AT&T mails its monthly flagship publication, *AT&T Focus*, to every employee's home. Imagine the competition for attention the publication must overcome when it reaches the 250,000 homes of AT&T's employees and their families. The usual goals of such publications include:

1. Keeping employees informed of the organization's lines of business, direction, and goals
2. Providing employees the information they need to perform their assignments proficiently
3. Encouraging employees to maintain and enhance the organization's standards for and commitment to quality improvement, increased efficiency, improved service, and greater social responsibility
4. Recognizing employees' achievements and successes

Each publication, each issue, each printed word is part of a coordinated employee communication program designed to achieve these and specific goals set in response to particular organizational settings and situations. Because of their impact, permanence, and reference value, printed words remain the "workhorses" of employee communication.

Organizational Publications

Estimates of the number of organizational publications in the United States range from 100,000 up to more than a million, if you count all the newsletters. Probably two thirds are internal, or employee, publications.

Their impact, formerly considered indirect—even "intangible"—is now viewed as direct and measurable.

An organizational publication can take the form of a simple newsletter, a tabloid newspaper, a "magapaper" that combines the format of a newspaper with the style of a magazine, or a magazine. Many are high-quality, four-color publications. A few carry advertising to help pay the costs of production. In Great Britain some industrial firms sell their organizational magazines rather than give them away. They take the position that employees tend to place more value on the publications if they have monetary worth. Two out of every three British coal miners, for example, buy the *Coal News* tabloid newspaper published by the National Coal Board.

All organizational publications have these characteristics in common: They satisfy the organizational need to go on record with its positions and to communicate information essential for achieving organizational objectives; they permit the organization to deliver messages to specific target publics; and they let the organization communicate in its own words, in its own way, without interruption or alteration. In short, they give the organization a means of controlled communications.

The organizational publication is versatile. It can be edited to serve the narrow interests of its sponsor. It can be edited to shed light on issues important to employees and other publics. Most often it combines editorial content that both espouses the sponsor's point of view and addresses concerns of targeted publics. (Without the latter, of course, it will die for lack of readers outside the inner circle of top management.)

Organization publications are directed to many publics, but the most common use is in employee communication. Practitioners responding to surveys usually rate employees as a primary audience for organizational publications. The major advantage of publications is their ability to deliver specific and detailed information to narrowly defined target publics. As a result of this characteristic, many organizations have several employee publications, each one designed to meet the information needs of particular employee groups. For example, because about half of Callaway Vineyards' employees speak Spanish, it prints its employee publication in both English and Spanish. Ciba-Geigy Canada Ltd. publishes its employee publications in both English and French. The front cover and pages to the center staple are in one language; flip the publication and the back cover becomes the cover for the half published in the other language.

There is a trend toward making publications two-way: inviting questions and conducting surveys, then reporting the results. (See Figure 9–2.) This requires the full cooperation of top management because of the time required to respond to questions and the expense of conducting surveys. Two-way communication also demands a climate of trust. Employees are often reluctant to submit questions or to write for publication. Nonetheless, internal publications provide an excellent mechanism for feedback and responsive communication.

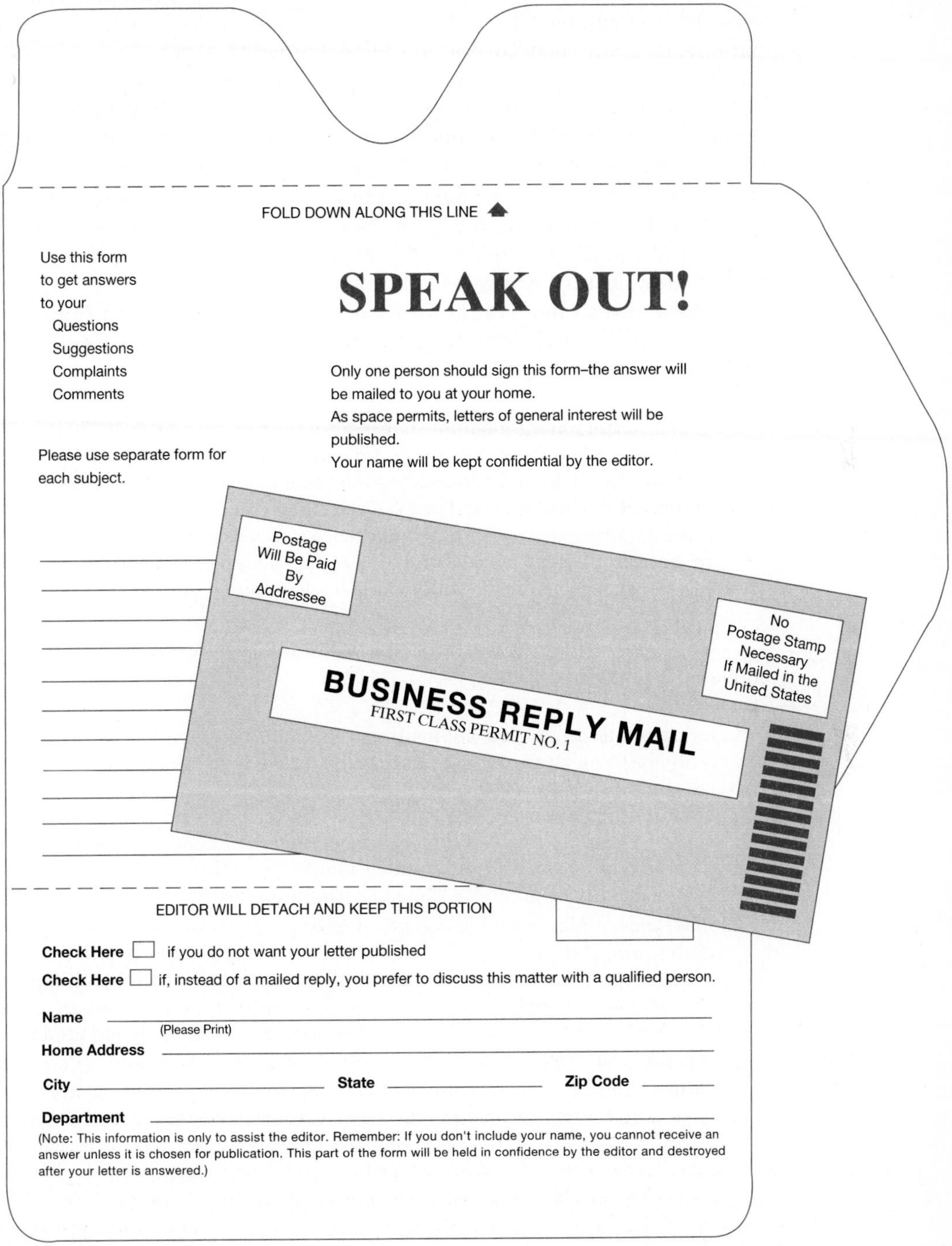

FOLD DOWN ALONG THIS LINE ⬆

Use this form
to get answers
to your
   Questions
   Suggestions
   Complaints
   Comments

Please use separate form for
each subject.

SPEAK OUT!

Only one person should sign this form–the answer will
be mailed to you at your home.
As space permits, letters of general interest will be
published.
Your name will be kept confidential by the editor.

Postage
Will Be Paid
By
Addressee

No
Postage Stamp
Necessary
If Mailed in the
United States

BUSINESS REPLY MAIL
FIRST CLASS PERMIT NO. 1

EDITOR WILL DETACH AND KEEP THIS PORTION

Check Here ☐ if you do not want your letter published

Check Here ☐ if, instead of a mailed reply, you prefer to discuss this matter with a qualified person.

Name _____
       (Please Print)

Home Address _____

City _____ **State** _____ **Zip Code** _____

Department _____

(Note: This information is only to assist the editor. Remember: If you don't include your name, you cannot receive an answer unless it is chosen for publication. This part of the form will be held in confidence by the editor and destroyed after your letter is answered.)

Figure 9–2

Cost effectiveness is a requirement for most organizational publications. Impact can be achieved without straining the budget or using special effects. Four-color covers and slick enameled papers are not essential. The primary requirements are for specific communication objectives that support organizational goals and meet the information needs of employee readers. Candor, intelligent selection of subject matter, simple format, and the constant goal of helping readers learn as much as they desire about matters of common interest all contribute to success.

Newsletters are the most common form of periodical publication. Because of readily available and inexpensive desktop publishing technology, newsletters are relatively easy, fast, and inexpensive to produce. As a result, most organizations rely on newsletters to communicate news in a timely and targeted fashion. According to Paul Swift, managing editor of the *Newsletter on Newsletters*:

> Newsletters are a medium that is here to stay . . . and grow. . . .
> There is more value being put on targeting communication with the corporate world and between associations and their members, as opposed to mass media. They [newsletters] are good for getting a specific message to a targeted audience in a specific context. Narrowcasting—what newsletters are, as opposed to broadcasting—is growing coincidentally with the desktop revolution.[7]

Supplemental publications—pamphlets, brochures, manuals, and books—have three major uses:

1. **Indoctrination.** These publications welcome new employees, members, students, or visitors. Indoctrination literature helps the newcomer get off on the right foot. It spells out the rules of the organization and the benefits of playing by the rules. It seeks to instill an attitude of team spirit by communicating that the newcomer has joined a winning team. ("Collateral materials" and product manuals for the consumer or product owner usually originate in the marketing function.)

2. **Reference.** Many publications deal with group insurance plans, pension plans, suggestion systems, hospitalization programs, profit sharing, housekeeping and safety, recreation programs and facilities, training and educational programs, and organizational policies and procedures. These handbooks give employees or members specific information and guidance.

3. **Institutional.** These typically spell out the organization's philosophy, values, and guiding principles. Messages relate to quality, competitiveness, environmental issues, the free-enterprise system, social responsibility, multicultural diversity, and the organization's role in the community. Other reports are tied to dedications, celebration, awards, history, organizational success, founders, and organizational "heroes." An example of this type of publication is Dow Chemical Canada's *Dow's Secret Weapons*, a book summarizing Dow's day-to-day operational philosophies. The content consists mainly of quotations from internal presentations and publications by Dow executives and directors, along with well-known authors on corporate management.

There are no "most effective" formats or methods for distributing handbooks. Dow sent *Dow's Secret Weapons* to selected executives and waited for others to request copies. It became a valued reference for hundreds of managers as the public relations staff filled orders. Sometimes books are written by authors commissioned to produce organizational books distributed in the commercial book market, in addition to serving internal institutional purposes. For example, *Schweppes, The First 200 Years* chronicles the history of the originator of carbonated mineral water and the soft-drink industry.

Organizational books are found in libraries, reception lobbies, wall racks, and employee lounges. They are usually mailed to leaders in community, business and industry, education, government, and the financial community. Employees and members get their copies either at work or in the mail at home. Dealers' copies are delivered by sales representatives. Books published by government agencies are available from the Superintendent of Documents. Associations often issue such books as part of convention or meeting packets, or they mail copies to members.

Books and lengthy booklets tracing the history of organizations or biographies of founders are usually subsidized by sponsors and published by commercial publishers. Sponsors distribute copies to libraries and selected influentials. Although high in initial cost, sponsored books can pay long-term dividends if they are accurate, well written, and distributed to appropriate libraries and individuals. Once catalogued into libraries, such histories become source material for writers, students, and others doing research on organizations and their founders.

Basic questions must be considered: (1) Does the type of book under consideration fit the needs it is designed to fill? (2) Will the nature and purpose of the book attract a capable outside writer? (3) Is the book to be sold commercially or given away? (4) Should it have a prestige hard cover or be a paperback? (5) What are possible tie-ins to promote it? (6) Does it further the organization's basic public relations objectives?

Letters

Even in the age of fax, E-mail, and cellular phones, *letters* remain the backbone of internal and external organizational communication. With the aid of computerized word processing, individualized letters are being used increasingly to establish direct, speedy communication with employees and other specific publics. Letters supplement the slower, less frequently published employee magazine. They offer an opportunity for the chief executive to communicate with employees and their families in a conversational, personalized, and newsy manner. Among their advantages are economy, direct and individualized approach, impressive appearance, impact, and speed. Letters support line communication by ensuring the accuracy of information, pointing out what is important and newsworthy in the organization's affairs, and adding importance to line communication. This support is increasingly important in large, diversified organizations.

Letters go from organization officials to community opinion leaders, to members of selected professions such as medicine or education, to legislators, suppliers, retailers, or media executives and reporters. Computers and high-speed printers have replaced typewriters, mimeograph machines, and offset presses for reproducing letters. The obvious advantage of individualized addresses and salutations, in addition to specific references in the body, make word processing the preferred method.

Even more important than periodic letters is an organization's daily correspondence. The normal flow of letters and memos constitutes an important and influential means of communication. The importance of effective letters that evoke pleased reactions, not irritation or confusion, is obvious. Yet many organizations continue in the rut of cold, stilted, hackneyed letters that do more to confuse and obscure than to clarify.

Inserts and Enclosures

Anyone who has received bills from utilities or oil companies knows about *inserts and enclosures*. A common form is the "payroll stuffer" that goes into paycheck envelopes. Typical uses range from news vignettes to offers of merchandise and services. The insert is an important public relations medium for appealing to natural constituencies for support and for important notices and news. Examples include calls for employees or stockholders to write legislators in support of an organization's stand on a public policy issue or notification of changes in benefits or procedures.

One obvious advantage of the insert is that the message goes to a favorably predisposed audience. Readership and receptivity can be high. Another advantage is economy. A small, lightweight printed insert need not add to the postage or change the classification of the mail.

Reprinted Speeches, Position Papers, and "Backgrounders"

Expressing an organization's position in reprints is a common method of communicating with select publics about controversial issues and public policy. The simple explanation is that as more organizations find their traditional policies and methods under investigation or challenge, they respond formally in speeches or by providing testimony in congressional hearings. Reprinting their responses in their entirety provides full disclosure of what was said and offers a rebuttal to the sometimes selective reporting by news media.

The major uses are to inform and reassure important individuals concerned about issues of mutual interest. Thus these materials are sent to employees, legislators and other government officials, financial analysts, leaders of pressure groups, the media, and community opinion leaders. The downside of this medium is that it sometimes serves primarily to massage the egos of executives espousing narrow interests and speaking in glittering generalities, or trying to win business for the organization by touting its products or services. Typically, readers see through these transparent uses.

A similar method of extending the reach of limited circulation materials is reprinting articles from publications. With permission from the original publications, favorable publicity, analyses of important issues, and other coverage of interest to an organization's publics can be reprinted and distributed. This adds control to what would otherwise be uncontrolled media coverage.

Bulletin Boards

The use of *bulletin boards* is widespread and here to stay. If there were no other reason, laws requiring the posting of an ever-increasing number of notices would preserve this medium. The nature of the medium is changing, however, as large numbers of employees in many organizations work at computer terminals that have the capability of "electronic bulletin boards" and messages. Their workdays often begin with a check of their E-mail for notices and messages on their terminals.

Bulletin boards offer a good place to corroborate information with brief messages publicly. They provide quick access for spiking rumors and for making desirable information stick. The dynamic board gets regular attention; it needs to be updated often. Seeing the same notice again and again becomes an annoyance and soon leads to inattention. In somewhat the same category are the *posters and placards* on walls or columns in work areas. The themes of such posters are usually safety, health, housekeeping, productivity, and security.

To work with all these publications, practitioners must know desktop publishing and be skilled in writing, editing, photography, layout, and design. For most, the monitor screen has replaced the paper page as the primary medium for producing "printed words" in the computerized information age.

The important thing to remember about publications is that they supplement, not replace, the face-to-face communication needed in successful work relationships. A handbook for the new employee is no substitute for the personal handshake, for a thorough orientation program and tour, or for regular and frequent communications from immediate supervisors.

Publications and the printed word are being redefined as communication technology makes new media available. T. Michael Forney predicted in 1982 that the information age would change public relations in ways similar to what Gutenberg's press did to calligraphers: "Within the next decade, the computer will be as commonplace in the home and office as the telephone is today." He was right. He also correctly predicted that organizational publications would be replaced by something that will take full advantage of new, enhanced communication linkages, including the following:

1. Instant contact, rather than the present cumbersome, time-consuming production process from typewriter, to printer, to mailroom, to desk.
2. Message flexibility, which allows information to be tailored automatically to different levels and types of employees.
3. Instant file and retrieval, which provides ready access to past information, at the touch of a key.
4. Interactivity, offering users the opportunity to get the information they want, in the form and detail they want, and ask for further clarification if they so desire.[8]

Paradoxically, the newspaper *USA Today* dropped paper entirely for its internal newsletters. It circulates four electronic letters, one for each of the paper's sections—News, Money, Sports and Life—by video display terminal. According to public relations manager Steve H. Anderson, "It's the easiest and most efficient way to get company news out to the employees."[9]

SPOKEN WORDS

New means of verbal communication also are changing and enhancing traditional face-to-face communication, but the oldest form of all still deserves first attention.

The Grapevine

The grapevine is neither a formal nor controlled medium, but word of mouth is often the quickest means for communicating some information. The grapevine is a potent line of communication. It carries information much more exciting than simple facts or truth.

Sometimes the grapevine is actually harmful, or threatens to be. Rumors of downsizing and layoff, of a hostile takeover by a competitor, of friction among officials, of sexual harassment charges, or of bad blood between factions can hurt. The word travels far beyond the local group, becoming more and more distorted as it spreads. Hints of trouble tend to breed trouble wherever there happens to be a chip on somebody's shoulder.

The public relations staff usually stays tuned in to the grapevine. When the gossiping and rumoring are harmless, nothing is done. When real trouble brews, the gossip is squelched by the release of full facts on the topic. Once in a while a counterrumor or an expose of the facts among the natural leaders of an organization is effected to offset a harmful rumor.

In either case, too many times the grapevine is the source of information for employees, even though it is not their preferred source. The lesson for the public relations practitioner is that *the grapevine will fill the information gaps left by an inadequate communication program*. The informal, uncontrolled channels will take over where the formal, controlled channels stop.

Meetings

Meetings bring people together, providing both opportunities to speak and opportunities to listen, a two-way communication. Work-group meetings, quality control circles, and participative management sessions are examples of small, task-oriented meetings. Such face-to-face get-togethers are expensive in time away from routine tasks, but economical in the long run because of both the ideas they produce and the team-building effects.

Just as with other communication strategies, a meeting requires specific objectives, careful planning and staging, and skillful direction. Exchange of viewpoints can be open but controlled so that the meeting does not drag or get diverted from its purpose. Effectiveness depends on the moderator's ability to lead and articulate. For some meetings, specially trained group-process facilitators serve this vital role while participants delve into important content issues. One school of thought is that important meetings involving people of different levels trying to resolve conflicts or make critical decisions should be guided by a process facilitator so that power, content, and process are not vested in one person, the boss. This approach may be useful only for special meetings or for training purposes, because part of any manager's role is to bring together the work group for problem-solving meetings and discussions.

For large gatherings, particularly those bringing together the entire employee force or important external publics, the public relations staff is called upon to plan the meeting. Annual meetings, for example, require a great deal of preparation time for top executives and a commitment of time from shareholders expecting a return on their time investment. Checklists for preparing such large meetings are extensive, so much so that many organizations contract with specialized firms to provide meeting management services.

Traditional meetings requiring face-to-face meetings in a single room are all but obsolete, according to one communication expert:

> New technologies such as PCs and digital audio-visual tools have
> created a whole new class of "electronic meeting." Conference calls,
> computer-interfaced meeting technologies, satellite connections,
> electronic bulletin boards and facsimile networks have forever
> blurred the meaning of meetings.[10]

To accomplish group decisions, many organizations now use the latest telecommunication and computer technologies to bring ideas and people together. One approach is to give members gathered around a table their own individual key pads connected to a single computer. Forcing communication through the computer screen enhances the exchange by giving timid group members and subordinates the same access as obnoxious talkers and opinionated bosses.

Some major global corporations have created state-of-the-art electronic meeting systems capable of connecting people around the world instantaneously to work together on a single problem. For example, IBM installed twenty "TeamFocus electronic meeting rooms" with personal computers and multimedia capabilities on a global network. Whether installed in a single room or designed as a multimedia global network, these new electronic "group decision support systems" are replacing traditional meetings.

Speeches and Speakers' Bureaus

There are few organizations of any size without some officials who can get on their feet and talk informatively and interestingly to select groups. *The Executive Speechmaker* lists these advantages for speeches:

1. Provides the most direct and persuasive means of communication since it involves face-to-face contact with a live audience.
2. Helps "personalize" an organization, particularly at a time when many people see large organizations as being excessively impersonal.
3. Often allows opportunity for give-and-take between speaker and audience, a two-way dialogue that can be informative for both parties.
4. Helps demonstrate the organization's openness and its desire to be a constructive participant in industry and community activities.
5. Brings prestige to both the speaker and the organization.
6. Gets the organization's views on public record.
7. Provides authoritative source material for other communications.[11]

Not all speeches accomplish these objectives effectively. Sometimes the blame can be attributed to public relations practitioners, because they are frequently called on to research a speech, prepare an outline, develop visuals, and sometimes write the entire speech. In addition to preparing materials for speakers, practitioners coach executives preparing for public appearances.

A *speakers' bureau* provides speakers on request. The subject matter usually represents a compromise between a desire simply to express organizational views on important issues and the need to provide requesting groups informative programs. As such, a speakers' bureau is a valuable medium for any organization with something important to say to key groups of influentials and community groups.

There are four points worth remembering in providing speakers:

1. First, carefully select and coach the lineup of speakers.
2. Second, select topics that serve the needs of potential audiences and carry the organization's story or positions on important issues of public debate.
3. Third, provide speakers visual aids: flip charts, slides, overhead transparencies, or videotapes.
4. Fourth, promote and publicize the availability of the speakers to appropriate groups.

IMAGES AND WORDS

The oft-predicted demise of printed and spoken words as major employee communication techniques has not happened. New technology simply expanded the reach and possibilities for communication and speeded up the process of distribution.

Teleconferencing

Technological advances in satellite communication have also expanded the range of possibilities for meetings and speeches. For example, key speakers unable to take time to travel to participate in person can be "beamed" to the meeting via satellite teleconferencing. Or, simultaneous sessions in several cities can be linked electronically with speakers shown on large-screen television equipment. The savings in travel time and costs, meeting facilities, and boarding of participants can more than offset the costs of using this new technology.

The primary reason for using teleconferencing is to reach people at a many locations all at the same time with the same message. AT&T Chairman Bob Allen's teleconference to discuss the company's special early retirement program reached some 100,000 managers at 250 U.S. locations. The chancellor of the California State University system used teleconferencing to keep administrators, faculty, staff, and students informed during the budget crises brought on by the faltering California economy of the early 1990s. (See Figure 9–3 for illustration of how the system works.)

Ford Motor Company's 275 manufacturing and sales offices all receive one-way video feeds from the Dearborn, Michigan, headquar-

Satellite Teleconferencing

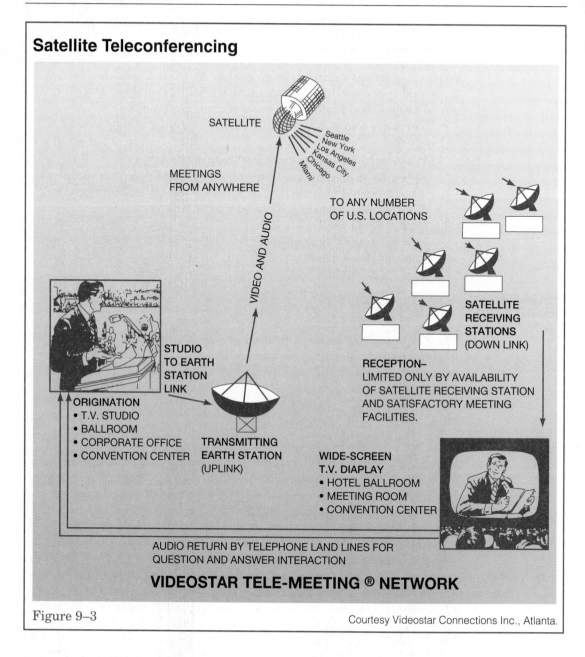

SATELLITE

Seattle
New York
Los Angeles
Kansas City
Chicago
Miami

MEETINGS
FROM ANYWHERE

TO ANY NUMBER
OF U.S. LOCATIONS

VIDEO AND AUDIO

STUDIO
TO EARTH
STATION
LINK

SATELLITE
RECEIVING
STATIONS
(DOWN LINK)

ORIGINATION
• T.V. STUDIO
• BALLROOM
• CORPORATE OFFICE
• CONVENTION CENTER

TRANSMITTING
EARTH STATION
(UPLINK)

RECEPTION–
LIMITED ONLY BY AVAILABILITY
OF SATELLITE RECEIVING STATION
AND SATISFACTORY MEETING
FACILITIES.

WIDE-SCREEN
T.V. DIAPLAY
• HOTEL BALLROOM
• MEETING ROOM
• CONVENTION CENTER

AUDIO RETURN BY TELEPHONE LAND LINES FOR
QUESTION AND ANSWER INTERACTION

VIDEOSTAR TELE-MEETING ® NETWORK

Figure 9–3

Courtesy Videostar Connections Inc., Atlanta.

ters. Twenty-five North American locations have two-way video transmission capabilities. The major U.S. facilities of General Motors (GM) are linked via satellite teleconferencing to facilitate the exchange of design, research, and production information among employees. Federal Express has one of the largest corporate employee satellite television systems:

A system with more than 1,000 downlinks in the U.S., Canada, Great Britain & Europe and 400-plus broadcasts a years. Its program places heavy emphasis on job-related information, including daily business updates, discussion of recurring-problem areas and ideas for improving performance at all levels.[12]

Not all satellite teleconferencing is limited to internal communication. During the Tylenol poisoning crisis, Johnson & Johnson used teleconferencing to hold national press conferences in 30 cities to answer reporters' questions and to keep media updated on developments. International Association of Business Communicators (IABC) conducted a teleconference for 1200 members in 22 cities. The National Safety Council held a meeting of almost 2000 participants in 45 cities across the United States on "Back Injury, Prevention and Rehabilitation." Part of the program consisted of a question-and-answer period in which participants engaged in two-way communication with the speakers.

Closed Circuit Television (CCTV)

GM's newest assembly plants have built-in CCTV capabilities. There are 60 "team centers," each seating 32 employees. The system makes it possible to telecast live or by videotape and film to almost 2000 employees at the same time. "Built to accommodate the strong emphasis on employees as business teams, each of these centers can also be split into rooms accommodating sixteen people, approximately the size of average work teams," according to the former director of corporate communications at GM, Alvie Smith. He is also cautious about the use of CCTV:

It is critical that the financial, personnel and equipment requirements be evaluated thoroughly—also factor in the availability of up-to-date videotape materials from within the organization and outside. And remember that if you decide to take employees off their jobs to watch CCTV shows, that's lost production and therefore expensive. So the programs have to be substantive to be worth the cost—not just a case of amateur TV producers having fun.[13]

Georgia-Pacific executives have grown accustomed to "going on camera" to keep thousands of employees in its many sites informed of developments in the forest products industry. The corporation's video production department produces about 70 training, sales, marketing, safety, and news programs each year. The broadcast-quality videotape productions eliminate the need to fly in hundreds of sales representatives to a central location or to various plants for product training and sales meetings.

The growing use of teleconferencing and television means that public relations practitioners have to understand these media that combine the spoken word with the visual image. Whereas the transmission technologies are relatively recent developments, these skills have long been part of the practice.

Videotape, Film, and Slide Presentations

Sponsored videotapes and films are those conceived within and commissioned by an organization for sales, training, or public relations purposes. The intent is not to reap direct, immediate monetary return "at the box office," but rather to develop favorable ideas, motivations, attitudes, or behaviors in viewing audiences.

Broadcast television provided the initial impetus, but cable television has greatly expanded the demand and opportunities for sponsored videotapes and films. Almost four generations have formed many of their impressions of the world from "the tube." Estimates are that by the time students graduate from high school, they have spent more hours watching television and movies than hours in the classroom.

The basic factors that gave television its great potential are used in videotape and film to transmit ideas, to stimulate imagination, and to produce action. With television and cinematography a tremendous audience awaits the timely, skillful presentation of a sponsor's story.

An example of the potential impact and audience for film is the Allstate Insurance Company short subject, *Ridin' the Edge*. Allstate campaigned vigorously to make air bags standard safety equipment on new cars, while some auto manufacturers resisted. A crash scene in the Hollywood movie *Moving Violation*, called for a stunt driver to crash into a concrete wall at almost 33 miles per hour. Allstate provided air-bag-equipped cars from their test fleet and technical advice in exchange for the right to use the scene footage in *Ridin' the Edge*. The film short was shown more than 125,000 times during the first 4 years and seen by more than 46 million people. Follow-up research on opinions toward air bags indicated that 27 percent more viewers approved of air bags than nonviewers. Only 2 percent of viewers disapproved of air bags, compared with 9 percent for nonviewers.[14]

The film was shown on commercial, public, and cable television; as a short in theaters; and to all types of groups and classes. Many police academies, driver education instructors, and insurance class teachers still use the film. Allstate public relations staff members think the short sponsored film helped keep air bags on the public agenda in spite of strong resistance by automobile manufacturers.

The public relations calling has its own sponsored videotape, "Communications That Count." Produced by the Institute for Public

Relations Research and Education in 1990, the videotape features case studies of how "public relations substantially contributes to the bottom line." The most widely seen company film celebrated its 35th year of distribution in 1993: Aero Mayflower Transit Company's *The Mayflower Story*.

Motion pictures and videotapes offer the following communication strengths:

1. They combine the impact of sight, sound, drama and movement, color, and music.
2. They present ideas involving motion that cannot be described effectively by print or audio means.
3. They attract sustained and exclusive attention to a message for the length of the showing.
4. They make explicit the time factor in any operation or series of events
5. They provide a believable record of events.
6. They show processes that cannot ordinarily be seen by the naked eye.
7. They bring the past and the distant to the viewer.
8. They enlarge, reduce, or simplify objects, as well as illustrate abstractions through the use of photography, cartoons, and graphics.
9. Above all, they let the viewers see with their own eyes: "Seeing is believing."

High-quality portable videotape recording equipment and computer-generated graphics increase the range of potential uses and reduce the production costs. Cable systems with insatiable programming needs increase exposure opportunities to audiences in their own homes. Increased use of closed circuit television and teleconferencing expand the potential internal audiences, but not without some reservations:

> One of the problems is finding time in the work day for employees to watch video programs. Managers are understandably reluctant to halt production lines and interrupt office work to watch video programs unless they are part of a training project. Therefore, we must be very selective in programs we ask managers to show to all employees.[15]

Many of the strengths and principles of videotape and film apply to slide presentations. If motion is not critical to the message, the less expensive slide presentation often can be as effective.

Displays and Exhibits

In almost every factory or hospital there is a reception room, showroom, cafeteria, or lounge. Every college has the equivalent of an "Old Main," student union, or reception or visitor's center. Every branch of the military has its sites to perpetuate its memories, receive guests, and show its progress. These places are natural areas for displays and exhibits. For anyone who has ever taken a plant tour or visited a major fair, the content of such exhibits needs no explanation. Displays must be conceived as part of the total public relations program designed to reach target publics.

"Fat Man" and "Little Boy" Exhibit, Bradbury Science Museum, Los Alamos National Laboratory, New Mexico

Figure 9–4

Another important use of displays and exhibits is the trade show or convention. Almost every major city has a convention center to host conventions and trade shows of all types. Exhibits at these gatherings often have marketing and sales objectives, but also include the following public relations uses:

1. Create or maintain a specific perception of the organization
2. Maintain contact with important audiences
3. Show depth and breadth of organization's operations
4. Generate inquiries for more information
5. Get feedback for evaluating strategies
6. Recruit personnel

Displays and exhibits are also distributed much like films and videotapes for use at special events and local gatherings. The U.S. Department of Agriculture and Cooperative Extension Service based at state land-grant universities have long provided displays and exhibits for local meetings and fairs. Many government agencies and corporations publish catalogues from which users order for local showings.

Permanent installations at theme parks, zoos, museums, airports, and other public attractions have become major public relations tools. Corporate displays now serve as both entertainment and information attractions at the major Walt Disney centers in Florida and California, as well as Sea Worlds in Florida, Ohio, and California. For years the University of Illinois College of Agriculture has provided educational exhibits for Chicago's Lincoln Park "Farm-in-the-Zoo" as a way to reach urban residents with information about agriculture.

Exhibitors know that the objective is to entice the footsore visitor to stop at the display, to retain attention long enough to study the presentation, and to impart information or stimulate immediate or future action. Usually displays and exhibits are constructed by specialized firms, but the purpose, concept, and message are typically the products of public relations programming and creativity.

This section has not covered all the controlled media available to practitioners. The intent here was to introduce a few of the major media over which the practitioner has a high degree of control. Controlled media are the primary media for communicating with internal publics. Moreover, they are the preferred means for reaching external publics when resources and time are available and when audience size and dispersion make use of controlled media possible. Because external publics are often large and dispersed, sometimes making controlled media impractical, uncontrolled media and other mass media are the topics in the sections that follow.

MEDIA FOR EXTERNAL PUBLICS

The economical, effective method of communicating with large and widely dispersed publics is through the mass media: newspapers, magazines, trade publications, AM and FM radio, television, cable, books, and so on. To handle this part of the job, practitioners must understand the role of information, the various media and their mechanics, and the values of those who control access to them. Practitioners also need to understand that media are constrained by their mechanical requirements, their values, their rules, and—for many—the necessity of delivering an audience to advertisers. Today's communicators are confronted with a paradox: Multiplying channels of communication permit a sharper focus of messages but greatly escalate competition for audience attention.

Mass media reach into nearly every home and workplace, showering citizens with far more messages than they can absorb. General and specialized media appear to represent an easily used means of disseminating ideas and information to publics, but this can be delusive. Just because these media have audiences and convey messages does not necessarily mean that those messages are received, accepted, or acted upon.

For example, print messages have no direct impact on the millions of illiterate Americans. Moreover, there are other nonreaders, either because of lack of interest or because they read and speak a language other than the one used in the publication.

For another thing, the public media have a relatively fixed capacity; newspapers and magazines have a limited number of columns for editorial matter, and there are only 24 hours in a broadcast day. Hence, these media cannot possibly accommodate all the messages fed into them. Receivers also have limited time and attention to give to the millions of messages. In a world stuffed with messages, only a tiny fraction gets past the door and into the home. Even fewer get attention.

Nonetheless, power in America is largely exercised through control of the means and content of mass communications. Mass media constitute the key components in the nation's public-information system, a system in which public relations practitioners play an important role. This public information system embraces all levels of government, staffed by public affairs and information officers; political parties, staffed by campaign experts, media consultants, and public relations experts; associations and other special-interest groups, staffed by lobbyists and other public relations specialists; corporations and nonprofit organizations, staffed by public relations practitioners and marketing communicators; and the media, staffed by reporters and gatekeepers. Each of these elements performs an important, integral function in the democratic process of attempting to debate issues and maintain the dynamic state of consensus required by both the governors and those governed. One element works in relation to other elements, so all may be lumped together under the rubric of "public information system."

The struggle to shape and manage the news has escalated in intensity as media power and political stakes have increased. Competition for access to media is spirited and becoming more so with each passing day. Practitioners must adjust their work to rapidly changing media, owing to a combination of the impact of computers, innovations in signal transmission, and new ways for sending and retrieving information and images. As one political public relations specialist advises:

> My advice is to watch *USA Today* and its imitators, pay attention to cable TV, and listen to the audio channels on transcontinental flights (where futurism/millennialism is in vogue). And remember, radio call-ins defeated the congressional pay raise.[16]

Newspapers

Although the number of daily and weekly newspapers declined in the 1980s, the newspaper remains the workhorse of the public information system. When people think of publicity, they almost instinctively think of the newspaper. American newspapers—daily, weekend, Sunday, weekly, semiweekly, ethnic, labor, religious, scholastic, and foreign language—are read by most literate people. Publicity in newspapers, day in and day out, forms the foundation of most information programs. Reading the newspaper is as much a part of the influential citizen's daily habits as are eating and sleeping. As a result, the influence of the world's great newspapers is great. Journalism scholar and educator John C. Merrill refers to these as "internationally elite newspapers":

> Such papers—mainly dailies—are read by the world's intellectuals, political and opinion leaders, and cosmopolitan, concerned citizens of various countries. They are directed at a fairly homogeneous audience globally and have a greater interest in international relations and the arts and humanities than the general run of mass-appeal papers. They are well-informed, articulate papers that thoughtful people the world over take seriously.[17]

U.S. papers included on Merrill's list of elite dailies include the *New York Times*, *Los Angeles Times*, *Washington Post*, and *Christian Science Monitor*. His European list includes *Le Monde* of France, the *Neue Zürcher Zeitung* of Switzerland, *El País* of Spain, the *Daily Telegraph* of England, and *Svenska Dagbladet* of Sweden. Asia's elite dailies include Japan's *Asahi Shimbun* and *Mainichi Shimbun* and India's *Times of India* and *Statesman*. According to Merrill, "The elite papers recognize that they will not reach many people, but they seek to have an impact that no other medium does on the serious, intellectual, opinion-leading segment of the world community."[18]

Newspapers are a moving force in society. The late Justice Felix Frankfurter once said, "To an extent far beyond the public's own realization, public opinion is shaped by the kind, the volume, and the quality of the news columns." Newspaper scholars have suggested that the power of the press comes from its dissemination of information and its impact on public interest in important issues (the agenda-setting function discussed in Chapter 8). Nor should editorial endorsement be totally discounted. Newspapers are a primary means of reaching community publics in these days of specialized media and fragmented audiences. Although no longer the primary news medium for the majority, newspapers are still a powerful force in shaping the public agenda and influencing the outcome of debate.

From the early part of the twentieth century until World War II, when newspapers were the prime source of news and entertainment, the number of *daily newspapers* declined. The number began to stabilize at mid-century and remained about the same through the mid-1970s. There were 1760 daily papers in 1950, for example, but only four fewer, 1756, in 1975. By 1992, however, the number had dropped to only 1570 dailies because of mergers and discontinued editions during the 1980s

EXHIBIT 9-1

What Happened to the Press ?

Obviously, the place of the daily paper in American life has changed. In my early days, we were the first purveyors of the news, but radio and television changed all that, and when the old man checks the next morning's newspaper for the latest locker room gossip on the baseball game he watched on television the night before, it merely says "Late Game" and doesn't even give him the score. What is more ominous for the future, the children are no longer picking up the newspaper habit by reading the comic strips, but find the latest TV murders much more exciting than "Little Orphan Annie" or even "Peanuts."

. . . I don't agree with those who think the newspaper is in decline, and I don't notice much red ink on their balance sheets.

In fact, I think we are witnessing the greatest expansion of information since the invention of movable type. On the three hundredth anniversary of America's first newspaper (Benjamin Harris's *Publick Occurences Both Foreign and Domestick*, published in Boston on September 25, 1690), there were 1,625 U.S. dailies with a circulation of over 62 million, and it was said that many of them were hauling in an average of 20 percent in profit before taxes—a record matched by few industries.

James Reston, *Deadline: A Memoir* (New York: Random House, 1991), 470-71. Used with permission of the author.

There were 1760 daily papers in 1950, for example, but only four fewer, 1756, in 1975. By 1992, however, the number had dropped to only 1570 dailies because of mergers and discontinued editions during the 1980s and early 1990s. In 1991 alone 42 evening dailies ceased publication. In 1992 only 33 cities had both morning and evening papers. Only 35 cities had two or more competing daily newspapers (only 17 were fully competitive, not joint operating agreements), compared with 57 in 1980. These figures pale when compared with the early 1920s—before radio and the Great Depression—when more than 500 cities had competing daily newspapers.[19]

Although the number of dailies declined during the 1980s and early 1990s, the average circulation for surviving papers increased and newspaper reading remained fairly stable despite increased media competition. Daily newspaper readership figures compiled by Simmons Market Research Bureau show that more than 115 million adults read a newspaper each weekday, and readership jumps to more than 126 million on Sundays. Approximately 63 percent of all adults say they read a daily newspaper; 68 percent on Sundays. Adults spend an average of 28 minutes with their daily newspaper. Among 18-to-24-year-olds, slightly more than half typically read a daily newspaper, but 59 percent do so on Sundays.[20]

A study of newspaper readers in Brazil identified five types. *Instrumental readers* use newspapers to get information they think will be useful for daily living. Reading is purely an information-seeking activity to understand what is happening and why it is happening. *Opinion makers* use newspapers to get advice and guidance for forming and validating opinion. Newspapers help them make up their minds on issues and provide insight on what others are thinking. *Pleasure readers* use newspaper reading as an enjoyable habit. They see newspapers as a source of enjoyment and reading as an end in itself, not as a means for accomplishing some other purpose. *Ego-boosters* use newspapers as a source of information for impressing others. They read to enhance their self-image and status with others. *Scanners* use newspapers for many and varied reasons, but no single motivation or pattern strong enough to suggest they belong in one of the other four types.[21]

There was a slight decline in the number of *weekly and semiweekly newspapers* in the 1980s. In 1980 there were 7954 weeklies with a circulation of 42.3 million. By 1993 the number had dropped to about 7406 weeklies, but *circulation* had increased to more than 55 million. Weekly *readership* is estimated at more than 120 million.[22] These newspapers offer an effective, direct, and intimate means of reaching the people of suburbs, small towns, and rural areas, who are often the source of grass-roots opinion. Readers of weekly newspapers are loyal and read their papers thoroughly. A weekly newspaper arguably exerts a far greater impact on readers' opinions than does the typical daily. And these opinions often count beyond their numbers.

Most weeklies emphasize news of local government, schools, public affairs, and personal news. Public relations practitioners, walled in by skyscrapers and stuck in traffic jams or crowded mass transit, should not forget the people of small-town and suburban America or the newspapers that help shape their opinions. In fact, many executives (with public relations assistance) write "op-eds" for the opinion-editorial page. These pieces, by design, focus on one subject—usually local and controversial—and openly express the organization's position on the issue. Key to placing op-ed pieces is timeliness. For example, if a bill being debated in Congress is not getting much media attention, an op-ed piece on how the bill will affect the local community or your company may catch the editorial page editor's eye.[23]

The *Sunday paper* generally gets a longer, more intensive and leisurely reading. It tends to emphasize feature material—stories without a time element—often more like a magazine than like a daily paper. Special features and pictures without a time peg are supplied early in the week. And because news can be relatively scarce on Sun-

developed by large-city newspapers for reaching large audiences. For example, more than 300 newspapers include *Parade* every Sunday, reaching some 70 million readers.

Newspaper space allocated to news has decreased in recent years, at least relative to the increased glut of newsworthy information pouring into newsrooms, including that from practitioners. Typically, newspapers devote about 50 percent of their space to editorial matter; some as little as 25 percent. The rest is advertising (about 46 percent) and unpaid public service (4 percent). Local news makes up the largest proportion of editorial content: about 75 percent of all news published. Financial, state, and international news typically receive the least amount of space. These figures reflect the increasing reliance upon network TV for national and international news. Many daily newspapers recently have greatly increased their business sections, as national attention focused on foreign trade deficits, the national debt, and the increasingly competitive global market. Business became big news in the early 1990s, as did science and technology and the environment.

The *strengths of newspapers are many.* No other medium offers comparable audience size and breadth day in and day out, or the range and depth of content. Most newspapers are produced in local communities and are indigenous to those communities. They have a firsthand intimacy with their local publics. The local YMCA can reach its community public through its local newspaper. The state health department can reach its publics through the state's daily and weekly newspapers. A commercial concern with regional distribution can reach its publics by a regional selection of newspapers. Similarly, a national organization can reach most national audiences with newspapers.

American newspapers—from the mass-circulation giants down to small weeklies with circulations of less than 2000—vary a great deal in content, character, and audience, yet all have a fairly standardized definition of news. The number, locale, and variety of newspapers enable practitioners to pinpoint the geography of publicity, as well as audiences, with precision. This capability has been enhanced by the development of city, state, regional, and national paid publicity wires.

There are other advantages. A person buys a newspaper as something that is wanted, not as something that is required. Newspapers constitute a medium of sustained interest and information. Readers are generally the interested, influential people. Because they reach most of their readers daily, major newspapers are the most acceptable medium for a cumulative publicity buildup and thus are especially valuable in promotional campaigns. Newspapers are read at the reader's leisure and convenience, in sharp contrast with the broadcast media, where a program missed is difficult to retrieve or gone forever. And finally, the perceived credibility of newspapers is hard to match.

Newspapers also have limitations. An important one is that the typical reader reads only one fifth to one fourth of the editorial content of his or her daily newspaper. Only 56 percent of readers say they read or scan all their daily newspaper's pages. Thus it is a mistake to assume that publicity printed is publicity read. As important as newspapers are, they cannot carry the information task alone. The press must be used in coordination with other channels of communication.

Another limitation is imposed by the newspaper journalists' fetish for speed and the resulting haste with which newspapers are put together. This pressure leads to many inaccuracies and fragmented, superficial coverage, a fact of life with which practitioners must cope. In contacts with the daily newspaper, practitioners quickly learn the importance of dealing with specialized reporters. If it is a sports-related story, work directly with the sports department. If it is a straight news story of local interest, deal with either the city editor or the reporter on the specific assignment. Newspapers have specialists covering the environment, health, science, international relations, business, and others areas too numerous to mention here. (Caution: No two newspaper organizations are exactly alike, so the same titles may mean different things at different newspapers.)

Wire Services and News Syndicates

For high reader-interest stories and spot news of state, regional, national, or international significance, the wire services offer the most economical and effective outlet. Publicity with a "local angle" can be directed to individual newspapers where that interest exists. For timely stories not limited to a locale, placing them on the wires increases the likelihood of immediate and widespread coverage. It also increases the acceptability of the practitioner's copy. Publicity racing into the newspaper's computer or spewing from a fast-speed printer is no longer "publicity." It is "news." A well-written wire story can reach newspaper readers, radio listeners, and TV viewers across the nation. Transmitting millions of words and pictures daily, the wire services are influential beyond calculation. Access to these networks is through the nearest bureau or "stringer" correspondent.

Each of the two major wire services in the United States operates with national trunk wires, regional wires, and state wires. In addition to their newspaper networks, both serve broadcast stations with wire copy and audio feeds. Associated Press, founded in 1848, has its headquarters in New York City with bureaus and clients around the world. The privately owned and scaled-down United Press International (UPI) is headquartered in Washington, D.C. It was formed in 1958 by the merger of United Press (founded in 1907 by newspaper magnate E. W. Scripps) and William Randolph Hearst's International News Service. UPI also provides worldwide service, although annual losses, reorganization in bankruptcy court, and restructuring have taken their toll.

United Press (founded in 1907 by newspaper magnate E. W. Scripps) and William Randolph Hearst's International News Service. UPI also provides worldwide service, although annual losses, reorganization in bankruptcy court, and restructuring have taken their toll.

Associated Press—better known as AP—is a cooperative owned by its member newspapers. Subscribers include almost 1600 daily and weekly newspapers and 5900 radio and television stations. In addition, AP markets its news services to nonmedia clients. Beginning in early 1993, AP began transmitting publicity photos for a fee, putting it in direct competition with the publicity wire services.

Newspapers also subscribe to news services from The *New York Times*, *Washington Post*, *Los Angeles Times*, Knight-Ridder, and newspaper syndicates such as King Features Syndicate, National Newspaper Syndicate, News America Syndicate, United Features Syndicate, and Newspaper Enterprises Syndicate.

Internationally, Reuters (United Kingdom), Agence France-Presse (France), New China News Agency (People's Republic of China), and Kyoto (Japan) are a few of the major news services providing news and features for not only newspapers, but also for radio, television, magazines, and private subscribers. These are large organizations with reporters, editors, and other staff in most major capitals and market centers. Reuters, for example, has a staff of almost 300 in its New York office, just one of its many offices.

Standing beside AP and UPI equipment in most of the nation's major newsrooms are high-speed teleprinters provided by commercial "PR wires." Practitioners use these distribution services to speed time-critical press releases simultaneously into newsrooms. Increasingly time-sensitive press relations brought on the dramatic growth of domestic and international publicity wire networks.

PR Newswire (PRN) introduced electronic distribution of news releases in New York City in 1954. Other local PR wires copied the concept. The idea quickly evolved into national systems in the United States, Canada, and England, followed by worldwide news-release distribution systems. Although they differ greatly in size, all these wires operate essentially the same: charging clients to transmit releases to the media, with fees based on extent and type of distribution ordered. For example, PRN offers more than 60 distribution options in the United States, ranging from "local coverage" to national distribution. Media receive these "news" services at no charge.

Because they offer fast, simultaneous transmission to all the media on a network, practitioners use these wires to flash news ranging from major corporate developments and earnings reports, sporting events, and obituaries to invitations to press conferences. They are especially useful in times of emergency. For example, within 36 hours of the big 1989 San Francisco Bay Area World Series earthquake, PR Newswire carried some 150 news releases from businesses and government agencies about grants, donations, other forms of aid, special telephone numbers, insurance, and other topics related to the disaster. Another example of an urgent need to distribute information to many media outlets quickly and simultaneously is a product recall, such as when a baby-food manufacturer found glass shards in one lot of food products!

PRN serves about 1500 media, covering every major area of the country. Operating from its headquarters in New York City, PRN transmits news releases and photos internationally through its Canada News-Wire and PR Newswire International Services. International distribution services include coverage in individual countries, as well as regional distribution packages such as European Financial Capitals, European General Pack, and Pacific Rim Pack.

PRN also offers selective distribution services to media, including features on the national overnight Feature News Wire; news about films, theater, records, music, and other entertainment topics on Entertainet™; announcements of satellite feeds and photo opportunities to 275 television stations and networks on PR/TV Newswire; and satellite transmissions of black-and-white and color images on Photos By Wire. National Affairs Newsline serves U.S. and foreign government offices, congressional offices, embassies, national associations, and media in Washington, D.C. Financial news transmissions over Investors Research Wire go to the news media and 15 minutes later to others in the investment community (in accordance with the "prompt disclosure" requirements discussed in Chapter 6). PRN reports that each year more than 15,000 news sources use these services to send 100,000 messages to newsrooms, trade publications, and selected offices.

Another large portion of newspaper content is supplied by the feature, photo, and specialized news syndicates. As in the case of the wire services, placement of a feature or a picture with a syndicate ensures wide, economical distribution and increases the acceptability of material. Most syndicates distribute columns and comics. For example, Universal Press Syndicate distributes both text features and comic strips, including Gary Larson's "The Far Side," Ted Martin's "Pavlov," and Jim Unger's "Herman." Syndicates charge fees based each client newspaper's circulation.

The world's largest feature news service, Newspaper Enterprise Association (NEA), provides news features, Washington columns, op-ed features, editorials, pictures, sports, family-page and food features, astrology columns, and crossword puzzles. It serves 750 daily newspapers in the United States and Canada. In addition, nearly 400 weekly papers use features distributed through the Suburban Features division of NEA. A carefully targeted story carried by the right syndicate can get nationwide coverage. Material can be channeled to the press through such syndicates as NEA, King Features Service, and United Feature Syndicate, to name but a few. Others deal in specialized news, such as Auto News Syndicate, Religious News Service, and Fashion 'n' Figure. A

material without charge. Clients pay the bill. Typical is the Derus Media Service, Chicago, which mails out a clip sheet, *Editorial PACE*, to dailies and weeklies. It also distributes individual releases. Another such service is North American Precis Syndicate, Inc. (NAPS), with offices in New York, Washington, Chicago, and Los Angeles. NAPS distributes news, features, and reprints to the nation's dailies and weeklies.

Magazines

More than 12,000 (some estimate more than 20,000) magazines and specialized publications published in the United States offer effective specialized channels of communication to narrowly defined audiences. Variations in the content and audience appeal of magazines are almost limitless, and ever-changing. Some 300 new magazines are started each year, but only one in ten is successful. Many never make it to the first issue. Others fail after the first year or two, disappointing enthusiastic publishers who had visions of attracting both subscribers and advertisers.

One author refers to magazines as "the first national mass medium," referring to Benjamin Franklin's *General Magazine*, published in February 1741. Technically, however, Andrew Bradford's *American Magazine* was the first American magazine because it appeared in print 3 days before Franklin's magazine. Historians, however, give Franklin credit for originating the concept of a magazine.[24]

Magazines' broad array and variety—from the circulation giants such as *Modern Maturity, Reader's Digest, TV Guide, National Geographic, Better Homes and Gardens, Family Circle, Time, Newsweek, U.S. News and World Report, Cosmopolitan,* and *Good Housekeeping;* more narrowly targeted magazines, such as *Ms, Rolling Stone, Sports Illustrated, PC World,* and *Architectural Digest;* and trade and business journals such as *Women's Wear Daily, Business Week, Fortune,* and *Forbes;* to such recreational magazines as *World Tennis, Video Review, Popular Photography,* and *Ski Magazine*—provide effective communication media to reach large audiences who share common interests. Thus magazines often enable communicators to target a specific message to a specific audience more economically than with other media.

The changing magazine market—from general to specialized publications—reflects the nation's changing interests and lifestyles. There is a magazine or periodical catering to almost every known interest, vocation, and hobby. Advances in offset printing and computerized production have stimulated circulation and advertising revenues by giving advertisers options for buying targeted portions of the total circulation. Regional advertising in such national magazines as *Time* or *Newsweek,* for example, allows advertisers to sell to a "market within a market," even local markets. *Farm Journal,* the first national magazine to publish regional editions (1952), now produces up to 9000 different versions of each issue. Specialized editions are tailored to match the information needs of selected groups of farmers, based on "the most complete database on farmers in the U.S.," according to the publisher.[25]

Several thousand business and professional publications serve the specialized needs of professional groups, trade associations, or business and industry. These publications generally use prepared news releases if the content serves their readers' economic or professional needs. Each of these publications caters to a carefully defined audience, usually representing the membership lists of the organization publishing the magazine. Examples include PRSA's *Public Relations Journal*, IABC's *Communication World*, and the American Medical Association's *American Medical News*. In addition to collecting subscription fees built into membership fees, many of these publications carry advertising of products and services specific to readers' occupations or professional practices.

A guide to the audiences and content of magazines is provided by two indispensable tools of the practitioner: *Writer's Guide* and *Writer's Market*. Audit Bureau of Circulation (ABC) publishes verified circulation figures of member magazines. Advertisers use these figures for making decisions about where to place advertisements. Public relations practitioners use these sources to estimate audience size and characteristics for magazine coverage.

The following facts illustrate the advantages of using magazines. Opinion leaders read many magazines. Magazines provide more durable information than do newspapers. Magazine readers have the opportunity to read, reread, discuss, and debate the information gleaned from this source. The trend is away from fiction and entertainment features toward more investigative and interpretative reporting of controversial issues. Readers with special interests turn to magazines for in-depth treatment of topics, such as when older citizens report that magazines are second only to health care specialists as a source for health information. The vitality and force of magazines in shaping opinions, creating fashions, designing houses, setting standards for professions or businesses, and enlisting political support have been demonstrated many times over since those first two American magazines appeared in 1741.

Publicity placement in a magazine should be preceded by a careful analysis of the publication's readers, its editorial formula, its advertising content, and the market it serves. The smart practitioner studies the magazine's topics, style, policies, trends, format, and so forth and then applies this knowledge by slanting news and features to the particular publication. Publicists generally do not submit unsolicited material, however. Rather, they work on a tip or query basis when they have something that would have reader appeal. They submit story outlines or feature suggestions. If one is accepted, they work with the magazine's staff or freelance writers to develop the story. The practitioner's jobs are to sell ideas to editors and then to cooperate with writers and photographers, who build the ideas into articles.

Magazine publicity placement is almost essential for organizations seeking to influence national or specialized audiences. Yet many practitioners fail in their efforts to get such publicity because they do not understand the long lead time of national magazines, the length of time it takes to put a story idea into final, publishable form, and the stiff competition for space; and also because they do not make adequate circulation studies so that material is targeted for the particular audience. The competition comes from editors and staff writers on the magazines, frequent contributors, and freelance writers who write regularly for national magazines.

An approach often used but sometimes overlooked is that of dealing with free-lancers. Free-lance writers who sell to national magazines are interested in an account of an institution, a person, or an event that possesses at least one of these three qualities: (1) national importance or significance; (2) elements of struggle, conflict, contest, or drama; or (3) anecdotal enrichment and entertainment value. It is common practice to give a freelancer a good story to develop. The freelancer gets a check; the practitioner gets a publicity placement in a magazine. The Society of Magazine Writers in New York City operates a Dial-a-Writer Service for those seeking writers for special projects.

Radio

Once thought to be fading because of television and cable, radio today serves a useful and pervasive role in our public information system. Radio offers a wide range of publicity possibilities. It is a mobile medium suited to a mobile people. It reaches the bedroom and breakfast table in the morning and rides to and from work in the car, lulls us to sleep at night, and goes along to the beach, to the woods, and on fishing trips, a flexibility no other medium can match. For example, in the aftermath of Hurricane Andrew, radio became the primary medium for communicating to the citizens of Florida's South Bay. No other medium reached the many citizens who had lost their homes, telephone and power lines, and transportation.[26]

There are close to 500 million radio sets, and radio listening has increased to more than 3 hours a day. The typical household has at least five radios. Almost 80 percent of all U.S. citizens listen to radio daily. As one radio specialist says, "It's the first source of news. It's there when you wake up. It's there when you go to sleep."[27]

There are more than 10,000 radio stations in the United States, of which 1,260 are public stations. About 5000 are AM, and 5000 are FM. There has been a marked shift in radio programming and listening patterns from AM to FM. In the early 1970s, AM stations attracted three fourths of the audience. By the early 1990s, more than three fourths of the total radio listening audience tuned to FM stations. The AM dial is so crowded that nearly half the AM stations—"daytimers"—have to shut down 15 minutes after sunset to avoid interfering with others. FM also gained listeners because of its high-quality stereo sound, which coincided with the development of noise-free recordings.

Radio news releases are usually fed to stations over telephone lines, sometimes to networks such as the Texas Radio Network and USA Radio Network. Audio news services, such as North American Network (based in Washington, D.C.) and News/Broadcast Network (Milwaukee and New York City), use telephone distribution to target stations by region and format. News/Broadcast Network, for example, reaches 2200 stations through its daily feeds on the Associated Press and Mutual Broadcasting wires. To increase airings on local stations, audio news services often localize national stories by including local interviews or sound bites.[28]

Even though it is a mass medium, radio possesses the qualities of a direct, personal touch, as it uses the spoken word, for the most part, to convey its message. Broadcast pioneer Arthur Godfrey put his finger on this intimate quality in describing the turning point in his career:

> Lying in that hospital listening to the radio, I realized for the first time how really intimate the medium is and how ridiculously ineffective most of the speakers were. . . . They were not *talking*, they were *reading*, and therefore convincing no one. . . . I decided I'd do things differently. . . . When I face a mike I have a mental image of only one person listening to me and I talk to that one person.

The practitioner should realize radio is a person-to-person medium that flourishes on conversation. Call-in talk shows now play a major role in setting the public agenda and in providing a forum for public debate. Writing in *New York Magazine*, Joe Klein said that radio talk-show hosts killed a proposed congressional pay raise:

> A gaggle of radio talk show hosts . . . rallied their listeners against the pay raise. They (along with consumer activist Ralph Nader) mounted the most effective lobbying campaign of the past decade— an effort that raised the daunting specter of radio populism on the rampage and talk hosts as the political organizers of the '90s.[29]

Talk shows certainly played a role in the 1992 Bush-Clinton presidential campaigns, with candidates and their spokespersons appearing on the nationally syndicated "Larry King Show" to make major announcements. Rush Limbaugh has a national radio audience, whereas Boston's Jerry Williams, another conservative, has political impact on listeners throughout New England. And almost every major city has its own radio all-talk shows capitalizing on local conflict, sensational topics, and legitimate public debate of important issues. Increased emphasis on the discussion type of program opens up many possibilities for practitioners. Talk shows and telephone interviews focusing on controversial issues have become increasingly popular and have an almost insatiable appetite for guests with a message—however controversial it may be.

Listener surveys show newscasts and talk programs at the top or near the top of programs preferred by most listeners. By providing news scripts or recorded interviews for radio newscasts, practitioners can get a wide hearing for stories within the audience limits of a given station or set of stations. Radio newsrooms want news prepared for radio, not copies of newspaper releases. They want news written for bulletin presentation. Radio news editors want all difficult names and words spelled out phonetically for the announcer. The lead story on a typical newscast is 100 words or fewer. News is written for the ear, not for the eye. Radio news must be informal, conversational, brief, to the point, and—above all—accurate. Once spoken, errors cannot be recalled and corrected; besides, one never gets exactly the same audience twice in radio. Radio journalists expect and deserve equal treatment with print journalists in releasing news and covering special events.

Many organizations provide stations with dial-access recorded newscasts, which are updated as news develops. Copy for these newscasts is prepared in the public relations office, then recorded on automatic playback systems. Stations are given an unlisted telephone number for these recorded newscasts. The AFL-CIO operates an automated telephone bulletin service to serve radio stations, as do many state highway patrol offices, weather reporting services, and stock and commodity brokers.

Public service time is seldom prime listening time, but it is not without value. Since the Federal Communications Commission relaxed its public service requirements for broadcasters, many stations have reduced the number of public service and other nonrevenue programs they broadcast. Yet most stations provide some free time to nonprofit agencies as part of the station's community relations program. In nonprime time the competition for air time is less intense than during the more desirable—and salable—drive time and other high-listenership hours. That is not to say, however, that an effective program cannot attract and hold listeners.

An effective way is to provide radio and TV *public service announcements* (PSAs) of 10 seconds, 30 seconds, or 60 seconds in length. A PSA is any announcement, for which no charge is made, that promotes programs and services of government and voluntary agencies. Stations set their own standards, but most use well-prepared PSAs. And they can be effective. For example, a PSA prepared by the Aluminum Association to urge recycling of cans was used by 244 TV stations more than 15,000 times, adding up to nearly 164 broadcast hours. The "Recycle and Save" PSA increased the number of logged toll-free calls from 433 a month to 9500 calls within 9 months.

Television

The communications phenomenon of the twentieth century, television, has great force and scope as a publicity medium. No other medium matches television's ability to provide a window on the world. What other medium could transmit live coverage of Patriot missiles intercepting Scud missiles above Saudi Arabia and Israel? Remember the live coverage of U.S. troops landing on the beach in Somalia? How could anyone ignore the human tragedies in Bosnia shown so vividly on the evening news? Many recall the soot-smudged faces of those fleeing New York's World Trade Center after the February 1993 terrorist bombing and the video of the March 1993 storm that devastated the East Coast. And long-lens cameras gave us live pictures of the Branch Davidian compound under siege outside Waco, Texas.

A medium that permits the use of the printed word, spoken word, pictures in motion, color, music, animation, and sound effects—all blended into one message—possesses immeasurable potency. It offers a vast range of possibilities for telling a story, from a terse, 60-second video on a TV newscast to a half-hour or 1-hour documentary film to a miniseries extended over several evenings. And with satellite transmission now commonplace, the powerful, pervasive impact of television is worldwide. Yet many practitioners do not fully capitalize on TV's power. Television took the lead from newspapers in 1963 as the primary source of news, a fact many practitioners, many of whom once worked in print media, fail to recognize.

More than 1500 TV stations broadcast almost around the clock to nearly every household. The number of cable channels now give viewers more options than they can carefully consider. The average time spent with television now approaches the length of a typical workday. Children spend more time watching TV than with their teachers in classrooms. They grow up using the remote-control clicker to explore a seemingly endless array of program services such as Disney, Discovery, Black Entertainment TV, TNT, HBO, CNN, and C-SPAN, to name but a few. As former FCC chairman Newton Minow says:

Choice has skyrocketed. The VCR means you can watch a program when you want to see it, not just when the broadcaster puts it on the schedule. If you are a sports fan, a news junkie, a stock market follower, a rock music devotee, a person who speaks Spanish, a nostalgic old-movie buff, a congressional-hearing observer, a weather watcher—you now have your own choice. The FCC objective in the early '60s to expand choice has been fulfilled—beyond all expectations.[30]

This is our most intimate mass medium, yet it can attract half the population to watch Michael Jackson perform during Super Bowl half time. It can entice advertisers to pay almost a million dollars to run a

30-second ad during the Super Bowl, or more than $100,000 for the same 30 seconds during the regular program schedule.

Television has become a dominant force in the rearing of our young, the prime source of news and entertainment for most Americans, and a powerful soapbox from which citizens' protests can be communicated to the nation and the world. This medium has greatly altered national election campaigns and has diminished the role of the political parties. Researchers in Germany, for example, found that TV newscasts not only caused changes in awareness of problems, but also had consequences on voting intentions.[31] National and international wire services and global TV news networks have created a truly global forum. Events made large by TV shape public opinion worldwide. What other explanation is there for the carefully scripted and choreographed TV appearances of both George Bush and Saddam Hussein during the Kuwait–Persian Gulf crisis?

Television greatly heightens citizen awareness of the conduct of public institutions and emphasizes the impersonal, interdependent nature of the environment. It also creates a sense of frustration for the citizen, who is witness to much that he or she cannot control, be it police beating Rodney King in Los Angeles, Coast Guard cutters intercepting boats overloaded with Haitian refugees, bloated stomachs of starving children in Somalia, pro-life protesters blockading the entrance to a health care clinic, the wretched life of homeless families, or developers scraping hillsides bare to build more look-alike houses. TV brings these and many more pictures of the world into our homes.

Those pictures of presidential candidates have changed the political process, for example. Scholars point out that public attitudes about presidential nominees have declined since the 1952 presidential election, which brought the Eisenhower 60-second spots. They attribute the decline to television "negative storytelling," which may have "reached an all-time high in 1992, but the phenomenon has been in the making for decades!"[32] Other political campaign scholars concluded that television news:

> has made us all more presidential, more political, more volatile and more cynical than we were in the era of traditional print, or even traditional radio. The new American electorate is, in part, a consequence of the new American media system.[33]

Likewise, in a study done in what was then West Germany, researchers found that the amount of television political news coverage parallels the relative importance of issues in public debate, what they called the "agenda-reinforcing effect."[34] In the United States, who can doubt the impact of Anita Hill's televised testimony in the U.S. Senate's confirmation hearings on Supreme Court Justice Clarence Thomas, or of the Clinton administration's TV appearances during the push to gain acceptance for the president's program to revitalize the nation's economy and reduce the national debt?

TV's influence is potent and pervasive because Americans spend more than 7 hours per day watching TV. But viewing habits and patterns are changing: The three major commercial networks now attract only about 60 percent of the viewing audience, compared with more than 90 percent in the early 1960s. The VCR has freed the viewer from being tied to program schedules. New transmission technology is expanding the channel-carrying capacity of cable networks, giving cable subscribers the choice of hundreds of program services and channels. As Newton Minow concludes, "The most important educational institution in America is television. More people learn more each day, each year, each lifetime from television than from any other source."[35]

Heavy reliance on TV news as a primary source of news disturbs thoughtful observers who know that the limits of time and dominance of dramatic pictures inevitably oversimplify and thus distort the news. For example, evening network shows, watched by more than 50 million people each night, must tell the story of the world in 4000 words or fewer, equivalent of four columns in a standard-sized newspaper. Fifty-eight seconds is a major story. Robert MacNeil of the MacNeil-Lehrer News Hour bluntly admits:

> In most of the stories television cares to cover there is always the "right bit," the most violent, the most bloody, the most pathetic, the most tragic, the most wonderful, the most awful moment. Getting the effective "bit" is what television news is all about.[36]

The compression involved in a TV news program, coupled with today's news values and technology, brings a compound of fiction and fact in terse fragments to viewers around the world. Adam Clayton Powell III says major TV networks have entered agreements with video news services around the world or formed alliances to get news once covered by their own foreign bureaus, "capturing images on videotape and distributing them within seconds to dozens or even hundreds of newsrooms around the country and around the world for immediate use."[37]

Even when doing news documentaries, television blurs the line between entertainment and objective journalism:

> The documentary's claims to offer unprejudiced rendering of objective reality were strained by a number of factors associated with the story-telling conventions of popular television, including considerations of plot, character, pursuit of an affective response from audiences, and conscious competition with entertaining programming. . . . Editing and camera techniques also suggested the malleable nature of the medium. Indeed, these techniques helped to generate debate over what is commonly referred to in the industry as "actuality," that is, material captured by photographic or audio equipment which "documents" the analysis of the producer.[38]

Success or failure of entertainment programs is determined by their ratings and consequent amount of advertising the programs can attract, not by their quality. These same criteria are applied all too often to television news programs. But according to one critic, shallowness and the emphasis on entertainment value are not necessarily givens of the medium itself:

> By its very nature, we are told, television emphasizes the visual over the ideational. Action events, national leaders, and political candidates have visual appeal; issues and policy analysis do not. Hence there is bound to be more surface than substance in the news.
>
> . . . . Rather than being a criticism, this "blaming the nature of the media" is a disguised defense. It gets everybody off the hook and treats television, or whatever medium, like a disembodied technological force all its own. However, it is not television as such that chooses to cling to surface events but the people who run it. With the right script and right intentions, visual media can offer engrossingly informative and penetrating presentations on vital subjects.[39]

Selling story ideas to TV producers is a common approach for using television. Producers are the ones who decide if an author's new book is reviewed or the author is interviewed or if a personality appears on shows such as NBC's "Today" and "Tonight" or on syndicated shows such as "Oprah" and "Phil Donahue Show." The most common technique, however, is providing video for news or documentary programs in the form of a *video news release*, or VNR.

TV Guide blew the whistle on the growing use of VNRs in newscasts without viewers being informed that the video was provided by an outside source. The magazine referred to the video press releases as "fake news," suggesting that VNRs blur the line between news and commercials.[40] Others have expressed concern that VNRs can be aired without first having passed journalistic standards for verifying accuracy, can be shown without identifying the source, can be used to manipulate media content in favor of the VNR source, and can violate generally accepted ethical principles in public relations and journalism.[41]

Responding to such concerns, a special committee of the Public Relations Service Council established a "Code of Good Practice for Video New Releases" (see Exhibit 9–2) and a logo to be used by those agreeing to abide by the code.

Virtually all the candidates in the 1992 presidential campaign used VNRs, meaning that campaign staff, not the station's videographers, likely shot the video of candidates used on local news programs. Estimates of the number of VNRs distributed each year range up to 5000, with about 80 percent of television news directors reporting that they use VNR material that they judge to have news value. Their news value is also the reason VNRs are being attacked by critics:

Code of Good Practise for Video News Releases

1. The objective of a VNR is to present information, pictures and sound that TV journalists can use and rely on for quality, accuracy and perspective.
2. Information contained in a VNR, to the extent possible, must be accurate and verifiable. Intentionally false or misleading information must be avoided.
3. A VNR must be clearly identified on the video's opening slate and any advisory material and scripts that precede or accompany tape distribution.
4. The sponsoring company, organization or individual must also be clearly identified on the video slate.
5. The name and phone number of a responsible party must be provided on the video for journalists to contact.
6. Persons interviewed in the VNR must be accurately identified by name, title, and affiliation on the video.

Used with permission of Public Relations Service Council.

At one time, VNRs were assailed by TV journalists because they too closely resembled advertisements. VNRs are under attack today, video experts say, because they deliver what they promise: news![42]

Practitioners are learning how to produce VNRs more acceptable to news directors. Bob Kimmel of News/Broadcast Network (a New York City VNR producer) lists techniques to avoid to increase the chances that stations will use a VNR:

1. Don't mix natural sound with voice-over narration.
2. Don't overuse stills as a substitute for action video.
3. Don't place titles of "supers" on the video news segment itself. Provide the information separately so stations can insert titles in their regular fonts and styles.
4. Don't use fancy special effects and repetitive dissolves not ordinarily used in news packages.
5. Don't commercialize the VNR with blatant product or service presentations.
6. Don't put your own reporter on the screen.
7. Don't produce a VNR unless you have a news story or a timely feature of general interest.[43]

Whether to reach specialized audiences or to place messages on the evening network news, VNRs are the 1990s video equivalent of the print press release. New York City–based Medialink's "Hispanic Telefeed" illustrates the versatility of VNRs in delivering targeted messages. The company distributes VNRs to 170 English-speaking and 25 Spanish-speaking television newsrooms in markets with large Hispanic populations.[44]

When there is not enough time to distribute a VNR on tape, satellite transmission makes it possible to instantaneously distribute public relations messages. Satellite media tours (SMTs), used so frequently in presidential campaigns, make it possible for candidates to appear on local television news and public affairs programs across the nation. The "tour," however, happens by satellite transmission technology without requiring the subject to move from the source station studio. The SMT no doubt will replace the time-consuming and expensive city hopping formerly part of political campaigns, crisis communication programs, and other breaking news stories calling for top management appearances on the global television medium.

Cable Television

The rapid growth of cable television has profoundly altered the nation's communication and viewing patterns. Cable was born in 1948 when the first community-antenna television (CATV) system was built in a small Pennsylvania community that suffered from poor television reception. The number of systems increased steadily until the early 1970s, but increased rapidly in 1975 when Time, Inc., put Home Box Office on the air and the FCC lifted restrictions on programming and advertising. It was Cable News Network's (CNN) live coverage of the 1986 *Challenger* disaster and the round-the-clock coverage of the 1991 Gulf War, however, that made cable news a major player in the global information system. For example, CNN had 125 staffers covering the Persian Gulf region when the war with Iraq began. ABC, CBS, and NBC each had between 60 and 80. CNN coverage was so much more complete that several network affiliates carried CNN reports rather than their own network feeds.[45]

As new technology expands the channel-carrying capacity of old and new systems alike, cable TV may become only part of the packages of services carried. For example, in 1993 two companies—International Cablecasting Technologies of Los Angeles and Digital Cable Radio in Hatboro, Pennsylvania—offered compact disk-quality music delivered by cable. Companies have experimented with interactive cable television services such as shopping and banking, information databases, and emergency alert connections to police and fire depart-

ments. *Videotext* and *teletext* systems link home television sets with central computers to give users access to their bank accounts, advertisements and other product information services, and news databases and libraries. With videotex, viewers are directly connected to a central computer by way of home terminals permitting viewers to call up or send information. In fact, futurists suggest that the line between the home television set and home computers will blur as both information and entertainment services are delivered to homes over cable systems.

Then again, there may be no wire or cable at all. Multipoint distribution systems (MDS) use microwave transmitters to distribute programs to subscribers. Satellite-delivered pay television was introduced in Australia in 1993. Widespread use of direct-broadcast satellite systems will occur when technology and economics converge to make it possible to replace the large home satellite dishes with small antennas mounted in attics or on windows. A small Texas town became the first wireless telephone community in 1993, changing its switch-and-wire system to digital wireless technology. The system reportedly gives the same quality, privacy, and data transmission capabilities of the old wire technology while lowering costs.[46]

In the meantime, telephone companies around the world are entering the video-transmission business. Using new asymmetric digital subscriber line (ADSL) technology, Bell Atlantic is experimenting with video-on-demand services in suburban Washington, D.C., over its existing copper-wire network. In the Tampa, Florida, area, GTE Corporation launched its fiber network in 1992 to carry video from city hall, performing arts theaters, and sports venues to local television stations and other carriers. Telcom Australia plans to have its fiber-to-home network installed by about 1996, with limited service testing beginning in 1994. The company already delivers CNN International and VIP Australian tourist information service to hotels and some businesses in major cities over its fiber-optic network.[47]

WORKING WITH THE MEDIA

Knowing about the media—knowing how to work with each medium, produce content for each, meet the deadlines of each, adhere to specific style requirements, and appeal to each medium's audience—is a major part of many practitioners' jobs. Practitioners responsible for dealing with the media and media gatekeepers must build and maintain relationships of mutual respect and trust. The relationship, although mutually beneficial, remains an adversarial relationship at its core, as journalists and practitioners are not in the same business and often do not have the same communication goals.

The Person in the Middle

To be effective in the go-between and mediating roles, practitioners must have the confidence of both their organization and the media. This is not an easy job. CEOs and other line managers are naturally suspicious of the media, just as journalists are by nature questioning and somewhat untrusting of those they put in the spotlight. Practitioners and others in organizations complain: "Why does the press always sensationalize things?" "Journalists never get things right." "I didn't say that!" "They take things out of context . . . or twist things to fit their story." Journalists counter with: "That organization never tells the truth!" "We don't get to talk with the person who has the real story and real news." "What we get is 'PR crap'." "You get the feeling they're trying to hide something."

The adversarial—even hostile—feelings that exist between practitioners and journalists often spill over into public debate. Herbert Schmertz, Mobil Corporation vice president of public affairs during the 1980s, criticized journalists and media performance by providing what he called "constructive, responsible criticism."[48] Mobil periodically uses its advocacy advertising to criticize the media (see Figure 9–5), to which Schmertz credits substantial progress in improving print coverage of his corporation and business in general. He saved his harshest criticism for television news and

> the questionable values that afflict TV journalism—the slavery to ratings . . . the pandering to the lowest common denominator . . . the emotional presentation to entice a larger audience . . . the subversion of news values to entertainment values . . . the ruthless compression of facts to fit preordained timetables.[49]

Schmertz is not alone in his criticism. Unhappy with television coverage of the B-2 bomber and the plane's price tag, veterans' organizations and the defense industry counterattacked:

> By its very nature, television news suffers from a variety of limitations and constraints. The process by which television editors, producers, and reporters compile, summarize, and synthesize complicated issues often leads to misrepresentations or outright distortions of the news. . . .

> Network television shies away from complicated events, focusing instead on simplicity. Entertainment. Images. . .

> Absent an image, television journalists do not seem capable of presenting the news. Even with an image, broadcast journalism is less serious, and oftentimes less responsible, than print journalism.[50]

Mobil Corporation's Advertisement on "The Myth of Open Airwaves."

4. The myth of the open airwaves

There is a simple, yet overwhelming, difference between the print media and television journalism. Newspapers and magazines offer regular access to their pages to those who wish to rebut what has been printed. The major television networks do not.

Access to television is supposed to be governed largely by the Federal Communications Commission's Fairness Doctrine. That doctrine owes its existence to the theory that the airwaves are a scarce resource and must therefore be allocated among potential users. The doctrine requires owners of broadcast licenses "…to encourage and implement the broadcast of all sides of controversial public issues…" and to play "…a conscious and positive role in bringing about the balanced presentation of the opposing viewpoints." In theory, the Fairness Doctrine doesn't preclude anything. In reality, the networks have turned it into a doctrine of unfairness.

Under a mandate to present all sides of a public issue, the networks confine debate through controls imposed by their own news departments. Through their news staffs, the networks exercise total control over the agenda of issues, and who may speak to the public. Unfortunately, the result of this network control, with no system or forum for rebuttal, has resulted in a narrow and selective discussion of major public issues—and the systematic exclusion or distortion of many viewpoints.

Mobil has often been denied the opportunity to rebut inaccurate television news broadcasts. Frequently, the broadcasts appeared at times when critical energy legislation was under debate in Congress—legislation regarding oil company divestiture, natural gas deregulation, oil decontrol, and the "windfall profit" tax. At such times, the networks' systematic exclusion of ideas and information impaired the public's ability to rationally decide fundamental policy issues.

Other companies have experienced similar frustrations in their attempts to gain adequate airtime to rebut erroneous television newscasts. Kaiser Aluminum & Chemical Corporation had to threaten a slander suit and had to ask the FCC to order ABC to give it time to respond to charges made on a 1980 *20/20* segment, before ABC finally gave the company the opportunity for an unedited reply. It took more than a year, however, before the rebuttal was aired on prime-time TV.

In response to a 1979 CBS *60 Minutes* broadcast, Illinois Power Company produced its own tape to point out the network's distortions. Called "60 Minutes/Our Reply," the power company's rebuttal exposed the bias of the broadcast by including CBS film footage not included in the original segment. The program has been widely shown to various groups across the country, but it has not been aired on television.

The networks not only block rebuttals, they refuse to air advertisements on "controversial" issues, and have rejected Mobil advocacy commercials since 1974—despite evidence that public support for issue advertising is strong. (Network policies would preclude the very message you are currently reading.) A 1980 survey by the Opinion Research Corporation found that 85 percent of the American public think corporations should be allowed to present their views on controversial matters in television commercials. And most independent stations and network affiliates have opened their doors to advocacy advertising, without creating the chaos the networks profess to fear.

As the Supreme Court affirmed in its 1978 *Bellotti* decision: "The press does not have a monopoly on either the First Amendment or the ability to enlighten."

Mobil®

Figure 9–5

General Motors counterattacked when in late 1992 NBC News reported a staged accident and fire involving GM's full-sized pickups manufactured from 1973 through 1987. The report aired on "Dateline NBC" under the title "Waiting to Explode." Exhibit 9–3 summarizes one case in which the media admitted fault and apologized to viewers and to GM.

EXHIBIT 9-3

General Motors versus NBC News

The Situation

In November 1992, a 16-minute segment entitled "Waiting to Explode" on the television news magazine "Dateline NBC" focused on what it called the unsafe design of GM full-sized pickups built from 1973 through 1987. The show included a 1-minute segment of "unscientific" demonstration crashes conducted by the Institute for Safety Analysis (ISA) in which one truck catches fire after being struck in the side by a car.

Seventeen million viewers saw apparent visual support for interviews with safety experts who claimed that the trucks were vulnerable to fires and explosions because of fuel tank design and placement. GM officially complained to NBC that the show was "grossly unfair, misleading and irresponsible."

The television segment also included interviews with the parents of a 17-year-old who was killed when his pickup was broadsided by a car driven by a drunk driver. GM officially complained to NBC that the show was "grossly, unfair, misleading and irresponsible."

In February 1993, the jury found GM "negligent" and awarded the parents $105.2 million. GM appealed, claiming that the 70-miles-per-hour impact into the cab, not the fire, killed the truck driver.

Although NBC and ISA claimed that the test vehicles had been destroyed after the demonstration crashes, GM investigators found them and got court approval to study the vehicles to recreate the demonstrations and results.

GM's Response

In a February 8, 1993, press conference in Detroit, GM's chief counsel presented a well-researched refutation of the "Dateline NBC" segment. GM locations throughout the world and North American dealers received the press conference via satellite. Hundreds of videotapes of the press conference were distributed. While displaying the crash truck fuel tank and slow-motion sequences of the crash, GM's counsel pointed out major deceptions in the report and test crash:

1. NBC did not tell viewers that incendiary rocket devices were taped under the trucks and timed to go off on impact to ignite any spilled gasoline.

2. The fuel tank had been "topped off" before the test and fitted with a nonstandard cap that allowed gasoline to escape as the incendiary device was fired.

3. There was no puncture of the gas tank, as had been claimed in the NBC report.

4. Impact speeds in the demonstration crashes were significantly higher than those NBC reported: one at 39 miles per hour, not 30, and the other at least 47, not 40.

GM filed a lawsuit against NBC and ISA for defaming its reputation. This was the first such action in GM's history.

NBC's Response

NBC carried highlights of GM's charges in its February 8 newscast, but NBC News President Michael Gartner defended the segment. On February 10, however, "Dateline NBC" coanchors Jane Pauley and Stone Phillips read a lengthy retraction negotiated by NBC and GM that day. NBC did not contest any of GM's accusations. "NBC deeply regrets using the one-minute crash segment," Phillips said. "We apologize to our viewers and to GM."

Results

GM accepted NBC's apology and dropped the lawsuit, with the provision that NBC pay GM's research expenses, about $2 million. Quick acceptance of NBC's apology and dropping legal action took the matter out of the media spotlight. In March 1993, Gartner resigned from NBC News and three other executives were fired. A group of independent lawyers hired by NBC had scathing criticism for the show's producers. NBC announced it would reorganize its procedures to ensure future accuracy and fairness. *Detroit Free Press* columnist Steven Brill wrote: "NBC's candid apology was a pivotal event in the annals of journalism—a refreshing reversal of the usual arrogance and stonewalling and hiding behind a justifiably permissive law."

Alvie L. Smith, APR
Director of Corporate
Communications (retired)
General Motors Corporation

Lest you think that all the acrimony is on one side of the practi-tioner-journalist relationship, Meg Greenfield, then–*Washington Post* editorial page editor, issued a memo barring practitioners from editorial offices: "We don't want any of that damned crowd around here." Subse-quently, *Post* executive editor Ben Bradlee extended the ban on talking to public relations sources to reporters, a directive quickly ignored because of reporters' dependence on public relations sources.[51] A schol-arly look at public relations "information subsidies" of news media led the study's author to conclude:

> In journalistic folklore there is a distrust, or mistrust, of public relations practitioners as biased "flacks" engaged in puffery and manipulations of information, and indeed public relations practitioners themselves are indoctrinated to expect that attitude of distrust from journalists.[52]

In fact, practitioners and journalists operate in a mutually depen-dent and mutually beneficial relationship, sometimes as adversaries, sometimes as colleagues cooperating in respective self-interest. Not as frequently, but occasionally, the news media are manipulated by the practitioner, who may have more resources, as well as control access to news sources. With at least equal frequency, news media frustrate prac-titioners in their attempts to get information to publics. In short, there is a dynamic tension in the relationship between practitioners and jour-nalists that is "firmly embedded in journalistic culture."[53] And all to often, neither practitioners' employers nor journalists understand prac-titioners' mediator role in establishing and maintaining media relations.

Guidelines for Good Media Relations

The underlying conflict of interests necessarily makes the practitioner-journalist relationship adversarial. The practitioner advancing a particular cause or organization stands in stark contrast to the journalist's drive to "dig up" news through good reporting and journalistic initiative. Given the experience of at least a century, the adversarial relationship appears to serve the public interest and the needs of the public information system.

The sound approach for organizations and practitioners is to view media relations as an investment. Accuracy and fairness in press cover-age does not result from reporters' work alone. Ultimately, however, the relationship between practitioners and journalists has an impact on the quality of new coverage about organizations.[54] Those relationships can best be achieved when practitioners follow a few basic rules: (1) shoot squarely, (2) give service, (3) do not beg or carp, (4) do not ask for kills, and (5) do not flood the media.

1. **Shoot squarely.** It is not just politically correct to counsel that "honesty is the best policy" in dealing with the press; it is good business and good common sense. Jerry Dalton, Jr., past PRSA president and manager of corporate communications at Vought Aircraft Company, says the practitioner's most important asset in dealing with the media is credibility: "It must be earned, usually over a period of time. It means simply that a reporter can trust [the practitioner] totally, and vice versa. It means never lying. If you can't, for some legitimate reason, speak the truth, then say nothing."[55] Journalists point out that good and bad news tends to even out over time, so if practitioners are honest with bad news, then they are more likely to be trusted with good news.

   Another fundamental principle is that a practitioner cannot favor one news outlet at the expense of others. The safest rule is that spot news should go out as fast as possible, letting the media determine the cycle in which it breaks. News and feature material should be alternated evenly among the competitors. As a corollary, practitioners must protect journalistic initiative. If a reporter gets a tip and asks for information, it belongs to the journalist. The same information should not be given to other outlets unless they come after it. This is a policy with which no reporter can justly quarrel, because each of them would demand the same protection for their "scoops."

2. **Give service.** The quickest, surest way to gain the cooperation of journalists is to provide them newsworthy, interesting, and timely stories and pictures that they want when they want them and in a form they can readily use. Journalists work with fixed and sometimes tight deadlines. Practitioners who hope to place stories in the news media must know and adhere to media "lead times" (see Exhibit 9–4).

EXHIBIT 9-4

Media Lead Times

"Lead time" means the amount of time needed by a medium to receive press materials and then turn a story around for publication or airing. Lead times also determine when you should (or shouldn't) send information to a medium.

So, the next time you're pitching a story or sending a news release, show editors you have publicity savvy by knowing their lead times. You'll not only score points, you'll also avoid missing a potentially "hot" media opportunity. The importance of meeting deadlines with the media can't be stressed enough. Once you've missed a deadline, there's no turning back—you can't recreate a story and use it a second time with the media.

Most lead times vary considerably among print, radio and television and are fairly consistent for each type of medium. For example, trade and consumer magazines generally have different lead times. But if a story qualifies as "breaking news," then lead times don't always apply. Faxes and overnight delivery services have made deadlines for lead times easier to meet if you are caught off guard. The bottom line, however, is that you should be aware of standard lead times.

When in doubt call a reporter and ask what the lead time is. In the meantime, here are a few guidelines:

By Roxanne Ruben
and Judy Lynes,
The Phelps Group
Los Angeles

Print / Lead Time

Print	Lead Time
Newspapers (some sections—food, travel, calendar listings—have longer lead times	One to two weeks (dailies) Three weeks (weeklies)
Trade Magazines (monthly)	Six weeks to two months
Consumer Magazines (monthly)	Five to six months
Metro Magazines (monthly)	Three to four months
Weekly Magazines	One to two months
Sunday Magazines (with Sunday newspapers)	Three to four months

Television

Television	
Public Service Announcements (PSAs)	Six to eight weeks
National Morning Shows	Two weeks to one month
Local Talk Shows	Two to three weeks
Local News	Two days

Radio

Radio	
Public Service Announcements	Six to eight weeks
Promotions	Two weeks to two months
Talk Shows	Four days to one month
News	Two days

Courtesy The Phelps Group, Los Angeles. (Photo by Mark Caroff.)

Journalists also count on and cooperate with the practitioner who willingly responds to a midnight call for a photo and biographical sketch of an executive who just died. News, a highly perishable commodity, occurs around the clock, as do news deadlines in the global village. Therefore, *practitioners must be on call around the clock.* As Dalton points out, "News doesn't wait—for anyone or anything. In many instances, it's now or never to respond on behalf of your organization. The well-written, properly-reviewed, thoroughly-coordinated reply or statement will never see the light of day unless it gets to the media in time for *their* deadlines."[56]

3. **Do not beg or carp.**   Nothing irritates journalists and their editors and news directors more than the practitioner who begs to have stories used or complains about story treatment. Journalists have finely developed senses of journalistic objectivity and news value. If information is not sufficiently newsworthy on its own merits to attract their interest, no amount of begging and carping can change the quality of that information. And do not ask journalists to send "tear sheets." Hire your own clipping service or monitor the media yourself.

Nothing, however, is more offensive to a journalist than a practitioner who tries to pressure the editorial side to use a story, change a story treatment, or kill a story by holding hostage the organization's advertising business. That kind of pressure does not work when up against journalistic integrity and will surely lead to resentment, or to an immediate public response. For example, a threat to "pull our advertising" can lead to a banner headline or the lead story on the evening news, pitting the media against a corporate bully. The rule of thumb is that advertising belongs in the advertising department, and news—good and bad—is for journalists to report in news columns or newscasts.

4. **Do not ask for kills.**   Practitioners have no right to ask the press to suppress or kill a story. It seldom works, is unprofessional, and brings only ill will. To journalists, this is a crude insult and an abuse of the First Amendment. It is asking journalists to betray their public trust. *The way to keep unfavorable stories out of the press is to prevent situations that produce such stories.*

There are occasions when it is perfectly legitimate to request a delay in publication or to explain to the press any part of the story that might be damaging to the public interest. As the Pentagon learned during the 1991 Gulf War, however, the press does not take such requests lightly. Imposing tight restrictions on journalists in press pools and requiring security reviews of all dispatches in the name of "national security" brought charges of censorship and reminders of California U.S. Senator Hiram Johnson's 1917 claim: "The first casualty when war comes is truth."[57]

However, if the press reports an inaccurate or misleading story, ask for a correction. Many news media, in the interest of their own public relations, have adopted policies of publishing or broadcasting corrections. At the same time, however, practitioners should also ask that the erroneous information be corrected in the computerized database, what used to be called the "morgue" or library. Some organizations provide updated background information about the organization, its finances, its products or services, or executives to media so it will be in the file when stories break. For example, the Pharmaceutical Manufacturers' Association sends a file of information to news outlets with this note: "If your files on the prescription drug industry don't include the information in this folder, your files

UCLA Media Guide

Figure 9–6

Courtesy UCLA Public Information Office.

may be incomplete." Many organizations send annual fact books to the media (see Figure 9–6).

5. **Do not flood the media.** Study and experience teach the boundaries of news worthiness, and common sense dictates respect for them. If a financial editor receives information appropriate for the sports or real-estate editor, the financial editor loses respect for the practitioner who engages in blanketing the media with releases. The best advice includes: (1) stick to what journalists will consider news, (2) keep media mailing lists current, and (3) send to only one—the most appropriate—journalist at each news medium.

To document how much his reporters and editors have to cull each day, Paul Steiger, the *Wall Street Journal*'s New York managing editor, asked the 17 domestic bureau managers to save all news materials they received on 1 day in July 1992. They sent him press releases, public relations wire stories, faxes, and letters, but not electronic news releases still in computer memory. The stack of boxes and bins in Steiger's office was more than 2 feet high and 10 feet long.[58] An avalanche of material similar to that at the *Wall Street Journal* occurs in news rooms around the globe. Journalists strike a bargain with their audiences to supply important and interesting information. These gatekeepers require that practitioners do likewise.

Guidelines for Working with the Press

Former CBS news reporter and experienced counselor Chester Burger says that the press "is often unfair, unreasonable, and simply wrong. But even if it isn't our friend, it is the best friend the nation has, and we should be thankful for it."[59] Based on notions of a free and independent press, as well as principles of sound public relations practice, seasoned practitioners offer the following guidelines for working with the press:

1. **Talk from the viewpoint of the public's interest, not the organization's.** The soft-drink bottler who launches a campaign to collect and recycle bottles can frankly admit that it does not want to irritate the public by having its product litter the landscape.

2. **Make the news easy to read and use.** Use a short, punchy headline to attract attention and give potential users an indication of the topic. Do not use jargon, unfamiliar acronyms, or technical terms. Personal pronouns, names, and quotations make your copy easier to read and more interesting. Put the name, address, and phone number of the news source and contact at the top of releases.

3. **If you do not want some statement quoted, do not make it.** Spokespersons should avoid talking "off the record," because such statements may well wind up published without the source. Some news organizations forbid reporters from accepting such information. And it is certainly too late to qualify something as off the record *after* you make a statement to a reporter.

4. **State the most important fact at the beginning.** A manager's logical presentation may first list the facts that led to a decision, but news reporters want the decision. The first-level response to a reporter's question is a short summary of your position or newsworthy announcement. The second-level response includes a concrete example or evidence to back up your first statement. If the reporter persists, return to the first-level summary statement.

5. **Do not argue with a reporter or lose your cool.**   Understand that journalists seek an interesting story and will go to great lengths to get the story. To paraphrase an old public relations maxim, do not argue with people who buy printers ink by the barrel or with people who own the transmitter or cable system; these people have the final say.

6. **If a question contains offensive language or simply words you do not like, do not repeat them even to deny them.**   Along the line of having final say, reporters also can select quotes, portions of quotes, or even single words for the final story. Reporters often use the gambit of putting words into subject's mouths, such as, "Do you mean . . . ?" or "Is what you are really saying . . . ?" For example, ABC-TV's Sam Donaldson is well known for his ability to goad subjects into saying headline-making statements using this technique.

7. **If the reporter asks a direct question, give an equally direct answer.**   Feeling pressure to say something more than what is called for by a question is a common error. If the appropriate answer is "yes" or "no," give the correct response and say no more. Some reporters will remain silent after getting an answer in hopes that the subject will volunteer more information. Assume that the camera is on at all times, otherwise the unguarded comment will be the "sound bite" on the evening news! Media adviser Roger Ailes's rule of thumb is that the tougher the question, the shorter the answer should be.

8. **If a spokesperson does not know the answer to a question, he or she should simply say, "I don't know, but I'll get the answer for you."**   This is a commitment to follow through by providing the information as quickly as possible. Better yet, prepare for the interview by anticipating what questions will be asked, by developing succinct answers, and by rehearsing with someone playing the role of the reporter.

9. **Tell the truth, even if it hurts.**   Do not think for a moment that bad news will go away or that the media will miss it. Treat it as you would any other story: prepare as if it were good news and take it to the media. Not only does that mean that you will keep some control over the story and how it is covered, but it means that you are not on the defensive, making yourself vulnerable to charges of trying to hide the facts or of having been "exposed" by the media. This may be the most difficult position to sell to those in top management who often see the practitioner's job as keeping bad news out of the media.

10. **Do not call a press conference unless you have what reporters consider news.**   When is a *news* conference justified? Seldom. In fact, call a news conference only when there is no other means to get an important breaking story to the media in a timely fashion. Examples include important controversial matters such as labor-management disputes and settlements, important political announcements, and major policy changes affecting large numbers of people. The determining factor is the need to give reporters an opportunity to ask questions and pursue the story, rather than simply issuing a statement or making an announcement. Complex matters that require backgrounding and detailed explanation, such as a technological breakthrough, may justify a press conference. Simple, straightforward, or noncontroversial announcements rarely justify the expense and effort of media coverage. And finally, if you do call a press conference, follow the suggestions outlined in steps 1 through 9.[60]

These suggestions can help practitioners build and maintain good relations with those in the news media. Because of the crucial gatekeeper role played by reporters and editors in both print and broadcast media, practitioners have little choice but to earn and keep the respect of journalists in the news media. At the same time, however, although the public has a right to *public* information, there are limits. Some information is confidential, and some information cannot be disclosed because of individual privacy. Knowing how to keep control of the agenda when dealing with the press is part of the media training required for all those acting as spokespersons.

In the final analysis, however, the practitioner-journalist relationship is an adversarial relationship. After being accused of doing something immoral by teaching people how to deal with the press, Roger Ailes told a journalism seminar:

> We always advise our clients to tell the truth. But the thing that disturbs me most is that you are here in journalism school learning how to ask the questions, yet you would deny a person the right to learn how to answer those questions.[61]

Part of the motivation for giving managers media training is that the top executives in many organizations are public figures without training or experience in dealing with this aspect of their public life. Some have suggested that the CEOs are obliged to deal with the media and face the public when their organizations make important decisions or are involved in crises that have impact beyond the organization. This obligation applies to leaders in corporations, nonprofit agencies, health and health care organizations, educational institutions, government, and all other organizations concerned about their relationships with publics.

Because a free press plays a central role in our free society, this is the era of the media-savvy top executive. Media training designed to help executives deal directly with the press is a responsibility of the public relations department and an essential investment in maintaining good media relations.

ADDITIONAL READINGS

Grunig, James E. "Symmetrical Systems of Internal Communication." In *Excellence in Public Relations and Communication Management*, edited by James E. Grunig, 531–75. Hillsdale, N.J.: Lawrence Erlbaum Associates, Publishers, 1992. Grunig concludes that internal communication does increase employee job satisfaction if the system is designed as a symmetrical, information-sharing system.

Howard, Carole and Wilma Mathews. *On Deadline: Managing Media Relations*. Prospect Heights, Ill.: Waveland Press, Inc., 1985. Summarizes how to deal with reporters, prepare spokespersons, and other aspects of making media relations effective.

Parker, Robert A. "Employee Publications—Dying?—Flourishing?" *IABC Communication World* 10, no. 1 (January–February 1993): 31–37. Findings show that employee publications (primarily newsletters, magazines, and magapapers) remain the primary media for employee communication.

Reichheld, Frederick F. "Loyalty-Based Management." *Harvard Business Review* 71, no. 2 (March–April 1993): 64–73. Reminds that efforts to build customer loyalty must take into account that customers build relationships with loyal employees, not executives.

Shaw, Donald L. "The Rise and Fall of American Mass Media: Roles of Technology and Leadership." *Roy W. Howard Public Lecture in Journalism and Mass Communication Research* 2 (April 4, 1991), School of Journalism, Indiana University, Bloomington. Traces the evolution of major media, concluding that media never regain the dominant position once it is lost. Rather, media innovate to find ways to better serve a loyal audience and develop new users.

Shoemaker, Pamela J. *Gatekeeping,* Communication Concepts No. 3. Newbury Park, Calif.: Sage Publications, Inc., 1991. Examines one of the oldest concepts in mass communication research, reviews previous research, and develops theories based on the findings reported in gatekeeping literature.

Shoemaker, Pamela J., and Stephen D. Reese. *Mediating the Message: Theories of Influences on Mass Media Content.* New York: Longman, Inc., 1991. Reviews research on the various influences on media content, including the impact of media professionals, media routines, organizational factors, outside sources, and ideological perspectives.

Weaver, David H., and G. Cleveland Wilhoit. *The American Journalist: A Portrait of U.S. News People and Their Work.* 2d ed. Bloomington: Indiana University Press, 1991.

Willis, Jim. *Journalism: State of the Art.* New York: Praeger Publishers, 1990. Synthesizes scholarly research on journalists, their work settings, their ethics, their relationships with news sources, and their decision-making processes. Written for those who would probably not chose to read the original scholarly reports.

NOTES

[1] Walter Lippmann, *Public Opinion* (New York: Harcourt, Brace and Company, 1922), 354.

[2] James G. Webster, "Audience Behavior in the Media Environment," *Journal of Communication* 36, no. 3 (Summer 1986): 83.

[3] Alvie L. Smith, letter to authors, March 28, 1993.

[4] Alvie L. Smith, "Getting Managers Off Their Butts and into the Communication Game," *Communication World* 9, no. 1 (January 1992): 35.

[5] Christopher Eschar, "Innovative New Strategies Enhance Employee Relations," *PRSSA Forum* 23, no. 3 (Spring 1991): 4.

[6] Linda Grant, "The Ascent of Delta," *Los Angeles Times Magazine,* June 16, 1991, pp. 17–19, 32–33.

[7] *pr reporter* 35, no. 50 (December 21, 1992): 1 and 3.

[8] T. Michael Forney, "The New Communication Technology," *Public Relations Journal* 38, no. 3 (March 1982): 22.

[9] Gene Goltz, "Making Harmony with House Organs," *Presstime* 13, no. 2 (February 1991): 33.

[10]Michael Finley,   "The New Meaning of Meetings," *IABC Communication World* 8, no. 4 (March 1991): 25.

[11]*The Executive Speechmaker: A Systems Approach* (New York: Foundation for Public Relations Research and Education, 1980).

[12]Alvie L. Smith,   *Innovative Employee Communication: New Approaches to Improving Trust, Teamwork and Performance* (Englewood Cliffs, N.J.: Prentice-Hall, Inc., 1991), 147. This "must-read" for those interested in employee communication details the Federal Express case and many other examples by former GM director of corporate communications.

[13]Ibid., 145.

[14]Don Costa,   "Winning with a Short-Subject Film," *Public Relations Journal* 38, no. 9 (September 1982): 24–26.

[15]Quote from former Johnson and Johnson public relations executive Larry Foster, in Smith, *Innovative Employee Communication*, 143.

[16]Frank Mankiewicz,   "From Lippmann to Letterman: The 10 Most Powerful Voices," in "The Opinion Makers," special issue of *Gannett Center Journal* 3, no. 2 (Spring 1989): 96.

[17]John C. Merrill,   "Global Elite: A Newspaper Community of Reason," in "World Media," special issue of *Gannett Center Journal* 4, no. 4 (Fall 1990): 93.

[18]Ibid., 101.

[19]Walt Potter,   "When Their Favorite Local Paper Dies, Where Do Readers Go?" *Presstime* 14, no. 4 (April 1992): 6–8 and 10; and Leo Bogart,   "Second Thoughts: The Prospects and a 'Modest Proposal' for Two-Paper Markets," *Presstime* 14, no. 12 (December 1992): 36. Also see *Facts About Newspapers '93*, published by Newspaper Association of America, The Newspaper Center, Reston, Va.

[20]Albert E. Gollin,   "Setting the Record Straight on Trends in Newspaper Readership," *Presstime* 14, no. 4 (April 1992): 42; and "Research: Good News," *Presstime* 14, no. 10 (October 1992): 28, "Newspaper Numbers," *Presstime* 14, no. 10 (October 1992): 48.

[21]A. Carlos Ruotolo,   "A Typology of Newspaper Readers," *Journalism Quarterly* 65, no. 1 (Spring 1988): 126–30.

[22]*Facts About Newspapers '93*, 21.

[23]Mary Jane Genova,   "Op-ed Articles Express Client's Point of View," *Public Relations Journal* 47, no. 9 (September 1991): 35.

[24]Shirley Biagi,   *Media/Impact: An Introduction to Mass Media*, 2d ed. (Belmont, Calif.: Wadsworth Publishing Company, 1992): 82–83.

[25]*PR Reporter* 34, no. 8 (February 25, 1991): 4

[26]According to Professor Joseph V. Trahan in a presentation to the New Mexico Public Relations Society of America Professional Development Seminar, Albuquerque, January 29, 1993. Trahan, also a major in the U.S. Army Reserves, coordinated on-site press relations for federal agencies responding to the Hurricane Andrew crisis.

[27]Keith Elliot Greenberg,   "Radio News Releases Make the Hit Parade," *Public Relations Journal* 48, no. 7 (July 1992): 6.

[28]Ibid.

[29]Charles Price,   "ATTACK of the Radio Talk-Show Hosts," *California Journal* 20, no. 9 (September 1989): 366.

[30]Newton N. Minow, "How Vast the Wasteland Now?" Address given at the Gannett Foundation Media Center (Now Freedom Forum Center for Media Studies), Columbia University, New York City, May 9, 1991 (the 30th anniversary of Minow's "Vast Wasteland" speech to the National Association of Broadcasters).

[31]Hans-Bernd Brosius and Hans Mathias Kepplinger, "Beyond Agenda-Setting: The Influence of Partisanship and Television Reporting on the Electorate's Voting Intentions," *Journalism Quarterly* 69, no. 4 (Winter 1992): 893–901.

[32]Maxwell E. McCombs, "Explorers and Surveyors: Expanding Strategies for Agenda-Setting Research," *Journalism Quarterly* 69, no. 4 (Winter 1992): 819.

[33]Michael J. Robinson and Margaret A. Sheehan, *Over the Wire and on TV: CBS and UPI in Campaign '80* (New York: Russell Sage Foundation, 1983), 262.

[34]Klaus Schoenbach and Holli A. Semetko, "Agenda-Setting, Agenda-Reinforcing or Agenda-Deflating? A Study of the 1990 German National Election," *Journalism Quarterly* 69, no. 4 (Winter 1992): 837–46.

[35]Minow, "How Vast the Wasteland Now?"

[36]Robert MacNeil, *The Right Place at the Right Time* (Boston: Little, Brown, 1982), 129.

[37]Adam Clayton Powell, III, "The Global TV News Hour" in "World Media" issue of *Gannett Center Journal* 4, no. 4 (Fall 1990): 119.

[38]Michael Curtain, "Packaging Reality: The Influence of Fictional Forms on the Early Development of Television Documentary," *Journalism Monographs* 137 (February 1993): 19.

[39]Michael Parenti, *Inventing Reality: The Politics of the Mass Media* (New York: St. Martin's Press, 1986), 9–10.

[40]David Lieberman, "Fake News," *TV Guide* 40, no. 8 (February 22, 1992), 10–14, 16, and 26.

[41]K. Tim Wulfemeyer and Lowell Frazier, "The Ethics of Video News Releases: A Qualitative Analysis," *Journal of Mass Media Ethics* 7, no. 3 (1992): 151–68.

[42]Adam Shell, "VNRs: In the News," *Public Relations Journal* 48, no. 12 (December 1992): 21.

[43]"Ten Tips on How to Get Your VNR Aired," *IABC Communication World* 9, no. 9 (September 1992): 10.

[44]"Suppliers Zero in on Growing Hispanic Market," *Public Relations Journal* 48, no. 7 (July 1992): 7.

[45]Patrick Mott, "New King of the Hill," *The Quill* 79, no. 2 (March 1991): 14–16.

[46]"Wireless City," *The Futurist* 27, no. 2 (March–April 1993): 5.

[47]Information about cable trends and developments, such as those reported here, are extensively reported in the weekly trade journal *Cable World*, Cable World Associates, 1905 Sherman Street, Suite #1000, Denver, CO 80203. Other sources include *Broadcasting* (weekly trade journal), 1735 DeSales Street, N.W., Washington, DC 20036, and *Journal of Broadcasting* (quarterly research journal), Ohio State University, Columbus, OH 43210.

[48]"Inquiry: Press Can't Have the Right to Lie," *USA Today*, November 4, 1983, p. 11A.

[49]Herbert Schmertz, "The Press and Morality." Remarks to Guild Hall Discussion Series, East Hampton, New York, July 12, 1983.

[50]Stephen Aubin, "The B-2 and Network News: A Case Study in Media Distortion." Report published by the Aerospace Education Foundation (an affiliate of the Air Force Association), Arlington, Va., January 1991, p. 1.

[51]"Flack Attack: The Post Spurns P.R. 'Wolves,'" *Time*, May 10, 1982, p. 101; and Carl Cannon, "The Great Flack Flap," *Washington Journalism Review* 4 (September 1982): 35.

[52]Judy VanSlyke Turk, "Information Subsidies and Media Content: A Study of Public Relations Influence on the News," *Journalism Monographs* 100 (December 1986): 26–27.

[53]Michael Ryan and David L. Martinson,   "Journalists and Public Relations Practitioners: Why the Antagonism?" *Journalism Quarterly* 65, no. 1 (Spring 1988): 139.

[54]Mark S. Cox,   "Media Relations and the Content of Business News" (Master of Science in Mass Communication thesis, San Diego State University, May 1983).

[55]H. J. Dalton, Jr., personal letter and enclosure "50 Basic Thoughts on Good News Media Relations" presentation to Veterans Administration public affairs training seminar.

[56]Ibid.

[57]Paul McMasters,   "Journalists Aren't Winning Their Gulf War," *The Quill* 79, no. 2 (March 1991): 8. See also Richard Zoglin,   "The Press: It Was a Public Relations Rout Too," *Time*, March 11, 1991, pp. 56–57.

[58]"News Is Stacked Up at *Wall St. Journal*," *Jack O'Dwyer's Newsletter*, August 26, 1992, p. 4.

[59]Chester Burger,   "Phony Communication Is Worse Than None at All." Arthur W. Page Society Hall of Fame induction speech, Amelia Island, Fla., September 23, 1992.

[60]Adapted from Roger Ailes (with Jon Kraushar),   *You Are the Message: Secrets of the Master Communicators* (Homewood, Ill.: Dow Jones-Irwin, 1988); Chester Burger,   "How to Meet the Press," *Harvard Business Review*, July–August 1975; Christel K. Beard and H. J. Dalton, Jr.,   "The Power of Positive Press," *Sales and Marketing Management*, January 1991: 37–43; and Dalton,   "50 Basic Thoughts on Good News Media Relations."

[61]Ailes, *You Are the Message*, 165.

CHAPTER 10

Step One: Defining Public Relations Problems

The old "flying by the seat of the pants" approach to solving public relations problems is over.

Dr. Edward Robinson wrote the obituary for the "seat-of-the-pants" approach to doing public relations in 1969. He saw the public relations practitioner as "an applied social and behavioral scientist" using "research to help in the problem solving process." He may have been a bit premature in his assessment, however, when he wrote this in the first public relations research book. Intuitive, individualistic approaches to problem solving often still guide the practice in many settings, even though, as Robinson wrote, research is "the most powerful tool available to the applied practitioner."[1]

The open systems approach discussed in Chapter 7 combines rational problem solving and proactive strategic planning. From its origins as the "art" of reacting to outside threats, public relations has evolved to an applied science. No longer do hunches, "gut feelings," and personal experiences, alone or in combination, serve as an adequate basis for public relations programs. And rarely do top managers or clients accept on faith alone a practitioner's recommendations or simple assertions that a program was successful.

MANAGEMENT PROCESS

In its most advanced form, public relations is a scientifically managed part of an organization's problem-solving and change processes. Practitioners of this type of public relations use theory and the best available evidence in a four-step problem-solving process:

1. ***Defining the problem (or opportunity).***   This first step involves probing and monitoring knowledge, opinions, attitudes, and behaviors of those concerned with and affected by the acts and policies of an organization. In essence, this is an organization's intelligence function. It provides the foundation for all the other steps in the problem-solving process by determining, *"What's happening now?"*

2. ***Planning and programming.***   Information gathered in the first step is used to make decisions about program publics, objectives, action and communication strategies, tactics, and goals. This involves factoring the findings from the first step into the policies and programs of the organization. This second step in the process answers, *"Based on what we know about the situation, what should we change or do, and say?"*

3. ***Taking action and communicating.***   The third step involves implementing the program of action and communication designed to achieve the specific objectives for each of the publics to accomplish the program goal. The questions in this step are, *"Who should do and say it, and when, where, and how?"*

4. ***Evaluating the program.***   The final step in the process involves assessing the preparation, implementation, and results of the program. Adjustments are made while the program is being implemented, based on evaluation feedback on how it is or is not working. Programs are continued or stopped after learning, *"How are we doing, or how did we do?"*

Each step is as important as the others, but the process begins with gathering intelligence to diagnose the problem. Information and understanding developed in the first step motivate and guide subsequent steps in the process. In practice, of course, diagnosis, planning, implementation, and evaluation cannot be as neatly compartmentalized, as the process is continuous and cyclical and is applied in a dynamic setting. Figure 10–1 illustrates the continuous, overlapping, and cyclical nature of public relations problem solving.

The four-step process is illustrated by how an oil company's public relations staff handled a problem situation some years ago: The company decided to close one of its sales divisions as part of a reorganization to increase efficiency. This meant that 600 employees would have to move or find new jobs, the community where the division was located would suffer economic loss, customers of the sales division would be concerned about getting equally good service under the new setup, and investors would be curious about the meaning of the move.

The first task was to marshal all the facts through research so that the move could be explained and justified in terms of those concerned. The next step was to plan the announcement. Timing was important. The news had to be broken swiftly, before rumors started, released simultaneously to all those affected, and communicated in such a way as to explain satisfactorily the necessity and wisdom of the change.

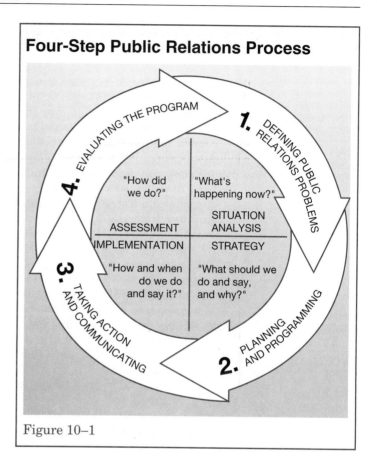

Four-Step Public Relations Process

EVALUATING THE PROGRAM

1. DEFINING PUBLIC RELATIONS PROBLEMS

"How did we do?"

"What's happening now?"

ASSESSMENT

SITUATION ANALYSIS

IMPLEMENTATION

STRATEGY

"How and when do we do and say it?"

"What should we do and say, and why?"

3. TAKING ACTION AND COMMUNICATING

2. PLANNING AND PROGRAMMING

Figure 10–1

Materials included a procedure memorandum to guide the staff, a presentation script for meetings, letters to several different groups of employees, letters to all dealers, a news release, a statement on banking arrangements for community banks, a general office letter, and plans for meetings. The news was released in a coordinated program of meetings, letters, and media coverage. Finally, evaluation focused on the department's original assessment of the problem situation, the techniques used, and the reactions of those affected, with an eye to improving procedures. The lessons learned were put to good use a few years later when the company closed a plant in another location, demonstrating how systematic research and evaluation improves the practice over time.

Obviously, this is an oversimplified presentation of what actually happened. The process includes many smaller steps within each of the four major steps represented in the model. These will be outlined in greater detail in this and the next three chapters. In this chapter, we will concentrate on the research and fact-finding methods necessary for beginning the strategic planning process.

ROLE OF RESEARCH IN STRATEGIC PLANNING

Monitoring the social environment is not only the first step in the process; it is the most difficult one. One is reminded of the fable of the elephant and the six blind men of Indostan: Each encounters only a single part of the beast and describes the elephant based on that limited information. For example, the one who grabs the trunk concludes, "The Elephant is very like a snake!" The one who feels the knee says, "'Tis clear enough the Elephant is very like a tree!" This process continues, with each experiencing only a portion of the elephant. In the end, each was partly right and mostly wrong about the nature of the beast, but argued "loud and long" based on their respective encounters with the elephant.[2] Without researching a problem situation, practitioners run the risk of acting like the six blind men from Indostan.

Surveys of practitioners routinely show that research training tops the list of needed professional continuing education. Surveys also show that practitioners often say that lack of funds and too little time are why they do not do more research. A better explanation of why so little research is used in public relations, however, is a combination of not understanding how to do and use research and many employers' and clients' views that research is not necessary. While in college, few practitioners studied research methods or anticipated that research would be part of their professional work. Once they began professional practice, they felt little pressure from employers and clients who often did not demand or fund research. As one corporate public relations executive responded in a Ketchum Public Relations survey: "The problem is not with research methodology, but with the inability—or perhaps laziness—of PR professionals who prefer to fly by the seats of their pants."[3]

For years, executives and practitioners alike bought the popular myth that public relations deals with intangibles that cannot be measured. With each passing day it becomes increasingly difficult to sell that position to results-oriented management (many with M.B.A. degrees) accustomed to making decisions based on evidence and objective analysis. A practitioner in a nonprofit organization attributes "the decline of PR . . . to the lack of monitoring and substantive evaluation of results. That's why PR is seen by CEO's as 'fluff'."[4]

Without research, practitioners are limited to asserting that they know the situation and can recommend a solution. With research and analysis, they can present and advocate proposals supported by evidence and theory. In this context, *research is the systematic gathering of information to describe and understand situations and to check out assumptions about publics and public relations consequences.* It is the scientific alternative to tenacity, authority, and intuition. Its main purpose is to reduce uncertainty in decision making. Even though it cannot answer all the questions or sway all decisions, *methodical, systematic research is the foundation of effective public relations.*

RESEARCH ATTITUDE

Computers and management information specialists have greatly increased organizations' capabilities to gather, process, transfer, and interpret information. The increase in M.B.A.-prepared, information-conscious middle and upper managers intensifies the pressure on public relations for accountability. In short, a research orientation is necessary for those practicing public relations in the information age. An early researcher who helped build the automotive industry, C. F. Kettering, once described this attitude toward research in these words:

> Research is a high-hat word that scares a lot of people. It need not. It is rather simple. Essentially, it is nothing but a state of mind—a friendly, welcoming attitude toward change. Going out to look for change, instead of waiting for it to come. Research . . . is an effort to do things better and not be caught asleep at the switch. The research state of mind can apply to anything. Personal affairs or any kind of business, big or little. It is the problem-solving mind as contrasted with the let-well-enough-alone mind. It is the composer mind, instead of the fiddler mind; it is the "tomorrow" mind instead of the "yesterday" mind.[5]

Research is no longer a specialized activity delegated to "chi-square types" tucked away in the bowels of an organization. As Rossi and Freeman put it: "It is also a political and management activity, an input into the complex mosaic from which policy decisions and allocations emerge for the planning, design, implementation, and continuation of programs."[6]

Modern managers are a fact-minded lot; they want figures. In many organizations, these executives tend to be isolated from problems by cadres of specialists and subordinates. When the public relations aspect of organizational problems must be brought home to them, the research-based approach is most effective. As other parts of organizations such as marketing, finance, and personnel have adapted a research-based approach, so must public relations. In fact, research findings suggest a strong linkage between doing research and earning one of the few seats at the management strategy table. Studies of practitioners show that participation in management increases when practitioners do research.[7]

LISTENING AS SYSTEMATIC RESEARCH

Effective public relations starts with listening, which requires openness and systematic effort. Too often, what purports to be communication is simply opposing ideas passing each other in different one-way channels, for example, in a management-versus-labor bargaining situation with each side merely wanting to score points, not listening to the other's views. As Wilbur Schramm explained, "Feedback is a powerful tool. When it does not exist or is delayed or feeble . . . then the situation engenders doubt and concern in the communicator, and frustration and sometimes hostility in the audience."[8] Also using his words, "Feedback tells the communicator how his message is being received."[9]

Listening is not an easy task. Channels from the worker out in the plant or from the alumnus in Seattle must be created and kept open. *Failure to listen often leads to purposeless "communications" on issues that do not exist to publics that are not there.* Unless you know the orientations, predispositions, and language of your audience—learned through empathetic listening—you are not likely to communicate effectively. Research is simply one method of structuring systematic "listening" into the communication process.

An able listener of another time, Abraham Lincoln, knew the importance of listening. Twice a week, Lincoln set aside a time for conversations with ordinary folk: housewives, farmers, merchants, and pension seekers. He listened patiently to what they had to say, no matter how humble their circumstances or how trivial their business. A military aide once protested to the president that he was wasting valuable time on these unimportant people. Lincoln rebuked him, saying, "I tell you, Major . . . that I call these receptions my public opinion bath . . . the effect, as a whole is renovating and invigorating."[10] Today the White House has sophisticated and elaborate methods for monitoring constituent opinion: daily analyses of media and mail content, sophisticated telephone voice-mail tabulations of calls, as well as regular polling of public opinion.

Prudence dictates the systematic listening to an organization's publics through scientific research. Yet many organizations fail to utilize this public relations tool fully. In some, two-way communication is seen as organized back talk and a potential threat, rather than an essential tool of modern management. More likely, systematic listening to obtain reliable feedback is limited because it takes effort and skill. The amount of information input, however, determines the extent to which an organization operates as an open versus closed system in dealing with problems.

DEFINING PUBLIC RELATIONS PROBLEMS

In closed systems, of course, problems are allowed to define themselves, often as crises. The public relations effort then necessarily reverts into "firefighting" rather than "fire prevention." Examples include spending millions of dollars to counter proposals made by dissident stockholders; paying millions of dollars for advertising time and space to apologize for past actions and to announce corrective measures; and suffering costly construction delays because active citizen groups resorted to legal action to stop proposed, yet unexplained, projects.

Such situations have long histories, and sometimes neither side recalls what caused the blowup. Heading off such blowups is part of the task. The earlier a complaint is caught, the easier it is to handle. Continuous fact finding uncovers many problems while they are still small enough to permit corrective action and communication before becoming major public issues. The same attentive listening catches rumors before they become widespread and part of the publics' perceptions of the organization.

The problem definition process begins with someone making a value judgment that something is either wrong or could soon be or that something could be better than it is. Implicit is the notion that organizational goals provide the criteria for making such judgments. Goal states serve as the bases for deciding if and when a real or potential problem exists. Once a judgment is made, however, the process becomes an objective, systematic research task designed to describe in detail the dimensions of the problem, the factors contributing to or alleviating the problem, and the publics involved in or affected by the situation. In short, research is used to determine, *"What's happening now?"*

Problem Statement

A useful problem statement summarizes what was learned about the problem situation. *Written in present tense, a problem statement describes a situation in specific and measurable terms.* It details most of or all the following:

> **What** is the source of concern?
> **Where** is this a problem?
> **When** is it a problem?
> **Who** is involved or affected?
> **How** are they involved or affected?
> **Why** is this a concern to the organization and its publics?

A problem statement does not imply solution or place blame, however. If it did, program strategies would be predetermined and limited, much like the cuttlefish's limited options for responding to its environment. The classic example of a problem statement that has an implied solution is the overused, "What we have here is a communication problem." Communication is part of the solution, not the problem! The real problem could be that *only 5 percent of new graduates join the alumni association during the first year following graduation, compared with 21 percent of all graduates, resulting in lost contact and reduced support for the university.* Or, in the case of a fund-raising effort for a new youth center, the problem could be stated as: *The building fund is $200,000 short of the amount needed to complete and equip the new gymnasium by* *the planned June 1 opening.* Or, if you had worked for one of the major oil companies a several years ago, you might have been concerned about the "divestiture problem": *A plurality (47 percent) of Americans agree with proposals to break up each of the major oil companies into four separate and competing operating companies, thus encouraging some in Congress to vote in favor of divestiture legislation.* Communication may be part of the solution, but it is not stated as part of the problem.

Notice that each of these problem statements contains concrete measures of the problem situation based on objective research and documentation. Notice also that solutions are not implied, meaning that no particular strategy is suggested in any of the problem statements. Finally, notice that the three examples describe the current situation— "What's happening now?"—not the future.

Situation Analysis

A problem statement represents a concise description of the situation, often written in a sentence or short paragraph. In contrast, a situation analysis is the unabridged collection of all that is known about the situation, its history, forces operating on it, and those involved or affected internally and externally. A situation analysis contains all the background information needed to expand upon and to illustrate in detail the meaning of a problem statement. In the process of analyzing the situation, one is able to clearly and specifically define and refine the problem statement. Typically, the definition process begins with a tentative problem statement, followed by investigation of the situation, which leads to refining the problem definition, and so on.

The situation analysis results in what some practitioners call their "fact book," often in the form of information assembled in three-ring binders or files. The section on *internal factors* deals with organizational policies, procedures, and actions related to the problem situation. Rather than direct all the attention to the publics and other external factors, a situation analysis begins with a thorough and searching review of perceptions and actions of key actors in the organization, structures and processes of organizational units relevant to the problem, and the history of the organization's involvement.

The internal situation analysis also includes a *communication audit, a systematic documentation of an organization's communication behavior for the purpose of understanding how it communicates with its publics.* One practitioner describes the communication audit as:

A complete analysis of an organization's communications—internal and/or external designed to "take a picture" of communication needs, policies, practices, and capabilities, and to uncover necessary data to allow top management to make informed, economical decisions about future objectives of the organization's communication.[11]

Consistent with the open systems model, practitioners do an audit to learn in detail how, what, and to whom they communicate. An audit provides decision makers a clear picture of what is currently done and a basis for deciding what changes need to be made.

Another essential part of the internal portion of a situation analysis is a constantly updated organizational almanac. This file not only serves as an essential organizational background reference when working on specific problems, but also provides ideas and information for speeches, pamphlets, special reports, exhibits, and media requests. Most organizations do not have librarians or historians, so public relations departments often handle queries that cannot be answered by others. Journalists expect and need quick answers. Ready access to complete and accurate information on an organization, its history, performance, and managers can give the public relations department a start on crises or rumors in the making.

After developing an understanding of the organizational side of the problem situation, an analysis focuses on the *external factors*, both positive and negative. The starting point may be a systematic review of the history of the problem situation outside the organization. A situation analysis also calls for detailed study of who is currently involved or affected and how. Much of what is done under the banner of public relations research includes gathering information about *stakeholders*: what they know, how the feel, and what they do that is related to the problem.

The process of identifying who is involved and who is affected in a situation is called "stakeholder analysis." Stakeholders are people—in the imagery of system theory—who are part of the same system as an organization. They are in interdependent relationships with an organization, meaning that what they know, feel, and do have impact on the organization and vice versa. In the interest of building and maintaining mutually beneficial relationships, organizations undertake periodic stakeholder analyses to monitor how organizational policies, procedures, decisions, actions, and goals affect others. The different stakeholder groups can be ranked or rated according to the extent to which each is interdependent with an organization in a particular problem situation. Notice that not all those identified as stakeholders necessarily become publics for a program designed to address a particular problem (more on defining publics in the next chapter).[12]

How could you set objectives for each of the publics if you do not know what they currently know, what their opinions are, and how they behave? How could you develop action and communication strategies without a detailed understanding of and empathy for the target publics? At least four additional questions must be answered through research:

1. *How much do people use information in the problem situation?* Communication is only effective if receivers see a need for information. The situation analysis research must determine to what extent different people actually feel a need for and use information related to a given problem situation.

2. *What kinds of information do people use?* Whereas "why" questions make up 20 to 35 percent of the questions people typically ask in situations, these are the ones least likely to be answered successfully in communication programs. Programs that respond to audience needs rather than the interests of the source are based on knowledge of what information different people want.

3. *How do people use information?* Information is rarely an end in itself because people use information in many different ways. Receivers see information as useful if they think that it relates to a specific action, topic, or plan they consider important. Rarely are they helped simply because they received "general information."

4. *What predicts information use?* Demographics or other cross-situational characteristics often do not predict how people use information. Rather, where receivers are in the decision-making process relevant to a problem, or how they see themselves in the situation, determines whether or not they will use the information. In other words, you must know how different individuals see themselves involved in or affected by the situation.[13]

The importance of situation-specific understanding of stakeholders is also evident in VanLeuven's theory of message and media selection that: "(1) the user selects media and messages for his or her own rational-appearing and personally relevant purposes; (2) the user will attach his or her own personal meanings to a selected message; (3) the user's behavior reflects anticipated future communication satisfaction as well as a history of prior motivation, intentionality, and reinforcement."[14]

Researching the stakeholders before planning program strategies tests the accuracy of assumptions about who they are, what they know, how they feel about the situation, how they are involved or affected, what information they see as important, how they use it, and even how they get information. With that information in hand—and only then—can program planners write objectives for each public and develop strategies to achieve them.

Systematic definition and study of the stakeholders are needed also to determine an order of priority. Rarely does a practitioner have the staff or money to mount programs directed to all stakeholders. Priorities must be assigned based on which of them are most central to the particular problem at hand, not in response to internal or external pressures not related to the problem situation.

Increased understanding of the stakeholders helps determine their information needs and uses: message content. Researching their communication patterns and media preferences helps practitioners select the most effective and efficient media strategy for delivering those messages.

Only after the situation has been completely analyzed can practitioners set realistic program goals. Lacking complete and accurate information, practitioners can be guilty of overpromises and under-delivery. Without a complete understanding of the problem situation, practitioners run the risk of developing programs that do not address the major causes of the problem. No amount of public relations communication can change bad performance into good performance or socially irresponsible action into responsible behavior. Neither can it compensate for lack of integrity or persuade publics that an unfair or self-serving policy is fair and unselfish. Overenthusiastic selling of the function often results from incomplete comprehension of the problem situation and leads to the appearance of program failure.

Situation analysis research gives practitioners and their employers and clients the timely, complete, and accurate information needed to understand the problem and to serve as a basis for decision making. (Exhibit 10–1 lists topics covered in a situation analysis.) Research is simply an attempt to reduce uncertainty, or as one executive put it, "to help really see what's there to be seen."

EXHIBIT 10-1

Content of Situation Analysis

I. INTERNAL FACTORS

1. Statements of the organization's mission, charter, bylaws, history, and structure
2. Lists, biographies, and photos of key officers, board members, managers, and so forth
3. Descriptions and histories of programs, products, services, and so forth
4. Statistics about resources, budget, staffing, sales, profits, stockholders, and so forth
5. Policy statements and procedures related to the problem situation
6. Position statements (quotations) by key executives regarding the problem situation
7. Description of how the organization currently handles the problem situation
8. Descriptions and lists of the organization's internal stakeholders
9. Lists of organizational media (two-way) for communicating with internal groups

II. EXTERNAL FACTORS

1. Clippings from newspaper, magazine, trade publication, and newsletter coverage of the organization and the problem situation
2. Reports, transcripts, and tapes of radio, television, and cable coverage
3. Content analyses of media coverage
4. Lists of media, journalists, columnists, talk-show hosts, freelance writers, and producers who report news and features about the organization and issues related to the problem situation
5. Lists of and background information on individuals and groups who share the organization's concerns, interests, and positions on the problem situation (including their controlled internal and external media outlets)
6. Lists of and background information on individuals and groups who oppose the organization's concern, interests, and positions on the problem situation (including their controlled internal and external media outlets)
7. Results of surveys and public opinion polls related to the organization and the problem situation
8. Schedules of special events, observances, and other important dates related to the organization and the problem situation
9. Lists of government agencies, legislators, and other officials with regulatory and legislative power affecting the organization and the problem situation
10. Copies of relevant regulations, legislation, pending bills, referenda, government publications, and hearing reports
11. Copies of published research on topics related to the problem situation
12. Lists of important reference books, records, and directories, as well as their locations in the organization

Detailed analyses of the internal and external factors in the problem situation provide practitioners with the information needed to assess organizational strengths (S) and weaknesses (W) and to identify the opportunities (O) and threats (T) in the external environment. In practice, practitioners refer to this approach to summarizing the situation analysis as "SWOT" or "TOWS" analysis. Several strategic implications logically flow from this analytic framework:

1. *SO strategies* build on organizational strengths to take advantage of opportunities in the external environment.
2. *ST strategies* also build on organizational strengths to counter threats in the external environment.
3. *WO strategies* attempt to minimize organizational weaknesses to take advantage of external opportunities.
4. *WT strategies* attempt to minimize both organizational weaknesses and environmental threats.[15]

Another analytic technique for summarizing the findings of a situation analysis is "force-field analysis." Before researching the situation, practitioners and others on the management team brainstorm the negative forces contributing to or causing the problem, as well as the positive forces alleviating or solving the problem. The research on the internal and external forces helps determine the extent to which each contributes positively or negatively to the problem situation. Just as with SWOT analysis, the results of a force-field analysis lead to strategic decisions designed to minimize or neutralize the impact of negative forces and to maximize or enhance the contributions from positive forces.[16]

RESEARCH PROCESS

The central roles of research in modern public relations, addressed further in Chapter 11, are demonstrated here. Sometimes practitioners do the research themselves. Other times practitioners hire research specialists or research firms to design the research, gather the information, or analyze the data. In either approach, practitioners must know the research process and concepts. Simply put, you cannot satisfactorily explain to someone else something you do not understand yourself. As Ann Barkelew, Dayton-Hudson Corporation's vice president of public relations, says, "You cannot practice public relations today—successfully or effectively—without research."[17]

Scientists have developed a generally accepted approach to research. The process begins with a clear statement of the problem under investigation. Some choose to phrase the problem in the form of a question. Others pose hypothetical relationships between observable phenomena for testing and theory building. The next step is to develop the research design, the plan for making the observations related to the research problem. Is a survey needed? An experiment? Or will the observations be taken from published census reports? This is followed by the specific methods for gathering, analyzing, and interpreting data.[18]

Whereas two research projects are seldom the same in the specifics of how they are implemented, they share a common goal of increasing our understanding of situations and society. The approach and methods chosen for a particular project will depend on the problem being addressed, the skills and preferences of the researcher, available resources, and the constraints imposed by others or as a result of the situation.

INFORMAL OR "EXPLORATORY" METHODS

Informal methods still dominate public relations research even though highly developed social science methods are available. Informal methods can be useful, however, if practitioners recognize their weaknesses and purposes. *The major problem—samples of unknown representativeness— results from how samples are selected.* The issue is the extent to which the results from samples represent anybody other than the few from whom information was gathered. For example, the results may represent only the opinions of a vocal minority, rather than the majority.

If viewed as good methods for *detecting* and *exploring* problem situations, and for pretesting research and program strategies, then informal methods serve valuable purposes. If the results are used as the basis for program planning and evaluation as if the findings are representative of target publics, then these methods are misused. "Exploratory" best represents the probing nature of informal methods.

The following sections describe some of the informal methods used in public relations.

Personal Contacts

In 1893 Lord Bryce said, "The best way in which the tendencies at work in any community can be best discovered and estimated is by moving freely about among all sorts and conditions of men." Politicians have been doing this for a long time. Skill in sizing up people's awareness, opinions, and attitudes has long been and always will be a prime qualification of public relations professionals.

For example, when management requested an employee communication campaign against drug abuse, a corporate practitioner, posing as a patient, checked into a drug treatment center and spent 3 days acquiring firsthand knowledge about drugs, their use, and their potential effects on employees. Others have worked in wheelchairs to gain perspective on what it is like to go for coffee breaks, to use the bathroom, or to complete other tasks in facilities not designed for easy access. Trade shows, community and professional meetings, or other occasions that attract stakeholders provide opportunities for practitioners to listen carefully and to gain understanding.

Feedback from periodic personal visits can be encouraged, extended, and amplified in many ways. For example, when former Los Angeles Mayor Thomas Bradley first took office, he opened his door to local citizens one day a month. They were given a chance to talk to the mayor about poor sewer facilities, increases in school vandalism, or whatever was on their minds. The mayor of Utica, New York, went a step further: To encourage people to drop in and air their complaints, he took his door off its hinges and put up a sign over his couch that read, "The Town's Living Room." The president of Delta Airlines maintains an open-door policy for employees.

A more structured use of personal contacts is exemplified by the annual shareholder meetings held each year by publicly owned corporations. For example, managers in one company visited shareholders in their homes after business hours. Each year management personnel in various locations personally talked with shareholders about the company's business. In another aggressive approach to getting feedback, a state highway department used a travel trailer as a mobile information center to collect citizens' views on proposed highway projects. The trailer provided an atmosphere for candid one-on-one discussions with highway personnel and gave people who are reluctant to speak in public meetings an opportunity to air their views.

Key Informants

Practitioners commonly talk with key informants, a variation on personal contacts. This approach involves selecting and interviewing knowledgeable leaders and experts. The interview typically takes the form of an open-ended discussion in which selected individuals are encouraged to talk about the problem or issue in their own terms. Because in-depth interviews with key informants take so long to complete and require such careful content analysis, the technique is limited to a relatively small number of respondents.

Many practitioners regularly consult influential people such as authors, editors, reporters, ministers, labor leaders, professors, civic leaders, bankers, and special-interest group leaders. Some have consulted bartenders and taxi drivers. The basis for selecting key informants is their perceived knowledge of an issue and their ability to represent others' views. The major limitation, of course, is that because they were selected purposely because they are seen to have special knowledge and leadership roles, by definition they do not reflect current views of followers. *In-depth interviews with key informants often yield early warning signals on important issues.*

Focus Groups and Community Forums

It is only a short step from personal contacts and key informants to asking groups for ideas and feedback. The range of groups runs from open town meetings, such as those used in the Ross Perot and Bill Clinton presidential campaigns, to the highly structured and videotaped focus group, a technique commonly used in both public relations and consumer marketing research. An effective moderator who is an able interviewer and facilitator of the group process is key to the success of this approach.

Practitioners use focus groups and community forums to *explore* how people will react to proposals and to gather information useful for developing questionnaires to be used in more formal research methods. Unexpected insights are gained from the sometimes spirited dialogue among participants. Researchers call such information "serendipitous findings," but unanticipated reactions may be the best reason for using these informal research methods. It is better to learn such things before going to the field with a full-blown survey or program test.

For example, the United Soybean Board (USB) developed a fruitful variation of the community forum when it held a series of "town hall meetings" for soybean producers. An influential producer was asked to invite neighbors to hear presentations and to comment on how the organization was spending producers' funds contributed through a mandatory checkoff on soybean sales. Producers hosted a total of 375 meetings in 28 states, providing USB useful feedback on its program and producers' interests. Similarly, the Chicago Welfare Council staged a "listen-in" for community leaders to get guidance and reactions for program planning. Government agencies have long used this exploratory strategy to solicit information and participation. The Forest Service, Army Corps of Engineers, and the Environmental Protection Agency regularly conduct public meetings and hearings to get information and reactions to various project and program proposals. One of the lessons learned from their experiences is that community input must be sought early and often to keep agencies responsive to citizen interests.

Focus groups represent a more structured approach. Typically, focus groups include six to 12 carefully selected representatives from a target public. They are asked to discuss a specific issue or program proposal in depth. Sessions are videotaped and the recordings carefully analyzed to catch the smallest detail in participants' comments. For example, one organization conducted focus-group research to learn what middle-school teachers want in curriculum materials provided by outside sources. One authority says the major strengths of focus groups is the open, spontaneous, and detailed discussions they generate, even among people who did not know each other before the session began.[19] They can be planned, conducted, and analyzed in a matter of days, providing insights and understanding that can be factored into program planning.

Even when members of a group are carefully selected, however, as with information gained from personal contacts, the results cannot be used to make inferences to a larger population or public. Because the group is small, selection is usually not truly random, and the group-discussion context introduces an artificial setting, the results are not representative—in a scientific sense—of a public or the publics from which the participants were selected. In fact, *focus groups are typically small groups of unknown representativeness.*

Moderators also can have an effect on what and how the group discusses. Those viewing the session filter what is said through their own subjective perceptions and interpretations. It is simply not appropriate to suggest that findings from this approach can be used in place of data gathered from scientifically selected samples. The major functions are to identify and explore issues for further study in formal surveys and to pretest program strategies before full-blown field testing.

Advisory Committees and Boards

A standing committee, panel, or board can sometimes be more useful than a single group session, particularly for long-running programs and issues. In some instances such a group can serve as a continuous feedback mechanism for detecting possible changes in public opinion on issues even before they would show up in polls and surveys. There is a price, however, in using advisory committees and boards. Their advice must be given earnest consideration, or this method will backfire. Members quickly sense when they are being "used" for cosmetic purposes or being showcased to demonstrate concern for community input. *Appoint such a committee or board only when the major motivation is to solicit input and guidance on a regular basis, and be prepared to act on the input.*

Nonprofit organizations use this approach to tap the professional public relations community for both expertise and services. Almost every chapter of the United Way, Arthritis Foundation, Easter Seals, and similar organizations has a public relations advisory committee. Committee service is one way public relations practitioners fulfill their public service obligation as professionals.

Other organizations, profit and nonprofit alike, use advisory committees and boards. For example, your city's childrens' hospital, chamber of commerce, and police department probably use this method of gathering information. The insurance industry created advisory committees and complaint bureaus to facilitate policyholder feedback in response to the consumer movement. An accounting firm set up a public review board to provide an outside perspective on operations. A board of education set up a 24-member community advisory committee to give the board a better sense of community attitudes and needs. The New York Stock Exchange created an advisory committee of 15 senior corporate officers to facilitate communication with the corporations listed on the exchange. The American Frozen Food Institute formed an advisory board on frozen goods made up of food editors and home economics instructors.

Advisory committees and boards provide valuable information and guidance, but they cannot substitute for formal approaches to determining the distribution of opinions and reactions among target publics. They provide effective forums for increasing interaction, participation, and in-depth probing of issues. In other words, they are exploratory techniques used to supplement more formal methods.

Ombudsman

The term *ombudsman* originated when the Swedish government established the first such position in 1713. Growing dissatisfaction with ever-longer lines of communication to increasingly isolated managers and bureaucrats has brought about widespread adoption of this informal information-gathering method in government agencies. In countless corporations the ombudsman concept has proved useful in providing feedback and ideas for solving problems while they are still manageable.

Two kinds of ombudsmen are used. One, true to the roots of the original, investigates and solves problems. The second, who at best parries problems, often is there to protect the bureaucracy and to create the illusion of a responsive organization. The former has independent authority to take action on complaints; the latter facilitates communication and seeks authority from others to implement remedies.[20]

The ombudsman's role and scope of its authority vary widely. Dow Chemical Company once established an "ombudswoman" to help promote the advancement of women in the company. At Bronx Community College the ombudsman, appointed by the president, acts as a conduit for student complaints but has no authority to make full-scale investigations. At the University of Nebraska–Lincoln, on the other hand, the ombudsman sees the job as "reporting to nobody and responsible to everyone." The U.S. Navy Family Ombudsman program, started in 1809, says the role is one of cutting governmental red tape and acting as liaison between interested parties and the Navy offices. The ombudsman "investigates organizational problems and makes recommendations for remedial action to improve the quality of administration and redress individual grievances." A large New York hospital employs, as do many hospitals, a "patient representative" to serve as an advocate of patients "to help them and their families find satisfactory solutions to problems." ARCO has an ombudsman to mediate problems dealers cannot get resolved through usual channels: "In a sense, I'm the court of last resort, so this office manages to resolve nearly all disputes."

In each of these settings, the ombudsman provides an effective means for facilitating greater management awareness of public reactions and views. If sincerely used and competently staffed, the ombudsman position can be an important means of obtaining organizational feedback, as well as for helping people get solutions for their problems and answers to their questions. But because this method relies on people who seek out the opportunity to make their feelings and complaints known—a self-selected sample—it also is an exploratory, informal approach to gathering information. Although *it can help identify and detect problems*, information gathered by an ombudsman may not accurately describe the frequency or distribution of problems or concerns among the larger group, particularly those of less assertive members.

Call-In Telephone Lines

Toll-free 800 numbers are commonly used to obtain "instant feedback" and to monitor the concerns and interests of various publics. Johnson & Johnson tracked telephone calls during the consumer panic associated with the seven deaths caused by cyanide-laced Extra-Strength Tylenol capsules. Similarly, Procter & Gamble (P&G) monitored more than 100,000 calls on its 800 number when a rumor was circulating that P&G promoted Satanism. The calls not only gave the companies opportunities to respond to concerned consumers, but also provided constantly updated information on public concerns and reactions.

Companies also recognize the public relations value of giving consumers and customers access to the corporation and of answering questions directly. By doing so, consumer and customer "hot lines" provide companies feedback on their products, service, facilities, and employees. For example, General Electric's customer-service Answer Center gets more than 6000 calls a day. Whirlpool Corporation, which initiated its "Cool Line" service in the late 1960s in response to growing customer dissatisfaction, found that about 70 percent of its calls were from customers who wanted information on repairs.

Some organizations use this method to field questions from employees; some hospitals use it to provide information and take complaints from patients and their families; other health care centers use toll-free numbers both to provide help and to determine the extent of health problems; and many government agencies use it to help citizens find their way through the bureaucratic maze. For example, the Internal Revenue Service Form 1040 publication lists toll-free 800 numbers for every state, the District of Columbia, and Puerto Rico. Taxpayers can ask IRS representatives how to complete tax forms or other tax questions. By dialing 1-800-TAX-FORM, taxpayers may order IRS forms. Both services help the IRS track taxpayer interests and needs.

To be effective, a call-in service must be used with sincerity. For example, the U.S. Bureau of Mines, acting in the wake of several major mine disasters, announced with great fanfare that it was installing "hotline" telephones at the entrance of every coal mine so that miners could alert the bureau if they found unsafe conditions. The bureau promised "instant action" on the reports. A few months later a *Wall Street Journal* reporter found that the bureau had not monitored the recorded calls for almost 2 months. The newspaper reported that bureau employees "had forgotten about the machine."

Nonprofit organizations also use analyses of telephone calls to track stakeholder concerns. For example, the American Red Cross analyzed more than 1700 calls about AIDS to determine information needs and which messages to target to different publics. In addition, program planners learned that many people did not understand some of the words used in AIDS educational messages. Based on their analyses of the telephone calls, program planners learned not only what questions needed to be answered, but also what words to use and avoid when answering.[21]

A pejorative description of radio talk shows, however, serves as a reminder of the danger in putting too much stock in analyses of telephone calls: SLOP, which stands for a self-selected listener opinion poll. Surely analyses of telephone calls can provide early evidence for detecting potential problems and public opinions. The caution, however, is that detecting problems and opinions cannot substitute for describing the frequency of problems or the distribution of opinions in an organizations' publics.

Mail Analysis

Another economical way of collecting information is periodic analysis of incoming mail. Stakeholders' correspondence reveals areas of favor and disfavor and information needs.

Keep in mind that letter writers tend to be critical rather than commendatory. Letters may serve as early warnings on sources of ill will or problem relationships, but they do not reflect a cross section of public opinion, or even the views of a particular public.

President John F. Kennedy borrowed a leaf from Franklin D. Roosevelt's book on keeping in touch with constituents. Kennedy directed that every 50th letter coming to the White House be brought to him. Periodic mail samples helped both these leaders bridge the moat surrounding the White House. Other chief executives in organizations of all kinds use daily or weekly reports on the mail to read the pulse of citizens' concerns and opinions. Many organizations file brief summaries of letters to track public concerns.

At its peak, Ford Motor Company's "We Listen Better" campaign brought in 18,000 letters a week from Ford owners. Letters were answered personally, not with form letters, thus requiring a large investment in money and human resources. Comments, suggestions, and criticisms were carefully coded and keyed into a computer file. Printouts of the running tallies provided Ford executives useful information, even though the data came from a self-selected sample. The exploratory nature of mail analysis nevertheless provided information useful for detecting concerns and problems before they became widespread. Those who feel so strongly about something that they take time to write letters may not be representatives of entire publics, but they may be the first of many to follow. In this role, those who write letters join those who call 800 numbers as early-warning signals of situations that need attention and may indicate a need for formal research.

Field Reports

Many organizations have district agents, field representatives, or recruiters who live in and travel the territories served. These agents should be trained to listen and observe and be given an easy, regular means of reporting their observations. In this way they can serve as the "eyes and ears" of an organization.

Studies of organizational intelligence and communication demonstrate, however, that such representatives tend to "gild the lily" and to report what they think will "set well" with their bosses. This is particularly true if field staff know that their reports will pass through a gauntlet of superiors, the same people who hold power over their futures in the organization.

For example, in an effort to assess the impact of a company's "progress week," management asked sales representatives to evaluate the program. Forty percent ventured no opinion. About half of those who did respond said the week's promotion had produced more favorable opinions of the company. A formal survey found that only about one in ten of the target population was inclined to be more favorable in their opinion of the company. After comparing the field reports with the survey results, it was clear that only 12 of the 42 grass-roots observers accurately assessed the results of the promotion. The comparison serves as a reminder that all subjective reports such as field reports must be used with caution. Like the other informal methods, field reports serve best as an early warning to detect situations that may call for more thorough investigation.

FORMAL METHODS

The purpose of both informal and formal methods is to gather accurate and useful information. *Formal methods are designed to gather data from scientifically representative samples.* Formal methods help answer questions about situations that simply cannot be answered adequately using informal approaches.

The danger is that practitioner-researchers can become more concerned about the methods used than the purpose of the study. As one writer put it, "In science as in love, concentration on technique is quite likely to lead to impotence." Those who get bogged down in research techniques at the expense of usefulness often spend time and resources to produce volumes of data that sit unused on shelves.

Formal methods are useful, however, only if the research question and objectives are clearly determined *before* the research design is selected (see Exhibit 10–2). Done correctly, each approach can yield information that describes phenomena and situations within established ranges of accuracy and tolerance for error. These approaches also make

EXHIBIT 10-2

Checklist for Starting a Research Project

1. *How will the results obtained from the research be used?* This may seem like an obvious question, but it is often easy, particularly in time of crisis, to jump into a research project without a plan for using the results.
2. *What is the specific population (public) being studied, and how should the sample be chosen?* In some studies, determining the population in question can constitute one of the more difficult aspects. Wise sample selection can minimize project costs and maximize the accuracy of results.
3. *What type of research technique is most appropriate in this instance?* Do not automatically assume that a survey is best. Perhaps a focus group or secondary research will yield better results.
4. *If a survey is to be used, what sort of field methodology will be most efficient?* There are three primary choices here: mail, telephone, and in-person interviews. The practitioner should be familiar with the pros and cons of each.
5. *Are closed-ended questions, open-ended questions, or a combination of the two recommended?* The response to the first question above will have a major effect on the types of questions used.
6. *What is the experience level of the research firm being considered, and what are the backgrounds of its personnel?* It is especially important to inquire into the firm's experience with the particular type of research being contemplated. Do not be afraid to ask for references.
7. *How will the data be analyzed and the results reported?* This is very important! Many practitioners have assumed that they were purchasing complete reports, only to be handed stacks of computer runs as the final product.
8. *How soon will the results be provided?* The luxury of proper planning, when available, can prevent a research project from becoming an unnecessarily costly undertaking.
9. *How much will it cost?* Professional research is expensive. It is wise to obtain written proposals from three firms. At the same time, many problems can be prevented by insisting that the proposals address each of these nine questions.

Courtesy David L. Smith. Adapted and reprinted with permission from June 1980 issue of *Public Relations Journal*. Copyright 1980.

it possible to use inferential statistics, the process of using data from representative samples to estimate characteristics of populations. In other words, systematic formal methods make it possible for practitioners to make accurate statements about publics based on evidence drawn from scientifically representative samples.

Successful public relations managers know about formal research methods and statistics. Public relations education at many universities now includes a research methods course as part of the curriculum. Continuing education programs for practitioners typically include offerings on how to use research in program planning, management, and evaluation. The following sections introduce some of the methods and issues in conducting formal research.

Secondary Analysis and On-Line Databases

Doing research does not always call for gathering data yourself. Secondary analysis reuses data gathered by someone else, often for other purposes.[22]

Numerous governmental and commercial organizations conduct national, regional, and local surveys. Some of these surveys track issues and trends. For example, the U.S. Bureau of the Census has a long history of developing standardized definitions, sampling techniques, sophisticated methods, and publications of findings. Within government, specialized departments have large research staffs tracking major developments and trends in agriculture, labor, business, the economy, and education, to name but a few of the areas under constant study.

Since the 1930s, major commercial polling firms such as those formed by A. C. Nielsen, George Gallup, Elmo Roper, and Louis Harris have made their names synonymous with measures of public opinion. Almost every major city has similar research firms tracking local public opinion trends and conducting marketing research. Major newspapers, television stations, and other news organizations regularly conduct and report surveys. The results of these surveys often can be segmented on the basis of geography, demographics, and other attributes relevant to public relations problem situations.

Sometimes overlooked are the survey research centers maintained by almost all major universities. Research conducted with public funds is often published and available for the asking. Most public agencies can provide listings of data sets and publications. For much less than the cost of conducting a survey, additional analyses of available data often can be done to help answer questions not asked in the original analysis.

Special-interest publications and scholarly journals regularly publish research data. A great deal of research is conducted to answer questions previously answered by competent researchers and reviewed by knowledgeable editorial boards. On-line searches now make it easy and cost-effective to search research literature for studies done on specific topics. It makes little sense to design and conduct research until after exploring the possibility that someone else has already done the work and published the results.

The most rapidly growing approach to information gathering in public relations, however, uses subscription on-line databases. Some of the most-used databases include Nexis, Dun and Bradstreet, Dow Jones News/Retrieval, NewsNet, Data Times, and Burrelle's Broadcast Database (all are brand names). Practitioners use these services to access and search through news and technical publications, business information services, market research, financial reports, government records, and broadcast transcripts. For example, the New York public relations firm, Chacma, Inc., conducts database searches for economic and political facts on foreign governments and clients dating back ten to 12 years. On-line feeds of international news wires allow the firm to track developments abroad, with summary printouts available each morning.[23]

Some on-line database companies customize services to meet the specific needs of subscribers. For example, to track the over-the-counter cold-remedy field, the manager of information services at Ketchum Public Relations in New York has Dow Jones fax relevant information to her office as soon as it goes on line. NewsNet and Nexis will set up special files for subscribers, making it easy for customers to access information without the usual cost of a conventional search of the entire database.[24]

Content Analysis

Content analysis is the application of systematic procedures for objectively determining what is being reported in the media.[25] Press clippings and broadcast monitor reports, all available from commercial services, have long been used as the bases for content analyses. They indicate only what is being printed or broadcast, *not* what is read or heard. And, they do not measure whether or not the audiences learned or believed message content. For example, a content analysis of newspaper clippings provides a useful measure of what messages are being placed in the media, but it does not indicate readership or impact.

Analyzing the editorials and letters to the editor may yield little more than the views of the editor and publisher. The range of letters sent is seldom represented by those chosen for publication.[26] And the editorial page does not represent public opinion, as is made abundantly clear when candidates receiving newspaper endorsements do not win elections. As agenda-setting researchers caution, media are better at telling us what to think about than they are at telling us what to think.[27]

As John Naisbitt demonstrated in his popular books on trends, however, content analysis can provide valuable insights into what is likely to be on the public agenda in the future. Recognizing the role of media in reporting and influencing trends, in 1968 Naisbitt began publishing a quarterly newsletter, *Trend Report,* based on content analyses of 206 metropolitan newspapers. By the late 1980s, his national and regional newsletters reported content analyses of more than 6000 newspapers. Based in Washington, D.C., but no longer owned by Naisbitt, these newsletters give corporate and government subscribers an early-warning system for forecasting social and economic conditions, often long before they are apparent to most observers.

Increasingly, public relations firms are helping their clients anticipate issues by either subscribing to issues tracking services or by doing their own media content analyses. It is important to note, however, that these media content analyses employ a more systematic, formal method than the usual informal approaches used for "monitoring" the media. The key differences are the representativeness of the content selected for analysis and the objectivity used in measuring and coding the content.

Surveys

Mailed questionnaires and in-person interviews are the two major approaches used in survey research. The adequacy of both depends on the sampling procedures used, what questions are asked, and how the questions are asked.

Advantages of *mailed questionnaires* include considerable savings of time and money, convenience for respondents since they determine when to answer the questions, greater assurance of anonymity, standardized wording, no interviewer bias, access to respondents not readily reached in person by interviewers, and opportunity for respondents to take time to gather information needed to complete the questionnaire.

The biggest disadvantages of many surveys are that researchers have no control over who responds and that low response rates are typical. Whereas the original mailing list may have been a randomly selected and representative sample, unless all respond there is no assurance of an unbiased sample. Even a 90 percent response rate could be inadequate if those not responding represent a significant and uniform segment of the population being studied. Remember that elections often are won by fractions of a percent. There is no basis for the conventional wisdom that a 50 percent return is adequate. The unanswered question remains, which half of the sample did or did not respond?

Other disadvantages include lack of control over the conditions under which the questionnaire is completed, no assurance that the intended respondent completed the questionnaire, lack of flexibility in how questions are asked if the respondent does not understand what is being asked, and difficulties in getting and maintaining current mailing lists.

A variation of the mailed questionnaire takes the form of a page included in publications or distributed with other materials. Whereas the cost of a separate mailing is saved, all the advantages and disadvantages of the mailed questionnaire apply and are in some cases are magnified.

In-person *interviews* give researchers increased control over the sample, but the increased cost of that control becomes the major disadvantage. Telephone interviews offer a fast and cost-effective way to complete interview studies while providing more anonymity to respondents. More than 95 percent of households have telephones, but not all are listed in directories. Computer-assisted random digit dialing (RDD) has helped solve the sampling problem caused by incomplete directory listings. But while the numbers selected for calls may be representative, answering machines and refusal rates have made it more difficult to obtain representative samples and have driven up costs.

For example, the research firm Survey Sampling, Inc., estimates that researchers must call five phone numbers to complete one interview in Chicago and three calls to complete one interview in Cincinnati. And although 36 percent of adults have refused to participate in a research study, they said inconvenience was the major reason for refusing. Notably, more people than ever are participating in surveys. Forty-two percent of all adults participated in some type of survey. Even 84 percent of those who had refused to cooperate in one survey said that they had participated in another survey.[28]

In-person doorstep interviews may be the most flexible and thorough method, but the costs are proportionately greater. In both telephone and doorstep approaches the interviewers themselves can influence the information gathered, so interviewer training is an essential element of this approach.

Advantages of interview studies include high response rates, greater flexibility in dealing with the respondents, more control over conditions under which the questions are asked, increased control over the order and completeness of questioning, and opportunity to observe and record reactions not covered by the questionnaire. In addition to the relatively greater cost and potential influence of interviewers, disadvantages include the inconvenience imposed on respondents, less anonymity for respondents, increased difficulty in contacting those selected in the sample, and respondents' negative reactions resulting from misuse of survey approaches by salespersons and other solicitors posing as researchers.

Usually, single surveys are conducted of *cross-section samples* of a population or public. If the study is designed to learn how people change over time or to track a process, however, a *panel study* may be the better approach. In panel studies the same respondents are interviewed several times during the study, are asked to complete a series of questionnaires on a fixed schedule, or are required to maintain a diary during the study period. Two problems common to this approach are that respondents drop out during the study ("panel mortality") and that respondents become more attentive to the issues being studied because of the repeated observations ("sensitization").

In summary, formal research methods follow the rules of science, use representative samples, and employ other systematic procedures for making the observations, taking the measurements, and analyzing the data. As with other skills based on specialized knowledge, doing formal research requires study and practice. Done correctly, however, formal research helps practitioners accurately describe reality. Research findings, combined with experience and judgment, provide the foundation for defining public relations problems and for designing programs to address those problems. In other words, research builds the information foundation necessary for effective public relations practice and management.

This chapter only highlights some of the approaches for gathering the qualitative and quantitative information needed to understand and define public relations problem situations. Whereas research is often viewed as a necessary step for evaluating program impact, it is equally necessary in the initial step of the problem-solving process: defining the problem situation. Not only does research provide the information necessary for understanding the problem, but this "benchmark" description serves as the basis for monitoring and evaluating program effectiveness. How do you plan the program if you do not know what you are dealing with? How do you determine how the program is working if you do not know where you started?

Practitioners know that research initiates, monitors, and concludes the problem-solving process. It is the essential ingredient that makes public relations a management function, as well as a managed function.

ADDITIONAL READINGS

Fowler, Floyd J., Jr., *Survey Research Methods*, 2d ed. Newbury Park, Calif.: Sage Publications, Inc., 1993. Covers essentials of survey research and adapts it to personal computers for data entry and analysis.

Hyman, Herbert H. *Secondary Analysis of Sample Surveys: Principles, Procedures and Potentialities.* New York: John Wiley and Sons, 1972. Considered the classic reference on doing secondary analyses.

Lavrakas, Paul J. *Telephone Survey Methods*, 2d ed. Newbury Park, Calif.: Sage Publications, Inc., 1993. Outlines the use of new technology for conducting telephone research, sampling techniques, supervising interviewers, and securing cooperation of respondents.

Miller, Delbert C. *Handbook of Research Design and Social Measurement*, 5th ed. Newbury Park, Calif.: Sage Publications, Inc., 1991. This may be the most complete manual on social science research methods. Most valuable are the guides to doing research and presentations of selected scales and indices.

Rossi, Peter H., and Howard E. Freeman. *Evaluation: A Systematic Approach*, 5th ed. Newbury Park, Calif.: Sage Publications, Inc., 1993. Discusses evaluation research concepts, techniques, and strategies.

Stewart, David W., and Prem N. Shamdasani. *Focus Groups: Theory and Practice.* Newbury Park, Calif.: Sage Publications, Inc., 1990. Compares the focus group method to other techniques and discusses how to do content analysis of focus group transcripts. See also "Appendix C: How to Conduct a Focus Group Study," in *Using Research in Public Relations*, Glen M. Broom and David M. Dozier, 325-30. Englewood Cliffs, N.J.: Prentice-Hall, Inc., 1990.

Williams, Frederick. *Reasoning with Statistics*, 4th ed. New York: Holt, Rinehart and Winston, 1991. Uses communication examples to introduce statistics.

NOTES

[1] Edward J. Robinson, *Public Relations Research and Survey Research: Achieving Organizational Goals in a Communication Context* (New York: Appleton-Century-Crofts, 1969). The first book devoted to using social science survey research methods in public relations.

[2] From the fable, "The Blind Men and the Elephant," by John Godfrey Saxe (1816–1887), quoted by Henry Mintzberg, "Strategy Formation: Schools of Thought," in *Perspectives on Strategic Management*, edited by James W. Fredrickson (New York: Harper Business Division of Harper & Row, 1990): 105–06.

[3] Quoted in Walter K. Lindenmann, "Research, Evaluation and Measurement: A National Perspective," *Public Relations Review* 16, no. 2 (Summer 1990): 14.

[4] Ibid.

[5] C. F. Kettering, "More Music Please, Composers," *Saturday Evening Post* 211, no. 32 (1938).

[6] Peter H. Rossi and Howard E. Freeman, *Evaluation: A Systematic Approach*, 4th ed. (Newbury Park, Calif.: Sage Publications, Inc., 1989), 27.

[7] David M. Dozier, "The Innovation of Research in Public Relations Practice: Review of a Program of Studies," *Public Relations Research Annual* 2 (1990): 3–28. See also Jon White and David M. Dozier, "Public Relations and Management Decision Making," in *Excellence in Public Relations and Communication Management*, edited by James E. Grunig (Hillsdale, N.J.: Lawrence Erlbaum Associates, Publishers, 1992), 91–108.

[8] Wilbur Schramm, *Men, Messages, and Media: A Look at Human Communication* (New York: Harper and Row, 1973), 51.

[9] Wilbur Schramm, "The Nature of Communication between Humans," in *The Process and Effects of Mass Communication*, rev. ed., edited by Wilbur Schramm and Donald F. Roberts (Urbana: University of Illinois Press, 1971), 26.

[10] Carl Sandburg, *Abraham Lincoln: The War Years*, II (New York: Harcourt, Brace and World, Inc., 1939): 236–37.

[11] Joseph A. Kopec, "The Communication Audit," *Public Relations Journal* 38, no. 5 (May 1982): 24.

[12] For more on the distinction between "stakeholders" and "publics," see James E. Grunig and Fred C. Repper, "Strategic Management, Publics, and Issues," in *Excellence in Public Relations*, edited by Grunig, 127–46.

[13] Adapted from Brenda Dervin, "Audience as Listener and Learner, Teacher and Confidante: The Sense Making Approach," in *Public Communication Campaigns*, 2d ed., edited by Ronald E. Rice and Charles K. Atkin (Newbury Park, Calif.: Sage Publications, Inc., 1989), 67–86.

[14] Jim VanLeuven, "Expectancy Theory in Media and Message Selection," *Communication Research* 8, no. 4 (October 1981): 431.

[15] Heinz Weihrich, "The TOWS Matrix: A Tool for Situational Analysis," in *Strategic Planning: Models and Analytical Techniques*, edited by Robert G. Dyson (Chichester, U.K.: John Wiley and Sons, 1990), 17–36.

[16] Kerry Tucker and Doris Derelian, *Public Relations Writing: A Planned Approach for Creating Results* (Englewood Cliffs, N.J.: Prentice-Hall, Inc., 1989), 41–46.

[17] Glen M. Broom and David M. Dozier, *Using Research in Public Relations: Applications to Program Management* (Englewood Cliffs, N.J.: Prentice-Hall, Inc. 1990). 20.

[18]For more detailed discussion of research methods, see Broom and Dozier, *Using Research in Public Relations*.

[19]Larissa A. Grunig, "Using Focus Group Research in Public Relations," *Public Relations Review* 16, no. 2 (Summer 1990): 36–37.

[20]For an account of the origins and uses of the ombudsman concept, see Donald C. Rowat, ed., *The Ombudsman: Citizen's Defender*, 2d ed. (London: George Allen and Unwin, Ltd., 1968).

[21]Meryl Davids, "Panic Prevention," *Public Relations Journal* 43, no. 3 (March 1987): 21.

[22]David W. Stewart and Michael A. Kamins, *Secondary Research: Information Sources and Methods*, 2d ed. (Newbury Park, Calif.: Sage Publications, Inc., 1993). Discusses how to locate information from various sources, including government agencies, on-line information search services, and CD-ROM delivery systems.

[23]*O'Dwyer's FARA Report* 1, no. 2 (March 1991): 5. (Monthly newsletter reporting developments under the Foreign Agents Registration Act.)

[24]John Masterton, "Discovering Databases: On-Line Services Put Research at Practitioner's Fingertips," *Public Relations Journal* 48, no. 11 (November 1992): 12–19 and 27.

[25]For more detailed descriptions of content analysis procedures, see Robert P. Weber, *Basic Content Analysis* (Beverly Hills, Calif.: Sage Publications, Inc., 1985); and Guido H. Stempel III, "Content Analysis," in *Research Methods in Mass Communication*, edited by Guido H. Stempel III, and Bruce H. Westley (Englewood Cliffs, N.J.: Prentice-Hall, Inc., 1981), 119–31.

[26]David L. Grey and Trevor R. Brown, "Letters to the Editor: Hazy Reflections of Public Opinion," *Journalism Quarterly* 47 (Autumn 1970): 450–56 and 471.

[27]For a good summary of two decades of agenda-setting research, see the special issue of *Journalism Quarterly* 69, no. 4 (Winter 1992); and Maxwell McCombs, Edna Einseidel, and David Weaver, "The Agenda-Setting Role of Mass Communication," chapter 2 of *Contemporary Public Opinion: Issues and the News* (Hillsdale, N.J.: Lawrence Erlbaum Associates, Publishers, 1991), 11–21.

[28]Pat Lewis, "Cooperation Rates, the Ups and the Downs," *The Frame* 14, no. 1 (1991): 2.

CHAPTER 11

Step Two: Planning and Programming

The best predictor of excellence in public relations is the ability to assume the manager role.

DAVID M. DOZIER

After a public relations problem or opportunity has been defined through research and analysis, practitioners must devise a strategy for coping with the problem or for capitalizing on the opportunity. This brings us to planning, in which basic strategic decisions must be made and plans of action set down. The effectiveness of the third step, taking action and communicating, depends on the sound planning done in this, the second step. Yet many practitioners do not take the time to give planning more than a glancing blow; they do "pseudoplanning."[1] Like the cuttlefish squirting ink, inadequate planning leads to routine responses whose origins and motivations are lost in history. Reactive programs based on inadequate planning may or may not be appropriate in the present context.

STRATEGIC THINKING

Strategic thinking involves predicting or establishing a desired future state, determining what forces will help and hinder movement toward the goal state, and formulating a strategy for achieving the desired state. When planning a program, an organization is, in effect, making tomorrow's decisions today. Skimping on the strategic planning step in the process results in programs that may reinforce controversy rather than resolve it, waste money on audiences that are not there, or add to misunderstanding and confusion instead of understanding and clarification.

, public relations problems were born of yesterday's
it decisions. For example, the American Heart Associ-
l "seal-of-approval" program for food products was can-
ivy pressure from the U.S. Department of Agriculture
rested parties. Another example is the public relations
resulted when Nestlé marketed in developing nations an
la substitute for breastfeeding. The company apparently
e into account that the formula would be mixed with water
: babies. Exxon's handling of the tanker *Valdez* oil-spill
in Prince William Sound on the Alaskan coast provides yet
case study of inadequate planning and programming for such a
r. One writer described Exxon's response in an article entitled
"Ex. n Valdez: How to Spend Billions and Still Get a Black Eye."[2]

In all three cases, program planners apparently made strategic
decisions based on inadequate situation analyses or without fully considering possible unintended consequences of their program tactics. In
effect, *programs represent strategic interventions for which both planners and their organizations are held responsible.*

Public Relations as Part of Strategic Thinking

A definition of strategy captures the essence of strategic thinking and
management expectations:

Strategy can be defined as the determination of the basic
long-term goals and objectives of an enterprise, and the
adoption of courses of action and the allocation of resources
necessary for carrying out these goals.[3]

Corporate-level strategy provides the overall goal and direction within
which an organization's divisions operate. *Business-level strategy* establishes the goals and directions for each division, each operating unit, or, in
diversified organizations, each business. In a *planning mode*, strategy
takes the form of a systematic plan and guidelines for achieving corporate-
and business-level strategies. In an *evolutionary mode*, strategies develop
over time, representing a pattern of decisions that respond to opportunities
and threats in the environment. Whereas the planning mode has been the
preferred model, the evolutionary mode is increasingly accepted as the
more appropriate approach for dealing with rapidly changing organizations and environments.[4] As such, plans that spell out the goals and
strategy—including the public relations components—become dynamic
documents that reflect the open systems approach discussed in Chapter 7.

Reliance on research findings as the basis for strategic planning to
achieve effective public relations varies widely. Walter Lindenmann,
senior vice president and director of research at Ketchum Public Relations in New York, surveyed practitioners to learn how many use

research as the basis for program planning. Seventy-five percent of all those surveyed reported that they "occasionally" or "frequently" do research specifically for the purpose of planning. Counselors were most likely to use research, 89 percent, whereas practitioners in nonprofit settings were least likely, 68 percent.[5]

Another study concludes that practitioners' use of strategic thinking and program evaluation are correlated with the number of social science, statistics, and computer courses taken by practitioners. "Seat-of-the-pants" approaches are not correlated with taking social science or statistics courses and are negatively correlated with course work in using computers. Also, the more that practitioners engage in various types of research, the more likely they are to approach their work as managers and to be involved in management decision making.[6] As one practitioner put it, "If you don't have information to take to the table, then you don't get invited to the table [management meetings]."

Management Expectations

In many organizations, top management limits public relations participation in management decision making. "Many public relations people fantasize their roles in strategic planning, but few are really involved in any meaningful fashion," according to a principal of a major public relations firm.[7] Responding to management expectations requires practitioners to think outside the boundaries of public relations by analyzing and understanding the needs and concerns of operating units. In short, line managers expect public relations efforts to help achieve organizational goals, or in the words of some managers, "affect the bottom line."

Long-time AT&T public relations executive, Ed Block, outlined a CEO's expectations of the chief public relations officer:

In this role, I need someone with an exquisite public relations "gut" combined with a comprehensive knowledge of the business and its external and internal environment. I want someone who is in touch with the "soul" of the business, someone who shares my vision and understands my sensibilities. I don't need a "handler" or a gate keeper. I need someone whose counsel, over time, will influence my thinking in broad terms, not someone who hectors me on ever piddling issue that crosses my desk. I also want someone whose counsel is sought out by others in top management because it is timely and thoughtful and helpful—not because it comes from someone who has special access to me.[8]

In the information age of instant computer communication and on-line databases, the days of playing hunches and simply replaying the past as the primary bases for planning are history. Others in the organization may make strategic decisions based on financial, legal, or technical considerations and data. It is the responsibility of the public relations practitioner to anticipate the impact of those decisions on various stakeholder groups. In the words of another telephone company executive, "We lead an issues management group that functions as an early warning sentinel for the corporation." He credits the environmental scanning and "up-front counseling" for public relations' company-wide acceptance in the strategic planning process. "Or to put it another way," he concludes, "we help plan the parade, not just carry the shovels afterward!"[9] AT&T's CEO and chairman, Robert E. Allen, made the same point, "I need PR people at my side not in my wake."[10]

Prudent long-range planning, anticipating conceivable developments, is more likely to result in the following:

1. An integrated program in which the total effort results in definite accomplishments toward specific goals.
2. Increased management participation and support.
3. A program emphasis that is positive rather than defensive.
4. Careful deliberation on choice of themes, timing, and tactics.

Even though the values of planning are evident and widely acknowledged, there is too little emphasis on this step in public relations. The following appear to be the main obstacles:

1. Failure of employers and clients to include the practitioner in deliberations that lead to policies and programs; a failure often born of lack of confidence in the public relations officer or counselor.
2. Absence of clearly agreed-upon objectives for implementing the public relations program.
3. Inadequate time because of the pressures of meeting daily problems.
4. Frustrations and delays that practitioners encounter in getting internal clearance and in coordinating with other departments.

With all the problems, however, in the final analysis management expects public relations to help manage threats from the environment, to enhance the organization's competitive edge (usually in the form of marketing support), and—most importantly—to protect an organization's most important assets, its good name and reputation. "Buildings depreciate, patents expire, but, properly managed, a company's name and reputation grow in value every year."[11]

Often the health of the "bottom line" depends on the health of an organization's reputation. An organization's market share, its ability to attract and retain valuable employees, its attractiveness to prospective donors and members, its autonomy and freedom to carry out its missions, and even its stock price are affected by its reputation among various stakeholders. Management expects the public relations unit to manage the organization's reputation and good standing with the same strategic thinking that goes into managing other assets.

STRATEGIC MANAGEMENT

Strategic management represents the open systems approach to public relations, rather than the closed systems, reactive approach. One counselor defines strategic management as "a process that enables any organization—company, association, nonprofit or government agency—to identify its long-term opportunities and threats, mobilize its assets to address them and carry out a successful implementation strategy."[12]

Strategic planning in public relations involves making decisions about program goals and objectives, identifying key publics, setting policies or rules to guide selection of strategies, and determining strategies. There must be a close linkage between the overall program goal, the objectives established for each of the publics, and the strategies selected. The key point is that strategies are selected to achieve a particular outcome (as stated in a goal or objective). On the other hand, if you don't care where you end up, any route will get you there.

Public relations practitioners work with other managers to develop strategic program plans. Although each program calls for specifically tailored and unique elements, the overall approach is similar from plan to plan. The planning and programming process typically includes the following steps:

1. *Defining roles and missions.* Determining the nature and scope of the work to be performed.
2. *Determining key results areas.* Determining where to invest time, energy, and talent.
3. *Identifying and specifying indicators of effectiveness.* Determining measurable factors on which objectives may be set.
4. *Selecting and setting objectives.* Determining results to be achieved.
5. *Preparing action plans.* Determining how to achieve specific objectives.
   A. Programming. Establishing a sequence of actions to follow in reaching objectives.
   B. Scheduling. Establishing time requirements for objectives and action steps.
   C. Budgeting. Determining and assigning the resources required to reach objectives.
   D. Fixing accountability. Determining who will see to the accomplishment of objectives and action steps.
   E. Reviewing and reconciling. Testing and revising a tentative plan, as needed, prior to commitment to action.
6. *Establishing controls.* Ensuring the effective accomplishment of objectives.
7. *Communicating.* Determining the organizational communications necessary for achieving understanding and commitment in the previous six steps.
8. *Implementing.* Securing agreement among all key people on who and what needs to be committed to the effort, what approach will work best, who needs to be involved, and what immediate action steps need to be taken immediately.[13]

Mission Statements

The four-step public relations process outlined in Chapters 10 through 13 is based on the assumption that the organization has clearly defined its overall mission and goals and that public relations is part of the plan to achieve them.

Most organizations have written statement of goals and objectives, long range and immediate. The purpose is to state succinctly why an organization exists, such as Merck Pharmaceutical's, "We are in the business of preserving and improving human life." Mission statements typically make public commitments of citizenship obligations and social responsibility. They often give the organization's attitude in dealing with its employees, members, clients, neighbors, and donors. They may state the organization's posture on government regulation or environmental issues, explain how it measures its own progress, and so on. In short, they are idealistic and inspirational statements designed to give those in the organization a sense of purpose and direction (Exhibit 11–1 gives some examples).

EXHIBIT 11-1

Mission Statements

Weyerhaeuser Company (Tacoma, Washington)

Our Vision. The Best Forest Products Company in the World.

Our Strategies. We shall achieve our vision by: Making Total Quality the Weyerhaeuser way of doing business. Relentless pursuit of full customer satisfaction. Empowering Weyerhaeuser people. Leading the industry in forest management and manufacturing excellence. Producing superior returns for our shareholders.

Our Values. **Customers:** We listen to our customers and improve our products and services to meet their present and future needs. **People:** Our success depends upon high-performing people working together in a safe and healthy workplace where diversity, development and teamwork are valued and recognized. **Accountability:** We expect superior performance and are accountable for our actions and results. Our leaders set clear goals and expectations, are supportive, and provide and seek frequent feedback. **Citizenship:** We support the communities where we do business, hold ourselves to the highest standards of ethical conduct and environmental responsibility, and communicate openly with Weyerhaeuser people and the public. **Financial Responsibility:** We are prudent and effective in the use of the resources entrusted to us.

New York Stock Exchange, Inc.

Mission Statement. Support the capital-raising and asset-management process by providing the highest quality and most cost-effective, self-regulated marketplace for the trading of financial instruments; promote confidence in and understanding of that process; and serve as a forum for discussion of relevant national and international policy issues.

Johnson & Johnson

Our Credo. We believe our first responsibility is to the doctors, nurses and patients, to mothers and fathers and all others who use our products and services. In meeting their needs everything we do must be of high quality. We must constantly strive to reduce our costs in order to maintain reasonable prices. Customers' orders must be serviced promptly and accurately. Our suppliers and distributors must have an opportunity to make a fair profit.

We are responsible to our employees, the men and women who work with us throughout the world. Everyone must be considered as an individual. We must respect their dignity and recognize their merit. They must have a sense of security in their jobs. Compensation must be fair and adequate, and working conditions clean, orderly and safe. We must be mindful of ways to help our employees fulfill their family responsibilities. Employees must feel free to make suggestions and complaints. There must be equal opportunity for employment, development and advancement for those qualified. We must provide competent management, and their actions must be just and ethical.

We are responsible to the communities in which we live and work and to the world community as well. We must be good citizens — support good works and charities and bear our fair share of taxes. We must encourage civic improvements and better health and education. We must maintain in good order the property we are privileged to use, protecting the environment and natural resources.

Our final responsibility is to our stockholders. Business must make a sound profit. We must experiment with new ideas. Research must be carried on, innovative programs developed and mistakes paid for. New equipment must be purchased, new facilities provided and new products launched. Reserves must be created to provide for adverse times. When we operate according to these principles, the stockholders should realize a fair return.

Mission statements without management commitment and support, however, become simply cosmetic additions to brochures, reports, and speeches. The challenge is to instill a sense of mission, values, and behavior standards throughout an organization. Each organization has to define its own unique mission, matching its strategy and values, and creating its own culture.[14]

Whether these documents are kept private for competitive or security reasons or whether they are open statements of mission, standards of conduct, or specific purposes, public relations staff are privy to them. In organizations where no such statements have been set down, there is an urgent need for the top public relations officer to propose one.

Mission statements of organizational goals, obligations, values, and social responsibility serve two important purposes in public relations: First, they commit the whole organization to accountability, and that means visibility or communication of some sort. Second, the attitudes expressed provide a framework in which public relations can devise its goals and objectives, build its budgets, direct its talents, devise its programs, and assess its impact.

The mission statement for the public relations function builds upon the organization's mission statement. Typically, the mission of public relations is to help the organization achieve its mission by:

1. Collecting and analyzing information on the changing knowledge, opinions, and behaviors of key publics and stakeholder groups.
2. Serving as the central source of information about an organization and as the official channel of communication between an organization and its publics.
3. Communicating significant information, opinions, and interpretations to keep an organization's publics and other stakeholders aware of organizational policies and actions.
4. Coordinating activities that affect an organization's relationships with its publics and other stakeholder groups.

To the extent that these activities and an organization's mission are connected to measurable goals and objectives, then public relations is part of management. To attain organizational maturity, the function must be mainstream in every sense, not a side show, and have management agreement of a clear-cut charter, or mission.

Management by Objectives

As executives have become sophisticated in the ways of public relations, they have become more demanding. Most organizations operate on the basis of management by objectives (MBO) or, as others term it, management by objectives and results (MOR). Simply put, MBO systematically applies effective management techniques to running an organization. It specifies the outcomes (consequences, results, impact) to be achieved, thereby establishing the criteria for selecting strategies, monitoring performance and progress, and evaluating program effectiveness.

As now applied, MBO operates at two levels of outcomes: goals and objectives. *Goals are summative statements that spell out the overall outcomes of a program.* Such a program may involve many different parts of an organization as well as many different strategies. Goals state what the coordinated effort is intended to accomplish and by when it will be accomplished. Goals establish what will be accomplished if the objectives set for each of the publics are achieved.

Objectives represent the specific knowledge, opinion, and behavioral outcomes to be achieved for each well-defined target public, what some call "key results." The outcome criteria take the form of measurable program effects to be achieved by specified dates. In practice, objectives:

1. Give focus and direction for developing program strategies and tactics.
2. Provide guidance and motivation to those implementing the program.
3. Spell out the criteria for monitoring progress and for assessing impact.

An organization's overall goals provide the outcome criteria for unit and individual goals, including those for the public relations department. Just as an organization has a written MBO plan, so should public relations have a long-range MBO plan on paper. A separate document should give guidance within the department. Just as managers or general officers are periodically subject to performance review by a superior officer, so is the public relations manager. If line departments and other staff functions hold annual conferences to reenergize the staff, so should public relations. Most important, however, public relations must operate within and as part of an organization's overall MBO plan, must be held accountable in the same way as other functions, and must show how public relations contributes to the achievement of the organization's mission and goals.

Strategy and Tactics

The terms *strategy* and *tactics* are often confused. Borrowed from the military, *strategy* involves the crucial decisions of a war or campaign, such as whether to rely on missiles or aerial bombardment. Strategy represents the overall game plan. *Tactics* are decisions made during the course of battle. Tactics represent on-the-spot decisions necessitated because of developments as the strategic plan is implemented. In effect, tactics are the decisions or actions taken to make the strategy fit the reality and contingencies of the field of battle.

In public relations practice, however, strategy typically refers to the overall concept, approach, or general plan for the program designed to achieve a goal. Tactics refer to the operational level: the actual events, media, and methods used to implement the strategy. For example, the Wisconsin Milk Marketing Board's (WMMB) successful program to pass a referendum illustrates the difference between strategies and tactics.

WMMB wanted to win dairy producers' support for increasing, from 5 to 10 cents per hundredweight of milk produced, the amount directed to state and regional promotions of dairy products. Congress mandated that dairy farmers nationwide contribute 15 cents for each hundredweight of milk they sell to do research and to promote the sale of dairy products. Of the mandatory checkoff, 5 cents goes to the National Dairy Promotion and Research Board and 5 cents goes to state or regional organizations. Dairy farmers then choose which organization gets the other 5 cents, often called the "middle nickel." WMMB wanted Wisconsin producers to direct the discretionary 5 cents to the state organization.

Program strategies included reinforcing the producers' belief in the need to build markets for Wisconsin dairy products; demonstrating WMMB's successes in marketing, research, and education; and enlisting influential third-party endorsements to reach targeted groups of producers. Tactics included check stuffers, newsletters, informational meetings, an 800 telephone number information service, the annual report, and exhibit booths at Farm Progress Days and the World Dairy Expo. Of the producers who cast ballots in the 1991 referendum, 93 percent voted in favor of directing the middle nickel to WMMB.

Reasons for Planning

Preparing a plan does not guarantee success, but it greatly enhances its chances. Strategic planning, however, is not universally accepted as part of public relations practice. The excuses practitioners give for not planning are similar to those offered by other managers:

1. *"We don't have time."* Practitioners who feel that they are already overloaded with work offer this excuse. Of course, they are missing the point that those with a plan typically make better use of their time, thus making time spent planning a wise investment.

2. *"Why plan when things are changing so fast?"* Plans get modified in light of changing circumstances; they are not cast in concrete. Having a plan, however, provides the baseline from which modifications can be made with full awareness that changes in strategy and direction are occurring. In fact, the more turbulent the environment, the greater the need to chart the changing course to the desired result, to have a plan.

3. *"We get paid for results, not for planning."* Public relations practitioners tend to be oriented more to activities than to strategic planning. A dollar spent on research and planning is often viewed as a dollar not available for implementing program activities. This orientation generally leads to counting activities rather than results that count. In fact, practitioners are paid for results that happen according to a plan.

4. *"We're doing O.K. without a plan."* Short-term success can change to failure if conditions change. For example, it is easy to see how an injury to a football team's star quarterback can change an entire football season. Such was the case in a business setting when the founder and CEO of a new and successful computer company died in an automobile accident the very day the company's stock went public. The stock offer was withdrawn until new management was in place. A few weeks later the company stock was again offered, but commanded a substantially lower price. Soon thereafter Eagle Computer went out of business. Part of planning involves building in strategies for handling contingencies such as industrial accidents and other operational crises; top management decisions that attract media and public scrutiny; changes in management and other key personnel; and charges by government agencies, consumer groups, unions, or whistle-blowers.[15]

Planning is for the purpose of making something happen or preventing it, for the purpose of exploiting a situation or remedying one. Public relations practice is engaged more often in trying to create a viewpoint or a happening than trying to prevent one and trying to take advantage of an opportunity more often than trying to remedy an undesired situation. There remain, however, many situations and occasions when remedial public relations measures are required because preventive measures were not taken.

Public relations calls for long-term planning and programming in many areas, such as public policy and social problems, but crises often give birth to public relations planning. *Preventive public relations is tied most often to long-term planning. Remedial public relations actions tend to be of short duration and with minimal time for planning.* The immediate need, quite often, is to pick up the pieces of a negative situation or to exploit a positive one. The latter works best if done within the framework of a long-term plan that includes strategies for such contingencies.

WRITING THE PROGRAM

Writing the program is a challenge. When the program meshes with organizational goals, the employer knows that the public relations practitioner understands what management is trying to do and is part of the management team.

The task of writing an overall program or a proposal would rarely fall on a new member of a staff. It is important, however, that all members understand how proposals and presentations evolve. By seeing how all the parts come together, each member is better able to perform his or her segment or specialty when programs are implemented. Plans and programs are generally infused with enthusiasm. That helps get approval by employers and clients. But overenthusiasm carries with it the serious danger of overpromising: "This employee communication program has everything necessary to eliminate the turnover problem." Those are dangerous words. Suppose the program falls short, reducing employee turnover by "only" 50 percent? Ordinarily, such a reduction might be considered an acceptable performance. But evaluated against the unrealistic earlier statement, it might be considered not up to the level promised.

The Program Plan

A public relations plan starts with the organization's mission statement. It proceeds from the specific role assigned to it in the form of a public relations mission. It engages in whatever fact-finding is indicated, as discussed in Chapter 10. An orderly investigative process involves the following four aspects of a situation analysis:

1. *A searching look backward.*   There is no organization, no problem, no opportunity without a history. Learning that history is the first step. In a newly created entity, who founded it? For what purpose? Is it time for an anniversary event, an institutional museum, a biography of the founder? Can public relations help? Background information is also essential if public relations is brought into a going entity to deal with a pressing problem. What is the background of the problem? What has happened that has caused public relations to be involved in a new or different way? Public relations problems, too, have a history.

2. *A wide look around.*   Where there has been no continuing monitoring of public opinion toward the organization, that is the next step. How do employees feel about the conditions of their employment, their leadership? How do the neighbors feel about the presence and conduct of the organization? Is there a breakdown in understanding between the organization and any of its constituent publics? Is there a resentment simmering somewhere? In a crunch, on whom could the organization depend? In that crunch, what groups would delight in the troubles or embarrassment of the organization?

3. *A deep look inside.*   Every organization has a character and a personality. Both tend to be reflections of those who control the organization by their ownership, management, votes, membership, or tenure or in some other way. Character can be discovered by examining the policies set down and by determining if day-to-day actions square with the words. Personality is evident in the style of administration: centralized authority or generous delegation, openness and candor or secretiveness and suspicion. It is portrayed by contemporary or traditional decor and equipment, open or closed doors on executive offices, symbols of stature, approachability of officials, and whether communication is formalized, as by memo, or casual, as by phone. The practitioner needs to know what makes the organization tick and whether it ticks with convictions, values, and standards that the practitioner can share and honestly promote.

4. *A long, long look ahead.*   Is the mission of the organization realistically attainable? Can public relations planning and programming fit in? Can they make a practical contribution? Will this organization be around in ten years? Will it be larger and more solidly entrenched, or will it be engaged in a slow retreat toward oblivion? What are the pros and cons? What are the forces that will affect the organization's chances for success or failure? Are the game and the outcome worth getting involved?

Implementing these steps has been greatly enhanced by advances in technology and resources. On-line databases, for example, as well as increasingly sophisticated issue-tracking techniques and services enable practitioners to meet executives' demands for data as a basis for planning. These data are used to build the foundation of the program: the problem statement and situation analysis (discussed in Chapter 10) and the program goal. The final plan (or proposal) typically includes the ten parts outlined in Exhibit 11–2.

The Role of Working Theory

A program plan represents someone's working theory of what has to be done to achieve a desired outcome. In the words and form of a theoretical statement, "If we implement these actions and communications, then we will achieve these outcomes with our publics, which should lead to accomplishing the program goal." Theory also determines the selection of tactics. Someone's working theory guides how a special event is designed, how a newsletter or press release is worded, and how a community function is conducted. The theory that guides how each tactic is executed represents the practitioner's idea of what will cause a desired result. So when people says a program is "all theory," they are right!

The role of theory is obvious, but not always made explicit, at every step of the planning process. Otherwise, how would decisions be made? For example, theory clearly guides the process when writing program objectives and determining the strategies to achieve them: Assume that the goal of an employee communication program is to reduce the number of employees seriously injured or killed while driving to and from work and while driving on the job. The situation analysis investigation shows that a surprisingly large percentage of employees do not wear seat belts while driving or when a passenger. Program planners decide to develop a program to increase seat belt use among employees. (Note that their theory is that increased seat belt use will lead to a reduction in serious injuries and deaths.)

The situation analysis also shows, however, that delivery drivers are the ones most frequently injured or killed in accidents and that the accidents occur during work hours. Program planners decide that, to have the greatest impact on solving the problem and achieving the program goal, the program should target delivery drivers and car parking-

EXHIBIT 11-2

Public Relations Strategic Planning Process

Four-Step Process	Strategic Planning Steps and Program Outline
1. Defining the Problem (Chapter 10)	**1. The Problem, Concern, or Opportunity** "What's happening now?"
	2. Situation Analysis (Internal and External) "What positive and negative forces are operating? "Who is involved and/or affected?" "How are they involved and/or affected?"
2. Planning and Programming (Chapter 11)	**3. Program Goal** "What is the desired situation?"
	4. Target Publics "Who—internal and external—must the program respond to, reach, and affect?"
	5. Objectives "What must be achieved with each public to accomplish the program goal?"
3. Taking Action and Communicating (Chapter 12)	**6. Action Strategies** "What *changes* must be made to achieve the outcomes stated in the objectives?"
	7. Communication Strategies "What *message content* must be communicated to achieve the outcomes stated in the objectives?" "What *media* best deliver that content to the target publics?"
	8. Program Implementation Plans "Who will be responsible for implementing each of the action and communication tactics?" "What is the sequence of events and the schedule?" "How much will the program cost?"

Four-Step Process	Strategic Planning Steps and Program Outline
4. Evaluating the Program (Chapter 13)	**9. Evaluation Plans** "How will the outcomes specified in the program goal and objectives be measured?" **10. Feedback and Program Adjustment** "How will the results of the evaluations be reported to program managers and used to make program changes?"

lot attendants. Planners then outline what each of the two publics must learn from the program, what opinions each must hold after the program, and what each must do to reach the goal of increased seat belt use: another complex theoretical model of what the program must achieve. Their working theory follows the "learn-feel-do" causal sequence that guides most public communication programs:

information gain ⟶ opinion change ⟶ behavioral change

The working theory is made explicit when stated in the form of objectives for the two target publics. After the objectives are written, planners then turn to developing strategies and tactics to cause the sequence of outcomes specified by the objectives. If during implementation or after the program, the expected (theorized) outcomes are not being achieved, then program planners must decide whether their theory was flawed or whether the program implementation was flawed.

It is indeed the wise practitioner who keeps track of the conditions under which theorized cause-and-effect relationships appear to work and when those assumptions about the linkages between program activities and program effects do not occur. For example, did the third-party endorsements used in the Wisconsin Milk Marketing Board referendum campaign actually make a difference in the number of votes cast in favor of the middle nickel checkoff? If so, maybe the strategy can be generalized to other programs. If not, are dairy producers unique and more resistant to such endorsements?

In summary, working theory drives every program decision, whether or not the assumptions about the causal relationships behind the decisions are made explicit. Practitioners are continually devising and testing their working theories.[16] Those who can bridge the gap between theory and practice are the one most likely to achieve management positions in the twenty-first century.[17]

Defining Target Publics

First of all, practitioners define publics; they are abstractions imposed by program planners. Planners must reify publics so as to develop the objectives, strategies, and tactics necessary for implementing a program. Reification is treating an abstraction as if it is exists as a concrete or material entity. The "general public" is the grandest and least useful reification of all; there simply is no such thing. Given unlimited resources, practitioners could avoid the need to reify by targeting individuals. Useful and practical definitions of publics, however, necessarily represent some degree of reification.

The usual demographic and cross-situational approaches to defining publics typically provide minimal useful guidance for developing program strategy. Simply listing general categories of potential stakeholder groups gives those planning and implementing a program little information about how people in each of the categories uniquely contribute to or are affected by the problem situation and organization.

Stakeholder categories such as employees, stockholders, alumni, consumers, community groups, government, and so forth, each may contain what public relations scholar James Grunig calls "nonpublics, latent publics, aware publics, and active publics."[18] *Nonpublics* are people who do not face a problem or situation in which they are mutually involved with or affected by either an organization or other people. Their level of involvement is so low that they have no impact on the organization and the organization has no recognizable impact on them. *Latent publics* include people who are simply unaware of their connections to others and an organization with respect to some issue or other problem situation. *Aware publics* are those people who recognize that they are somehow affected by or involved in a problem situation shared by others, but have not communicated about it with others. When they begin to communicate and organize to do something about the situation, they become *active publics.*

Useful definitions describe program publics based on how people are involved or affected by the problem situation or issue, who they are, where they live, what relevant organizations they belong to, what they do relevant to the situation, and so forth. The definitions derive from the particular situation for which a public relations intervention is being planned.

For example, suppose that a university has the goal of increasing the number of incoming freshmen for the next academic year. The target publics for the program might include staff members in the admissions and academic advising offices (internal publics); high-school students and others who have written or called academic departments requesting information about particular majors; high-school seniors with grade points of at least 3.0 in high schools within 100 miles of the university and their parents; and high-school guidance counselors in those same schools. When a local newspaper accuses two starting football players at the same university of receiving bogus academic credit for summer work experience, however, the public relations office will define different target publics for the university's response. It is obvious that different people, with different kinds of connections to the university, are involved in and affected by the potential crisis in the university's football program.

Following are approaches used alone and in combination to define target publics from among the various stakeholder groups:

1. *Geographics*—natural or political boundaries—indicate where to find people, but give little useful insight about important differences within the boundaries. This approach is useful for selecting media and allocating program resources according to population density. ZIP codes, telephone area codes, city limits, county lines, and so forth, are examples of the geographic approach to defining publics.

2. *Demographics*—gender, income, age, marital status, education—are the most frequently used individual characteristics, but provide little understanding of why or how people are involved or affected. Demographics and geographics help practitioners make the first "cut," but without additional information about how people are involved or affected by an issue, problem, or situation, they usually give little guidance to developing strategy and tactics.

3. *Psychographics*—psychological and lifestyle characteristics (cross situational)—widely used under the name "VALS," segment adults based on "psychological maturity." Knowing about lifestyle and values is useful, but typically only when combined with other attributes that tie the segments to something related to a particular situation.

4. *Covert power*—behind-the-scenes political/economic power—describes people at the top of a power pyramid who operate across situations. They exert power over others on a wide range of issues, but often not in ways easily observed. Identifying these people requires a combination of careful observation over time, interviews with others in the problem situation, analyses of documents that record or tract the exercise of covert power, or any combination of the three.

5. *Position*   uses the positions held by individuals, not attributes of the individuals themselves, to identify target publics. People are identified as important in a particular situation because of the roles they play in positions of influence in particular situations. The positions they hold make them important players in the efforts to achieve program goals and objectives.

6. *Reputation*   identifies "knowledgeables" or "influentials" based on others' perceptions of these individuals. These publics are referred to as "opinion leaders" or "influencers," but they are defined as such by people in the situation of interest and are not to be confused by the cross-situational covert power group or defined as opinion leaders by the observer using some cross-situational definition.

7. *Membership*   uses appearance on an organizational roster, list, or affiliation as the attribute relevant to a particular situation. For example, membership in a professional association or special-interest group signals a person's involvement in a situation, not the individual attributes of the member. Usually members receive controlled media from the organization with whom they affiliate.

8. *Role in decision process* calls for observing the decision-making process to learn who plays what roles in influencing decisions in a particular situation. This approach helps identify the most active among the active publics, those who really make decisions, take action, and communicate. Again, knowing their individual attributes can be less important than knowing how they behavior in the process that leads to decisions related to the issue or problem of interest.

The key to defining publics is to identify how people are involved and affected in the situation for which the program intervention is being developed. Program planners can develop specific and responsive program objectives and strategies if they know what different people know about an issue or situation, how they feel about it, and what they do that is either contributing to or reacting to it. This understanding of what they know, how they feel, and what they do, combined with who and where they are, provides the basis for writing useful program objectives for each target public.

Writing Program Objectives

Objectives spell out the key results that must be achieved with each public to reach the program goal. In practice, objectives:

1. Give focus and direction to those developing program strategy and tactics.
2. Provide guidance and motivation to those charged with implementing the program.
3. Spell out the outcome criteria to be used for monitoring and evaluating the program.

All too often, however, public relations program objectives either describe the tactic, or means, rather than the consequences, or ends, to be achieved. For example, "To issue 12 monthly issues of . . ." and "To inform people about . . ." both describe activities, not results. Objectives should outline the intended impact of the 12 issues and of the effort to inform.

Objectives also make concrete the working theory behind the program, usually in the "learn-feel-do" causal sequence. Program objectives for each public specify the desired outcomes, in what sequence, by what dates, and in what magnitude, needed to achieve the program goal. (See Exhibit 11–3.) The more specific the objectives, the more precise everything that follows. Following are examples of useful program objectives for the three levels of outcomes:

1. *Knowledge outcome:* By July 1, to increase the number of local homeowners from 13 percent to 27 percent who know that wildland fires destroyed 2500 homes during the past three fire seasons.

Sample Program Goal and Objectives

Goal: To reduce the number of delivery drivers seriously injured or killed while driving on the job from a five-year average of five per year to no more than two in the next fiscal year.

Program Objectives for Delivery Drivers

1. To increase, within 6 weeks after starting the program, the percentage of drivers from 8 percent to at least 90 percent who are aware that in a typical year four company delivery drivers are seriously injured and one is killed while driving on the job.

2. To increase, within 2 months after starting the program, the percentage of drivers from 5 percent to at least 80 percent who know that 55 percent of all fatalities and 65 percent of all injuries from vehicle crashes could be prevented if seat belts were used properly.

3. To increase, within 2 months after starting the program, drivers' awareness to at least 85 percent that 95 percent of all city employees, police, and emergency vehicle drivers use shoulder restraints and seat belts any time they drive on the same city streets.

4. To reduce, within 3 months after starting the program the number of drivers from 67 percent to less than 25 percent who feel that using seat belts while driving adds to delivery time and extends the time needed to complete routes.

5. To decrease, by the end of the third month after the program begins, the number of drivers from 70 percent to less than 35 percent who "agree" or "strongly agree" with the statement that their own safe driving prevents serious driving accidents to the point that seat belts are not necessary.

6. To increase the percentage of drivers who use seat belts from the current 51 percent to at least 70 percent within 3 months after the program begins, to at least 80 percent within 5 months, and to at least 90 percent by the end of the first year.

7. After the 90-percent level use is achieved, to maintain that level of seat belt use among all permanent and all temporary replacement drivers.

2. *Predisposition outcome:* To increase neighboring property owners' confidence in our ability to conduct field tests safely from a mean confidence rating of 2.7 to 3.5 by January 15.

3. *Behavioral outcome:* To increase the percentage of employees who use seat belts when driving on the job from the current 51 percent to at least 70 percent within 30 days after the program begins.

These examples illustrate the elements and form of useful program objectives:

1. *Begin with "to" followed by a verb describing the direction to the intended outcome.* There are three possibilities: "to increase," to decrease," and "to maintain."

2. *Specify the outcome to be achieved.* Again, there are three possible categories of what is to be maintained or changed: what people are aware of, know, or understand (knowledge outcomes); how people feel (predisposition outcomes); and what people do (behavioral outcomes). Each objective should spell out a single, specific outcome.

3. *State the magnitude of change or level to be maintained in measurable terms.* To provide useful and verifiable outcome criteria, objectives must be stated in quantifiable terms. Surely, the levels must be realistic and consistent with the resources available to those implementing the program. Experience and judgment, plus evidence from the situation analysis research, provide the bases for setting the levels of outcomes to be achieved. Without benchmark data, judgment dominates when setting the outcome levels.

4. *Set the target date for when the outcome is to be achieved.* Dates stated in the objectives follow the working theory of the sequence of what has to happen. Typically, outcomes must be achieved in order, with one necessary before another. Each successive outcome is a logical consequence of the previous outcomes. Dates also provide guidance for those developing strategy and tactics, even down to deciding when to schedule communications and events.

Objectives should be in writing, with copies available to each person working on the program. Objectives become the primary basis for developing and implementing program strategy and tactics. Because they provide the guidance for planning, managing, and evaluating program elements and the overall program, *objectives should be discussed frequently*. As the topic of staff discussions, objectives keep the program on track. As conditions change, program planners change the objectives to reflect the different program environment.

Without objectives, programs drift according to the whims and desires of clients and employers and the intuitions and preferences of practitioners. People in power choose program strategy and tactics because they "like" them, not because they are logically related to intended outcomes. Practitioners select strategy and tactics because of habit, comfort based on previous experience, or because "they worked last time." In effect, objectives provide a road map, derived from the working theory, to the desired goal.

PLANNING FOR PROGRAM IMPLEMENTATION

Plans, if they are to be carried out effectively, must be monitored at each step of the way. Preparation and follow-up support are necessary to ensure a return on the investment made in planning and programming. Anticipation and follow-through on plans are just as important in the practice of public relations as in sports.

Writing Planning Scenarios

Writing planning scenarios is the art of forecasting and describing the range of possible future states. Scenarios provide either longitudinal or cross-sectional summative statements about the future for the purpose of planning. Forecasters working in the Rand Corporation in the 1950s were the first to refer to "scenario writing" when describing their more qualitative approach to forecasting the future. The process differs from more traditional quantitative forecasting in that planners develop a number of plausible predictions of the future, rather than relying on a single projection, as the bases for charting strategy.[19]

The origins of scenario writing are more qualitative than quantitative. In fact, the pioneer of the technique said that the most important parts of the process are "simply to think about the problem" and to engage in "systematic conjecture."[20] The goal is to help clients anticipate more than one possible future state and plan for events that may have no history upon which to build.

Futurists generally agree that the range of useful scenarios is two to four, but that the idea number is three. And while the labels may vary, they represent high-, low-, and middle-ground future states, with the middle-ground scenario often viewed as the one most likely to occur. Some experienced planners, however, argue that, to avoid the appearance of assigning probabilities, scenarios should be titled according to some major theme or major attribute. Still others suggest "optimistic, surprise-free, and pessimistic" labels, again without suggesting probabilities. These planners point out that futurists cannot predict an uncertain future with certainty, so they cannot attach probabilities to scenarios.[21] Catastrophic events, political revolutions, and other dramatic and unanticipated changes in the social, political, economic, and technological environments demonstrate that scenarios represent possibilities. In contrast, the vision of hindsight reported in case studies gives the appearance of predictability; but note that case studies describe the past, not the future.

The danger of labeling one scenario as "most likely" or "probable" is that program planners tend to develop strategy for only that one possible future state, thereby defeating the purpose of having developed scenarios. After all, the purpose of writing scenarios is to construct descriptions of possible future states so that contingency planning can help prepare for the range of possibilities. The greater the future uncertainty, then the greater the need for planning scenarios. Predictions based on historical data, traditional forecasting models, and trend analyses may not meet the needs of public relations planners who must be prepared for the unexpected. This is not to say that one would be wise to abandon traditional quantitative methods, however.

Anticipating Disasters and Crises

Whereas public relations practitioners typically cannot predict a specific disaster or crisis, they can anticipate that the unexpected will occur. First, though, practitioners must determine the types of crises, because the response depends in part on the type and duration of possible scenarios.

1. *Immediate crises,* the most dreaded type, happen so suddenly and unexpectedly that there is little or no time for research and planning. Examples include a plane crash, product tampering, death of a key officer, fire, earthquake, bomb scare, and workplace shooting by a disgruntled former employee. These call for working out in advance a consensus among top management for a general plan on how to react to such crises to avoid confusion, conflict, and delay.

2. *Emerging crises* allow more time for research and planning, but may suddenly erupt after brewing for long periods. Examples include employee dissatisfaction and low morale, sexual harassment in the workplace, substance abuse on the job, overcharges on government contracts, and the GM pickup fuel tank. The challenge is to convince top management to take corrective action before the crisis reaches the critical stage.

3. *Sustained crises* are those that persist for months or even years despite the best efforts of management. Rumors or speculation get reported in the media or circulated by word of mouth, outside the control of public relations. No amount of denial or countering seems to stop the rumor or purge the news database, meaning that reporters working on a new story will see the old story and may repeat the misinformation. Examples include persistent rumors of eminent downsizing, suggestions that Procter & Gamble's logo contains Satanic symbolism (this paragraph is an example of how such rumors get repeated to new audiences!), and the charges of promiscuity that plagued candidate Bill Clinton in his ultimately victorious presidential campaign.[22]

Practitioners who prepare for the worst are anticipating and responding to the needs of top management. For example, in the insurance industry, a string of catastrophic loss years and the politicization of insurance issues helped establish the role of public relations in planning and management. In an industry in which disasters and crises are part of the business, senior managers regard public relations as essential to maintaining the industry's public franchise.[23]

Most organizations know how to deal with operational crises internally. It is the "unplanned visibility" following such crises, however, that can turn them into events that threaten reputation, credibility, and market position.[24] Some crisis management experts attribute the seemingly heightened interest in crisis management to what *Time* magazine called the "magazining of TV news" and fierce competition for "high-impact, hot-button stories":

> And everyone in magazineland seems to agree on what the good stories are: consumer rip-offs, miscarriages of justice, teary tales of people victimized by bad doctors or trampled on by insensitive government agencies. Like the one-hour dramas they have replaced on the prime-time schedule, the magazines serve up morality tales of black hats vs. white hats, with the reporter as avenging U.S. marshal. Instead of a six-gun, his or her weapons are a hidden camera (for the inevitable undercover exposé) and a hand-held mike, thrust at reluctant witnesses before they slam the car door. It's "Gotcha!" journalism.[25]

Common mistakes in handling crises include:

1. *Hesitation*, which leads to public perception of confusion, callousness, incompetence, or lack of preparation.
2. *Obfuscation*, which leads to the perception of dishonesty and insensitivity.
3. *Retaliation*, which increases tension and intensifies emotion, rather than reducing them.
4. *Prevarication or equivocation*, which creates the biggest problem, because nothing substitutes for truth.
5. *Pontification*, which creates vulnerability by taking a high-handed approach without really dealing with the issue at hand.
6. *Confrontation*, which provides others visibility by keeping the issue alive, by giving them a platform, and by giving them more to respond to.
7. *Litigation*, which guarantees even greater visibility and may eliminate more reasonable solutions.[26]

The key to anticipating and avoiding crises is assessing what can go wrong, what can affect people or the environment, and what will create visibility. Guidelines for preparing for public relations crises include:

1. Identify things that can go wrong and become highly visible; assess vulnerabilities throughout the organization.
2. Assign priorities based on which vulnerabilities are most urgent and most likely.
3. Draft questions, answers, and resolutions for each potential crisis scenario.
4. Focus on the two most important tasks—what to do and what to say—during the first critical hours following a crisis.
5. Develop a strategy to contain and counteract, not react and respond.[27]

A fire on the then-new $200-million luxury liner *Crystal Harmony* demonstrated the value of crisis planning. The Los Angeles–based ship's captain called by radio phone to report that a fire in the ship's auxiliary engine room had disabled the ship. There were no deaths or injuries among the 920 guests and 540 crew members, but the ship was dead in the water. Public relations director Darlene Papalini turned to the company's 61-page "Crisis Communication Manual." It covers five types of emergency scenarios: (1) trade: labor strike or delayed sailing; (2) business page: "bad press," unfavorable financial news, or sale of a company; (3) shipboard: natural catastrophes, such as a hurricane or accidents such as a ship running aground; (4) media: a bomb threat, fire, or threat of sinking; and (5) international: terrorist or other attack. Each executive member of the crisis management team has a copy of the manual at home as well as a copy at the office. The crisis was successfully handled with passengers, media, port agents, employees, vendors, and suppliers in part because such a crisis had been anticipated as a possible scenario and plans had been put on paper. According to Papalini, "We certainly do not want to go through such a thing again, but we were most pleased that people understood the plan and followed it; it worked."[28]

Successful handling of this and other crises requires an ability to anticipate possible emergencies and vulnerabilities, skills in planning strategy for responding to possible emergency scenarios, recognition of the early stages of crises, and the capacity to respond immediately as part of a systematic crisis management plan. (See Exhibit 11–4.)

EXHIBIT 11–4

Checklist for Crisis Communication

Do the Following:

▶ Get out your prepared crisis plan, call together the crisis management steering committee, call in experts to help analyze and explain the crisis, and open the lines of communication.

▶ Notify top management and refer them to the crisis plan. Give them the task of making impact projections in preparation for inquiries from employees, government agencies, and the media.

▶ Channel all inquiries to the designated spokesperson, who was selected and trained in advance as part of the crisis planning preparation. Notify receptionists, operators, secretaries, and others to direct all inquiries to the designated spokesperson *without giving their own versions or opinions*.

▶ Set up a news center for media and begin providing information as quickly as it becomes available. Provide information background packets, telephones, computers and printers, fax machines, and a place for television interviews away from the crisis scene.

▶ Be open and tell the full story. If you do not, someone else will and you will lose control as journalists turn to other sources and outside experts to fill in gaps in the story.

▶ Demonstrate the organization's concern for what is happening and for the people who are involved and affected. At the same time, explain what the organization is doing or planning to do to solve the problem.

▶ Have someone on call 24 hours a day and stay with the story as long as the media are interested.

▶ Reconvene the crisis management team afterward to summarize what happened, to review and evaluate how the plan worked, and to recommend improvements in the crisis plan.

On the Other Hand:

▶ Do not speculate publicly about what you do not know to be fact. And do not respond to reporters' questions designed to solicit speculation.

▶ Do not minimize the problem or try to underplay a serious situation. The press will find out the truth soon enough.

▶ Do not let the story dribble out bit by bit. Each new disclosure becomes a potential headline or lead story.

▶ Do not release information about people if it will violate their privacy or if it blames anyone for anything.

▶ Do not say "no comment" or make off-the-record comments. If you cannot say something on the record, then explain why and tell reporters when they can expect the information. If information is simply not available, say so and assure reporters that you will get it to them as soon as you can.

▶ Do not play favorites among the media or the reporters. Respect reporters' work by not undercutting their scoops and enterprise.

▶ Do not try to capitalize on media attention and interest by trying to promote the organization, cause, products, or services. Do not do what will be perceived as a self-serving pitch while in the crisis spotlight.

Adapted from Claudia Reinhardt, "Workshop: How to Handle a Crisis," *Public Relations Journal* 43, no. 11 (November 1987): 43–44. Used with permission of *Public Relations Journal*.

Establishing an Information Center

Many organizations have discovered the dangers of rumors and the need to provide authentic information. When a crisis arises, it suddenly becomes apparent that some seemingly unimportant facets of an operation have been overlooked and must be given hurried attention. Inevitably, one such area of weakness is the availability of information. A knee-jerk response usually results in a jerry-built rumor center that operates through the crisis period, then fades away without serious thought until the next crisis comes.

There are three major points to remember in planning for a information center. *First*, the center must be recognized for what it is: a place where information moves from the institution directly to an organization's publics. It is not a press operation. To saddle an organization's press office with an added responsibility of answering questions from other publics reduces the effectiveness of both functions. Press and public information centers must be closely coordinated, but where it can be afforded, they must be separate entities, each directed toward its own specific function.

Second, the center should be in two parts. Rumor centers are almost exclusively telephone operations. Of course, there must be an answering service or information center. So, one group deals directly with the publics, taking questions and providing answers. If that group does not have the information, they promise to have it within a certain period of time. The second group, however, is a coordinating agency: the point of contact between the information center and the institution's staff and agencies. The coordinating agency goes to the institution's staff for information and checks material with the highest level of the administration for accuracy, coordinates it with the press office, and relays it to the center for use. Hence, all information flows through the coordinating agency, where it can be accounted for and logged. In addition to raw information—the factual material used to answer direct and simple questions—the coordinating agency should have qualified people available to speak on policy or to conduct philosophical discussions of current issues. As the sole source of material for the information center, this agency controls the center and what is being said to the various publics. Although not an official spokesperson, it does provide for "one-voice" response to the institution's problems.

Third, and perhaps the most important, any such center must have credibility established long before any crisis; it must be the accepted source of accurate information. This cannot be accomplished during the period of crisis alone. The flow of credible information must be established during routine times. The function must become an accepted part of the institution on a full-time, continuing basis, identical in crisis or routine situations. It must, over an extended period, encourage both internal and external publics to use it with faith and confidence. This amounts to more than establishing a reputation for truth; it involves education. Internally, all agencies of the institution must be made aware that such a system exists and must be encouraged to use it to make information for which they are responsible available.

Procter & Gamble

Old

New

Such a information or fact center, operating normally over a long period of time, sets the pattern within an institution for quickly and efficiently moving information. If the institution is tuned to such an operation in routine times, the transition in troubled times is far less shattering.

What appeared to be an effective response to a devastating rumor can be studied in Procter & Gamble's handling of a wild rumor that it was in "league with Satan" and giving part of the corporation's money to the "church of Satan." Evidence for such claims was Procter & Gamble's logo, which had evolved over more than a century, showing the man in the moon and stars. To deal with this rumor, the company went to the press, the pulpit, and the courts to stop the wild charges emanating from religious fanatics. But in April 1985, Procter & Gamble gave up the fight and announced that it would remove the logo from its products. In 1991, Procter & Gamble modernized its logo for the first time since 1930, but did not use it on products or in advertising.

Budgeting

There is as much art and artistry in public relations budgeting as there is science. Available literature on the subject is sparse. Few practitioners study accounting and finance as part of their professional education. Surveys of practitioners reveal that they typically use their computers for word processing and desktop publishing, but not to manage financial data. For example, Canadian practitioners rate budgeting as their weakest skill, with 60 percent reporting that they have never received financial training. Yet two thirds of these same practitioners said that they manage budgets greater than $500,000, and about 30 percent indicated that they management budgets of $1 million or more.[29]

No doubt, practitioners in other countries suffer from the same deficiency in their professional preparation. At professional seminars the most frequently mentioned guideline seems to be, "Always ask for more than you need." Of course, the deliberate, habitual padding of budget requests is not peculiar to public relations. It has become part of "the system," but is not recommended.

In established departments, budgets generally relate to one of four control factors. One is the total income or funds available to the enterprise, the second is the "competitive necessity," the third is the overall task or goal set for the organization, and the fourth is the profit or surplus over expenses.

When *total income* or *funds available* is the basis, as in marketing or fund-raising activities, public relations is generally allocated a percentage. The percentage relates to organization's total operating budget, to gross sales, to funds raised, or to funds allocated from taxes. When *competitive necessity* is the criterion, the amount spent by a similar charity or a competing organization is matched or exceeded. This method is very risky. The *task* or *goal* basis usually provides for public relations to have a share of the funding set aside to achieve the desired end result. For example, to achieve a fund-raising goal, a museum might increase the percentage of the operating budget allocated to "development" activities. The final approach—based on how much money is "left over"—usually sets a fluctuating figure that can go up or down, depending on "the point at which we break even," or, in a nonprofit operation, "the point at which we cover all expenses." Not only is it difficult to plan and staff under this option, but it also reinforces the impression that public relations is something you do if you have money to spend after covering the essentials.

Budgeting is rarely a one-person job. Each specialist is called on to estimate and itemize variable costs that will be incurred to implement the public relations plan during the next budget year. Variable costs are those associated with projects and activities, such as printing, rent for special events facilities, speakers' fees, photographers, advertising, travel, and entertainment. The department head, or someone designated, adds the estimated variable costs to the unit's fixed costs, including such expenses as salaries and benefits, overhead for office space, phone, service, equipment leases, supplies, subscriptions, and service contracts. The next executive up the line evaluates the budgets from the departments for which he or she is responsible, negotiates and adjusts the budget requests to fit the total available or needed, and finally either approves or forwards the budgets to the next level for approval. (See Figure 11–1.)

Three guidelines may be helpful:

1. *Know the cost of what you propose to buy.*   If you plan to do a special mailing, find out the exact costs for photography and artwork, printing and folding, mailing lists, labeling and sorting, delivery, postage, and everything else needed to complete the job. Do not guess, because you will have to live within the budget that gets approved and deliver what was promised.

2. *Communicate the budget in terms of what it costs to achieve specific results.* The actual details of actual variable and fixed costs used to develop the budget may not be of interest to management or to a client. Managers who must approve the budget typically want to know how much it will cost to achieve goals and objectives. They look to you to manage the process in a cost-effective fashion.

3. *Use the power of your computer to manage the program.*   Develop a master spreadsheet, as well as spreadsheets for individual projects. By tracking each project and linking each to the master spreadsheet, you can estimate cash-flow requirements in advance and monitor expenditures against cost estimates.

Public Relations Budgeting and Planning Process

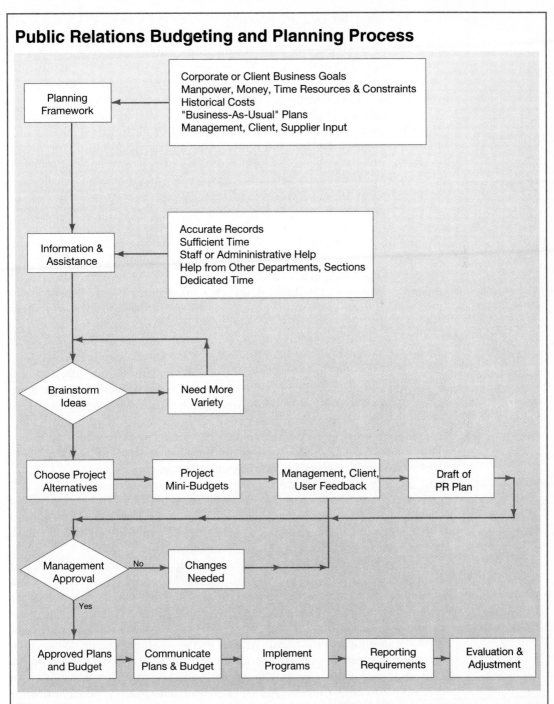

Figure 11–1   Bob Delaney and Michael Lewis, "Planning and Budgeting for Public Relations Professionials," paper presented to the 1990 Annual Conference of the Canadian Public Relations Society, June 1990, p. 8. Used with permission.

Too often, budgets are put aside after they are approved and are not used as management tools. Used in conjunction with other elements of program planning, however, budgets provide guidance for scheduling staff resources, contracting for services, tracking project costs, and establishing accountability. Individual staff members, as well as the entire unit, should refer to the budget when assessing performance against expectations.

Budgets often play an important part in shaping and maintaining the relationship between the public relations staff and their clients and top management. In the final analysis, practitioners must have realistic budgets, must use them to direct staff efforts, must review them frequently with clients and top management, and must be able to link costs to performance and outcomes.

Pretesting Program Elements

Once the strategic plan is formulated, it should be tried on a pilot basis. Marketers have been doing this for decades. Only recently has pretesting a plan of action and communication become somewhat routine in public relations.

Many qualitative and quantitative tools are available: interviews with opinion leaders, focus groups, controlled laboratory tests, and field tests in pilot communities. Careful pretests of strategy, tactics, and program materials provide estimates of how they will work, provide comparisons of alternatives to determine which works best, and detect possible backlash effects of unanticipated, unfavorable results.

Backlash effects can be avoided by conducting a response analysis. This means using a sample audience to observe immediate reaction to specific communication content. As an example, the Occupational Safety and Health Administration (OSHA) would have been spared much embarrassment had it pretested its 16-page booklet, "Safety with Beef Cattle." A pretest would have eliminated such nonsense as, "Be careful not to step into the manure pits," "If your ladder is broken, do not climb it," and "Beams that are too low can hurt you."

Message pretesting also can help increase the understandability of the information for its intended audience. The symbolism chosen for a public relations document may represent perfect clarity to its creator but be both uninteresting and unintelligible to the reader. Or the symbol may be inappropriate, as when Caterpillar Tractor Company sent 10,000 calendars to its Saudi Arabia dealer, Zahid Tractor. When government inspectors opened the shipment they found that the calendar contained a picture of a village in Iceland showing a church with two crosses. Workers blotted out the crosses with heavy black markers because Christian symbols are forbidden in the devoutly Islamic nation. The blotches created 10,000 reminders of the need to pretest even the smallest detail in program communications and activities.

A few years ago an experimental program of health education was undertaken in an isolated Peruvian community high in the Andes. As part of the program, a film on the transmission of typhus by lice, featuring graphic close-up shots, was prepared and shown to the villagers. It became apparent that the message was not getting through. A survey of the people who had seen the film revealed that although they had many lice in their homes, they had never been bothered by the "giant" kind shown on the screen. To get results, appeals and symbols must be appropriate and understood.

A cautionary note on pretesting must be inserted. The stream of public opinion rushes along swiftly. An idea that worked well in a pretest might prove a fiasco upon widespread use because of a time lag. Seasons change and with them change people's concerns, recreational pursuits, and so forth. Overpowering events can quickly alter the public opinion climate overnight with an unexpected news event; for example, the United Way of American national headquarters scandal dramatically changed the climate for fund-raising campaigns run by local United Way organizations. When using pretest results as a guide to communication programs, practitioners need to be as certain as possible that program conditions are similar to those that existed during the pretest and that pretest subjects are representative of the program target publics.

Selling the Plan

Research, analysis, precedents, and experience must be converted into program forms acceptable to those who are not public relations executives and to clients. Some are not sensitively attuned to public opinion. Some are cost oriented, or publicly gun-shy, or both. Some do not commit comfortably to speculative expenditures with no guarantee of return. Some are nervous about issuing information to news media. Goals and objectives not tied directly to sales or profits are ephemeral to many. The more specific the institutional goals, the more specific and effective the public relations plan can be.

Selling the program proposal puts the practitioner's persuasive and technical communication skills to the test. It calls for effective writing, persuasive speaking, skillful use of presentation audiovisual materials, and careful reading of those around the conference table. But effective selling begins with an effective program proposal.

After a program has been approved at the policy level, it becomes necessary to indoctrinate colleagues in what is to follow. Otherwise, these important collaborators may wind up uninformed, like an outside counselor who is not allowed to participate in the planning. They would not be able to do their part. They would not be in a position to solicit support from the people under their supervision.

Some generally accepted tenets related to introducing others to the program merit noting. Explain the basic problems in terms of the harm that can be done if they are left unattended. Then, explain the immediate remedial measures in relation to long-term plans. Use similar case examples, precedents, and survey results to substantiate the plan. Eliminate personal opinion except as it applies to special knowledge of related cases. Relate the program to the climate in which the organization operates and that it hopes to enjoy in the future. Stress that the activities will have a desirable ultimate effect on public opinion. Keep explanations short and to the point. Be decisive and have conviction in the plan, qualities highly respected by administrators.

Staff orientation and indoctrination are best handled through informal sessions in which people can air their views and talk things out. Quite often, meetings are arranged in which the practitioner presents the program, and then throws the meeting open to discussion. When this is done, a summary should be supplied afterward to all participants in the discussion. It can take the form of meeting minutes, a program timetable, a roster of projects, or a report explaining the plans. It is important for future relationships that the programming agreed upon be a matter of record. Getting it down on paper tends to make the planning and programming steps real and tangible for those charged with implementing the program.

ADDITIONAL READINGS

Cantor, Bill, and Chester Burger, eds.   *Experts in Action: Inside Public Relations*, 2d ed. New York: Longman, Inc., 1989. Contains useful chapters on dealing with crises, CEOs' expectations, strategy, and accountability.

Kendall, Robert.   *Public Relations Campaign Strategies*. New York: Harper Collins, 1992. How-to approach to applying four-step public relations process and campaign principles to public relations.

Nager, Norman R., and T. Harrell Allen.   *Public Relations Management by Objectives*. Lanham, Md.: University Press of America, 1984. (Originally published by Longman, Inc.) Still the most comprehensive effort to date to apply MBO to public relations.

Rayfield, Robert E., Lalit Acharya, J. David Pincus, and Donn E. Silvis.   *Public Relations Writing: Strategies and Skills*. Dubuque, Iowa: William C. Brown Publishers, 1991. Approaches public relations writing as the application of communication and other social science theory.

Rice, Ronald E., and Charles K. Atkin, eds.   *Public Information Campaigns*, 2d ed. Newbury Park, Calif.: Sage Publications, Inc., 1989. Useful reference for students and practitioners with interests in government and politics, and public health.

Salmon, Charles T., ed.   *Information Campaigns: Balancing Social Values and Social Change*. Newbury Park, Calif.: Sage Publications, Inc., 1989. Merges communication and "social marketing" thinking to develop theory *of* and theory *for* information campaign.

Tucker, Kerry, Doris Derelian, and Donna Rouner.   *Public Relations Writing: An Issue-Driven Behavioral Approach*, 2d ed. Englewood Cliffs, N.J.: Prentice-Hall, Inc., 1994. Cited in footnotes, but worth mentioning again because it applies theory to developing public relations strategy and tactics.

U.S. Department of Health and Human Services, Office of Cancer Communications. *Making Health Communication Programs Work: A Planner's Guide.* National Institutes of Health Publication No. 89-1493 (1989). Discusses principles and processes for developing health communication programs. Includes examples and specific step-by-step guidelines applicable in other contexts.

NOTES

[1] David M. Dozier and Larissa A. Grunig,   "The Organization of the Public Relations Function," in *Excellence in Public Relations and Communication Management*, edited by James E. Grunig (Hillsdale, N.J.: Lawrence Erlbaum Associates, Publishers, 1992), 412–13.

[2] William J. Small,   "Exxon Valdez: How to Spend Billions and Still Get a Black Eye," *Public Relations Review* 17, no. 1 (Spring 1991): 9–25.

[3] Stephen P. Robbins,   *Organization Theory: Structure, Design, and Applications*, 3d ed. (Englewood Cliffs, N.J.: Prentice-Hall, Inc., 1990), 121.

[4] Ibid., 121–23.

[5] Walter K. Lindenmann,   "Research, Evaluation and Measurement: A National Perspective," *Public Relations Review* 16, no. 2 (Summer 1990): 8.

[6] David M. Dozier,   "The Innovation of Research in Public Relations Practice: Review of a Program of Studies," *Public Relations Annual* 2 (1990): 15–21.

[7] Robert W. Kinkead and Dena Winokur,   "How Public Relations Professionals Help CEOs Make the Right Moves," *Public Relations Journal* 48, no. 10 (October 1992): 19.

[8] Ed Block,   "Expectations of PR: A Colloquy," *Arthur W. Page Society Newsletter* 7, no. 2 (June 1991): 4.

[9] David M. Bicofsky of New York Telephone Company, quoted in Kinkead and Winokur,   "How Public Relations Professionals Help CEOs," 23.

[10] Quoted in Dena Winokur and Robert W. Kinkead,   "How Public Relations Fits into Corporate Strategy," *Public Relations Journal* 49, no. 5 (May 1993): 23.

[11] Kinkead and Winokur,   "How Public Relations Professionals Help CEOs," 21.

[12] Paul S. Forbes,   "Applying Strategic Management to Public Relations," *Public Relations Journal* 48, no. 3 (March 1992): 32.

[13] Adapted from George L. Morrisey,   *Management by Objectives and Results for Business and Industry*, 2d ed. (Reading, Mass.: Addison-Wesley Publishing Company, 1982), 107, 216–20.

[14] Andrew Campbell,   "The Power of Mission: Aligning Strategy and Culture," *Planning Review* 20, no. 5 (September/October 1992): 10–12 and 63.

[15] Adapted from Patrick J. Below, George L. Morrisey, and Betty L. Acomb,   *The Executive Guide to Strategic Planning* (San Francisco: Jossey-Bass Publishers, 1987), 17–19; and Robert B. Irvine,   "The Crisis Outlook for '92 and Beyond," *Public Relations Journal* 48, no. 10 (October 1992): 8 and 34.

[16] See Kerry Tucker, Doris Derelian, and Donna Rouner,   *Public Relations Writing: An Issue-Driven Behavioral Approach*, 2d ed. (Englewood Cliffs, N.J.: Prentice-Hall, Inc., 1994) for a detailed discussion of how working theory guides strategic planning in public relations.

[17] Winokur and Kinkead,   "How Public Relations Fits into Corporate Strategy," 23.

[18] James E. Grunig and Fred C. Repper,   "Strategic Management, Publics and Issues," in *Excellence in Public Relations and Communication Management*, edited by James Grunig, (Hillsdale, N.J.: Lawrence Erlbaum Associates, Publishers, 1992), 127.

[19]Steven P. Schnaars, "How to Develop and Use Scenarios," in *Strategic Planning: Models and Analytical Techniques*, edited by Robert G. Dyson (Chichester, U.K.: John Wiley and Sons, 1990), 153–67.

[20]Herman Kahn, *The Japanese Challenge* (New York: Thomas Y. Crowell, 1979), 5, as quoted in Schnaars, "How to Develop and Use Scenarios," 160.

[21]Schnaars, "How to Develop and Use Scenarios," 158–65.

[22]Adapted from Claudia Reinhardt, "Workshop: How to Handle a Crisis," *Public Relations Journal* 43, no. 11 (November 1987): 43–44.

[23]Robert J. Gore, "In a High-Profile, Crisis-Laden Business, Insurance CEOs Rely on Public Relations," *Public Relations Journal* 49, no. 5 (May 1993): 21.

[24]James E. Lukaszewski, "How to Handle a Public Relations Crisis," *World Executive's Digest* 12, no. 6 (June 1991): 68.

[25]Richard Zoglin, "The Magazining of TV News," *Time* 142, no. 2 (July 12, 1993): 50–51.

[26]Adapted from Lukaszewski, "How to Handle a Public Relations Crisis," 68–69.

[27]Ibid.

[28]Norman Sklarewitz, "Cruise Company Handles Crisis by the Book," *Public Relations Journal* 47, no. 5 (May 1991): 34–36.

[29]Bob Delaney and Michael Lewis, "Planning and Budgeting for Public Relations Professionals." Paper presented to the 1990 Annual Conference of the Canadian Public Relations Society, June 1990.

CHAPTER 12

Step Three: Taking Action and Communicating

> Words are merely words, and they can be purely cosmetic if they aren't backed by convictions, actions and policies.[1]
>
> **HAROLD BURSON**

In the third step of the public relations process, the function moves into the implementation stage based on the fact-finding and planning of the first two steps. Once a problem has been defined and a solution worked out, the next steps are *action* and *communication*.

ACTION AND COMMUNICATION

Public relations has matured into the role of helping organizations decide not only what to say, but what to do, according to Harold Burson. In its infancy and into the 1960s, public relations simply crafted and distributed the message handed down from management. Indicating their view of the role of the function, management asked, "How do I say it?" In response to the social changes of the 1960s, organizations and their CEOs were increasingly held accountable on such issues as public and employee safety, equal opportunity, and the environment. In addition to how to say something, management asked public relations, "What shall I say?" Beginning in the 1980s, however, public relations entered a third stage, in addition to being asked communication questions; management now asked, "What do I do?"[2]

Burson attributes this new role to unavoidable and increasingly detailed public scrutiny of what organizations do and say. Public

379

response also happens quickly because of almost instantaneous worldwide communication. Modern communication technology closes the loop between message and behavior to the point that they are almost one and the same: What an organization does can be reported as quickly as what the organization says. As a result, *all organizations need public relations more than ever, first to help determine what to do, and then to work out what to say and how to say it.*[3]

THE ACTION COMPONENT OF STRATEGY

In the words of the old adage, "Actions speaker louder than words." Yet, many people in management, and even some in public relations, unfortunately believe the myth that communication alone can solve most public relations problems. Typically, however, public relations problems result from something *done*, not something *said*. The exception is when the "something said" becomes an event itself, such as when someone in authority or in a prominent position makes a sexist remark, racial slur, or other bigoted comment. Even more problematic is when such a comment appears in official organizational communications.

Acting Responsively and Responsibly

It stands to reason that if something that was done caused the problem, then something must be done to solve the problem. In other words, corrective action is necessary to eliminate the original source of the problem. An example of the need for corrective action is the university that had difficulties attracting freshmen. Investigators discovered that the word was out, "Don't go to State, freshmen can't get classes." Sure enough, freshmen had the lowest priority for registering for classes. Only after the university gave freshman registration priority did the number of freshmen increase significantly.

Another example is the "wild horse problem." The Bureau of Land Management (BLM) runs the Department of the Interior's mandated program to manage the wild horse and wild burro populations on federal lands. Protected under the Wild Horse and Burro Act of 1971, the wild herds grew too large for the range and invaded the grazing land leased to ranchers. The BLM rounded up horses and burros and made them available through the successful "Adopt-a-Horse" program. Because not all horses and burros are desirable to potential adopters who pay a $125 adoption fee, the BLM waived adoption fees for ranchers who took large numbers of the surplus animals. Animal-protection protesters charged the BLM with condoning the slaughter of wild horses, "our national heritage." They alleged that the ranchers shipped the animals directly to slaughterhouses, making a handsome profit in the process. BLM officials disavowed any role in the commercial slaughter of wild horses and burros for pet food, but questioned the wisdom of spending $7 million a year to board surplus captured horses at a time when government programs for the poor were being cut. Still the angry protests continued. No amount of communication strategy appeared to ease the problem. When BLM officials recognized that their fee-waiver program was a major contributing factor, the program was canceled. Also, beginning in April 1988, ranchers did not take title of adopted horses and burros for 1 year. For that year, even though the rancher was responsible for care and feeding, the animals remained public property. Again, actions spoke louder than words.

The classic case study of responsive and responsible public relations actions, however, remains Johnson & Johnson's handling of the Tylenol crisis (review Exhibit 1–3).

Coordinating Action and Communication

The Tylenol poisoning crisis also illustrates the need for coordinated action and communication: Late in 1982, McNeil Consumer Products, a subsidiary of Johnson & Johnson, was suddenly confronted with a crisis when seven persons on Chicago's West Side died mysteriously. Authorities determined that they had died from cyanide poison that had been inserted in Tylenol capsules. The news spread rapidly over television and the news wires. Panic among consumers, hospitals, doctors, and pharmacists ensued nationwide. The crisis called for an immediate action response supported by communication. The following are the *action components* of the company's response:

1. Alert consumers nationwide, via the media, not to use capsules until the extent of tampering could be determined. (It was unclear at first that the tampering was limited to the Chicago area.)
2. Stop production of Tylenol capsules and halt advertising.
3. Establish liaison with the Chicago police, the FBI, and the Food and Drug Administration.
4. Recall all Tylenol capsules: 31 million bottles with a retail value of more than $100 million dollars.
5. Design and produce tamper-resistant packaging.
6. Return Tylenol capsules to the market with a stepped-up marketing effort to assure users of the product's safety.

Communication strategy supports the action program: (1) to inform internal and external target publics of the action; (2) to persuade those publics to support and accept the action; and possibly (3) to instruct publics in skills needed to translate intention into action. The following highlights summarize the communication components of Johnson & Johnson's strategy:

1. **Publics:**   Consumers, pharmacists, management and staff of food chains, hospital administrators and staff, doctors, the Food and Drug Administration contacts, FBI contacts, medical press, and general press.

2. **Message strategy:**   Intensive effort to gather facts on production of the lot of capsules in Chicago market. Full cooperation with the Food and Drug Administration. Assurance to alarmed inquirers of the company's determination to solve the mystery and to ensure the purity of its products.

3. **Media strategy:**   Full, candid cooperation with the media to get facts to the public as quickly as possible, including the use of a 30-city press conference conducted via television satellite. Centralized release of all information. Appearance of Johnson & Johnson chairman on television, including *60 Minutes*.

EXHIBIT 12-1

Coordinating Action and Communication

Few corporate management decisions are as difficult as a decision to relocate a company's headquarters. Southern Railway System and its parent company, Norfolk Southern Corporation, made such a decision in 1983. Several publics were affected by the decision, so the reasons for the move and its ramifications had to be explained to them as effectively as possible.

Southern Railway had been headquartered in Washington, D.C., since its founding in 1894. Although Atlanta had always been the operational center of the Southern system, the company's top management and up to 700 key officers and support staff were headquartered in Washington.

Southern Railway and Norfolk and Western Railway consolidated in June 1982, under joint ownership of the newly formed Norfolk Southern Corporation. In the first stage of the new partnership, the holding company was established at Norfolk, Virginia; the executive and operating headquarters of the Northern and Western were retained at Roanoke, Virginia; and Southern retained its executive offices in Washington and its operational headquarters in Atlanta.

As implementation of the merger plans unfolded, management determined that the maximum efficiency of operations could be achieved by consolidating Southern's executive and operating headquarters. Atlanta, as the operating "heart" of this 13-state, 10,000-mile railroad, was the logical site. Thus, the decision was made to close the Washington office and to relocate the personnel either to Norfolk or to Atlanta.

Except for a relatively few personnel who would remain in Washington, all employees would be involved in the relocation, so hundreds of employees and their families would be affected.

The first priority of management, then, was to inform employees of the move officially, before they read about it in the paper.

Once the decision to move was final, department heads in the headquarters building were briefed on the decision, and then told to advise the personnel in their departments immediately. Everyone used a general letter signed by the president of the parent company as the authoritative source for information about the move. They were told the reasons for the move, were advised that new offices would be constructed in Atlanta to accommodate them, were told that they would be given adequate time to plan an orderly relocation, and were informed that the company offered an extremely generous relocation assistance program.

On the obvious assumption that word of the decision would soon spread, the decision was made to inform key news media in both Washington and Atlanta. The wisdom in this approach, in contrast to saying nothing and then having to handle a "leak" situation, was borne out by universally favorable coverage of the relocation. Not a single negative word appeared in news or editorial coverage.

As word of the pending move spread through the media and other channels, favorable results continued. Southern's public relations department responded to numerous requests for information on the company's traditional relationship with Atlanta and Washington, details on who would move to Atlanta and when, and related questions. All inquiries were answered promptly, and thoroughly.

Further evidence of the effectiveness of communicating the move came at a major conference of government, transportation, and business leaders in Atlanta. The mayor of Atlanta gave a resounding official welcome to Southern and told Southern's president, before television cameras and media representatives from around the country, that Atlanta would do everything it could to make the move comfortable and mutually profitable.

"This transition undoubtedly could have been made without a word being uttered," one company public relations officer noted. "But we discovered once again, as we have so many times in the past, that the results are much more positive when you 'talk about it now' rather than have to 'defend it later.'"

Action as an Open Systems Response

Public relations action is "socially responsible acts taken by public relations departments or other parts of the organization with your counsel."[4] Action strategy typically includes changes in an organization's policies, procedures, products, services, and behavior. These changes are designed to achieve program objectives and organizational goals, while at the same time responding to the needs and well-being of an organization's publics. In short, corrective actions serve the *mutual* interests of an organization and its publics.

Action strategy results from knowing how an organization's policies, procedures, actions, and other outputs contribute to public relations problems. As pointed out in the situation analysis section of Chapter 11, a thorough understanding of the problem situation is essential for designing the action strategy. For example, when the Atlanta Bureau of Police Services (ABPS) tackled the problem of not enough police for public safety and security, it began by studying its own recruiting and training program. Before developing any external recruitment communications, ABPS changed how it operated its recruiting program. First, ABPS expanded the search area from the metropolitan Atlanta area to all Georgia. Second, it staffed an office specifically to handle recruiting. Third, ABPS equipped the office with the computer equipment necessary for expediting applications. These internal changes and the communication campaign resulted in more than 1800 applicants and a net gain of 80 new officers on the force in 1 year. Previous attempts at statewide recruiting without the other changes in structure and processing had not reversed the attrition problem.

Action strategy concentrates on adjustment and adaptation within the organization. Opportunity to implement such changes, however, requires that both top management and practitioners define public relations as something much more than publicity and persuasive communication. As pointed out by Harold Burson, in its mature form public relations is involved in determining what is done, as well as what and how something is said. The case of the Sybron Chemical Inc. provides yet another illustration.

Sixty neighbors of the Birmingham, New Jersey, manufacturer of water purification resins were evacuated following an accidental release of a noxious chemical. A month later, two plant workers were seriously burned during a process accident. These accidents and the resulting publicity only heightened public concerns about odors from the plant, about plant safety, and about the lack of information about plant operations. Neighbors and a U.S. senator called for new state and federal controls. Some in the community demanded that the plant be closed.[5]

With public relations counsel, Sybron devised a strategy to "take immediate, effective and credible action regarding each of the concerns identified by neighbors, local officials and state regulatory officials." The company also decided to break with past practice and begin regularly communicating both what was happening and the results of corrective actions. Action strategy included hiring an independent engineering firm to solve odor and chemical-handling safety problems and to upgrade plant facilities. Communication strategy included forming the Sybron Neighborhood Involvement Council to promote face-to-face communication; issuing a quarterly newspaper, *Sybron Community Update*; holding the first Sybron open house and plant tour; and installing a computerized 24-hour phone system (PINS Hotline®) that calls neighbors' homes if there is a problem and allows neighbors to call any time of day for updated information (See Figure 12–1).[6] A follow-up survey of neighbors indicated that

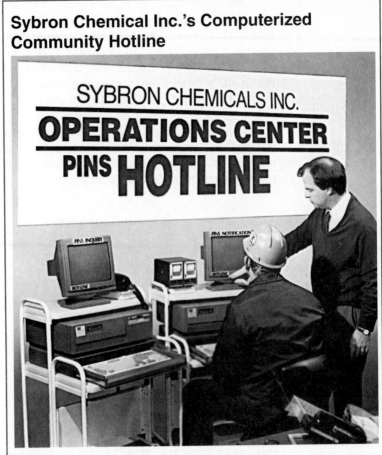

Sybron Chemical Inc.'s Computerized Community Hotline

Figure 12–1   Courtesy Environmental Affairs Institute, Edison, New Jersey

nine of ten felt more secure about Sybron as a neighbor and almost all believed that the company had improved communication with its neighbors. A report describes the award-winning program as "the story of how a new commitment to corrective action and communications resulted in a complete turn-around, in just seven months, with state regulators praising Sybron's actions as a model for the entire chemical industry."[7]

"Sybron is certainly a textbook example of how a company can turn neighborhood fear and anger into trust and credibility," according to Christine Foschetti, account executive at Sybron's public relations firm, Holt and Ross, Inc. Sybron's management first had to mount an action strategy that included significant odor-reduction efforts and substantial environmental improvements. According to Foschetti, "Without these two very important elements, the company's public outreach program would have been doomed to fail."[8]

Action strategy puts into practice what Chapter 7 refers to as the open systems model, or what James Grunig calls "two-way symmetrical" public relations.[9] The first assumption basic to this approach is that change is as likely within the organization as it is on the part of the organization's publics. Another assumption of this approach is that changes result in "win-win" outcomes, meaning that both sides in an organization-publics relationships can benefit. A third assumption that drives action strategy is suggested by the quote in Chapter 7, "Clean up your act, not just your image." If public relations is to have an impact in shaping the mutually beneficial relationships necessary for organizational survival and success, it must participate in developing the action strategy and in coordinating this strategy with the communications that follow.

THE COMMUNICATION COMPONENT OF STRATEGY

Action strategy necessarily makes up the main thrust of a program but represents the part of the public relations iceberg that might not show above the surface. Communication, typically the more visible component, serves as the program catalyst to interpret and support the action strategy. Chapter 8 outlines relevant communication theory and concepts that serve as the foundation for this section. What follow are fundamentals and principles for applying the theory to the practice.

Framing the Message

The first principle of framing message content for the communication effort is to know the client's or employer's position and the problem situation intimately. The second principle is to know the needs, interests, and concerns of the target publics. In the words of one practitioner, "Get smart and put yourself in the other party's shoes."[10]

Attempting to establish any single set of sure-fire rules for framing message content would be disappointing, if not futile. Such rules might appear perfect in principle, yet be rendered ineffectual by an unseen characteristic of the audience; for example, a religious belief that bans certain foods. The timing could be bad. A carefully timed announcement of a new stock offering by an oil company was smothered in the news by revelations that it had used corporate funds for political campaigns in the United States and for bribes abroad. The audience could harbor an unspoken prejudice, such as confronts a Democrat campaigning in a Republican precinct. The wording of the message could be such that it does not square with the images in the heads of the audience. Or, perhaps the audience is not in a listening mood. Regardless of the specific barrier, results from standardized programming are generally frustrating and futile.

Effective communication must be designed for the situation, time, place, and audience. It means careful selection of media and technique. For example, the annual spring migration of college students to Florida's beaches poses health problems for that state, among them the spread of venereal diseases. One year the Florida Health Department gave frisbees carrying messages on how to recognize and prevent venereal diseases to these students as they swarmed the Florida beaches. This is targeted communication.

Advances in technology and specialized media are opening up a wealth of possibilities for serving the needs of special audiences. Practitioners would be well advised to think in terms of smaller and more circumscribed patterns of communication as they seek to modify or mobilize opinions. No communication or action, simply because it worked once before in a given situation, can be carted about like a trunk full of clothes and fitted to a new situation. With rare exception, the clothes will not fit the second wearer. If nothing else, they will be out of style.

All public relations problems, however, do have people as a common denominator and require communication to bring the people and their viewpoints closer together. This applies whether the programming calls for news releases, institutional advertising, meetings, or any other tool of contact. Continuity is required in communication. So are repetition of a consistent message in simple form, careful selection of time, place, and method, and a variety of media that converge on the audience from several avenues.

Public relations, with its powerful and varied means of selectively disseminating targeted information, suffers from an overcapacity. Simon and Garfunkel sang to us, in "The Sounds of Silence," that our problem is people talking without speaking, people hearing without listening. As repeatedly suggested in this book, there is an urgent *need to target specific messages to specific audiences to achieve specific results.*

Practitioners must define audiences with great precision and must use different strategies and techniques to accomplish different goals. For example, different concerns and different levels of intensity about an issue call for different message strategy. The following time-tested techniques help reduce the discrepancy between the communicator's position and the audience's attitudes:

1. Use the media most closely identified with the audience's position.
2. Use a communications source that enjoys high credibility for the audience *on the topic of communication.*
3. Play down the differences between the positions in the communication and those of the audience.
4. Seek identification in vocabulary and anecdote with the audience *in an area removed from the issue.*
5. Establish the communicator's position as being the majority opinion, defining the majority from the audience itself.

6. Bring the audience's group identifications into play, when those identifications will help develop a positive response. The converse is also true.

7. Modify the message to fit the organization's need.[11]

Framing the message for the media and media gatekeepers also requires attention to news value. Traditional criteria applied by gatekeepers, who see their role as acting on behalf of media audiences, include:

1. **Impact:** the number of people affected, the seriousness of the consequence, the directness of cause and effect, and the immediacy of the effect. This criterion applies not only to news, but also to other information.

2. **Proximity:** the distance between the audience and the problem or issue of concern. This criterion simply suggests that local connections or news angles increase news value.

3. **Timeliness:** perishability, or like bread, news gets stale. This criterion also explains why journalists and media compete to be first with the news, but why print media cannot compete with broadcast media on timeliness. As a result, print media may be more interested in "why" and "how" than in "when," although daily newspapers remain concerned with the timeliness of information.

4. **Prominence:** recognizable and well known. Almost by definition, celebrity and celebrities are of interest to large numbers of people; they are newsworthy. Prominence means that journalists and their audiences are interested in the private lives of public organizations and figures.

5. **Novelty:** the unusual, bizarre, deviant, and offbeat. Some even define news as deviation from the normal. Journalists and editors know that people are attracted by and interested in what is new, unique, and unexpected.

6. **Conflict:** strikes, fights, disputes, wars, crime, politics, and sports. All too often, conflict is the major ingredient in news, not only because of its appeal to journalists, but because of media pandering to public interest in the sensational and uncertain. Conflict situations often have issues that are not clearly defined, uncertainty about what is right or wrong, and oversimplified versions of winners and losers.[12]

Defining news may not be that simple, however. Some contend that news is anything that affects the lives and interests or stimulates the concern and curiosity of a significant number of people. In the final analysis, the distinction between hard news and soft news changes to accommodate audience interests in an ever-expanding range of topics, including science, culture, environment, social change, and education, to name but a few. Day-to-day news selection by gatekeepers, however, may result more from routine, deadline pressures, mechanical requirements, and their perceptions of what other journalists are saying and doing.[13]

Public relations practitioners must frame their messages to make them *newsworthy*, by whatever standard (hence the requirement to know the media and media gatekeepers). Messages also must be *under-*

standable: uncomplicated, free of jargon, and simple to grasp. They must also be *topical* or *local* to take advantage of audience interest in information that is both timely and close to home. Most important, however, is that the message must be immediately *actionable*. In the same way that the action strategy must be mutually beneficial, so must messages. The content should be framed in such a way that the information answers questions, responds to audience interests and concerns, and empowers members of the audience to act on their interests and concerns. The actionable quality deserves special attention.

Journalists systematically tend to shy away from including "mobilizing information" in their news stories. This is the information about identification, location, and instruction or direction audience members would need so as to act on their predisposition. One could speculate that journalists might feel that providing such information would be a departure from their perceived role of objective news reporters. When they include mobilizing information in stories about charities, other community drives, and crises, journalists may see this either as a forgivable departure, given the positive context, or as acceptable professional behavior.[14]

Another useful approach to framing the message is to use the "30-3-30" formula devised by long-time author-scholar Clay Schoenfeld.[15] The first number means that many in the audience will give you no more than 30 seconds, no matter how attractive or interesting you make the presentation. You can count on no more than 30 seconds to get your message across, meaning that your key points must be strong, positive, and dominantly displayed. The second number indicates that some will give you up to 3 minutes, meaning that you can count on bold lines, subheads, illustrations, photo captions, and even highlighted summary statements to carry the message. Thirty-minute audience members will spend the time necessary to get message content, even though the details are reported in small type. Maybe a 3-30-3 formula should replace the optimistic Schoenfeld's 30-3-30 formula when framing most public relations messages.

Finally, framing the message strategy requires attention to four fundamental facts. *First, the audience consists of people.* These people live, work, worship, and play in the framework of social institutions in cities, in suburbs, in villages, or on farms. Consequently, each person is subject to many influences, of which the communicator's message is typically only one small source of influence. *Second, people tend to read, watch, or listen to communications that present points of view with which they are sympathetic or in which they have a personal stake. Third, mass media create their separate communities.* For example, those who read *Soldier of Fortune* and The *National Enquirer* are not likely to read *Scientific American* and *Architectural Digest. Fourth, mass media have a wide variety of effects on individual and collective knowledge, predisposition, and behavior, not all of which are readily measurable.* Careful framing must take into account both the intended and unintended effects of message content.

Semantics

Semantics is the science of what words mean. Language is constantly changing, with new words appearing (such as *faxed*) and words dropping from use (such as *groovy*). The meanings of words can change (such as *politically correct*). Others take on so many meanings that they become almost meaningless (such as *bottom line* and *strategic planning*, according to some in public relations!).

Here we have space only to acknowledge the importance of semantics in public relations. Do not be misled, however; the subject really deserves and gets a great deal of attention from men and women in public relations. For in communicating and interpreting, practitioners live by words and make their living by them. For example, Edward Bernays referred to the "semantic tyranny" represented by the title of what is widely recognized as one of history's greatest special events, "Light's Golden Jubilee," the celebration of the 50th anniversary of Thomas Edison's invention of the incandescent light bulb. There is no escape for communicators from what T. S. Eliot described as "the intolerable wrestle with words and meanings." Practitioners seek mastery of word meanings.

In the midst of the "wrestle with words" is the public relations practitioner. Studying the words that leap out of people's mouths, stare up from newspapers, and smile out from a television tube, the practitioner is expected to react and then to be able to tell what those words mean, *not what they say, but what they really mean.* Then, the public relations specialist is expected to combine words and actions that will correct misunderstandings, educate where there is a lack of knowledge, and in general clear up confusion.

Practitioners are constantly making decisions about word meanings, so the basic importance of semantics must not be overlooked. Deciding what the refusal of people to work should be called represents a decision in semantics. Is it a strike, a work stoppage, or an outrage against the people? Cutbacks are referred to as "downsizing" or "rightsizing." Procter & Gamble called its July 1993 announcement that it was cutting 13,000 jobs and closing 30 factories, "the global initiative announcement." Weapons of mass destruction are called "peacekeepers," military invasions are referred to as "police actions," and new taxes are camouflaged as "revenue enhancements." Clearly, there is no one-to-one ratio between a word and its meaning. The same signs and word symbols have different meanings for different people.

In addition, they have two different kinds of meaning: *denotative* and *connotative*. Denotative meaning is the common dictionary meaning, generally accepted by most people with the same language and culture. Connotative meaning is the emotional or evaluative meaning we read into words because of our experience and background. For example, all people will agree that *dog* denotes a four-legged, furry, canine animal. For most people, the word *dog* connotes a friendly, faithful pet and usually awakens nostalgic memories about a childhood pet. To others, however, the word connotes a dangerous animal to be feared. Another example is the word *bullfight*. North and South Americans fully agree on what the term denotes, but its connotative meaning differs sharply north and south of the U.S.-Mexico border.

Our political language has become an integral part of events and helps shape their meaning. The campaign for national prohibition made *saloon* a dirty word; so today, those who drink do so in *taverns* and *lounges*. Incidentally, the Drys were too wise to campaign for *prohibition*, a harsh word; they advocated *temperance*. Another great coup in semantics was scored in coining the term *life insurance* to describe what could be called, more properly, *death insurance*, but the latter would be harder to sell. A ten-strike in semantics has been the successful effort of bowling promoters to change *bowling alleys* to bowling *lanes* and bowling *centers*. *Educational* television became *public* television, which has a more popular ring to it. Semantic manipulation is an old art.

Words can excite and inflame. For example, there is evidence that a mistake in translating a message sent by the Japanese government near the end of World War II may have triggered the bombing of Hiroshima and thus ushered in atomic warfare. The word *mokusatsu*, used by Japan in response to the U.S. surrender ultimatum, was translated as "ignore" instead of its correct meaning, "withhold comment until a decision has been made." And some years ago, semantic difficulties caused a crisis between the United States and Panama: Panamanians interpreted the English verb *negotiate* as a commitment to negotiate a new treaty, the meaning of the Spanish verb *negociar*. The U.S. State Department intended it simply in its noncommittal sense of "to discuss."

Words often become "code words" to convey an unspoken but unmistakable meaning; for instance, "right to life," "law and order," "reverse discrimination," and "ethnic purity of neighborhoods." Even the meaning of commonplace words cannot be taken for granted. For example, one of the authors used the word *fallacy* on an exam, only to find that many students did not know what the word meant.

Public relations people must be able to select and to transmit for various audiences words that will be received as kinfolk. Think of the harm that has been done, the confusion created, by legal language. The same is true for the language of doctors, educators, the military, and government. Each has a special jargon not readily understandable to others: legalese, educationese, militarese, and governmentese. And besides jargon are slang, dialects, slogans, and exaggerations. Practitioners must work with their counterparts in the press, radio, and television and on the platform to help straighten things out for their publics.

Poet Anne Sexton cautioned that, "Words, like eggs, must be handled with care; once broken, they are beyond repair." Practitioners must have a flair for the picturesque, memorable term and a feeling for words.

Symbols

Communication involves more than semantics; in large measure it uses *symbols* and *stereotypes*. The symbol offers a dramatic and direct means of persuasive communication with large numbers of people over long lines of communication. Symbols have been used since the dawn of history to compress and convey complex messages to the multitudes. The Star of David and the Cross of Christ remind us of this. Most people need the shorthand of symbols to deal with whatever is abstract, diffuse, or difficult.

Years ago, Lippmann explained the need met by symbols and stereotypes as "introducing (1) *definiteness* and *distinction* and (2) *consistency* or *stability* of meaning into what otherwise is vague and wavering. . . . We tend to perceive that which we have picked out in the form stereotyped for us by our culture."[16] Here is a current example of Lippmann's point: "Pro-life" is a powerful symbol because it condenses an enormous amount of meaning, information, and experience.

The value and use of a venerated symbol is seen in the British monarchy. The British Commonwealth of Nations today is a free association of independent nations shakily held together, not by legal ties, but by the symbol of the Queen of England. She symbolizes the traditional loyalties, the common interests, the traditional institutional forms held more or less in common, and the family ties.

Symbols play an important role in the public relations and fundraising programs of health and welfare agencies. Probably the best-known symbol of the kind is the Red Cross, from which that agency takes its name. The Red Cross originated in Switzerland and created its symbol by reversing the white cross and red background of the Swiss flag. The upright sword of the American Cancer Society, chosen in a nationwide poster contest, was created to portray its crusading spirit. Another crusade, that of the National Tuberculosis Association, is symbolized by the Cross of Lorraine that dates back to the Crusades.

One of the most effective symbols ever created is that of Smokey Bear, used by the U.S. Forest Service, the Association of State Foresters, and the Advertising Council to promote forest-fire prevention. The idea originated with a group of foresters and advertising specialists concerned about the need to protect our forests. After experimenting with drawings of deer, squirrels, and other small animals to carry fire-prevention messages, they had the idea of using a bear. A bear—with its humanlike posture, its way of handling itself, and its universal appeal to young and old—seemed ideal to build into a persuasive symbol. (See Figure 12–2.)

The Smokey Bear symbol changed over the years, as did the appeals used in the public service announcements. In 1976 a public awareness campaign showed almost universal awareness of Smokey Bear, with 98 percent aided recall. But even though the symbol enjoys widespread recognition, many of the young urban children exposed to Smokey Bear in

Smokey the Bear

Figure 12-2

Recycle Symbol

school programs do not know what to do to prevent forest fires. The bear, however, remains a credible symbol of forest-fire prevention.[17]

Increasingly, profit and nonprofit organizations emphasize symbols (designs and logos) to create a "public image" and instant recognition or to capitalize on widespread public awareness and acceptance. A current example of the latter is the symbol for recycling, which marketers and organizations use to demonstrate their concern for the environment. In fact, another new term—*green*—has entered the language to describe communication and action strategies shaped to demonstrate sensitivity and commitment to protecting the environment.

Surely symbols should be distinct, different, and in character for the institutions using them. However, a changing public climate governed by new and different values can make symbols obsolete, or offensive. For example, new public sensitivity for the rights and feelings of minority groups has forced Dartmouth College, Syracuse University, and Stanford University to abandon Indian symbols and names for their athletic teams. The University of Illinois and Florida State University, as well as the Atlanta Braves and Cleveland Indians, face the same pressure to drop their long-standing Indian symbols and mascots.

Barriers and Stereotypes

Barriers to understanding and to clarity of messages exist in the communicator and the audience alike. As Lippmann noted, each person lives in the protective shelter of a cocoon of his or her own spinning. This cocoon insulates the individual from the incessant communication babble that is steadily increasing in intensity. There are social barriers, age barriers, language or vocabulary barriers, and political and economic barriers. There is also the race barrier; the barriers and distortions that block communication are seen starkly in the gulf between racial and ethnic groups in the multicultural American society. There is peer pressure exerted within groups, where "reality" is shared and interpreted. There is also the often overlooked barrier of the audience's ability to absorb messages. Finally, there is the constant roar of competition for people's attention in the noisy public arena. Barriers are not the only complications in communication, however.

People have impressions about everything that touches their consciousness. Everyone lives in a world of his or her own symbols. Public figures, for example, during their lifetimes and afterward, are known partly through a personality created by images fixed in the public imagination. Astronauts, politicians, rock stars, and sports heroes are good examples. Their families and associates know them as people entirely different from their public personalities. People who live on one side of town tend to know people on the other side of town, as well as those in remote cities, in a half-fictional, half-imagined way. The only feeling that anyone can have about an event he or she does not experience or a person he or she does not know is by his or her own mental image of the event or person, developed from fragmentary, secondary sources.

In communication, nothing raises more problems than the reality that most in mass media audiences have limited access to the facts. With limited access, and with some information tending to confuse as much as it clarifies, people rely heavily on stereotypes. Specific and significant impressions become generalities. As Lippmann pointed out, the "pictures in our head" derive mainly from what we see and hear in the mass media. Certainly our impressions of what happened in Bosnia, Somalia, and Kuwait, as well as our stereotypes of the people in each situation, came from cable and network television, news magazines, newspapers, and radio.

For example, readers looking at a magazine cover picture entitled "Criminal" may pick out two or three sharply defined features. Perhaps they select a low forehead, a squinting eye, a scarred face, or a mouth that curls at the corner. From then on, the impression may be so deeply rooted that readers feel sure that they know the "criminal type" whenever they see it. They can classify everyone, including friends, as to whether or not they are criminal types. Indeed, people have classifications into which they can fit almost everyone they see or hear about. These distorted stereotypes pose public relations problems. The newly elected president of the California State Bar, for example, announced that she would make addressing negative and distorted public stereotypes of lawyers her highest priority. Unfortunately for lawyers everywhere, however, cartoonists took advantage of her announcement by exploiting stereotypes in a new rash of cartoons portraying lawyers as snakes, vultures, wolves, sharks, and so forth. The media are constantly helping to create new stereotypes by reducing complex people, groups, countries, and situations to their simplest and most general—sometimes distorted—attributes.

Lippmann emphasized the sacrosanct regard that people have for stereotypes as "the core of our personal tradition, the defense of our position in society."

> They may not be a complete picture of the world, but they are a picture of a possible world to which we are adapted. In that world people and things have their well-known places, and do certain expected things. We feel at home there. We fit in. We are members. We know the way around.
>
> . . . The stereotypes are, therefore, highly charged with the feelings that are attached to them. They are the fortress of our tradition, and behind its defenses we can continue to feel ourselves safe in the position we occupy.[18]

Stereotypes, then, serve as a defense mechanism against having to exert the effort required to learn about and understand the uniqueness and details of each person, group, and situation. They also form a moral code from which personal standards of behavior are derived. Practitioners must learn to recognize the influence and the presence of symbols and stereotypes in what appear to be the contradictions and contrariness of public opinion. *Symbols are used to counter symbols, and stereotypes are used to counter stereotypes.*

There is yet another side to stereotypes, however. In the context of a multicultural society, media are trying to be more sensitive and respectful of differences based on age, gender, sexual preference, race, body shape, and ethnicity. Some criticize efforts to purge the language of stereotypes as yielding to the "politically correct language" movement. They say the movement is headed by the kind of "thought police" George

Orwell warned us about. Others see eliminating words and phrases that are pejorative stereotypes as a way to promote acceptance of diversity and to make media content more inclusive and less offensive.[19]

To avoid having the words themselves become a public relations problem, practitioners must be sensitive to word choice. A good reference on words to avoid is the *Dictionary of Cautionary Words and Phrases*, published by the University of Missouri, which includes a checklist of offense words and stereotypes.[20] In the final analysis, language changes carried to extremes can debase the language by substituting euphemisms for accurate and meaningful descriptions. Responding to every charge of "oppression" without care can take away from the real effort to rid language of sexist, racist, and other insensitive stereotypes. Paradoxically, "political correctness" has taken on many different connotations to many different people in many different contexts, robbing the term itself of real meaning.

Putting It All Together in a Campaign

The difficulty of public information campaigns can be clearly seen in the battle to save us from polluted air, polluted water, and chemically dangerous foods. America's pioneer ecologist, Aldo Leopold, thought in his early years that "if the public were told how much harm ensues from unwise land-use, it would mend its ways." In his twilight years, he knew that this conclusion was based on three mistaken assumptions: (1) that the public is listening or can be made to listen; (2) that the public responds, or can be made to respond, to fear of harm; and (3) that ways can be mended without any important change in the public itself.[21]

In a much-quoted article, Hyman and Sheatsley codified the major reasons why many information campaigns fail:

1. There exists a hard core of chronic "know-nothings." These people are difficult to reach, no matter what the level or nature of the information.
2. Interested people acquire the most information. Motivation is essential to learning or assimilating knowledge, yet there are large groups in the population who admit that they have little or no interest in public issues.
3. People seek information that is compatible with their prior attitudes and avoid exposure to that which is not compatible.
4. People interpret the same information differently. Selective perception and interpretation of content follows exposure: Persons perceive, absorb, and remember content differently.
5. Information does not necessarily change attitudes. Changes in views or behavior following exposure to a message may be differentially affected by the individual's initial predisposition.[22]

Another researcher, Harold Mendelsohn, countered with an analysis of why information campaigns can succeed:

What little empirical experience we have accumulated from the past suggests that public information campaigns have relatively high success potentials:

1. If they are planned around the assumption that most of the publics to which they will be addressed will be either only mildly interested or not at all interested in what is communicated.

2. If middle-range goals which can be reasonably achieved as a consequence of exposure are set as specific objectives. Frequently it is equally important either to set up or to utilize environmental support systems to help sheer information giving become effective in influencing behavior.

3. If, after middle-range objectives are set, careful consideration is given to delineating specific targets in terms of their demographic and psychological attributes, their life-style, value and belief systems, and mass media habits. Here, it is important not only to determine the scope of prior indifference, but to uncover its roots as well.[23]

That public-information campaigns can succeed has been demonstrated by numerous campaigns against smoking in public places, the highly successful effort by Mothers Against Drunk Drivers (MADD), the Stanford University communication experiments in preventing cardiovascular diseases, and American Cancer Society efforts promoting cancer detection and prevention, to name but a few. The jury is still out on campaigns to prevent HIV infections, to reduce drug abuse, and to promote social tolerance.

One persuasion theorist described the plight of campaign planners this way: The person beginning to design a public communication campaign is like a person lost somewhere in a dense forest of possibilities. He or she can find a way out by following old scout training to keep calm and keep moving in one direction, and sooner or later will reach the clearing; the only real dangers are freezing in place or losing all sense of direction and wandering around in circles. Even when the chosen theory is not optimal for the situation (in that an alternative direction would have led us out more easily), it suffices to lead us out to terra cognita with deliberate speed.[24]

Disseminating the Message

Gaining acceptance of an idea or an innovation is more than simply beaming it to an audience through a mass medium or internal publication. To illuminate, communication must be aimed with the precision of a laser beam, not cast in all directions in the manner of a light bulb. Even after many years of research, there is still not definitive evidence of a single model of how ideas are disseminated among people. Elmo Roper, after nearly 30 years of opinion research, formulated a hypothesis that has some value as a guide. His "concentric-circle theory" says that ideas penetrate to the whole public very slowly through a process similar to osmosis. Histories of public campaigns substantiate this. They move out in concentric circles from great thinkers to great disciples to great disseminators to lesser disseminators to the politically active to the politically inert. This hypothesis assumes that American society can be stratified as indicated and emphasizes the importance of using opinion leaders in the public relations process.

The rate of flow in the transmission and acceptance of ideas, however, is governed by many factors other than the characteristics of the people involved. These include Lippmann's "barriers to communication" and George Gallup's "regulators of absorption rate" illustrated in Figure 12–3.

The communication step in the public relations process often requires influencing knowledge, opinions, and actions among sizable and distant groups. The accelerating rate at which innovations are being invented, developed, and spread makes it vital that communicators be able to transfer information to those who need it. Examples include gaining public acceptance of using sunscreen lotions to protect against skin cancer; overcoming fear of technology, such as programming a VCR or paying bills electronically; and getting high-risk publics to get blood pressure checkups. *Diffusion* is the term for the process by which new ideas and practices are spread to members of a social system. The U.S. Department of Agriculture has been working at this task longer than most. It learned from experience that getting new ideas accepted involves more than simply discovering a new grain and publicizing it. It took 13 years to gain widespread adoption of hybrid seed corn on America's farms, for example. Out of their long experience and *evaluation research*, agricultural sociologists have concluded that acceptance goes through five stages:

1. **Knowledge:**   People learn about an innovation and some gain understanding of what it is.
2. **Persuasion:**   Potential adopters develop interest in the innovation. They seek more information and consider its general merits.
3. **Decision:**   Potential adopters decide to adopt or reject the innovation after weighing its merits for their own situation.
4. **Implementation:**   Those willing to try the innovation actually apply it to their situation, usually on a small scale. They are interested in the practice, techniques, and conditions for application.
5. **Confirmation:**   Adoption is ether reinforced or the decision to adopt is reversed based on the evaluation.[25]

Mass media have their greatest impact and usefulness in creating *awareness* in the knowledge stage. For farmers, at least, the mass media become less and less influential as the acceptance process advances toward confirmation of the adoption. Interpersonal influence increases with each

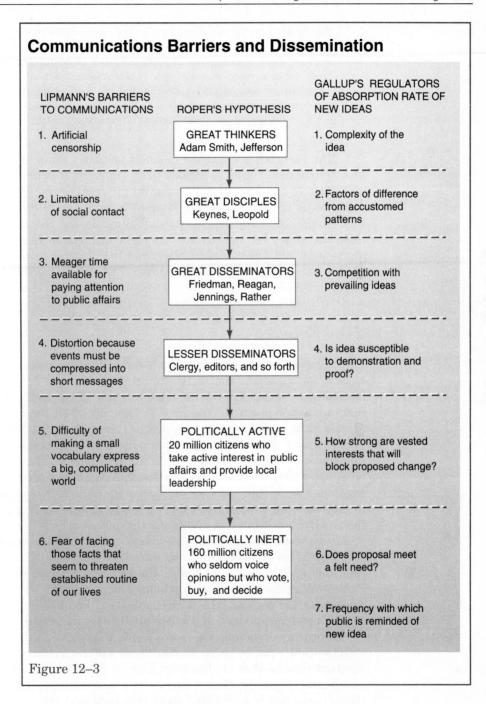

Communications Barriers and Dissemination

LIPMANN'S BARRIERS TO COMMUNICATIONS	ROPER'S HYPOTHESIS	GALLUP'S REGULATORS OF ABSORPTION RATE OF NEW IDEAS
1. Artificial censorship	GREAT THINKERS Adam Smith, Jefferson	1. Complexity of the idea
2. Limitations of social contact	GREAT DISCIPLES Keynes, Leopold	2. Factors of difference from accustomed patterns
3. Meager time available for paying attention to public affairs	GREAT DISSEMINATORS Friedman, Reagan, Jennings, Rather	3. Competition with prevailing ideas
4. Distortion because events must be compressed into short messages	LESSER DISSEMINATORS Clergy, editors, and so forth	4. Is idea susceptible to demonstration and proof?
5. Difficulty of making a small vocabulary express a big, complicated world	POLITICALLY ACTIVE 20 million citizens who take active interest in public affairs and provide local leadership	5. How strong are vested interests that will block proposed change?
6. Fear of facing those facts that seem to threaten established routine of our lives	POLITICALLY INERT 160 million citizens who seldom voice opinions but who vote, buy, and decide	6. Does proposal meet a felt need?
		7. Frequency with which public is reminded of new idea

Figure 12–3

step. This diffusion model, developed through extensive research among rural families, was supported in subsequent studies in other settings. Chaffee suggests that there are several reasons for this pattern of diffusion:

> The media are comparatively rich in news content, whereas personal associates are likely to have had relevant "consumer" experience. Further, since consumption is partly a matter of defining one's social "self," other persons would be able to offer normative social guides to appropriate consumption patterns that the media cannot. Finally, some matters may not be dealt with by the media in sufficient depth or detail to satisfy personal information needs.[26]

The research conclusions demonstrate that communicating a new idea or practice is a long, tedious task. Different communication tactics are effective at different points and in different ways. The influence of influentials or opinion leaders is great in many situations. It is important for the communicator to know what media and techniques to use at different stages and how to mobilize these influences effectively. In summary, however, *effective communication is expensive in research, preparation, attention, and implementation. The cost is higher than is commonly supposed.*

Reconsidering the Process

The three elements common to all communication are the source or *sender*, the *message*, and the destination or *receiver*. A communication breakdown can involve one or more of these three elements. Effective communication requires efficiency on the part of all three. The communicator must have *adequate information*. He or she must have *credibility* in the eyes of the receiver. The communicator must be able to transmit information in codes the receiver can *comprehend*. The communicator must use a channel that will carry the message to the receiver. The message must be within the receiver's *capacity to comprehend* and *relevant* to the receiver's interests or needs. Finally, the message must motivate the receiver's self-interest and cause a *response*.

Wise communicators see receivers not as passive subjects but as selective users of information for their own purposes. Too many public relations programs do not gauge the individual's role in the process. Public relations educator and scholar Doug Newsom says that practitioners should not use "the term 'audiences,' because it implies 'recipients' of messages instead of participants in communication."[27]

Words are symbols. There are words that serve as symbols for real objects—table, chair—thing words. There are words that are symbols of abstract ideas—such as freedom, love—nothing words. Children are taught, for example, that a furry little animal with long ears and a short, fuzzy tail is a "rabbit." Once the word and the little animal are associated, the word will always evoke the image of that creature. Word symbols for real objects are readily understood and agreed upon. This is not so with symbols for abstractions. Abstractions such as "pro-choice"

or "pro-life" have no simple or universally accepted referents in the real world of objects. It is difficult for people to agree on an image of "free trade" when they cannot see, touch, hear, taste, or smell it. This difficulty goes right to the heart of the communications problem.

To communicate effectively, the sender's words and symbols must mean the same thing to the receiver that they do to the sender. The word *communication* is derived from the Latin *communis,* meaning "common." So, "communication" means to establish a commonness. A veteran practitioner, Don Hill, combined these fundamental principles to formulate the model of congruent communication illustrated in Figure 12–4.

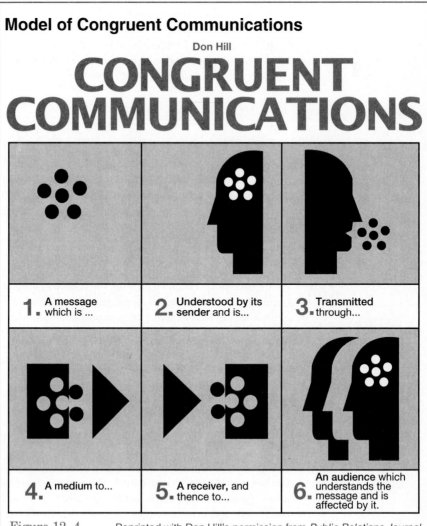

Figure 12–4   Reprinted with Don Hill's permission from *Public Relations Journal.*

A sender can encode a message and a receiver decode it only in terms of their own experience and knowledge. When there has been no common experience, then communication becomes virtually impossible. This explains a layperson's inability to understand an Einstein; it explains why, despite the tremendous flow of words to and from China, Americans and Chinese still have little understanding of each other. Common knowledge and experience provide the connection links. The greater the overlap in common interest and common experience, the easier it is to communicate. There are many barriers to achieving this overlap of commonness. Commonness in communication is essential to link people and purpose together in any cooperative system.

Public relations communication provides the climate for an action's acceptance and implementation, but is only one element. For example, successful public campaigns against smoking, unsafe sex, drinking and driving, drug use, and careless use of fire in forests must be accompanied by action strategy that changes the problem situation and provides enforcement and social support.

IMPLEMENTING THE STRATEGY

The purpose of this chapter is to introduce some of the major considerations and principles of implementing public relations programs. However, entire books devoted to the topic cannot adequately cover the range of issues and practices related to putting the program in place. This chapter concludes with the seven Cs of public relations communication.

1. **Credibility.**   Communication starts with a climate of belief. This climate is built by performance on the part of the institution, reflecting an earnest desire to serve stakeholders and publics. Receivers must have confidence in the sender and high regard for the source's competence on the subject.

2. **Context.**   A communications program must square with the realities of its environment. Mass media only supplement the words and deeds of daily living. The context must provide for participation and playback. It must confirm, not contradict, the message. Effective communication requires a supportive social environment, one largely set by the news media.

3. **Content.**   The message must have meaning for receivers, and it must be compatible with their value system. It must have relevance to the receivers' situation. In general, people select those items of information that promise them the greatest rewards. The content determines the audience.

4. **Clarity.**   The message must be put in simple terms. Words must mean the same to receivers as to the sender. Complex issues must be compressed into themes, slogans, or stereotypes that have simplicity and clarity. The farther a message has to travel, the simpler it must be. An organization must speak with one voice, not many voices.

5. **Continuity and consistency.**   Communication is an unending process. It requires repetition to achieve penetration. Repetition—with variation—contributes to both learning and persuasion. The story must be consistent.

6. **Channels.**   Established channels of communication should be used, channels that receivers use and respect. Creating new ones can be difficult, time-consuming, and expensive. Different channels have different effects and serve effectively in different stages of the diffusion process. Selective channels are called for in reaching target publics. People associate different values with the many channels of communication.

7. **Capability of the audience.**   Communication must take into account the capability of the audience. Communications are most effective when they require the least effort on the part of receivers. This involves factors of availability, habits, reading ability, and prior knowledge.

Communication and action are not the end, but only the means to ends. The ends of public relations are the outcomes spelled out in program goals and objectives. Assessing the effectiveness of program strategy, the fourth step, is the topic of the next chapter.

ADDITIONAL READINGS

Bivins, Thomas.   *Handbook for Public Relations Writing*, 2d ed. Lincolnwood, Ill.: NTC Business Books, 1992. One of several good how-to books on preparing public relations and publicity materials.

Brody, E. W., and Dan L. Latimore.   *Public Relations Writing.* New York: Praeger, 1990. Covers basics of writing, writing for the print media, and writing for electronic media as a "process within a process."

Budd, John F., Jr.   *Street Smart Public Relations.* Lakesville, Conn.: Turtle Publishing Co., 1992. Veteran practitioner's down-to-earth instruction on "how to get things done."

Kendall, Robert.   *Public Relations Campaign Strategies.* New York: Harper Collins, 1992. How-to application of the four-step public relations process outlined in Chapter 11 of this book.

Newsom, Doug, and Bob Carrell.   *Public Relations Writing: Form and Style,* 3d ed. Belmont, Calif.: Wadsworth Publishing Company, 1991. Instructs on how to prepare and present information in the wide variety of public relations media.

Rayfield, Robert E., Lalit Acharya, J. David Pincus, and Donn E. Silvis. *Public Relations Writing: Strategies and Skills.* Dubuque, Iowa: William C. Brown Publishers, 1991. Practical application of communication and other social science theory to public relations writing.

Smith, Alvie L.   *Innovative Employee Communication.* Englewood Cliffs, N.J.: Prentice-Hall, Inc., 1990. Discusses action and communication strategy in the context of employee communication.

Tucker, Kerry, Doris Derelian, and Donna Rouner.   *Public Relations Writing: An Issue-Driven Behavioral Approach.* Englewood Cliffs, N.J.: Prentice-Hall, Inc., 1994. Applies state-of-the-art knowledge about anticipating issues and strategic planning to public relations writing.

Wilcox, Dennis L., and Lawrence W. Nolte.   *Public Relations Writing and Media Techniques.* New York: Harper and Row, 1990. Addresses a wide range of public relations writing assignments, including advertising, special events, conferences, meetings, and audiovisual presentations.

NOTES

[1]Speech to Raymond Simon Institute for Public Relations, Utica College, Syracuse University, March 5, 1987.

[2]Harold Burson,   "Beyond 'PR': Redefining the Role of Public Relations," 29th Annual Distinguished Lecture of the Institute for Public Relations Research and Education, Inc., New York, October 2, 1990.

[3]Ibid.

[4]Norman R. Nager and T. Harrell Allen,   *Public Relations Management by Objectives* (Lanham, Md.: University Press of America, 1984), 241–42. (Originally published by Longman, Inc.)

[5]Caron Chess, Michal Tamuz, Alex Saville, and Michael Greenberg,   "Reducing Uncertainty and Increasing Credibility: The Case of Sybron Chemicals Inc.," *Industrial Crisis Quarterly* 6, no. 1 (1992): 55–70.

[6]PINS Hotline is the registered trademark for the Prompt Inquiry and Notification System of the Environmental Affairs Institute, Inc., Edison, N.J.

[7]Public Relations Society of America, "1990 Silver Anvil Winners: Index and Summaries," New York, 1990, 1–2.

[8]Christine S. Foschetti, Edison, N.J.,   correspondence to the authors, July 15, 1993.

[9]James E. Grunig,   "Communication, Public Relations, and Effective Organizations: An Overview of the Book," in *Excellence in Public Relations and Communication Management*, edited by James E. Grunig (Hillsdale, N.J.: Lawrence Erlbaum Associates, Publishers, 1992), 18–19.

[10]A. C. Croft,   "Delayed Action Allows Informed Response," *Public Relations Journal* 48, no. 5 (May 1992): 31.

[11]Eugene F. Lane,   "Applied Behavioral Science," *Public Relations Journal* 23, no. 7 (July 1967): 6.

[12]Adapted from Brian S. Brooks, George Kennedy, Daryl R. Moen, and Don Ranly,   *News Reporting and Writing*, 3d ed. (New York: St. Martin's Press, 1988).

[13]Pamela J. Shoemaker,   *Gatekeeping*, Communication Concepts 3 (Newbury Park, Calif.: Sage Publications, Inc., 1991), 50–52.

[14]James B. Lemert and Marguerite Gemson Ashman,   "Extent of Mobilizing Information in Opinion and News Magazines," *Journalism Quarterly* 60, no. 4 (Winter 1983): 657–62.

[15]Clay Schoenfeld,   "Thirty Seconds to Live," *Writer's Market*, February 1977, p. 29.

[16]Walter Lippmann,   *Public Opinion* (New York: Harcourt, Brace and Company, 1922), 81.

[17]Eugene F. McNamar, Troy Kurth, and Donald Hansen,   "Communication Efforts to Prevent Wildfires," in *Public Communication Campaigns,* edited by Ronald E. Rice and William J. Paisley (Beverly Hills, Calif.: Sage Publications, Inc., 1981), 143–60. Later summarized in *Public Communication Campaigns,* 2d ed., edited by Ronald E. Rice and Charles K. Atkin (Newbury Park, Calif.: Sage Publications, Inc., 1989), 215–18.

[18]Lippmann,   *Public Opinion*, 95–96.

[19]Natasha Spring,   "Freedom of Speech vs. Politically Correct Language," *IABC Communication World* 9, no. 5 (April 1992): 34–38.

[20]This useful reference was compiled by the 1989 Multicultural Management Program Fellows at the University of Missouri School of Journalism. It lists derogatory and offensive terms, as well as preferred substitutes.

[21]For the story of Leopold's career as an innovator and environmentalist, see Susan Flader, *Thinking Like a Mountain* (Columbia: University of Missouri Press, 1974).

[22]Herbert H. Hyman and Paul B. Sheatsley, "Some Reasons Why Information Campaigns Fail," *Public Opinion Quarterly* 11 (1947): 412–23.

[23]Harold Mendelsohn, "Why Information Campaigns Can Succeed," *Public Opinion Quarterly* 37 (Spring 1973): 50–61.

[24]William J. McGuire, "Theoretical Foundations of Campaigns," in *Public Communication Campaigns*, edited by Rice and Atkin, 65.

[25]Everett M. Rogers, *Diffusion of Innovations*, 3d ed. (New York: Free Press, 1983).

[26]Steven H. Chaffee, "The Interpersonal Context of Communication," in *Current Perspectives in Mass Communication Research*, edited by F. Gerald Kline and Phillip J. Tichenor (Beverly Hills, Calif.: Sage Publications, Inc., 1972), 103.

[27]Doug Newsom, Texas Christian University, as quoted in *pr reporter* 36, no. 17 (April 26, 1993): 4.

CHAPTER 13

Step Four: Evaluating the Program

When you can measure what you are speaking about, and express it in numbers, you know something about it. But when you cannot measure it, when you cannot express it in numbers, your knowledge is of a meager and unsatisfactory kind.[1]

LORD KELVIN

No topic dominates the practice as does program evaluation—the final step in the process. Actually using systematic measures of program effectiveness, however, lags behind practitioner interest in program evaluation. In the words of educator-scholar David Dozier: "Although considerable lip service is paid to the importance of program evaluation in public relations, the rhetorical line is much more enthusiastic than actual utilization."[2] But, there are encouraging signs that the field is changing to make evaluation research more central to the process.

For example, Walter K. Lindenmann, senior vice president for research at Ketchum Public Relations (New York), reports that 48 percent of the practitioners he surveyed in 1992 conducted evaluation research to assess program impact, up from only 30 percent only a couple of years earlier, and only 16 percent in 1988:

Clearly, the heat is on in the public relations field; more and more public relations practitioners are being asked to be accountable for what they do, and that is being reflected in the types of public relations research assignments that organizations like ours are being asked to carry out.[3]

Increasingly practitioners are being asked to document measurable results and returns that are commensurate with program costs. Public relations, like other staff and line functions, is being evaluated by how much it contributes to advancing the organization's mission and achieving organizational goals. Executives in all types of organizations, from the largest corporations to the smallest nonprofit groups, ask for evidence of program *impact*—particularly when budgets are reviewed, when new budgets are negotiated, or when organizations are downsized to be more competitive.

THE PUSH FOR MEASURABLE RESULTS

A "results orientation" of top management accounts for much of the increased use of computers to track program progress and of evaluation research to measure impact. Many executives look at unsupported claims with suspicion. More sophisticated use of measurable outcome criteria in public relations objectives (see the "Management by Objectives" section of Chapter 11) also makes it possible to measure program impact. Fewer and fewer practitioners get by with the claim that program impact cannot be measured: "It's intangible." The following exchange captures the essence of the problem in taking the position that public relations results are not measurable:

"Why not?"

"They're intangible. You can't actually see the results of public relations."

"Why should I pay you for something that can't be detected—what you call 'intangible results'?"

"Because public relations is different and can't be held to the same performance standards as other departments."

"Well, O.K. Here's your money."

"Where? I don't see any money."

"Of course not. It can't be detected—it's what you call 'intangible'."

Surely, knowledge outcomes, predisposition changes, and behaviors can be measured. So what excuse justifies not knowing if the action and communication strategies are making progress toward achieving program objectives? What justifies not documenting how the program worked? What justifies not being able to answer whether or not the problem has been solved?

Concurrent with increased interest in evaluation is rapid development of supportive literature. For example, Sage Publications has become the leading publisher of books and journals devoted to the general field of evaluation research. The 1990s began with the publication of two books devoted to using research in public relations programs.[4] *Public Relations Review* has devoted entire issues to the topic.[5] Both the *Review* and *Journal of Public Relations* periodically publish scholarly articles related to evaluation research. The February 1993 issue of *Public Relations Journal* features articles on measuring the impact of public relations. This professional journal, as well as *IABC Communication World* and *Public Relations Quarterly*, regularly publish articles and how-to features on research and evaluation. Clearly, lack of available published guidance is not a defense for not using research.

This body of literature serves as the basis for evaluation research courses now taught at many universities and included in a growing number of public relations curriculums. As noted in Chapter 5, the Commission on Undergraduate Public Relations Education identified research for planning and evaluation as one of five areas of study in the core curriculum. Among practitioners, however, are many who did not study research methods. As Ketchum's Walter Lindenmann said, "Most public relations people have heard of these techniques and have occasionally used them, but are not that thoroughly aware of them."[6]

On the other hand, an increasing number of public relations firms build evaluation research into the services they offer clients. Among major New York–based firms, for example, Lloyd Kirban built Burson-Marsteller's long-standing research department. Lindenmann heads research at Ketchum Public Relations, and Frank Walton directs Ruder and Finn's research subsidiary, Research and Forecasts. Similar research and evaluation departments exist in smaller public relations firms across the United States, Canada, and worldwide. A parallel development, however, is "outsourcing" (the 1990s euphemism for contracting with outside vendors and suppliers) for research services. For example, since Hill and Knowlton closed its Group Attitudes Corporation research subsidiary, it contracts for much of its U.S. research with the Worthlin Group in Washington, D.C., and in Canada with an Hill and Knowlton–owned Toronto subsidiary, Decima Research. Senior vice resident and general manager, Margaret Buhlman, supervises Decima's staff of 20 research professionals. Ruder and Finn's Research and Forecasts no longer staffs a telephone survey center or keeps data entry specialists on payroll, choosing instead to contract with outside research firms to do most of its data gathering and compilation.

In the early 1990s, the trend appeared to be toward specialized research companies providing formative and summative evaluation research services. Miami-based Strategy Research and San Diego–based Market Development Inc. (MDI) illustrate why public relations firms turn to specialized research companies. These are the two largest research companies specializing in Hispanic population research. Former Burson-Marsteller (Chicago) research specialist Roger Sennott manages MDI's 35 professionals and 50 part-time bilingual telephone interviewers. MDI conducts the quarterly Hispanic Poll for 1250 clients and other users; the quarterly Hispanic Teen Poll, based on a sample of 750 teens in Los Angeles, Miami, Houston, New York, and San Antonio; and the semiannual MDI Mexico Poll, which reports findings from 750 in-home interviews conducted in Mexico City, Guadalajara, and Monterrey. Similar research companies develop databases and expertise in specialized niches based on ethnicity, occupation, geography, demographics, or other categories of interest to clients. Farm Research Institute, based in Urbana, Illinois, for example, provides research results for agricultural companies, associations, agencies, and firms.

Some clients, some line managers, and even some public relations practitioners still do not budget for research or see research as an integral part of the process. Too many are content with the "warm fuzzy feeling they get from counting their media clips," according to many who work in public relations. "If they feel it's working, they don't want to spend the money to get the data," says another. The trend is clear, however, as more are budgeting for research "because top management is asking them to be more accountable," according to Lindenmann. He thinks that there will be more research and evaluation because "students of public relations will see measurement and evaluation techniques built into their curriculums."[7]

An early indication of this trend is that research is increasingly vital to firms seeking new business accounts. The ability to document baseline data and results gives firms a competitive edge. In short, good research is fundamental, not an extra. As practitioner Gary Barton, Monsanto Company (St. Louis), put it:

In general, public relations people are being asked more and more by either their management or their clients to justify the expenditures for a project or the program. For example, after spending $200,000 or whatever for a program, they ask, "Did that change people's minds? Do they think differently now? Are they more aware of the company?" In other words, did it accomplish the objectives you said you were going to accomplish? That is the evaluative use of research at the end of the program. Without research, it is much harder to show results.[8]

EVALUATION RESEARCH PROCESS

The process of evaluating program planning, implementation, and impact is called "evaluation research." Rossi and Freeman use the terms *evaluation research* and *evaluation* interchangeably to represent "the systematic application of social research procedures for assessing the conceptualization, design, implementation, and utility of social intervention programs."[9] They outline the basic questions in evaluation:

> *Program conceptualization and design*
> What is the extent and distribution of the target problem and, or, population?
> Is the program designed in conformity with intended goals; is there a coherent rationale underlying it; and have chances of successful delivery been maximized?
> What are project or existing costs and what is their relation to benefits and effectiveness?
> *Monitoring and accountability of program implementation*
> Is the program reaching the specified target population or target area?
> Are the intervention efforts being conducted as specified in the program design?
> *Assessment of program utility: impact and efficiency*
> Is the program effective in achieving its intended goals?
> Can the results of the program be explained by some alternative process that does not include the program?
> Is the program having some effects that were not intended?
> What are the costs to deliver services and benefits to program participants?
> Is the program an efficient use of resources, compared with alternative uses of the resources?[10]

Evaluation research is used to learn what happened and why, not to "prove" or "do" something. For example, one organization set up an evaluation project for the sole purpose of justifying the firing of its senior communication officer. In other cases, evaluation research is done to delay or justify decisions or to persuade someone to support or not support something. The major distinction is that true evaluation research is done to gather information objectively, whereas *symbolic* uses are to support positions already held or decisions already made.[11]

Program managers use such "pseudoresearch" for three reasons:

1. *Organizational politics:* Research is used solely to gain power, justify decisions, or serve as a scapegoat.
2. *Service promotion:* Pseudoresearch is undertaken to impress clients or prospects that the sponsor is sophisticated, modern, or sincere.
3. *Personal satisfaction:* Research is done as an ego-bolstering activity to keep up with fads or to demonstrate acquired skills.[12]

In the long haul, these spurious efforts are self-defeating.

Figure 13–1 illustrates the basic steps in the evaluation process:

Evaluation Process

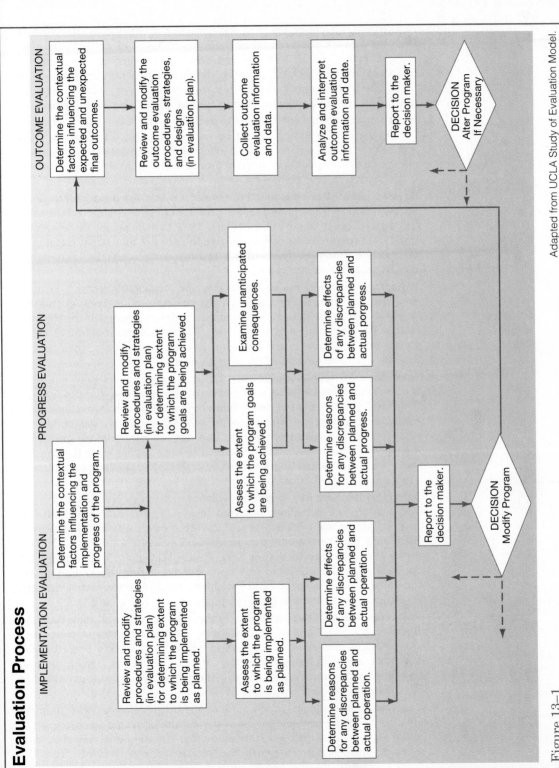

Figure 13–1

Adapted from UCLA Study of Evaluation Model.

1. **Establish agreement on the uses and purposes of the evaluation.**   Without such agreement, research often produces volumes of unused and often useless data. Commit to paper the problem, concern, or question that motivates the research effort. Next, detail how research findings will be used. Such statements are doubly important when outside research specialists are hired to avoid buying "canned" or "off-the-shelf" services.

2. **Secure organizational commitment to evaluation and make research basic to the program.**   Evaluation cannot be tacked on as an afterthought. Build research into the entire process, with sufficient resources to make it central to the problem definition, planning and programming, implementation, and evaluation steps.

3. **Develop consensus on evaluation research within the department.**   Even practitioners not eager to trade in their notions of public relations as "intangible" must be part of the effort. They have to accept the concept of evaluation research long enough to give the process time to work and must feel secure that research will not replace completely the lessons and insight gained from experience.

4. **Write program objectives in observable and measurable terms.**   Without measurable outcomes specified in the program objectives, evaluation research cannot be designed to evaluate program impact. If an objective cannot be evaluated, it is not useful. The evaluation imperative forces clarity and precision in the planning process, particularly when writing specific objectives for each of the target publics.

5. **Select the most appropriate criteria.**   Objectives spell out intended outcomes. If increasing *awareness* of an organization's support of local charities is stated in an objective, for example, then column inches and favorable mentions in the media are inappropriate measures of the *knowledge* outcomes sought. Identify what changes in knowledge, opinions, attitudes, and behaviors are specified in the objectives before gathering evidence. The same applies when the program seeks to maintain existing levels of desired states. (Review the "Writing Program Objectives" section of Chapter 11.)

6. **Determine the best way to gather evidence.**   Surveys are not always the best way to find out about program impact. Sometimes organizational records contain the evidence needed. In other cases, a field experiment or case study may be the only way to test and evaluate a program. There is no single right way to gather data for evaluations. The method used depends on (1) the questions and purposes motivating the evaluation; (2) the outcome criteria specified in the objectives; and (3) the cost of research resulting from the complexity of the program, setting, or both.

7. **Keep complete program records.**   Program strategies and materials are real-world expressions of practitioners' working theories of cause and effect. Complete *documentation* helps identify what worked and what did not work. Records help reduce the impact of selective perception and personal bias when reconstructing the interventions and events that contributed to program success or failure.

8. **Use evaluation findings.**   Each cycle of the program process can be more effective than the preceding cycle if the results of evaluation are used to make adjustments. Problem statements and situation analyses should be more detailed and precise with the addition of new evidence from the

evaluation. Revised goals and objectives should reflect what was learned. Action and communication strategies can be continued, fine-tuned, or discarded based on knowledge of what did and what did not work.

9. **Report evaluation results to management.**   Develop a procedure for regularly reporting to line and staff managers. Documented results and adjustments based on evidence illustrate that public relations is being managed to contribute to achieving organizational goals. Evaluation reports also help demonstrate the essentiality of the function.

10. **Add to professional knowledge.**   Scientific management of public relations leads to greater understanding of the process and its effects. Most program evaluations tend to be organization- and time-specific, but some findings are cross-situational. For example, findings about how many employees learned about a proposed reorganization from an article may be relevant only to that one article and organization. On the other hand, learning that employees want more information about organizational plans provides not only guidance for future issues of a particular newsletter, but may apply in other organizations. Sharing the knowledge gained from relevant research distinguishes the professional practice from the aggregate of technical crafts practiced under the public relations rubric.

The evaluation process is not new; the need has long been recognized. To illustrate, here is what an early publicity specialist, Evart G. Routzahn, told the 1920 National Conference of Social Work:

After the returns are all in—when the last meeting has been held, the final distribution of printed matter made, and all activities of the immediate effort have been recorded as history—is the time to put yourself and your methods through the third degree . . . with prayerful solicitude that you will be able to untangle the lessons to be applied to the next project.[13]

His counsel only recently has been fully accepted—if not always applied—in public relations, even though its merit has long been obvious.

LEVELS OF PROGRAM EVALUATION

Evaluation means different things to different practitioners. To some it is the "best annual report" award plaque, a letter from the boss or client complimenting the writing and photographs in a new brochure, IABC's Gold Quill Award for publication design, or a PRSA Silver Anvil trophy for a community relations program. To some it is clippings from newspaper around the world. To others the only meaningful evaluations are scien measures of increased awareness, or changed opinions, attitude behaviors. To those concerned about public policy or social probl evidence of economic, political, or social change satisfies their r for program evaluation. In fact, these all represent differ complete program evaluation: *preparation, implementatio*

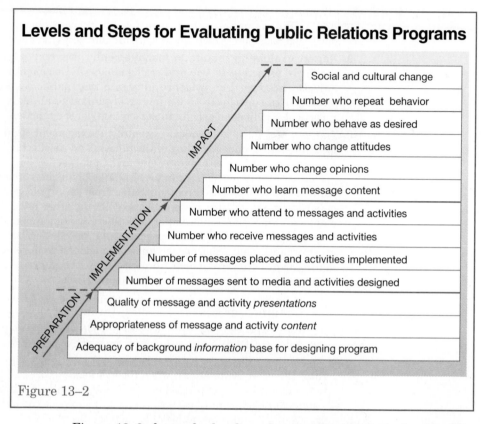

Levels and Steps for Evaluating Public Relations Programs

IMPACT
- Social and cultural change
- Number who repeat behavior
- Number who behave as desired
- Number who change attitudes
- Number who change opinions
- Number who learn message content

IMPLEMENTATION
- Number who attend to messages and activities
- Number who receive messages and activities
- Number of messages placed and activities implemented
- Number of messages sent to media and activities designed

PREPARATION
- Quality of message and activity *presentations*
- Appropriateness of message and activity *content*
- Adequacy of background *information* base for designing program

Figure 13–2

Figure 13–2 shows the levels and steps of program evaluation. The sequence represents typically *necessary*, but not *sufficient*, program elements leading to problem resolution and social change. *The most common error in program evaluation is substituting measures from one level for those at another level.* This is most clearly illustrated when practitioners use the number of news releases sent, brochures distributed, or meetings held (implementation efforts) to document program "effectiveness" (impact). Or, if asked to document program impact, they substitute publicity placements, in the form of column inches or air time, for the changes in target publics' knowledge, predisposition, and behavior spelled out in ___ objectives. Evaluation researchers refer to this as the "substitu-___." Somewhat analogously, to create an illusion magicians talk of ___ting" audience attention from what is really happening.

___h step in program evaluation contributes to increased under-___ and adds information for assessing effectiveness. Program ___ion evaluation assesses the quality and adequacy of information ___tegic planning. *Implementation evaluation* documents the ade-___ the tactics and effort. *Impact evaluation* provides feedback on ___sequences of the program. No evaluation is complete without ___ng criteria at each level.

Preparation Criteria and Methods

During a program, practitioners periodically find that vital information was missing from the original situation analysis. Done systematically and recorded, this assessment represents an evaluation of the *adequacy of the background information* used for planning the program. Were key publics missed in the original determination of stakeholder groups? What assumptions about the publics proved to be in error? Did journalists request information that was not readily available in the background packet or fact book? What last-minute crises called for additional research and organization of information? Had all the key actors in the situation been identified? In effect, this part of the evaluation assesses the adequacy of the information-gathering and intelligence steps in the preparation phase of the process.

The second step in evaluation addresses the *organization and appropriateness of program and message strategy and tactics.* Critical review of what was said and what was done with the advantage of hindsight gives guidance for future program efforts, but only if done with the motivation of constructive criticism. In politics, for example, campaign planners study their candidate's statements in speeches and televised debates in light of media reactions and voter responses in follow-up polls. Did program message content match the problems, objectives, and media? Were communications accurate, timely, and appropriate for the intended publics? Were there adverse reactions to messages or actions? Did the events, corrective actions, and other activities support the program effort? Was enough done? Did the communications capitalize on and complement the action components of the program? Were staff and budget adequate for the task? This phase of the evaluation calls for a review of how well the program matched the demands of the situation.

Content analyses of materials produced, speeches and other presentations, press clipping, and broadcasts also provide evidence for evaluating how closely program efforts match the plan (see Figure 13–3). Practitioners use the results of content analyses of media placements to make changes in how the program is being implemented, as well as for reassessing planned strategy and tactics (preparation). Public relations and research firms are able to customize content analyses of what is published or aired about clients or issues.

In addition to the usual media names and types, cities, amount of coverage, and nature of coverage, new media databases such as Dialog, Nexis®, and Lexis® make it possible to identify the sources quoted in stories, key message points in the content, the names of journalists or writers, content devoted to other organizations or opposing points of view, and what other subjects the media are reporting. According to Ketchum's Lindenmann, "When we do content analyses for our clients, we build 36 to 40 variables into the computer program."[14] Computer analysis makes it possible to cross-tabulate content by geographic areas, by types of treatment, by audience characteristics, and even by reporters and writers.

Examples of Media Content Analysis in Evaluation

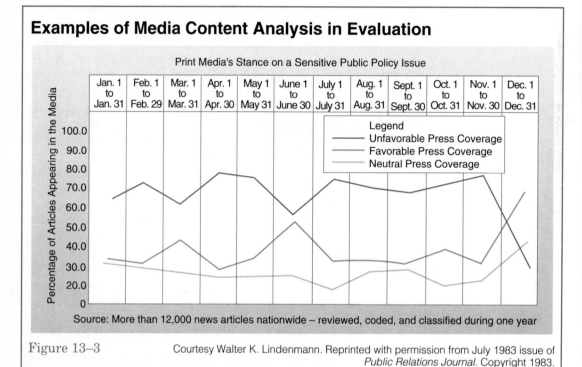

Print Media's Stance on a Sensitive Public Policy Issue

Source: More than 12,000 news articles nationwide – reviewed, coded, and classified during one year

Figure 13–3

Courtesy Walter K. Lindenmann. Reprinted with permission from July 1983 issue of *Public Relations Journal.* Copyright 1983.

Quality of message and other program element presentations constitutes the final step of preparation evaluation. The awards programs of many professional societies and groups employ criteria from this step. Often the "best" annual report, the "most effective" overall program, and even the "outstanding" professional are picked on the basis of style, format, and presentation of program materials. Best graphic design, best use of photographs, or best multimedia presentation are but three of literally dozens of categories in which awards are given on the basis of production values and judgments of presentation merit. These are the attributes that communication techniques courses and professional workshops emphasize. This step in program evaluation considers the quality of professional performance in light of conventional wisdom and consensus among practitioners as to what is good and bad technique. Presentation quality is not judged by subjective criteria alone, however.

Readability tests are frequently used to assess message preparation objectively. Readability tests, however, take into account only the approximate ease with which printed material can be read and comprehended; they do not consider the content, format, organization, and other elements of writing style. These factors, coupled with an understanding that what writers bring to their writing and readers bring to their reading, all shape the reception and impact of printed words. If used with this perspective in mind, readability tests are useful guides for making copy more readable and for increasing comprehension.

Three commonly used methods for measuring readability include:

1. **The Flesch Formula.** Dr. Rudolf Flesch's Readability Score provides an indication of reading difficulty and approximate educational level required to read the material. Calculations require at least two 100-word randomly selected samples of text (or an entire short manuscript).[15]

   A. Count the sentences, words, and syllables (count numbers, abbreviations, symbols, and hyphenated words as single words).

   B. Compute the *average sentence length* by dividing the number of words by the number of sentences.

   C. Compute the *average word length* by dividing the number of syllables by the number of words.

   D. Use these averages in the *Readability Score Formula*. Multiply average sentence length by 1.015. Multiply average word length by 84.6. Subtract the sum of these two numbers from the baseline value of 206.835.

   $$\textit{Readability Score} = 206.835 - [(\text{average sentence length} \times 1.015) \\ + (\text{average word length} \times 84.6)]$$

   E. Estimate the relative reading difficulty using Table 13–1. According to Flesch, "plain English" scores at least 60 and conversational English scores at least 80.

TABLE 13–1

INTERPRETATION OF FLESCH READABILITY SCORE

Score	Readability	Grade Level
90–100	Very easy	5th
80–90	Easy	6th
70–80	Fairly easy	7th
60–70	Plain English	8th and 9th
50–60	Fairly difficult	10th to 12th
30–50	Difficult	College
0–30	Very difficult	College graduate

Source: Adapted from Rudolph Flesch, *How to Write Plain English: A Book for Lawyers and Consumers* (New York: Harper & Row, 1979), 25–26.

2. **The Gunning Formula.** Robert Gunning's Fog Index measures reading difficulty based on average sentence length and the percentage of words with three or more syllables.[16] The index is based on the number of whole sentences in at least two samples of text containing 100 words. Divide the number of words in the sentences by the number of whole sentences. Next count the number of words with three or more syllables (but not counting capitalized words; those ending in *es*, *er*, or *ed*; and those that combine simple words, such as "heretofore"). Enter the counts into the following formula.

$$Fog\ Index = 0.04 \times (\text{average number of words per sentence} + \text{number of long words per 100 words})$$

The Fog Index provides an indication of the number of years of education needed to find copy easy to read (see Table 13–2).

TABLE 13–2

INTERPRETATION OF FLESCH READABILITY SCORE

Fog Index	Grade Level	
17	College graduate	
16	College senior	
15	College junior	
14	College sophomore	
13	College freshman	
		"Danger line"
12	High-school senior	
11	High-school junior	
10	High-school sophomore	
9	High-school freshman	
8	Eighth grader	"Easy-reading range"
7	Seventh grader	
6	Sixth grader	

Source: Adapted from Robert Gunning, *The Technique of Clear Writing*, rev. ed. (New York: McGraw-Hill, 1968), 40.

3. **The Fry Formula.**   Edward B. Fry's graph produces results similar to Flesch's Readability Scores.[17] It also is based on sentence length and number of syllables.

   A. Start at the beginning of a sentence in each of three randomly selected passages. Count exactly 100 words in each sample passage, including proper nouns, initializations, and numerals. (A word is any group of letters with a space before and after, such as "USDA," "1993," and "&.")

   B. Count the number of sentences in each of the three 100-word samples, estimating the fractions of the last sentences to the nearest tenth.

   C. Count the number of syllables in each of the 100-word samples. (A syllable is defined as a phonetic unit. For example, "asked" is one syllable, but "often" is two. For numerals and initializations, count each symbol as a syllable. For example, "USDA" is four syllables, "1993" is four syllables, and "&" is one syllable.)

   D. Enter the graph in Table 13–3 using the average sentence length and average number of syllables, putting a dot where the two values on the chart intersect. The dot falls in the area representing the approximate grade level required to find the material easy to read.

TABLE 13–3 FRY'S EXTENDED GRAPH FOR ESTIMATING READABILITY

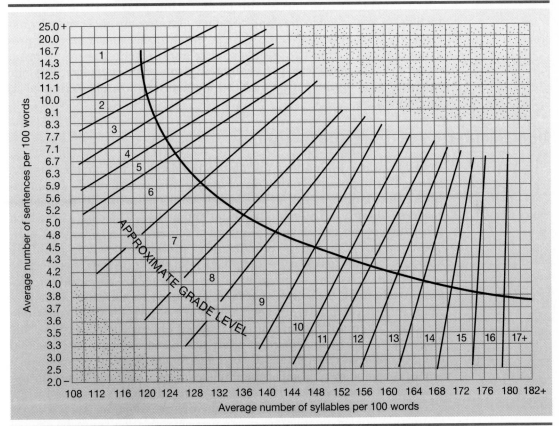

Source: Edward Fry, "Fry's Readability Graph: Clarifications, Validity, and Extension to Level 17," *Journal of Reading* 21, no. 3 (December 1977): 149. Used with permission.

Irving Fang's Easy Listening Formula (ELF) provides a comparable measure for estimating the "listenability" of broadcast copy, speeches, and other scripts. In fact, scores correlate highly with Flesch scores ($r = 0.96$). Simply calculate the average number of syllables (*above one per word*) in sentences. Like the Flesch Readability Score, the ELF score represents the approximate grade level required to follow and understand what is being said easily. Fang found that good television news copy averages below 12 on the ELF.[18]

Readability and listenability scores provide only rough indicators of how comprehensible messages are to target publics. Jargon, technical terms, and even dialect may make written material difficult to understand even when the Flesch, Gunning, Fry, or Fang indices indicate otherwise. These measures can help writers gauge the extent to which their copy matches audience needs for easy-to-read-and-understand messages. The measures simply give quantitative and objective indicators useful for monitoring one aspect of writing style.

Clearly, evaluation of the preparation phase of the program includes a mix of subjective and objective assessments of (1) the adequacy of the background research, (2) the organization and content of program materials, and (3) the packaging and presentation of program materials. The next phase of evaluation deals with how effectively the program gets implemented and communications are disseminated to target publics.

Implementation Criteria and Methods

Public relations evaluations are most often done on the implementation phase. This approach typically involves counting the numbers of publications printed; news releases distributed; stories placed in the media; and readers, viewers, or listeners (potential and actual). The ease with which practitioners can amass large numbers of column inches, broadcast minutes, readers, viewers, attendees, and gross impressions probably accounts for widespread use—and misuse—of evaluations at this level.

Whereas records of program implementation are essential for program evaluation, measures at this level cannot be substituted for program impact. Evaluation researchers warn of substituting "countable activities" or recorded effort for achievement of program objectives. This amounts to using the amount of effort and resources expended (means) in place of measures of intended outcomes (ends). Without complete documentation and evaluation of the implementation phase of the program, however, practitioners cannot track what went right or wrong, and why.

Criteria and some methods for evaluating the communication portions of program implementation follow. Analogous evaluations must be done of the action components to complete the assessment of implementation.

The phase begins with keeping records of the *number of messages sent*, or *distribution*. This step is a straightforward documentation of how many letters, news releases, feature stories, publications, public service announcements, and other communications were produced and distributed. It also includes how many speeches, broadcast appearances, audiovisual presentations, and exhibits were used in the program. In other words, this step calls for documenting all the materials and activities produced and distributed. During the program, such records provide evidence that the program is being implemented as planned. Unsatisfactory results identified in subsequent steps may be traced back to the amount of the program directed to specific publics or to the program placement, the next criterion.

Regardless of how much is produced and distributed, the *number of messages placed in the media* determines whether or not target publics have an opportunity for exposure. Clippings and broadcast logs have long been used to measure how many and what portions of news releases and public service announcements were used by media. Similarly, the number of organizations using a speakers' bureau, audiovisual presentations, and exhibits indicate effectiveness in getting messages placed in the intended channels of communication.

Evaluations at this level sometimes detect fatal flaws in program procedures. Lindenmann reports the case of a client who launched an expensive publicity campaign that produced little use of the materials sent to media. A poll of the media found that the materials were not being used because the right people were not receiving them:

> The press contact list that the client had been using was sorely out of date. Editors and reporters whose names appeared on the list were no longer covering those assignments, had left those newspapers or magazines, or had retired or died. Since the individuals to whom the materials were being sent were no longer at the media at which they were addressed, most of the materials were ending up in the garbage.[19]

Even the most effectively written materials have no chance of impact if they are not available to the intended publics.

Clipping and monitoring services such as Bacon's PR and Media Information Systems (Chicago), Burrelles's Press Clipping Service (Livingston, New Jersey), the Delahaye Group (Hampton Falls, New Hampshire), Luce Press Clippings, Inc. (New York), and PR Data Systems, Inc. (Wilton, Connecticut) track national and international print and broadcast media placements for clients. Similar regional and local services in many areas provide documentation of media placements. Specialized services track publicity placements in selected trade or special-interest print media, help clients monitor crises or other breaking news with same-day customized clipping services, and verify VNR placements on television news programs. One such service that monitors VNR placements, for example, puts an invisible code onto a client's video and then monitors stations to see if any or all of the VNR is aired. The monitor signal decoder is capable of detecting and recording air time and date, station, and exact content aired.[20]

Services vary in how they operate, but the general procedure calls for the client to provide key words and topics to watch for: organization's name, staff names, products or services, and even similar or competing organizations. Typically, the client also sends its monitoring service copies of news releases and broadcast scripts sent to the media. As noted in the second step in "Preparation Criteria and Methods," computerization of media placements and coverage makes possible any number of analyses of the quality and quantity of publicity content resulting from program efforts.

Most local organizations maintain their own clipping files and placement records. Interns and entry-level practitioners often find "clipping the media" in their job descriptions. Rather than being a dreaded chore, however, it should be viewed as an opportunity to systematically study content and style preferences of the various media. Maintaining the clipping files also gives beginning practitioners opportunities to practice media surveillance and to learn about issues relevant to their organizations.

Clippings and similar media placement records have gotten a bad name in public relations because they too often are misrepresented as measures of program impact. Used properly, they are important elements of program implementation evaluation.

The next step is determining how many in the target publics received the messages, that is, the *number of people potentially exposed to program messages*. Care must be taken to separate the *delivered audience* from the *effective audience*. The delivered audience includes all potential readers, viewers, listeners, or those attending. The effective audience represents only those who are in the target publics. Audience size is seldom the major consideration; rather, the makeup of the audience is more important to program evaluation. For example, placement in a prestigious publication not read by the intended target public may make the boss happy but probably contributes little to program success. Practitioners can capitalize on the placement, however, by reprinting the article (with permission) and distributing it themselves to key publics. The expense of such a strategy usually makes placement in appropriate media initially a more cost-efficient practice.

Circulation figures and audience-size data are readily available for most publications and broadcast media. Most newspapers and major magazines belong to the Audit Bureau of Circulation (ABC), which publishes guaranteed circulation figures for member publications. Circulation departments of local newspapers and magazines regularly report the number of paid subscriptions, as well as audience size and characteristics. A. C. Nielson Company and the Arbitron Company report audience estimates for television stations in more than 200 market areas. Arbitron does most of the ratings research for local and network radio. Local television and radio stations often selectively report audience data in their own promotional materials, forcing practitioners to survey all stations in an area to get the complete picture of audience size and demographics.

Traffic Audit Bureau and Simmons Market Research Bureau report audience reach and frequency figures for outdoor advertising, whereas local transportation authorities and commissions provide ridership figures for estimating audience size for transit public service advertising placed inside buses, subways, and trains. Attendance figures for events, meetings, and exhibits are also part of the record used to measure potential exposure to program messages.

Although publicity is not the whole of public relations, it is a large segment of most programs. Astute practitioners have developed tracking systems for evaluating effectiveness in delivering messages to target publics. Ketchum Public Relations uses its own "publicity-tracking model," which it claims goes beyond traditional accounting methods to produce indices of publicity exposure and value (see Figure 13–4). The firm's literature describes the process:

> In planning a publicity campaign to be evaluated . . . the client and agency establish mutually agreed upon standards of performance in two areas in advance of the campaign. First, the number of gross impressions within the target audiences to be achieved. Second, the key messages to be delivered to the target audience. In both cases, the value of the placement is determined by its relations to length, size and media environment.

"Publicity Tracking Model" Report

PLACEMENT TYPE	DMA TARGET AUDIENCE*	AVG. SIZE/ LENGTH	AVG. MEDIA UNITS	PUBLICITY EXPOSURE UNITS	AVG. IMPACT FACTOR	PUBLICITY VALUE UNITS
NEWSPAPERS	4,552,000	1/9 page	.93	4,233,000	1.26	5,334,000
MAGAZINES	268,000	1/2 page	1.66	455,000	1.47	656,000
TELEVISION, network	95,000	5:10 min	1.93	183,000	.81	149,000
TELEVISION, local	504,000	6:05 min	2.13	1,073,000	1.81	1,946,000
RADIO, local	200,000	10:00 min	2.60	520,000	1.40	728,000
TOTALS	5,619,000		1.15	6,454,000	1.37	8,813,000

Publicity Exposure Norm* – Orlando DMA 5,960,000
Publicity Exposure Index – 6,464/5,960   1.08
Publicity Value Index – 8,813/5,960   1.48–

The Publicity Exposure Index suggests that the campaign's exposure was 1.08 as good as expected on a Normal* (= 1.00) basis.

The Publicity Value Index suggests that the impact value of the campaign was 1.48 times as good as expected on a Normal* (= 1.00) basis.

The Publicity Exposure Norms are established by estimating the target audiences, (adults 18-49, weighted 60% male, 40% female) exposure of a "good" hypothetical placement schedule.

Figure 13–4   Courtesy Ketchum Public Relations.

Calculations of potential audience size produce huge totals that must be interpreted with care. Some evaluation reports boast of literally billions of potential exposures to program messages. Surely few managers and clients are so naive as to think these figures alone indicate program effectiveness. Not unexpectedly, their next question should be, "Of those potentially exposed, how many actually paid attention to the message?"

The number of people who attend to the message, then, constitutes the next criterion in program implementation evaluations. Readership, listenership, and viewership studies measure audience attention to media and messages. *Readership studies identify how many read, and what they read, how much they read, as well as who reads and who does not.* Studies of broadcast audiences produce similar findings.

Readership studies of employee publications are commonplace. Weyerhaeuser Corporate Communications tracks *Today* readership (see Figure 13–5) to learn how many employees read each of the stories, their interest in stories, the magazine's readability and appearance, and the perceived balance in how issues are reported. Sometimes readership studies produce surprising results. For example, when Jim McBride surveyed San Diego Kaiser Permanente hospital and clinic employees, he found that fewer than half read anything in the employee newsletter. Readership was high among those who received the publication, but about half of all employees did not receive the newsletter! His findings prompted changes in the method of distribution, not changes in the content, which received high marks from readers. This case illustrates the necessity of evaluating every step in the program implementation process.

The best-known print advertising readership technique is Daniel Starch's recognition method, as now used by Starch INRA Hooper, Inc. Results divide readers into three levels of readership. *Noted* readers simply recall having seen the advertisement. *Associated* readers also remember the name of the advertiser. *Read most* readers say that they read at least 50 percent of the copy and recall enough of the content to support their claim. This method is called "aided recall" because respondents are shown the advertising or other published material and then asked if they recall having read the material. Simmons Market Research Bureau is one of several firms providing magazine and newspaper readership data. Magazine Publishers Association and American Newspaper Publishers Association commission numerous readership studies to track audience characteristics and reading habits.

Radio and television audience research employs four primary methods:

1. **Diary.** The diary method requires some member (or members) of the household to keep a written record or log of listening or viewing. Recent research findings indicate that this method has a built-in bias, as those who agree to participate may differ significantly from nonrespondents.[21]

2. **Meter.** The meter method electronically records individual set tuning by frequency or channel and time of day. The information is sent over telephone lines to a central computer. This is the method used by both Nielson and Arbitron in major cities for the "overnight" ratings reported for major television programs. A major problem with this method is that the meter cannot always reliably detect who (if anyone, or how many people) is watching or listening.

3. **People meter.** Since 1987, audience measurement companies have used more sophisticated meters in an attempt to solve the missing-information problem of audimeters and television meters. Each person in a metered home has his or her button to push when watching television. The meter records who in the household is watching what program and feeds the information over telephone lines to the base computer. The people meter

Weyerhaeuser *Today* Tracking Report

Figure 13–5   Courtesy Weyerhaeuser Company.

also is used in marketing research to report purchasing behavior and then to correlate purchases with television viewing. Not surprisingly, people tire of having to "punch in" and "punch out" and of entering all the other information requested, such as entering for small children too young to manage the technology that goes with living in a metered home. Another problem is that not all television sets in a home are metered, so the people meter yields incomplete reports of household viewing.

4. **Telephone interview.**   The telephone interview method involves calls either during or following a given program to determine audience size and composition. The most common approach is the *telephone coincidental survey,* meaning that calls are made while the program is running. Answering machines and abusive and high-pressure telemarketers causing non-responses are making it increasingly difficult to obtain representative samples using this technique.

Combinations of these and other methods are used by audience research firms to measure broadcast audiences for clients. Notice, however, that these, and assessments of print media audiences, are discussed under the *implementation* section of the evaluation process, as they provide no evidence of program effects on target publics. *Impact* is the next level of program evaluation.

Impact Criteria and Methods

As a practitioner once put it, "We must not only seek results, we must be able to measure them." But 83 percent of all organizations responding to a survey conducted by the Wyatt Company marked "no formal review" when asked how often they measure the return on investments made in employee communication.[22] The company report of the survey concluded:

> Communication will no longer be effective simply because it looks good and reads well. It will be effective when it influences action of employees to meet the organization's business objectives and we can demonstrate this influence. . . . We'll have to document our goals and collect data proving that we have met those goals. In short, we will have the same bottom-line accountabilities as other organizational functions.[23]

Impact measurement documents the extent to which the outcomes spelled out in objectives for each target public and the overall program goal were achieved. In Chapter 10 the term *benchmark* was used to describe how *formative* research findings define the problem situation and establish the starting point for the program. *Intermediate* impact assessments monitor progress toward objectives and goals while the program is being implemented. Why wait until the end to find out that the program did not work? Frequent monitoring of progress toward achieving intended outcomes can indicate where changes need to be made. *Summative* impact assessments provide evidence of success or failure in reaching the planned ending point.

The benchmark model in Figure 13–6 illustrates the program evaluation cycle, showing how summative evaluations (Time$_2$) serve as formative evaluations (Time$_1$) for the next program cycle. Here we are limited to discussing only general guidelines and methods for impact assessments, because intended outcomes are unique to each program. Specific criteria for evaluating program effects should be clearly stated in the objectives that guided program preparation and implementation. For impact evaluation, these same criteria identify both the nature and magnitude of changes in or maintenance of knowledge, predisposition, and behaviors of internal and external publics. These criteria were chosen because they were viewed as essential steps to achieving the overall program goal (working theory). The first impact assessment deals with what people learned from the program.

The *number of people who learn message content* is clearly the logical follow-up to measures of how many attended to the message. Most programs seek to communicate information to increase knowledge, awareness, and understanding among internal and external target publics. Increasing knowledge is often critical to increasing their interest or motivation, a sequence leading to taking action. What people know about your organization—regardless of where they got the information—affects how they feel and act, and, therefore, the organization's relationships with them. What they do not know may be even more critical: As long as explorers believed that the world was flat, they dared not sail too far toward the horizon. Similarly, what people know or do not know about issues and events may influence opinions and behaviors relevant to organization-public relationships.

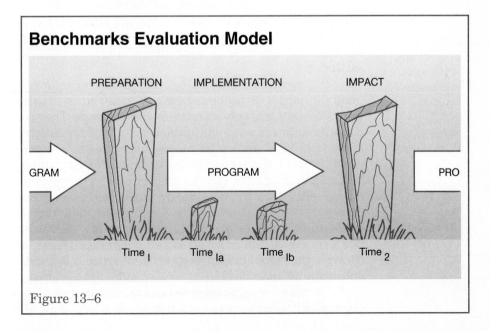

Benchmarks Evaluation Model

PREPARATION   IMPLEMENTATION   IMPACT

GRAM   PROGRAM   PRO

Time$_1$ Time$_{1a}$ Time$_{1b}$ Time$_2$

Figure 13–6

The key to evaluating what people learned from a program (or concurrent sources) is to measure the same knowledge, awareness, and understanding variables measured before the program began. To determine change, comparisons must be made between at least two comparable measures: by repeating the measures on the same or similar people or by making comparable measures in a control group of similar people not exposed to the program. This same principle applies to all assessments of program impact.

For example, a gas and electric utility evaluates an energy conservation information program designed in part to increase knowledge of how much energy is saved with proper insulation. The research design calls for comparing survey results from a sample of homeowners who received the information ("treatment group") with results from a similar survey of homeowners who did not receive the information ("control group"). An employee communication specialist in a manufacturing organization evaluates a program to increase production employees' awareness of safety procedures by comparing precampaign and postcampaign survey results. Similar research designs are used to assess changes in opinions and attitudes.[24]

The gas and electric utility may also want to know the *number of people who change their opinions* about the value of home energy conservation efforts. The manufacturer conducting the safety information program could be interested in increasing employee *interest* in on-the-job safety. The same surveys used to measure changes in knowledge, awareness, and understanding can be used to determine if the programs had an impact on audience predisposition. Different questions would be required, however, as increased knowledge and opinion change are different outcomes, and one can occur without the other. Similarly, changes in opinions that are specific to a particular issue or situation may or may not reflect changes in more basic underlying attitudes.

The *number of people who change their attitudes* is a higher-order program impact. Attitudes represent broad, cross-situational predisposition. They are less subject to short-term change. They result from a lifetime of reinforcement and experience, so they typically require time and effort to change. And, what you see expressed in a situation may or may not represent the underlying attitude. For example, just because a homeowner holds the *opinion* that adding attic insulation will save on energy bills does not necessarily mean that the person qualifies as a "conservationist" *attitudinally*. Determining whether or not a person holds an attitude about energy conservation requires measuring his or her predisposition across many energy-use issues and situations. (Review the "Orientation" section of Chapter 8 for distinction between opinions and attitudes.)

The *number of people who act in the desired fashion*—behavioral change—likewise may or may not follow a sequence of knowledge and predisposition changes. Chain-link fences, for example, negate the need for informational and persuasive communications designed to keep all but the most determined people from entering restricted areas. Seldom do public relations programs have such powers, so typically people must be informed and persuaded before behavioral changes occur. Assessments of program impact on behavior include self-reports of behavior through surveys, direct observation of people's actions, and indirect observation through the examination of official records or other "tracks" left by those engaging or not engaging in the behavior.

Surveys sometimes yield unreliable measures of behavior, especially if respondents are asked to report sensitive or socially acceptable actions. Not surprisingly, few employees willingly report that they ignored management policy. Folks tend to claim more viewing of public television programs than detected by other audience measures. Imagine how many students would admit not doing assigned readings on the professor's class survey, or how many taxpayers would mark, "Yes, I cheated on last year's income taxes" on an IRS questionnaire! With validation questions built into the survey, however, many types of behavior can be measured using survey methods.

Examples of direct observation are turnstiles at events, head counts at meetings, tallies of telephone or mail responses, and participant observation. The local Red Cross or blood bank does not need to develop an elaborate measurement technique to determine how many people respond to a call for donations of a rare blood type. Nor does an organization hire a research consultant to learn if protesters stopped picketing in the main lobby.

Indirect methods for observing behavior include a social service agency's records of client appointments, a museum's maintenance records showing where worn floor tiles are most frequently replaced, and library check-out records. By studying these byproducts of behavior, assessments are made about how many people used agency services, which areas or exhibits in the museum are most popular, and how many students checked out assigned public relations reference books. This type of observation technique is called "unobtrusive measures."[25] This approach to assessing impact does not depend on the cooperation of those being observed, and the measurement technique does not contaminate the behavior being observed.

In summary, measures of behavior call for a combination of research skills and ingenuity to get valid evidence for the evaluation and to avoid influencing the behavior of those being observed.

Public relations programs are usually designed to increase *the number of people who repeat or sustain the desired behavior*. Counts of the number of people who give up smoking on the day of the Great American Smoke Out are not sufficient measures of program success for those wanting to decrease the number of people engaging in this health-threatening habit. As any reformed smoker will attest, success in quitting cannot be determined by checking only once shortly after a "quit smoking" program. Evaluation must include follow-up measures sometimes continuing for months or even years. United Nations family-planning programs are more interested in repeated use of contraceptive methods, not just short-term trials motivated by an educational movie and samples. The same applies to those interested in assessing the impact of safe-sex education programs among at-risk high-school and college populations. Evaluating program success in changing long-term behavior calls for an extended period of observation and measurement to document program impact.

At some point in this series of impact levels, *the program goal is achieved or the problem solved*. Election and referendum results, legislative victories or defeats, and fund balances all provide summative indications of the success or failure of political, lobbying, and fund-raising programs, respectively. The program goal spells out the appropriate summative evaluation criteria. It should also be clear that evaluation must extend to this level, as it is possible that some or many of the intermediate impact outcomes may occur without the program goal being achieved.

For example, the goal of an energy conservation program was to reduce total energy consumption. Increased knowledge of cost-saving practices, increased interest in energy conservation, and even changes in energy-use habits do not indicate success or failure in achieving the overall program goal. The utility reported program success this way:

> The average cost of all conservation advertising to provide you with information on how to save energy is about 11 cents per month per customer. An analysis conducted on the actual savings realized by customers through conservation indicates that the savings averaged $10 for each $1 spent on conservation advertising.

The utility's suggestion that the conservation advertising *caused* the savings illustrates a major problem in program evaluation the tentative nature of cause-and-effect claims. To list but a few alternative explanations for reduced consumption, the drop in energy consumption occurred during a period of escalating energy costs; energy conservation was a topic of many news stories and features in the national and local media; and manufacturers were introducing more energy-efficient appliances. In the uncontrolled environment of most public relations programs, evaluation research only helps answer questions about impact. Definitive answers are elusive, but objectively and systematically gathered evidence certainly beats assertions and strengthens the case for or against claims of program success or failure.

The ultimate summative evaluation of programs and the practice of public relations is their contribution to positive *social and cultural change*. To complete the range of impact assessments, we conclude with this step. Evaluation at this level is confounded by the passage of time and the existence of other causal factors and is usually left to scholars in sociology and anthropology. Early programs promoted settlement in the West. Health and nutrition education programs have both reduced infant mortality and extended life. Programs that resolved conflicts and built new relationships maintained the dynamic public consensus necessary for meeting human needs. *Those in the calling derive their professional motivation and fulfill their social responsibility by being concerned about the impact of their work on society and culture.* Accordingly, both individual practitioners and the practice of public relations will be judged by future generations.

INTERPRETING AND USING RESULTS OF EVALUATION

In open systems public relations, evaluations are not limited to measures of external change. Implicit to all the evaluation steps discussed in this chapter is that the evaluation criteria refer to both inside and outside the organization. Complete summative evaluation calls for measuring program impact on publics, the organization, and their shared social and cultural environments. The magnitude and complexity of the task probably explain in part why so little evaluation research is done in the closed systems programs that still dominate the practice.

Demonstrating program effects can be a difficult task. Professor Byron Reeves summarizes the requirements for demonstrating program effects as including:

> (1) knowledge of the stimulus material; (2) control of its application; (3) assessment of impact; and (4) understanding of the mechanism or process underlying the effect. In question form: What's having an effect, who's affected, what changes, and when and how does it change?[26]

Evaluation is continuous and central to the process. After only *summative* research showing that program effects did or did not occur is of little value. *Formative* research before and during the program provides the information necessary for comparing summative research findings with conditions at the beginning of the program and for making midcourse corrections. Even armed with evidence, however, care is required when interpreting and using evaluation results. Three major interpretations are possible when expected impact is not detected in the evaluations:

1. Even though preparation and implementation were adequate, *the theory behind the program strategy was faulty.* This type of failure is typified by the common notion that "telling our side" will win agreement.
2. If the theory guiding the program was useful, then the absence of impact may be attributed to *program failure: errors made when preparing and, or, implementing the program.*

3. It is also possible that the program succeeded in all respects, but that the *evaluation methods did not detect program impact*. Observations were made on the wrong people, the observations were not valid or used unreliable measures, or the effect was so elusive that it could not be detected using conventional measurement techniques.

In the final analysis, program evaluation involves a great deal of knowledge beyond familiarity with traditional scientific research techniques. Sometimes an in-depth case study in which both qualitative and quantitative data are gathered is the only reasonable approach.[27] *The principle in practice is to gather the best available evidence to manage and evaluate public relations programs.*

Top management support and acceptance by practitioners are primary among the many structural, process, and organizational factors influencing the utilization of evaluation research in public relations. Following are recommendations for increasing the probability that research will become central to managing public relations:

1. Show how research findings relate to potential users' current concerns, policies, procedures, and practices before discussing long-term applications.
2. Maintain frequent and direct participation of and communication with potential users and other stakeholders throughout the research.
3. Limit reports of research findings to either those with immediate application or those with implications for long-term changes. Save the other type of findings for another report and setting.
4. Report only implications that are logically derived from and supported by the data.
5. Use researchers with established credibility and integrity, and avoid using people who might be seen by others as having a vested interest in the results.
6. Use research designs and methods that conform to rigorous scientific standards and technical soundness.
7. Emphasize corroborating information over information that contradicts users' expectations and frames of reference, minimize negative surprises, and avoid early closure on politically sensitive recommendations.
8. Enlist sponsorship of key managers in encouraging serious consideration and use of what was learned from the research.
9. Take the time and effort necessary to persuade potential users to consider and understand the findings and to help them apply what was learned from the research.
10. Conduct the research and use the findings in an ethical and socially responsible manner; respect basic human and civil rights.[28]

Useful program evaluations call for planning from the beginning to the end of their process. Effective program planning and effective program evaluation are inseparable:

> The sins of the program are often visited on the evaluation. When programs are well-conceptualized and developed, with clearly defined goals and consistent methods of work, the lot of evaluation is relatively easy. But when the programs are disorganized, beset with disruptions, ineffectively designed, or poorly managed, the evaluation falls heir to the problems of the setting.[29]

Equally important is viewing research as central to the management of public relations, not seeing it as only the means by which practitioners are held accountable and the worth of their programs is assessed. As the benchmark model suggests, today's impact evaluation is tomorrow's baseline. In the words of long-time public relations executive Kalman B. Druck: "I have found that research is too frequently used as an odometer rather than as a speedometer. Research is often used to tell us where we have been, not where we are going."[30]

To conclude, we repeat the important point made in Chapter 10: *Research initiates, monitors, and concludes the problem-solving process. It is the essential ingredient that makes public relations a management function, as well as a managed function.*

ADDITIONAL READINGS

Broom, Glen M., and David M. Dozier.   *Using Research in Public Relations: Applications to Program Management.* Englewood Cliffs, N.J.: Prentice-Hall, Inc., 1990.

Green, Paul E., Donald S. Tull, and Gerald Albaum.   *Research for Marketing Decisions*, 6th ed. Englewood Cliffs, N.J.: Prentice-Hall, Inc., 1988. Useful reference demonstrating that marketing research methods and techniques are not significantly different from those used in public relations. Also introduces language and applications unique to the marketing function.

Grunig, James E., ed.   *Excellence in Public Relations and Communication Management.* Hillsdale, N.J.: Lawrence Erlbaum Associates, Publishers, 1992. See, in particular, David M. Dozier and Fred C. Repper, "Evaluation of Public Relations Programs: What the Literature Tells Us About Their Effects," pp. 159–84; and William P. Ehling, "Estimating the Value of Public Relations and Communication to an Organization," pp. 617–38.

Lindenmann, Walter K.   *Guide to Public Relations Research.* New York: Ketchum Public Relations, 1993. Seventy-page booklet written by one of the leaders in using research in practice.

Miller, Delbert C.   *Handbook of Research Design and Social Measurement*, 5th ed. Newbury Park, Calif.: Sage Publications, Inc., 1991. An encyclopedic presentation of research methods, measurement scales, and references.

Rossi, Peter H., and Howard E. Freeman.   *Evaluation: A Systematic Approach*, 5th ed. Newbury Park, Calif.: Sage Publications, Inc., 1993. Essential reading for those engaged in program evaluation.

Smith, Mary John, *Contemporary Communication Research Methods.* Belmont, Calif.: Wadsworth Publishing Company, 1988. Addresses how to do communication research in naturalistic settings, combining traditional empiricism with analytical and critical methods of the arts and humanities.

Wimmer, Roger D., and Joseph R. Dominick. *Mass Media Research: An Introduction,* 3d ed. Belmont, Calif.: Wadsworth Publishing Company, 1991. Useful research methods reference for understanding and interpreting media research.

NOTES

[1] Lord Kelvin, more correctly, First Baron Kelvin, was the British physicist, mathematician, and inventor William Thompson (1824–1907).

[2] David M. Dozier, "The Innovation of Research in Public Relations Practice: Review of a Program of Studies," *Public Relations Research Annual* 2 (1990): 5.

[3] Walter K. Lindenmann, as quoted in *pr reporter* 36, no. 9 (March 1, 1993): 3.

[4] See reviews of Glen M. Broom and David M. Dozier, *Using Research in Public Relations: Applications to Program Management* (Englewood Cliffs, N.J.: Prentice-Hall, Inc., 1990), and E. W. Brody and Gerald C. Stone, *Public Relations Research* (New York: Praeger Publishers, 1989), in *Public Relations Journal* 47, no. 1 (January 1991): 32–33. See also James Grunig's review of Broom and Dozier's book in *Public Relations Review* 16, no. 2 (Summer 1990): 78–79.

[5] *Public Relations Review* 16, no. 2 (Summer 1990), devoted entirely to "Using Research to Plan and Evaluate Public Relations"; *Public Relations Review* 10, no. 2 (Summer 1984), featured articles on "Measuring Public Relations Impact"; and *Public Relations Review* 3, no. 4 (Winter 1977), published papers from the 1977 National Conference on Measuring the Effectiveness of Public Relations held at the University of Maryland and sponsored by AT&T.

[6] Deborah Hauss, "Setting Benchmarks Leads to Effective Programs," *Public Relations Review* 49, no. 2 (February 1993): 16.

[7] Ibid.

[8] Quoted in Broom and Dozier, *Using Research in Public Relations*, 11.

[9] Peter H. Rossi and Howard E. Freeman, *Evaluation: A Systematic Approach*, 5th ed. (Newbury Park, Calif.: Sage Publications, Inc., 1993), 5.

[10] Ibid., 34–41. The questions appeared in earlier editions.

[11] Broom and Dozier, *Using Research in Public Relations*, 299.

[12] Stewart A Smith, "Research and Pseudo-Research in Marketing," *Harvard Business Review* 52, no. 2 (March/April 1974): 73–76.

[13] Routzahn (1869-1939) was a social worker and foundation executive, associate director of the Russell Sage Foundation, 1912–1934. He also was the founding chairman of the Social Work Publicity Council, one of the first professional public relations groups. The quotation is from the 1920 National Conference of Social Work proceedings.

[14] Quoted in Hauss, "Setting Benchmarks Leads to Effective Programs," 15.

[15] Rudolf Flesch, *How to Write Plain English: A Book for Lawyers and Consumers* (New York: Harper & Row, 1979), 23–26.

[16] Robert Gunning, *The Technique of Clear Writing*, rev. ed. (New York: McGraw-Hill, 1968), 38–40.

[17] Edward Fry, "Fry's Readability Graph: Clarifications, Validity, and Extension to Level 17," *Journal of Reading* 21, no. 3 (December 1977): 242–52.

[18]Irving E. Fang,   "The 'Easy Listening Formula,'" *Journal of Broadcasting* 11, no. 1 (Winter 1966–67): 63–68.

[19]Walter K. Lindenmann,—"Dealing with the Major Obstacles to Implementing Public Relations Research," *Public Relations Quarterly* 28, no. 3 (Fall 1983): 12–16.

[20]"Hi-Tech VNR Tracking Service Comes of Age," *Public Relations Journal* 47, no. 12 (December 1991): 23 and 28.

[21]H. Leslie Steeves and Lloyd R. Bostian,   "A Comparison of Cooperation Levels of Diary and Questionnaire Respondents," *Journalism Quarterly* 59, no. 4 (Winter 1982): 610–16.

[22]"The Changing Role of Today's Communicator," *IABC Communication World* 9, no. 6 (May–June 1992): 39.

[23]Ibid., 38.

[24]For more information about research designs for evaluating program impact, see Chapter 5, "Designing the Research," in Broom and Dozier,   *Using Research in Public Relations*, 89–113.

[25]Eugene J. Webb, Donald T. Campbell, Richard D. Schwartz, and Lee Sechrest, *Unobtrusive Measures: Nonreactive Research in the Social Sciences* (Chicago: Rand McNally, 1966).

[26]Byron Reeves,   "Now You See Them, Now You Don't: Demonstrating Effects of Communication Programs," *Public Relations Quarterly* 28, no. 3 (Fall 1983): 17.

[27]Robert K. Yin,   *Case Study Research: Design and Methods*, rev. ed. (Newbury Park, Calif.: Sage Publications, Inc., 1989).

[28]Broom and Dozier,   *Using Research in Public Relations*, 302–13.

[29]Carol H. Weiss,   "Between the Cup and the Lip," *Evaluation* 1, no. 1 (1973): 54.

[30]*Arthur W. Page Society Newsletter* 4, no. 1 (April 1988): 4.

Business and Industry

All business in a democratic country begins with public permission and exists by public approval.

ARTHUR W. PAGE

Although the downsizing of the late 1980s and early 1990s made an indelible mark on organizations throughout the world, nowhere were these new economic realities felt more strongly than in corporate America. Millions of workers lost their jobs as businesses sought ways to pare overhead, to cut costs, and to compete with foreign goods in a global recession.

In this frightening atmosphere of change and uncertainty, public relations professionals working for increasingly cost-conscious companies sought ways to maximize their contributions to the bottom line. "Working harder, working smarter" became the motto as professional journals reflected these concerns in myriad articles on keeping and finding jobs, working more efficiently, cutting costs, and being part of management's goals.

PUBLIC RELATIONS IN THE COMPETITIVE SETTING

Public relations in any organization dependent on profit must be cost-effective and part of the formula for successful competition. Thus the competitive nature and the profit imperative of business make public

This chapter was written in collaboration with Professor William C. Adams, Fellow, PRSA, Florida International University. Professor Adams spent more than two decades in corporate public relations at Standard Oil Company (Indiana), now Amoco Corporation; Phillips Petroleum Company; and ICI Americas Inc.

relations work extremely demanding. Add to this the increasingly global nature of business (with more foreign ownership of "American" corporations) and its potential clash of cultures, as well as the possibility of a corporate takeover, merger, or acquisition. In the mid-1990s, the "think globally" manifesto proclaimed by many in the late 1980s rings true.

The public relations function in business is subject to continuing evaluation—as are marketing, finance, and manufacturing—with the ultimate yardstick being progress toward goals and objectives set by management. Other evaluations of the function are made in terms of "organizational loyalty," being "on the team," and being "in tune with the objectives."

In times of stress, economic downturn, or increased competition, management often increases its concern for the survival of the business and demands greater commitment to organizational goals. The public relations practitioner must be alert to these conditions, must understand that internal dissent and criticism of communications policies may be regarded as "disloyal," and must yet continue to act professionally in the roles defined in Part I of this text.

For public relations to survive in business, it must do more than build and maintain relationships with employees and neighbors. *Public relations must help business create an environment in which owners or investors are satisfied with return on their invested capital.* This motivation usually means that much of what is called public relations is designed to help the marketing function attract new customers and keep present customers satisfied with products or services. Simply put, *public relations must contribute to achieving the profit goal of business in a competitive environment.*

The competitive and private nature of the business system and the demands placed on each function make for variety in the role and stature of public relations. Its place in the organization is often determined by top management's concept of the function; hence the ongoing education process some practitioners find necessary in making the function part of the management team and professionalizing the practice.

TITLES IN CORPORATE SETTINGS

Some top business executives simply do not like the term *public relations*. Many years ago, distaste for the term at IBM led to titles such as "manager, community affairs" and "director, community programs." Today, IBM's top public relations executive has the title "vice president, communications," and there is still nary a title on the organization chart that includes "public relations."

On the other hand, the overall function at Kaiser Aluminum and Chemical Corporation and Goodyear Tire and Rubber Company is headed by a "vice president of public relations." Readers Digest Association, Inc., calls it "vice president and director—public relations and communications policy." AT&T uses the title "senior vice president–public relations."

Nonetheless, the trend has been to move away from the "public relations" title at the top corporate level and towards an amalgam of terms such as "vice president, corporate communications" (Pacific Gas and Electric Company and Coca-Cola Company); "vice president, public affairs" (Chevron Corporation and the Detroit Edison Company); and "vice president, corporate relations" (Kemper Group and Manville Corporation). The list of corporate titles includes many other terms and combinations. At Ford Motor Company, for example, there is a "vice president—external affairs"; Eaton Corporation has a "vice president—corporate affairs"; and Control Data Corporation and Wisconsin Electric Power Company both have a "vice president—communications." All these titles cover the public relations management function in the corporate setting.

In some corporations, public relations is a subfunction of marketing, personnel, human resources, or even the legal department. In others, it reports directly to the CEO. Each industrial or commercial organization tailors its public relations function to reflect the character and personality of its management, its corporate culture, and its tradition.

CORPORATE SOCIAL RESPONSIBILITY

As ethical standards change and commitments to corporate social responsibility grow, the role of public relations in business has become more clearly defined as helping corporations "do the right thing," as well as say the right thing.

Apparently, some in business still agree with a remark attributed to President Calvin Coolidge that "the business of America is business" or even the claim made by a former head of General Motors that what was good for the car maker was "good for America." The 1980s and early 1990s definitely brought about a reassessment of such one-dimensional viewpoints. Companies began to "act green," invest heavily in socially responsible programs, and come under what one major company's CEO called "unprecedented scrutiny" and "unprecedented governmental regulation."[1]

In the past, many business leaders resisted the notion that their corporations should seek to fulfill social responsibilities beyond providing jobs, earning a profit with which to pay investors and underwrite growth, paying taxes, and voluntarily supporting nonprofit health, welfare, and education activities. A number of eminent economists and observers of the social scene agreed with this assessment of the limited role of business.[2]

The number of business leaders who still subscribe to the view that business is only for profit and the "bottom line" is dwindling, even in an era of consciously cutting costs. With the help of public relations counsel, corporations are targeting their philanthropic contributions, becoming "greener" through environmentally sound products and programs for plant-location communities, and teaming with local agencies and governments to improve schools, employment training programs, and food and shelter programs for the needy. Or they may take a stance as a "health-conscious company" through AIDS research underwriting; as an arts-oriented company through sponsorships of local, regional, or national programs; or as a company committed to education, with funding, contributions of staff time and equipment to schools and universities, or both.

Years ago, the notion of corporate social responsibility centered around only the stakeholders directly involved with the company: employees, stockholders, customers, and the community. While the debate over the extent and nature of corporate social responsibility continues today, it has become increasingly clear that public relations practitioners in corporate settings find themselves center stage in helping to formulate policy and programs for carrying out their organizations' social responsibility.

Caterpillar's Code of Worldwide Business Conduct and Operating Principles

To Caterpillar People:

In 1974, Caterpillar published its first "Code of Worldwide Business Conduct and Operating Principles," a code based on ethical convictions and international business experience dating back to the turn of the century.

This fourth revision of the Code still has the purpose of guiding Caterpillar people in a broad and ethical sense, in all aspects of our worldwide business activities. Experience has demonstrated the practical utility of this document.

The Code isn't an attempt to prescribe actions for every business encounter. And it isn't published out of any doubt about the desire of Caterpillar people to comply with its contents. Rather, we believe that the worldwide reach an complexity of our business—and the fact that ethical conduct isn't always subject to precise definition—argue strongly for our development of standards.

To the extent our actions match these high standards, such can be a source of pride. To the extent they don't, this Code should be a challenge to each of us.

No document issued by Caterpillar is more important than this one. I ask that you give this Code your strong support as you carry out your daily responsibilities.

Donald V. Fites	Issued October 1, 1974
Chairman of the Board	Revised September 1, 1977
	Revised May 1, 1983
	Revised May 1, 1985
	Revised August 1, 1992

(Excerpts from 12-page Code.)

Business Ethics. The company's most valuable asset is a reputation for integrity. If that becomes tarnished, customers, investors, suppliers, employees, and those who sell our products and services will seek affiliation with other, more attractive companies. We intend to hold to a single high standard of integrity everywhere. We will keep our word. We won't promise more than we can reasonably expect to deliver nor will we make commitments we don't intend to keep....

We seek long-lasting relationships—based on integrity—with all whose activities touch upon our own.

Protection of the Environment. Caterpillar's continued competitiveness and leadership in a global marketplace require individual and corporate dedication to a clean and safe environment wherever it conducts business. We will establish, maintain, and follow environmentally responsible policies and practices comply with applicable laws and regulations in both "letter and spirit" and respond openly and promptly to responsible inquiries about environment issues as they relate to Caterpillar and its products.

Public Responsibility. All Caterpillar employees are encouraged to take part in public matters of their individual choice. Further, it is recognized that employee participation in political processes—or in organizations that may be termed "controversial"—can be public service of a high order.

Just as Caterpillar supports the notion of <u>individual</u> participation, it may, to the extent legally permissible, support committees aimed at encouraging political contributions by individuals. The company itself will not normally make political contributions, even where it is legally permissible and common practice....

Overall, it's our intention that Caterpillar's business activities make good social sense—and that Caterpillar's social activities make good business sense.

Figure 14–1

Prelude to the Present: The Uneasy 1960s and 1970s

In the 1960s, business came under scrutiny, the likes of which most executives had never experienced. Increased government regulations, investigations by government agencies, and more intense reporting requirements threw the media spotlight on business activities, once relegated only to the financial pages.

With insider-trading scandals, conflicts of interest, bribery, price collusion, and illegal political contributions surfacing, the environment was ripe for a new kind of journalism, a new era of muckraking, as it were: "investigative reporting."

Business tried to fight back, but legal defense was time-consuming and costly. Many corporations began to look hard at internal affairs and sought to get their houses in order; the result was the introduction of "codes of conduct," and early efforts to operate "in the public interest." (See Figure 14–1 for a contemporary version of the Caterpillar Inc. code of conduct.) Externally, some businesses maintained a low profile, while a few took their cases to the "court of public opinion." Former Mobil Oil public relations executive Herb Schmertz's book, *Good-bye to the Low Profile: The Art of Creative Confrontation*, outlined and exploited this aggressive reincarnation of the "tell-our-side" approach to public relations.[3] While some corporate practitioners enjoyed seeing one of their own striking back at the media, others understood that engaging the media in any form of combat—verbal or otherwise—was not wise. As an observer once counseled, "Don't argue with people who buy printer's ink by the barrel." The same counsel applies for those who control broadcast and cable distribution systems.

Still, the 1960s and much of the 1970s was a time of public distrust of business. Public interest groups were on the rise, and many activists spawned during the anti–Vietnam War, antibusiness years on college campuses worked in government, where they had an opportunity to promulgate laws and regulations involving the very companies they sought to restrain. Investigative journalists were helping not only to bring down a corrupt government during the Watergate crisis, but were prying open the doors to corporate board rooms long locked to an inquisitive outside world.

A 1972 Opinion Research Corporation survey found that 60 percent of adults held business in "low esteem," highlighting a growing problem for business. The Washington-based Media Institute published a book about media treatment of business in the 1970s, pointing out that almost half of all media portrayals of business were of illegal activities and two-thirds of all business leaders in television entertainment programs were shown to be greedy, foolish, or criminal.[4]

For businesses, the problems continued into the 1970s. The Organization of Petroleum Exporting Countries (OPEC) oil embargo of 1973–1974 and the Iranian Revolution of 1978–1979 each disrupted oil prices. Economic shock waves resulting from skyrocketing oil prices produced public frustration and increased media coverage, with the energy industry taking the brunt of the charges. The oil companies, especially, were targeted by Congress through hearings and peered at by the news media as never before. Companies were accused of "perpetrating a hoax, profiteering, withholding supplies, or other devious actions."[5]

Out of this seemingly chaotic public relations environment came several organizations dedicated to helping business and the news media meet on common ground, to help each understand the other's jobs. On one hand was a need to educate business executives about the role of the journalist and on the other to help educate reporters who might be covering the energy beat for the first time. The Foundation for American Communications and the Media Institute were pioneers in this effort, born during the mid-1970s. Even Harvard University joined in, hosting a series of seminars on "Business and the Media."

Despite these efforts, the 1970s ended with a communication and environmental bang as Three Mile Island became a buzzword for bungled public relations and a suspect nuclear-energy industry. Metropolitan Edison's poor crisis planning and mangled communication efforts earned the company a nation's wrath and exposed a lack of candor and trustworthiness that many Americans—including reporters—had suspected throughout business.[6]

Ironically, the 1970s had seen an almost imperceptible shift by some businesses away from the "traditional" dependence on media to "tell our story" to the use of more "controlled" media (booklets, corporate advertising, speech reprints, and corporate mission statements). Businesses directed more efforts to influencing legislation and its implementation and increased its reliance on trade associations. "Issue management" became a hot buzzword in the corporate setting. Washington, D.C., corporate offices saw unprecedented growth in the 1970s, with most major companies having at least one Washington representative. That growth continued virtually unabated into the 1990s.

The corporate credibility gap cited by an economist in 1974 summed up the era for many corporations that operated under the guise of withholding information because of "privacy rights," or fear of "trying a case in public," or simply, "no comment." He stated the problem simply: "The reason the public is so suspicious is because our large corporations so habitually do engage in clever public relations instead of telling the truth."[7]

A New Era of Corporate Social Responsibility: The 1980s

The 1980s introduced a new era of public relations and corporate social responsibility. For example, Johnson & Johnson's classic handling of the Tylenol poisonings in 1983 became a textbook case in how to respond to a crisis (review Exhibit 1–2). Unlike Three Mile Island, Johnson & Johnson responded to all media requests for information and generally fulfilled the company's responsibility to the public interest.

Also early in the decade, Dow Chemical's former chairman outlined some basics of corporate social responsibility:

> The business community's efforts to solving social problems must be
> integrated with long-term profit growth. If done properly, solving
> social problems is both good business and good citizenship, for the
> two goals are wholly compatible.[8]

By the time the 1980s drew to a close, the rest of the chemical industry had caught up with Dow's philosophy and instituted an across-the-industry program of social responsibility. "Responsible Care" is the title of the self-policing code of conduct by which all members of the Chemical Manufacturers Association abide.

Also in the 1980s, churches and universities began scrutinizing their investment portfolios, selling holdings in companies that might conflict with public (and constituency) perceptions of corporate insensitivity to social concerns. Interest groups prodded American companies to pull out of South Africa. A simmering issue for years, it boiled over with a vengeance at corporate annual meetings and on the sidewalks outside corporate headquarters. Companies throughout the world heard the protests, and hundreds of millions of dollars in plants, equipment, and jobs were removed from South Africa in the 1980s. The pros and cons of those actions are still being debated today. In fact, the issue has become localized to the extent that in some states, companies doing any kind of business with South Africa are forbidden from bidding on state government contracts.

Even with increased efforts by business to become more socially responsible in the 1980s, public confidence in major institutions—as measured in surveys by the University of Chicago Opinion Research Center—showed that only about 25 percent of Americans expressed a "great deal of confidence" in major corporations, banks, and financial institutions.[9]

Business and industry continued to labor under many government regulations imposed a decade or more earlier because of public and governmental concern about the treatment of the environment, product quality, equal employment, and workplace safety. Public perception was that American corporations were not assuming leadership roles in dealing with social problems and that increased (or continued) regulation was necessary.

News media continued reporting on corporate bribes to foreign government officials, antitrust and product safety violations, cancer-causing drugs and chemicals, and "lemon law" cases involving defective automobiles. All further undermined public confidence in business and industry.

When the Reagan administration began deregulating various industries, corporate social responsibility was again tested as airlines, railroads, banks, and savings and loans were given greater freedom to set rates and compete. While the deregulation debate continues, it became increasingly clear with bank, savings and loan, and airline failures of the late 1980s and early 1990s that simply easing government regulations was not a panacea for social responsibility.

Beginning in the mid- to late 1980s, economic conditions brought about what some termed a "new federalism." Simply put, cuts in federal funds for social, cultural, educational, and welfare programs began to put increased pressure on corporations to carry an even larger share of the financial burden for these activities in their communities. Business leaders and public relations practitioners began to take center stage in the public arena as the times called for a new spirit of volunteerism, such as President Bush's "Thousand Points of Light"; new forms of public and private partnerships, such as adopt-a-school and adopt-a-highway programs; and innovative private sector initiatives for solving social problems, such health care and insurance reform.

The professional ethics of business leaders and public relations practitioners, along with the social responsibility of their organizations, began to be scrutinized as never before on a worldwide basis. Union Carbide's Bhopal (India) chemical manufacturing accident, Perrier's tainted bottled water, and *Exxon Valdez's* oil spill into Alaska's Prince William Sound all became news in every corner of the world. Toxic substance accidents, environmentally hazardous manufacturing processes, and human rights violations cannot be exported and hidden from instantaneous global news reporting.

Public Relations Challenges in the 1990s

Former PRSA president James Fox accurately foresaw three major forces shaping the role of public relations in corporate settings:

> 1) The identification and tracing of issues within corporate staff before legislation is proposed. 2) The formulation of corporate policies and the communication of these policies to modify or forestall restrictive legislation—the management of industry's response to change. 3) The emergence of the CEO as corporate spokesman, . . . and the assumption by chief executives of responsibility for direct involvement in public-policy issues.[10]

As he predicted, issues management began to catch on across all business lines in the late 1980s.

Today, although not an exclusively public relations task, issues management plays a major role in strategic planning in most companies. Lessons learned in corporate America during the 1970s and 1980s make it clear that businesses must actively monitor issues likely to impact their ability to reduce risk, make a profit, serve stakeholders, and operate in the public interest. Yet, a panel of experts concluded that public relations has not responded fully to the challenge because:

1. The connection to the bottom line is long-term and not well understood.
2. Many issues require organizational changes, not just communication. As a result, practitioners have to move past their traditional communication boundary to develop broader strategy.
3. The profession as a whole has not embraced issues management by defining it as part of public relations and by providing practitioners the training needed to assume the new roles.

4. Issues management is a high-level management function that requires mature judgment, depth of experience, and sophisticated understanding of business, social-political environment, and stakeholders.[11]

Certainly, the concept of the CEO as corporate spokesperson has taken hold in the 1990s, along with unprecedented public interest in the inner workings of business and the private lives of top executives. Increased public interest and scrutiny can be traced to media coverage of what appeared to be outrageous salaries, compensation packages, stock options, and "golden parachutes" for retiring and terminated corporate executives. Added to these are the seemingly endless stream of industrial accidents, corrupt savings and loans dealings, the scandalous Wall Street junk-bond world of Ivan Boesky and Michael Milken, and defense contractors' fraudulent billings and defective products. This was not a pretty picture as business entered the 1990s, but one that apparently stirred public curiosity in the candidacy of H. Ross Perot in the 1992 presidential campaign and the success of the book and HBO movie, *Barbarians at the Gate*, depicting the Wall Street personalities and shenanigans involved in the leveraged buyout of RJR Nabisco.

Some observers believe that increased public interest has been fueled by the CEOs themselves.[12] More and more CEOs play the spokesperson role in company advertising campaigns, write autobiographies or agree to be the subjects of popular "success-and-power" books, and respond to media requests for interviews, talk-show appearances, and business magazine features. Some CEOs even see themselves as CCOs: the chief communication officers for their corporations. After admitting that others in the organization probably know more about the business side, and some know more about management, one CEO said: "Most importantly, you need to be able to communicate your ideas and thoughts. . . . I think that's why I'm here today and not in some lower position."[13] Many CEOs see explaining company-related issues, such as layoffs, year-end results, and product recalls, as their primary obligation.

> Just as President Clinton relies every day on a corps of public relations–savvy advisors to assist him as he prepares for his daily interface with the press and the public, so too will tomorrow's CEOs become more dependent on communications advisors who bring valuable insights and useful techniques to the executive suite.[14]

The late 1980s concept of increased social responsibility calls for increased public accountability, whether voluntary or imposed by the government. New demands on corporate performance at all levels cast the public relations function as a major player in the process of organizational and social change on a global scale. Clearly, the 1990s present even more challenges for corporate public relations professionals helping to merge corporate bottom-line goals with environmentally friendly and socially sound business practices. Continued pressure on profits, downsizing, global competition, new technology, and government regulation will test corporate commitments to social responsibility. But as a corporate CEO once wrote:

> The basic goal of private enterprise remains what it has always been—to produce needed goods and services, earn a fair return on investment, and succeed as an economic institution. But the new dimension that must be observed—a new "bottom line" for business, really—is social approval. . . . A successful business organization must possess a moral sense as well as an economic sense.[15]

Recent corporate public interest publications and foundation annual reports reflect a continuing commitment to the "second bottom line," fulfilling social responsibility:

> We believe we have a special responsibility to enhance the quality of life for our customers, employees and community at large. This responsibility goes beyond producing high quality products. It also involves conducting our business in accordance with the highest ethical standards, treating our employees sensitively and fairly, and helping to meet critical community needs. . . . We would not consider ourselves successful as a corporation if we were to fall short as a good corporate citizen.
>
> Ralph S. Larsen, *Chairman and CEO, Johnson & Johnson*[16]

> Today, concern for the future of the environment has become one of the most important issues on the public agenda. More importantly, the issue has become a personal matter for the great majority of people who now classify themselves as "environmentalists." The special challenge for companies like General Motors is to do everything possible to minimize the negative effects of our products and processes on the environment.
>
> Roger B. Smith, *former Chairman, General Motors Corporation*[17]

> Our policy is to donate the equivalent of at least 2% of our U.S. pretax income to nonprofit organizations. In our 1992 fiscal year, we exceeded that goal, just as we have for the past nine years. . . . Our giving, like our management style is decentralized. The Sara Lee Foundation makes contributions on behalf of Sara Lee Corporation. In the same way, our divisions—around the country and around the world—work with community agencies to find the best local programs for local needs. Financial aid, food and clothing product donations, and—perhaps most importantly—the personal involvement of our employees are the tangible results of our resolve to make a difference.[18]

Every indicator suggests that nothing has changed this view as we approach the year 2000. In fact, public scrutiny and demands for corporate responsiveness is increasing. What some have called the Big Green

Brother—a collection of activist, regulatory, media, and consumer interests—now monitors business and industry to make sure that products
and processes are environmentally friendly. "Greenness" and "green marketing" now get top priority when developing any environmental program.
According to the *Good Housekeeping* Institute, to be environment-friendly,
marketers must address four issues: water conservation, energy conservation, solid waste reduction, and reduction of environmental hazards.[19]

Social Investment Forum, an organization that monitors investments, reports that almost 10 percent of all investments (more than
$500 billion) are made on the basis of how "green" and otherwise socially
responsible companies are. The environment is a criterion for 78 percent
of "green-minded" and "socially responsible" investors. As the president
of an environmental investment counseling firm said, "Quite aside from
their responsibility as part of our society, companies who ignore the
half-trillion dollars in potential capital that they could be attracting if
they weren't polluting do so at their peril."[20]

Examples of corporate "greenness" include Procter & Gamble's program to reduce solid waste by using recycled plastic in bottles and by
developing more compostable disposable diapers, McDonald's switch
from polystyrene foam cups and packaging to more "eco-friendly" materials, and 3M Company's pioneering "Pollution Prevention Pays" program. 3M's program began in 1975, well before the current green movement, making it the first formally organized corporate effort to control
pollution at the source rather than at the end of the production line. It
called for reformulating products, modifying manufacturing operations
and equipment, and recycling. The program had saved 3M $500 million
by mid-1991, garnered widespread public recognition, and earned
PRSA's Silver Anvil Award in 1978. The updated program goal is to
reduce pollution in the year 2000 by 90 percent from 1987 levels.[21]

Clearly, the conflict between corporate America and what some
called "eco-freaks" and "tree huggers" that officially began on Earth
Day, April 22, 1970, has ended. The environmentalists not only won, but
made environmental protection "a core American value." The debate
now centers on which policies and practices most effectively achieve the
goals of the new environmental ethic.[22]

CORPORATE PHILANTHROPY

The major tactics for expressing and demonstrating corporate social
responsibility include mission and value statements, speeches, advertising, and philanthropy, or contributing to education, health care,
welfare, and the arts. Chapter 12 covers the communication tactics,
so here we will limit our discussion to corporate philanthropy.

Although corporations gave charitable contributions totaling
some $6 billion in 1992, that seemingly hefty sum represented just
under 5 percent of all charitable giving ($124.3 billion). Corporate giv-

ing was also down by almost 4 percent from the 1991 total, after adjusting for inflation.[23]

While many top managers willingly participate financially in causes preferred by their corporations, a philosophic debate continues as to whether business has an obligation to "give away" its hard-earned profits to social and cultural programs. Social responsibility based on "enlightened self-interest" links philanthropy to organizational goals: "Our intent is to tie the grants program to our business and technical interests," according to the executive director of E. I. du Pont de Nemours and Company Committee on Educational Aid.[24] Others define enlightened self-interest as, "You must do well in order to do good." They employ a participative approach, in which employees, customers, and opinion leaders help select which projects receive funds. In this approach, volunteerism, gifts, and services in-kind are often more important than money for building relationships with key publics in communities.[25]

Corporate leaders view philanthropy as a way of giving something back into local communities, improving the quality of life for employees, and practicing corporate citizenship. They give to improve schools because they are experiencing or anticipate problems with low-skill levels in the work force; they give to organizations in the arts, culture, and humanities because it enhances the quality of community life; and they give to hospitals and clinics because the quality of health care helps attract others to the community.

As the demand for corporate support increases as government support decreases, however, many companies are formulating targeted corporate giving "missions," concentrating on health, environment, education, or even more specific causes. The trend is to focus giving in a particular area to increase giving effectiveness. For example, DuPont Stainmaster Carpet™ provided carpeting for all Ronald McDonald Houses in the United States. These homes provide temporary residence for families of children being treated at nearby hospitals. As Figure 14–2 illustrates, a 3-foot-square portrait of Ronald McDonald carved from Stainmaster Carpet provided a permanent reminder (and photo backdrop) of DuPont's philanthropy.

Education has always been a prime recipient of corporate philanthropy. Contributions are usually measured in dollar value, although in-kind assistance (facilities and equipment, teaching aids, employees' time in teaching and training, internships, grant and matching gifts made by employees) has grown in recent years. Corporate executives see an increased need to support public education at all levels as part of their social responsibility. Some have almost made it a corporate mission. Phillips Petroleum Company, for example, has for decades focused company resources and personnel on aid to education at the secondary and university level (see Exhibit 14–1).

Often, the public relations practitioner plays a key role in the corporate philanthropy function (and in some organizations is *responsible* for it), assisting in several ways:

Ronald McDonald Portrait in Carpet

Figure 14–2

Courtesy DuPont.

1. Staging appropriate events for making a decisive contribution, as in a welfare fund drive or the creation of a scholarship fund
2. Assisting in a charitable campaign or endeavor, with communication-strategy counsel, preparing printed or audiovisual materials, and advertising support or publicity placement
3. Heading a project or campaign or serving as the alternate for a corporate senior official
4. Auditing various community causes to determine where and how a corporation might best be of assistance
5. Guiding, not directing, the participative approach that involves community constituencies in allocating corporate contributions

EXHIBIT 14-1

Phillips Petroleum Support of Education

PHILLIPS PETROLEUM COMPANY
BARTLESVILLE, OKLAHOMA 74004

April 1992

Phillips Petroleum Company's philanthropic activities are consistent with good corporate citizenship.

Phillips strives to identify and support those charitable organizations which most effectively and efficiently address issues and problems facing our society and which present the best promise for the future. We are especially concerned with education and workforce preparedness, the environment, opportunities for women and minorities, ethics as a lifelong experience and the enhancement of the quality of life through the arts and the humanities.

The majority of the grants approved by Phillips go to organizations in areas where the company has large concentrations of employees and to educational institutions where the company actively recruits. Grants are often in the form of a challenge.

Contributions from Phillips Petroleum Company and Phillips Petroleum Foundation,Inc. are funded through corporate earnings and are a reflection thereof. Funding varies from year to year but Phillips commitment to good corporate citizenship remains constant.

C. J. Silas
Chairman and CEO

PHILLIPS PETROLEUM CONTRIBUTIONS
1988 THROUGH 1992

CATEGORY	1988	1989	1990	1991	1992
EDUCATION	$2,933,926	$2,641,121	$3,249,804	$5,100,403	$4,766,201
CULTURE AND THE ARTS	444,708	580,915	648,125	633,014	470,585
HEALTH AND WELFARE	468,624	740,186	722,160	1,011,836	633,108
YOUTH	459,232	620,003	715,956	665,692	641,736
CIVIC	639,628	1,257,167	1,020,390	1,102,704	2,960,147
TOTAL	$4,946,118	$5,839,392	$6,356,435	$8,513,649	$9,460,642

Courtesy Phillips Petroleum Company.

Corporate philanthropy, once thought of by many as extraordinary generosity, is increasingly viewed as an *obligation* and necessary component of corporate citizenship. It has also moved to center stage a part of the public relations mission in building relationships with key corporate publics.

CORPORATE FINANCIAL RELATIONS

In the 1980s, economic conditions and the prevailing "fast-buck" atmosphere of the era placed financial relations in the forefront of public relations activities. "Benign neglect," one business journalist wrote, "facilitated a wave of takeovers that piled up corporate debt . . . and cost thousands of workers their jobs."[26]

Corporations began to understand who *really* controlled their stock. It was not individual investors anymore, but huge, multibillion-dollar retirement funds and pension plans wanting maximum return on their investments. When takeovers were imminent, these money managers tended to eschew loyalty in favor of whoever had the most cash. For a few years, Carl Icahn, T. Boone Pickens, and their like ruled the land, instilling fear and loathing into hundreds of board rooms across America, providing solid employment for legions of investment bankers and putting the skills of public relations practitioners to the extreme test.

During the takeover mania of the 1980s, investor relations became an integral part of many corporate communications programs, in many cases working closely with public relations professionals for the first time.

Public relations plays an integral part in most financial relations programs, assisting with analyst presentations, preparing speeches to shareholders, and working with the news media during "road shows" (visits by top corporate officials with analysts and financial editors, often covering many cities in a relatively short period of time; hence, careful planning and coordination is needed).

With large pension plans and investment funds holding more and more shares of corporate stock, individual shareholders often feel powerless. In the late 1980s, there were efforts to organize shareholders, ostensibly to give them "more of a voice" in how "their" corporations should be run, what social enterprises should be supported, even what products should and should not be marketed. For the large part, however, these attempts to put together coalitions of smaller shareholders had no effect on corporate policies, since it is difficult to organize shareholders into common-interest groups with collective voices. The small investor continues to feel awed by the large corporation; their 50, 100, or even 1000, shares pale in comparison with the huge blocks of stock bought by investment funds and trusts. Their only contact with management is through printed materials, such as quarterly and annual reports, company publications, and the news media. The small investor feels helpless; to some management, they may even seem apathetic. Meanwhile, many heads of large investment trusts meet face-to-face with corporate executives. The financial public relations practitioner must be aware of these conditions and work closely with top management to address shareholder concerns.

Much of financial relations is governed by law, as described in Chapter 6, by SEC rules and regulations, by stock-exchange requirements, and by management attitudes toward of disclosure. Implementation of policies and financial relations plans falls largely to financial officers with advice and support from the public relations staff or specialized outside counsel.

The usual assignments given to public relations in the financial arena include:

1. Measuring opinions toward the company, the industry, or free enterprise, held by shareholders, financial analysts, federal agency executives, and legislators
2. Recommending communication strategy, particularly with respect to corporate goals
3. Assisting with preparation of financial literature, such as letters to new stockholders, interim and annual reports, dividend enclosures, and information for brokerage-firm research reports
4. Making arrangements and preparing informational materials for financial meetings, facility tours, and presentations for investor groups, analysts, and the financial media
5. Writing financial news releases and handling of inquiries from financial media

A company's first contact with new shareholders is extremely important. The public relations practitioner can work with management to create a *letter of welcome*, enclosing recent financial reports, and booklets or brochures about the company. Likewise, there is correspondence *from* investors. Often, investors request information about products, sales, research, stock prices, number of shares owned, or the company's stand on social, political, or ethical issues.

These letter exchanges with stockholders can function as a useful two-way communications tool. Some top corporate executives handle selected responses personally.

The keystone of any financial relations program is the *annual report*, a "window," in effect, through which varied constituents view the company and its operations. According to one annual report design firm executive, "Annual reports have gone from being a simple reporting tool to a document used to strategically position a company."[27]

In some companies, the annual report is the most used external communications tool, sent to a wide range of publics, from employees to analysts, educators, and business media. This tool has evolved to a high degree of technical and graphic excellence, due in a large part to its public relations objectives for so many different publics. In recent years, however, reflecting tighter economic times, many companies have been taking a closer look at the expenses connected with producing the annual report and have begun issuing slightly less glossy and expensive models. "Some companies cut back from 6-color reports to 2-color reports, pruned mailing lists and eliminated photographs altogether."[28] Others cut other departmental budgets to maintain or increase the annual report budget.

The annual report does more than merely present financial results from the previous year, information reported on the 10K form, as required by the SEC (review the Chapter 6 section on disclosure). Some reports also discuss the company's impact on the economy of plant cities, reflect on the firm's international scope, show concern for social problems, and indicate ways in which environmental issues are being addressed. Others may convey management's position on various public issues crucial to the company's well-being. Overall, today's annual report places increased emphasis on the role of the modern corporation in society.

Since the early 1980s, some companies have produced supplemental annual public interest and social responsibility reports detailing environmental activities; programs to meet community and employee needs; support for the arts, health, and welfare, and other social quality-of-life concerns. The reports often are as well produced and as costly as the financial annual report. (See Figure 14–3.)

In some large corporations, the annual report is the primary responsibility of a specialized public relations professional working within an internal communications division or as an expert counsel in an outside firm. In either case, this specialist maintains close contact with company financial executives. For most of those charged with producing the annual report, it is at least a half-time job for up to 6 months each year.[29] It can be a frustrating, politically charged task, requiring excellent writing (and editing) skills, an understanding of corporate finance, and the ability to work with top management in all lines of business. Not surprisingly, investor relations is the highest-paid specialty in public relations, with a 1993 median salary of almost $67,000 and with three out of four in this specialty earning at least $45,000 (see Chapter 2).[30]

Current economic conditions and management direction dictate the content, graphics, and style of annual reports. And although there are no tried-and-true "formulas," effective annual reports contain all or most of the following:

1. A distinctive cover to attract interest and reflect corporate character
2. An inviting design that helps the reader get the main message points easily and quickly by scanning the report
3. A table of contents and/or highlights
4. Identification of members of the board of directors and top corporate officers
5. A statement or letter from the CEO, generally summarizing the past year's events and emphasizing goals for the future

Johnson & Johnson and General Motors'
Special Annual Reports

WORLDWIDE CHILD SURVIVAL
PROGRAM

SOCIAL RESPONSIBILITY
IN ACTION
WORLDWIDE

Figure 14–3

6. Consolidated balance statements of earnings, shareholders' interest, and operating cash flows for the year

7. Financial highlights and comparisons with at least the previous year, but often with the past 5 to 10 years

8. Auditor's statement of independence and adherence to accepted accounting principles

In addition, public relations practitioners often create communications to be attached to the reports, targeting financial news media, analysts, educators, and other constituents. These take the form of news releases, personalized letters, or fact sheets detailing highlights of the report for specific audiences.

Another important component of investor relations is the *annual meeting*. Largely a ritual prescribed and governed by SEC regulation, the annual meeting symbolizes corporate democracy in action. While these yearly gatherings (usually held at corporate headquarters or at a venue in the headquarters city) provide opportunity for face-to-face contact, it is often only those who live nearby or who represent huge blocks of shareholders who take the time and effort, and who can afford the time and expense, to attend. Therefore, postmeeting communications have become increasingly important if all shareholders are to be reached.

In conjunction with annual meetings, the public relations department typically supports the event by:

1. Helping with physical arrangements
2. Creating hand-outs and other on-site communications
3. Assisting with tours and souvenirs
4. Accommodating the news media, including arrangements for computers, telephones and modems, fax machines, photo opportunities, and postmeeting interviews
5. Generating publicity support
6. Preparing question and answer sheets for top executives, in anticipation of shareholder questions

For the last task, practitioners are often charged with anticipating the tough questions likely to be asked of the CEO and other company officials during and after the meeting. Many an annual meeting has come to a halt by shareholders seeking simple answers to extremely difficult questions or asking embarrassing questions about company operations, disappointing earnings, executive compensations and "perks," or alleged misdeeds by top executives. Management must be ready to respond satisfactorily not only to shareholders, but to news media covering the event as well. Some executives rehearse their responses by having the public relations staff role play as audience members or reporters asking the tough questions.

CONSUMER AFFAIRS AND THE "MARKETING MIX"

Public relations has long been an essential supplement to the marketing effort, particularly in consumer product and services companies. In fact, for many counselors and staff professionals, participation in the "marketing mix" is their "bread and butter," it pays the bills. As one practitioner noted, "By being involved early and regularly with the client marketing functions, public relations can help assure totally integrated, strategically focused and cost-effective marketing communications."[31]

Another public relations practitioner says that "public relations cannot simply be slipped into a marketing communications program. It must be integrated when marketing plans are conceived and developed."[32]

Public relations support for marketing includes:

1. Publicizing news and events related to launching new or improved products or services
2. Promoting established products or services
3. Creating a favorable reputation or "image" of the company behind the product or service
4. Arranging and publicizing public appearances of marketing spokespersons
5. Probing public opinion in market areas (research)
6. Attracting news-media coverage of sales conferences, trade shows, and other sales promotion events
7. Assisting in programs concerning consumerism

The subject of *consumerism* in the marketplace has been discussed in business and trade circles almost to the point of exhaustion. The debate came into sharp focus in the 1960s, with government intervention in the form of many consumer protection laws. Books, articles, congressional hearings, and public interest group actions followed in great numbers over the next two decades, culminating in the appointment of an assistant to the president for consumer affairs in the early 1970s. Shortly thereafter, the National Business Council for Consumer Affairs was created to encourage self-regulation.

While there continues to be distrust in the fragile business-consumer relationship, recent years have seen an increased effort by business to practice two-way communication with its crucial marketing publics, listening more closely to complaints and seeking to instill quality in the workplace and resulting products.

Practitioners play an integral role in the marketing mix, promoting the sale of products and services while helping to ensure more attention to truth and accuracy of claims. In the 1990s, the emphasis has shifted to communication projects and vehicles for product-problem alerts and recalls, consumer education programs, and easier redress for settlement of grievances by private arbitration. But most important, corporations have become seemingly obsessed with satisfying customers by improving the quality of products and services.

THE QUEST FOR QUALITY

Business and industry got a wake-up call during the 1980s: produce high-quality, reliable products at a reasonable price or consumers will find somebody else, often in another country, who will. Corporations worldwide mounted programs under the banners of "total quality management" (TQM) and "ISO 9000." In a bit of semantic tyranny, TQM became the hot buzzword of the 1990s: Who could be against creating quality? Companies stopped buying from suppliers that did not meet ISO 9000 standards. Quality is not a passing fad. It is an international revolution.

TQM means near-zero defects in every task performed in the production and delivery of products and services, with total customer satisfaction as the goal. At Motorola, for example, the goal was to reach "Six Sigma" by 1992. Six Sigma stood for six standard deviations from the usual result, or "a defect rate of 3.4 parts per million for each and every process step or procedure. That's 99.9997 percent perfect."[33]

Motorola developed a course call "Six Steps to Six Sigma" to introduce TQM to all its employees. The six steps are:

1. Identify the product you create or the service you provide. In other words, answer the question, "What is my mission?"
2. Identify the person who actually pays for the products and services that the company produces.
3. Identify what you need so as to provide a product or service that satisfies the customer.
4. Identify the process for doing your work. In other words, break down operations into steps and tasks, chart the flow of work from supplier to customer, spot tasks that are prone to error, and measure the defect rate and cycle time.
5. Redefine the process so that it is mistake-proof and so that wasted effort is eliminated. If a task adds no value, throw it out.
6. Ensure continuous improvement by measuring, analyzing, and controlling the process.[34]

TQM is not just an internal matter either:

For example, soon after Motorola won the Malcolm Baldrige National Quality Award in 1988, its thousands of suppliers were asked to pledge that they, too, would apply for the award within five years. Those refusing to sign the pledge were dropped from the rolls of qualified suppliers unless they did not qualify as an applicant due to size or other exclusions, or there were some extenuating circumstances.[35]

TQM dominated U.S. business and industry during the late 1980s and early 1990s, but ISO 9000 became a worldwide movement. The International Association for Standardization (ISO) published a set of five standards used to document, implement, and demonstrate quality management and assurance in 1987. Since then, 55 countries have adopted the standards. Worldwide, 30,000 companies are certified on one of the ISO 9000 standards. By early 1993, 855 company sites had been registered with ISO, meaning that an independent third party had conducted an on-site audit of company operations against ISO standards.[36]

ISO 9000 was originally designed to be a voluntary guide for ensuring quality products and services, but it has become an imperative in the competitive marketplace. According to one consultant, "Industry wails about government imposing regulations, and here we are imposing them on ourselves." For some companies doing business abroad, ISO 9000 has become an informal requirement. A certified ISO assessor says, "There's a fear of being shut out. They're told they must get certified if they want to export to Europe, but that is stretching the truth." But meeting ISO 9000 standards is a requirement for doing business with an increasing number of European Community companies, many of which refuse to buy or accept bids from suppliers who do not. According to the manager of quality systems at Union Camp Container Division, "I seriously doubt anyone who's not registered to ISO 9000 in five years will be doing business with any of the heavy hitters."[37]

The TQM and ISO 9000 revolutions demonstrate a worldwide commitment to quality, but some have suggested that the focus on customer satisfaction and employee participation is "simply a dramatic return to the basics."[38] The critical role that communication plays in the quest for quality puts public relations square in the middle of this revolution, even it is only a glorified return to the basics of good business.

CORPORATE PRACTICE AS THE MODEL

It is in business and industry that the public relations function is most often held up for public scrutiny and evaluation. Individual practitioners and the profession as a whole are often judged on the basis of how those in business and industry discharge their duties and fulfill their social responsibility.

Corporate practitioners must assume an even greater share of the burden in anticipating long-term consequences of their companies' policies, balanced with professional crisis planning and response to social concerns. Public relations executives must counsel management that the public interest and corporate interest converge in the long run and that this approach to corporate social responsibility must take precedence over—or at least *balance*—concerns about immediate profit and loss. Such an approach is demonstrated in Chevron Corporation's (San Francisco) public affairs mission statement:

> Our mission is to maximize the company's ability to conduct its
> worldwide business in the best interests of its stockholders. These
> are served when we perform responsibly toward the environment,
> our employees, our customers, and our neighbors. To that end, we
> will look ahead, anticipate change and develop innovative responses
> to environmental, public and governmental concerns.

Tim Traverse-Healy, long-time public relations leader in Europe, holds a similar notion of the mission and future of corporate public relations:

> A company will see nothing unusual in being quizzed and in respond-
> ing fully and quickly on matters such as, its employment record and
> practices; its environmental policies; the quality of its products; the
> safety of it products; and the effectiveness of its services. Discussion
> and debate will be encouraged, rather than feared; sought rather
> than avoided. One measure of a corporation's social acceptance will be
> the professionalism of its two-way communications and the degree of
> genuine dialogue it encourages and entertains.[39]

ADDITIONAL READINGS

Barton, Laurence.   *Crisis in Organizations: Managing and Communicating in the Heat of Chaos.* Cincinnati: South-Western Publishing Company, 1993. Presents "how-to" guide for dealing with a crisis, a step-by-step approach to creating a crisis management plan, and case studies illustrating experiences of practitioners.

Beauchamp, Tom L.   *Case Studies in Business, Society, and Ethics.* Englewood Cliffs, N.J.: Prentice-Hall, Inc., 1993.

Buchholz, Rogene A.   *Principles of Environmental Management: The Greening of Business.* Englewood Cliffs, N.J.: Prentice-Hall, Inc., 1993. Traces growth of environmentalism, environmental public policy and regulation, and strategies for "managing" environmental issues.

Budd, John F., Jr.   *Street Smart Public Relations.* Lakesville, Conn.: Turtle Publishing Company, 1992. Recounts lessons learned by a respected corporate practitioner and counselor.

Caywood, Clarke, and Raymond Ewing, eds.   *The Handbook of Communications in Corporate Restructuring and Takeovers.* Englewood Cliffs, N.J.: Prentice-Hall, Inc., 1992. Presents papers and discussions from the Arthur W. Page Society–Northwestern University seminar.

Harris, Thomas L.   *The Marketer's Guide to Public Relations: How Today's Top Companies Are Using the New Public Relations to Gain A Competitive Edge.* New York: John Wiley and Sons, 1991. Adds to the confusion between public relations and marketing by defining "marketing public relations" as "programs to encourage purchase and consumer satisfaction," or, more precisely, marketing.

Harrison, E. Bruce.   *Going Green: How to Communicate Your Company's Environmental Commitment.* Homewood, Ill.: Business One Irwin, 1993. Outlines a participative approach to building "sustainable communications" with core environmental constituencies; "green listening."

Thompson, Louis, Jr. "The Fight for Good Governance." *Harvard Business Review* 71, no. 1 (January–February 1993): 76–83. Discusses the expanded role of boards of directors in investor relations, reforms in how directors relate to CEOs, and the push for greater accountability.

Treacy, Michael, and Fred Wiersema. "Customer Intimacy and Other Value Disciplines" *Harvard Business Review* 71, no. 1 (January–February 1993): 84–93. Reports findings from 3-year study of 40 companies on achieving operational excellence, building customer intimacy, and product leadership.

NOTES

[1] C. J. Silas, "The Environment: Playing to Win," *Public Relations Journal* 46, no. 1 (January 1990): 10. Silas is chairman and CEO of Phillips Petroleum Company.

[2] Most notable among those holding the "business-for-business" view are economist Milton Friedman and Wall Street commentator Louis Rukeyser.

[3] Herbert Schmertz (with William Novak), *Good-bye to the Low Profile: The Art of Creative Confrontation* (Boston: Little, Brown, 1986). See Philip Lesley's review in *Public Relations Review* 12, no. 3 (Fall 1986): 59–60.

[4] *Crooks, Conmen and Clowns: Businessmen in TV Entertainment* (Washington, D.C.: Media Institute, 1981).

[5] Leonard J. Theberge, ed., *TV Coverage of the Oil Crises: How Well Was the Public Served?*, I (Washington, D.C.: Media Institute, 1982); p. xii. Three-booklet series of quantitative and qualitative analyses and commentary.

[6] For more information about the Three Mile Island case, see Richard C. Hyde, "Three Mile Island: PR's Balaklava," *Public Relations Journal* 35, no. 6 (June 1979): 10–14.

[7] Irving Kristol, "The Credibility of Corporations," *Wall Street Journal*, January 17, 1974.

[8] As quoted by Donald R. Stephenson, "Internal PR Efforts Further Corporate Responsibility: A Report from Dow Canada," *Public Relations Quarterly* 28, no. 2 (Summer 1983): 7–10.

[9] Seymour Martin Lipset and William Schneider, "The Decline of Confidence in American Institutions," *Political Science Quarterly* 98 (Fall 1983): 379–402, or the same authors' book, *The Confidence Gap: Business, Labor, and Government in the Public Mind* (New York: Free Press, 1983).

[10] James F. Fox, "The Politicizing of the Chief Executive," *Public Relations Journal* 38, no. 8 (August 1982): 23.

[11] Adapted from summary report of the "Public Relations Colloquium 1992—Issues Management," held January 20–21, 1992, at Northwestern University, cosponsored by Nuffer, Smith, Tucker, Inc. (public relations firm) and San Diego State University Department of Journalism. See also *pr reporter* 35, no. 4 (January 27, 1992): 1 and 2.

[12] J. David Pincus, Robert E. Rayfield, and Michael D. Cozzens, "The Chief Executive Officer's Internal Communication Role: A Benchmark Program of Research," *Public Relations Research Annual* 3 (1991): 1 and 5.

[13] Quote from J. David Pincus, Robert E. Rayfield, and J. Nicholas DeBonis, "Transforming CEOs Into Chief Communications Officers," *Public Relations Journal* 47, no. 11 (November 1991): 24.

[14] Dena Winokur and Robert W. Kinkead, "How Public Relations Fits Into Corporate Strategy," *Public Relations Journal* 49, no. 5 (May 1993): 23.

[15]Thornton F. Bradshaw, then-president of Atlantic Richfield Company, in the introduction to *Participation III: Atlantic Richfield and Society*, edited by Nita B. Whaley (Los Angeles: Atlantic Richfield Company, undated).

[16]From interview printed in *Social Responsibility in Action Worldwide* (New Brunswick, N.J.: Johnson and Johnson, undated). Included as part of "Johnson and Johnson Programs in Philanthropy: 1990 Report on Contributions."

[17]Quote from Smith's introduction to *General Motors and the Environment* (Detroit: General Motors Corporation, April 1990).

[18]*Sara Lee Foundation Programs and Application Procedures* (Chicago: Sara Lee Corporation, undated). Reports grants and programs made during fiscal 1992.

[19]Susan Schaefer Vandervoort, "Big 'Green Brother' Is Watching: New Directions in Environmental Public Affairs Challenge Business," *Public Relations Journal* 47, no. 4 (April 1991): 14–19, 26.

[20]"Investing in the Environment: Options Appeal to Green-Minded Investors," *CALPIRG Citizen Agenda* 7, no. 4 (Spring 1991): 6. CALPIRG is the California Public Interest Research Group, a consumer and environmental activist organization.

[21]Lowell F. Ludford, "3P Program Pays Off in Cost Savings of $500 Million for 3M," *Public Relations Journal* 47, no. 4 (April 1991): 20–21.

[22]A. Joseph LaCovey, "Business Changes Its Ways," *Public Relations Journal*, 47, no. 4 (April 1991): 23.

[23]Julie L. Nicklin, "Charitable Giving Rises 6.4%; Education Gets $14 Billion," *Chronicle of Higher Education* 39, no. 38 (May 26, 1993): 25 and 27.

[24]Julie L. Nicklin, "Many Fortune 500 Companies Curtail Donations to Higher Education," *The Chronicle of Higher Education* 39, no. 38 (May 26, 1993): 25 and 26.

[25]"12 Trends That Are Steering Public Relations Practice," *pr reporter* 36, no. 11 (March 15, 1993): 4.

[26]Dan Cordtz, "American Business: The Golden Century," *Financial World* 160, no. 13 (June 25, 1991): 54.

[27]Audrey Balkind, quoted by Adam Shell in "Designing Messages: How Annual Reports Reflect Your Image," *Public Relations Journal* 47, no. 10 (October 1991): 15.

[28]Adam Shell, "Communicating in Tough Times," *Public Relations Journal* 48, no. 8 (August 1992): 23.

[29]Robert K. Otterbourg, "Managing the Annual Report," *Public Relations Journal* 48, no. 8 (August 1992): 24.

[30]Nicholas J. Tortorello and Elizabeth Wilhelm, "Eighth Annual Salary Survey," *Public Relations Journal* 49, no. 7 (July 1993): 15.

[31]Anthony J. Tortorici, "Maximizing Marketing Communication through Horizontal and Vertical Orchestration," *Public Relations Quarterly* 36, no. 1 (Spring 1991): 20.

[32]Michael O. Niederquell, "Integrating the Strategic Benefits of Public Relations into the Marketing Mix," *Public Relations Quarterly* 36, no. 1 (Spring 1991): 23.

[33]Charles A. Sengstock, Jr., "The Quality Issue in Public Relations." Paper presented to the Arthur W. Page Society Meeting, Northwestern University, Evanston, Ill., May 31, 1991.

[34]Ibid. Adapted with permission of the author.

[35]Charles A. Sengstock, Jr., "Pursuing the Not-So-Elusive Goal of Perfection," *Public Relations Journal* 47, no. 8 (August 1991): 22.

[36]Robin Tierney, "ISO 9000 Unmasked!" *World Trade* 6, no. 4 (April 1993): 47–48, 50, 100, and 102.

[37]Ibid., 48 and 50.

[38]Dan Koger and Greg Brower,   "If Total Quality Seems Like a Revolution, That's Because It Is," *IABC Communication World* 9, no. 10 (October 1992): 21.

[39]Tim Traverse-Healy, O.B.E.,   "Riding Point." Hall of Fame Award Lecture presented to the Arthur W. Page Society Annual Meeting, Orlando, Fla., September 16, 1990.

15

Government and Politics

A popular government without popular information or a means of acquiring it, is but a prologue to a farce or tragedy, or perhaps both.

JAMES MADISON

The role of public relations in government varies widely. The diversity of goals and activities in government is greater than in any other area of public relations practice. While one practitioner assists in selling a product such as commemorative postage stamps, another promotes a service such as youth basketball at the local community center. As one practitioner seeks to gain public compliance with mandatory use of child safety seats in cars, another attempts to interpret national public opinion to assist in domestic policy formulation. Yet another practitioner may publicly defend controversial art created with taxpayers' money, while another explains troop movements and reports the number of casualties in a major battle.

THE ROLE OF PUBLIC RELATIONS IN GOVERNMENT

Government touches every aspect of society, and virtually every facet of government is closely tied to and reliant upon public relations. In a

This chapter was written in collaboration with Mark S. Cox, APR, Director of Public Relations, City of Chesapeake, Virginia. Cox also serves as the city's liaison to the Virginia General Assembly. He began his government public relations career as the first coordinator of public information for the City of Chula Vista, California.

very real sense, the purpose of government itself closely matches the purpose of public relations. Successful government maintains responsive, mutual understanding based on two-way communication with citizens. Democracy in the United States is structured upon principles that mandate effective public relations, with public apathy and ignorance its greatest enemies.

Without an informed and active citizenry, elected and appointed officials may lose touch with the true needs and interests of their constituents. Programs costing millions of dollars may be undertaken to address public needs that have been overestimated, while real needs remain hidden. Special-interest politics may dominate decision making. Citizen discontent may linger just under the surface, but once it appears it can be fueled by simplistic rhetoric in place of a deeper understanding of issues.

Government is intended to provide services that would otherwise be impractical for individuals to provide, such as police and fire protection, wildlife preserves, national defense, transportation systems, justice systems, social programs, and national museums. The problems and pressures of society increasingly strain the machinery of government.

As the needs of society have expanded in scope and complexity, government at all levels has also grown. Now some see government as no longer an extension of the people, but as rather an adversary, or "big brother." A labyrinth of bureaus, offices, departments, agencies, divisions, authorities, commissions, councils, boards, and committees has developed. Millions of tons of forms and reports are generated annually, most containing technical terms and jargon that inhibit many citizens' understanding and confidence in working with government effectively.

Much of the expansion of government can be attributed to two basic trends in America. First, increased population, social movements, business and economic activity, and technology have created new problems and issues that require regulatory attention. A few examples include the actions of the Federal Communications Commission, Food and Drug Administration, Immigration and Naturalization Service, Federal Trade Commission, Department of Transportation, state health departments, local zoning boards, and many other agencies created to address increasing complexities of modern society.

Second, U.S. citizens have increasingly grown to expect more from all levels of government. What may start as an off-handed remark such as, "There ought to be a law against that!" often leads not just to new regulations but to agencies set up to ensure that new laws are obeyed. In the simpler times of our agrarian past, neighbors often worked together to build community projects, families were extended to include elderly grandparents, and food was grown locally. Today, government is viewed more than ever as the primary mechanism to address injustices and inequities in virtually all human activities, from the bedroom to outer space.

As a result, government at all levels has grown to heretofore unimagined proportions. In state and local government, the growth rate for the number of employees has increased faster than the rate of population growth. New York City added 76,000 employees to the payroll from 1980 to 1990, bringing the total to 395,000, an increase of 24 percent. During that same time, New York City's population grew by only 3.5 percent. In some cities, such as Washington, D.C., the number of government employees increased to about 48,000 while the population actually decreased. Nearly 4.5 million people are employed by state governments in the United States. California, the largest state employer, maintains a payroll of 325,000 people, and other states are not very far behind. Reporting on the "shrink-proof bureaucracy," journalist Jonathan Walters concluded that the number of employees is only one aspect of the problem of dealing with government:

> A further complication is the intricate system of job classification within civil service. New York State has 7,300 different job categories for its 285,000 state employees. Iowa has 1,254 different job titles for 44,000 employees; of those job titles, 364 apply to positions held by one individual. Under Florida's current civil service system, there are 23 categories of administrative assistant, none interchangeable.[1]

As government becomes more complex and ubiquitous, the challenge of maintaining citizen involvement and ensuring that government is responsive to societal needs becomes more difficult. Elected officials often claim credit for their election on their ability to keep a finger on the pulse of constituents. However, because of the sheer magnitude and complexity of the job, most of that responsibility falls to government public relations specialists.

The complexity of public relations work is most apparent in local government. This level is closest to its constituents, both in the services it provides and in the accessibility of elected and appointed officials. However, it is often subject to the actions of higher levels of government. For example, in 1992, Danville, Virginia, spent 40 percent of its budget on meeting mandates from the state and federal governments. These mandates passed down to local government frequently cause problems in funding and affect citizens directly.[2]

One example is storm water management regulations that require localities to remove pollutants from rainwater runoff before it enters rivers or lakes. The cost of containing and treating rainwater is enormous, and local government must collect the taxes or fees to pay for the program. As a result, local officials must administer a program they may have not requested or even supported.

Government public relations activities, many embraced by terms such as *public affairs* and *public information*, have developed as a political and administrative response to achieve various organizational goals.

They are a key component of the administrative system, specifically designed to bridge the gap between popular and bureaucratic government. The number of people employed as government public relations practitioners is difficult to pinpoint because of varying job titles and the reluctance of some government agencies to acknowledge the function's existence. Too often this vital part of the government process is referred to as "just PR," "publicity budgets," "propaganda machines," or "spin doctors."

The National Association of Government Communicators estimated in 1992 that there were about 40,000 government communicators in the United States at all levels of government.[3] In Washington, D.C., alone, CBS News identified almost 11,000 public affairs specialists working in federal agencies.[4] However, difficult economic conditions often affect the size of public relations staffs. The recession of the early 1990s brought with it government cutbacks in many areas, including government public relations. In Georgia in 1991, 29 of the 40 communication specialists in the state's Cooperative Extension Service lost their jobs, and the Arizona State Extension Service eliminated its entire communication staff. Other similar instances showed that government policy-makers often view public relations as a "soft" service that can be cut more easily than the core services such as police protection, road building, and human services. In response, National Association of Government Communicators President Russell Forte wrote to the governors of every state emphasizing the importance of maintaining the public information function in government:

> When we cut back on communication offices and staff, we dilute the ability to provide the flow of information Americans need to make basic decisions for this country. In the end, the public does make the basic decisions that guide our governments. With inadequate information, those decisions are sometimes off target, wasteful and disruptive.[5]

Often, but certainly not always, government public relations programs deal with one-way communication directed to constituents. However, when viewed this way by policy makers, whether in government or in the private sector, the perceived impact of cutting public relations budgets is reduced to making publics themselves more responsible for obtaining information about the organization. When budgets get tight, this is a regrettable but acceptable consequence for many government leaders. For example, a California legislator apparently was serious when he proposed in 1993 a bill that would have eliminated all public affairs and public information specialists in state government "to eliminate waste." However, even when the full benefit of public relations is not realized and the function is seen as only public information, it nevertheless serves a vital function in government. In *Communicating for Results in Government*, James L. Garnett discussed the importance of straightforward communication with citizens:

Whether a government job is primarily managerial or technical, involves preparing budgets or analyzing educational progress, or is routine or nonroutine, effective communication is crucial to solid performance. Yet communication is not important for its own sake. As with planning, budgeting, program evaluation, and other managerial tools, communication is important because it affects people's control over government. It influences employee morale and productivity and permeates all facets of government. Because government decisions and actions often affect more people and with greater consequences, communicating in government tends to be more important and often more difficult than communicating in business.[6]

Specific public relations objectives will vary from agency to agency, but the basic justification for government public relations rests on two fundamental premises: (1) that a democratic government must report its activities to the citizens and (2) that effective government administration requires active citizen participation and support. Even the staunchest critics of "government propaganda" concede that the first justification is a valid one. However, effective government administration is sometimes construed by critics to mean protection of the bureaucracy at all costs.

Overall goals for government public relations programs, regardless of the level of government, have at least three things in common:

1. Informing constituents about the activities of the government agency;
2. Ensuring active cooperation in government programs (for example, voting, curbside recycling), as well as compliance in regulatory programs (for example, mandatory seat belt use, antismoking ordinances); and
3. Fostering citizen support for established policies and programs (for example, foreign aid, welfare). (See Figure 15–1 for examples of program materials.)

MAINTAINING AN INFORMED CITIZENRY

The primary job of government public relations practitioners is to inform. A multitude of other roles and responsibilities are assigned to specific government practitioners, many of enormous importance and scope, but ensuring the constant flow of information to persons outside and inside government is, generally speaking, the top priority. The information task is global, as the need to inform extends well beyond U.S. borders.

United States Information Agency (USIA)

The United States Information Agency coordinates America's informational and educational efforts in more than 120 countries. It also inter-

Examples of City Public Public Relations Materials

Figure 15–1

Courtesy City of Chesapeake, VA.

prets public opinion overseas and provides analysis and feedback to the federal government. USIA, an independent agency within the executive branch, reports directly to the president. It is perhaps best known for its radio broadcast network, Voice of America, which began in World War II and was responsible for providing information to American troops and citizens in war areas. In addition, USIA operates Worldnet, a satellite television service, and various other programs and services.

Overseas, USIA is known as the United States Information Service, or USIS. In American embassies, the chief USIS officials are the public affairs officers. They advise ambassadors and other diplomats on relevant public relations issues affecting U.S. interests and policy and on embassy operations and relationships within host countries. President Jimmy Carter said that the USIA role is to "build two-way bridges of understanding between our people and the other peoples of the world."

A vital responsibility of USIA is to correct information or to counter adverse propaganda that might have a detrimental effect on the United States. For example, in the early 1980s, USIA had to respond aggressively to a story planted by the Nigerian press claiming that the United States was developing a weapon that would kill blacks but not whites.[7]

It remains to be seen how the end of the Cold War between the United States and the former Soviet Union will affect USIA. Since World War II, the United States has been concerned with the problems of international communication, particularly in getting the people of other nations to understand America's foreign policy motives and goals. USIA has the responsibility of presenting to the world "a full and fair picture" of the United States. America's overseas public relations program has had two main goals: (1) countering divisive propaganda disseminated by hostile nations and fostering in other countries a fuller and friendlier understanding of American policies and (2) making technical knowledge available to assist developing countries.

More than once, the agency has been subjected to philosophical debates concerning its role overseas in advancing foreign policy objectives that resulted in reorganization and restructuring. The agency often suffers from a "split personality" as it attempts to maintain credibility abroad through objective reporting while dealing with domestic political demands to disseminate persuasive or even biased, unbalanced information. The philosophy of the organization is best summarized in the Voice of America charter written into Public Law 94-350 and signed by President Gerald Ford in July 1976:

1. VOA news will be accurate, objective, and comprehensive.
2. VOA will present a balanced and comprehensive projection of significant American thought and institutions.
3. VOA will present the policies of the United States clearly and effectively.[8]

To achieve its purposes, USIA employs more than 8500 specialists. In addition to personal contact, the agency uses print media, radio, television, film, libraries, books, the arts, and exhibits to communicate the

U.S. message abroad. To facilitate two-way communication, agency programs include cultural and educational exchanges of scholars, journalists, students, and cultural groups around the world.

Citizen Participation

An important but often overlooked responsibility of government practitioners is soliciting and motivating involvement of citizens in government, including decision-making processes. Often the major obstacle is internal, as elected officials and administrators may be reluctant to have their carefully formulated plans altered by the multitude of interests and viewpoints citizen involvement inevitably generates. Writing in *Policy Studies Review*, Mary Kweit and Robert Kweit discussed the trade-offs inherent in encouraging citizen input:

> In the ideal bureaucracy there is no place for citizen participation. Citizens lack the technical expertise, are unfamiliar with bureaucratic routines, and are emotionally involved in issues rather than being detached and rational. Citizens are outside the hierarchy and therefore hard to control. As a consequence, participation may increase the time needed to reach decisions as well as the level of conflict.[9]

Public involvement typically slows and complicates the process, but it nonetheless increases government responsiveness. Bill Davis advises city administrators:

> Often the best advice on both problems and solutions comes from those within the community who are most affected. Viewing a neighborhood, or a group of people as "the problem" is almost always a mistake, but it is never an error to view them as essential to "the solution."[10]

Scientific surveys of citizens are increasingly used in government. Politicians, especially those running for national office, have long relied on the Roper and Gallup polls, as well as privately commissioned surveys, for guidance in formulating campaign strategies. More recently citizen surveys have been used for identifying priorities for government. In addition, surveys are being used as the bottom line for government, whereby citizens' ratings of various services are the barometer of organizational success. In some cases, citizens' ratings have been directly tied to employees' performance and their salary increases.

When used to set goals and priorities, citizen surveys prove to be an equalizer against well-funded special interests and lobbying groups. "The greatest strength of citizen surveys is that they have the potential to sample the viewpoints of all citizens—not simply those who choose to participate."[11] Conducting surveys of citizens can prove counterproductive when not properly administered. For example, surveys that ask citizens to answer questions on subjects they have little or no knowledge about, such as how best to design a major highway or how to solve complex financial problems facing government, can have negative results.

> A second serious problem with citizen surveys is that they can have some serious political repercussions. The public may express a negative view of whatever services are dutifully provided. Pressures may develop to enact whatever recommendations the public might suggest. And then, apart from the issues of effectiveness and political advisability, there is always the issue of cost. With budgets getting ever tighter, a citizen survey might easily seem like an unnecessary frill. The costs could be particularly onerous to small governments.[12]

Surveys also provide only a snapshot in time of public opinion. This is clearly evident prior to nearly every presidential election, when polls show drastic changes in voters' preferences in response to events such as national conventions and domestic or international crises. Surveys take on greater credibility the more often they are repeated, allowing trends to be charted and previous findings to be validated.

Increasing involvement in programs and activities leads many government practitioners to use other tools and tactics often identical to private public relations and advertising firms. Products and services are "sold" whether they are free or user fee-supported, voluntary or mandatory.

For example, in 1991 Hampton, Virginia, faced escalating costs of garbage disposal, inadequate landfill space, and new state requirements for recycling. The city council appointed a citizen group to work with city staff in developing a plan to address these problems, a key part of which was a public relations program that would lead to at least 80 percent of eligible households participating in the curbside recycling program. The process began with primary and secondary research, including a random sample telephone survey of residents to identify current behaviors and attitudes toward recycling, a review of the most successful curbside recycling programs in the nation, and studies of theories relating to acceptance of new ideas and strategies proven effective with environmentally conscious consumers.

The city used various strategies to approach the problem from several perspectives. Two of the city's environmental commissions that were previously at odds with each other, the Clean City Commission and the Solid Waste Commission, were convinced to join forces. The city, in cooperation with the Hampton Roads Chapter of the Public Relations Society of America, produced television and radio public service announcements to emphasize the regional nature of the campaign, thereby generating maximum air time through regional broadcast media. Printed material, newspaper ads, a speakers' bureau, special events, recycling resource

"Ralphy Recycler" Program Materials

Figure 15–2

Courtesy June McPartland, City of Hampton, VA.

kits for schoolteachers and other vehicles promoted the theme, "Recycling Makes You Feel Good." "Ralphy Recycler," a friendly, green character, made the campaign message more memorable (see Figure 15–2). Volunteers produced and wore Ralphy costumes at various events, and this image appeared on stickers, advertisements, and fliers.

Results of the campaign were impressive. Research had shown that appealing to children was one of the best and quickest ways to encourage new habits to protect the environment, and this was confirmed in the resulting high recycling participation rates in homes with children. The goal of 80 percent overall participation in curbside recycling was surpassed by 10 percent, and Hampton achieved the highest participation rate of any city in the region. The success of the campaign and the process used to achieve the results were recognized nationally when the city's public relations staff was awarded the Silver Anvil award by the Public Relations Society of America.[13]

BARRIERS TO EFFECTIVE GOVERNMENT PUBLIC RELATIONS

Public relations practitioners in government shape much of the meaningful dialogue necessary to make democracy work. Their work carries with it a civic obligation to serve as intermediaries between elected officials and staff and their citizen constituencies. Yet the work of building and maintaining government and citizen relationships is hampered by two major factors: public apathy and legislative hostility.

Public Apathy

Unlike most business operations, it is usually not possible for government practitioners to target small segments of broad publics to achieve desired results and to ignore the rest of the people. An automobile manufacturer, for example, may be satisfied with achieving success with 10 or 20 percent of the car-buying adults in the country. Government seeks to serve all taxpayers, or at least as great a portion as possible. This is an extremely difficult task, made nearly impossible because of the lack of interest among many citizens.

Public apathy is an indisputable fact of public life. The percentage of eligible voters who participate in major national elections is invariably low, and the percentage of those voting in state and local elections is even lower. Even in large- and midsized cities, candidates are often elected by slim margins. Only 50 percent of adult Americans voted in the 1988 presidential election, and only 36 percent voted in 1990 elections. One writer said that public apathy is a "ground swell" among Americans:

> The hard fact is that most Americans are contemptuous of politicians and cynical about the motives of government and business. The U.S. now ranks 23rd in voter participation among Western democracies, and the share of adults who vote in presidential elections has dropped 20 percent since 1960.[14]

Voter turnout did rise slightly in the 1992 presidential election, to just over 55 percent. Voter interest increased because of a severe economic recession, increasing discontent with government gridlock, and the emergence of H. Ross Perot as a national political figure.

> Thanks in part to Perot, the 1992 campaign saw forms of communication develop between candidates and voters that aroused widespread interest. Perot had his town meetings and "infomercials." Clinton played his saxophone on "The Arsenio Hall Show" and toured the country by bus. Bush took to the train. All three candidates appeared on Larry King's TV talk show, and one of the presidential debates featured audience questions.[15]

Political author Ruy A. Teixeira also credits the increase to the news media's focus more on issues and less on negative campaign tactics. But like many other political commentators, he is only cautiously optimistic about future voter turnout:

> Thus, while we should take heart from the 1992 election results— turnout can go up, not just down—much remains to be done. Absent a combination of substantial registration and political reforms, turnout is unlikely to rise much above its level in 1992 and may even fall again.[16]

City councils, county boards of supervisors, citizen advisory boards, and commissions all struggle with apathy each time a public hearing is scheduled, frequently cutting meetings short when few, if any, citizens show up to voice an opinion. Local government agencies who appoint citizens to serve on advisory boards often have woefully few candidates from which to choose.

Lack of interest and a basic knowledge of government is not new, however. The *New York Times* reported in 1989 that Americans' "factual knowledge about civics and politics has improved only marginally in the past 40 years, and many Americans still lack basic knowledge of the country's political system."[17] This conclusion was based on the results of a survey conducted in 1989 by the Survey Research Laboratory of Virginia Commonwealth University that found, among other things, that only 25 percent of those surveyed could name the two U.S. senators representing their state and only 46 percent knew that the first ten amendments to the Constitution are called the Bill of Rights.[18]

Despite its unique role and responsibilities in the American system of checks and balances, the explosion of news media, talk shows, public affairs programs, and special-interest publications has done little to make Americans better informed about government. Commenting on the performance of the broadcast media during political campaigns, Bernard Shaw, anchor of Cable News Network, refused to blame the media for the lack of interest among citizens:

> The juice of a democracy is information, and that is what we [the news media] are about. One of the reasons journalists do not point out what we do, especially what we do successfully—we all have PR departments that specialize in that—is we feel that it is self-serving. We feel we are there to serve the people. I would like to turn the mirror around and say that just as we have a responsibility in our democracy, the American people have a responsibility. And when you consider that at least 73 to 75 percent get our information from television, we know instantly that most Americans are underinformed.[19]

At the local level, many citizens simply do not know much about their government. For example, in surveys conducted by the city of Chesapeake, Virginia, in 1991, only 14 percent of heads of households even knew how many members there were on the locally elected city council (nine). And in 1992, only 13 percent knew that the city had a storm water management program for which each household would be billed, even though there had been considerable public discussion over many months.[20]

Lydia Bjornlund, citizenship education coordinator for the International City Management Association, stated:

> Government leaders are aware of the frustrations of dealing with an apathetic and poorly educated citizenry. Many have been confronted by irate citizens who do not understand the issue, the problem, the reasons behind unpopular decisions. Officials at one level of government are blamed for policies enacted at another. Citizens vote down government proposals in referenda because they do not understand the proposed actions or the alternatives. And, too often, citizens are shaken from their apathy only when a problem directly affects them.[21]

Contributing to public apathy are citizen frustration and a general sense of impotence toward government at all levels. Correct or not, the popular perception of government is one of gridlock, a maze of red tape, special interests, corruption, ineptitude, and partisan politics. A law degree is virtually a prerequisite for elected officials at the federal and state levels. The system has grown too complicated for most citizens either to understand or to gain access to services easily. Despite the annual rhetoric calling for simplifying the filing of personal income tax forms, millions of Americans must seek the assistance of accountants and tax-preparation experts. Adding a simple room or a back porch to a home often requires the help of an architect or development consultant to ensure that proper permits are acquired and that no environmental regulations are violated.

Citizen frustration found an outlet in the 1992 presidential campaign. Polls revealed that the cavalier, unaffiliated Texas tycoon H. Ross Perot at times led both incumbent President George Bush and Democratic challenger Bill Clinton in the race for the White House. Party loyalty and identification with a particular political platform became secondary for many Americans who saw in Perot a chance to flush out the system, cut some red tape, and inject a Texas-size dose of common sense into a bureaucracy smothering itself and ignoring the public it was designed to serve. Unrealistic or not, even the possibility of such actions drove millions of Americans to abandon, at least temporarily, the two-party system that they viewed as no longer responsive to the people.

As the American population became older and better educated, some predicted that voter participation in general would increase; however, this has not occurred. Despite advances in media and communication, an increasing number of young, poor, and uneducated citizens have become less active than in previous generations:

> They no longer believe their votes have an effect on government. Vietnam, Watergate, a huge federal deficit, and the savings-and-loan nightmare have convinced many Americans that politicians make promises only to break them.[22]

Legislative Hostility to the Function

The public relations function has been established longer in government than in any other field of practice, yet it has never been totally effective or given the respect enjoyed by practitioners in the private sector. *In government, as in other organizational settings, public relations is a legitimate management function that helps make agencies, departments, and other public entities responsive to the citizens they were created to serve.* However, government practitioners often face more hostility and suspicion than do other practitioners. This hostility stems from four fundamental and long-standing conflicts of interest embedded in our democratic government:

1. The continuing struggle between the press, fighting for "the people's right to know," and the officials of government, who insist upon discretion in certain sensitive areas of the public business.
2. The unrelenting struggle for balance of power between the legislative and executive branches of government. This contest is present whether it is between mayor and council, governor and legislature, or president and Congress.

3. The continuing struggle for power between the major political parties. The "out" party fears the power of an army of "propagandists" in keeping the "ins" in and the "outs" out.

4. The protests of industries, institutions, and other vested interests when threatened by proposed legislation or government regulation. They often disparage the use of public funds and government machinery to carry the day against them.

Beyond these conflicts is the inevitable association of government information programs with the word *propaganda*. Americans have long been deeply suspicious of anything with that label, particularly so since this powerful technique has been used in other countries to gain and hold despotic control. Thus public suspicion of information as "nothing but propaganda" is especially strong when the information comes from the government. This is reflected in a fear that government communication could become little more than tax-supported propaganda designed to persuade taxpayers to spend even more tax dollars.

Also involved in this opposition is the double standard that many citizens have for government and for private enterprise. The public generally accepts the propriety of business to publicize and advertise even though the customer pays for it. On the other hand, many people regard government information work as a waste of tax dollars; they see no need for government to sell itself or its products and services. There is no way of telling just how deep-seated and widespread this citizen attitude is, but some politicians think that they win votes when they flay "government propaganda."

The public relations function in government has been handicapped by the opposition of legislators, which prevents maximum effectiveness and accurate accounting of the function's cost and performance. Attacks on public relations by legislators are less frequent than those by the press, but perhaps more damaging.

Legislative opposition is often stimulated by other sources of hostility. At the turn of the nineteenth century, the Roosevelt-Pinchot campaign for land conservation sparked congressional reaction, thanks in large part to the efforts of spokespersons of lumber interests, mine operators, and cattle grazers who had been exploiting the nation's public lands. Congressman Franklin Mondell of Wyoming, spokesman for sheep and cattle ranchers, won adoption in 1908 of an amendment to the agricultural appropriation bill dealing with the Forest Service, which read:

> That no part of this appropriation shall be paid or used for the purpose of paying for in whole or in part the preparation of any newspaper or magazine articles.[23]

Thus the first effective use of public relations to promote acceptance of an administration's policies brought congressional restriction of the function in the executive branch.

Congressional ire next erupted in 1910, when Joseph T. Robinson, representative from Arkansas, demanded an investigation of the Census Bureau for employing a special agent at $8 per day in 1909. The agent was to explain to the public the purpose of the 1910 census. Census Bureau Director E. Dana Durand insisted that it was essential, if the census was to be complete, that all citizens and aliens be reached— through newspapers, the foreign-language press, and agricultural weeklies—and be assured that their replies would not be used for taxation purposes. The committee, after hearing this, tacitly approved.

By 1912 the number of "publicity agents" employed by executive departments was growing, and some campaigns were not beyond reproach. In May 1912, Congressman John Nelson of Wisconsin gained passage of a House resolution to investigate meat inspection in the Department of Agriculture's Bureau of Animal Industry. Early in the hearings, Nelson was angered by a circular criticizing the resolution and defending the department; the pamphlet had been published before the hearings opened. He charged that the department was using publicity to discredit one of its accusers, and he introduced a House resolution to investigate "the expenditure of public moneys for press bureaus, postage, stationery, and employees by the Department of Agriculture and by other departments; and that said committee be directed to make recommendations to the House as to what steps are necessary to protect public funds from newspaper exploitations."[24] The resolution did not pass.

A year later the Civil Service Commission advertised for "a press agent to help boom the good roads movement" in the Office of Public Roads. The circular called for a "publicity expert" whose "affiliations with newspaper publishers and writers is extensive enough to secure publication of items prepared by him." The circular prompted Representative Frederick H. Gillette to offer an amendment to an appropriations bill specifying that no money could be spent for publicity unless specifically authorized by Congress. It passed.

The 1913 Gillette Amendment remains embedded in law and the source of much confusion. As one government public affairs officer explained: "The amendment does not prohibit the use of publicity; it merely states that such funds be clearly identified." He went on to say that the 1913 amendment continues to intimidate those who work in government public relations.[25]

The Gillette Amendment is only one of six restrictions on the function that have been written into U.S. codes. These laws cloud and confuse the practice in the federal government:

1. An act of Congress, passed in 1913, forbids spending for "publicity experts" any part of an appropriation unless that money is specifically appropriated by Congress (38, U.S.C. 3107).

2. The "gag law" of July 11, 1919, prohibits using any part of an appropriation for services, messages, or publications designed to influence any member of Congress in his or her attitude toward legislation or appropriations (18, U.S.C. 1913).

3. Another law passed in 1919, but not strictly enforced until 1936, requires that all duplicating of material, including multilith and multigraph, must be done by the Government Printing Office, or at least farmed back to the department for reproduction by the GPO (44, U.S.C. 501).

4. Restrictions on the privilege of executive departments and independent establishments in the use of the free-mail frank prohibit executive departments from mailing material without a request (Title 39, U.S.C.A. Sec 321n).

5. No part of any appropriation contained in Public Law 92-351 or any other act, or of the funds available for expenditure by a corporation or agency, shall be used for publicity or propaganda purposes designed to support or defeat legislation pending before the Congress (Pub. Law 92-351, Sec. 608 [a], enacted July 13, 1972).

6. No part of any appropriation contained in Public Law 93-50 or any other act, or of the funds available for expenditure by any corporation or agency, shall be used, other than for normal and recognized executive-legislative relationships, for publicity or propaganda purposes, for the preparation, distribution, or use of any kit, pamphlet, booklet, publication, radio, television, or film presentation designed to support or defeat legislation pending before the Congress, except for the presentation to Congress itself (Pub. Law 93-50, Sec. 305, enacted July 1, 1973).[26]

Legislative opposition to the function at all levels has led to legal restrictions, circumvention of budgetary procedures, and wasteful practices designed to conceal legitimate government functioning. Legislative hostility and self-serving posturing by elected and appointed officials also causes many competent professionals to shy away from government service.

GOVERNMENT-MEDIA RELATIONS

Since the very beginning of American government, the First Amendment to the Constitution has guaranteed freedom of the press. This freedom was vital to the founders of the new nation, so much so that Thomas Jefferson said, "Were it left to me to decide whether we should have a government without newspapers or newspapers without government, I should not hesitate a moment to prefer the latter."

Media Access to Government

In more recent times, the constitutional freedoms guaranteed to the press have been expanded and clarified. Access to government information, in addition to the freedom to speak out or write freely about government, has been codified in freedom of information legislation, or "sunshine laws." Except for well-defined areas, such as national security, litigation, certain personnel records, and so forth, virtually every piece of information maintained by government is open to inspection by the press, and by the public for that matter. In most cases, a reporter can demand to see unfinished drafts of reports and handwritten notes if the reporter has specific knowledge of these and can request them with adequate specificity.

The right of access to government information and meetings is of paramount importance. Beyond just informing citizens about the official actions of government, the indispensable role of the press as the watchdog of government helps guarantee accountability, reduce corruption, and crystallize public issues and opinions, and it places the press in the position of being the citizen's representative in the broad system of checks and balances. Almost by definition, government-press relationships are adversarial. Government frequently argues that any large organization is more effective if it has a degree of privacy in formulating strategies. For example, in labor and contract negotiations or the purchase of land, privacy is needed to avoid giving the other side, who is often exempt from freedom of information laws, an unfair advantage. The press counters that the public's business should be conducted in the open to ensure that all activities are conducted ethically and in the public interest.

Many attribute the strained relations between reporters and government officials to events surrounding the Watergate scandal of the mid-1970s. President Richard Nixon was openly hostile to reporters and made it as difficult as possible for them to obtain information about his administration. Others argue that *Washington Post* reporters Bob Woodward and Carl Bernstein, who were in large part responsible for the resignation of Nixon, marked a drastic change in journalism's approach to government reporting. Several government officials were exposed as ruthless, Machiavellian, and at times, liars. Although the Justice Department and the FBI were responsible of uncovering the majority of information about the break-in of the National Democratic Party's headquarters, the news media affirmed their role as the guardian of the public trust.

Years later, the historic events referred to as Watergate serve as a reminder and a model to reporters of what might be lurking behind the doors of city halls, state capitols, and the halls of Washington. The ultimate effect of the Watergate scandal is still debated, and in the last few decades Watergate is only one of the many factors affecting the press' and the public's perception of government. Michael Schudson observed in the *Columbia Journalism Review*:

Did Watergate lead to an increase in investigative reporting? This depends on what investigative reporting is. Of course, Watergate was not the beginning of the adversarial relationship between the government and the Washington press corps. The key event was Vietnam, not Watergate, and the "credibility gap" that drew the press toward deep distrust of government voices first came to a head in Johnson's administration, not Nixon's.[27]

Competition among news organizations has intensified, and many seem to be searching for the next Watergate. However, by the time Ronald Reagan became president, the emphasis on investigative reporting had lessened, and "the relationship between public officials and the press in Washington is, for the most part, comfortable and cooperative."[28] Nevertheless, from city halls to Capitol Hill, reporters and government communicators today continue to work together in a volatile environment of caution and, in many cases, mutual distrust about each other's motives and tactics. Journalists criticize public officials for not being candid and honest in public statements; government officials point to the press' habit of looking only for what government is doing wrong, and they condemn reporters for their lack of knowledge in the areas they cover and for their lack of simple objectivity. Christopher Lasch, writing in the *Gannett Center Journal*, counters that the press is, in fact, too unbiased in government coverage:

> The job of the press is to encourage debate, not to supply the public with information. But as things now stand the press generates information in abundance, and nobody pays any attention. It is no secret that the public knows less about public affairs than it used to know. Millions of Americans cannot begin to tell you what is in the Bill of Rights, what Congress does, what the Constitution says about the powers of the presidency, how the party system emerged or how it operates. A sizable majority, according to a recent survey, believe that Israel is an Arab nation. . . . But since the public no longer participates in debates on national issues, it has no reason to be better informed.[29]

Government Dependence on Media

The relationship between journalists and government is simultaneously an unquestioned necessity and an obstacle to government communication with citizens. A shortage of media attention is rare, but it usually comes when government agencies want it least. Mark Hughes, public information officer for the city of Phoenix, describes media attention as unrelenting: "We get shelled on a daily basis. We have four full-time reporters who spend eight hours a day trying to catch us screwing up."[30] But when government needs to just "get the word out" on routine issues, the news media are often only mildly interested.

During the economic recession of the early 1990s, all levels of government became desperate to communicate to their constituents the ways they were attempting to deal with shrinking revenues when public demand for services was still increasing. New concepts were being discussed to trim budgets, but news reports centered almost exclusively on the increasing deficits, government waste, deteriorating levels of service, and individual suffering brought on by government and industry layoffs. While government hoped to solicit active support and economic optimism from individuals and business, the news of the day provided a disincentive. Many in government felt that reporters were perhaps not interested in interpreting the events and factors influencing the actions and decision-making of government.

It is difficult for the average citizen, who must rely on the mass media to interpret events, to make heads or tails of these changes. Their substance is all but invisible, in part because they take place outside the glare of publicity that shines on Washington. They also stubbornly refuse to fit into the traditional liberal versus conservative categories through which the media views [sic] the world. Because most reporters are asked to provide instant analysis, they have little choice but to fall back on the tried and true lenses of past practice. And because their standard formula relies on conflict to sell a story, they look for heroes and villains rather than innovation and change. In the process, they inevitably miss much that is new and significant.[31]

The standards used by reporters and government communicators to define news are usually quite different. It is not surprising that much information considered by individual agencies to be of vital importance gets lost in the mountains of information generated by public relations staffs. Anne Groer, national correspondent for the *Orlando Sentinel* who is based in Washington, described the challenge of sorting through the barrage of publicity from just one government agency:

NASA led the hypesters with seven faxes, including three concerning personnel changes that I, personally, would have combined into one—except that I am not a government information specialist wedded to the notion that every GS-Whatever deserves his/her own release. . . . The one truly useful release announced an April 13 press conference to unveil a report from NASA's Aerospace Safety Advisory Panel, created after the horrific 1986 Challenger disaster. My colleague, Chris Reidy, covered the story, which went out on the Chicago Tribune-Knight Ridder wire and was picked up by several papers, including the *Washington Post*.[32]

In just five days, Groer had collected 228 pieces of printed matter weighing more than 16 pounds:

How many daily stories sprang directly from that pile? One.
How many long-range ideas or follow-up calls? Perhaps three.
How many pieces would we normally have saved for more
than a day or two? Maybe 20 out of the 228 pieces (which,
for all I know, is a terrific ratio).[33]

Despite the difficulties, government relies heavily on the press to pass on important information. And regardless of its use of brochures, speakers' bureaus, cable television, and many other methods of disseminating information, government's communication vehicles will never match the effectiveness of the privately owned mass media. Perhaps more important, the power of the press to set the agenda for public debate, while often under emphasized by reporters and editors, is unmistakable. "Everyone in politics turns to the press, if only to manipulate it or deflect it," asserts William Greider, former assistant managing editor of the *Washington Post*.[34]

> What matters to the press matters perforce to politicians. What the press ignores, the politicians may safely ignore too. What the newspapers tell people, whether it is true or false or cockeyed, is what everyone else must react to, since alternative channels of political information are now weak or nonexistent for most Americans.[35]

The news media do not have the resources to cover all that is the public's business in government. *First*, there are not enough journalists on all the news media payrolls to adequately track all the developments in the many agencies and activities at all levels of government. *Second*, there is a dominant set of news values that prefers and rewards the negative, controversial, and sensational aspects of government. Critics condemn the media for "elections by sound bites" and for an overemphasis of issues not relevant to the performance of government.

> Because government is seen as the "public's business," citizens as individuals or organized in interest groups justifiably deem it their right to know what government does. News media correspondingly consider it their duty to report on virtually every facet of government judged to be newsworthy because it involves politics, scandal, tax dollars, or simply the public interest. For these reasons, the decisions, thoughts, and even the life-styles of public officials and administrators are far more likely to receive public scrutiny than is the case for their business sector counterparts, Donald Trump notwithstanding.[36]

Public officials have grown more and more accustomed to living "life in the fishbowl."

> As for the private lives of public officials, adultery, drug dependency, abortion, mental health and sexual preferences are all potential news material. There are no longer any skeletons too personal to remain in the closet.[37]

Media Reporting on Government

The news media are grappling with the task of reporting government activities under the heavy hand of news values fashioned in frontier days and with too few reporters. In days gone by, news of government was a relatively simple matter of personalities, oratorical political campaigns, trust busting, and the like. It was entirely different from reporting government finance, world affairs, nuclear energy, mental health, space travel, controversies over issues affecting equal opportunity, the environment, and other complex subject matters. Interpreting the complexities of government requires trained specialists and often takes more time than news media deadlines permit. Hence, government public relations specialists play an essential role in working with journalists to communicate with citizens.

Much progress has been made by the media in government reporting. But the need for government to strengthen and supplement today's reporting by the media is greater than ever. Problems in the media coverage of federal government are not always the fault of either the media or individual journalists. Rather, shortcomings in coverage are due to the magnitude of the task, and the size of the job is staggering. Washington dominates the nation's news system. News organizations, write Grossman and Kumar, "have become one of the principal forces on the national political scene, influencing the other major forces—the President, Congress, the bureaucracy, the parties, and the pressure groups—and in turn being influenced by them."[38]

Many in government do not think that the media measure up to their task. David Brown asserted in 1976:

> On the reportorial side, I find the media have become society's follower, not leader. The media lack understanding of the complexity of government and dwell on exceptions, which all too often disguise the rule. The media tend to judge the nation's capital by the White House, The Congress, the State Department, and the Defense Department. These are but four of the some 200 Federal entities in Washington.[39]

Washington's dominance of government reporting often comes at the expense of state and local governments, thus making the job of state and municipal practitioners more difficult. Stephen Hess, an astute student of Washington journalism, observed: "Given the limits to the size of news holes, a rise in Washington stories presages a decline in news of municipal and state governments, most often the latter."[40]

MILITARY PUBLIC RELATIONS

The actions of the military have long been covered by news reporters, in times of both peace and war. For just as long, military leaders have attempted to limit the flow of information that could potentially benefit their adversaries. The conflict between reporters and the military can be traced at least as far back as the Civil War.

During the Civil War the horrors of war were vividly brought to the folks back home. Mathew Brady and his assistant Alexander Gardner documented major battles throughout the war. Brady's black wagon, which served as his darkroom, became a dreaded sight on the battlefield. Brady seemed to know where the action would be the heaviest, and soldiers soon learned that when Brady's wagon came on the scene, heavy fighting would likely follow. Brady took more than 3500 photographs of the war, and these had a profound impact on the civilian population of the day and the way that war in general was perceived.[41]

By the Vietnam War, same-day coverage had become the norm. The American people saw not only the consequences of war but could witness much of the actual fighting. As the popularity of the war decreased among many Americans at home, the pictures of burning villages and body bags fueled the growing antiwar sentiment. Extensive coverage of antiwar demonstrations on college campuses contributed to public distrust of U.S. involvement in the affairs of Southeast Asia and the escalating military actions. Military leaders who once criticized the press for potentially revealing sensitive information faced a new, more complex problem. News coverage was influencing public opinion against them, and many in the military viewed the media as adversaries set on undermining the entire war effort.

> Since Vietnam, when the military thought its conduct of the war had been impaired by negative media coverage, people in the Pentagon had been simmering, planning and talking. In sessions there and in the war and naval colleges, the issue of "handling" the media was widely discussed and carefully understood. While the military assessment of the media's role in Vietnam and other wars may have been wrong—some of the most critical reporters in Vietnam, for example, were hawks, not doves—there was nonetheless a determination to be ready for the next war not only in strictly military terms but also in terms of public opinion.[42]

In subsequent years, the military has placed much greater emphasis on preparing for dealing with the media in times of war. During the brief Grenada conflict in 1983, reporters were not allowed to cover the invasion as it began. Although members of the news media were highly critical of the military, national polls showed that most Americans did not share their outrage.

The news media's reporting of the Persian Gulf conflict in early 1991 was unlike anything previously experienced. According to H. J. (Jerry) Dalton, Jr., corporate public relations specialist and former Air Force brigadier general in charge of Air Force public affairs: "We are witnessing for the first time the phenomenon of live TV coverage of a

war. The problem is that there's absolutely no time to put the report in perspective and explain how it fits into the big picture."[43]

So immediate was the coverage that military leaders on both sides, including Iraqi leader Saddam Hussein, relied heavily on news reports—particularly that of Cable News Network (CNN)—to follow initial military activities as they occurred. And unlike previous military engagements, the military was well prepared for the onslaught of reporters, perhaps too well prepared, according to some reporters. Department of Defense Assistant Secretary for Public Affairs Pete Williams became a regular on the evening news as he was often the only authoritative source on events in the Persian Gulf (see Figure 15–4).

In 1992, 20 news organizations, including the Associated Press, the *Washington Post*, CNN, and others, proposed to the Pentagon a set of principles for wartime news coverage. The principles provided that public affairs officers should act as liaisons but should not interfere with the reporting process, journalists would be allowed to ride on military vehicles and aircraft whenever possible, and journalists will make every effort to assign experienced reporters to cover combat operations. Although many in government endorsed the principles, the Pentagon

MacNelly Cartoon of CNN Persian Gulf War Coverage

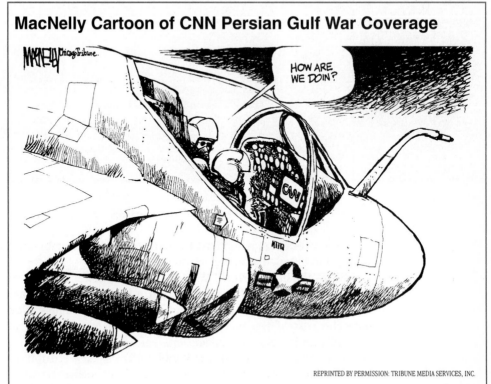

REPRINTED BY PERMISSION: TRIBUNE MEDIA SERVICES, INC.

Figure 15–3   Reprinted by permission: Tribune Media Services, Inc.

Assistant Secretary of Public Affairs, Pete Williams, Conducting Press Briefing in the Pentagon

Figure 15–4   Official Department of Defense photo. Used with permission.

insisted on retaining the right to review battlefield reports prior to their publication or release to reporting pools.[44]

Since the end of World War II, a key component of U.S. military policy has been based on the precept that a high state of military readiness is an effective deterrent to war, but only if that readiness is communicated to the rest of the world. To that end, an increasingly professional cadre of public relations specialists serves in every branch of the military, usually under the title of "public affairs" (see Exhibit 15–1.) Many of the enlisted "journalists" and public affairs officers trained for their public relations roles at the Defense Information School, Fort Benjamin Harrison, near Indianapolis, Indiana, or at universities offering undergraduate and graduate curricula in public relations and journalism.

EXHIBIT 15-1

PUBLIC RELATIONS, NAVY STYLE

Military public relations is no different from any other public relations, just our product is different. We use the same tools, we compete for the same news space, and we approach public relations problems in the same way as practitioners in the private sector do. The basic process is the same: research, planning, implementation, and evaluation.

There is a greater emphasis on internal audiences in the military. There is also a more complex organizational structure to deal with in the military, and more people are usually involved in addressing public relations issues. Often our activities are scrutinized by local, national, and international news organizations. The result is that doing public relations work in the military is often more demanding than in the private sector.

Today's environment requires a high degree of professionalism among military public affairs officers, including high ethical standards as well as a solid educational foundation. When I first entered the Navy, there were many excellent public affairs officers doing their jobs very effectively. However, most of them were former news reporters who had no formal public affairs training. The demands of the field today require professionals specifically trained in military public affairs. The Navy has tremendous respect for public relations as a discipline, and it takes a strong, aggressive approach to public affairs issues.

The military attracts more media attention than most other organizations. There are more military reporters than ever before, and many—if not most—have very little experience with military operations when they first come to us. It requires a constant educational process. During Vietnam and the Persian Gulf War, Americans had a war in their living rooms. Coverage of a crisis is virtually instantaneous. We have to be well prepared, and we have to act and react very quickly.

The primary goals of Navy public affairs are (1) keeping the American public informed about Navy operations in a timely, complete and accurate fashion; (2) coordinating Navy participation in special events and community affairs: and (3) supervising the Navy's internal communications activities. In addition, every public affairs officer—from the Chief of Information to the information officer on a ship—is constantly a part of the decision-making process. He or she is an indispensable member of the leadership team. When important decisions are made in the Navy, the public relations ramifications of those decisions are carefully considered in advance.

Rear Adm. Kendall Pease
Chief of Information
Department of the Navy

GOVERNMENT AS BUSINESS

Significant events in the early 1990s may have altered the basic philosophy of government for a long time to come. These included:

1. a serious economic recession, which caused nearly every government entity to tighten its belt;
2. the popularity of Texas businessman H. Ross Perot, who for several months of the 1992 presidential campaign captured Americans' attention by effectively asserting that government should be run more like a business; and
3. publication of perhaps the most widely read book ever on the subject of government management: *Reinventing Government: How the Entrepreneurial Spirit Is Transforming the Public Sector* by David Osborne and Ted Gaebler.

Osborne and Gaebler said that government needs to go back to square one, evaluate its basic goals, and establish concrete, achievable objectives. The cornerstone of their approach was integrating government management with the real needs of constituents effectively, and the authors asserted that much could be accomplished toward improving government's image among citizens through one-to-one contact. "The greatest irritant most people experience in their dealings with government is the arrogance of the bureaucracy. People today expect to be valued as customers—even by government."[45]

Osborne and Gaebler point out that unlike businesses, however, most public agencies do not get their funds from their clients or customers. Rather, funding decisions are made by city councils, legislatures, or elected boards. Agency heads, therefore, aim to please these bodies, not those they are designed to serve. Besides, their clients—unless they move to another city or state—have little choice for the services provided by government. Most businesses, on the other hand, must remain competitive and attempt to please their customers just to stay in business.[46]

Some see inherent similarities but important differences between government and business. According to the chief executive officer of Eugene, Oregon, Mike Gleason:

> First, these businesses are *owned by their customers*. Second, to that end, they must be operated in the light of day and in a democratic fashion. Third, in addition to producing products and services, as any private corporation would, they have major responsibilities regarding legislation.[47]

In several other aspects, government operates in a competitive, businesslike environment, and public relations plays a key role. States and cities launch massive promotional campaigns to attract tourists and conventions. Tourism is a relatively clean industry that brings millions

of dollars into communities. These dollars support local businesses, which in turn pay more taxes, and keep the general tax rates down for residents. For many communities, tourism is the key source of revenue. State and local governments also compete to attract new industry, thereby creating more jobs and opportunities for their residents and diversifying their tax base.

PUBLIC RELATIONS IN POLITICS

Early in his administration, President Bill Clinton recognized effective communication as essential to his proposals for reform in health care and foreign policy. Much to the surprise of many in his administration and party, in May 1993, President Clinton named an adviser to three Republican presidents and former *U.S. News and World Report* columnist David Gergen as top communication counselor in the White House.

> Both in his writings and by the trajectory of his career, Gergen perfectly embodies the polished figure of the Washington courtier— a man who seldom stays too late or says too much, who regards himself as "a facilitator," and who never confuses a stratagem with a conviction or an expedient policy with a passionate belief.[48]

Gergen's appointment was initially met with distrust by many Democrats and disbelief by many Republicans. Newspapers reported that some Republicans would no longer talk to Gergen and quoted a former associate as saying, "He doesn't have any particular principles. He just wants to be in power."[49] The appointment made clear, however, Clinton's view of how important effective communication and public relations counsel are to government effectiveness and to achieving his administration's goals.

Cynicism about public relations in government is greatest when associated with elected officials, or "politicians." Within an environment of skepticism, many view communication from elected officials as mere propaganda. Often many question when the work of government is purely politics and running for reelection.

For example, members of Congress use their franking privileges (free mailing) to communicate to their constituents back home. However, as one newspaper report illustrates, such communication can be an easy target for critics:

> You know that chatty newsletter your local congressman mails you? The one that leaves a lingering impression of how hard-working your federal representative has been over the past few months?

> Well, read it carefully, because you're paying for it.
>
> Last year, the 435 members of the House of Representatives spent
> $44 million on such mailings, says the National Taxpayer's Union.
> That's enough to buy 44 million school lunches for poor children. And
> it was all at taxpayers' expense.[50]

Voters decided in California in 1988 that many elected officials were taking advantage of their agencies' publications to gain recognition and popularity. Proposition 73 was aimed at limiting campaign contributions as well as prohibiting elected officials from using public funds to gain political advantage. Included in the new law was a provision that prohibited government agencies from mailing newsletters and other mass-produced publications if the publication included "the name, office, photograph, or other reference to an elected officer affiliated with the agency which produces or sends the mailing." The California Fair Political Practices Commission, the agency responsible for enforcement, later clarified the law to prohibit any publication that "features" an elected official. The term *features*, by their definition, "singles out the elected officer by the manner of display of his or her name or office in the layout of the document, such as by headlines, captions, type size, typeface, or type color."[51] Elected officials' photographs and signatures were also prohibited.

Leaders in both government and business share a concern about political interference:

> Government agencies are also more likely to experience intervention
> from political party officials, legislators, public interest groups, and
> other political actors than are typical business firms. While politics
> tends to be underrated as a force in business, it can hardly be over-
> rated as the dominant driving force in government agencies.[52]

In fact, politics and government cannot be separated. Likewise, the role of public relations in politics and government is inextricably interrelated. At no level of government is public relations more important than in our cities, where government provides schools, fire and police protection, safe streets and public transportation, recreation facilities and programs, housing, and a host of other vital services. Yet, even with cities in crisis, public relations has been slow to develop and is often the target of tax protesters and politicians looking for easy targets to exploit.

As the practice in government matures and becomes more professional, however, it has demonstrated its ability in making government more responsive to citizen needs and concerns, gaining acceptance of necessary programs, and making services widely available to those who need them. In short, the public relations function in government is increasingly recognized as an essential element of effective government.

**ADDITIONAL
READINGS**

Books, John W., and Charles L. Prysby.   *Political Behavior and the Local Context.* New York: Praeger, 1991. Scholarly review of research on politics, political information, and people in neighborhoods, counties, communities, and regions.

Brody, Richard A.   *Assessing the President: The Media, Elite Opinion and Public Support.* Stanford, Calif.: Stanford University Press, 1991. Correlates the results of public opinion polls on approval of the president with the cumulative effect of news coverage; the number of "good-results" stories versus the number of "bad-results" stories.

Kotler, Philip, Donald Haider, and Irving Rein.   *Marketing Places: Building a Future for Cities, States, and Nations.* New York: Free Press/Macmillan, 1993. Suggests that there is hope for places in crisis through strategic marketing approaches to economic renewal.

Pedersen, Wesley, ed.   *Leveraging State Government Relations.* Washington, D.C.: Public Affairs Council, 1990. Fifth in a series of handbooks published by the Public Affairs Council, this edition outlines the history of the public relations function in state government, organization and management of the function, dealings with elected officials and lobbyists, and grass-roots participation.

Pfau, Michael, and Henry C. Kenski.   *Attack Politics: Strategy and Defense.* New York: Praeger, 1990. Details how attack ads were used in political campaigns in the 1980s, as well as the results of two studies testing "inoculation" strategy to counter advertising messages that emphasized candidate weaknesses.

Yankelovich, Daniel.   *Coming to Public Judgment: Making Democracy Work in a Complex World.* Syracuse, N.Y.: Syracuse University Press, 1991. One of the leaders in public opinion polling discusses problems in how opinion polls are conducted and used, defines different levels of public opinion, and outlines steps for achieving resolution of issues in public debate.

NOTES

[1] Jonathan Walters,   "The Shrink-Proof Bureaucracy," *Governing* 5, no. 6 (March 1992): 36.

[2] Mayor F. Seward Anderson, City of Danville, Virginia, speaking to the Governor's Advisory Commission on the Dillon Rule and Local Government, Danville, Va., March 24, 1992, as quoted by Christine A. Everson in "Virginia Municipal League Letter," April 1, 1992.

[3] Robin Pan-Lener,   "There's Room to Grow," *Government Communications* (publication of the National Association of Government Communicators), March 1992, p. 3.

[4] "CBS Evening News," September 7, 1993, in a report by Erik Engberg in which he refers to the "Flack Attack" in the nation's capital.

[5] Russell Forte,   "More Communicators Get the Ax," *The Communicator* (October–November 1991): 3.

[6] James L. Garnett,   *Communicating for Results in Government* (San Francisco: Jossey-Bass, Inc., 1992), 14.

[7] Clinton L. Doggett and Lois T. Doggett,   *U.S. Information Agency* (New York, Chelsea House Publishers, 1989), 25.

[8] Robin Grey,   "Inside the Voice of America. Government Radio Has Gone to War—with the Soviets and with Itself," *Columbia Journalism Review* 21 (May/June 1982): 26.

[9]Mary Grisez Kweit and Robert W. Kweit, "The Politics of Policy Analysis: The Role of Citizen Participation in Analytic Decision Making," *Policy Studies Review* 3, no. 2 (February 1984): 32.

[10]Bill Davis, "Coping with Change: Communities Learn Keys to Effective Problem Solving," *Nation's Cities Weekly* 15, no. 25 (June 22, 1992): 5.

[11]Gregory Streib, "Dusting Off a Forgotten Management Tool: The Citizen Survey," *Public Management* 72, no. 7 (August 1990): 17.

[12]Ibid., 18.

[13]Information supplied by June McPartland, APR, director of Marketing and Communications, City of Hampton, Va.

[14]Mark D. Uebling, "All-American Apathy," *American Demographics* 13, no. 11 (November 1991): 30.

[15]Rhodes Cook, "'92 Voter Turnout: Apathy Stymied," *Congressional Quarterly Weekly Report* 51, no. 20, (May 15, 1993): 1258.

[16]Ruy A. Teixeira, "Turnout in the 1992 Election," *Brookings Review* 11, no. 2 (Spring 1993): 47.

[17]Michael R. Kagay, "Public's Knowledge of Civics Rises Only a Bit," *New York Times*, May 28, 1989, p. 31.

[18]Ibid.

[19]Bernard Shaw, comments made during "The Press and Politics," Joan Shorenstein Barone Center, New York, July 12, 1992.

[20]Figures from reports of citizen surveys conducted for the City of Chesapeake during November 1991 and November 1992 by Continental Research Associates, Inc., Norfolk, Va.

[21]Lydia Bjornlund, "Citizen Education," *Management Information Service Report* 23, no. 6 (June 1991): 2.

[22]Kagay, "Public's Knowledge," 33.

[23]*Congressional Record*, 60th Congress, House Rules Committee, 1st sess., 1908, vol. 42, p. 4137. Historical data provided by Felice Michaels Levin.

[24]U.S. Congress, House Rules Committee, *Hearing on H. Res 545 Department Press Agents*, 62nd Cong. 2d sess., 1912, pp. 3–4.

[25]David H. Brown, "Government Public Affairs—Its Own Worst Enemy," *Public Relations Quarterly* 26 (Spring 1981): 4.

[26]For debate on this measure, see *Congressional Record*, May 31, 1973, S10129–31.

[27]Michael Schudson, "Watergate: A Study in Mythology," *Columbia Journalism Review* 31, no. 1 (May/June 1992): 32.

[28]Ibid., 35.

[29]Christopher Lasch, "Journalism, Publicity and the Lost Art of Argument," *Gannett Center Journal* 4, no. 2 (Spring 1990): 1–2.

[30]Comments from workshop at PRSA 1991 national convention, "Handling Issues, Crises and Emergencies in Local Government," quoted in "At City Hall, Every Day's a Crisis," *Public Relations Journal* 48, no. 2 (February 1992): 7.

[31]David Osborne and Ted Gaebler, *Reinventing Government: How the Entrepreneurial Spirit Is Transforming the Public Sector* (Reading, Mass.: Addison-Wesley Publishing Company, 1992), 19.

[32]Anne Groer, "Paper Madness in Washington," *Gannett Center Journal* 4, no. 2 (Spring 1990): 72.

[33]Ibid., 80.

[34]William Greider,   *Who Will Tell the People: The Betrayal of American Democracy* (New York: Simon and Schuster, 1992), 299.

[35]Ibid., 287.

[36]Garnett,   *Communicating for Results,* 17.

[37]Judy Leon,   "The News Business: It's Not What It Used To Be and Neither Is Your Job," *Government Communications*, December 1991, p. 15.

[38]Michael Baruch Grossman and Martha Joynt Kumar,   *Portraying the President* (Baltimore: Johns Hopkins Press, 1981), p. 16. An insightful analysis of the relationship of political leadership and the power of the media.

[39]David Brown, in a speech to American Business Communicators Association, San Diego, Calif., December 30, 1976.

[40]Stephen Hess,   *The Washington Reporters* (Washington, D.C.: Brookings Institution, 1981), 133. Also see David Morgan, *The Capital Press Corps: Newsmen and the Governing of New York State* (Westport, Conn.: Greenwood Press, 1978).

[41]Edwin Emery,   *The Press and Americans: An Interpretive History of the Mass Media,* (Englewood Cliffs, N.J.: Prentice-Hall, Inc., 1972), 239.

[42]Everette E. Dennis,   "The Media at War: The Press and the Persian Gulf Conflict," conference report edited by Craig LaMay, Martha FitzSimon, and Jeanne Sahadi, Gannett Foundation Media Center, New York City, June 1991, p. 1.

[43]Adam Shell, ed.,   "Military PIOs Direct 'Theater' of War," *Public Relations Journal* 47, no. 3 (March 1991): 9.

[44]"Wartime News Coverage Guidelines Are Okayed," *O'Dwyer's Washington Report* 2, no. 10 (June 8, 1992): 4.

[45]Osborne and Gaebler,   *Reinventing Government,* 167.

[46]Ibid., 166–67.

[47]Mike Gleason,   "The Business of Government: Serving the Customer," *Nation's Cities Weekly* 15, no. 10 (March 9, 1992): 3.

[48]Lewis H. Lapham,   "Notebook: Cosmetic Surgery," *Harper's,* 287, no. 1719 (August 1993): 5.

[49]Michael Kranish (*Boston Globe*),   " 'Spin Doctor' Gergen in Never-Ending Whirl," *San Diego Union-Tribune*, August 14, 1993, pp. A1 and A20.

[50]Alex Marshall,   "Big spender: Pickett's Mailings Cost $205,000," *Virginian-Pilot*, April 1, 1992, p. D1.

[51]Information supplied by the League of California Cities in March 1990 letter to California city managers. Also see California Government Code Sections 82041.5 and 89001.

[52]Garnett,   *Communicating for Results,* 16.

CHAPTER 16

Nonprofit Organizations, Health Care, and Education

We've gotten a wake-up call from America. They want greater accountability.

ELAINE CHAO, PRESIDENT,
UNITED WAY OF AMERICA[1]

More so in the United States than in any other country, the "third sector"—an array of voluntary nonprofit organizations—assumes responsibility for providing many social, educational, cultural, and welfare services. In effect, it is the nonprofit sector that fills the gaps in meeting the needs of society left unattended by for-profit corporations and government agencies. As recognition of the role and importance of nonprofit organizations continues to grow, recent events have highlighted the need for effective public relations.

Charitable agencies within the nonprofit sector are still reeling from exposés in the early 1990s of six-figure executive salaries and charges of financial mismanagement and lavish spending. Ethics and accountability dominate hallway discussions, staff meetings, and convention programs. Public trust has eroded as a result of headlines about former United Way of America President William Aramony's $360,000 annual salary and lavish lifestyle and a spate of follow-up stories reporting that top executives in many nonprofit organizations make $100,000-plus salaries. Reform-minded critics call for more effective policing of charitable fund-raising and fuller disclosure of how nonprofit organizations spend their funds. Public relations is charged both with helping to rebuild credibility and

This chapter was written in collaboration with Kenneth G. Trester, APR, director, Office of Planning and Marketing, University of Michigan Medical Center, Ann Arbor, and Catherine J. Smillie, director of sales and marketing, MCARE, Inc., Ann Arbor.

with trying to restore public confidence in the many charitable agencies and voluntary groups that serve the needs of so many people.

The Clinton administration put health care reform at the top of the list of national domestic policy issues, with the goal that every person will have access to essential health care covered by comprehensive, government-regulated insurance programs. Health care reform became the hottest topic of national debate, resulting in increased scrutiny of health care costs and calls for increased accountability within the health care delivery system. Headlines and lead stories on the evening news keep health care at or near the top of the public agenda. Debates cover why health care costs so much; who will pay; who will be covered; what care will be available; and what are the roles of government, health insurance companies, health maintenance organizations (HMO), private hospitals, doctors, nurses, psychologists, and other care givers such as midwives and nurse practitioners. Talk shows feature politicians, executives of public health agencies, hospital administrators, doctors, insurance company executives, and representatives from too many special-interest groups and associations to list. Public relations plays a central role in shaping both the national agenda and health care reform.

Education reform closely follows health care reform on the public agenda, with questions about cost and quality also dominating public discussion and debate. Public concern and controversy almost caused a major change in California's educational system and public policy. For example, in the November 1993 general election, California voters defeated Proposition 174, the education vouchers initiative. "Prop 174" would have allowed parents to transfer tax dollars from public schools to qualifying private schools by using state-funded vouchers. Each child would qualify for a voucher, regardless of financial need. Parents would have the right to cash the vouchers at the school of their choice, public or private. Proponents said that ineffective, administratively bloated public schools would have to shape up to compete successfully for state funds in the new educational marketplace. Voucher critics said that the initiative would deplete an already financially strapped system and would lead to state subsidies of segregated, elitist private schools. Even though the ballot initiative failed, it spurred serious reassessment of the education system and served as a wake-up call for public schools across the country. Education administrators invited public relations specialists to join the management team and work more closely with the executive offices of school districts, colleges and universities, and educational associations. Educational reform was a real threat, or opportunity, depending on the views of top administrators in school systems.

In short, following an historic pattern, public relations is added, expanded, and elevated in stature when organizations are confronted by outside forces, threatened with funding cuts or outright elimination, or otherwise pressured to change or reform. The nonprofit sector faces all these in an environment of economic uncertainty, diminished government tax revenues, and increased demand for services.

As social and economic conditions require, and as the need for public support grows, public relations helps create the public policy environment, volunteer participation, and philanthropic support crucial to the survival of charitable organizations. (See Figure 16–1.) In other words, *the role of public relations in the nonprofit sector is to establish and maintain relationships necessary to secure the organizational autonomy and resources needed to achieve their humanitarian missions.*

Examples of a Small Community Hospital's Public Relations

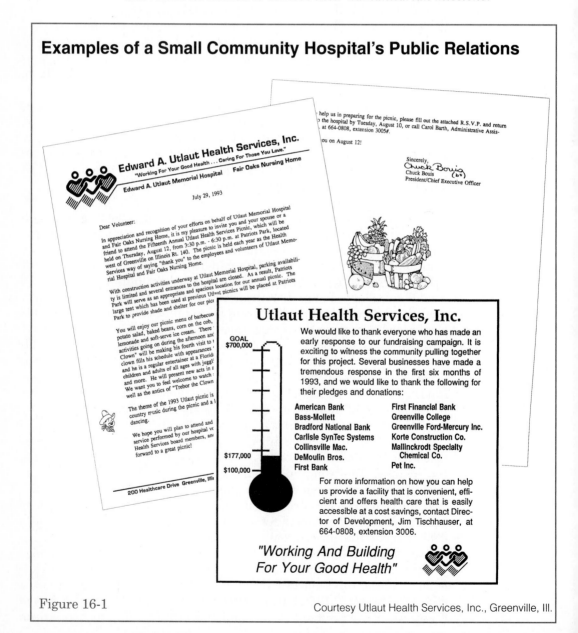

Figure 16-1

Courtesy Utlaut Health Services, Inc., Greenville, Ill.

THE ROLE OF PUBLIC RELATIONS IN NONPROFIT ORGANIZATIONS

Nonprofit organizations in different fields approach public relations programming with diverse tactics, but promoting public service and building public trust are common to all. Health care agencies, social welfare organizations, churches, educational institutions, or fine arts and performing arts groups all depend on public support. All are also caught in the conflicting crosscurrents of social, political, and economic trends that require managerial and public relations efforts of the highest order. There can be neither the intent nor appearance of "putting something past the public" or "getting the public off our backs."

To the contrary, public relations in most nonprofit agencies aims:

1. To gain acceptance of an organization's mission,
2. To develop channels of communication with those an organization serves,
3. To create and maintain a favorable climate for fund-raising,
4. To support the development and maintenance of public policy that is favorable to an organization's mission, and
5. To inform and motivate key organizational constituents (such as employees, volunteers, and trustees) to dedicate themselves and work productively in support of an organization's mission, goals, and objectives.

Whereas these missions are common to most nonprofit organizations, the tactical approach and level of sophistication of public relations practice differs greatly. Compared with other nonprofit organizations, for example, hospitals often invest relatively more net resources in public relations and associated programs, such as marketing and development. In fact, some hospitals have converted to for-profit organizations. They often take an integrated approach to public relations and marketing similar to and every bit as sophisticated as that found in other corporate settings. As a result, these hospitals often set the pace for other hospitals that must compete to survive.

Many social welfare agencies, on the other hand, have neither the financial resources nor expertise necessary to mount sophisticated efforts. Some nonprofit organizations depend on inexperienced practitioners or nonprofessional volunteers to conduct their public relations programs.

Thus the public relations practice in nonprofit institutions encompasses a wide variety of approaches and services. At one extreme is a lone practitioner implementing a simple, unstructured publicity campaign. The other end of the spectrum is a large professional, management-level department following a research-based strategic plan with adequate funding and the support of outside consultants. The practice in nonprofit organizations mushroomed during the 1980s and continues to grow, just as the charitable nonprofit sector has.

Voluntarism and Philanthropy

The role of nonprofit organizations was not always as large or significant as it is today. There were only 12,500 charitable tax-exempt organizations not affiliated with churches in 1940, and only 32,000 in 1950. Now there are more than 700,000, with most of the increase occurring since 1970. Nonprofit organizations exist as a special category in the tax code in recognition that society is "delegating public tasks to private groups." And although debate continues over whether or not the wide variety of charitable tax-exempt organizations truly represents a category that can be meaningful defined, there is little question about the interdependence of government and the nonprofit sector.[2]

For example, in 1989 President George Bush asked Congress for $425 million to support his "Points of Light Initiative." Designed to fight drug abuse, illiteracy, homelessness, and other critical social problems, the program's objective was to recognize and to promote volunteer public service a part of the life and work of every individual, group, and organization. Bush recognized that nonprofit organizations are essential to the quality of life and, in some instances, the very survival of many citizens. Indeed, volunteers and philanthropic donations are the only sources of support for many social, health, cultural, and arts programs in many communities.

Each year, almost 40 million people volunteer for work without pay. The Internal Revenue Service reports that there are more than one million tax-exempt organizations in the United States, which are divided into private foundations reporting revenues of $20 billion and a broad range of nonprofit organizations with revenues of more than $300 billion. Despite these impressive numbers, however, the number of volunteers and donated dollars are seldom enough to meet the increased demand for nonprofit organizations' services. Public relations, therefore, has become more critical in the nonprofit sector as a turbulent economic, social, and political climate presents new challenges each year.

Across the country, state and local governments are struggling with budget deficits. Localities, both large and small, are slashing budgets and hiking taxes and user fees. Government cutbacks to deal with these deficits mean fewer staff and reduced resources for social services. At the same time, corporate philanthropic contributions remain about level at almost $6 billion in both 1991 and 1992. In those years, corporate donations actually declined, after adjusting for inflation. Individuals, on the other hand, increased their giving during the same period from about $95 billion to almost $102 billion. Total charitable giving increased 6.4 percent in 1992 to $124 billion (see Figure 16–2 for how much each nonprofit segment received).[3]

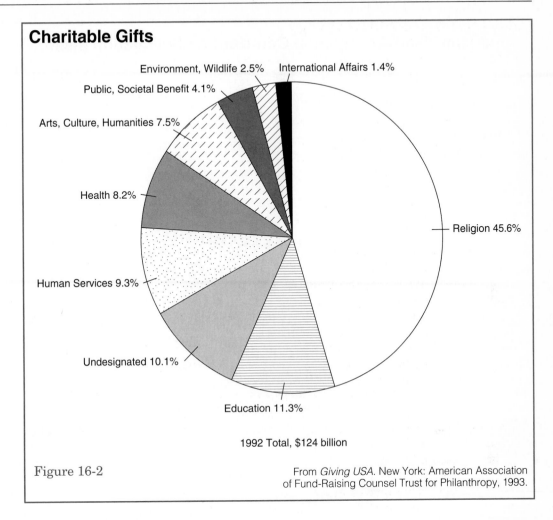

Charitable Gifts

Environment, Wildlife 2.5%   International Affairs 1.4%

Public, Societal Benefit 4.1%

Arts, Culture, Humanities 7.5%

Health 8.2%

Religion 45.6%

Human Services 9.3%

Undesignated 10.1%

Education 11.3%

1992 Total, $124 billion

Figure 16-2

From *Giving USA.* New York: American Association of Fund-Raising Counsel Trust for Philanthropy, 1993.

Changing Climate

The nonprofit sector operates within a climate of change, which includes:

1. Shifting responsibility for public service and assistance from government programs to voluntary organizations
2. Increasing competition among charitable groups for financial and volunteer support
3. A growing public concern about the credibility and accountability of tax-exempt organizations (see Figure 16–3)
4. Increasing cost and difficulty in raising funds
5. A lessening of community ties on the part of corporate leaders and professional staff who tend to move frequently for career advancements.

American Heart Association Contribution Solicitation Insert

76% of every dollar we spend goes directly towards research, education and community service programs.

American Heart Association
California Affili[a]

To reduce administrative costs, all gifts are processed at a central facility. Rest assured your contribution supports research and programs in your local area. For more information, please call your local American Heart Association. Thank you.

American Heart Association

Figure 16-3

Courtesy American Heart Association.

Changing Function

This climate has resulted in profound changes for public relations practitioners in nonprofit organizations:

1. Marketing concepts and management by objectives have emerged as important parts of communication strategy.

2. Technology has extended communication selectivity and reach, but in some instances, such as electronic ministries, has raised questions about ethics, privacy, and legitimacy.

3. Paid advertising has emerged as a major controlled communication tactic for nonprofit organizations, particularly for the health care industry.

4. There is mounting pressure from nonprofit sector leaders (boards of directors or trustees and program managers) to engage professional public relations assistance.

5. Building coalitions in communities and empowering those being served call for different skills than those learned in traditional public relations curricula. (See Exhibit 16–1 for principles of fund-raising.)

HEALTH CARE

In a watershed 1991 political event, Pennsylvania college professor and Democratic state official Harris Wolford scored a stunning U.S. Senate victory over his White House–endorsed opponent by making health care reform a centerpiece of his campaign. The election demonstrated how hospitals and health care agencies, nonprofit and profit alike, are caught in the vise of rising public expectations and demands on one side and escalating costs, limited access, and stiff competition on the other.

Health care became *the issue* when President Bill Clinton appointed First Lady Hillary Rodham Clinton to head his administration's effort to reform national health care policy and delivery systems. After several earlier efforts to put health care reform on the public agenda, public opinion now agreed with what labor and business leaders alike, academicians, and others had long been diagnosing: the health care system is critically ill.

Health Care in Crisis

Driving this ascendancy to public attention were two increasingly critical problems: cost and access. The cost of health care has grown ever more burdensome. In the early 1960s, the United States spent no more than 5 percent of its economic resources on health care. By the early 1990s, health care costs almost tripled as a percentage of the nation's total spending. U.S. health care costs almost twice as much in the United States as in Germany and Japan, with an average of $1200 of the cost of an American-made car traced to health insurance premiums to cover workers and pensioners. Some economists have predicted that the percentage of national spending on health care could reach 20 percent without major reform. In the meantime, 37 million U.S. citizens are not covered by health insurance; with layoffs and shifts to part-time, per diem, and "temp" employment arrange-

EXHIBIT 16-1

PRINCIPLES OF FUND-RAISING

Preparation

1. The five essentials of a successful campaign are a strong case, effective leadership, conscientious workers, prospects willing and able to give, and sufficient funds to finance the campaign. These five essentials should be weighed with scrupulous care before outlining a strategic plan.
2. Committee work and publicity work should be mapped out in advance. The coordination of these two lines of activity, all designed toward bringing a trained and enthusiastic worker face to face with sympathetic and well-informed prospects, is fundamental to the success of any fund-raising effort.
3. The cost of a campaign, within reasonable limits, should be estimated in advance.
4. All campaign activities should be given a time limit. Deadlines provide the only insurance for proper coordination of committee work, publicity, and canvassing.

Committee Work

1. The originating group, whether a committee or a board of directors, should be a representative body.
2. The necessity for strong leadership is inversely proportional to the strength of the appeal.
3. The effectiveness of the group is conditioned by the degree to which individuals will accept responsibility.
4. The activity of the originating group determines the activity of all subordinate groups: The originating group is the inevitable yardstick, both for giving and for working.
5. Committees are better at critiquing than creating. Before asking any group for ideas on a plan of action or for suggestions on a list of prospects, give each member of the group a copy of the plan.

Publicity

1. The case must be bigger than the institution. The first objective of publicity is to sell the idea; the second objective is to sell the means of its accomplishment.
2. Publicity materials should appeal both to the emotions and to the intellect.

3. Publicity must have continuity, with all elements of a campaign tied together with a theme of common appeal.

4. Publicity should proceed from the general to the specific. Interest in an idea proceeds from an appeal of general application.

5. Cheap publicity is expensive. Quality in publicity efforts pays dividends.

6. Publicity should be positive and not negative. Effective publicity always plays up elements of strength.

Campaign Operation

1. A campaign should not only solve immediate financial needs, but should lay a firm foundation for the future campaigns.

2. Solicitation should proceed in six steps: listing, rating, assignments, cultivation, canvassing, and follow up.

3. Effective canvassing answers six questions: why, where, who, what, when, and how.

4. Campaigns should periodically reach a climax. The climax is essential to arouse and maintain interest in the campaign.

5. All canvassing, even for special gifts, should be conducted in an atmosphere of universality. Prospects typically ask, "What are others doing?"

6. Campaigns should be conducted under a steady and constant pressure and sense of urgency.

7. The time spent on a campaign varies directly with the size of the goal and inversely with the popularity of the appeal.

8. The direct appeal for help should be made when the interest is at its peak.

9. Ask for ideas, not for money. The canvasser should first interest prospects in an idea.

10. There are four tests of the effectiveness of campaign operations: quality, quantity, cost, and time.

11. Campaign impact is judged by success or failure in achieving the campaign objectives and the overall goal.

ments rapidly increasing the number of uninsured people. Individual insurance premiums put coverage out of reach for most not covered at work. Health care is in crisis.[4]

These disenfranchised Americans are joining business and labor leaders (who represent the mechanism that funds those who are insured) in demanding that hospitals, physicians, and other health care providers explain why the system is not working for many. Donna E. Shalala, secretary of the U.S. Department of Health and Human Services, says that the crisis represents a "crossroads in the history of our health-care system":

It is a modern-day tragedy that in the next two years *one of four* Americans will lose the health insurance that he or she has today. It is an American tragedy that *85 percent* of the uninsured come from working families. It is an American tragedy that one-year-old children are less likely to have two shots of polio vaccine than children of the same age in *eighty-eight* other countries. It is an American tragedy that our senior citizens should now face the terrible choice of whether to purchase prescription drugs or food.[5]

Public Relations as Marketing

The hospital industry is increasingly embroiled in public policy debates and in aggressively pursuing patients. Reforms in government and insurance coverage reduced both the number of patients and the length of time each stayed in the hospital. These two factors led to aggressive public relations and marketing campaigns that have attracted both new business and criticism.

Competition for consumers' favor poses another challenge in that some make decisions about health care needs on the basis of the *hospital* they want to go to, rather than on their choice of physicians. Still, the majority of people report that their physicians referred them to a particular hospital. However, if their physicians are affiliated with several hospitals, then individuals make the choice based on their perceptions of the quality of medical and staff care and the hospital's reputation, along with location.[6] Competition also has intensified as health care moves from the traditional not-for-profit community hospital model to the corporate hospital chain operated to return a profit to investors.

Harvard Medical School professor and former editor of the *New England Journal of Medicine*, Arnold S. Relman, M.D., refers to the commercialized system of health care as the "medical-industrial complex."[7] Relman estimates that at least one third of all nonpublic health care facilities are investor-owned businesses. These include nursing homes, psychiatric hospitals, and clinics. Two of three health maintenance organizations (HMOs) operate as investor-owned health care businesses. These commercial enterprises compete with traditional acute-care general hospitals that "originally were philanthropic social institutions with the primary mission of serving the health-care needs of their communities."[8] Now, as a "matter of survival," even a community hospital with more than 100 years of history must "position itself in a very competitive health care market" to ensure "making a fair return" on services by addressing "prospective customers."[9] Public relations in many hospital settings has assumed a marketing or "integrated marketing communication" orientation similar to that in business and industry.

An excess of hospital beds in most large cities forces hospitals to compete to keep beds occupied, or as one practitioner put it, albeit crudely, "My job is to put butts in beds." The occupancy rate, the "census," has dropped to an average of less than 70 percent as the average number of days a patient stays in a hospital has been shortened to reduce cost. As a result, staff layoffs are becoming common, as are once-rare hospital closings and sales to for-profit chains.

Many for-profit hospital chains as well as not-for-profit hospital groups have formed multihospital systems. These new chains and merged systems are organized to combine management know-how and financial strength. As hospitals become more competitive and businesslike, however, much of the old goodwill from the time they were viewed as a paternalistic cottage industry has waned. Under the new customer-centered approach to patient care, hospitals are now expected to be more responsive to their "market" wants and needs. The emphasis on marketing in health care is pervasive:

1. Marketing is defined as identifying the wants and needs of a hospital's constituents and guiding the organization toward effectively satisfying those wants and needs. It includes a diagnosis of the environment using tools and techniques founded in behavioral and social science research.

2. Hospital marketing differs from marketing in most other business and industry for three reasons: (1) Generally the payer for health services—an insurance company—has limited or no control over the purchase or cost of service; (2) selection of the hospital and the decision to order services generally are not made by the consumer, but rather by a supplier, usually a physician; and (3) the services rendered can be painful and unpleasant, clearly making the distinction between wants and needs.

3. Health care professions and the insurance industry play important roles as intermediaries in dealing with the consumers of health care. Consequently, a growing number of public relations practitioners work for the American Medical Association, American Nursing Association, Blue Cross, HMOs, preferred provider organizations (PPOs), and similar groups at the national, state, and local levels.

4. Prospective customers do not have to be sold on their need for hospitals, doctors, and nurses. They want assurance of ready access to them when needed. They worry most about financing their health care needs. Unless the financial concern is addressed, other issues matter little.

In the final analysis, however, hospitals need both marketing and public relations, because they seek to achieve different essential outcomes:

> The careful analysis and planning, demand forecasting, feasibility analysis, and input given to pricing, access, channeling (distribution), and product design, which marketing provides, are essential in this era when the financial risks are great and the competition is intense. And . . . hospitals, which are considered community resources regardless of their ownership and are held very accountable to the public for their decisions, increasingly must balance price and quality, sound communication and issues management are needed. . . .[10]

Role of the News Media

Media coverage of health care increased sharply after the 1992 presidential election. One study found an increase in the number of published stories of more than 46 percent in the first quarter of 1993, with the tone of coverage having shifted from positive to slightly negative.[11] With increased media scrutiny and a more critical treatment of health care issues, practitioners in health care face unprecedented challenges, according to Bruce Vladeck, president of the United Hospital Fund: "Of all the tasks of leadership in health care organizations, maintaining communications between the organization and its communities is perhaps the most important."[12]

Even though personal contact and publications distributed to patients and others who have contact with a hospital are the most effective methods for reaching community publics, the mass media play an important role in setting the health care agenda and in conveying messages about individual hospitals and health care issues. Hospital administrators who maintain cooperative relationships with the press are virtually ensured access to the community through media. Each hospital should have available at all times an authorized spokesperson to answer inquiries from the media. Honesty and good service are the keys.

The public relations officer also must prepare medical personnel for press interviews and provide adequate background information to reporters. Health care is a complicated, technical beat, so time spent orienting and educating reporters is a good investment. A well-informed reporter increases the likelihood of accurate, complete, and fair media coverage of complex health care issues in public debate.

Another area of news media interest—patient information—requires special attention. Simply put, there is often a gap between what health care professionals can reveal about patients and what the press wants for publication about personal injuries and illnesses, especially when the patients are celebrities or are otherwise in the news. Press demands for news and "the public's right to know" collide with laws protecting an individual's privacy, the medical profession's code of ethics, and the confidential relationship between doctor and patient. In part to respond to this conflict, medical societies and hospitals have devised "confidentiality of medical information" codes outlining the principles guiding both the press and hospital staff when dealing with news about patients, which include the following goals:

1. To safeguard the private rights of the individual, so that no hospital patient will be caused unnecessary embarrassment or discomfort or be made the object of scorn or ridicule.
2. To report the news accurately, authoritatively, and promptly.
3. To cooperate sincerely in all relationships.

Unless there is a written request by the patient to the contrary, the guidelines typically allow hospitals to release the name, age, sex, general description of treatment, reason for treatment, and general condition of a patient. Medical information protected by the confidentiality guidelines includes a patient's medical history, mental or physical condition, and details of treatment. The guidelines also recommend that every hospital should have a designated person or staff available to the media on a 24-hour basis.

But care must be taken even when following the guidelines. In the era of tabloid journalism and increased litigation, hospitals and other health care organizations find themselves the target of patient charges. Again, the legal and ethical considerations limit how health care organizations can respond in the media. Again, however, any response must take into account the press' obligation to report medical news adequately and accurately and a health care organization's obligation to serve as a cooperative news source while protecting the right to privacy and professional reputations of those both inside and outside the organization. Exhibit 16–2 outlines one public relations practitioner's advice for when patients take complaints to the media.

No longer a low-profile, low-status function, public relations in health care has moved into the management function. In the debate over health care reform, Steven V. Seekins, a vice president of the American Medical Association and an accredited member of PRSA, identifies an increasingly important role for practitioners in health care settings: "To make public relations indispensable to senior management, practitioners must stake out issues management as an area of expertise."[13] No doubt, the complex and hotly contested public debate on how to make quality health care both affordable and available to all in need will continue for years. All parties in the debate will call on public relations practitioners to help set the agenda and to contribute constructively to shaping public policy in health care.

SOCIAL WELFARE

The work of social welfare agencies is society's response to the consequences of its social disorganization. These agencies are an outgrowth of the conflicts and maladjustment produced by America's high-speed, urbanized living and of the recognition that not everyone has equal access to services or the resources to acquire services. To gain support for their programs, such agencies must convince their many constituencies collectively and individually that the agencies are "doing for others what I would like to do if I could."[14]

Federal and state government spending on social welfare programs totals more than $800 billion annually. In many communities, government spending on social welfare programs is being cut in

EXHIBIT 16-2

WHEN PATIENTS TAKE COMPLAINTS TO THE MEDIA

Confidentiality of a patient's medical record is a right that is guaranteed by law. As public relations practitioners who work in health care and research settings know, it is our responsibility to guard this right and to use appropriate guidelines and consents when we release condition reports on accident victims or when we pitch patient stories to illustrate the excellent care our organizations provide.

But there are also instances when patient confidentiality can be a sticky issue. This can occur when a patient or volunteer for medical research alleges ill treatment and takes the story to the media. If the story is compelling and the reporter or producer pursues it, what can the institution say in its defense? If the patient has filed or threatened a lawsuit, should you avoid talking to the media altogether?

Media response is complicated because confidentiality laws prohibit the health care organization from talking about a case even when the patient talks about the case in the media and charges malpractice, wrongdoing, or misconduct. Unless the patient is willing to sign a release, the public relations practitioner may not reveal any details about the case.

The situation poses an interesting public relations challenge. Although specific information that would undoubtedly help to explain the situation cannot be divulged, we can still reinforce openness and concern by providing more general information and effective spokespersons in a timely and responsive manner.

Initial communications can diminish the impact of negative allegations when a high-level spokesperson comes forward to reassure the public that the organization cares about the well-being of all patients and that they are looking into the charges.

If a problem exists, disclosure early in the game will help to maintain public trust and keep the story contained and short-lived. Plans to correct the problem should be implemented and announced as soon as possible.

Also, because general information about medical treatment and programs can be easily distorted and confused, it is critical to provide accurate information to reporters, in the form of fact sheets and backgrounders. To keep the rumor mill at a minimum, similar materials may be distributed to patients, staff, and outside audiences who may be affected by the adverse publicity.

When the charges have little or no merit and media interest remains intense, the public relations practitioner may need to recommend additional strategies. For example, an internal- or external-conducted investigation could help to demonstrate due concern and ultimately alleviate the appearance of guilt. Meeting with key leadership in health care advocacy, research, and government could also broaden support and media focus.

During the critical period of media scrutiny, when there is great temptation to pull back and bury our heads, we must always remember our obligation to represent the public's concerns among administrative, legal, clinical, and research leadership in our organization. If media response is based on litigious or other administrative concerns, without due concern for public trust, the ultimate loss of public faith in the organization could be far greater than any courtroom defeat.

Vicki Hoffman Beck
Assistant Director, Communications
Center for Health Sciences
University of California, Los Angeles

response to budget deficits, shifting the burden to community nonprofit agencies. Apart from Medicaid, where spending keeps rising, poor people are especially vulnerable. Governors are using the current fiscal crisis to work their versions of welfare reform. *Business Week* (April 22, 1991) reported two examples: In Ohio, which faced a $1.5 billion revenue shortfall for 1992–1993, Governor George Voinovich suggested turning over welfare support for able-bodied adults to local governments and cutting the program by $50 million. Michigan's Governor John Engler wanted to cut benefits to families whose children drop out of school. He also ended general assistance to some 100,000 people who he said were able to go out and find work.

Charitable contributions to the "human services, public, and society benefit" categories of nonprofit groups and causes totaled $17 billion in 1992.[15] And although individual philanthropic giving continues to increase slightly each year, funding for social service agencies has not kept pace with community needs. "In addition, current frictions between publics splintering along demographic and ethnic lines tend to adversely affect agencies which depend on gifts and volunteers."[16]

Social agencies are hit hard during economic recessions. Yet the demand for their services multiplies in hard times even as sources of funds shrink. Public and private agencies represent a less-than-adequate response to social welfare needs and pose public relations problems of awesome complexity. At the very times of greatest need, citizens are hounded by the demands for funds by a seemingly multiplying number of causes and agencies. At the same time, citizens see their tax bills increase to pay for some of the same services through government agencies. More effective two-way communication with all constituencies will be required to build and maintain the relationships needed to achieve public interest goals through nonprofit social service agencies. Figure 16–4 shows the "United Way Wheel," graphically illustrating the components of United Way of America's public relations effort.

Donor-supported agencies must get the bulk of their budgets from the upper- and middle-income groups. It is in the middle-income group that a strong sense of responsibility must be built. The alternative is to transfer the burden to government; then all will pay, through compulsory contributions in the form of taxes. The donor-supported, volunteer-staffed agency has an important innovative

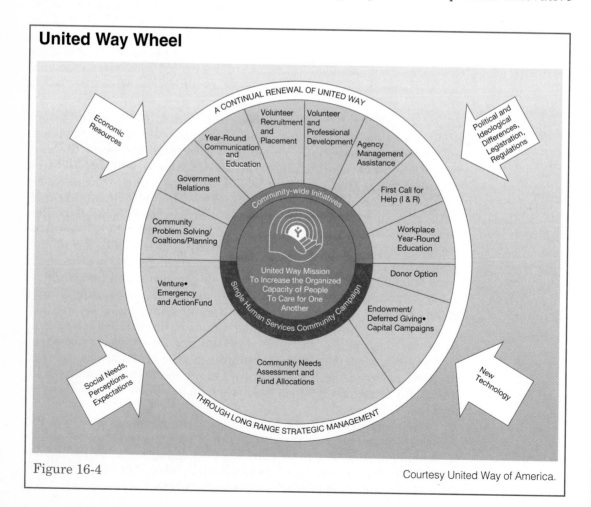

United Way Wheel

Figure 16-4

Courtesy United Way of America.

function that must be maintained, however. Leaders of these agencies must strive even harder to muster public support through public relations, support that will endure in good times or bad.

A welfare agency starts out in an enviable position, however. Its sole reason for existence is to help people. Yet the public is ambivalent in its attitude toward welfare. The term *welfare* has come to have a pejorative ring. Poll after poll shows public opinion deeply antagonistic to the concept of public welfare, but strongly supportive of what welfare programs do.

Part of the difficulty results because social agencies often deal with intangibles. The United Way has widely proclaimed, "Thanks to you, it works for all of us," but still many people regard these agencies as existing for the "other fellow." Some in need shun the service provided by social agencies because "it's charity." Many who could use these services simply do not know of their availability. Potential supporters often will not find concrete illustrations of tangible benefits to individual citizens in agency publications and presentations because of the confidential relationship that must exist between agency and client.

Welfare agencies must tightly link their programs to educating the public to accept enlightened social concepts in fields such as poverty, mental health, crime and correction, child welfare, problems of aging, and drug addiction. Planned, consistent programs are required to break the barriers of public apathy, superstition, and the deadweight of indifference on these fronts.

Among the difficult problems facing health and welfare agencies is that of building a communication bridge among ethnic communities and between the inner city and the outer city. Traditional "come-and-get-it" services and communication messages fail to reach many in need, particularly those in the inner city. The public relations challenges are to make communication and programs more effective through greater empowerment and involvement of inner-city residents in the affairs of social agencies.

EDUCATION

Education touches the lives of virtually every citizen. It employs 3.1 million teachers and administrators. Federal, state, and local government spend almost $300 billion dollars a year for elementary and high-school education and higher education. According to the U.S. Census Bureau, state governments pay the greatest share, about 55 percent.

Surveys repeatedly show that education ranks among the most valued symbols in American life. In fact, many Americans expect too much from education, presuming it to be the panacea for all the ills that beset the nation. And yet, with all these high expectations, Americans remain ambivalent toward education.

Accountability

Growing public dissatisfaction with the performance and cost of schools has led to widespread demands for more accountability. Demands for accountability have moved far beyond student achievement scores to include calls for teacher competency tests and the institution of merit-based incentive pay. Tenure is under siege at every level of education. And both taxpayers and legislators reject the notion that schools and universities will improve if given more funds. Educators' and their institutions' responses to these new and stricter demands for accountability will require greater attention and more adequate information programs for most school systems.

Accountability requires keeping good records and making actions public. An "accountable school" is one that (1) discloses its activities, (2) makes good on its promises, (3) assigns staff responsibility for each area of public concern, and (4) monitors its teaching and learning.[17] Accountability also includes gathering evidence to document progress on meeting public expectations and using research to explain both strengths and weaknesses. The demand for accountability in education is a relatively recent development:

Whereas business for years has been the bad guy in terms of the public's acceptance of the credibility of its actions, education and the nonprofits have been ranked with apple pie and motherhood. That's no longer true. We, too, are now expected to be efficient, productive, purposeful and accountable in our work.[18]

Basic to effective public relations in any setting is performance that the public deems satisfactory. Central to the difficult task facing public education officials is widespread concern that the money American taxpayers have spent on their schools and universities has not been effectively used. The progress of any educational system depends, in the final analysis, on public support.

Public Relations for Public Schools

The major general objectives of public relations for public schools include:

1. Increasing awareness of education and head off misinformation and rumor.
2. Building public support necessary to obtain adequate funds.
3. Gaining public acceptance and cooperation in making educational changes.
4. Building amicable working relationships with news executives and reporters.

Public relations for education is expanding in scope, concept, and utilization. It has taken on increased importance as officials try to persuade taxpayers to raise school levies to cope with inflation or to pass bond issues for new buildings because of shifting enrollment patterns. In fact, most school public relations practitioners regard the financing of public education as the issue that will present the greatest communications problem during the next several years.

For example, when the Dayton, Ohio, board of education voted to put a tax levy on the ballot, it took an all-out campaign focused on positives to win voter support. Based on research findings showing that voters were reluctant to vote for higher taxes, but concerned about economic issues, the strategy focused on positive outcomes of the proposed education tax: (1) how schools attract jobs and provide qualified workers, (2) the link between good schools and stable property values, (3) the contribution schools make to order and discipline, and (4) the how good Dayton schools are and the prospects for getting better. The system's public information officer, Jill Moberley, said:

> Key to success was that we did our research and targeted our messages. Also our superintendent was upfront, available to answer voters' questions, doing door-to-door literature drops and talking one-on-one with people in neighborhoods. We made it personal. And we're continuing to tell our story, after the campaign. It's important to apprise people of how dollars are being spent, what changes are occurring and how schools are benefiting the community.[19]

Other major issues include a return to the "basics," discipline, religion and theory of creation, violence and weapons, substance abuse, sex education, pupil achievement, parental concern and participation, teacher competence and performance, negotiations with teachers' unions, and students' right of free expression.

Essential aspects of a school-community relations program designed to anticipate, to avoid, and to respond to these problems include:

1. Commitment to public partnership on the part of school boards, administrators, and teachers;
2. Competence in the school-community relations staff;
3. Centralization of community relations policy making;
4. Free-flowing communication from and to publics: up, down, and across; and
5. Coordination of all efforts to ensure the accomplishment of predetermined goals.

The relationships between educational institutions and the people are many, diverse, and complex. Key internal and external publics for public schools include the following groups.

1. **Parents** play a key role in the educational process and in building support for adequate budgets. A strong parent association also serves as a buffer against extremist groups. Good relationships with parents start with frequent, frank communication between teacher and parents. Communication means conferences, encouragement of parent observation of normal classroom situations, special programs for parents, and home visits by the teachers to help resolve students' problems.

2. **School staff** from principal and teacher to bus driver, custodian, and school nurse, must be brought into a public relations program. Teachers, in their day-to-day activities, are in a position to relate effectively to students, parents, and others. As a result, they are able to provide valuable feedback to administrators and those responsible for the curriculum and other programs. Many superintendents have found it desirable to organize advisory councils that include representatives from all categories of employees (teacher advisory council, food-service advisory council, and so on). Superintendents are also using employee newsletters to keep staff informed about the school system.

3. **Students** represent what may be the school system's most important public. Public relations truly starts in the classroom. In public opinion surveys, parents say that they rely most on their children for information about the schools. School executives should determine students' views of their school experiences, see that pupils are well informed about policies, make sure that courses satisfy their needs and challenge their abilities, arrange that individual attention is provided for those who need it, and create an overall atmosphere that engenders pupil and parent pride in the school.

4. **Business community** and school partnerships take many forms. These include adopt-a-school programs, resource-sharing for professional training of staffs, consultation in management and technology to improve school system effectiveness and to promote innovation, and advocacy with state and local governments to increase support of public schools. School systems recognize the necessity for assistance and support from business and industry. Likewise, business and industry communities recognize that they have a high stake in the public schools.

5. **Community groups**—include many groups: parents, taxpayers, and other citizens concerned about "what our schools ought to be teaching." These groups can be reached through parent-teacher associations, press, service clubs, church groups, and countless other ways. Periodic surveys of parents and community groups not only provide benchmarks for evaluation of a system's public standing, but also, and more importantly, provide feedback that improves education.

6. **Local news media** are the primary means of informing the public of what schools are doing and with what they contend in doing it. This requires continuous reporting, so schools must take the initiative with a planned information program directed by a trained practitioner. Most local news media have neither the staff resources nor the expertise to cover public education adequately. The press typically covers administrative changes, school conflicts, and school sports, but will not assign reporters to the more time-consuming assignments to cover curriculum changes, educational policies, and the like. Thus school systems must, in their own self-interest, provide broad, constructive coverage of education at the local level.

   Cable television can provide almost unlimited opportunity for communicating with the community publics: school-community bulletin boards, board meetings and public hearings, student and school system news programs, fine arts and other cultural events, athletic contests, school closing and crisis announcements, and school leader interviews and panel programs.

School Public Information Literature

Figure 16-5

7. **Board of education members** act as intermediaries between school publics and the professional administrators. It is essential that board members agree on an adequate statement of public relations policy. The board must serve its function of interpreting the community to the school staff and, in turn, interpreting staff ideas and policies to the community.

Nationally, advances are being spearheaded by the National School Public Relations Association, whose membership includes most school practitioners, as well as many school administrators. Other national educational organizations include the National School Boards Association, the American Association of School Administrators, the National Association of Elementary School Principals, the National Association of Secondary School Principals, and two major teachers' unions: the National Education Association and the American Federation of Teachers.

Higher Education

Each year American society invests about $160 billion in higher education, with almost half coming from federal, state, and local governments. An analysis of the return on Massachusetts taxpayers' investments in higher education at the University of Massachusetts at Boston conservatively concluded that "for every $1 the state spends on the university, it will receive $1.57 in return."[20] The total state subsidy for a student's 4-year program was estimated to be $13,253 for the 1991 entering class. The average expected return in income and sales-tax revenues above the average of what high-school graduates contribute, after excluding the 11 percent of undergraduates and 18 percent of graduate students who leave the state after graduation, will total $20,832.[21]

Sectors of society with greater political clout and with more sophisticated lobbying techniques than those possessed by higher education compete for funding from state governments. As a result, many states in recent years have not increased higher-education budgets in proportion to increased costs and increased demands for research and off-campus services. In too many states, an increasing share of the cost is being placed on the student by tuition hikes, raising concerns about access and equal opportunity in tough economic times. Today, many qualified young people are excluded from the benefits of higher education, in some instances because of sex, race, or religion, but mostly because of the escalating cost of college.

Higher education faces four continuing problems.

1. Academic freedom is frequently in question, if not in danger, from within and from without.
2. Financial support is insufficient and precarious.
3. Competition for qualified students is spirited, and their selection difficult.
4. Constraints and regulations that make university administration difficult and costly are being imposed by agencies of the federal government.

Additionally, just as in other organizations, taxpayers demand broader accountability by state colleges and universities for how tax dollars are spent. According to Roger Williams, assistant vice president and executive director of university relations, Pennsylvania State University, University Park:

> We had a nice, protected status until the late 1980s, when a series of unrelated incidents from misreporting the use of government funds to scientific fraud, animal welfare, and so-called tuition price-fixing began to undermine public confidence in higher education. Now we have to begin work on the long road back toward (regaining) public trust.[22]

This emerging demand for more accountability underscores the need to provide feedback from students, faculty, townspeople, taxpayers, and other constituent-claimant publics. People want to know what institutions of higher education are doing to keep costs under control and to eliminate wasteful programs. At the same time, taxpayers also demand that colleges and universities maintain quality and remain accessible to an increasingly diverse population. Higher education must "meet these issues head on," according to Gail Raiman, vice president for public affairs, National Association of Independent Colleges and Universities:

> Just as the media are being more aggressive in covering education, we must be more aggressive in educating the public and opinion leaders. We need to use clear language, not academic jargon. We have to go to these opinion leaders instead of waiting for them to come to us.[23]

The ingredients of a system of accountability include:

1. A clear mission statement of goals with an ordering of priorities
2. Allocation of resources toward maximum return in relation to goals
3. Cost and benefit analysis, including allocation of costs and benefits to each institution and to programs within institutions
4. Evaluation of actual results
5. Reporting on the evaluation to governing boards to sources of financial support—including constituents throughout the region served—and to the faculty and administrative staff.

Current responds to demands for accountability draw on a long history of public relations in higher education. Institutions of higher learning were among the first to set about winning public favor on a systematic basis. The University of Michigan led the way when it established a publicity office in 1897. Increased competition for funds and students forced private institutions to counter with similar programs. As classical education gave way to curricula responsive to the needs of the twentieth century, as the demand for extension and research grew, and as the need for money increased sharply, the college administrator turned, sooner or later, to the use of publicity and, ultimately, to public relations.

The 1974 merger of two associations, the American College Public Relations Association and the American Alumni Council, brought together public relations practitioners working in alumni relations, fund-raising, government relations, and publications and periodicals, and student recruitment, as well as administrators. The merger formed the Council for Advancement and Support of Education (CASE), based in Washington, D.C. The broad goals of the organization are to build public understanding of higher education, to step up the level of alumni involvement and support, to improve educational government relations, to strengthen communication with internal and external campus audiences, and to increase private financial support for education. Membership includes approximately 14,000 individuals representing 3200 colleges, universities, independent elementary and secondary schools, and other educational organizations such as museums and teaching hospitals.

To maintain quality and access in the face of declining state support, public institutions of higher education must look to private sources for an increasing portion of their financial support. State universities and colleges actively compete with private universities and colleges for donor dollars. Caught in the vise of rising costs and rising public demands on one side and declining enrollments and government support on the other, colleges face public relations tasks unparalleled in the history of higher education. Therefore, a sound public affairs program has improving the climate for fund-raising as a primary goal.

Public relations in higher education typically targets the following key publics, although programs vary with the size, base of support, and philosophy of the institution.

1. **Students.**   Students are both the most important public and most important public relations representatives, first as students and later as alumni. Student opinions and conduct are powerful factors in determining public opinion about higher education. A university must develop an enthusiastic, responsible body of students as goodwill ambassadors.

    Fundamental to effective student relationships is maintaining, regardless of the institution's size, free-flowing channels between administrators and students. Likewise, students who have good teachers and who are given wise counsel and helpful individual attention generally become loyal alumni.

    To bring quality and diversity to their student bodies, most colleges and universities now have special recruitment programs for National Merit Scholars, National Achievement Scholars, and minority students. These programs, usually directed by a full-time person in admissions, require a strong public relations backup.

2. **Faculty and staff.**   Professors are also an important internal public, both because of their critical roles in education and governance and because of their role as representatives of the university to external constituencies. Yet many faculty members remain aloof, others merely indifferent, and a few plainly hostile to assuming any role or responsibility in effectively representing the university to external groups and the media.

Unions and collective bargaining have changed the nature of relationships between faculty and administration on many campuses. As a result, some campus public relations offices now have the task of dealing with the press during contract negotiations. As a result, it is imperative that administrators keep open channels of communication with the faculty and provide freedom, adequate pay, research support, and competitive fringe benefits.

Today, faculty members insist on a voice in college policy making. If this participation is to be meaningful, they must be kept informed by the administration so that they can take informed positions. The best way to win the faculty's cooperation is through patient internal education; input and participation in decision making; and empowerment in determining the mission, values, and governance of the university.

3. **Alumni.**   Contributions from alumni are the single most important source of voluntary support in higher education. It is no surprise, then, that colleges and universities strive to gain loyalty, interest, and counsel from their alumni. Win those, and the dollars will follow. The function of the director of alumni relations is to see that alumni are appreciated rather than exploited, cultivated rather than coerced, frankly informed rather than party-lined, and above all interested in and organized for more than money making (see job description in Figure 16–6). The alumni association must be kept harnessed to its basic objective, supporting the alma mater through organized effort.

Liberal arts colleges receive more than 10 percent of their total annual revenues from alumni giving, while for all colleges and universities the average is almost 6 percent. First, larger institutions get more dollars from alumni; smaller institutions average about 25 percent more per alumnus. The inverse relationship between the size of the university and the average amount contributed by each alumnus suggests that large colleges and universities must take steps to establish a strong feeling of affinity between students and the institution. Second, private institutions do not receive more from their alumni than do public institutions of comparable size, scope, and perceived quality. "Given the importance of graduates' pride in their alma maters, a fund-raising strategy should begin at the time students are enrolled."[24] Just as in other settings, relationships begin to be formed at the time of first contact. Too many institutions wait until graduation to begin building good alumni relations.

4. **Community groups and business leaders.**   The "town-gown" relationship has always been a set of complex and symbiotic relationships. Colleges and universities lag behind industry in recognizing the importance of good community relations. As state funding does not keep pace with increased costs on campuses, many are turning to the business sector to build new, mutually beneficial relationships. Support can be won by giving the citizens a voice and a sympathetic hearing, through consultation, on college matters directly affecting the community, such as campus expansion and building projects that have direct impact on traffic, property values, and ambiance in neighborhoods near campus.

The tax-exempt status of educational institutions may appear as a sign of partiality or bias in favor of the campus. Municipalities, however, are increasingly hard-pressed to find adequate revenues to pay for expanding demand for services from all parts of the community, including the campus. When metropolitan campuses must expand in already built-up areas, the growth ultimately greatly benefits the community. In the short term, however, campus expansion means removal of property from the tax rolls and, hence, reduced revenues to the campus host community. Part of the role of public relations is to remind townspeople and business leaders that the campus can and does offer many positive advantages to the community.

Alumni Relations Job Description

THE STATE UNIVERSITY OF NEW JERSEY

RUTGERS

ASSISTANT VICE PRESIDENT
OF ALUMNI RELATIONS

Rutgers, The State University of New Jersey, invites applications and nominations for the position of University Assistant Vice President of Alumni Relations with responsibilities for planning, directing, and coordinating a comprehensive program of activities and communications designed to inform and engage alumni worldwide on behalf of the University. In this capacity, the Assistant Vice President serves as the principal liaison between the alumni, faculty, administration, students, and the Rutgers University Foundation. The Assistant Vice President will also work with the leadership of the Alumni Federation, as well as a growing number of school-based alumni associations and regional alumni clubs to develop programs and services that will both advance the University's goals and objectives and encourage alumni support. The Assistant Vice President shall also have editorial responsibility for the 24-page alumni supplement in RUTGERS MAGAZINE, the University's quarterly magazine for alumni and friends.

Founded in 1766, Rutgers today has campuses in New Brunswick, Camden and Newark and has an enrollment of 49,000 students in 26 degree-granting units. The University has an alumni population of 225,000 graduates and graduates 10,000 students each year. Rutgers is a member institution of the Association of American Universities and is linked through athletics to the Big East and Atlantic 10 Conferences.

The Assistant Vice President reports to the President of the Rutgers University Foundation, the University's chief development and alumni relations officer. Candidates for the position must have senior-level management experience in alumni relations or some other advancement area. The position requires strong organizational and interpersonal skills and an ability to write and speak effectively on behalf of the University. Knowledge of computer records systems and standard management and accounting practices is desirable.

Rutgers, The State University of New Jersey, is an Equal Opportunity, Affirmative Action Employer.

Interested candidates are invited to contact Bruce D. Newman, President, Rutgers University Foundation, Winants Hall, 7 College Avenue, New Brunswick, New Jersey 08901-1261.

Figure 16-6   Courtesy Rutgers University.

5. **Government.** Building understanding and support in federal and state executive branches and agencies—mainly in departments of education, in legislative bodies, and in the voter public—has become a major public relations task in higher education. Many universities and state systems now maintain full-time or part-time public relations officers in Washington and in their state capitals, where their tasks are fact finding, troubleshooting, and lobbying, primarily providing information about higher education and their universities. Their concerns range from funding levels to legislative and executive interference and regulation, and include all public policy issues that affect campuses directly or indirectly through other campus constituencies.

6. **Media.**   Building good media relations is an investment that pays off over the long term, but can be destroyed in an instant, as pointed out in Chapter 9. Centralizing and coordinating the news flow from the campus is an almost impossible task. A college or university speaks with many voices and has many media specialists, from the information office to the student newspaper and radio station, the publicity-seeking professor, and campus sources with whom reporters have developed special relationships. The most frequent sources of news are college presidents, other administrators, athletic directors and coaches, and professors.

Colleges remain the center of youthful discontent, sometimes in terms of legitimate complaints about the deficiencies of the institution and other times as a convenient tactic for assault on the general society. Given the news values and methods of media reporting, dealing with these activities is difficult. Public opinion is influenced by the news media spotlighting protests but neglecting quiet academic achievement. Often the job of public relations is to help balance media coverage by giving reporters examples of achievements and contributions to the community.

7. **Parents and others.**   Parents are a ready-made nucleus of support. They have a vital stake in the institution and thus can be welded into an effective group of allies. Other publics include prospective students, parents of prospective students, present and prospective donors, opinion leaders, philanthropic foundations, similar educational institutions, the armed forces, and various agencies of the federal government, particularly those with research programs.

The College President's Public Relations Role

College and university presidents must lead, not direct, faculties, students, and governing boards. Leaders in higher education are caught in the crunch of conflicting values and demands from stakeholder-constituent publics. To thread their way through these conflicts, presidents must be effective communicators and mediators. In fact, they spend as much time practicing public relations as they do on the other aspects of administering their institutions:

> Thirty-nine percent of the presidents said they spent between 21% and 40% of their time over the past year on public relations. Twenty-seven percent said they devoted 41% to 60% of their time to public relations. Only 10% said they spent more than 60% of their time on public relations activities.[25]

Almost a third of the presidents said they met more frequently with their public relations officers than with any other member of the management team.[26]

A president personifies the institution. A strong personality can bring prestige, stature, and public confidence. Given the many demands being made on institutions of higher learning—to do more and better with less—the president's role in public relations is more important than ever before. The president is the key to establishing the relationships and public support needed to fulfill higher education's mission in the new global society. But as one university president observed, the U.S. vision of higher education is not shared globally: "We are unique in this country in having made higher education such an achievable goal. We are the only country in the world to do so."[27]

CHURCHES AND OTHER NONPROFIT ORGANIZATIONS

Space does not allow detailed analysis of all nonprofit settings. But brief descriptions of some of the issues and pressures on churches, libraries, museums, and arts groups illustrate how the practice of public relations is both as complex and as essential in these settings as in other nonprofit settings.

Even a church is not immune to public relations crises. Few Seventh-Day Adventist church members among the seven million worldwide had ever heard of cult leader David Koresh and the group in Waco, Texas, who called themselves "Branch Davidian Seventh-Day Adventists" until February 28, 1993. Suddenly, television satellites around the globe carried the horrifying pictures of a botched U.S. Treasury Department Bureau of Tobacco and Firearms raid and the subsequent fire that killed men, women, and children. It was the beginning of a crisis for Seventh-Day Adventist public relations departments across the nation.[28]

Some Episcopalians see the new age movement as a threat to religion, some Catholic priests are charged with sexual misconduct, and some television evangelists and faith healers are exposed as lavish spenders and frauds. Polls conducted by the Gallup Organization for the National Catholic Evangelization Association show that the percentage of Americans who identify themselves as members of a church or synagogue is the lowest—65 percent—since Gallup polls began tracking membership in 1937. The National Conference of Catholic Bishops broke tradition in 1990 and retained Hill and Knowlton, then the nation's biggest public relations firm, and former President Ronald Reagan's pollster, the Wirthlin Group, to help design a counterattack against growing public support for abortion.

On top of such crises and activism, churches face increased competition for volunteer commitment and dollars. Slightly less than half the nation's population are regular churchgoers. Declining participation and the financial squeeze have underlined the importance of public relations to many church leaders, but churches face some unique obstacles:

1. The intangible nature of many religious activities;
2. The sacred nature of many activities, which demands a dignified approach;
3. The problem of showing the practical worth of religious values; and
4. The difficulty of finding which level to project ideas so that they will appeal to many.

Organized religion has not escaped the vortex of change, crisis, and confrontation, so it has become top news. Whereas churches have long been comfortable using the media in the cause of religion, they are not experienced or comfortable in the spotlight of evening news and tabloid exposés. But as a major force in society and social change, churches cannot avoid the spotlight. Increased media attention and a range of other relationship problems suggest an important and growing role for public relations in churches and synagogues.

Although apparently much less controversial by their very nature and missions than churches, libraries, museums, and arts groups compete for public support in the form of volunteers, donations, and public funding. Many of these important institutions, which contribute much to the quality of American life, live in a financial straitjacket that does not permit adequate funding for either their programs or professional public relations assistance.

Most public libraries in major cities have public relations departments, usually called public information departments. But in smaller cities and suburbs, public libraries may have very small staffs that do not include public relations expertise. At best, these libraries may take advantage of volunteer support and special events such as National Library Week to achieve limited public relations objectives. To provide effective public relations support to its many small libraries, Wisconsin established the Coordinated Library Information Program, which provides the counsel of a public relations specialist to libraries in that state.

Like libraries, arts groups in this nation are faced with a constant battle to keep the financial wolf from the door. In recent years, both foundations and the government have cut support of cultural institutions and museums. The early 1990s recession made many question the relevance of arts and cultural organizations: "When families begin to choose tangibles over intangibles in their budgets, relevance becomes increasingly important when planning activities, fund raising and launching drives for new members."[29]

Always confronted with the challenges of attracting individual volunteers and donations and funding from other public and private sources, nonprofit organizations rely more on good public relations than any other sector in society. The recession has only made this sector more vulnerable, as the base of support has diminished while need has expanded. Without effective public relations, many of these organizations will not survive the recession and what many see as a permanently downsized economy. Without these organizations, many needs not now addressed by either business and industry or government will go unmet. At stake are the very existence of some nonprofit organizations and the continuing vitality of the "third sector."

"Meet J. Robert Anderson, Philanthropist"

Meet J. Robert Anderson, philanthropist.

He's not a millionaire. In fact, he's not even rich. But he gives.

Most of the giving in this country doesn't come from the wealthy. Almost half of it comes from people who earn less than $20,000 a year. Everyday, ordinary people. Like the guy down the street. Or your next-door neighbor. Or 100 million others who, every year, give unselfishly just to help people.

And while those who give may sometimes go unnoticed, their contributions don't. Because in this country, when a lot of people give, it adds up to a lot.

It helps fund important research. It helps run community church programs. It helps support local charities.

It helps people out.

There are so many things in this country that could use your hand. Your time, your tal-

ents, your money. What you give isn't so important. That you do give is. Because you don't have to

be rich to be a philanthropist. You just have to care.

 A Public Service of This Publication & The Advertising Council

Figure 16-7   From the Advertising Council.

ADDITIONAL READINGS

Backer, Thomas E.   *Designing Health Communication Campaigns: What Works?* Newbury Park, Calif.: Sage Publications, Inc., 1992. Describes what has worked and not worked in health promotion campaigns designed to reduce substance abuse, smoking, teen-age pregnancy, heart disease, and AIDS.

Badaracco, Claire.   "Public Relations and Religion," special issue of *Public Relations Review* 18, no. 3 (Fall 1992). Articles analyze the convergence of religion and politics, using rhetorical, political, and communication perspectives.

Cutlip, Scott M.   *Fundraising in the United States.* New Brunswick, N.J.: Transaction Publishers, 1990. Reprint of the 1965 classic history of how fund-raising evolved to become big business, its early pioneers, and campaigns that had a major impact on society.

Kelly, Kathleen S.   *Fund Raising and Public Relations: A Critical Analysis.* Hillsdale, N.J.: Lawrence Erlbaum Associates, Publishers, 1991. Argues that fund-raising should be a part of the larger public relations function in charitable, educational, and other nonprofit organizations, with the main purpose to give these organizations the autonomy they need to achieve goals.

Kotler, Philip, and Alan R. Andreasen. *Strategic Marketing for Nonprofit Organizations,* 4th ed. Englewood Cliffs, N.J.: Prentice-Hall, Inc., 1987. Outlines the application of marketing principles and practices to building interest in programs offered by churches, government agencies, schools, health care organizations, and fine arts and performing arts groups.

Kotler, Philip, and Eduardo Roberto.   *Social Marketing: Strategies for Changing Public Behavior.* New York: Free Press, 1990. Outlines government and nonprofit campaigns to encourage safe sex and to discourage smoking, alcohol consumption, and drug abuse.

Lewton, Kathleen Larey.   *Public Relations in Health Care: A Guide for Professionals.* Chicago: American Hospital Publishing, 1991. Outlines strategic planning, program implementation, measurement and evaluation, and legal and ethical considerations for public relations in the health care setting. Published for the American Society for Health Care Marketing and Public Relations of the American Hospital Association.

Magat, Richard, ed.   *Philanthropic Giving: Studies in Varieties and Goals.* New York: Oxford University Press, 1989. Presents essays on the methods of, influences on, and sources of private giving. Represents another installment in the continuing Yale Studies on Nonprofit Organizations.

Rabinowitz, Alan, ed.   *Social Change Philanthropy in America.* New York: Quorum Books, 1990. Addresses the category of philanthropy that aims explicit to bring about change in social institutions and economic arrangements in society.

Ray, Eileen Berlin.   *Case Studies in Health Communication.* Hillsdale, N.J.: Lawrence Erlbaum Associates, Publishers, 1992. Provides helpful and detailed case studies of health communication programs.

Skolnik, Rayna.   "Rebuilding Trust: Nonprofits Act to Boost Reputations," *Public Relations Journal* 49, no. 9 (September 1993): 29–32. Describes efforts by nonprofit organizations after the United Way of America scandal to deal with public scrutiny of how funds are spent and demands for proof that objectives are achieved.

NOTES

[1]Pamela Sebastian,   "Nonprofit Groups Seek to Set Standard for Ethics in Aftermath of Scandals," *Wall Street Journal*, October 30, 1992, p. A7C.

[2]Peter Dobkin Hall,   *Inventing the Nonprofit Sector and Other Essays on Philanthropy, Voluntarism, and Nonprofit Organizations* (Baltimore, Md.: Johns Hopkins University Press, 1992): 13, 14, and 82.

[3]Julie L. Nicklin,   "Many Fortune 500 Companies Curtail Donations to Higher Education," *Chronicle of Higher Education* 39, no. 38 (May 26, 1993): A25–27.

[4]Sara Fritz,   "U.S. Cautiously Awaits Clinton Health Program," *Los Angeles Times*, September 19, 1993, pp. A1, 21–22.

[5]Donna E. Shalala,   "The Future of Health-Care Reform in America," *National Forum* 53, no. 3 (Summer 1993): 10.

[6]"How Is a Hospital Selected?" *pr reporter* 36, no. 24 (June 24, 1993): 2.

[7]Arnold S. Relman,   "What Market Values Are Doing to Medicine," *National Forum* 53, no. 3 (Summer 1993): 18.

[8]Ibid., 19.

[9]Susan L. Fry,   "Century-Old Hospital Complex Repositioned as Medical Center," *Public Relations Journal* 47, no. 8 (August 1991): 13.

[10]Rebecca H. Christian,   "A Personal Look at the Marketing/PR Evolution," *Hospital Marketing and Public Relations* 15, no. 4 (July–August 1989): 6.

[11]"Media Coverage of Health Care Rebounds," *Issue Scan* 3, no. 1 (First Quarter 1993): 1. *Issue Scan* is a quarterly media report on health care issues and trends published by S. D. Searle and Co., a pharmaceuticals manufacturer.

[12]Quoted by David Kirk in "Briefings: Hospital Research Targets 'Key Leaders,'" *Public Relations Journal* 49, no. 3 (March 1993): 12.

[13]Steven V. Seekins,   "Forecast 1993: System Reform Looms," *Public Relations Journal* 49, no. 1 (January 1993): 21.

[14]Richard T. McCartney,   "Forecast 1992: Gain Community Support," *Public Relations Journal* 48, no. 1 (January 1992): 24.

[15]Julie L. Nicklin,   "Charitable Giving Rises 6.4%; Education Gets $14-Billion," *Chronicle of Higher Education* 39, no. 38 (May 26, 1993): A25 and A27. See *Giving USA*, published annually by the American Association of Fund-Raising Counsel Trust for Philanthropy (New York) for detailed description of philanthropic giving each year.

[16]McCartney,   "Gain Community Support," 24.

[17]Robert E. Stake,   "School Accountability Laws," *Journal of Education Evaluation*, 4 (February 1973).

[18]Karen L. Cedzo,   "Forecast 1993: Increased Scrutiny of Nonprofits Ups Stakes," *Public Relations Journal* 49, no. 1 (January 1993): 18.

[19]"School Case Shows How Tough Selling Tax Hikes Is Today," *pr reporter* 36, no. 29 (July 26, 1993): 1 and 2.

[20]Barry Bluestone,   "States May Be Making a Healthy Profit on Their Public Colleges and Universities," *Chronicle of Higher Education* 40, no. 7 (October 6, 1993): A52.

[21]Ibid.

[22]Judith R. Phair,   "1992 Education Report Card," *Public Relations Journal* 48, no. 2 (February 1992): 22.

[23]Ibid., 23

[24]Robert A. Baade and Jeffrey O. Sundberg,   "Identifying the Factors that Stimulate Alumni Giving," *Chronicle of Higher Education* 40, no. 6 (September 29, 1993): B1 and B2.

[25]"Briefings: Campus CEOs Say Public Relations' Role Will Increase," *Public Relations Journal* 47, no. 8 (August 1991): 12.

[26]"'In' Box," *Chronicle of Higher Education* 37, no. 47 (August 7, 1991): A9. For the complete report, see Commission on Institutional Relations, *Survey of College and University Presidents' Perceptions of the Public Relations Function* (Washington, D.C.: Council for Advancement and Support of Education, 1991).

[27]Michele Tolela Myers, president, Denison University, quoted in the *1989–1990 Annual Report,* Council for Advancement and Support of Education, Washington, D.C., p. 1.

[28]Marilyn Thomsen,   "Briefings: Church Distances Its Name from Waco Cult," *Public Relations Journal* 49, no. 8 (August 1993): 10 and 12.

[29]Robert H. Woodroof,   "Forecast 1992: Find a Niche That's Relevant," *Public Relations Journal* 48, no. 1 (January 1992): 20.

CHAPTER 7

Trade Associations, Professional Societies, and Labor Unions

The concept of a business or professional association is a highly civilized one. It calls for what people do least well, subordinating their self interest to the betterment of all. And when members of the group are competitors, it seems an unnatural alliance that won't work. Yet it does, as the proliferation of associations has demonstrated.

HOWARD PENN HUDSON

Trade associations, professional societies, and labor unions exist to advance the interests of their members. They accomplish this in three ways: They provide information and services to members, they promote high standards of self-discipline, and they present the members' case to important publics and to government bodies at various levels.

TYPES OF ASSOCIATIONS

Professional associations and *professional societies* typically represent individuals, as do the American Nurses' Association, the American Bar Association, and the Public Relations Society of America. *Cause groups* and *special-interest groups* function as associations of individuals with a common interest or goal. Examples include the National Audubon Society and the American Automobile Association, the nation's largest association with more than 34 million members.[1]

Producer associations and *commodity boards,* such as the National Dairy Promotion and Research Board (with the fifth largest advertising

budget among U.S. associations in 1992, $73 million), National Live-
stock and Meat Board (eighth, with a budget of more than $33 million),
and the Illinois Pork Producers Association, represent the interests of
their members and promote consumption of their commodities.[2]

Membership in *trade associations* usually includes companies,
firms, or other organizations engaged in similar activities. Otherwise
competing members associate to organize and implement mutual-assis-
tance efforts and to expand or protect their industry. Examples include
the National Association of Manufacturers and the General Motors Corporation Dealer Association, which spent more than $250 million in
1992 on advertising in major media, making it the association with the
largest advertising budget in the United States.[3]

Members of *federations*—also referred to as councils or institutes—
typically include other associations. Examples are the Federation of
National Associations, the National Cotton Council of America, and the
Transportation Institute.

Organized labor has a similar structure in that *unions* represent
individual workers, as in the case of the Screen Actors Guild and the
Communication Workers of America. *Federations* of labor unions, such
as the Teamsters and the American Federation of Labor and Congress of
Industrial Organizations (AFL-CIO), represent many different occupational, trade, and craft unions. AFL-CIO, for example, includes more
than 90 different unions with almost 14 million members. It was formed
in 1955 when the two labor federations—the Congress of Industrial
Organizations and the American Federation of Labor—merged under
the leadership of the late George Meany.

ASSOCIATIONS AND SOCIETIES

Associations and societies have proliferated. The 28th edition of Gale
Research's *Encyclopedia of Associations* lists more than 25,000 national associations, more than 53,000 regional, state, and local associations, and more than 11,000 international associations, including
many headquartered outside the United States[4] The American Society
of Association Executives (ASAE) estimates that there are approximately 2500 business and professional associates headquartered in the
Washington, D.C., area alone, making associations the third largest
industry in the nation's capital, after government and tourism.
Approximately 1800 associations are based in the New York City area
and 1400 in the Chicago area.[5]

Associations nationwide employ more than 500,000 people. Thirty-
eight percent employ at least one lobbyist, 35 percent have political
action committees (PACs), 79 percent hold annual conventions, and 79
percent conduct educational seminars apart from national conventions.
Association chief executive officers earn average annual salaries of

almost $84,000, and the public relations officers average just under $48,000, based on ASAE's 1992 compensation survey.[6]

According to 1993 ASAE member records, approximately 80 percent of its member associations have staffs of 20 or fewer.[7] In contrast, the American Medical Association has a staff of approximately 1000 in its Chicago headquarters, 35 in the Washington, D.C., office, and 12 in a New York office. There are 33 on the public relations staff in Chicago and two each in Washington and New York offices.[8] The 296,000-member American Institute of Certified Public Accountants has a staff of 700 in its New York headquarters and 75 in Washington, D.C. The vice president of communications supervises a staff of ten professionals with a budget of more than $5 million.[9]

The number of members is not the only basis for influence and power. Some associations have small but mighty memberships. The Aluminum Association, for example, has only 84 members, but each is a corporation. The same applies to the American Tobacco Institute, which represents a relatively small number of corporations but is one of the most powerful associations in the United States. The powerful American Medical Association represents almost 300,000 dues-paying physician members. And what some call the most powerful association in the United States, the American Association of Retired Persons (AARP), represents more than 32 million members aged 50 and over and 4000 local chapters, making it the second largest association. AARP's membership and influence no doubt will continue to grow because its represents the interests of the fastest-growing segment of U.S. society.

At the state level, the California Milk Advisory Board has a budget of $20 million to promote consumption of dairy products. Another statewide dairy association, the Dairy Council of California (DCC), conducts nutrition education programs financed by the 2200 California producers and more than 100 handlers of milk and milk products. In 1992, DCC had a budget of $4 million, five offices, 30 professionals working in nutrition education, and the services of the San Diego public relations firm of Nuffer, Smith, Tucker, Inc. Their educational programs are presented in secondary school classrooms and directed to the medical and nutrition communities.

The resources dairy associations are able to direct to such activities illustrates the power of producer groups: Congress mandated that dairy farmers nationally contribute a 15-cent checkoff on every 100 pounds of milk produced to promote dairy products. Five cents of the checkoff goes to the National Dairy Promotion and Research Board, 5 cents goes to state or regional promotion organizations, and the remaining 5 cents (sometimes referred to as the middle nickel) can go to either the national or state organization, depending on which one individual diary farmers designate. When 93 percent of the Wisconsin dairy farmers casting ballots in a 1991 referendum voted in favor of directing the discretionary 5 cents to the Wisconsin Milk Marketing Board (WMMB), $10 million was added to the WMWB budget for promoting dairy products, consumer and trade relations, and nutrition education programs in Wisconsin.[10]

The Problem of Serving Many Masters

In contrast to corporations and many other organizations with relatively monolithic interests and hierarchical structures, associations serve membership interests that may differ widely. Association staffs must attempt to meet membership demands and serve their interests externally, but often must do so with little centralized power and authority to act. Any difficulties corporations have in marshaling employees or gaining support of a few publics pale by comparison with the task in associations seeking to satisfy a diversity of members and public opinion groupings. Differences can result from regional influences; narrow concerns particular to specialties within the broad membership category; and varying political, ethnic, or proprietary interests. The challenge for public relations is to find the common ground and unifying position that best represent member interests.

A corporation's management can decide with comparative ease whether—and the degree to which—corporate interests are affected by high or low tariffs, a change in public policy, a new regulation, a strike in the coal industry, or a change of administration in Washington. But such decisions are much more complex for an association's executives and elected officials. The views of all members, and perhaps an evaluation of which ones count most, must somehow be synthesized, represented, and weighed in decisions. This can be a lengthy process. This problem is reflected in a statement of policy of the National Council of Farmer Cooperatives:

> We recognize the wide divergence of political opinion among our employees, member cooperative personnel, and farmer-owners. It would be inappropriate for us to express a partisan viewpoint. Therefore, we will support non-partisan programs, as far as is practicable, and will encourage employee participation in partisan programs of their choosing.

Thus associations are by nature limited to areas of action in which there is an obvious, predetermined unanimity of opinion or a substantial majority in support of any initiatives taken on behalf of membership.

Many times this characteristic of associations does not present a problem, particularly when the greater public interest is involved. For example, when cyanide-laced Tylenol capsules caused seven deaths in Chicago, an association that represents many competing manufacturers—the Nonprescription Drug Manufacturers (NDM)—took the lead for the industry as a whole. NDM representatives met with Food and Drug Administration staff to investigate ways to improve packaging and to develop federal legislation to require safer packaging. The association also launched an education campaign to teach consumers how to protect themselves from product tampering.

The Electronics Industries Association project to develop common standards for equipping television sets with captioning devices for the hearing impaired is another example of competitors cooperating and collaborating through an association. A group of engineers who worked for competing television manufacturers worked together to respond to the requirements of the Americans with Disabilities Act. As a result, today every television set sold is equipped with a captioning device.

An Era of Change and Gain

Traditional inclinations and public postures are changing. While normal, noncontroversial services to members continue as a mainstay for associations, the element of public advocacy is growing. The need first became evident in the 1960s with the passage of many regulatory laws. Legislators began to respond to growing public concerns about civil rights, the environment, and public safety. The wave of government regulations and consumer activism spurred even more rapid change through the 1970s. A climate of growth, competition, and deregulation encouraged even bolder advocacy in the 1980s. The 1990s brought changing technology, growing diversity, economic recession, and increased demands to address social and environment concerns.

From a member's viewpoint, a more aggressive stance might be seen as necessary to counter government intervention in the natural forces of commerce and competition. An executive in a regulatory agency might hold that there has been too little self-discipline within the trades and professions. To a bystander it might seem that there has been too little responsiveness by private entrepreneurs to the needs and standards of the consuming, voting public.

Whatever the rationale, the crunch of controversy seems to have left little choice for associations in the 1990s. The mounting tide of social and environmental concerns, protests, boycotts, and litigation simply could not be treated as routine business, as exceptions, or as nuisances. Response would not wait for an association consensus to develop. Nor would adversaries accept silence. Making matters worse, some situations were unexpected. Some involved only a few members. Some had implications far beyond the scope of the association's franchise. Many associations learned from bitter experience that an aggressive public relations program is a better investment than waiting until the situation calls for a "legislative fire-fighting operation."[11]

Another lesson from experience is that the reputation and effectiveness of an association or society often depend on the public actions of individual members. Individual members taking a posture that is purely defensive, defiant, or protective serves neither the public interest nor the ultimate collective goals of association members. As a result, associations and professional societies have been increasingly willing to serve as advocates and media contacts rather than leaving such actions and responses to individual members.

Not all associations and societies have had to assume an aggressive stance, however. The degree of advocacy and public response to criticism or protest usually reflects the example set by those members who dominate a given association. As a generalization, however, more and more industrial and professional leaders are speaking up in efforts to shape public opinion when their interests are at issue. Public relations staffers in associations and societies have been following suit. Additionally, the increasing number of PACs and political education campaigns make these organizations important power groups in the political process.

The Growing Importance of Public Relations

With such heavy stakes riding on effective communications and strategy in a climate of public skepticism and opposing advocacies, public relations counsel and skill assume major importance. In many associations, public relations practitioners design and implement programs to serve the following needs:

1. To provide members with helpful information (see Figure 17–1 for samples of association publications)
2. To expand the association itself by recruiting new members
3. To harmonize member viewpoints by promoting positive positions
4. To promote the industry or profession
5. To influence government legislation and regulation
6. To improve products and services collectively
7. To gain popular support and combat adverse publicity
8. To train recruits and provide programs of continuing education for all members
9. To contribute to social progress by sponsoring public service programs
10. To promote acceptable public behavior among members so as to gain public credit and stave off government regulation.

To achieve these purposes, public relations practitioners in associations are playing increasingly important roles in dealing with issues in the news that affect their members. For example, as health care reform took center stage in public debate, the American Medical Association public information staff was responding to more than 1100 calls each month, with about 75 percent of the calls from reporters:

Associations have an advantage when it comes to dealing with the news media and other audiences. To the media and other publics, associations often have more credibility than individual companies or public relations firms because, correctly or not, they are perceived as less self-serving.[12]

Examples of Association Publications

Figure 17–1   Courtesy American Society of Association Executives.

ASAE's president, R. William Taylor (Figure 17–2), explains that public relations is even more important for associations in the 1990s as government, media, and many citizens attribute negative motives to "special interests":

> Each of us has some interest that is special to us, whether it be a farmer concerned about his business, a manufacturer interested in marketing his product, or a teacher worried about salary and benefits. Each of these people can work through their association to make sure his or her interests are protected. Effective public relations combined with government relations will ensure that the correct message is expressed and the members' needs have been addressed. This is where good public relations can combat the image that "special interest" is bad.[13]

Ironically, ASAE did not have a public relations department until 1982. It was formed after an audit by its public relations firm, Hill and Knowlton, and an ASAE Foundation study of association members

EXHIBIT 17-1

ASSOCIATION PUBLIC RELATIONS PROGRAMS

The following examples were selected from winners of the 1991, 1992, and 1993 ASAE "Associations Advance America" Campaign Awards Program.

The *National Association of Life Underwriters* (NALU) initiated a "Million Hour Pledge" to involve actively its 140,000 members in public service and volunteerism. The pledge was for 1 year, yet NALU members far exceeded the goal and completed 1.6 million hours of public service.

The *Cosmetic, Toiletry, and Fragrance Association Foundation* conducted a national program called "Look Good . . . Feel Better" to teach female cancer patients, through make-over workshops, techniques to help restore appearance and self-image. The program, in conjunction with the American Cancer Society and the National Cosmetology Association, has helped 20,000 women each year since 1989.

The *National Mental Health Association* created a "Coping with War" resources packet during Operation Desert Storm, with fact sheets on topics such as coping with war-related stress, helping children handle grief, and understanding military resources for families in crisis. Five thousand kits were distributed through local community organizations.

The *California Podiatric Medical Association* created "Shoes for the Needy," which provides 3000 to 5000 pairs of shoes each month to eight homeless shelters in San Francisco. Volunteers acquired a warehouse and solicited donations of shoes from shoe companies. In addition, members provide free foot screenings monthly in the shelters.

The *Society of Automotive Engineers* created "A World in Motion," a supplemental science program for students in grades 4, 5, and 6. Volunteer engineers team with teachers to stimulate students' interest in science through classroom experiments.

The *Houston Automobile Dealers Association* sponsors "Earning by Learning" to give young readers the incentive to read by giving them a monetary reward for each book read. In 1992, 1179 children read 9432 books and earned $18,864.

The *American Public Health Association* collaborated with the American Academy of Pediatrics to develop the first-ever standards for out-of-home child care facilities. After 5 years of development and review by many professionals, the standards were distributed to child care directors and advocates in every state.

Summarized by Lorri Lee, APR, Director of Public Relations, American Society of Association Executives, Washington, D.C.

R. William Taylor, President American Society of Association Executives

Figure 17–2 Used with permission. Photo courtesy American Society of Association Executives.

found that public relations was one of the lowest rated among a list of functions performed by their associations. Public relations plays a major role in associations in that both internal service programs for members and external advocacy functions involve a great deal of communication support and sound public relations counsel. In fact, *the major goals of associations parallel those of public relations: to establish and maintain mutually beneficial relationships among internal publics and between the membership collectively and their many external publics.*

The Nature of Programming

Much of what associations and societies do in the name of public relations follows an annual cycle: seeking new members, making reports to them, and holding conferences. Most associations engage in some of or all the following:

1. Preparing and disseminating technical and educational publications, videos, and other public information materials
2. Sponsoring conventions and meetings, instructional seminars, and exhibitions
3. Handling government contacts and interpreting to members the legislative and administrative actions of government agencies
4. Compiling and publishing relevant statistics
5. Preparing and distributing news, information, and public service announcements to the media
6. Planning and implementing public service activities (see Exhibit 17–1 for examples of association public service programs)
7. Establishing and enforcing codes of ethics and standards of performance
8. Disseminating governmental and other standards to members
9. Conducting cooperative research: scientific, social, and economic
10. Placing institutional and product advertising on behalf of an entire industry, profession, or business endeavor; or in furtherance of such matters as public health, safety, or welfare (see Figure 17–3 for example of American Medical Association advocacy advertising)
11. Promoting good employee relations, accident prevention, and cooperation within an industry, profession, or other special-interest membership.

The public of first importance is members, with public officials second, the voting public third, and consumers or customers fourth. Trade associations typically rank consumers higher in the list. By design, associations facilitate the exchange of information among members and externally to publics who are affected by, involved with, or have an impact on members' activities. Nine out of ten associations conduct educational programs for both their members and external publics. The American Chamber of Commerce Executives (ACCE), the national association of chamber management professionals based in Alexandria, Virginia, for example, lists more than 100 books and other reference publications available to members. ACCE also offers members access to a comprehensive electronic information center, ChamberNet$_{TM}$, via computer and modem. Members can call up information about chamber management, membership databases, case studies, abstracts of chamber-related articles published in national and regional periods, and other commercial information services. See Figure 17–4 for an example of a search to learn about member-retention methods used by the Holland (Michigan) Area Chamber of Commerce.

Trends include growing emphasis on public affairs and advocacy communication and on the use of computers, communication technology, and on-line databases to meet the information needs of constituents and members. After interviewing a panel of technology consultants, the editor of ACCE's monthly journal to members, *Chamber Executive*, concluded that "providing information transcends all chamber functions and the future simply holds more of the same."[14] The panel of technology experts' observations about chambers apply to all associations:

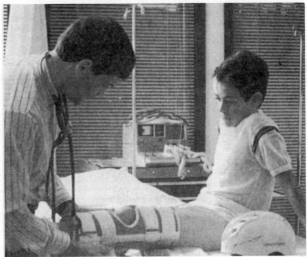

Figure 17–3   Courtesy American Medical Association.

Chambers will have to become more information-driven if they want to impact legislation, do economic development, educate folks. Traditional (chambers of commerce) have been in the middle, moving information. Now there are so many sources of information that chambers must figure out how to tie-in, how to become a leading source of information and deliver that information faster, cheaper, easier. Otherwise, chambers will be usurped by technology.[15]

ChamberNet Search Menus

How Does ChamberNet Work?

It takes just a few minutes to learn how to use the service. For instance, to access the Chamber Management Database, you simply follow a few menus:

At this point, you will see a listing of documents on the topic of your choice, and you may choose whichever documents you would like to read:

After you choose a number, you'll see the text of the article.

CHAMBERNET MAIN MENU

Selection:	Service	At Command?
1.	ChamberNet Mail	
2.	ChamberNet Bulletin Boards	check (board)
3.	All Information DATABASES	goto local
4.	Special Delivery Services	c acce.msg.svc
5.	Commercial Information Services	goto oag (news)
6.	U.S. Congress Listing	c us.congress
99.	Exit ChamberNet	bye

Type EXIT at Command? to return to this Main Menu.

Please enter selection: 3

CHAMBER MANAGEMENT DATABASE - CATEGORY MENU

Categories

1 — > All Chamber Management Database
2 — > Chamber Administration: Finance
3 — > Communications; Membership
4 — > Economic Development; Global Economy; Research
5 — > Government Relations; Public Policy Issues
6 — > Small Business
7 — > Misc.- Community Leadership; Convention & Visitors Bureau
8 — > Category Descriptions
9 — > Searchable Words
10 — > Help
98 — > Return to Previous Menu
99 — > Return to Opening Menu
BYE — > Disconnect from Service

Option ===> 1

CHAMBERNET DATABASE MENU

1 — > ACCE's Chamber Management Database
2 — > ACCE's Who's Who Directory of Members
3 — > ACCE's Computer Updates
4 — > NAMD's Membership Databases
5 — > LEX's (Local Exchange) Local Government Solutions
6 — > LEX's Urban Affairs Abstracts
7 — > LEX's Health, Human & Youth Services
A — > All Databases
D — > Databases Descriptions
99 — > Return to Opening Menu
BYE — > Disconnect from Service

Option ===> 1

DATABASE SEARCH MENU

1 — > Database Search
2 — > Searchable Words
3 — > Help
98 — > Return to Previous Menu
99 — > Return to Opening Menu
BYE — > Disconnect from Service

Option ===> 1

Enter search term(s) (or RETURN for Main Menu)
> membership and retention

. . . .

147 Document(s) Qualified

Display Index (Y / N) > Y

1 Chamber Membership Retention: Decatur, IL
2 Membership Club Earns Dues: Sacramento, CA
3 Retention For Small Business Members: Lawrence, KS
4 Statewide Membership Campaign: Sanford, ME
5 Operation Thank You is a Big Hit: Anniston, AL
6 Annual Incentive for Retention: Tulsa, OK
7 Motivating Volunteers: Naples, FL
8 Member Retention Program: Wilmington, DE
9 Membership Anniversary Calls: Sioux Falls, SD
10 Member to Member Sales: Dayton, OH
11 Retention Takes Hard Work: Kansas City, MO
12 Member Retention Through Telemarketing: Dayton, OH
13 Retention Methods: Indianapolis, IN
14 Recognizing the Member of the Month: Farmers Branch, TX
15 Strategic Plan for Marketing: Albuquerque, NM
16 Retention Methods: Detroit, MI
17 Membership Retention: Lower "Drop Rate": Cleveland, OH
18 Non-dues Sources of Revenue: Alexandria, VA
19 A More Service Oriented Chamber: Montreal, QU
20 Emphasis on First Year Members: Stockton, CA
21 More Tips On Retention: Scranton, PA
22 Membership Campaign: Salt Lake City, UT
23 Member Retention Methods: Holland, MI

Enter number(s) from entries listed or Press RETURN to enter new keyword(s)
>23

MEMBER RETENTION METHODS: HOLLAND, MI
NAMD-Award for Excellence-Application- Member Retention Methods
GOAL-
Achieve a renewal rate among existing members of at least 86%

BACKGROUND/KEY ELEMENTS OF STRATEGY:
Retention is a key measure of our success at the Holland Chamber. To keep our "customers" happy, we have developed a variety of successful practices. Each new member is invited to their first Early Bird Breakfast free of charge. They are given a special name-tag, introduced to the audience, and presented with their membership plaque. Each new member is also invited to a New Member Reception and is "adopted" by an Ambassador to encourage participation in chamber activities. Monthly communications with all members include the newsletter plus all members are contacted in the newsletter plus all members are contacted during "Operation Thank You."

RESULTS:
As a result of the above efforts, 856 members out of 971 or 88.1% of our existing members renewed their membership. One-third of those dropping their membership did so because they went out of business or relocated out of the area.

Date: June 1992
Holland Area Chamber of Commerce - Holland, Michigan
Size: MED

Figure 17–4

LABOR UNIONS

Organized labor unions, with a total membership of less than 19 million in 1993, represent only about one of every six of the nation's wage earners and salaried employees. In 1983, one of every five employed workers belonged to a union.[16] (See Table 17–1.) These levels are significantly lower than in 1945, when one in three workers was a union member. Because of the generally acknowledged collapse of the U.S. steel industry, union membership among steel workers dropped from 1.2 million members in 1980 to only 560,000 members in 1993.[17]

TABLE 17-1	UNION AFFILIATION		
	Percentage of Union Members		
	1983[1]	**1988[2]**	**1992[3]**
Percentage of *all employed workers* in unions	20.1%	16.8%	15.8%
Percentage of employed *men* in unions	24.1	20.4	18.7
Percentage of employed *women* in unions	14.6	12.6	12.7
Percentage of *full-time* workers in unions	22.9	19.1	17.8
Percentage of *part-time* workers in unions	8.4	6.6	7.2
Total number employed workers (16+ yrs.)	97,450,000	111,800,000	117,600,000

[1] "Union Affiliation," *Employment and Earnings* 32, no. 1 (January 1985): 208.
[2] "Union Affiliation," *Employment and Earnings* 36, no. 1 (January 1989): 225.
[3] "Union Affiliation," *Employment and Earnings* 40, no. 1 (January 1993): 238.

Despite the decline in membership, organized labor still symbolizes and speaks for working men and women in the United States. Suggestions that the labor movement is dead are exaggerated, according to Lynn Williams, president of the United Steel Workers of America (USWA):

> The figures on unionization rates in the private sector are quite misleading. . . . When you look at the Northeastern states, such as New York and Pennsylvania, the percentage of the unionized work force is quite respectable by world standards. It's not the 90%-plus figure of Sweden or the 50%-plus of Germany or even the 40% figure of Canada. But at 34%, it's quite respectable.[18]

The American labor movement is credited with helping bring about many of the changes and legislation in civil rights, health, education, and employee rights that have occurred since the death of President Franklin Roosevelt. Its clout has diminished recently, however, as a result of changes in the work force and declining public support of labor unions. The critical turning point may have been in 1981 when President Ronald Reagan ordered the firing of striking air traffic controllers, effectively breaking their union, the Professional Air Traffic Controllers Organization (PATCO).[19] Since that time, employers have used various tactics to counter powerful unions, including filing for protection under the bankruptcy laws, using company lock-outs of striking workers, and following through on threats to replace striking workers.

The power of labor's voice in shaping national public opinion and policy goes far beyond what might be suggested by its modest numerical share of the popular electorate. One reason is that the movement's specific and deeply held convictions hold strong attraction for adherents. In the words of an early 1900s union organizer who was sentenced to be executed, "Don't mourn, organize."[20] Strong convictions get translated into cash that is dispersed to selected candidates by organized labor's powerful PACs.

Another reason unions remain powerful is that union leadership traditionally has been able to leverage concessions for members because of leadership's ability to deliver a majority of their members' votes as a bloc in local, state, and national elections. Even this traditional voting bloc power was threatened after the PATCO case. PATCO had broken ranks and joined the Teamsters in supporting Reagan over Jimmy Carter in 1980. But in the 1992 presidential election, some credited union support with having made the difference in President Bill Clinton's bid for the White House.

The Role of Public Relations

In pursuing their stated goals, unions and their leadership share in the burden of responsibility for the health of the economy. With serious problems besetting the economy in the 1990s, it follows that there has been a decline in public confidence in unions as well as in business, government, and most professional groups.

Understandably, then, public relations has taken on added emphasis as the movement's political, educational, and community involvement has increasingly supplemented its traditional role in labor-management relations. The skills of public relations specialists and others have been augmented and honed to meet the needs of expanded, more sophisticated programs. Indicative of this trend, most unions now have a "public relations director" rather than a "publications director" who simply responds to news media inquiries between putting out union newsletters and other publications directed to members.

Awareness of the need to be more responsive constitutes a major change for the labor movement from the early days of George Meany, who served as first president of the AFL-CIO. Meany's early notions of dealing with the media, for example, reputedly included the directive, "Kick the damn reporters down the stairs." For much of the mid-1950s until the 1970s, no group in American society had a more identifiable, outspoken, and unquestioned spokesperson than labor's Meany. He strongly backed the Vietnam War, provided lukewarm support for Democratic Senator George McGovern's presidential candidacy, and led the AFL-CIO call for President Richard Nixon's impeachment. For 25 years, he was the chief public relations spokesman for labor.

Labor's primary public relations orientation remains to print media, both within and outside the labor movement. Labor public relations uses press contacts, preparation and distribution of materials on specific subjects, television spots (see Figure 17–5), and interviews and press conferences to get labor's point of view across (see Figure 17–6). Of increasing importance are the estimated 5000 union publications on the national and local level. Many of these have improved their format and writing quality and toned down their rhetoric, often publishing articles from the International Labor Press Association about issues affecting the labor movement.

The Problem of Strikes

Labor has had its problems in developing and sustaining a broad base of sympathetic support from the nonunion lay public. This results, in part, from strikes, the strategic use of work stoppages to gain concessions from employers. Stoppages are typically timed for maximum inconvenience, thereby exerting the greatest pressure for settlement on the employer.

Despite the inconveniences and costs involved, the strike weapon is considered essential to labor's success. It is visible, in contrast to management's policies and reactions. It also takes advantage of management's need not to appear to be bullying workers and not to portray employees as enemies. Media coverage tends to feature picket lines, angry strikers, and vocal labor leaders. Management, on the other hand, is somewhat restricted by law as to what can be said and done. (Review the section in Chapter 6 on the National Labor Act of 1935 and the Taft-Hartley Act of 1947.)

Explaining public inconveniences caused by strikes is part of the role public relations plays in organized labor. But in times of a bad economy, downsizing, layoffs, and high unemployment, it is a story that must be told with less frequency: The number of major work stoppages and idleness in 1992 was at its lowest levels since record keeping began in 1947. There were 35 work stoppages and four million days of idleness in 1992. A total of 364,000 workers were involved in major stoppages, with most—230,000—involved in a national railroad stoppage that lasted 2 days. In the longest work stoppage of 1992, the Teamsters Union struck the *Pittsburgh Press* from May until November, shutting down the *Press* and its rival *Pittsburgh Post-Gazette*. The strike idled 1400 workers at the two papers.[21]

In a typical year, contract negotiations involve almost three million workers under 700 major collective bargaining agreements (those covering 1000 or more workers).[22] On the surface, it would be easy to advise unions not to go on strike because of the impact on public opinion and

American Federation of State, County, and Municipal Employees' 60-Second Television Spot, "Social Security"

When I began working as a young man the government had just started Social Security.

Part of every worker's paycheck would be matched by the boss and sent to the government. When we retired, we'd get enough of our money back to help us get by.

It was sort of a contract between working people and the government.

Now the administration wants to cut out some of the benefits you'd get at 65. And at 62 they want to cut your benefits . . . from 80% to 55%.

SOCIAL SECURITY.
A CONTRACT, NOT A HANDOUT.

AFSCME.

Figure 17–5   Courtesy American Federation of State, County, and Municipal Employ

AFL-CIO President Lane Kirkland Addressing National Press Club, Washington, DC

Figure 17–6   Used with permission. Courtesy AFL-CIO.

relations with management. But unions have as their primary obligation to meet the needs of the people they represent. Strategic public relations in the labor movement often calls for leveraging labor's position of power in ways that will not be universally popular, but that will achieve labor's goals for members.

Even under the pressures of a weak economy and the perceived threat of the North American Free Trade Agreement (NAFTA), the need for unions is as valid today as in the past, according to USWA President Williams:

> All across the United States, one sees that workers need to have their economic interests represented in order to be able to bargain with their employers to ensure that they receive the best wages and working conditions. Look at what has happened in the last dozen years: the decline in real wages, barely maintainable family incomes despite the fact that both partners now work as a rule, the increase in temporary workers and companies contracting out.[23]

The Challenge for Labor

The challenges of public relations in the labor movement are basically the same as in all other settings: to establish and maintain mutually beneficial relationships with those upon whom success or failure depends. It is labor's position that its success should be measured not on a barometer of public opinion of its "image," but on results. Similarly, labor public relations efforts should be measured by the quality and persuasiveness of information presented to union members and to other publics on important issues, rather than on image-building advertising campaigns that ignore a union's inescapable responsibility to its members.

Members of the work force in the twenty-first century will be largely younger than members today, female, and multicultural. Therefore, the greatest challenge facing the largely older, male, and white union leadership is not unlike the challenge facing leaders in other institutions: Labor must attract the next generation of leaders from females and people of color.

To that end, the AFL-CIO Organizing Institute has mounted an annual 6-month internship program that prepares young, potential leaders for careers as union organizers. After only 4 years, the program has surpassed its goal of placing 20 to 25 new organizers in the field annually, with diversity in the leadership ranks as a priority. Seventy percent of the interns have been female or people from under-represented groups.[24] In the final analysis, the labor movement is also a social movement.

ADDITIONAL READINGS

"Association Public Relations," special issue of *Public Relations Quarterly* 37, no. 1 (Spring 1992). Features a collection of articles on professional, ethical, legal, and management issues in association public relations.

Ballot, Michael. *Labor-Management Relations in a Changing Environment.* New York: John Wiley and Sons, 1992. Covers the broad field of industrial relations, including the changing relationship between unions and employers, the future of organized labor, and public sector unionization.

Bradley, Joseph F. *The Role of Trade Associations and Professional Business Societies in America.* University Park: Pennsylvania State University Press, 1965. Assesses the historical role of national business associations in a free society and economic system.

Close, Arthur C., and others, eds. *Washington Representatives: 1993,* 17th ed. Washington, D.C.: Columbia Books, 1993. Lists "who does what for whom in the nation's capital," illustrating the presence of associations, unions, and other special interests.

Dunlop, John T. *Industrial Relations Systems,* rev. ed. Boston: Harvard Business School Press, 1993. Presents a general theory of industrial relations, outlining the formal and informal ways management organizations, workers, and government agencies are organized.

Washington, D.C.: Columbia Books, 1993. Lists "who does what for whom in the nation's capital," illustrating the presence of associations, unions, and other special interests.

Dunlop, John T.   *Industrial Relations Systems,* rev. ed. Boston: Harvard Business School Press, 1993. Presents a general theory of industrial relations, outlining the formal and informal ways management organizations, workers, and government agencies are organized.

Lynn, Leonard H., and Timothy J. McKeown.   *Organizing Business: Trade Associations in America and Japan.* Washington, D.C.: American Enterprise Institute for Public Policy Research, 1988. Examines how business associations in the United States and Japan help coordinate economic and political activity and differences in the flow of information and influence between corporations and trade associations.

Robinson, Archie.   *George Meany and His Times: A Biography.* New York: Simon and Schuster, 1981. Details the life and personality of the man who shaped the American labor movement, and the political events and social changes during his 63 years in labor unions.

Schlossberg, Stephen I., and Judith A. Scott.   *Organizing and the Law,* 4th ed.

NOTES

Washington, D.C.: Bureau of National Affairs, 1991. Guides readers through the process of a union organizing campaign and a National Labor Relations Board election, including the ground rules for union organizers.

Turner, Lowell.   *Democracy at Work: Changing World Markets and the Future of Unions.* Ithaca, N.Y.: Cornell University Press, 1991. Compares labor movements in six developed nations, concluding that unions still have roles to play in the competitive global economy.

[1]"Association Fact Book," pamphlet published by the American Society of Association Executives, Washington, D.C., May 1993, p. 21.

[2]Ibid.

[3]Paul H. Alvarez,   "Overall Media Buying Stagnates But Targeted TV Booms," *Public Relations Journal* 49, no. 8 (August 1993): 16.

[4]Peggy Kneffel Daniels and Carol A. Schwartz, eds.,   *Encyclopedia of Associations*, 28th ed. (Detroit: Gale Research, 1994), inside cover table in vol. 1, part 3.

[5]"Association Fact Book," 25.

[6]Ibid., 17–23. Salary figures are also found in *Association Executive Compensation Study*, 8th ed. (Washington, D.C.: American Society of Association Executives, January 1993): xii.

[7]Personal communication with Lorri Lee, APR, director of Public Relations, American Society of Association Executives, October 25, 1993. Lee helped update this chapter by providing useful suggestions, data, examples, and illustrations.

[8]Personal communication with Thomas G. Tofty, director of Public Information, American Medical Association, Chicago, October 26, 1993.

[9]*Jack O'Dwyer's Newsletter* 23, no. 24 (June 13, 1990): 1.

[10]From "Wisconsin Milk Marketing Board 'Middle Nickle,' 1991," unpublished case study summary distributed at "Firehouse Tech," professional development seminar, Morgan and Myers (Jefferson, Wisc.) public relations firm, June 3 and

4, 1993, Oconomowoc, Wisc.

[11]Helen Frank Bensimon and Patricia A. Walker, "Associations Gain Prestige and Visibility by Serving as Expert Resources for Media," *Public Relations Journal* 48, no. 2 (February 1992): 16.

[12]Bensimon and Walker, "Associations Gain Prestige," 16.

[13]R. William Taylor, in speech to the International Convention Center Conference, October 29, 1993, San Antonio, Tex.

[14]"Changing Technology—How Can We Keep Up?" *Chamber Executive* 20, no. 9 (September 1993): 1.

[15]Ibid. Quote from Mike Herron, president, Humanomics, Sandy, Ore.

[16]Data on union affiliation found in the January issues of *Employment and Earnings*, published monthly by the U.S. Department of Labor, Bureau of Labor Statistics, Washington, D.C.

[17]Barbara Presley Noble, "Reinventing Labor: An Interview with Union President Lynn Williams," *Harvard Business Review* 71, no. 4 (July/August 1993): 115.

[18]Ibid., 116.

[18]Mark Shields, "What PATCO Did to Labor," *Washington Post National Weekly Edition*, January 2, 1984, p. 26.

[20]John Hill, as quoted by Barbara Presley Noble, "Organizing the Future," *Harvard Business Review* 71, no. 4 (July/August 1993): 124.

[21]"Labor Month in Review," *Monthly Labor Review* 116, no. 3 (March 1993): 2.

[22]Lisa M. Williamson, "Collective Bargaining in 1993: Jobs Are the Issue," *Monthly Labor Review* 116, no. 1 (January 1993): 3.

[23]Noble, "Reinventing Labor," 121.

[24]Noble, "Organizing the Future," 124.

Index

-A-

Abbott Laboratories, 77
ABC, 172
Aburdene, Patricia, 202
Accreditation, 144-45
Action:
    communication and, 379-80
    component of strategy, 380-86
    open systems response and, 383-86
Adams, Samuel, 91, 92
Adams v. Tanner, 143
Adjustment and adaptation:
    cybernetics in open systems, 214-19
    ecological approach, 199-200
    open and closed systems, 212-14
    open systems model of public relations, 219-24
    systems perspective, 206-12
    trends and changes, 200-206
Advertising:
    agencies, 75-76
    definition of, 10
    examples of, 10-11
    readership techniques, 424
Advertising Age, 76
Advisory committees/boards, 332-33
Aero Mayflower Transit Co., 277
AFL-CIO, 528, 540-41, 544
Agenda-setting theory, 13, 239-40
AIDS, 202
Alcoa, 73
Allen, Ben, 111
Allen, Robert E., 273, 348
Allen, Ronald W., 261
Allen, Walter S., 108
Allstate Insurance Co., 276
Aluminum Association, 529
American Alumni Council, 518
American Association of Engineers, 114
American Association of Retired Persons (AARP), 529
American Association of School Administrators, 516
American Automobile Association, 527
American Bar Association, 156, 527
American Cancer Society, 392, 397
American Chamber of Commerce Executives (ACCE), 536

American College Publicity Association, 116
American College Public Relations Association, 116, 518
American Council on Public Relations (ACPR), 103, 146
American Express, 77
American Federation of Teachers, 516
American Heart Association, 346, 500
American Hospital Association, 149
American Institute of Certified Public Accountants, 529
American Medical Association (AMA), 99, 289, 529, 532, 536
American Newspaper Publishers Association, 424
American Nurses' Association, 173, 527
American Public Health Association, 535
American Public Relations Association (APRA), 141, 146
American Red Cross, 72, 109, 335
American Revolution, 91-92
American Society of Association Executives (ASAE), 528-29, 533, 535
American Society of Hospital Marketing and Public Relations, 149
American Society of Personnel Administrators, 72
American Stock Exchange, 179-80
American Tobacco Institute, 529
Amnesty International, 204
Anderson, J. Robert, 524
Anderson, Steve H., 270
Annual meetings, 454
Annual reports, 451-54
Anti-Digit Dialing League, 90
Anti-Saloon League, 111
Antonini, Joseph, 67
Apple Computer, 261
Appropriation, 188, 189
Aramony, William, 494
Arbitron Co., 422
ARCO, 333
Arizona Economic Council, 80
Arnold, H. H., 119
James E. Arnold Consultants, 78
Arts, public relations in, 523
Arvida Corp., 178
Associated Press (AP), 285, 286, 485

Association of American College News Bureaus, 116
Associations (*see also under name of*):
    changes in, 531-32
    growth of, 528-32
    problems with, 530-31
    programs of, 534-37
    role of public relations in, 532-37
    types of, 527-28
AT&T, 101, 107, 108, 114-15, 218-19, 263, 273, 437
Atlanta Bureau of Police Services (ABPS), 384
Attitudes, 248
Audience:
    delivered versus effective, 422
    measuring, 422-26
Audit Bureau of Circulation (ABC), 289, 422
Automobile industry, 106
Availability of staff practitioners, 65
N. W. Ayer, 76, 101, 107

-B-

Bacon's PR and Media Information Systems, 421
Baer, George F., 104
Daniel H. Baer, Inc., 78
Baker, Joseph Varney, 117
Baker, Ray Stannard, 101-2
Baker v. Daly, 143
Baldwin, William, 113
Banking, 93-94, 115-16 (*see also* Financial relations)
Bank Marketing Association, 116
Bank Public Relations and Marketing Association, 116
Barbarians at the Gate, 444
Barkelew, Ann, 328
Barnes Hospital, 77
Barnum, Phineas T., 94, 95
Barriers:
    communication, 394-96, 398
    to effective government public relations, 472-78
Barry, David S., 105
Barton, Gary, 409
Baumgartner, J. Hampton, 106
Baxter, Leone, 118
Beck, Vicki Hoffman, 509
Beckley, John, 96
Beeman, Alice L., 116
Bell, Eugene C., 220-21
Bell, Sue H., 220-21
Bell Telephone System, 90
Benchmarks, 426-27
Benton & Bowles, 76
Bernays, Edward L., 2, 100, 111, 112, 136, 142-43, 223, 390
Bernstein, Carl, 479
Bhopal, India, 443

Biddle, Nicholas, 90, 93-94
Bjornlund, Lydia, 474
Blackmun, Harry, 167
Black Public Relations Society, 149
Blacks, 117
Bleyer, Willard G., 107-8
Block, Ed, 347
Blythe, Richard, 113
Boesky, Ivan F., 181, 444
Boorstin, Daniel, 134
Boulware, Lemuel R., 176
Bradford, Andrew, 288
Bradlee, Ben, 304
Bradley, Thomas, 329-30
Brady, Mathew, 484
Brennan, William J., 183
Bridge, C. A., 103
Brisbane, Arthur, 104
British Institute of Public Relations, 2
Broadcast media, access to, 183-85
Brochures, 266
Howard Bronson and Co., 178
Brown, David, 483
Bruno, Harry A., 113
Bryan, William Jennings, 96
Bryce, Lord, 329
Buckley, Walter, 214-15, 222
Buckley v. Valeo, 169, 171
Budgeting, planning process and, 371-74
Buhlman, Margaret, 408
Bulletin boards, 269-70
Burger, Chester, 78, 309
Burger, Warren, 183
Burke, James E., 23
Burrelles's Press Clipping Service, 421
Burson, Harold, 379, 384
Burson-Marsteller, 23, 28, 29, 74, 75, 408
Bush, George, 443, 475, 498
Business and industry:
    competition, 436-37
    consumer affairs, 455-56
    financial relations, 450-54
    government as, 488-89
    philanthropy, 446-50
    quality issues, 456-57
    social responsibility, 438-46
    titles in, 437-38
Business Week, 509
Byoir, Carl, 110, 111
    Carl Byoir and Associates, 75

-C-

Cable News Network (CNN), 298, 485
Cable television, 298-99

Calhoun, John C., 93
California Milk Advisory Board, 529
California Podiatric Medical Association, 535
Callaway Vineyards, 264
Call-in telephone lines, 334-35
Campaigns, public information, 396-97
Canadian Public Relations Society (CPRS), 44, 147
Cantor, Bill, 50, 51-53
Carnation Co., 181
Carnegie-Frick Steel Co., 97
Carter, Jimmy, 468
Caterpillar, 77, 374, 439
Cause groups, 527
CBS, 172
C-Cube Microsystems, 77
Celler, Emanuel, 174
Central Hudson, 168
Chacma, Inc., 339
Chaffee, Steven H., 399-400
Chandler, Donna, 37-38
Channel, 233-35
Chase, W. Howard, 16
Chemical Manufacturers Association, 442
Chevron Corp., 438, 457-58
Chicago Edison Co., 106
Childs, Harwood L., 2-3, 223
Churches, 108-9, 115, 522-23
CIA, 186
Ciba-Geigy Canada Ltd., 264
Citizens Against Rent Control v. City of Berkeley, 171
Civil rights, 204-5
Civil War, 98, 484
Clarke, Edward Y., 114
Clarke, Joseph Ignatius Constantine, 106
Clarke, Mathew St. Clair, 93, 95
Cleveland, Grover, 103
Clinton, Bill, 475, 489, 501
Clinton, Hillary Rodham, 501
Clipping services, 420-22
Closed circuit television (CCTV), 275-76
Closed systems, 212-14
Club Med I, 215-16
Coca-Cola Co., 193, 438
Cold War, 120, 468
Collective bargaining, 175-76
Commercial speech, 167-68
Commission on Public Relations Education, 136, 408
Committee on Public Information (CPI), 2, 109-10
Commodity boards, 527-28
Communicating for Results in Government (Garnett), 465
Communication (see also Media):
    action and, 379-80
    barriers/stereotypes, 394-96
    between labor and management, 175-76

commonness in, 400-402
component of strategy, 386-402
disseminating the message, 397-400
dissemination versus, 228-30
effects of, 238-42
elements of the communication model, 230-38
employee, 260-63
facilitator role, 43
framing the message, 386-89
global, 203-4
model of congruent, 401
relationships, 236-37
semantics, 390-91
seven C's of, 402-3
social setting and, 237-38
symbols, 392-94
technician role, 42
Communication, methods of:
    cable television, 298-99
    closed circuit television (CCTV), 275-76
    displays and exhibits, 277-79
    magazines, 288-90
    newspapers, 280-85
    organizational publications, 263-67
    radio, 290-92
    teleconferencing, 273-75
    television, 120-21, 234-35, 293-98
    verbal, 270-73
    videotapes, films, slides, 276-77
    wire services and news syndicates, 285-88
Communication Briefings, 141, 142
Communication Workers of America, 528
Communication World, 139, 147, 289, 408
Communique, 147
Community forums, 330-32
Competition, 436-37
Concentric-circle theory, 398
Consensus, coorientational, 250-51
Consolidated Edison Co., 171
Consumer affairs, 455-56
Content analysis, 339-40
Continuing education, 138
Control Data Corp., 438
Cooke, Jay, 98
Coolidge, Calvin, 438
Coorientation, public opinion and, 249-54
Copyright, 190-92
Corporate political expression, 168-69
Cosmetic, Toiletry, and Fragrance Association Foundation, 535
Council for the Advancement and Support of Education (CASE), 116, 518
Council on Public Relations Education, 121-22
Counseling firms:
    advantages of, 82-83

Counseling firms (*continued*)
  advertising agencies, 75-76
  checklist for selecting, 78
  client-firm relationship, 79-82
  cost of, 84-86
  disadvantages of, 83-84
  public relations firms, 74-75
  reasons for retaining, 78-79
  specialization in, 76-78
Cox, Mark S., 38-40, 67
Creel, George, 2, 109-10, 118
Crises, anticipating, 366-69
Crockett, Davy, 13, 94-95
Crystal Harmony, 368
Crystallizing Public Opinion (Bernays), 112, 136, 223
Cunard Hotels and Resorts, 77
Cunningham Communication, Inc., 77
Curti, Merle, 97
Cybernetics in open systems, 214-19

-D-

Dairy Council of California (DCC), 529
Dalton, H. J., Jr., 485
Davis, Arthur Vining, 178
Davis, Bill, 469
Davis, Elmer, 118
D-A-Y, 102
Deaver, Michael, 77
Decima Research, 408
Decision-making role, 62-63
Defamation, 187-88
Delahaye Group, 421
Depression, 116-17
Deregulation, 442
Derus Media Service, 288
Detroit Edison Co., 438
Development, 20-21
DeVries, Henry, 22
Dewey, John, 245, 246
Diary method, 424
Dictionary of Cautionary Words and Phrases, 396
Diffusion of information, 240-41, 398-400
Digital Research, Inc., 217
Dilenschneider, Robert, 86
Disasters, anticipating, 366-69
Disclosure, 177-78
Walt Disney Co., 172
Disney World, 13
Displays, 277-79
Disseminating the message, 397-400
Dissemination versus communication, 228-30
Dissensus, 250
Dominant coalition, 62
Domination, 66

Douglas, William O., 165
Dow Chemical Canada, 266-67
Dow Chemical Co., 333, 441
Dowling, James H., 75
Dozier, David, 406
Drexel Burnham Lambert, 181
Druck, Kalman B., 433
Dryden, John F., 101
Dudley, Pendleton, 102, 109, 150
Dudley-Anderson-Yutzy Public Relations, 102
DuPont, 447
DuPont Powder Co., 107
Durand, E. Dana, 477

-E-

Eastern Railroad Presidents Conference v. Noerr, 174
Eastman Kodak Co., 10, 64
Eaton Corp., 438
Ecological approach, 199-200
Edelman Public Relations Worldwide, 75, 82
Edison, Thomas A., 98, 390
Edison General Electric Co., 98
Editing, 33
Education:
  accountability in, 512, 517
  continuing, 138
  corporate philanthropy for, 447
  degree programs, 136-38
  public relations for public schools, 512-16
  public relations in, 511-22
  public relations in higher education, 516-21
  reform in, 495
  research development, 138-40
  role of college presidents, 521-22
Elections:
  contributions to, 169-70
  labor, 175
Electronics Industries Association, 531
Eliot, Charles W., 107
Eliot, T. S., 390
Elliott, Frank R., 136
Ellsworth, James Drummond, 101, 107
E-mail, 269
Emerson, Guy, 110
Employee communication, 260-63
Employment and Earnings, 27
Enclosures, 268
Encyclopedia of Associations, 528
Engineering of Consent, The (Bernays), 2
Engler, John, 509
Environmental issues, roles and, 45-46, 200-201, 208-9, 445-46
Equal time rule, 184-85

Ethics, 129
  code of, 151-57
  corporate, 438-46
  future of, 157-60
  professional, 130
  professional privilege, 131-32
  social responsibility, 132-34
  trust, 130-31
Evaluation (*see also* Programs, evaluation of):
  research process, 410-13
Executive Speechmaker, The, 272
Exhibits, 277-79
Expert prescriber role, 42-43
External relations, 20
Exxon, 79, 172, 346, 443

-F-

Fairness doctrine, 183-84
False consensus, 251
False light, 188, 189
Family, trends/changes in, 204
I.G. Farben, 105
Farm Research Institute, 409
FBI, 186
Federal Communications Act (1934), 183
Federal Communications Commission, 183-85, 463
  F.C.C. v. League of Women Voters, 183
Federal Election Campaign Act (1971), 169
Federal Express, 274-75
Federalist, 92
Federal Regulation of Lobbying Act (1946), 172
Federal Trade Commission (FTC), 151, 168, 463
Federation of National Associations, 528
Federations, 528
Felton, John, 156
Ferguson, Donald, 17, 156
Field reports, 336
Film, 276-77
Financial Advertising Association, 115
Financial public relations, 176-82
Financial Public Relations Association, 115-16
Financial relations, 19
  corporate, 450-54
Financial Relations Board, 77
First Amendment, impact of, 165-72
First National Bank of Boston v. Bellotti, 170-71
Fleischman, Doris E., 112
Fleishman-Hillard, 29, 75
Flesch, Rudolf, 417
Flesch formula, 417
Florida Public Relations Association, 149
Focus groups, 330-32
Food and Drug Administration (FDA), 463
Foote, Cone and Belding, 75

Forbes, 217
Force-field analysis, 328
Ford, Gerald, 468
Ford, Henry, 106
Ford Motor Co., 190, 273-74, 335, 438
Foreign Agents Registration Act (1938), 77, 174
Forney, T. Michael, 270
Forte, Russell, 465
Foschetti, Christine, 385
Foster, Lawrence G., 23
Foundation for American Communications, 441
Foundation for Public Relations Research and
      Education, 122, 139-40, 141
Fowler, George, 139
Fox, James, 443
Franco, Anthony, 156
Frankenberg, T. T., 116
Frankfurter, Felix, 281
Albert Frank-Guenther Law, 76
Franklin, Benjamin, 288
Fraud in securities trading, 180-82
Freedom of Information Act (1966), 185-86
Freeman, Howard E., 410
Frenzied Finance (Lawson, Thomas W.), 100
Frick, Henry Clay, 97
Fry, Edward B., 418
Fry formula, 418
Fulbright Act (1946), 120
Fund raising, 98-99
    principles of, 502-3

-G-

Gaebler, Ted, 488
Gallup, George, 117, 338, 398
Gallup poll, 117, 522
Gardner, Alexander, 484
Garnett, James L., 465-66
Garrett, Paul, 114
General Electric (GE), 176, 334
General Mills, 77
General Motors (GM), 113-14, 274, 275, 302-3, 445, 453
    Dealer Association, 528
Georgia-Pacific, 275
Gergen, David, 489
Gillett, Frederick H., 477
Gillett Amendment, 14, 477
Glass ceiling effect, 46-47
Gleason, Mike, 488
Global communication, 203-4
Globalization, 202-4
Goals and objectives, writing, 362-64
Godfrey, Arthur, 291
Goldman, Eric F., 97, 104
Golly, Jeanne, 67

Good-bye to the Low Profile: The Art of Creative Confrontation (Schmertz), 440

Goodyear Tire & Rubber, 437

Gorney, Sondra, 30

Government, public relations in:
    barriers to effective, 472-78
    citizen participation, 469-72
    flow of information, 466-72
    legislative hostility, 475-78
    role of, 462-66

Government as business, 488-89

Government information, access to, 185-86, 479

Government in the Sunshine Act (1976), 185, 186

Government-media relations, 478-83

Grapevine, 270-71

Grass-roots lobbying, 173-74

Greenfield, Meg, 304

Greider, William, 482

Grenada conflict, 484

Groer, Anne, 481

Grossman, Michael B., 483

Grunig, James, 140, 245-46, 360, 386

GTE, 79

Gunning, Robert, 417

Gunning formula, 417-18

-H-

Hamilton, Alexander, 92

Hamilton, Richard F., 95

Hampton, Virginia, 470-72

Handy, Moses P., 95

Harllee, William C., 109

Harlow, Rex F., 3, 103, 122, 141

Harlow's Weekly, 103

Harper, William Rainey, 108

Harris, Louis, 338

Harvard College, 91, 107

Harvard University, 441

Hayes, Glenn G., 113

Hayes, Loeb and Co., 113

Hayworth, Rita, 13

Health care reform, 201-2, 495
    media role in, 506-7, 508-9
    public relations in, 501-7

Hearst, William Randolph, 285

Heilbroner, Robert, 133-34

Heinrichs, E. H., 98

Henegen, Ronald, 180

Hepburn Act, 102

Hess, Stephen, 483

Hewlett-Packard, 77

Hill, Don, 401

Hill, John W., 113, 150

Hill and Knowlton, Inc., 29, 75, 77, 79, 80, 84, 113, 408, 522, 533

Hispanic Public Relations Association, 149

History of the Standard Oil Company (Tarbell), 100

Hogan, Hulk, 13

Homeostasis, 213-14

Home Placement Service v. Providence Journal, 182

Hoover, Herbert, 111

Horton, Robert, 118

Hospital Marketing and Public Relations, 149

Houston Automobile Dealers Association, 535

Hovland, Carl I., 230, 232

Howard, Edward D., II, 113

Edward Howard and Co., 113

Howe, Louis McHenry, 99, 116

How We Advertised America (Byoir), 110

Hughes, Mark, 480

Human relations, definition of, 1

Human resources, relationship with public relations, 72-73

Hunter, Barbara, 102

Hurst, Willard J., 135

Hyman, Herbert H., 396

-I-

IBM, 64, 78, 272, 437

Icahn, Carl, 450

Illinois Pork Producers Association, 528

Image, The (Boorstin), 134

Immigration and Naturalization Service, 463

Informants, key, 330

Information campaigns, 396-97

Information center, establishing an, 370-71

Information diffusion, 240-41

Inserts, 268

Institute for Public Relations Research and Education, 122, 140, 276

Institute of Public Relations (IPR)(United Kingdom), 147

Insull, Samuel, 98, 106-7, 114

Interdepartmental relationships, 68, 70-74

Internal department, 64-68

Internal relations, 20

International Association for Standardization (ISO), 456, 457

International Association of Business Communicators (IABC):
    description of, 147
    educational background of members, 29, 30, 138
    role research, 44
    salary survey, 31-33
    teleconferencing and, 275

International Labor Press Association, 541

International organizations, 150

International Public Relations Association (IPRA), 3, 121, 141, 148
International Public Relations Review, 141, 142, 148
International relations, definition of, 1
International Technologies Corp., 178
Interpersonal relations, definition of, 1
Interstate Commerce Act, 106
Interviews, in-person, 341
Intrusion, 188, 189
Investor relations, 19
IRS, 334
Issue management, 16-17, 441

-J-

Jack O'Dwyer's Newsletter, 141, 142, 155
Jackson, Andrew, 93
Janis, Irving L., 232
Jay, John, 92
Jefferson, Thomas, 478
Job descriptions, 33-41
Johnson & Johnson, 23, 59, 60, 275, 334, 351, 381-82, 441, 445, 453
Jones, F. F., Jr., 107
Jones, John Price, 110, 113
Jones and Laughlin Steel Co., 107
Journal of Public Relations Research, 139, 141, 142, 408
Jungle, The (Sinclair), 100
JWT Group, 113

-K-

Kaiser Aluminum & Chemical Corp., 437
Kemper Group, 438
Kendall, Amos, 93
Kendall, Marilyn, 36-37
Kennedy, John B., 115
Kennedy, John F., 335
Ketchum Public Relations, 319, 339, 346-47, 408, 422-23
Kettering, C. F., 320
Kimberly Clark Corp., 192
Kimmel, Bob, 297
Kinko's Graphics, 192
Kirban, Lloyd, 408
Kissinger, Henry, 186
Klein, Joe, 291
Kmart Corp., 67
Knights of Columbus, 115
Knowledge, organizational, 64-65
Knowlton, Don, 113
Koresh, David, 522
Ku Klux Klan, 114
Kumar, Martha J., 483
Kweit, Mary, 469
Kweit, Robert, 469

-L-

Labor, communication between management and, 175-76
Labor Management Relations Act (1947), 169
Labor unions, 528
    challenge for, 544
    decline in affiliation, 539-40
    problem of strikes, 541-43
    role of public relations in, 540-41
    statistics on, 539
Ladies Home Journal, 100
Lanham Trademark Act (1946), 192
Larsen, Ralph S., 445
Larson, Cedric, 110
Lasch, Christopher, 480
Lasswell, Harold D., 111
Lawson, Thomas W., 100
Lee, Ivy, 71, 102, 103-5
Lee, Spike, 130
Legal counsel, relationship with public relations, 71-72
Legal issues:
    access to government information, 185-86
    access to the media, 182-85
    commercial speech, 167-68
    communication between labor and management, 175-76
    copyright, 190-92
    corporate political expression, 168-69
    elections, 169-70
    financial public relations, 176-82
    First Amendment, 165-72
    libel and slander, 187-88
    licensure, 143-44
    lobbying, 172-74
    privacy, 188-90
    referenda and political issues, 170-72
    trademarks, 192-93
Legislative hostility, 475-78
Leopold, Aldo, 396
Letters, 267-68
Levine, Dennis, 181
Lewis, David, 106
Lewis, Fred, 103
Lewis-Seabrook Co., 103
Libel and slander, 187-88
Liberty Loan drives, 110
Libraries, public relations in, 523
Licensing and accreditation, 142-44
Lincoln, Abraham, 321
Lindbergh, Charles A., 113
Lindenmann, Walter, 346, 406, 408, 409, 415, 421
Line-staff management model, 60-62
Lippmann, Walter, 112, 228, 238-39, 241, 392, 394, 395, 398

Listening, role of, 320-21
Littlejohn, Stephen W., 214
Lobbying:
    definition of, 17
    description of, 172-74
    growth of, 17-18
Loeb, Sidney C., 113
Long, Richard, 50
Lowell, Charles Russell, 95
Lowell, James Russell, 242
Luce Press Clippings, Inc., 421
Lugosi, Bela, 190

-M-

MacArthur, Douglas, 119
McBride, Jim, 424
McCammond, Donald B., 160
McDonald, Forrest, 98
McDonald's, 201, 446
Machiavelli, 90
MacLeish, Archibald, 118
McLuhan, Marshall, 234
MacNeil, Robert, 295
McNeil Consumer Products Co., 23, 381
Madison, James, 92
Magazine Publishers Association, 424
Magazines, 288-90
Mail analysis, 335
Management:
    communication between labor and,
        175-76
    issue, 16-17, 441
    planning and programming and expectation of,
        347-48
    process, 316-18
    role of top, 59-60
    strategic, 349-55
Management by objectives (MBO), 63, 352-53
Management by objectives and results (MOR),
    63, 352
Managers, technicians versus, 44-46
Manning Selvage and Lee, 82
Manuals, 266
Manville Corp., 438
Market Development Inc. (MDI), 409
Marketing:
    consumer affairs and, 455-56
    in health care, 504-5
    public relations versus, 6-8
    relationship with public relations, 70-71
Marvin, Thomas O., 101
May, Carl, 90
Mayflower Story, The, 277
Meany, George, 540-41

Media (see also under type of):
    access to, 182-85
    controlled versus uncontrolled, 259
    for external publics, 279-99
    -government relations, 478-83
    guidelines for working with, 299-311
    health care and, 506-7, 508-9
    images and words, 273-79
    influence of, on public opinion, 227-28
    for internal/employee publics, 260-63
    printed words, 263-70
    relations and placement, 33
    verbal, 270-73
    World War I and use of, 99, 109-11
Media Institute, 440, 441
Medium/channel, 233-35
Meetings:
    annual, 454
    verbal communication at, 271-72
Megatrends 2000: Ten Directions for the 1990's
        (Naisbitt and Aburdene), 202
Mellett, Lowell, 118
Mendelsohn, Harold, 396-97
Merck Pharmaceutical, 350
Merrill, John C., 281
Message, 231-33
    disseminating the, 397-400
    framing the, 386-89
Metaphor Computer Systems, 77
Meter method, 424
Metropolitan Edison, 441
Metropolitan Life Insurance Co., 113
Michaelis, George V. S., 101
Midler, Bette, 189-90
Military public relations, 483-87
Milken, Michael, 181, 444
Miller, James G., 210-11
Minnesota Law Review, 11
Minorities as practitioners of public relations,
    46-47
Minow, Newton, 293
Mission statements, 350-52
MIT, 72
Moberley, Jill, 513
Mobil Oil, 11, 70, 172, 300, 301, 440
Mock, James O., 110
Mondell, Franklin, 476
Monolithic consensus, 250
Morphogenesis, 214
Mossman, W. T., 107
Mothers Against Drunk Drivers (MADD), 397
Motorola, 456
Muckraking journalism, 2, 100-101
Mutual Life Insurance Co., 98

-N-

Naisbitt, John, 122-23, 202, 339-40
National Association of Elementary School
    Principals, 516
National Association of Government Communicators
    (NAGC), 149, 465
National Association of Life Underwriters (NALU),
    535
National Association of Manufacturers, 528
National Association of Public Relations Council
    (NAPRC), 103, 146
National Association of Secondary School Principals,
    516
National Audubon Society, 527
National Business Council for Consumer Affairs,
    455
National Catholic Evangelization Association,
    522
National Communication Council for Human
    Services, 146
National Conference of Business Public Relations
    Executives, 150
National Conference of Catholic Bishops, 522
National Cotton Council of America, 528
National Council of Farmer Cooperatives, 530
National Dairy Promotion and Research Board,
    527-28
National Education Association, 516
National Film Preservations Act (1988), 190
National Labor Relations Act (1935), 175
National Labor Relations Board (NLRB), 175-76
National Livestock and Meat Board, 77, 528
National Lutheran Council, 115
National Mental Health Association, 535
National Publicity Council for Welfare Services,
    115
National Safety Council, 275
National School Boards Association, 516
National School Public Relations Association, 516
National Tuberculosis Association, 109, 392
NBC, 172, 302-3
Nelson, John, 477
Nestlé, 181, 346
Nevins, Allan, 93
New Deal, 116-17
New England's First Fruits, 91
Newsletters, 266
Newsom, Doug, 400
Newspaper Enterprise Association (NEA), 287
Newspapers, 280-85
News reporters, 102
News syndicates, 285-88
New York Mutual Life Insurance Co., 101
New York Public Service Commission, 171

New York Stock Exchange, Inc., 351
New York Times, 110, 115, 473
New York Times v. Sullivan, 166
A.C. Nielsen Co., 338, 422
Nixon, Richard, 479
Nofziger, Lyn, 77
Nonprescription Drug Manufacturers (NDM), 530
Nonprofit organizations, public relations in, 494-95,
    497-501
Norfolk Southern Corp., 382-83
North American Free Trade Agreement (NAFTA),
    543
North American Precis Syndicate, Inc. (NAPS), 288
Northern States Power Co., 217-18

-O-

Objectives, writing, 362-64
Objectivity, 65-66
Occupational Safety and Health Administration
    (OSHA), 374
O'Dwyer's Directory of Corporate Communications,
    66, 67
O'Dwyer's Directory of Public Relations Firms, 74
O'Dwyer's PR Services Report, 141, 142
Office of War Information (OWI), 118, 120
Ogilvy & Mather, 102
Ogilvy Public Relations Group, 76, 82
Ombudsman, 333-34
Omnicom Group, 76
Omnicom PR Network, 76, 82
On-line databases, 338-39
OPEC, 440
Open systems, 212-14, 219-24
    action and, 383-86
Opinion Research Corp., 261, 440
Organizational development (OD), relationship with
    public relations, 73-74
Organizational publications, 263-67
Organizational structure:
    changes in, during the 1980s and 1990s, 56
    decision-making role, 62-63
    integration of functions, 86-87
    interdepartmental relationships, 68, 70-74
    internal department, 64-68
    origins of, 57-59
    outside counseling firm, 74-86
    staff role, 60-62
    titles and reporting relationships, 66-68
    top management, 59-60
Organization and Publicity Counsel, 113
Organization charts, 68, 69
Orientation, public opinion and, 247-49
Osborne, David, 488
Outsourcing, 408

-P-

Pacific Gas & Electric Co., 437-38
Page, Arthur W., 114-15
Arthur W. Page Society, 115, 150
Pamphlets, 266
Panel studies, 341
Papalini, Darlene, 368
Parker, Alton, 102
Parker, George F., 102, 103-4
Parker & Lee, 102, 103
Pate, Thomas F., 178
Patrick, Dennis, 184
Payne Fund studies, 234, 238
People for the Ethical Treatment of Animals (PETA), 206
People method, 424, 426
Perot, H. Ross, 444, 473, 475, 488
Perrier, 59, 60, 443
Persian Gulf War, 484-85
Personal contacts, 329-30
Personnel department, relationship with public
    relations, 72-73
Pertinence, 247
Peters, Thomas J., 212
Philanthropy:
    corporate, 446-50
    public relations in, 498-501
Philip Morris, 172
Phillips, David Graham, 100
Phillips Petroleum Co., 447
Pickens, T. Boone, 450
Pierce, Lyman L., 109
Pinchot, Gifford, 105
Pittsburgh Post-Gazette, 541
Pittsburgh Press, 541
Planning and programming:
    anticipating disasters/crises, 366-69
    budgeting, 371-74
    defining target publics, 360-62
    establishing an information center, 370-71
    four-step process, 357-58
    for implementation, 365-76
    management expectations, 347-48
    pretesting, 374-75
    reasons for, 354-55
    selling of, 375-76
    strategic management, 349-55
    strategic thinking, 345-48
    writing planning scenarios, 365-66
    writing the program, 355-64
Pluralistic ignorance, 251
Policy Studies Review, 469
Political action committees (PACs), 170
Political campaigning, 96, 117-18, 120-21
    contributions to elections, 169-70

Political expression, corporate, 168-69
Political issues:
    public apathy, 472-75
    referenda and, 170-72
Politics, public relations in, 489-90
Polling firms, 338
Popcorn, Faith, 200
Popoff, Frank, 123
*Posadas de Puerto Rico Associates v. Tourism
    Company of Puerto Rico*, 167
Powell, Lewis, 170-71
Practitioners of public relations:
    education and preparation of, 29-30
    glass ceiling effect, 46-47
    job descriptions, 33-41
    location and types of employment, 27-29
    minorities as, 46-47
    number and distribution of, 26-27
    professionalism, 48-49
    requirements for success, 50-53
    roles, 42-46
    salaries, 31-33
    women as, 30-31
PR Data Systems, Inc., 421
Presley, Elvis, 190
Press, guidelines for working with, 309-11
Press agentry, 11, 13, 94-95
Pretesting, 374-75
Pride and Alarm, 150
Print media:
    access to, 182-83
    types of, 263-70
Privacy, right to, 188-90
Privilege, 131-32
PR Newswire (PRN), 286-87
Problem-solving:
    defining problems, 321-28
    facilitator role, 43-44
    formal methods, 336-42
    informal/exploratory methods, 329-36
    problem statement, 322-23
    process, 317-18
    situation analysis, 323-28
Procter & Gamble (P&G), 334, 371, 390, 446
Producer associations, 527-28
Professional Air Traffic Controllers Organization
    (PATCO), 540
Professional associations, 527
Professionalism, 48-49, 135, 157-60
Professional organizations, 145-50
Professional societies, 527
Programs, evaluation of (*see also* Planning and
    programming):
    impact criteria and methods, 426-31
    implementation criteria and methods, 420-26

Programs, evaluation of (*continued*)
   levels of, 413-31
   preparation criteria and methods, 415-20
   results of, 431-33
   trends in, 407-9
Propaganda, 476
Prosser, William L., 188
PR Quarterly, 146
PR Reporter, 31, 64, 73, 82, 141, 142
Prudential Insurance Co., 101
PR Week, 74, 141, 142
Pseudoresearch, 410
Public affairs, 14-15
Public apathy, 472-75
Public disclosure, 188, 189
Publicity, 2
   definition of, 8-9
   examples of, 9-10
   original use of the term, 104
   right of, 189-90
Publicity Bureau, 101-2, 107
Publicity Methods for Engineers, 114
Public Law 92-351, 14
Public Law 94-350, 468
Public opinion (*see also* Publics):
   coorientation and, 249-54
   definition of, 243-45
   dissemination versus communication,
     228-30
   influence of, 242-43
   influence of the media on, 227-28
   orientation and, 247-49
Public Opinion (Lippmann), 112, 228
Public relations:
   definitions of, 1, 3-6
   evolution of concept, 2-3, 89-90
   parts of function, 8-21
   social utility of, 21-23
   sources of information on, 140-42
   versus marketing, 6-8
Public Relations, 147
Public relations, history of:
   early years, 91-94
   middle years, 94-99
   1900-1917, 99, 100-109
   1917-1919 (World War I), 99, 109-11
   1919-1929, 99, 111-16
   1930-1945 (World War II), 99, 116-19
   1945-1965, 99, 120-22
   1965-present, 100, 122-23
Public Relations Consultants Association (PRCA)
   (United Kingdom), 148
Public relations firms, 74-75
Public Relations Journal, 103, 122, 135, 139, 141,
   142, 146, 289, 408

Public Relations News, 3, 141, 142
Public Relations Quarterly, 141, 142, 146, 408
Public Relations Research and Education, 141
Public Relations Research Annual, 141
Public Relations Review, 139, 140, 141, 142, 408
Public Relations Seminar, 150
Public Relations Society of America (PRSA), 527
   accreditation, 145
   Body of Knowledge Project, 139
   code of ethics and professional standards, 151-57,
     159-60
   Counselors Academy survey, 82
   creation of, 103, 122, 146
   description of, 145-47
   educational background of members, 30, 136, 137,
     138
   financial public relations defined, 176
   Official Statement on Public Relations, 4-5
   role research, 44
   salary survey, 31-33
   statistics on, 27
Public Relations Student Society of America
   (PRSSA), 150
Publics:
   defining target, 360-62
   definition of, 245-46
   measuring, 422-23
   media for external, 279-99
   media for internal/employee, 260-63
   situational theory of, 246
   types of, 246
Public service announcements (PSAs), 292

-Q-

Quality issues, 456-57
Quarterly Review of Public Relations, 146
Questionnaires, 340

-R-

Radio, 290-92
   measuring audiences, 424, 426
Railroads, 95, 101-2, 106, 113
Railway Age Gazette, 106
Raiman, Gail, 517
Ralston Purina, 77
Randall, Clarence, 67-68
Rand Corp., 365
Raucher, Alan, 94, 105
Readability tests, 416
Readers Digest Association, Inc., 437
Readership studies, 423-24
Reagan administration, 442, 539-40
Receivers, 235, 400-402
Recycle symbol, 393

Reed's Worldwide Directory of Public Relations Organizations, 26
Reeves, Byron, 431
Regier, C. C., 100
Reich, Robert B., 122
Reinventing Government (Osborne and Gaebler), 488
Relman, Arnold S., 504
Reporting relationships, 66-68
Research, 33
  attitudes toward, 320
  checklist for starting a project, 337
  development, 138-40
  evaluation, 410-13
  formal methods, 336-42
  informal/exploratory methods, 329-36
  listening and, 320-21
  process, 328-29
  pseudo-, 410
  role, 44-46
  in strategic planning, 319
  trends in, 407-9
Responsively/responsibly, acting, 380-81
Ridin' the Edge, 276
RJR Nabisco, 206, 444
Robinson, Edward J., 316
Robinson, Joseph T., 477
Rockefeller, John D., Jr., 104, 106
Rogers, Henry, 11, 13
Rogers and Cowan of Shandwick, 29
Roles:
  confusion of, 66
  decision-making, 62-63
  of practitioners of public relations, 42-46
  staff, 60-62
  top management, 59-60
Romans, 90
Roosevelt, Franklin D., 99, 116-17, 118
Roosevelt, Theodore, 101, 102, 105
Roper, Elmo, 397-98
Roper poll, 117, 338
Ross, T. J., 150, 158
Rossi, Peter H., 410
Routzahn, Evart G., 115, 413
Routzahn, Mary Swain, 115
Rowland Worldwide, 82
Ruder Finn, 84, 408

-S-

Sage Publications, 408
Salaries, 31-33
  glass ceiling effect, 46-47
Salience, 247
San Diego Gas & Electric (SDG&E), 11

San Diego Kaiser Permanente hospital, 424
Sass, Hans-Martin, 158
Scalia, Antonin, 166
SCEcorp (Southern California Edison), 11
Scenario writing, 365-66
Scheff, Thomas J., 250, 251
Schlanger v. Four-Phase Systems, Inc., 181
Schmertz, Herbert, 300, 440
Schoenfeld, Clay, 389
Schoonover, Jean, 102
Schramm, Wilbur, 229, 321
Schudson, Michael, 479
Schweppes, 267
Screen Actors Guild, 528
Scripps, E. W., 285
Seabrook, William, 103
Sears, Roebuck and Co., 113
Securities Act (1933), 177
Securities and Exchange Act (1934), 177, 178
Securities and Exchange Commission (SEC), 156, 176-81
Securities trading, 178-80
  fraud in, 180-82
Seduction of the Innocent, 234
Seekins, Steven V., 507
Seifert, Walter, 150
Seitz, Don C., 109
Semantics, 390-91
Sender, 230-31, 400-402
Sennott, Roger, 409
Sentry Insurance, 71
Seventh Day Adventist Church, 108, 522
Sexton, Anne, 391
Shalala, Donna E., 503-4
Shandwick, 29, 74, 75
Shannon, Claude E., 229
Shaw, Bernard, 474
Sheatsley, Paul B., 396
Shipp, Thomas R., 103
Siemens, 79
M. Silver Associates, Inc., 77
Simmons Market Research Bureau, 282, 422, 424
Simons, William Joseph, 114
Sinclair, Upton, 100
Six Sigma, 456
Slander, 187-88
Small, Herbert, 101
Smith, Alvie, 260-61, 275, 303
Smith, Charles J., 98
Smith, Rea, 30
Smith, Roger B., 445
Smith, William Wolf, 102, 103
Smith-Mundt Act, 120
Smokey Bear, 392

Social Investment Forum, 446
Social responsibility, 132-34
    corporate, 438-46
Social setting, communication and, 237-38
Social support, defining, 241-42
Social welfare, public relations in, 507, 509-11
Societies. (*see* Associations)
Society for Human Resources Management, 72
Society of Automotive Engineers, 535
South Africa, 442
Southern Publicity Association, 114
Southern Railway System, 382-83
Spanish-American War, 99
Speakers' bureaus, 273
Speaking, 34
Special-interest groups, 527
Speeches:
    advantages of, 273
    reprinted, 268-69
Spiral of silence theory, 241-42
Staff role, 60-62
Standard Oil, 106
Stanford University, 72, 397
Starch, Daniel, 424
Starch INRA Hooper, Inc., 424
State organizations, 149
Steffens, Lincoln, 100
Steiger, Janet, 168
Stereotypes, 394-96
Stokes, Anson Phelps, 107
Storm, Joette, 40-41
Stouffer Presidente Hotels, 77
Strategic management, 349-55
Strategic thinking, 345-48
Strategy:
    action component of, 380-86
    communication component of, 386-402
    definition of, 346
    versus tactics, 353-54
Strategy Research, 409
Student organizations, 150
Success, requirements for, 50-53
Surles, Alexander, 119
Survey Research Laboratory, 473
Surveys, 340-42, 469-70
Survey Sampling, Inc., 341
Swift, Paul, 266
Sybron Chemical Inc., 384-85
Symbols, 392-94
Systems:
    cybernetics in open, 214-19
    open and closed, 212-14
    open systems model of public relations,
        219-24
    perspective, 206-12

-T-

Tactics, strategy versus, 353-54
Taft-Hartley Act, 169, 175
Tarbell, Ida, 100
Task Force on the Statute and Role of Public Rela-
        tions, 62
Taylor, R. William, 533
Alan Taylor Communications, Inc., 77
Team membership, 64
Teamsters, 528, 541
Technicians versus managers, 44-46
Teixeira, Ruy A., 473
Teleconferencing, 273-75
Telephone interview, 426
Telephone lines, call-in, 334-35
Television, 120-21, 234-35, 293-98
    cable, 298-99
    closed circuit (CCTV), 275-76
    measuring audiences, 424, 426
Texas Gulf Sulphur, 181
J. Walter Thompson Co., 75, 76, 113
3M, 446
Three Mile Island, 441
Time, 367
Time v. Hill, 144
Time Warner, 31
Titles, 66-68
    in corporate settings, 437-38
Toffler, Alvin, 199
Tornillo, Pat, 182-83
Toshiba Corp., 11
Total quality management (TQM), 456-57
Towers, Perrin, Forster and Crosby, 262
Trade associations, 528
Trademarks, 192-93
Traffic Audit Bureau, 422
Training, 34
Transportation Institute, 528
Traverse-Healy, Tim, 148, 458
Trend Report, 340
Trinity Episcopal Church, 108-9
Truman, David, 92
Trust, 130-31
Tucson Electric Power (TEP) Co., 11
Tylenol, 23, 59, 334, 381, 441, 530
Tyler, Bessie, 114

-U-

Uhlman v. Sherman, 182
Union Camp Container Division, 457
Union Carbide, 443
Unions. (*see* Labor unions)
Unisys, 233
United Press International (UPI), 285

United Soybean Board (USB), 331
U.S. Bureau of Land Management (BLM), 380-81
U.S. Bureau of Mines, 334
U.S. Bureau of the Census, 338, 511
U.S. Department of Agriculture, 346, 398, 477
U.S. Department of Defense, 64
U.S. Department of Labor, 27, 30, 47
U.S. Department of Transportation, 463
U.S. Golf Tour, 77
U.S. Information Agency (USIA), 28, 118, 120, 466-69
U.S. Information and Educational Exchange Act
      (1948), 120
U.S. Information Service (USIS), 468
U.S. Marine Corps, 99, 109
U.S. Navy, 201, 333, 487
U.S. Office of Personnel Management, 28
U.S. Postal Service, 90
U.S. Supreme Court. (see Legal issues)
United Steel Workers of America (USWA), 539, 543
United Way of America, 208, 210, 375, 494, 510, 511
University of Chicago, 442
University of Massachusetts, 516
University of Michigan, 517
University of Pennsylvania, 107
University of Wisconsin, 108, 140
USA Today, 270
Utilities, 106-7, 114

-V-

Vail, Theodore N., 97, 101, 107
Van Hise, Charles R., 108
VanLeuven, Jim, 325
Verbal communication, 270-73
Video news releases (VNRs), 296-98, 421
Videotapes, 276-77
Vietnam War, 484
Virginia State Board of Pharmacy v. Virginia Citizens
      Consumer Council, 167
Visual Artists Rights Act (1990), 190
Vladeck, Bruce, 506
Voice of America, 467-68
Voinovich, Goerge, 509
John Volk Co., 77
Voluntarism, 498

-W-

Walking the Tightrope (Rogers), 11, 13
Walters, Jonathan, 464
Walton, Frank, 408
Wang Associates Health Communications, 77
War Advertising Council, 119
Ward, Charles Sumner, 109
Warner-Lambert, 77
Washington Post, 485

Watergate, 479
Waterman, Robert H., Jr., 212
Weaver, Warren, 229
Welfare, social, 507, 509-11
Westinghouse, George, 99
Weston, Charles K., 107
Weyerhaeuser, 201, 217, 350, 424
Whirlpool Corp., 334
Whitaker, Clem, 118
Williams, Frederick, 199
Williams, Lynn, 539, 543
Williams, Pete, 485
Williams, Roger, 517
Wilson, Woodrow, 109-10
Wire services, 285-88
Wirthlin Group, 522
Wisconsin Electric Power Co., 438
Wisconsin Milk Marketing Board (WMMB), 354, 359,
      529
Wise Men, 150
Wolford, Harris, 501
Women:
      glass ceiling effect and, 46-47
      as practitioners of public relations, 30-31
Women's Tennis Association, 77
Wood, Leonard, 104
Woodward, Bob, 479
Words That Won the War (Mock and Larson), 110
Work assignments, 33-41
Working theory, role of, 358-59
Worldcom Group, Inc., 75
Worldnet, 468
World War I, 99, 109-11
World War II, 99, 116-19
WPP Group PLC, 75, 76, 113
Wright, Donald, 157
Wright, Hamilton Mercer, 102
Wright, Joseph F., 136
Hamilton Wright Organization, Inc., 102
Writing, 33, 34
      planning scenarios, 365-66
      programs, 355-64
Wyatt Co., 73, 262, 426
Wylie, Frank, 157

-X-

Xerox, 192

-Y-

Yale University, 107
YMCA, 109
Young, James Webb, 119
Young & Rubicam, Inc., 76, 189